1104   ǂ 12

THE HISTORY OF THE
ROYAL
AIR FORCE

THE HISTORY OF THE
ROYAL
AIR FORCE

Consultant: John D.R.Rawlings

Temple Press
Aerospace

TEMPLE · PRESS
𝍢𝍢𝍢𝍢𝍢𝍢𝍢𝍢
NEWNES·BOOKS

Published by Temple Press
an imprint of Newnes Books
84/88 The Centre, Feltham, Middlesex TW13 4BH, England
and distributed for them by
The Hamlyn Publishing Group Limited
Rushden, Northants, England

Created by Stan Morse
Aerospace Publishing Ltd
179 Dalling Road,
London, W6 0ES

© Aerospace Publishing Ltd 1984

Colour profiles and line diagrams © Pilot Press Ltd

First published 1984
Second impression 1985

ISBN: 0 600 34990 X

All correspondence concerning the content of this volume
should be addressed to Aerospace Publishing Ltd.
Trade enquiries should be addressed to Temple Press.

Printed in Italy

Editor: Trisha Palmer
Editorial production: David Donald
Three-view artist: Keith Fretwell

Filmsetting: SX Composing Ltd, Rayleigh, Essex
Colour reproduction: Bright Arts Ltd, Hong Kong
Film work: Precise Litho Ltd, London

Picture acknowledgements

The publishers would like to thank the following individuals and organisations for their help in
supplying photographs for this book.

Avro: pages 194, 219
British Aerospace: jacket, pages 301, 309, 310, 313, 317, 319, 321, 322, 323, 326, 333
British Aircraft Corporation: pages 188, 196
Charles Brown – RAF Museum, Hendon: pages 79, 86, 91, 127, 158, 180, 278
de Havilland: pages 293
Flight: pages 52, 65
Peter Foster: page 316
Fox Photos: jacket, pages 67, 87
Hawker Siddeley: page 288
Imperial War Museum: jacket, pages 9, 10, 14, 15, 19, 20, 24, 60, 62, 63, 67, 68, 69, 70, 71,
72, 74, 75, 76, 77, 78, 81, 84, 85, 86, 87, 88, 89, 90, 92, 93, 94, 96, 98, 99, 100, 101, 104, 105,
107, 108, 109, 110, 111, 112, 113, 116, 117, 118, 119, 120, 121, 123, 124, 126, 127, 128,
129, 131, 134, 135, 136, 137, 138, 139, 140, 141, 142, 143, 144, 145, 146, 147, 148, 149,
150, 151, 152, 154, 156, 157, 158, 159, 160, 161, 165, 167, 170, 171, 172, 174, 175, 176,
226, 227, 228, 229, 230
MoD: jacket, pages 14, 16, 32, 179, 181, 182, 183, 184, 185, 187, 190, 191, 192, 193, 195,
196, 197, 200, 201, 202, 203, 204, 205, 206, 210, 211, 212, 213, 214, 215, 218, 219, 220,
221, 222, 223, 229, 230, 231, 232, 233, 234, 235, 236, 237, 238, 239, 240, 241, 242, 243,
244, 245, 246, 247, 248, 249, 250, 251, 252, 253, 254, 255, 256, 257, 258, 259, 260, 261,
262, 263, 265, 266, 267, 268, 269, 270, 271, 274, 275, 276, 277, 278, 279, 282, 283, 284,
285, 286, 287, 288, 289, 292, 293, 294, 295, 296, 297, 298, 299, 300, 301, 305, 306, 318,
320, 322, 323, 324, 325, 327, 328, 329, 330, 331
Matthew Nathan: page 155
Popperfoto: pages 124, 129
Press Association: jacket, pages 303, 304, 307, 308
RAF Ballykelly: page 216
RAF Coningsby: pages 17, 21, 297
RAF Tengah: page 241
RAF Waddington: page 187
RAF Wittering: page 302
RAF Museum, Hendon: pages 8, 15, 16, 23, 24, 30, 31, 37, 39, 49, 54, 55, 57, 61, 62, 73, 74,
75, 76, 80, 86, 95, 107, 122, 124, 130, 135, 163, 172, 173, 176, 203, 205, 206, 217, 218
John D. R. Rawlings: pages 11, 15, 17, 18, 21, 22, 23, 25, 28, 29, 33, 36, 38, 40, 41, 42, 43,
44, 45, 46, 47, 48, 50, 51, 53, 54, 55, 56, 57, 58, 59, 60, 64, 66, 95, 97, 119, 162, 164, 166,
168, 169, 178, 179, 183, 185, 186, 203, 207, 223, 234, 242, 264, 265, 290, 291, 292, 296,
318, 326
US Air Force: page 153
US Navy: page 106

CONTENTS

Authors

John Rawlings

Paul Jackson

Francis K. Mason

Paul Wood

INTRODUCTION

The British Army and the Royal Navy are old-established organisations with their roots deep within the heart of Great Britain and with many centuries of service and tradition behind them. Not so the Royal Air Force, which was formed only in 1918 and is still in the process of forging its own traditions. Nonetheless, the reader will find in the following pages a fast-moving spectacle of development from a tiny élite to a giant air force, which fought the largest war the world had ever seen and went on to display the great flexibility demanded by post-war technological and political change.

Born as an unwanted complication in the middle of conflict, the new service had, in the ensuing peace, to battle against its elder relations, who wanted to swallow it up. Only the steadfastness of its originator, Hugh Trenchard, and his administrative genius in forming the core on which the new service could grow enabled it to withstand the pressures. His vision was projected by his lieutenants who followed him into high command, so that when the new, vast conflict of World War II loomed they built on solid foundations an edifice which more than fulfilled expectations. In that war the Royal Air Force came of age – in double-quick time. The tenacity and professionalism of its permanent personnel were infused into thousands of wartime servicemen, and together they caried this fine spirit throughout the war; men and women who are still proud to wear the RAF tie. With the end of World War II the Royal Air Force had earned a right to hold its head high amongst the Armed Services of the United Kingdom, and it has done so ever since.

The challenges facing a contracting service after the war did not destroy the essential Royal Air Force. Rapid technological progress required even higher professionalism from all its members, adding a new dimension to those vibrant qualities which have stood the service in good stead throughout its existence: the qualities of adaptability and downright common sense. These qualities again came to the fore when all three services were plunged unexpectedly into a fighting war in the South Atlantic; the Royal Air Force of the 1980s showed itself to be a worthy successor to the generations which had gone before. It is this Service which we have humbly endeavoured to chronicle in this short space, and it is this Service to whom we dedicate this volume.

John Rawlings

Prelude to an Air Force

When the Royal Air Force was founded in 1918, it became the first major air arm to be created independently of the British Army and Royal Navy, setting a precedent amongst the warlike nations which stood alone for many years. But the Royal Air Force itself was not the first such creation and, in fact, the first practical military aviation organisation had taken place six years earlier in Britain.

As so often happens in Britain, something worthwhile only comes about because of a scandal, or because a situation has become so bad that drastic remedial action needs to be taken. And this was the case with the early attempts to fit matters aeronautical into the British Armed Services. By the end of 1911 the British Army and Royal Navy between them could muster approximately three airships and between four and eight aircraft with 19 competent aviators. By comparison France had over 200 aircraft and 263 aviators, whilst Germany mustered a fleet of 30 airships. Something had to be done. The Committee of Imperial Defence set up a technical sub-committee (a typical British reaction) to look into British military aviation. But this committee outperformed most of its type: its findings were speedily formulated with complete agreement, and issued in a White Paper in 1912 which set up a unified flying service called The Flying Corps. However, His Majesty the King decided that as flying, let alone fighting in the air, was a hazardous occupation, he would issue a royal warrant to grant it the title The Royal Flying Corps (RFC). This was at the time a most revolutionary step for, before ever aeroplanes had fought in action, here was the concept of an air force which would be independent of both Army and Navy while serving them both – in fact, the germ of the Royal Air Force itself. This Royal Flying Corps would have a Central Flying School, a Military Wing to work with the Army, a Naval Wing to work with the Navy, a Reserve, and the Royal

Aircraft Factory (RAF, at Farnborough) to build its military aircraft.

Not often has a government body made such a far-sighted start on a major new project. But its implementation rested on other government departments, and the War Office and the Admiralty (particularly the latter) had their own views on the Royal Flying Corps. From the start, the Admiralty had no intention of allowing its air affairs to escape from under its own control, and in fact the name Royal Flying Corps, Naval Wing, never really appeared anywhere other than on a few official documents. A new title, Royal Naval Air Service (RNAS), gained rapid currency and, by the time that World War I broke out in August 1914, it had received official sanction. With only a token participation in the Central Flying School, the Admiralty carried on with its own aviation affairs, training its own aviators and ordering its own aircraft direct from the manufacturers, thereby spurning most of the products of the Royal Aircraft Factory at Farnborough. It was therefore almost inevitable that Farnborough should concentrate its efforts on producing aircraft for the army's needs. By 1914 the RFC had effectually become a part of the army rather than an independent arm, and almost all of British aviation entered World War I as a component of either the British Army or of the Royal Navy.

In the 18 months or so of preparation which Britain had enjoyed before the horrors of World War I began, the Royal Flying Corps, firmly wedded to the Army and with most of its bases around the perimeter of Salisbury Plain, put in much research into establishing its squadrons on a battle footing, ensuring that they would be fully mobile down to the last piece of equipment. Originally the corps had one balloon squadron and three aeroplane squadrons, but the balloons were transferred to the Royal Navy in 1913 and the RFC then con-

Where it all began: Farnborough airfield before World War I, where the Royal Flying Corps first established itself alongside the Royal Aircraft Factory. Many of the buildings shown here are still in existence, including the 'black sheds' in the foreground, the HQ building approximately in the centre of the photo and the building to its right. Next to that is the Beta shed for the second British airship and further airship sheds in the distance. On the right is the Spinning Tower.

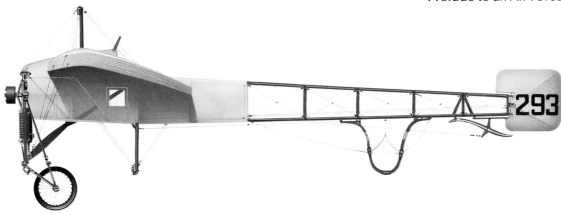

In 1912 the British aircraft industry was in poor shape to supply the new RFC with aircraft. Many were bought from France, including many Blériot Type XIs such as 293 here, which served with No. 3 Squadron, RFC.

The first important product of the Royal Aircraft Factory for the new Royal Flying Corps was the B.E.2 biplane, designed by Geoffrey de Havilland. A sight of wonderment to local Farnborough inhabitants, it awaits its test flight. Designed to be inherently stable as a good observation platform, the B.E.2 and its derivatives served operationally in all theatres throughout World War I.

centrated on building up its aeroplane squadrons; to do this it gathered in a whole medley of types, many from French constructors, a sprinkling from British manufacturers but a growing contingent from Farnborough. Principal amongst these was the Geoffrey de Havilland-designed B.E.2, a two-seater tractor biplane and with the accent on aerial stability. As it was thought that the aeroplane would be used for reconnaissance and little else, the most stable observation platform possible would be most suitable – hence the B.E.2.

By contrast the Royal Navy was pursuing quite other lines of aeronautical application. The Navy

had traditionally been responsible for the safety of British shores, and so it was decreed that the aerial defence of the United Kingdom should be vested in the Royal Naval Air Service. So the RNAS busied itself setting up a chain of naval air stations around the UK coastline, to be used by airships and aeroplanes. The vision of aircraft to fly off ships was a natural one for a sailor, inasmuch as if aviation was to be of any use to him, it must accompany him at sea. Much effort, therefore, went into developments which would enable aircraft to land on and take off from water. The Navy had a more direct approach to its particular brand of warfare; anything which served with the Navy would be expected to fight and so, even before World War I broke out, bombs up to the size of 100 lb (45 kg) and torpedoes had been successfully dropped from naval aircraft. But because the problems to be overcome by the Royal Navy were greater and more intractable, it was natural that when the test of war came both the Royal Flying Corps and the Royal Naval Air Service (especially the latter) were less than ready to play an immediate part in the day-to-day activities of the war.

On paper the RNAS had grown by August 1914 to 128 officers and approximately 700 ratings with 10 bases, seven airships and 71 aircraft. On this basis, the RNAS mounted North Sea patrols from Killingholme in Lincolnshire, used two of its airships to escort the troopships taking the British Expeditionary Force (BEF) to France, and set up its own No. 2 Wing over the English Channel in the Dunkirk area with nine aeroplanes of five different types. Commander C. R. Samson was in control of

It was the Naval Wing that first went in for airships, in this case Naval Airship No. 3 (an Astra-Torres design) during 1913.

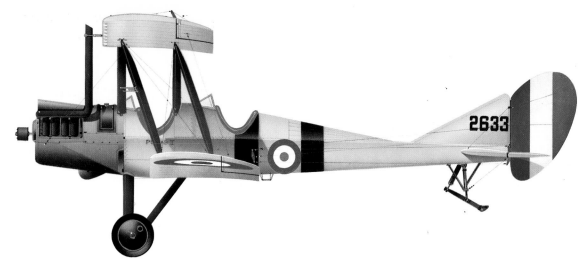

The B.E.2c was the mass-produced aircraft of the early World War I period which was designed (largely by Geoffrey de Havilland) at the Royal Aircraft Factory at Farnborough. Designed with great stability as an observation platform, it became easy meat for the German fighters of 1915–16 and was shot down in great numbers. 2633 is shown with the black bands used as a marking by No. 16 Squadron, RFC in 1915.

this Wing, and its exploits in the early days of the war were legion, extending far beyond the mere use of aircraft. Such flying operations as it carried out were almost all of an offensive nature, such as carrying small bombs to drop on enemy naval installations up the coast. One such attack must go on record as the first highly-successful aerial bombing raid, when Flight Lieutenant R. L. G. Marix in a Sopwith Tabloid flew all the way to Dusseldorf and dropped two 20-lb (9-kg) bombs on the airship sheds with the remarkable result that the roof of one fell in and a brand new Zeppelin went up in flames.

How different to these cavalier and highly original exploits by the Royal Navy were the contributions of the Royal Flying Corps; less flamboyant but, for the moment, more practical and lasting. With war declared, the Royal Flying Corps went to France with the BEF. Numerically the RFC had seven aeroplane squadrons, although the seventh existed only in embryonic form, and four of these were quickly established in France together with an Aircraft Park (a maintenance and supply depot). This force comprised 105 officers, 63 aeroplanes and 95 motor vehicles to provide mobility, a factor which was soon needed. On 19 August 1914 the RFC began its air war with two reconnaissances, one by Captain Philip Joubert de la Ferté of No. 3 Squadron in a Blériot, and the other by Lieutenant G. W. Mapplebeck of No. 4 Squadron in a B.E.2. The value of aerial reconnaissance was quickly made crystal clear with the German advance and the Allies' hurried withdrawal, the RFC squadrons keeping the troops posted with information on the Germans' latest strength, location and movement. Allied casualties could well have been higher without the advantage of this new method of reconnaissance. But the hurried withdrawal also showed the foresight of the RFC in making its squadrons fully mobile for, without such provision, its few squadrons could have been engulfed early in the fighting. Within a month the RFC had started to use both photography and W/T operationally, the latter being of particular potential now that the early squadrons were spotting for the guns of the Royal Artillery, a task which became abbreviated to Art/Obs in the jargon of the day.

In the meantime the RNAS had been carrying the war to the enemy in a style more akin to that of World War II. In November three naval officers set off from Belfort in southern France in Avro 504s,

Typical of the offensive activities of the RNAS early in World War I was the attack by Squadron Commander Bigsworth on Zeppelin *LZ39* over Ostend in this Avro 504B in May 1915.

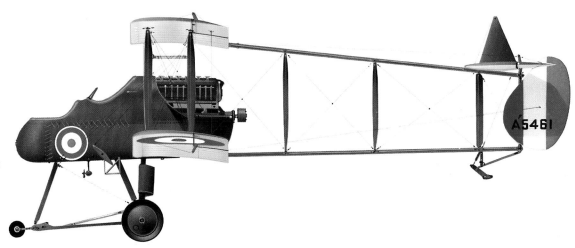

The Royal Aircraft Factory's answer to air fighting was to provide pusher aircraft giving a forward facing gun a wide field of fire. The big two-seater design was the F.E.2b and, surprisingly, this began life as a successful fighter until superseded by more conventional and faster scouts. It was then transferred to night bombing, at which it was most successful until the arrival of the D.H.4 and Handley Page O/100 rendered it obsolete. The aircraft depicted served in this latter role with No. 101 Squadron in France.

By 1916 the B.E.2c was the standard corps reconnaissance aircraft of the RFC, serving in greater numbers than any other type. Running up in the long grass at La Gorgue airfield is this aircraft of No. 16 Squadron, with the observer about to climb into the front seat before a patrol.

each fitted with four 20-lb (9-kg) bombs. Their target was the Zeppelin factory at Friedrichshafen on Lake Constance, and their diminutive bombs caused damage out of all proportion: a Zeppelin in flames, the workshops badly damaged and the gas plant out of action. One Avro was forced down and its pilot, Squadron Commander E. F. Briggs, taken prisoner. The other two returned to Belfort. In December Commander Samson from Dunkirk made the first night bombing raid in history and, more significantly perhaps, there occurred the first naval air attack, i.e. a raid by aircraft operating from ships. In this case, three seaplane carriers launched their seaplanes by lowering them on to the sea, from which they took off, and were then recovered

from the water on their return. This was really a dead end as far as future development was concerned because the method could only be used when the sea was calm, but at this stage it seemed the only practical method of ship operation. The purpose of the operation was to attack the airship sheds at Cuxhaven, and the three ships took three seaplanes apiece which, before dawn on Christmas Day 1914, they hoisted into the North Sea off Heligoland. Of the nine seaplanes two failed to start, so the remaining seven set off individually for Cuxhaven, which they were unable to find. So they sought targets of opportunity, ranging from the centre of Wilhelmshaven to sundry ships and a seaplane base. The only tangible result was that two warships, horrified at the sight of British seaplanes, collided, but damage from the raid itself was negligible. Only three of the aircraft made rendezvous with their parent ships, the other four running short of fuel and force-landing in various places. One crew was interned in the Netherlands, whilst the rest were picked up by a British submarine. Although a failure, this raid set a precedent and taught valuable lessons which became the inheritance of later RNAS flyers and of the Royal Air Force itself.

As 1915 progressed, the build-up in air activities took place mainly on the Western Front. Back in November 1914 the RFC had been reorganised on the basis of the Wing formation, and by the Spring of 1915 the RFC in France, under its general officer commanding, Major-General Sir David Henderson, KCB, DSO, comprised three Wings with eight squadrons, their operational strength being between 80 and 90 aircraft with 18 in reserve at the Aircraft Park at St Omer. By now the War

Generally it was the rule for the British services not to fly monoplanes, but so desperate was the need for aircraft to combat the German scouts that the French-built Morane Parasol was pressed into service. The type served with success for two years with No. 3 Squadron, whose line-up is seen here at Longavesnes in the summer of 1917, by which time the Morane was outclassed.

Sopwith Tabloid

The Sopwith Tabloid was already in service with the RFC and RNAS in small numbers on the outbreak of war. Effectively it was the first single-seater scout used by both services, and it was used on more warlike enterprises than simply reconnaissance in the early days. Although unarmed, one RNAS Lieutenant (Norman Spratt) took steel darts with him when flying, and managed to force a German machine to land by flying rings around him. Then there were the amazing exploits of Squadron Commander Spenser Grey and Flight Lieutenant Marix of the Eastchurch Squadron at Antwerp. They set out to bomb the Zeppelin sheds at Cologne and Düsseldorf in two Sopwith Tabloids – Spenser Grey hit Cologne Railway Station and Marix bombed and set on fire the airship shed at Düsseldorf, destroying a Zeppelin (the Z.IX) inside. The aircraft shown here, No. 394, was built for the RFC and served as a scout with one of the early reconnaissance squadrons.

The Airco D.H.2 was a first attempt at beating the Fokker menace in 1915 and was the first RFC type to equip scout squadrons entirely. It was immediately a success because it was fast and very manoeuvrable, but was soon outclassed by more conventional aircraft. 5925 served with No. 24 Squadron, RFC, the first unit to be fully equipped with one type of scout aircraft at Bertangles.

in the Air was moving out of the purely passive phase: the joy of simply sitting up in the air watching the land battle below had been spoilt by one or two pilots taking their revolvers aloft with them and taking pot shots at the enemy's aircraft. By October the French had already armed a Voisin with a machine-gun and shot down a German reconnaissance aircraft – war in the air was on. So the complement of each RFC squadron now included one or two 'scouts': small single-seaters which were marginally faster and certainly more manoeuvrable than the B.E.2s, Farmans and Blériots used for reconnaissance. The Royal Aircraft Factory had produced the S.E.2a, but there existed only one example, which served briefly with No. 3 Squadron. The RFC had to look to the independent manufacturers (to whom the RNAS were already going for most of their aircraft) and so Vickers, Martinsyde and Bristol Scouts took their place in small numbers as escorts to the slower reconnaissance aircraft. But No. 3 Squadron, under Major W. G. Salmond, DSO, was almost totally equipped with Morane-Saulnier Parasol monoplanes, and these, with a fixed machine-gun on the upper wing, began to serve both for reconnaissance and for scouting. The aircraft over the battlefield was beginning to make its presence felt. As early as March 1915 the assault on Neuve Chapelle benefitted from the availability of tactical maps based solely on aerial photographs. Up until now the RFC had largely been observers of the battle scene, but in that same month the B.E.2s and other suitable aircraft were bombed up and sent in to attack behind the enemy lines to prevent reserves from moving up to the front line.

It was out of these bombing attacks that the first

To combat the growing menace of the Fokker monoplane fighters, new 'scouts' were designed for the RFC. Farnborough produced this pusher fighter, the F.E.8, which went into service in small numbers at Abeele with No. 41 Squadron.

aerial Victoria Cross was won. Flying a B.E.2, Lieutenant W. B. Rhodes-Moorhouse attacked Courtrai railway station in an effort to delay German reinforcements moving up to the Front. He descended to 300 ft (90 m) to drop his 20-lb (9-kg) bombs in the centre of the station and was mortally wounded in the process. He flew his aircraft back to his base at Merville, succumbing to his wounds the next day. He had been one of the RFC's most experienced pilots, having been flying for six years. Within two months the RNAS had 'drawn equal' when Flight Sub-Lieutenant R. A. Warneford destroyed a Zeppelin in the air for the first time. He had set off from Dunkirk in a Morane-Saulnier to bomb the Zeppelin sheds at Berchem but, seeing Zeppelin *LZ.37* airborne, he climbed above it and dropped his bombs on the airship, which exploded, almost blowing him up as well. The explosion dislodged the petrol pipe on his aircraft, so Warneford forced-landed behind the lines, repaired it himself

An early operational 'aircraft-carrier' with the Royal Navy was this seaplane carrier, HMS *Ark Royal*. Note the two steam-driven cranes to winch the seaplanes on and off the hangar deck.

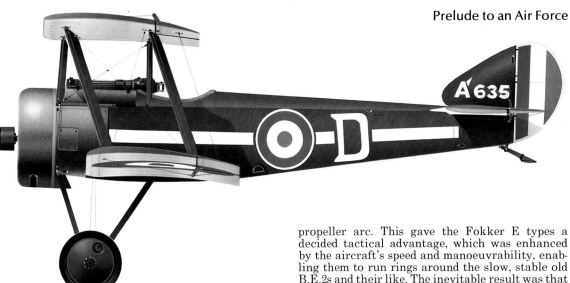

One of the most delightful types emanating from World War I was the Sopwith Pup fighter. Ordered originally for the RNAS, it soon found its way to RFC squadrons, the first being No. 66, which took the type to France in March, 1917. A635 was one of No. 66 Squadron's aircraft, distinguished by the lengthwise white band along the fuselage.

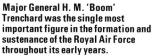

Major General H. M. 'Boom' Trenchard was the single most important figure in the formation and sustenance of the Royal Air Force throughout its early years.

Above right: The RFC was engaged overseas as well as on the Western Front, including Africa, India and the Middle East, where the ubiquitous B.E.2c flew on whatever task was required. No. 14 Squadron mechanics manhandle this specimen out of its hangar at Ismailia in Egypt, ready for the day's flying.

propeller arc. This gave the Fokker E types a decided tactical advantage, which was enhanced by the aircraft's speed and manoeuvrability, enabling them to run rings around the slow, stable old B.E.2s and their like. The inevitable result was that RFC losses went up alarmingly, and the expression 'Fokker Fodder' was soon applied to most of the reconnaissance aircraft in the Allied inventory. True, No. 3 Squadron had been using its Moranes more and more for fighting; and in July 1915 the first fighter squadron of the RFC (No. 11) arrived in France, but this was equipped with Vickers F.B.5 GunBus aircraft – heavy pusher two-seaters which were scarcely faster than the aircraft they were to escort and certainly no match for the Fokker monoplanes. The writing was clearly on the wall; until the RFC could find a match for the Fokker (and other scouts that Germany had coming into production) it would be increasingly hampered in its operations and its casualty rate would continue to soar.

But whilst all this was happening on the Western Front, the RNAS had been tackling its problems with verve if not with complete success. It was in 1915 that it mounted its first truly overseas operation, when the Eastchurch Wing was sent to the melancholy campaign in Gallipoli. In terms of later naval equipment it was an ideal naval operation, but with the rudimentary ships, aircraft and equipment to hand it was attempting the impossible. HMS *Ark Royal* sailed out, with six seaplanes which could only be launched in calm water and which were unreliable aircraft in themselves. Even Commander Samson was hard put, with his ex-Dunkirk Wing which was also out there, to gain any success from the situation, apart from providing a valuable photographic service to the land and naval forces, which made for valuable mapping amongst other things. All the wing's ingenuity could not make up for the shortcomings of the campaign, which in the end failed and to which the RNAS was unable to make the contribution it would have wished. Nearer home, though, it was

and then flew back to base. Thus the RNAS gained its first VC; 10 days later Warneford was killed. Life expectancy of the military and naval fliers had already taken a drop, and this factor was to become worse as 1915 progressed. The leisurely days of aerial warfare were soon over for ever, and the most spectacular symbol of this change was the Fokker Eindecker (monoplane). Both sides in the struggle had progressed towards scouts armed with machine-guns for the express purpose of aerial combat, but none so far had approached the effectiveness of the Fokker Monoplane. This aircraft could have fought with the British, for Anthony Fokker, a Dutchman, had offered his services first to the Allies, only to be spurned. He then moved to Germany where his Monoplane was evolved, being the first production aircraft successfully to solve the problem of firing the machine-gun through the

The RNAS used a large number of small non-rigid airships for coastal patrolling, including *C.23A* seen here being manhandled into position.

The RNAS bought its own aircraft early on from private manufacturers, although the edict had gone out that military machines must come from Farnborough. One of the navy's early purchases was the Sopwith Triplane, with which it equipped its scout squadrons to great effect. Foremost amongst these squadrons was No. 8, 'Naval Eight' as it was known, and N5493 was one of its aircraft, shown in Naval Eight's markings.

faced with a bigger problem. The submarine had become a potent menace and the RNAS was finding that its coastal air stations, with their cumbersome seaplanes with unreliable engines, were not finding and destroying the underwater menace in any sort of practical way; so they turned to the airship once more and the brilliant little SS.1 was conceived. It was itself a makeshift design, being the Willows airship with a B.E.2 fuselage slung underneath, but it was put into production and slowly a practical submarine hunter moved into service. The SS.1 could do little at this stage to destroy the submarine, but by patrolling with the convoys and on the shipping routes it kept the U-boats submerged and thus prevented them from attacking. The real answer was to have ships from which aircraft could operate, but this ultimate dream was still some time from fulfilment. True, steps were being taken and HMS *Campania* was already in service with a flying-off deck forward from which aeroplanes could take off, but as yet no answer had been found to landing them on again. This was even longer in coming.

Probably one of the most significant events in military aviation that took place in 1915 occurred on 19 August when Colonel Hugh Trenchard was given command of the total RFC in France. It was evident already that the types of aircraft the RFC had on the squadrons in France were totally un-

suitable to oppose the German machines, and yet the policy was to equip the Corps mainly with aircraft emanating from the Royal Aircraft Factory. At this time these were largely updated variants of the old B.E.2, with the same outmoded concepts and little if any improvement in performance. What was needed, urgently, was a successful fighter aircraft for real aerial fighting, and a two-seater for bombing and reconnaissance, which could defend itself. Such designs were in prospect amongst the independent aircraft companies but could not be purchased because of official policy. So, more and more B.E. variants were churned out of the factories, sent to France and almost immediately shot down, each taking two good RFC airmen to their deaths. Scandalous indeed, but given the monumental casualties on the ground this fact had little impact on the Great British Public, and Trenchard had to battle in governmental corridors to remedy the situation.

1915 also saw the RFC moving farther afield. It had established an aerial presence in Egypt in November 1914 with three Maurice Farmans.

The Royal Navy had decided it would rather buy aircraft from sources other than those used by the RFC in order to get the best; thus it brought into production some of the finest aircraft, which were also used by the RFC. First of these was the Sopwith 1½-Strutter, a general-purpose machine which could be used as a two-seater fighter, reconnaissance or bomber aircraft or a single-seater bomber. No. 3 Wing, RNAS, was one of the earliest units to receive these aircraft at Dunkirk.

The Farnborough factory seemed hooked on the pusher principle and produced the F.E.2b as a two-seater fighter. At first it achieved some success, but was soon outclassed; however, it was transferred to night-bombing, where it played a significant role in preparing the way for the Independent Bombing Force.

The Sopwith 1½-Strutter was one of the types ordered in 1916 by the RNAS from the Sopwith Company, and this initiative was quickly followed by the RFC. A993 was one of the aircraft serving with No. 70 Squadron, RFC.

When the Turks set out for the Suez Canal in January 1915 these, plus two other Farmans bought locally, provided reconnaissance facilities for the Army, which repelled the attack and provided the nucleus for a slow build-up of air power in the Suez Canal area. In Mesopotamia a similar force of Farmans was instrumental in providing the reconnaissance information to enable General Barrett to take the initiative and accomplish a rapid advance of 100 miles (160 km). It was in this area that the RFC and RNAS fought together for the first time, No. 30 Squadron, RFC combining with an RNAS Flight for the attack on Kut. Eventually Kut was surrounded by Turkish troops and the RFC found itself pre-dating the Berlin Airlift by flying rations into the beleaguered garrison. Of necessity, all that could be done was too little, and eventually Kut fell to the enemy – but the RFC had learnt a new lesson in supply-dropping from the air.

Trenchard did what he could to remedy the situation on the Western Front whilst the inter-service rivalry hotted up in Whitehall throughout 1916. He first introduced a degree of specialisation in the reconnaissance squadrons by setting some aside more specifically for the task of bombing the enemy troops and supplies. Then he set about decentralisation by forming Brigades and allotting these to different ground armies, which would use these on their own affairs. Each Brigade had two Wings, one whose specific task was 'Corps' work (artillery observation, battlefield reconnaissance etc.), the other for fighting, bombing and other more specialised tasks. It was during 1916 that more scouts came to the rescue. The only suitable aircraft coming from the Royal Aircraft Factory was the F.E.2, a large two-seater pusher aircraft with a machine-gunner in the very nose. Despite its cumbersome size it was remarkably successful and proved a dogged fighter aircraft, especially when the squadrons flying F.E.2s formed a 'fighting circle' in which each defended the tail of the aeroplane in front when attacked by the German flying circuses which were beginning to roam the skies. De Havilland had left the Royal Aircraft Factory and was designing for the Aircraft Manufacturing Co; he produced a mini-F.E.2 in the Airco D.H.2, a single-seat pusher fighter which also helped to stem the flood of Fokker victories. The RFC bought both this and the Nieuport 11 single-seat scout, despite the policy of using only Factory-produced aircraft, so great was the need for fighting aircraft.

For the RFC in France, 1916 was largely the Battle of the Somme. In this, the greatest land battle to date, the RFC's strength was 47 squadrons with 421 aircraft available, divided amongst four Brigades; during the Battle eight more squadrons joined this strength. At first the RFC achieved air superiority and was able to provide all the corps flying, reconnaissance and bombing necessary to cover the pushes by the ground forces, D.H.2s and F.E.2bs providing sufficient fighter cover for this. During this battle the first regular use of 'contact patrols' was made: B.E.2s, flying at low level in touch with the troops, were able to direct aspects of the fighting to the advantage of spot situations on the battlefield itself. However, by September the air picture over the Somme altered drastically. Jagdstaffel 2 of the German air force had been formed as a large fighter 'circus' under the dynamic

Geoffrey de Havilland left the Royal Aircraft Factory to design for the Aircraft Manufacturing Co. His answer to the Fokker was another pusher design, the D.H.2. No. 29 Squadron's hangar at Abeele shows the canvas hangar doors, the windsock attached to the roof (thus giving an erroneous indication); flying for the day has obviously ended, and the machines are being pushed back into the hangars.

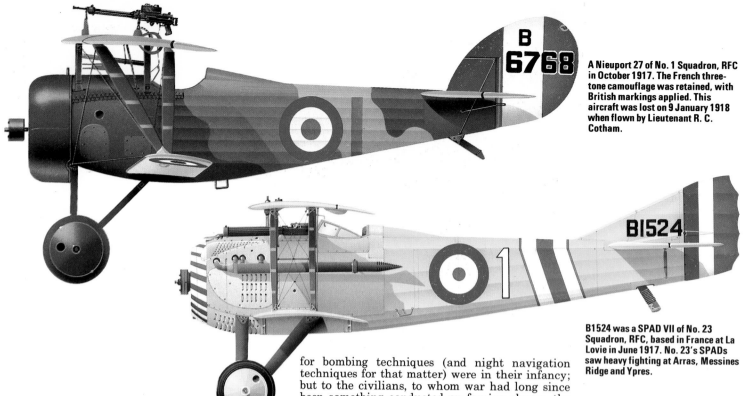

A Nieuport 27 of No. 1 Squadron, RFC in October 1917. The French three-tone camouflage was retained, with British markings applied. This aircraft was lost on 9 January 1918 when flown by Lieutenant R. C. Cotham.

B1524 was a SPAD VII of No. 23 Squadron, RFC, based in France at La Lovie in June 1917. No. 23's SPADs saw heavy fighting at Arras, Messines Ridge and Ypres.

leadership of Oswald Boelcke, and this unit flew large fighter formations of the new Albatros D I and D II fighters, causing a sharp upsweep in RFC casualties, robbing the British of air superiority, and depriving the Army of its 'eyes' by seriously hampering the reconnaissance squadrons. The RFC fought valiantly, but was no real match for the Albatros-equipped Jagdstaffeln; once again the pendulum in the air war had swung in the Germans' favour.

At home mastery was slowly being achieved over another problem which had been an embarrassment to both air services since December 1914. Air defence had been vested in the RNAS, who saw it as a secondary duty to be performed by the coastal air stations. Thus, when the Germans sent their Zeppelins against England they were opposed by a collection of maritime reconnaissance landplanes and seaplanes armed for the most part only with anti-shipping bombs. Ground defences were, at first, a mere four effective anti-aircraft guns.

Little wonder, then, that for the most of 1915 the Zeppelins roamed at will over England and were deterred more by weather than by armed opposition. The damage they caused was relatively minor,

for bombing techniques (and night navigation techniques for that matter) were in their infancy; but to the civilians, to whom war had long since been something conducted on foreign shores, the threat of aerial bombardment and such attacks as took place assumed a terror out of all proportion to the actual threat. Certainly the sight of a huge, sinister slug of a machine sliding across the sky in the dusk or plunging in and out of searchlight beams was something to set the heart pounding; and so there was complaint and uproar and much loss of man-hours as a result of people refusing to go to their places of work. By February 1916 the Cabinet limited the RNAS to interception over the sea and gave the landward duty to the RFC. Accordingly Home Defence squadrons were set up around the country, equipped with the inevitable B.E.2c, and a more advanced system of organisation was set up for reporting the movements of raiders. This began to pay off the following month when a combination of hits from anti-aircraft guns and an aircraft brought a Zeppelin down in the sea off Westgate, in Kent. The next victory was not until 2 September 1916, when Second Lieutenant William Leefe Robinson shot down the Schutte-Lanz airship SL.11 in flames at Cuffley (for which he gained the VC), and later that month another airship was shot down. The combination of aircraft and guns so deterred the Zeppelins from reaching their targets, three more being brought down before the end of the year, that the menace of the

The private-venture stablemate to the S.E.5 was the famous Sopwith Camel, which served with great distinction on the Western Front. Originally bought by the RNAS, it is seen here in service with a naval squadron which had become No. 208 Squadron when the RAF was formed.

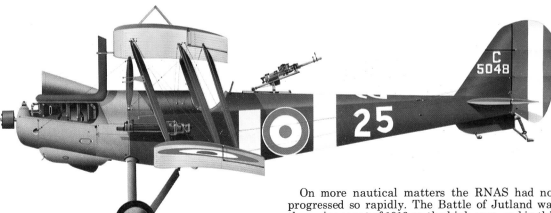

The R.E.8 served in very great numbers for Corps duties over the Western Front. C5048 served with No. 16 Squadron. It carries the two white bands, which were No. 16 Squadron's identity markings, and the number '25' denotes the aircraft's number in the squadron.

Zeppelin receded from the home scene.

For the Royal Navy 1916 had, oddly enough, seen the greatest advance in those units more particularly applied to the land war from its Dunkirk complex. This resulted from the Navy's policy of buying the best aircraft available, mainly from British independent constructors. In particular, the Navy had great faith in the designs coming from the workshops of 'Tommy' Sopwith at Kingston-on-Thames. It was two of his designs which moved the RNAS ahead in 1916. First of these was the aircraft that became universally known as the Sopwith 1½-Strutter. It could be either a single- or a two-seater and either a fighter or a bomber (the original multi-role combat aircraft?), and the Royal Navy used it principally in the latter role, following up its policies of tactical and strategic bombing as essentials. But the 1½-Strutter could easily outperform any of the RFC's aeroplanes. The other aircraft was the Sopwith Pup, a pretty little scout which was a delight to fly and was the only effective answer to Boelcke and his Albatros. So, whilst the tide of battle was turning against the RFC in the south, up north in Dunkirk the RNAS had the answer. Whilst serious questions were being asked at home about the inadequate Farnborough designs and the slaughter of RFC crews, the RNAS was ordering large quantities of effective aeroplanes. As a result the government stepped in and transferred many of the 1½-Strutter and Pup orders from the RNAS to the RFC, and arranged for Naval squadrons in Dunkirk to be lent to the RFC until such time as the RFC squadrons were adequately equipped. In fact one Naval squadron, No. 8, was formed specifically to serve with the RFC.

On more nautical matters the RNAS had not progressed so rapidly. The Battle of Jutland was the major event of 1916 on the high seas, and in this the part played by the RNAS was, through no fault of its own, inconspicuous. Of the two seaplane carriers only HMS *Engadine* sailed with the Fleet, the new HMS *Campania* being delayed as a result of confusion over signals. At this time, and for a long time afterwards, the traditionalists in the Royal Navy regarded the aviation enthusiasts with at best contempt and at worst hostility. Consequently they were not called upon to make any great participation in the Battle and, of course, were then castigated for being of little use. *Engadine* did put up a seaplane flown by Flight Lieutenant F. J. Rutland and Paymaster G. S. Trewin, who flew close enough to the enemy fleet to draw fire from the ships and reported position, numbers and direction with great clarity. But although *Engadine* passed the reports on, they were never received by the fleet commanders, and Rutland's gallantry had availed nothing. However, one development in the North Sea air war which began to make strides in 1916 was the arrival of the flying-boat. For long overwater patrolling the naval air stations had proved that landplanes were unsatisfactory and current seaplanes underpowered and too fragile for sea operations. However, a naval officer by the name of John Porte had experience of the Curtiss flying-boats which had been made for the projected pre-war Atlantic crossing, and eventually interested the Admiralty sufficiently to purchase some. The first boats were little improvement on the seaplanes, but during 1916 Porte worked away with modifications to make them seaworthy and this effort blossomed during 1917 into a viable force of long-distance overwater fighting and reconnaissance flying-boats.

In 1916 there had come to light two factors that, as noted above, pointed to the fact that much was not at all well with the British air services: the slaughter of many British airmen by the Fokker

Roy Fedden at the Royal Aircraft Factory produced Farnborough's finest aircraft and arguably one of the best scouts of World War I, the S.E.5. No. 56 Squadron was the first squadron to receive the type, which it used on home defence for a while in June 1917 (here at Bekesbourne) before going to the Western Front.

The Naval Squadrons were more garish in their markings, as exemplified by this Sopwith Camel of No. 10 Squadron, RNAS. The Camel achieved much fame over the Western Front; it had vicious handling qualities, however, and the novice found it a handful.

Monoplane and its successors had revealed a serious deficiency in the procurement of suitable warplanes; and the regular flight of Zeppelins, almost at will, over the UK brought a call for something to be done to investigate and remedy the situation. 'When in doubt, appoint a committee' is a good British maxim, and the Prime Minister did just that. The committee's first chairman, Lord Derby, soon resigned because the body's very constitution rendered it useless. Lord Curzon tried to remedy the situation and established an Air Board to investigate and recommend, with a view to setting up an Air Ministry. But the Service Ministries were equally opposed, particularly the Admiralty, who was determined to lose not one whit of control over its own air service. So sharp was the clash that the Air Board was given sweeping scope to discuss policy, to control design and to ensure adequate supply of aviation materials. The writing was now on the wall – the two older Services could not be trusted to administer the air on a broad enough scope to ensure that the country's best interests would be served, so sooner or later there would have to be a British Air Force.

By now Britain's aeronautical fortunes were beginning to swing upwards anyway, and 1917 saw the RFC beginning to get the numbers and types of aircraft it needed and the RNAS moving on towards the accomplishment of many of its goals. British air power expanded rapidly in many fields.

On the Western Front, the RFC at the beginning of 1917 was seeing the way forward, but was as yet hampered by lack of the right equipment. The successful experiment of Boelcke's 'Circus' had led to the formation of other élite German fighter units, led by aces, and these roamed far and wide attacking British aircraft with great effect. Only the Sopwith Pups were any real answer and there were only two squadrons of these, one with the RNAS. But more were on the way and, what is more, new and improved types of aircraft were coming into service in greater numbers. SPAD fighters had been bought from the French but from England came the Sopwith Camel, a potent fighting machine which was adored or hated by its pilots (for it could have vicious handling qualities for the tyro). The Royal Aircraft Factory, stung by the criticism of its products, produced two fine aeroplanes: the R.E.8, which replaced the B.E. variants in the Corps squadrons, and the S.E.5, a Folland-designed fighter which flew alongside the Camel, rather like the Hurricane and Spitfire in the Battle of Britain, to such good effect that by that September air superiority, which at the beginning of 1917 had rested firmly with the Germans, was just as decidedly in British hands. Another development of 1917 was the growing use of bombing aircraft by the RFC. De Havilland's D.H.4 was the aircraft which proved suitable, and bomber squadrons were formed with the express purpose of taking the war beyond the confines of the battlefield, a dictum which had been expounded by the RNAS from 1914 onwards. But not only day-bombing was envisaged, and the first RFC night-bomber squadron went to France in March 1917, equipped with the F.E.2b in a bombing role. Then, when Britain howled for revenge against the Germans for their daylight raids on England, the 41st Wing was formed in France in October for the purpose of bombing industrial targets, and it was equipped not only with D.H.4s and F.E.2bs but with another product of the Royal Navy's foresight, the Handley Page O/400. Back in 1914, after the RNAS's heady successes in its early bombing raids, Captain Murray

Bombing as a specialist task came into operation in 1917, and the ideal long-distance bomber of those days was the D.H.4, of which No. 18 Squadron was one of the early operators.

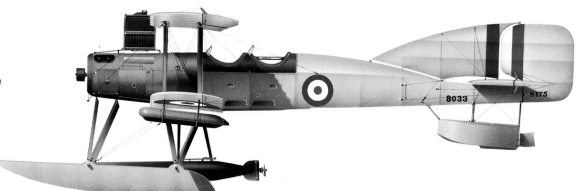

No real aircraft carriers saw service in World War I, but several seaplane carriers operated in various theatres. It was a cumbersome operation, the seaplanes having to be hoisted outboard and inboard before and after flying off the sea. HMS *Vindex* was one such seaplane carrier and Short 184, 8033, was part of its fleet. The Short 184 was the most successful of the navy's seaplanes and was almost universally used in 1917 and 1918, both by the seaplane carriers and the coastal stations around the coasts.

In World War I there was no such thing as an electric starter: propellers had to be swung. Where the powerful engines had a high compression it was sometimes necessary for added force as with this No. 79 Squadron Sopwith Dolphin.

boat came into service in numbers and was now a practical fighting aircraft in which the crews had much greater confidence, destroying both Zeppelins and U-Boats. The RNAS was moving slowly nearer to the true aircraft-carrier with the commissioning of HMS *Furious*, which had a foredeck for flying off and a platform abaft the superstructure. This was far too turbulent for landing on and attempts were made to land on the foredeck. Squadron Commander E. H. Dunning accomplished this in a Sopwith Pup, but several days later was killed trying to repeat the procedure.

Overseas things were hotting up, too. Squadrons had been transferred earlier from the Western Front to Italy to back up the Italians, and fought on for the rest of the war there. In Palestine, too, the war against the Turks was taking more and more RFC units, with a devastating effect on Turkish morale.

But it was in the UK that the decisive aerial events were taking place. Though 1916 had seen a number of successes against Zeppelins, the Germans now started a combined campaign using both Zeppelins and Gotha twin-engined bombers by day and night. Although the defence forces put up many aeroplanes they were almost entirely ineffectual, and the indignation of the country rose with every attack. During the year methods of dealing with these raids improved considerably (and would bear fruit in 1918), but the country was unimpressed so once again fuel was added to the flames for those who saw a need to make drastic alterations to British air services. As a result Lieutenant General J. C. Smuts was appointed in the summer of 1917 to make a thoroughgoing examination of the situation, and just under nine months after he produced his recommendation the Royal Air Force came into being.

Sueter had approached Frederick Handley Page with the idea of building a very large bomber. This emerged as the Handley Page O/100, which entered service with the 3rd Wing, RNAS in April 1917, being used for shipping attacks. These were incomparably the largest and finest bombers of the day. The O/100 and its development, the O/400, became the heavyweights of squadrons of both the RNAS and RFC which entered into strategic bombing during 1917.

In the sea battle, too, things were looking up. The Porte-modified Curtiss Large America flying-

As the war drew on aircraft became more specialist, and one of the earliest ground-attack machines was the D.H.5, a curious aircraft with back-staggered wings. This example, a gift from the women of New South Wales was, appropriately, in service at Baizieux with No. 68 Squadron, an all-Australian unit which later became No. 2 Squadron, Australian Flying Corps.

A Laboured Birth

It cannot be said that the birth of the Royal Air Force as the third service of the British armed forces was an auspicious event. Only those with great vision for the future were hopeful that this was a great step forward, and it was fortunate for the Royal Air Force that one such enthusiast had been appointed as Chief of Staff of the new venture. And to add insult to injury, the thoughtless minions of the Civil Service had deemed that this new Service should be born on 1 April 1918 – to all Englishmen the day known as All Fools' Day – and there were not a few in the War Office and very many in the Admiralty who could see in this date a fitting omen for the new Service's future. How wrong they were!

After the failure of the committee headed by Lord Derby and then Lord Curzon, on 22 December 1916 the Air Board had been finally formed under Lord Cowdray, and its practical outcome was the co-ordination of the supply of aircraft, aero engines and materials to the air arms of both services. It had no hand in operational policy, however, and hardly had the Air Board set up in business than the air raids of 1917 on London (and other United Kingdom targets) caused a public furore, for it was now transparently obvious even to the most Whitehall-bound civil servants that the problems with the conduct of the air war were not simply questions of supply but also matters of deployment, tactics and even strategy. At this moment there arrived in England the South African Lieutenant General Jan Smuts. As an enemy of Britain he had conducted the Boer War with great brilliance but now, as a subject of the British Empire, his allegiance was to the King. He was respected for his ability, and he had no axe to grind for he had no connections with the policies and prejudices that prevailed in the British corridors of power.

He acted with typical speed, foresight and application by setting himself three questions to answer, all concerning organisational policy: departmentally, should there be one Ministry to administer air affairs; operationally, should there be one single Air Service to cover all the flying activities of the nation at war; and practically, if the answers to the first two questions were in the affirmative, what sort of structure should be set up so that this Service could relate to the British Army and Royal Navy in such a way that their air needs would be met? The evidence Smuts had before him was almost all one-sided. Obviously aerial bombardment was here to stay, and was likely to become the foremost factor in future hostilities; and most of the shortcomings which had bedevilled the aerial arms of the British services appeared traceable to the fact that these Services were acting, if not in direct competition, at least on their own and so narrowing the use of their aircraft to their own particular interests. There could therefore be no alternative but to give affirmative replies to his first two questions, and this Smuts did on 17 August 1917. But because of the need to come to an early conclusion, the third (and probably most difficult) question remained unanswered for at least two decades, causing many headaches and loss of operational efficiency in peace and war. With the gift of hindsight, it is easy now to say how important it should have been to retain a separate air arm for both the Army and Navy in addition to the separate Royal Air Force. However in mid-1917, with the pressure of time and public opinion upon him, Smuts made an historic decision; as a result of his report the Air Force (Constitution) Bill was prepared for Parliament and was passed on 29 November 1917. The first Air

The transfer to the RAF from the RFC made little difference to the personnel at the operational end of things. All the squadrons on the Western Front carried on with the offensive all through the summer of 1918 towards the final successful conclusion in the autumn. At Conteville were the S.E.5a fighters of No. 24 Squadron.

Typical of the many World War I airfields is Wyton in Huntingdonshire, a small field alongside a road with the name and a white circle in the middle of the field, hangars along two sides, and the accommodation and offices, including tented encampments (presumably for the airmen) amongst them.

With the ability of German Zeppelins and bombers to fly at will over southern England, the RFC was forced to form home defence squadrons and to convert various types of aircraft for night-fighting. Even the Avro 504 trainer was given a new landing gear and forward-firing guns for this task. One such squadron was No. 33 at Kirton-in-Lindsey.

the 1918 campaign would be the arrival of the American forces, and this engendered different policies on opposite sides of the lines. The Allies decided that it would be futile to attempt any offensive until the American troops arrived, and so adopted a policy of attempting to hold their lines and little else. The Germans realised that it was now or never, for the arrival of Americans might tip the balance, so they planned a series of final offensives for spring 1918 which opened on the night of 20/21 March 1918. The RFC was assigned to the defensive role, largely providing cover for the corps squadrons, although some of the scout squadrons harassed the advancing German hordes with very low-level attacks with bomb and gun. The increasing number of bomber squadrons, equipped mainly with F.E.2bs and D.H.4s, were directed to bomb enemy installations immediately behind the lines, hampering the bringing up of supplies and reinforcements, but this was largely ineffectual as a result of an inflexible order which decreed that such bombing attacks must be made from 15,000 ft (4570 m), and no bomb-aiming equipment of the period could ensure accurate bombing from that height.

Ground attack

The main German drive was directed against Amiens, and the British were forced to give much ground. Aircraft were thrown into the battle with all flying, apart from the night bombing, directed to corps and ground-attack work. Once the RFC had learnt to concentrate its aircraft in small areas rather than dissipate them along the whole front, it began to make a contribution to holding back the streams of German troops. As March turned into April the Germans reckoned that this front was stabilising, so they transferred their attention to the north, a fact discovered by reconnaissance aircraft but disbelieved by the generals. This was the point at which the RFC/RNAS merger into the RAF occurred. On 9 April the German attack took place and broke through with great advances for several days – only on 12 April was the situation held, though the Amiens front opened up again. But these were the final throes, and Germany had no further fight left. Its armies had not broken through, though they had struck back. Now it would be the Allies' turn.

As on the Western Front, British fighting airmen engaged in North Sea patrols and the sideshows in various parts of the world were far more concerned with getting on with their war than with bothering

Council was formed on 3 January 1918, and even at the eleventh hour there were unseemly ructions. Lord Rothermere had been appointed as President, Sir David Henderson as Vice-President and Major General Sir Hugh Trenchard as Chief of Staff. The last-named found it impossible to work with Lord Rothermere, so he resigned. Major General Sir Frederick Sykes was substituted, whereupon Sir David Henderson resigned. To solve the dilemma Lord Rothermere stepped down, his place being taken by Lord Weir.

The stage was now set organisationally, and on 1 April 1918 the Royal Flying Corps and the Royal Naval Air Service ceased to exist, both becoming integral parts of the Royal Air Force. It is not really surprising that this historic creation of an independent air service, setting a pattern for other nations in the years ahead, went largely unnoticed by most of its members, particularly those who were engaged in the fighting in which both the RFC and the RNAS were engaged, not only in Europe but in the Middle East and Africa.

By this time the Western Front in particular had erupted into violent and dangerous action. At the end of 1917 both sides were exhausted by the gigantic tussles which had taken place and which, for the loss of thousands of lives, had gained but little advantage for either side; the futility of it all was more than apparent, but neither side could see a way out. The greatest factor likely to play a part in

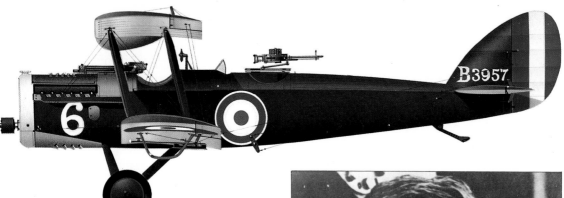

The Airco D.H.4 supplemented the F.E.2b in the long-range strategic bombing role, and served with both the RFC and the RNAS with some success during 1917. It was mass-produced and served with many squadrons. It is not known with whom B3957 served; this particular aircraft was built by Westland at Yeovil and was originally an RNAS contract, but was converted to the RFC.

With the advent of successful scouts, some of the British pilots began to mount good scores and thus became classified as 'aces'. One of the most famous was Captain Albert Ball, VC, who was credited with 44 victories at the time of his death in May 1917.

about the nature of the change which had overtaken them. Only at home were there feuds and fuss: arguments about new rank titles, provisional new uniforms (some of which looked more suitable for a Gilbert and Sullivan opera than for a fighting force) and other ancillary but (to some) important matters.

One of the immediate operational developments which was to have a lasting effect not only on future Royal Air Force policy, but on military aviation strategy the world over, took shape soon after the formation of the RAF. It had its beginnings in the early raids of the RNAS at the start of the war when, for a very small expenditure of aircraft and bombs, much destruction was wrought by bombing, principally on Zeppelin bases. Captain Murray Sueter had soon after contacted Frederick Handley Page and asked him to produce a truly strategic bomber or, to use Sueter's famous phrase, 'a bloody paralyser of an aeroplane'. Whilst this aircraft was being developed, the Royal Navy began other plans to build up a strategic bombing force. Commander Samson's No. 3 Wing, which had returned from the Dardanelles in January 1916, was reconstituted at Manston with the specific purpose of forming a strategic bombing Wing to serve in France. The fact that it was not in action by that summer was due to the fact that the aircraft destined to equip it, Sopwith 1½-Strutters, were almost all transferred to the RFC because of

the latter's critical shortage of effective aeroplanes. However, the Wing did begin its allotted task in October and through that winter made its contribution by attacking German industry within its reach, using 1½-Strutters and the bigger Short Bomber, an aircraft which was really too big for its single engine. These were soon followed by the

The Royal Navy had always had an eye on the possibility of strategic bombing, and early in the war had ordered a giant bombing aeroplane from Frederick Handley Page. This really came into its own as part of the RAF's Independent Bomber Force, and the Handley Page O/400 became the precursor of the RAF's later heavy bombers. At Coudekirke, mechanics go about the laborious process of fuelling an O/400 of No. 207 Squadron on 1 June 1918.

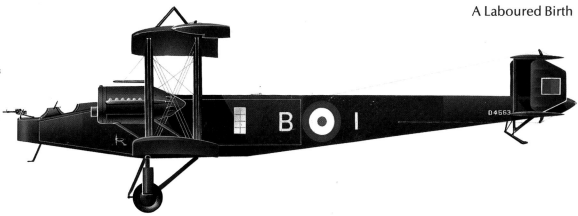

At the time the RAF was formed, the RFC's standard day bomber was the Handley Page O/400. This aircraft was flown by No. 207 Squadron at Ligescoult, France, in 1918.

early Handley Page O/100s, at first with No. 5 Wing which used the type principally against naval targets.

During 1917 these beginnings of bomber power made little further progress, for a variety of reasons, most of the Handley Pages being put to purely naval targets. But in October 1917 the RFC formed the 41st Wing at Ochey to begin its own bomber offensive. This Wing comprised one squadron of D.H.4s (No. 55), one squadron of F.E.2bs, now transferred from the fighter role (No. 100) and an RNAS unit, No. 16 Squadron, with Handley Pages. These big aircraft could uplift 16 112-lb (51-kg) bombs, a bigger load than any other British aircraft, and were destined to become the UK's first practical heavy bomber. These three squadrons resumed the strategic offensive begun by the Royal Navy, partly as a retaliation for the German raids on England, and during the winter of 1917–8 built up their effectiveness slowly and surely. In February 1918 the 41st Wing became the VIIIth Brigade and soon after greater things were planned.

Trenchard takes over

With the formation of the RAF there was now even more appreciation of the role of the bomber, and in June 1918 the VIIIth Brigade was expanded into the Independent Bombing Force, almost an air force within an air force, charged with the strategic bombing of Germany and, by August, consisting of nine bomber squadrons, five of which had Handley Page O/400s, the developed version of the O/100. To command this new and important force was the man who had resigned from the post of Chief of Staff under Lord Rothermere, Major General Sir Hugh Trenchard. No single man has had more effect in shaping the destiny of the Royal Air Force, and we must now consider him in order to understand what took place in the next few important years.

Hugh Trenchard came into the RFC after an Army career which had not shown him at his best.

This was not wholly his fault, because he suffered from ill-health; but it has to be said that he was a difficult man to get on with, and was blunt to the point of rudeness with his superiors. He carried the DSO for his activities in the Boer War, in which he was badly wounded and in 1912 at the age of 39 after a severe and nearly fatal dose of a pneumonic-type fever in Nigeria he had been found a staff job in the Army to see him through to retirement. With the advent of flying in the Army he soon arranged to qualify for his pilot's licence and move into this sphere of military activity, becoming Station Staff Officer to the embryo Central Flying School and ending up as Assistant Commandant. When war broke out most of the RFC went to France. What little was left was put under Trenchard's command to build up a training organisation and to feed out to France a growing supply of reserves of men, machines and equipment. His flair for administration enabled Trenchard to set the machinery in motion within three months, whereupon he was posted to France himself to command the 1st Wing, and nine months later he commanded the whole of the RFC on the Western Front. It was Trenchard who, seeing the mounting losses of British aircraft and crews, had to battle with those at home for better aircraft with which to prosecute the air war, and it was here that he began to learn the art of inter-departmental warfare. He was not naturally gifted at this for he was a gruff man, and he had to rely on the power of his personality. It was this gruff forcefulness which acquired him the nickname 'Boom', which stuck to him throughout his career; whilst such a personality did not advance him well in the more traditional branches of the Army, in the new sphere of aviation, which he entered in a fairly formative and influential position, it built him up a coterie of subordinates who respected him and were in awe of him. Many of these were to follow him to high rank within the Royal Air Force.

This was the man, then, who took command of the Independent Force in June 1918 and began to work out the theory that air power was an indepen-

One of the overseas theatres where aircraft soon became a major asset was Mesopotamia, where No. 63 Squadron flew its R.E.8s on reconnaissance duties in 1918.

Sopwith Camel

The Sopwith Camel was one of the most successful of the single-seat scouts of World War I and served in two versions, the F1 (shown here) and the 2F1, used by the RNAS for shipboard use. F6314 was built by Boulton and Paul at Norwich and was fitted with a 130-hp Clerget engine. It carries the markings of No. 3 Squadron, RFC, for the period October 1917/March 1918, when No. 3 Squadron was flying from Warloy Baillon on the Western Front. The two vertical bars indicate the identity of No. 3 Squadron and the 'B' shows the aircraft's letter in the squadron. These are the markings carried by the Sopwith Camel in the RAF Museum, Hendon.

dent force which, of itself, could fight and win a battle. Of course the limited forces he had for bombing (numbers of men, types and numbers of aircraft, and the primitive navigational and bomb-aiming aids available) meant that the raids he could lay on could not be construed as terror bombing or bombing which brought the German industrial machine to a standstill. But progress was made, and in the five months of war that were left, 550 tons (559 tonnes) of bombs were dropped on enemy targets, most of which could be considered strategic. Whilst, as his detractors claimed soon after the war was over, the IBF did not shorten the conflict by as much as one day, it did make some contribution to final victory and, more importantly, learnt lessons which were to be of use in the decades ahead. For Trenchard himself it meant the opening up of a whole new field of warfare and although he had, earlier in his career, been critical about the independent use of aircraft and the creation of a separate air force, he was now, to use a later expression, completely 'sold' both on a separate air force and on the fact that air warfare could be the predominant means of fighting a future war. In practice, given a man of Trenchard's temperament, once convinced of an idea he would bend all his energies to prosecute that idea, ignoring even a reasoned argument against it. In later years this had outstanding results for the nation, both good and bad.

Numerical superiority

But what of the fortunes of the Royal Air Force, newly created out of veteran fighting stock, in the war? On the Western Front the die was now cast, although there was much to be done before victory was assured. The logistics problem had long since been solved and by August, when the 'last great battle in the West' began, there were approximately 800 British aeroplanes lined up for battle against between 300 and 400 German machines, with French aircraft topping the 1,000 mark. This became the era of the great air battles, with large formations of Allied scouts (Camels and S.E.5as predominantly in the RAF squadrons) roaming the skies as escort to reconnaissance and bombing formations, and embroiling themselves in vast dogfights with the German circuses. However, and not surprisingly, the RAF was still fighting an Army battle and, instead of attempting to give the smaller German aerial forces a knock-out blow and then turning its attention to the land battle, it flew mainly in conjunction with the Army's activities; once again the aerial fighting was dissipated rather than concentrated, and because the Germans had magnificent aeroplanes (Fokker D VII and Albatros D V scouts in particular) the disparity in numbers was made up for by lack of cohesion in fighting the air battle on the part of the RAF commanders.

The war ends

One interesting development which pre-dated close-support operations in World War II was the establishment, in the Battle of Bapaume, of a Central Information Bureau which, well up in the front of the battle, selected the most important targets for ground attack and quickly passed the information back to the RAF squadrons (an embryo cab-rank system). This, needless to say, was evolved by junior commanders in the thick of the fighting, for the generals were too far back to see what was lacking. This made possible a greater concentration of the RAF's efforts where they were most needed. Now the Army was advancing steadily, and the RAF had almost forgotten about mobility in the field, so static had the trench warfare been over the last three years. The battle moved relentlessly on into the autumn with the Germans fighting ever more recklessly as the end drew near; this ensured that the RAF's casualties were never light during the final phase of the struggle. New aircraft had been brought in: the Sopwith Snipe appeared as a successor to the Camel, but was just too late to get into its stride; and the D.H.9 bomber was to have replaced the D.H.4, but the new aircraft was a failure because of its chronically unreliable engine. Still, the Allied war machine moved on and by 11 November it was all over – all at last was quiet on the Western Front.

But how had the war in the air fared elsewhere?

Another type which came into service just at the end of World War I was the D.H.9A, and this was soon in extra service for postal and VIP flying between the UK and the British Army of Occupation.

The most successful two-seat fighter of World War I was the Bristol Fighter, which doubled as a reconnaissance aircraft. This gaudily-painted machine belonged to No. 139 Squadron on the Italian Front, based at Villa Verla.

defile and subjected to very low bombing and machine-gun attacks – it was a massacre, and the remnants of the army were incapable of any further fighting. Two days later the 7th Army was caught in a similar situation and the retreat was turned into a rout. From daybreak until dusk the slaughter went on, 9¼ tons (9.4 tonnes) of bombs and 56,000 rounds of machine-gun fire being spent in destroying this army; the carnage appalled even those soldiers who, next day, moved into the defile. Never before had the potential for destruction by naked air power been more forcibly demonstrated, and this was a lesson which spelt volumes to those who, already, were seeing a vision of warfare conducted principally by aerial forces. One such visionary was soon to command the whole of the Royal Air Force.

Naval contribution

Of the ex-RNAS units, now in the Royal Air Force with 200 added to their squadron numbers, many were involved in the final land battle on the European continent. In fact there goes to a Captain Roy Brown of one of these squadrons, No. 209 (ex-naval No. 9) the distinction of probably shooting down the German's greatest 'ace', Manfred von Richthofen, although this fact was hotly disputed by some Australian gunners who claimed him for themselves. Elsewhere, in the U-boat war, the sea patrols and the research into the use of flying aircraft with the Fleet continued. In fact this latter problem came up for solution just before the war ended, when HMS *Argus*, the world's first flush-decked aircraft-carrier, joined the Fleet in October 1918. At last the agony of flying aircraft off fore-decks and having to land them in the sea would be over. In the meantime an immediate expedient, flying off lighters towed behind destroyers, had enabled Lieutenant S. D. Culley to use his Camel to shoot down Zeppelin *L.53*. The first effective anti-submarine flying-boat, the Felixstowe F.2A, built to John Porte's ideas, had also come into service and became the forerunner of that most exclusive part of the future RAF, the flying-boat force.

And so the newborn Royal Air Force had proved lusty and full of fight, and was weaned in the testing environment of war. But now, scarcely seven months old, it faced a battle of a very different kind.

In Italy the small RAF force was primarily supporting the Army, although at one point a Camel squadron found and bombed an Austrian attack which was rushing across the Piave river; this application of initiative and determination stabilised the front and enabled the offensive to be contained. On the minor fronts there was little activity, as a result largely of the inadequacy of supplies coming out from the UK. However, in Palestine there happened one of the most significant events, from the point of view of air power, of the whole war. General Allenby, in the summer of 1918, mounted an offensive with the intention of removing Turkey from the war. The RAF forces soon established air superiority over the battlefield, denying the German fliers the ability to reconnoitre. This was possible because a sizeable force of RAF units had been slowly built up with its own training and reserve units in Egypt. Towards the end of September both the Turkish 7th and 8th Armies were in retreat, and their paths lay through narrow defiles in the desert. By noon on 19 September the Turkish 8th Army was found in one such

The RNAS spent World War I developing the flying-boat into a practical long-range reconnaissance and anti-submarine aircraft which became more and more successful. The RNAS squadrons became part of the RAF on its formation, and the RAF carried on the tradition. N4490 was a Felixstowe F.2A serving with No. 267 Squadron in Malta.

The Difficult Twenties

At the close of 'The Great War' a feeling of loathing permeated all levels of society. The carnage and horror of four years of static trench warfare, the scale of death when thousands were wiped out for the gaining of a few yards of ground and, at sea, the terrors of U-boat warfare, added up to such revulsion that when the war ended most people wanted to get straight out of uniform and forget it all. And when the British Army found that it could not just do this but was committed to Army of Occupation duties in Germany, and that the demobilisation plans were unfair, emotions sometimes erupted into mutiny.

For the Royal Air Force this was a time of great insecurity. On Armistice Day (11 November 1918) the RAF comprised 27,333 officers and 263,837 other ranks, with about 25,000 women in the Women's Royal Air Force as well. Total inventories showed that it possessed 22,647 aircraft, 3,300 of which were in front-line categories and 103 of which were airships. Never before or since was the RAF in possession of so many aircraft, but almost immediately it was apparent that there was little or no use for such a fleet: no future outbreak of war on a grandiose scale could be seen, for the major protagonists had been exhausted, and the British public was enamoured neither of the aeroplane nor of the Royal Air Force. The aeroplane, to quote Winston Churchill, was 'this cursed hellish invention' which now struck terror in the hearts of innocent civilians, and the Royal Air Force was so new and untried that it had won little understanding and no affection from the public who paid for it. For the first few months quite a sizeable contingent of flying units remained, but 1919 was a year in which squadron after squadron was reduced to cadre strength and then disbanded. And if this was not enough, the new Service knew that in the

wings were the big guns of the War Office and, perhaps more significantly, the Admiralty waiting to wrest the RAF apart and resume control over their own air services.

Then circumstances took a turn which could have been neither foreseen nor planned. December 1918 saw a quick election and David Lloyd George re-arranged his ministers. Prominent amongst these was Winston Churchill, who was offered either the Admiralty or the War Office, but was to take the Air Ministry with him in either case. With mutiny erupting in the Army, he felt duty bound to take the War Office and, because the opposition there was nowhere near as strong as in the Admiralty, he was able to maintain a separate air force. Not only that but, as future events showed only too well, if Churchill was 'on your side' things would get done. The second factor was the movements of Sir Hugh Trenchard, who found himself out of a job when the Independent Bombing Force was dissolved at the end of the war. He was seriously considering the Colonial Office for a job overseas when the Army asked him to do something about its mutineers. Trenchard stepped in and quelled an ugly situation at Southampton so effectively that Churchill took note, remembering also his already not inconsiderable experience of air matters. So it was that Churchill invited Trenchard back into the post of Chief of the Air Staff. No move could have made more sure the future of the Royal Air Force as an independent entity. In some respects Trenchard resembled Churchill in that he bent all his energies to whatever responsibilities he was given. Unlike Churchill, though, he could not remove himself from his own situation and see the logic of other people's arguments, but once he was commited to a responsibility his whole being was given to it. For example, as head of the RFC

One of Trenchard's innovations was to form the RAF's own college. This was at Cranwell in Lincolnshire (an ex-naval aerodrome). It was unique in having two separate aerodromes divided by the camp. Ever since the early 1920s, when this photograph was taken, Cranwell has been a hive of training activity. Although many modern buildings have been put up, the hangars in the foreground are still in use on the south airfield.

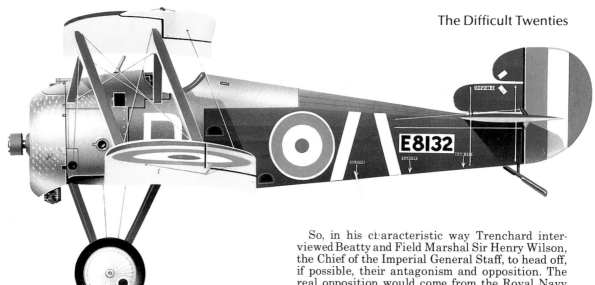

No. 208 Squadron received Sopwith Snipes in October 1918 and became the third squadron to re-equip with the type. They saw little service during the war, but remained overseas under the Army of Occupation until August 1919, when the squadron was disbanded.

in France in World War I he had opposed the formation of the Independent Bombing Force, but once made its commander his total loyalty was given to fostering it. Thus the RAF had now at its head the one man who could ensure its future, and backing him one of the most forceful personalities of British politics of this century. Whilst this augured well for the immediate future, Trenchard's blinkered attitude to anything that did not agree with his own views and responsibilities meant that built into his regime were certain weaknesses which were to rebound on the nation in the next large conflagration.

At a time of economic stringency, many a lesser man than Trenchard would have simply bargained to retain as much of the remains of the large air force as possible and, in so doing, lost a viable force completely to the onslaught of the Treasury and the other Service Chiefs. But Trenchard was not a man just to preserve a status quo or to be content with working on anything but his own terms, so he set out to build a new Air Force, a permanent edifice which would stand the test of future trends in war and be the sort of force that could be rapidly expanded from a core whose basic organisation was sound. And what he built was the work of a visionary; that it was built at all was the result of his dogged sense of purpose allied to sound common sense in dealing with others at high level. The Government would inevitably be lukewarm towards the continuance of the RAF because of the monetary drain a third service would entail. The other services were anxious to regain their own air arms and in the post-war climate could easily gun Trenchard's Air Force out of existence, and Trenchard knew that, because Admiral of the Fleet Lord Beatty headed the Royal Navy and was a popular figure, he had a formidable opponent.

So, in his characteristic way Trenchard interviewed Beatty and Field Marshal Sir Henry Wilson, the Chief of the Imperial General Staff, to head off, if possible, their antagonism and opposition. The real opposition would come from the Royal Navy so Trenchard extracted from Beatty a promise to give him (Trenchard) a year's grace 'out of a sense of fair play', and Wilson agreed to go along with this; Wilson was too apathetic to take action on his own. Beatty had underestimated Trenchard's ability, for that year was enough – having headed off this attack he could now apply all his superabundant energy to securing the Royal Air Force over that year. This pact was made in December 1919. In that same month there appeared a White Paper which was in effect Trenchard's Memorandum as to how the new Air Force should be established. It contains informative and enlightening statements and ideas, more so as read with hindsight, and the core of it all, the *raison d'être* for the peacetime Royal Air Force, can be summed up in these words of Trenchard from the preface:

'The principle to be kept in mind in forming the framework of the Royal Air Force is that the main portion of it will consist of an Independent Force, together with service personnel required in carrying out aeronautical research. In addition there will be a small part of it specially trained for work with the navy, and a small part trained for work with the army, *these two small portions probably becoming, in future, an arm of the older service.* It may be that the main portion, the Independent Air Force, will grow larger and larger and become more and more the predominating factor in all types of warfare...'

Had the portion italicised by the author, put in by Trenchard as a sop to Wilson and Beatty, come to pass sooner than it did, the next war might have been more successfully waged. But for all that these words were prophetic indeed.

Training facilities

Trenchard could see that a Royal Air Force could only survive and achieve its future if it built its own traditions on its own foundations, and so rightly he spurned the overtures of the other services to provide training in their cadet and staff colleges; the building of the new RAF Cadet College at Cranwell went ahead. It was recognised that the RAF would require a much higher proportion of officers than the other two services, so Trenchard proposed a system of short-service commissions for two-thirds of his officer force, a system which thus would ensure a favourable rate of promotion for the one-third core of permanent officers. To cope with the fact that the RAF would be a highly technical service he inaugurated an apprentice scheme for boy entrants ('Trenchard's Brats' as they were known) and the big camp at Halton became the centre of technical training for this purpose. He also inaugurated a scheme for a territorial arm which blossomed into the Auxiliary Air Force in the years ahead. Trenchard was building for permanence and for excellence, and so he was content to build small; never was quality sacrificed for quantity, and this was the foundation on which the peacetime RAF was built.

But with all this going on in Whitehall, what had

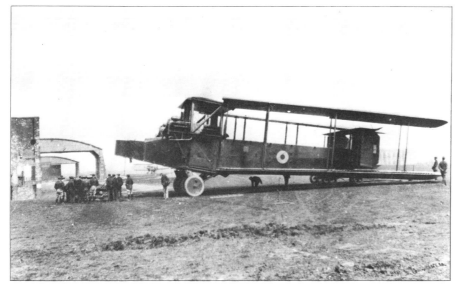

Coming into service just too late to become operational was the RAF's first four-engine heavy bomber, the Handley Page V/1500. Two squadrons, Nos 166 and 167, formed at Bircham Newton in Norfolk to bomb Berlin but the armistice intervened and little use was found for the V/1500s after that.

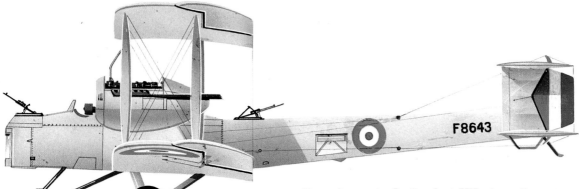

The Vickers Vimy served from late 1918 until 1931. This example flew with No. 70 Squadron, based at Heliopolis in 1921.

F8643

been happening on the seemingly innumerable airfields and camps where the RAF existed? At many of them it was a sad story, for the Royal Air Force had now to be reduced to a minimal size which meant the disposal of aircraft, stores, equipment, bases and personnel; and there is no situation where morale can drop more quickly than on an airfield which is to be closed, with equipment waiting to be sold and personnel waiting to be posted or 'demobbed'. But this was the situation throughout, and Trenchard, ever the realist, would slip away from his office betimes and visit one station or another unannounced to find the temper of the officers and men, and to lift their hearts beyond the depressing present to the more hopeful future. Small wonder, then, that this gruff and uncommunicative man yet found a way of winning the hearts of those men who were to form the core of his early peacetime RAF. This loyalty to Trenchard and the traditions he was fostering were the hidden foundations upon which the RAF stood when war again engulfed the world.

The proponents of aviation were quicker to expect the blossoming of civil flying than it actually appeared. True, the Royal Air Force had formed No. 86 (Communications) Wing at Hendon in December 1918 to provide a budding airline between London and Paris for the peace conference and the travels of civil servants between the two capitals. But the Department of Civil Aviation, formed a month later (and providing Churchill with a suitable post into which to move Major General Sir Frederick Sykes, so as to enable Trenchard to take his place as Chief of Air Staff) was more involved in setting up its own rules and regulations than in administering a booming new civil aviation for some time yet. Because civil aviation was slow off the mark, the Royal Air

Force began to fly the first UK air mail service. The service was inaugurated in March 1919, and the two terminals were Folkestone and Cologne, the mail carried being for the Army of Occupation which was still holding in Germany a good number of soldiers and airmen, many of whom were anxious to become civilians once more. The RAF at home was temporarily reorganised into three areas (the Southern Area, the Northern Area and the Coastal Area), the last embracing most of the home shore-based units which had been part of the RNAS and whose task was co-operation with the Royal Navy. A month later, in October 1919, Trenchard founded the RAF Benevolent Fund to cater for the needs of all those within or attached to the new service whose lives were tragically affected by the misfortunes of peace or war, an organisation which is with us today and through whom thousands have found not only relief and material comfort but companionship as well.

Somaliland

As part of the memorandum of December 1919, Trenchard listed the order of battle for his immediate peacetime Royal Air Force. No one could have accused Trenchard of building up an independent striking force at home at the expense of units for working with the Army and Navy – his once-proud Independent Bombing Force now consisted of two squadrons. The most surprising feature, and one on which the critics fastened, was the high proportion of the RAF's strength being overseas. To all such criticism the Chief of Air Staff's answer was brief and to the point: 'The first duty of the Royal Air Force is to garrison the British Empire.' And it was in India, Mesopotamia, and all points east and south that independent air power now began to show its great potential.

In British Somaliland there existed a bandit who, since the beginning of the century, had been a festering sore in the side of the civil administration and thus of the Colonial Office. Known as 'The Mad

The Avro 504K had been the universal trainer in service during World War I, and it soldiered on in the newly-formed flying training schools in the 1920s. One such school was established at Abu Sueir in Egypt, and it was to that unit which this particular machine belonged.

Mullah', he had used World War I as an opportunity to consolidate his position and the issue had become so fraught that either a full-scale military expedition was needed to winkle him and his supporters out of their well-built forts, or the territory would have to be abandoned to him. In the first two decades millions of pounds and many lives had been spent in inconclusive and often disastrous fighting (to quote the Colonial Under-Secretary). In Somaliland were a battalion of the King's African Rifles and, more importantly, a compact force of 500 men comprising the Camel Corps. Into this situation Trenchard suggested he send bombers and take over the campaign. The Army was horrified but, wearying of mounting a full-scale campaign, allowed him to try. So in January 1920 12 D.H.9 aircraft under the command of Group Captain R. Gordon (calling itself 'Z' Force) sailed to Somaliland in HMS *Ark Royal*, and, beginning on 21 January, bombed the Mullah's main camp and one other fort. Seven days later the Mullah was in full retreat and the Camel Corps moved in to occupy his forts. By 9 February, as a result of the bombing, the campaign was over and the Mullah's forces reduced to four men. Eventually he was killed over the border in Abyssinia. Here was a resounding success for the Royal Air Force – Trenchard and Churchill hailed it as such and the Colonial Office also acknowledged it. For £77,000 and three weeks' action there had been resolved a situation which had looked unanswerable on a small scale. Somaliland was to enjoy undisturbed peace until World War II brought the Italians.

Imperial expansion

Of course one small campaign did not prove everything, but it gave the Royal Air Force the confidence to see a way ahead, a justification for its presence in the farthest parts of the British Empire. One such part was the North West Frontier of India, where there were stationed squadrons of general-purpose two-seaters, Bristol Fighters which had been prominent as fighters in the last two years of World War I. There had been two squadrons (Nos 31 & 114) in India during that war, battling with the Pathan tribesmen raiding in the hills; now that the Third Afghan War had begun these two were reinforced by two others (Nos 20 and 48, the latter being the original Bristol Fighter Squadron) and by June there were over 36 'Brisfits', as they soon became known, in action on the North

West Frontier. A complication here was that the money for the RAF forces in India was voted by the Indian Government, and consequently it was negligible compared with that supplied to home units. As a result the crews were flying on operations with aircraft having only one magneto, no tyres on the wheels etc. This was eventually remedied by an investigation by Air Vice Marshal Sir John Salmond but not until 1922 – for two years the situation festered and at least one squadron commander, later to make a name for himself as head of wartime Bomber Command – Arthur Harris – refused to send his crews out on operations and attempted to resign from the RAF.

Back at home developments moved on apace. On 5 February 1920 the RAF College opened at Cranwell near Sleaford in Lincolnshire, with one of Trenchard's men, Air Commodore C. A. H. Longcroft, as Commandant. This cocked a snook at the Admirals and Generals who had patronisingly recommended that they could provide officer training for the fledgling Air Force to enable it to get on with the flying; Trenchard knew that the Royal Air Force would only prosper by forging its own traditions. Quality was of the utmost importance and so, when the RAF Central Band was formed at Uxbridge on 1 April 1920, it contained musicians of a very high standard indeed. But as far as the British public was concerned, the RAF event of the year, and the one which began to put the Service on the map and in people's hearts, was the RAF Tournament which took place at Hendon on 3 July.

Sir John Salmond had supervised the flying display, much practice going into the efforts of the small band of RAF aviators. On the day, which was sunny and dry, the crowds flocked in (official figures being 60,000) but countless more watched from the hill opposite. All the emphasis on quality now paid off, for the flying display of aerobatics, bombing raids and formation flying was something that the British public had never seen on this scale or to such a high degree, and the Press was impressed – and said so. Even Admiral Beatty, who was still in his 'year of restraint', congratulated Trenchard. But it was not simply those at the top for whom the Tournament did something. The Royal Air Force had had a hard time since the Armistice with demobilisation, recession and uncertainty; its members knew that to most people the RAF was an upstart and inferior to the older services. So the Tournament gave a great fillip not

An early post-war attempt at a long-range bomber, albeit single-engined, was the Avro Aldershot which saw limited service with No. 99 Squadron for just over a year in 1924.

Vickers Vimy

The Vickers FB.27 Vimy bomber arrived in RAF service just too late to see action in World War I. It continued in production, however, and became the standard heavy bomber for the beginnings of the 1920s. Several aircraft were sold for civilian use and were used for trail-blazing long-distance flights – across the Atlantic and from England to Australia being just two such feats. Those in RAF service were used mainly in the Middle East, with Nos 45, 58, 70, 216 Squadrons and No. 4 Flying Training School, whilst Nos 7 and 9 Squadrons in the UK together with 'D' Flight of No. 100 Squadron also flew them until re-equipped with Virginias. The aircraft shown, F3184, served in Egypt with No. 70 Squadron.

F
3184

F 3184

only to the aircrew and groundcrew taking part, but to all members who saw in their papers next day the complimentary remarks which even those newspapers formerly dedicated to its demise (principally the Northcliffe and Beaverbrook press) produced.

But what aircraft did the public see at Hendon? The RAF at this time was equipped with the many excellent aircraft with which it ended the war and a few which were just about to come into service when hostilities were concluded. For fighter duties the Sopwith Camel and RAF S.E.5a which had fought so successfully in France were all but extinct, their places being taken by Sopwith's more powerful fighter, the Snipe. Army Co-operation, for long the province of the aircraft from the Royal Aircraft Factory (now renamed Royal Aircraft Establishment) at Farnborough, was now being taken over by the many surplus Bristol Fighter two-seaters, although some R.E.8s remained. Bombing, which had been in the hands of the Handley Page O/400s, quickly passed to the Vickers Vimy, a new bomber just about to appear at the end of the war and which leapt into worldwide fame when Alcock and Brown crossed the Atlantic in one. Handley Page had built a superbomber, the four-engined V/1500, designed to bomb Berlin from the UK, and a wing of these large aircraft had been working up when the war ended; but peacetime requirements found them too large and uneconomical so they also soon disappeared. Light bombing became the prerogative of the de Havilland stable. The D.H.4 had gone, except with the American forces, its successor the D.H.9 was in service, but unsatisfactorily so because of its unreliable engine, and the definitive light bomber became the D.H.9A, the same aircraft re-engined with a 400-hp (298-kW) Liberty engine. For torpedo-bombing there was the Sopwith Cuckoo, whilst the coastal units forged on with Felixstowe flying-boats and a variety of floatplanes. Training was ubiquitously in the cockpits of the Avro 504K. These were the types with which the Royal Air Force cut its teeth as a permanent service, and three of them (the Avro 504K, Bristol Fighter and D.H.9A) were still in service at the end of the decade.

But now further trouble arose overseas, this time in Iraq where Great Britain had been given a mandate to develop the new state until it could itself form its own entity. This was not recognised by some of the powerful Arabs of the day or by Turkey, and so there was much fighting, largely in the form of border incursions and riots. This, by a strange coincidence, now came into Winston Churchill's province, for he had lately moved from the War Office to the Colonial Office. With Somaliland in mind, Churchill achieved Cabinet agreement that the RAF should take over from the Army the policing of Iraq; the overriding considerations were those of finance, this being the language that talked most accommodatingly to politicians then as now. Churchill immediately called a conference in Cairo, where he told all concerned in the Middle East that this plan would be put into effect, despite their protests, and the Royal Air Force (from March 1921) had to take over control from the Army within the course of 18 months.

Political struggles

Now the RAF had a specific responsibility which underlined its existence. This was more than fortunate, for the year of restraint with Beatty and Wilson was now over and both War Office and Admiralty were turning their guns on the Royal Air Force with the vigour of a year of repression. The battle was on, and it became primarily a contest between Beatty and Trenchard: the War Office opposition did not really come to very much. This was probably just as well, for the Army was in fact not so badly off with its Army Co-operation Squadrons of the RAF as was the Navy with its air force contingents; the various squadrons allotted to the army co-ordinated well with the ground units to which they were attached. This was not so with the Navy, which was in a difficult position anyway, for when the RAF had been formed most of the naval pilots had transferred to the new service while other aircrew members had preferred to stay within the Navy. The Navy's body of experience on aviation matters, therefore, came largely from the Observers who remained within its ranks. This situation was worsened when the arguments were settled in 1923: Trenchard, maintaining his 'Unity of the Air' policy, stuck to his idea that the air power needed by the Navy should be provided by the RAF, a fallacious argument which has been proved wrong on other occasions since but which descendants of Trenchard still put forward today as an argument to get their share of Treasury pickings in these days of stringency. Beatty affirmed that the true flush-decked aircraft-carriers, developed by 1923, needed RN aircraft and RN crews in order to provide the Royal Navy's own air cover and air power and, knowing how nearly

One of the earliest examples of the RAF's mobility to meet crises in different parts of the world was the Chanak crisis in Turkey in 1922. No. 208 Squadron, flying Bristol Fighters in Egypt, flew across and maintained patrols. The squadron's aircraft carried cartoon characters on their fins.

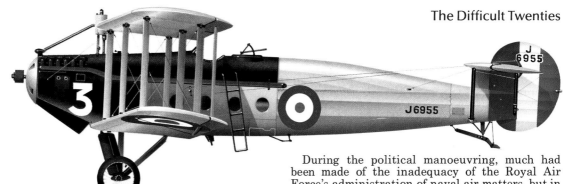

The Avro 549 Aldershot III single-engined heavy bomber was built only in small numbers, the only squadron equipped with the type being No. 99.

Commander Samson had pioneered the use of armoured cars in World War I, and such vehicles became an integral part of the RAF overseas in Egypt and Iraq, where one is seen leading a convoy up a pass during the 1920s.

Britain had been defeated by the U-Boat campaign in World War I, he argued that sea power was still the key to the British Empire's defence. Trenchard, however, faithful to his vision, saw the air becoming the primary battlefield with nations subdued by 'repeated incursions on a large scale by hostile aircraft'. In those days no one could say for sure who was right; now it can be seen that events of World War II went to prove that Beatty was nearer the mark although, had the country not had the Royal Air Force to fight the Battle of Britain, who knows but that Trenchard's fears of Britain's downfall to hordes of enemy bombers might not have come true. Even now the answers are by no means conclusive.

The protagonists came to a deadlock in their bitter quarrels in mid-1921 and Lord Balfour with his Committee of Imperial Defence was called in to establish a verdict on the claims and counter-claims; he came down heavily on the side of an autonomous air force. But the battle was not over, and for the next two years all manner of means were raised to pull down the building that Trenchard had created. Later in 1921 the Geddes Inquiry into government expenditure almost halted the building programme upon which the RAF was dependent. All through 1922 the arguments, like a desultory thunderstorm, rumbled on in Parliament and Whitehall; the Chanak crisis in Turkey was the one factor which united the Chiefs of Staff in having to prepare for the immediacy of war, but that same crisis forced a general election, and with a new prime minister, Arthur Bonar Law, the whole question of the necessity or not of an Independent Air Force was raised once again. Eventually in 1923 Lord Balfour was again called upon to head the committee which had, again, to arbitrate between Beatty and Trenchard. Before this committee, however, the Navy overstated its case, with the result that the recommendations went in favour of retaining the Royal Air Force (but made some important suggestions as to improved naval/air co-operation). Beatty and the Board of Admiralty thereupon threatened to resign en masse if the government took up the Balfour Committee's recommendations, but when the Cabinet endorsed the recommendations this threat was proved to be a bluff. And so at last the wrangle was settled, at least for a decade and a half; Trenchard could now concentrate upon the more positive task of building his Royal Air Force.

During the political manoeuvring, much had been made of the inadequacy of the Royal Air Force's administration of naval air matters, but in reality how had things progressed since the RNAS had dissolved?

Probably the most important factor in naval aviation at this time was the arrival on the scene of HMS *Argus*. This vessel was the final solution in the long quest for a ship which could be used with full practicality for aircraft landing and taking off. It had a flush-deck and the boiler exhausts were aft so that nothing impeded the passage of the aircraft. The problem now became one of arresting aircraft after landing, but this did not prevent the practical operation of aircraft – the Royal Navy now had a real aircraft-carrier. As soon as financial conditions permitted, HMS *Furious* went in for rebuilding with a flush-deck, and in the meantime a Chilean battleship was converted to become HMS *Eagle*, which differed from the other two in having a superstructure on the starboard side with a conning tower and two funnels, aerials and the like, but a flying deck unobstructed from stem to stern. She came into commission in 1923. Supporting these two were sundry seaplane carriers still working on the restricted principles of the wartime flights, and on these ships disported the one squadron for spotting and reconnaissance, the Fleet Fighter Flight, the half squadron of torpedo-bombers, and the seaplane flight which was all the Royal Air Force possessed for naval co-operation except for the Flying-boat Flight, which was shore-based. Like the rest of the RAF, the 'Coastal Area' was in the main using wartime aircraft, although special deck-landing aircraft were soon produced and in many cases soon discarded. Because most of the Royal Navy's expertise on air matters came from observers, the specifications for their new FSR (Fleet Spotter Reconnaissance) aeroplanes centred around the job of the observer and looked for all the world like flying chartrooms, with wings appended and the pilot perched up on top as an afterthought. In any case, to design an aircraft for carrier operation is an exacting task and some of the answers to the Royal Navy's well-nigh impossible requests were odd in the extreme. Of course, at carrier level interservice rivalry was at its minimum, the sailors and airmen by and large worked together with a good will, albeit spiced with good-humoured badinage. The Balfour Committee ruled that all the observers in naval aircraft should be naval officers, but the squadrons themselves were part of the Royal Air Force and most of the pilots belonged to that junior service. Between them the officers and men of the two services worked together to hammer out the remaining problems of carrier operations.

Overseas skirmishes

Once again it was overseas that the developments were taking place which pushed the RAF forward operationally. Iraq was the area where this was worked out, and it was here that the early beginnings in Somaliland were developed to great effect. As previously mentioned, the RAF was to take over complete responsibility for the control of Iraq from October 1922, and the method of air policing which the RAF evolved was quite revolutionary. Hitherto policing had been a costly army affair, involving the holding down of comparatively large numbers of troops to keep an eye on the warring and highly mobile tribes. This was expensive not only in terms of money but of lives, for the desert heat and disease, as well as the opposition, took their toll of the soldiers. However, the RAF managed things differently; where a group of dissidents was making a nuisance of itself, the RAF would deliver a note to the villagers to the effect that unless they toed the line, their village would be bombed on such and such a day, giving them plenty of time to evacuate it. From then on the life of hostile natives was completely interrupted with the minimum of damage and little or no casualties to either side. This method was highly successful, providing a more stable situation for a fraction of the cost and trouble, in Iraq, where the League of Nations' mandate had reckoned without the opposition of the local sheikhs, who would much rather have been left to their own lawlessness, and without the latent ambitions of Turkey, eager to regain its lost territory.

These two features came to the boil in many a small skirmish but, with the activities of Sheik Mahmud in Kurdistan, affairs were more than just a skirmish. This man had been in official power on and off since World War I, having been appointed by the British and then dismissed after open revolt. This had happened not once but several times, and by early 1923 he had gathered a large force who advanced on Kirkuk in north east Iraq. The RAF immediately flew in troops to bolster the garrison; they arrived in the nick of time as the town was already being invested, but the sight of several hundred troops fresh into battle drove the invaders away without a pitched battle. From then on Mahmud was harassed by the RAF and he, and his Turkish supporters who had had an eye for the main chance of furthering their own interests, had no peace and security of tenure, being confined to making occasional raids over the border from Persia – a far cry from the repossession of the land which was their primary aim. Their raids continued on and off for more than a decade, but never did they become a serious threat whilst the RAF had control over Iraq. Air Marshal Sir John Salmond was in charge and had a large HQ airfield at Hinaidi where there were stationed some five squadrons, one squadron down the Persian Gulf at Shaibah, one station at Mosul in the north and one at Kirkuk in the north east, each with one squadron. Most of these squadrons were flying World War I aircraft, the only exception being the two transport squadrons, Nos 45 and 70, which operated the Vickers Vernon, an aircraft which came about as a result of Vickers' wish to produce an early airliner. What the company had done, in essence, was to take the proven Vimy bomber and put a new voluminous fuselage on the airframe. This had a cabin capable of holding 11 people and was called the Vimy Commercial. When it appeared with RAF roundels it was renamed the Vernon and was equipped with stretcher facilities as well for casualty evacuation. The RAF bought the type to fulfil a basically peaceable task in 1921: when the Iraq responsibility fell on RAF shoulders it was obvious that a regular transport service between Egypt and Baghdad would be essential, and that this could not be flown around the corners of the Arabian peninsula. To fly the 800 miles (1290 km) or so across the featureless desert between Cairo and Baghdad was beyond the capabilities of the navigation equipment of the day, so the RAF ploughed a track right across the desert and set landing grounds at intervals along this track. Fuel installations were dug into the sand and a force of armoured cars patrolled the track's length. All the pilots had to do was to follow the furrow and, if in difficulty, land at the nearest landing ground. The simplicity of it all meant that a regular service could be maintained over impossible terrain with little or no trouble, and the Vernons were acquired for this task. It was found that in the prevailing hot climate their engines were not powerful enough, but once the Rolls-Royce Eagles had been replaced by Napier Lions all was well. So Nos 45 and 70 Squadrons opened up a weekly mail service between Cairo and Baghdad with the inaugural flight on 23 June 1923. Originally these aircraft were intended for troop transport only, but when they arrived in Iraq their user squadrons rigged them up as bombers as well and they were soon classified as bomber-transports. As such they were a great success, having an overawing effect on the Arab tribes lacking in the smaller D.H.9As and Bristol Fighters. This class of aircraft, peculiar to this type of situation, persisted until mid-World War II, the Vernons being succeeded by Vickers Victorias and then by Vickers Valentias and finally by Bristol Bombays.

The '52 squadrons'

So successful had the Iraq operation been that the similar policy was laid down for other areas where Great Britain had mandates for supervision: in April 1924 a similar but smaller organisation was set up in Palestine, and in February 1928 Aden Command was formed, both successfully applying the lessons learnt in Iraq. Had similar responsibilities been given on the North West Frontier of India a similar success story might have taken place, but there the army retained control with the RAF simply in the role of army co-operation.

Developed from the Vimy of transatlantic fame came the Vickers Vernon. Two squadrons, Nos 45 and 70, flew these from Hinaidi in Iraq to maintain an air route across the Arabian desert to Egypt, presaging the Imperial Airways routes of later years.

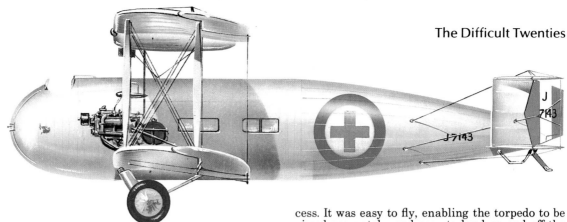

The Vickers Vernon was the first aircraft designed specifically as a troop carrier to enter service with the RAF, in 1921. Illustrated is one of the Vernon IIIs equipped specially for ambulance duty.

At Ziza in 1924 are seen the two arms of the RAF together; the armoured cars and the D.H.9A aircraft both carry No. 30 Squadron's insignia.

As the 1920s progressed, so the RAF gained ground. In June 1923, following the Salisbury Report, the Prime Minister authorised a Home Defence Force of 52 squadrons, a far cry from the two which Trenchard had allowed himself only three years before. However, even a decade later these 52 squadrons had not appeared, and the promise needed the scares of the 1930s before it came to pass. Trenchard's Short Service Commission Scheme came into being at the outset of 1924, with the Air Ministry calling for 400 officers. It was in this year, too, that the first positive steps were taken to advance the research and development side of the RAF with the setting up of the Aeroplane and Armament Experimental Establishment at Martlesham Heath (from where it moved to Boscombe Down on the outbreak of World War II) and the Marine Aircraft Experimental Establishment at Felixstowe, a base where all the flying-boat developmental work which Porte had put in during World War I was now officially recognised and expanded. It was to these two establishments that came the first generation of new aircraft which replaced the veterans from World War I, which were still providing the backbone of the growing RAF.

It was at this time, too, that the official Fleet Air Arm of the Royal Air Force was formed, resulting from the Balfour Committee and its 1923 recommendations. Instead of returning the old RNAS squadrons, now renumbered in the 200 series, the whole organisation was set up on the basis of Fleet Flights, now numbered in the 400 series, based principally at Leuchars in Scotland and Gosport in southern England. At first there were two Fleet Fighter Flights, flying the Nieuport Nightjar, a post-war fighter not unlike the Sopwith Snipe; three Fleet Spotter Reconnaissance Flights with the Westland Walrus at Gosport (the Walrus was basically a D.H.9A which had been modified to fly naval tasks and looked not only pregnant but with a goitre as well!); a flying-boat flight at Leuchars with the Supermarine Seagull amphibian together with two flights of Parnall Panther spotter aircraft; at Gosport two torpedo bomber reconnaissance flights with the Blackburn Dart; and at Calshot seaplane base the one Flying-boat Flight, equipped with the Felixstowe F.5. The Parnall Panther was a tiny little hump-backed biplane with a folding fuselage for shipboard operation, flotation bags in the bottom wings and a hydrovane in case of forced landings. It did not last long and was chiefly notable as a pioneer in the development of deck-landing. The Blackburn Dart, however, was a more lasting proposition and was the first post-war aircraft for fleet use that was an unqualified suc-cess. It was easy to fly, enabling the torpedo to be aimed accurately, and easy to land on and off the carriers, so it served with the Fleet Air Arm for a whole decade.

Following hard on the heels of this reorganisation came Trenchard's new look at the Home Defence line-up, which was now entitled Air Defence of Great Britain. This had four divisions (the Bombing Area, Fighting Area, Special Reserve and Auxiliary Air Force). The two latter need some explanation, and arose out of Trenchard's desire to exploit the potential of retired officers and airmen into the equivalent of a Territorial Army, together with others, of a high quality, who would take up military aviation as a weekend occupation. The Special Reserve Squadrons, of which there were at one time five, were approximately one-third regular personnel and two-thirds local volunteers. The Auxiliary Air Force comprised 16 squadrons which had a small core of regulars and the rest 'weekend airmen'. They were based at military airfields adjoining towns where they would find sufficient volunteers, and were associated with the local county or city. The very first actually to form was No. 602 (Auxiliary) Squadron (City of Glasgow), which came into being at Renfrew on 12 September 1925, but within a month three others had formed, two at Hendon in the form of No. 600 (City of London) and No. 601 (County of London), and one at Turnhouse in the form of No. 603 (City of Edinburgh). The contribution that these units made to World War II is well known, and we shall refer to them again later. At this stage they were very much an unknown quantity and had to prove themselves to a sceptical public and regular air force.

University Air Squadrons

Another of Trenchard's bright ideas came to fruition in 1925. He was anxious, as always, to attract the finest type of officer into the RAF for his permanent commissions, and to do this he had intense competition from the older services. So he set up at the universities what were known as University Air Squadrons, with the object of providing early training in flying and RAF matters to undergraduates, with the opportunity of moving on into the RAF as a career. Not only did these Air Squadrons catch many good men for the RAF, but they also played a very prominent part in spreading that vital quality – airmindedness – amongst one of the most important sectors of the nation. The first two University Air Squadrons sprouted in 1925 at Oxford and Cambridge but by the late 1930s no self-respecting university was without one.

And so by the mid-1920s the Royal Air Force could begin to relax. Its beginnings had been in the heat of war but its development had been in another climate, that of feud and intrigue between those to whom it would look for support, and for five years its whole being had virtually rested in the strength of one man, 'Boom' Trenchard, called the Father of the RAF. But he and his loyal subordinates had won through and produced an altogether unexpectedly sturdy youngster to take its place in the triumvirate of Britain's defence forces. By the end of 1925 the RAF had found its position in the country and its popularity was at last in the ascendant, as could be seen at the now-annual Hendon Pageants. Now the young service could afford itself a modest expansion into the carefree atmosphere of the late 1920s.

A Decade of Peace and Development

Although there were still alarums and excursions in the political field for the Royal Air Force during the years from 1925 to 1935, these were not of the magnitude of its early days and boiled down in essence to financial restrictions as a result of the sombre economic climate of those years – the General Strike of 1926 and the following Depression. These were times when Treasury cuts faced the services, and each service fought the others to preserve its own programmes; the old call for the dismemberment of the RAF was heard in the background, but never with the force or insistence of the past. So the outcome of these pinch-penny days was to slow the RAF's expansion towards the 52-squadron goal established in June 1923.

At the level of the average RAF station, life was now taking on a much more secure form and the service was already beginning to respect and foster its own traditions. In many realms, not least in sport, the Royal Air Force was showing that its men and methods were second to none. The Locarno Pact had produced an air of peace in Europe and peacetime life in the RAF was good, very good; it was divided between rigorous training combined with generous leisure activities. For the officers particularly the social scene developed, but for all there was the excitement of participation in the annual Hendon Pageants and an increasing number of air displays at which invariably the RAF's aircraft were the most exciting present, coupled with the development of new types and new equipment.

The basic types of aircraft which the RAF was flying at the end of the 1920s differed little from those it inherited at the end of World War I. The fighters were still single-seat biplanes with two machine-guns firing through the propeller disc, the day bombers differed little from the D.H.9A (in fact many of them still were D.H.9As) and the night bombers and flying-boats followed the same general configuration and performance as the Handley Page O/400 and Felixstowe F.5.

The first post-war generation of fighters comprised the Armstrong Whitworth Siskin III and the Gloster Grebe II, which between them equipped seven home fighter squadrons. Neither manu-

Between the world wars the Gloster Aircraft Company produced a fine range of radial-engined fighters for the RAF. The second such type was the Gloster Gamecock, seen here in service with No. 23 Squadron at Kenley in 1927.

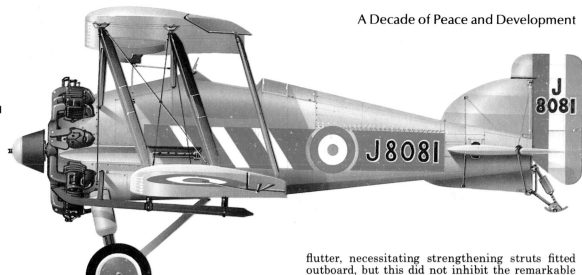

The most potent fighter in the RAF in the early 1920s was the Gloster Gamecock, a pilot's aeroplane and responsible for many fine aerobatic displays. J8081 served with No. 32 Squadron at Kenley between 1926 and 1928 and carries the squadron's blue band with white diagonal insignia.

To overcome the perennial chore of prop-swinging and to speed up the process for fighters needing a speedy take-off, the Hucks Starter was brought into service. It was a spindle attached to the drive of a car which rotated the hub of the aircraft's propeller at the same time as the pilot switched on. It is seen here in operation on a Siskin Mk III of No. 111 Squadron.

flutter, necessitating strengthening struts fitted outboard, but this did not inhibit the remarkable aerobatic displays with which squadron pilots displayed their Gamecocks.

On the bomber side the D.H.9A was still to the fore but was rapidly overhauled by the Fairey IIIF; this latter was a refined development of the Fairey III series which had started back in 1917. Powered by a close-cowled Napier Lion XIA engine of 570 hp (425 kW), the Fairey IIIF became the general-purpose aircraft *par excellence* of the late 1920s and early 1930s. Not only did it equip the day-bomber squadrons, but it also served the Fleet Air Arm with distinction, both with wheels and floats. Over a period of six years more than 600 were built, a large total for those years. From the same stable, too, came the Fairey Fox. Richard Fairey had acquired a Curtiss D.12 engine from America and built around it an airframe which cut drag to the minimum by careful design and attention to detail; the result was a day bomber with a higher performance than that of current fighters. When Sir Hugh Trenchard saw it he ordered a squadron at once, but only that one squadron could be wrung out of the Treasury. So No. 12 Squadron became the proud possessors of the Fairey Fox in the RAF, a fact commemorated in their badge (today to be seen on the side of their BAe Buccaneers). 'Shiny Twelve', as it was called because of its highly-polished aircraft, proved an acute embarrassment to the fighter squadrons during the annual exercises for quite a few years to come by being un-catchable.

The heavy bombers largely came from two stables, Frederick Handley Page's works at Crickle-wood and the Vickers Company at Weybridge, where the latter's designs flew from inside the Brooklands racing track. Handley Page continued its line of large aircraft producing a basic airframe which became the W.8 airliner, or the Hyderabad

facturer was resting on its laurels, however, and successors soon entered service. The Siskin III was replaced by the Siskin IIIA, which was the first all-metal aircraft (fabric-covered) to enter the service. It had a much more powerful version of the Armstrong Siddeley Jaguar engine, the Mk IV, which gave it a maximum speed at sea level of 156 mph (251 km/h) and a climb to 5,000 ft (1525 m) in 3 minutes 30 seconds. Such figures were almost exactly equalled by Gloster's Gamecock which, engined with the Bristol Jupiter VI, embodied much of what Gloster had learned with the Grebe and was a magnificent pilot's aeroplane evoking much affection from those who flew it. Both the Grebe and the Gamecock had troubles with wing

The D.H.9A was one of the RAF's 'maids of all work' of the 1920s. Particularly valuable service was flown in India and Iraq on patrol and policing duties, and No. 8 Squadron's 'Nine-Acks' were operated from Hinaidi on just such missions.

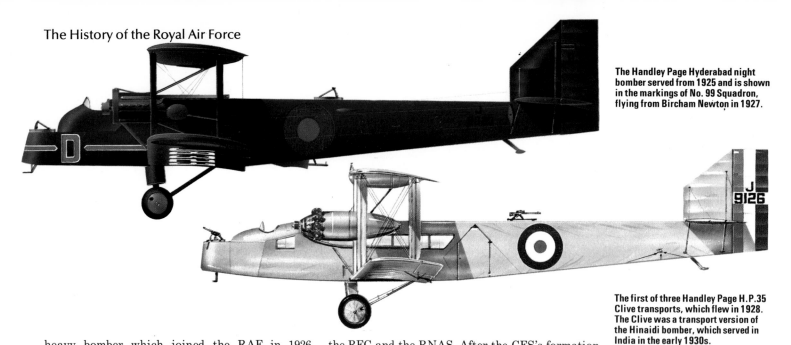

The Handley Page Hyderabad night bomber served from 1925 and is shown in the markings of No. 99 Squadron, flying from Bircham Newton in 1927.

The first of three Handley Page H.P.35 Clive transports, which flew in 1928. The Clive was a transport version of the Hinaidi bomber, which served in India in the early 1930s.

heavy bomber which joined the RAF in 1926, replacing the single-engined Avro Aldershot. The Hyderabad had two Napier Lion engines totalling 908 hp (677 kW). This aircraft was further developed by going from wooden construction to metal and re-engining with Bristol Jupiter radial engines, so becoming the Hinaidi with marginally improved performance and serving with the RAF until the end of 1933. Vickers developed from the Vimy and Vernon a heavy bomber (known in those days as night bombers) which lasted right through until World War II and was produced in 10 different marks: this was the Virginia, a Napier Lion-engined stalwart which first entered service in 1924 and in its time equipped most of the RAF's heavy bomber squadrons.

For army co-operation duties Armstrong Whitworth had produced the Atlas, which served satisfactorily with the one Egypt-based and three home-based squadrons, replacing Bristol Fighters. But in Iraq and India the wartime D.H.9As and Bristols continued to reign supreme, joined by the Westland Wapiti. This aircraft was typical of the stringencies of the period, for Westlands had been ordered to design a new aeroplane to use up surplus D.H.9A wings and the Wapiti, with its Bristol Jupiter engine, was just that – a general-purpose biplane which served faithfully in Iraq and India. Transport work was carried out by the balloon-fuselaged edition of the Virginia called the Victoria, whilst training was still the prerogative of the Avro 504, now re-engined with the Lynx radial, and the Bristol Fighter.

Mention of training inevitably focuses attention on one aspect of the RAF which is often overlooked, but which was and still is one of the greatest factors in the success of the Royal Air Force. When British military aviation began, the necessity for training was paramount but was seen then as merely the adapting of aviators for military flying, these aviators having already obtained their own flying certificates from the Royal Aero Club. For this purpose the Central Flying School had been established at Upavon on Salisbury Plain in the summer of 1912, to meet the training needs of both

the RFC and the RNAS. After the CFS's formation the Navy paid little more than lip service to it, using its own training organisation because the CFS was administered by the War Office and the Navy felt, with some degree of reason perhaps, that such an establishment could not train men adequately for naval flying.

Demand for pilots

Under the spur of war, with a great demand for new pilots for the rapidly expanding aerial services, the training of pilots became something which was considered a necessary evil and became the responsibility of pilots resting from their exertions over the Western Front or those who were not sufficiently capable for war flying – it was almost true of the training scene to use Bernard Shaw's old adage: 'Those who can, do; those who can't, teach.' The job of instructing had neither status nor recognition, and was heartily loathed. Consequently those who did it had little enthusiasm, their only desire being to get out of the job as quickly as possible. The result of this was that new pilots arrived for action with only the barest ideas of how to get the best from their machines or how to get out of difficult situations, and with little enthusiasm for pure flying as such. The Central Flying School had become just one of many pilot training schools and its emphasis shifted rather to experimental work, testing new aircraft and equipment. The standards of instruction which it had set up originally for training already-qualified pilots were by no means adequate for the proper instruction of *ab initio* pupils. It fell to one of the great characters of the RFC to alter all this and set up the finest system of flying instruction of the time, one which has not only stood the test of time but formed the basis on which most other air forces around the world have trained their pilots.

The man concerned was Robert Smith-Barry who had himself gone through the CFS course in 1912, had fought on the Western Front until breaking both legs in a crash and had then gone back to command a scout squadron. In this task he was appalled by the standard of flying shown by the

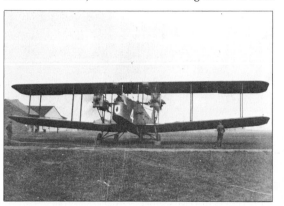

Far left: Handley Page continued to build on the reputation of its wartime bombers and built the Hyderabad which entered service in the 1920s. Some of the production went to the newly-formed Special Reserve squadrons, another of Trenchard's brainchildren. One of these was No. 502 Squadron at Aldergrove, its aircraft carrying the red hand of Ulster.

Left: The most widely used heavy bomber of the RAF in the 1920s was the Vickers Virginia, which was continually updated. This aircraft was flown from Worthy Down by No. 7 Squadron.

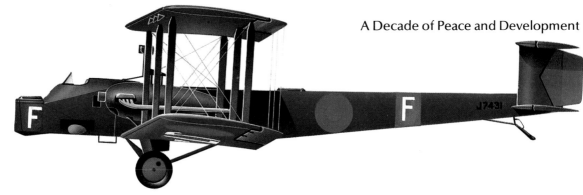

The Vickers Virginia night bomber was in service from 1924 to 1937. Illustrated is a Virginia VII of No. 7 Squadron based at Worthy Down.

Armstrong Whitworth produced a sturdy biplane for army co-operation duties, and such squadrons all flew the Atlas at some time in the late 1920s and early 1930s. Most of these squadrons were stationed around Salisbury Plain but one, No. 26, was at Catterick to co-operate with the army units in the north.

velop their skills to the point where hitherto improbable feats of flying became the common-place. Up till now the only communication between instructor and pupil in the air had been by gesticu-lations, so Smith-Barry evolved a flexible tube down which the instructor could bellow into head-phones that the pupil wore and known thereafter as a 'Gosport tube'. From this came the establish-ment of standardised instructional 'patter' which the instructor passed to the pupil as the aircraft performed its evolutions. A strict disciplinarian, Smith-Barry insisted that his aircraft were im-maculately clean, and each flight had distinctive markings to promote rivalry between flights of the squadron, which by now had been renamed the School of Special Flying.

Smith-Barry's school must have been an em-barrassment to nearby airfields and a cause of alarm to the citizenry of Gosport and the sur-rounding towns, for it was nothing for his pilots to 'buzz' passing cars, landing on the road in front of and behind them, or to beat up local aerodromes. But Smith-Barry's aim was not simply undiscip-lined 'fun' flying. His intention was to make the pupil so much the master of his machine in every situation that his judgement and knowledge would enable him to fly it successfully down to the finest limits. The stall and the spin had been manoeuvres to be avoided at all costs, for they could lead to uncontrollability with fatal results. Smith-Barry deliberately stalled and spun his pupils and, through the Gosport tube, told them how to recover. When inspectors came to examine his pupils' abilities they were so far ahead of other pilots that without hesitation his methods were applied throughout the whole service, and his school became henceforth a school to teach in-structors how to instruct.

It was this pattern of training that the Central Flying School had taken up at about the time the Royal Air Force was born, and the CFS has fostered and developed the pattern to meet current needs ever since, maintaining the RAF's training ahead of the rest of the world's until, even today, the RAF-

pilots sent out to him from home, and by their lack of enthusiasm. At the end of 1916 he began writing letters to Training Division not only complaining about the state of affairs but also airing his views on remedying this situation practically. Fortu-nately these letters came to the notice of General John Salmond, who had been instructing at the CFS when Smith-Barry was there and, knowing the man, pulled him back to take charge of one of the training units, the Reserve Squadron at Gosport, where he was given a free hand to try out his ideas. At first he reorganised the equipment, standardis-ing on the Avro 504J aircraft because of its control features, which would teach pupils how to cope with more advanced aircraft. Then he gathered around him kindred spirits from the front-line squadrons and imbued them with his enthusiasm, raising the status of instructor thereby. Up till then the whole training philosophy had been to teach pilots to avoid getting into dangerous and difficult situations in the air; Smith-Barry worked on the principle of putting the pupil into such positions and teaching him how to get out of them, at first with an instructor and then without. He instilled a principle of daring into flying, which encouraged pupils and instructors alike to de-

To replace the wartime D.H.9A and Bristol aircraft serving in Iraq and India, the Westland company was enjoined to produce a general-purpose aircraft but it had to have D.H.9A wings. The result was the Wapiti which did valiant service, some still being operational in India during World War II. This Wapiti Mk IIA is from No. 27 Squadron at Kohat in India – notice that the crew wear solar topees ('Bombay Bowlers') instead of flying helmets.

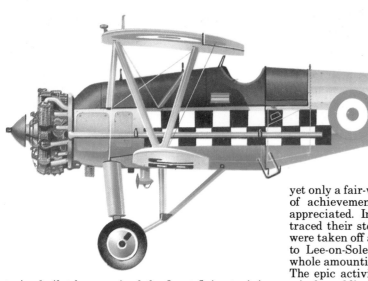

The Armstrong Whitworth Siskin IIIA equipped No. 43 Squadron ('The Fighting Cocks') from June 1928 until June 1931. These flew from Tangmere alongside the Siskins of No. 1 Squadron.

trained pilot has received the finest flying training in the world.

This period of the RAF's history saw the service's star so in the ascendant as to enable its pilots and aircraft to reach out across the globe and to the extremes of performance – it was the era of record-breaking flights. Some of these were part of routine training, some were special efforts but all of them served to further the confidence and ability of the Royal Air Force. For example, in October 1925 three D.H.9As, led by Squadron Leader A. Coningham, left Cairo on a flight to Kano (Nigeria), returning three weeks later. This having been successful, a much more ambitious flight began on 1 March 1926 under the command of Wing Commander C. W. H. Pulford, four Fairey IIID aircraft leaving Cairo for Cape Town. It is probably difficult to imagine today the complete lack of facilities, even of accurate maps, the less reliable engines, and the fact that the RAF was as

yet only a fair-weather force, and so the magnitude of achievement of these flights is not readily appreciated. In fact these four Fairey IIIDs retraced their steps to Cairo by 27 May, the wheels were taken off and floats put on, and they then flew to Lee-on-Solent in Hampshire by 21 June, the whole amounting to a 14,000-mile (22530-km) flight. The epic activities of the RAF in those years did stir the public, however, and none more so than the series of three participations in the Schneider Trophy races.

The Schneider Trophy race had begun in quite a small way in 1913, when Jacques Schneider put up his trophy to encourage the development of marine aircraft. It was a speed race and the outright winner would be the nation which won it three successive times. Britain won it in 1914, but then sterner things prevented further races until after the Armistice. Britain again won the trophy in 1922 but the contest moved on, gaining more international kudos year by year, and in the mid-1920s far-seeing men in the Air Ministry decided to take British participation out of the hands of individuals and companies and go in for it on a national basis. Accordingly they ordered aircraft for the 1927 race (it was now being held every two years) and deputed service pilots to fly them. The result was a great success for Britain; the aircraft used had

One of the prestige events of the inter-war years was the Schneider Trophy contest. This was finally won by the RAF's High Speed Flight at Calshot in 1931 using the Supermarine S.6B. Two of these are shown flanking the S.6 at Calshot Castle.

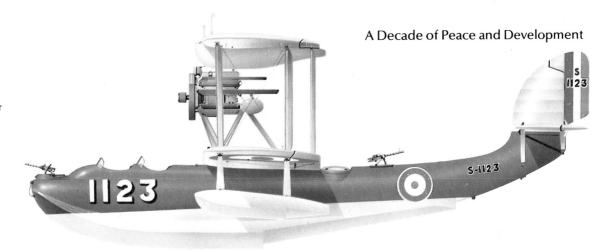

S1123 was a wooden-hulled Supermarine Southampton Mk 1 of No. 480 (Coastal Reconnaissance) Flight based at Calshot. It was later converted to a metal-hulled (silver finished) Mk II.

been specially designed by R. J. Mitchell of Supermarine from experience gained from his S.4 aircraft used in the 1925 race. Three S.5s were built for the 1927 race. Two of them participated, and Flight Lieutenant S. N. Webster won the event at an average speed of 281.65 mph. He went on to take the 100-km (62.1-mile) closed-circuit record at 283.66 mph (456.5 km/h), only to have this beaten by Flight Lieutenant D. D'Arcy Greig in 1928 on the S.5, taking it to 319.57 mph (514.28 km/h).

The flying was done by RAF pilots belonging to the High Speed Flight, specially formed for participation in the Schneider Trophy contests, and for them Mitchell produced the S.6 for the 1929 contest. Victory again came to the RAF team, Flying Officer H. R. D. Waghorn being the winner at 328.63 mph (528.86 km/h). This type was subsequently flown to capture the World Speed Record by Squadron Leader A. H. Orlebar, AFC at 357.7 mph (575.65 km/h). Now Britain had two consecutive wins, so there was only the 1931 contest to win for the trophy to reside permanently in the country. But now the government, in the throes of the Depression, felt unable to find the money; however, an indefatigable lady, with Britain's interests at heart, one Lady Houston, offered to provide the money if the RAF would provide the pilots. This was a happy arrangement and R. J. Mitchell pulled out all the stops to provide a superb machine, the S.6B; Rolls-Royce did likewise with the 2,300-hp (1716-kW) 'R' engine. This combination was all set for the contest, but when it came to it the other challengers France and Italy asked for a postponement which was not granted. Not to be outdone, the High Speed Flight crews flew the course fully, and Flight Lieutenant J. N. Boothman achieved first place at 340.08 mph (547.29 km/h). Shortly afterwards Flight Lieutenant G. H. Stainforth used

this type to take the World Speed Record up to 407.5 mph (655.79 km/h). So the Schneider Trophy was permanently British (and resides in the custody of the Royal Aero Club), but what was more important was the pitch to which the RAF's crews had been trained, the experience of high speed flight they had obtained and, probably most of all, the design expertise that Mitchell had acquired for, directly from this line of monoplane seaplanes was developed one of the thoroughbreds of the RAF, the Spitfire.

The other record the RAF set out to achieve in the late 1920s was the world long-distance record. For this a special aircraft was built, the Fairey Long-Range Monoplane, designed for a range upwards of 5,000 miles (8047 km). It first flew in November 1928, and by the following spring was ready for its first attempt. Flown by Squadron Leader A. G. Jones-Williams and Flight Lieutenant N. H. Jenkins it left Cranwell on 24 April and flew on without landing until it reached Karachi 4,130 miles (6646 km) away in a time of 50 hours. But this was not far enough to break the world record. A second attempt, to South Africa, was made in 1929 but ended in tragedy when the aircraft crashed fatally in Tunisia. A second aircraft of this type was built and eventually, after another failed attempt in October 1931, the world record was obtained in February 1933 when Squadron Leader O. R. Gayford and Flight Lieutenant G. E. Nicholetts flew from Cranwell to Walvis Bay in South Africa, a distance of 5,309 miles (8544 km) covered in 57 hours 25 minutes.

It was also during this era that the flying-boat really came into its own. Hitherto it had been used mainly as a patrol aircraft for the North Sea and the Western Approaches but in the 1920s development had come on apace. On 1 April 1924 the

Far right: The most universal general purpose type to enter service in the 1920s was the Fairey IIIF. This came as a landplane or seaplane and served in bombing squadrons at home, in policing squadrons in Egypt and Aden, with the Fleet Air Arm aboard the Royal Navy's carriers and for maritime reconnaissance. This last was the role in which these five aircraft of No. 202 Squadron were employed from Malta.

Right: Under the joint auspices of the Royal Navy and RAF, the Fleet Air Arm began to expand in the 1920s. One of the first 'real' aircraft-carriers, with the now classic configuration of a clear flying deck and superstructure on the starboard side, was HMS *Eagle*. A Blackburn Baffin is taking off, with three more and two Fairey IIIFs to go.

Hawker Horsley day bomber, as operated in 1929 by No. 33 Squadron at Netheravon. The Horsley showed good climb and manoeuvrability, and was used for a number of long-distance flights.

Marine Aircraft Experimental Establishment had been formed at Felixstowe and here, not far from the similar establishment for landplanes and armament at Martlesham Heath, every floatplane or flying-boat was rigorously tested. This provided a spur for the four main maritime constructors (Fairey, Blackburn, Short and Supermarine) to produce of their best, and the Coastal Area of the RAF received a succession of fine biplane flying-boats which enabled it to spread its wings. The first of these boats was the Supermarine Southampton; it entered service at Calshot in September 1925 with No. 480 Flight, and very quickly it became the standard maritime reconnaissance aircraft of the service. The Southampton will always be remembered for the Far East Flight. This began at Felixstowe in 1927 when four metal-hulled Southamptons were fitted out to fly out to Singapore and establish themselves as a permanent unit there. The Flight was commanded by Group Captain H. M. Cave-Browne-Cave, DSO and left Plymouth on 17 October 1927, setting course for Naples, and then over Italy, Greece and Crete to Aboukir in Egypt. From there it was across the desert to Baghdad, some 480 miles (772 km) of dust and rain for which these open-cockpit boats were far from ideal. From there the route went down the Gulf to Karachi, where the Flight spent three weeks so that the aircraft could be thoroughly overhauled. The course now closely followed the coastline of India and Ceylon, and the beaches were crowded with Indians who had never before seen an aeroplane. Thence it was Calcutta, Rangoon, Penang and so on down to Seletar, which was to be the Flight's permanent base. All the way through the boats had behaved well and, when they were hauled up on the slipway for inspection, surprisingly little was found necessary. But this was not the end of the venture; now the Flight set out on a flag-waving tour of the Dutch East Indies, Aus-

tralia, Borneo, the Philippines, Hong Kong and Siam. This extended touring took up most of 1928, and after its conclusion the unit settled in at Seletar to become, on 1 January 1929, No. 205 Squadron. Some 27,000 miles (43450 km) of flying had been covered without mishap, flying with minimal or no radio facilities and often without any accurate maps at all. The RAF's presence had become a living thing for many people who had never seen an aircraft, and the Flight had become an excellent ambassador for Britain.

Fleet Air Arm

The other aspect of the RAF's maritime aviation was the Fleet Air Arm of the RAF. The governing control of this aspect of aviation had long been the most bitter of the bones of contention between the three services, and it was not until Lord Haldane was appointed in March 1924 to bring the Air Ministry and the Admiralty together to determine a common policy that at last the inter-service feuding abated. Although the Navy had not obtained what it wanted, there was at least a workable arrangement until such time as they could make a 'putsch' to regain control of naval aviation for themselves. It was under this truce agreement that the Fleet Air Arm got down to the more serious business of developing the fleet's aviation. The mean base for naval aviation strength has always rested in its aircraft-carrier force, and in this respect the Fleet Air Arm progressed logically. Beginning simply with HMS *Argus*, the fleet gradually built up with HMS *Eagle* commissioning in 1923, *Hermes* in 1924, the rebuilt *Furious* in 1925 and then the two biggest, *Courageous* and *Glorious*, in 1928 and 1930 respectively. In addition to these floating airfields many of the battleships and cruisers of the Navy were equipped with trainable catapults to launch floatplanes, so extending the eyes of the ships over the horizon. On both types of ship the Fairey IIIF became the ubiquitous general-purpose aircraft, on wheels or on floats. Torpedo-bombing was left to the successful Blackburn Dart and its later development the Ripon, whilst the defence aspect was carried out by one of the most delightful aircraft of the inter-war years, the Fairey Flycatcher fleet fighter, a manoeuvrable

Hawker really came into its own in the early 1930s with the Kestrel-engined Hart bomber. It took over the concept of the Fairey Fox and was rushed into mass production, serving with many light bomber units such as No. 57 Squadron, three of whose aircraft are seen here.

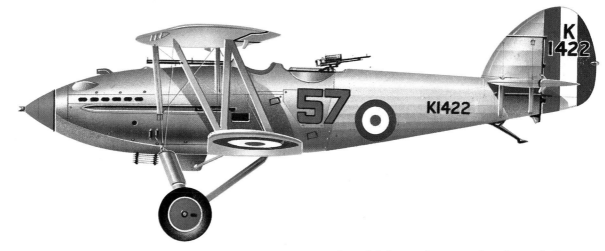

The RAF acquired some 450 Hawker Hart day bombers, used from 1930 onwards. They saw service in many parts of the world and continued in limited service for many years. K1422 flew from Upper Heyford in 1934 with No. 57 Squadron.

little aircraft which delighted its pilots.

This was the period when the problems of landing aircraft on carrier decks were largely solved, at least for 30 or so years. The only form of arrester in general use in the early 1920s was the arrangement of fore-and-aft wires combined with hooks on the undercarriages of the aircraft which in theory engaged the wires and slowed the aircraft to a standstill, but in practice more often than not tipped them on their noses or wingtips – or both. These were so damaging that for a while no form of arrester was used and it was entirely up to the pilots to accomplish a safe conclusion to each flight. But with the coming of HMS *Courageous* in 1928 attempts to use transverse arrester wires were renewed, and after five years of experiments a practical system was eventually adopted. Aircraft could engage a hook, let down from the rear of the fuselage, with a hydraulically damped transverse wire on the ship, and so effect a deceleration that neither tipped the aircraft on its nose nor tore out the rear end. This system was quickly standardised.

Carrier operations

During this period, too, the now-traditional role of the carrier in subduing local uprisings had its beginnings, with *Hermes* and *Argus* dashing off to China to deal with banditry and piracy ashore and afloat in 1926, and *Courageous* in 1928 involved in Jewish/Arab troubles at Jaffa, which she reached from Malta within three days of being ordered to embark the army. For those in the close intimacy of naval aviation it could be seen that with the carrier a weapon of great power could be forged which would quickly make the battleship as dead as the dodo, that developments were in hand which expanded the performance envelope of

operations (night carrier operations began before 1930), and that many uses of the carrier could be found for which there was no other reasonable substitute. But despite these encouragements, the odds against these developing within the British forces were too great. First of all, the Navy itself was still preoccupied with the idea that all naval power operations would resemble Jutland and therefore the battleship was 'the greatest' – no high-ranking naval officers of the period had much experience of or respect for naval aviation. And in any case, as a result of Trenchard's dictum that all flying must be under the umbrella of the Royal Air Force, the Admiralty could not develop it the way it wanted, and the Royal Air Force saw the Fleet Air Arm as an ancillary force with lesser priorities than its own bomber and fighter activities. So naval aviation fell between two stools and, for all the brilliance and devotion of the men carrying out the task at sea, British naval aviation fell seriously behind that of other maritime powers during the 1920s and 1930s, an error that nearly cost Britain its life when the U-boats again took up the battle in 1939.

Of course, throughout this period of peace in Europe the RAF was still at war. In Iraq, on the North West Frontier of India and, from February 1928, in Aden, the RAF was busy policing dissident areas. The setting up of Aden Command in 1928 was a most successful instance of the RAF having complete control of a vast area of southern Arabia and maintaining the peace by air patrol, No. 8 Squadron being allocated this task and beginning a link with Aden which was to last on and off until Aden was abandoned in 1967. But it was in Afghanistan where the most energetic uprising was taking place in 1928. So successful was Kabibullah Khan

In 1925 Richard Fairey had built an aeroplane around the Curtiss D-12 liquid-cooled engine and this was bought on a small scale by the RAF as the Fairey Fox. It only equipped one squadron, No. 12, but it was a sensation because, although a bomber, it easily out-performed all the RAF's fighters.

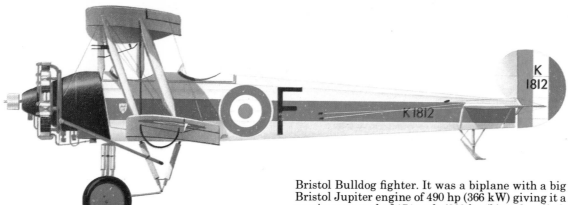

and his rebel tribesmen that the city of Kabul was completely surrounded; amongst the people cooped up there were nearly 600 civilian men, women and children. The decision was made to evacuate them by air, and No. 70 Squadron, flying Vickers Victoria bomber-transports, flew to and fro, over 10,000-ft (3050-m) mountains in severe weather bringing out 586 refugees and clocking up 28,160 miles (45320 km) of flying within two months. For the first time air evacuation had become a proven possibility.

The biplane formula continues

All this time the RAF had been seeking and receiving new equipment, for the British aircraft industry was anxious to keep alive and well and so was constantly improving its products in order to squeeze that extra ounce of performance out of its aircraft. The general configuration of the aircraft, however, remained the same. For example, they all had to be biplanes; some time before World War I the RFC and RNAS had had one or two structural failures with monoplanes, and the edict went out that no further monoplanes should be bought for the British services. This doctrine stuck and, apart from a small batch of Bristol Monoplane Scouts and a few special-purpose aircraft such as the Fairey Long-Range Monoplane and the Schneider Trophy racers, remained in force even 20 years later, when the construction of monoplanes was no longer a matter of structural suspicion. For the most part, too, the aircraft were powered by air-cooled engines which, for the single-seaters, meant radial engines; exceptions were such aircraft as the Fairey IIIF with its close-cowled Napier Lion liquid-cooled engine and, of course, the Fairey Fox. So the idea was to improve the traditional aircraft and perhaps one of the most successful examples of this arrived in RAF service at this time: the

Bristol Bulldog fighter. It was a biplane with a big Bristol Jupiter engine of 490 hp (366 kW) giving it a maximum speed of 174 mph (280 km/h) and a climb to 20,000 ft (6095 m) in 14 minutes 30 seconds. It entered service in 1929 and soon became the RAF's predominant fighter, so liked was it by all in the service. The Bulldog was used by 10 fighter squadrons in the eight years of its front-line service.

At this stage it is perhaps appropriate to mention the name of the H. G. Hawker Engineering Co. Ltd. This company had been formed in 1920, almost as a resurrection of the famous Sopwith Company which had produced such splendid warplanes in World War I as the Pup, 1½-Strutter, Camel, Dolphin and Snipe. The company set out, under its new name, to continue in aviation business after the war. But its first efforts were none too inspiring, although it secured three RAF contracts during the latter half of the 1920s: one for the Horsley, a heavy single-engined bomber which doubled up as a torpedo-bomber with five regular and one Special Reserve squadrons; one for the Woodcock, a lumbering fighter which equipped two squadrons; and one for the Tomtit, a two-seat trainer aimed at replacing the Avro 504N. However, the arrival of the rival Fairey Fox in service had set Hawker on the right lines and it set about designing a family of aeroplanes tailored around the new liquid-cooled engine which Rolls-Royce was producing as a direct result of participation in the Schneider Trophy races, and which was later named the Kestrel. In 1928 the first two prototypes appeared; one was a two-seater bomber, very like the Fox, which was in competition with the Fox Mk II for Air Ministry orders, and the other was a delightful single-seat fighter. Both these types won their competitions and were ordered into production, the two-seater becoming the Hawker Hart and the single-seater the Hawker Fury. The Hart entered service in January 1930 and that year could not be caught by any of the RAF's fighters; the Fury came a year later, the first in-service RAF fighter with a top speed of over 200 mph (322 km/h). The Hart caught on and many new contracts were issued; sub-versions were pro-

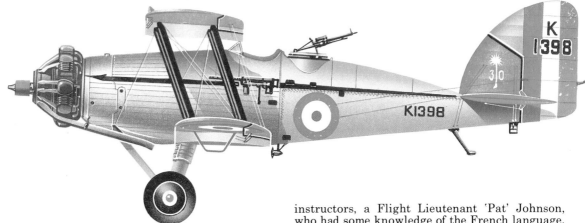

The Westland Wapiti was the most important aircraft overseas in the 1930s. K1398 served with No. 30 Squadron in Iraq, the red wingtips and fin being for identity purposes should the aircraft force-land in the desert.

duced for communications duties, and for operation in India and in the Middle East. And from the Hart came a family of aircraft, with the same basic airframe, but modified in different ways: the Demon was developed from the Hart Fighter as a two-seater fighter, the Audax was an army co-operation variant which was also used as a general-purpose aircraft, the Hart Trainer was produced for advanced training, the Hardy appeared as the definitive overseas general-purpose aircraft, the Hind was a second-generation day bomber, and the Hector was an Audax with a Napier Dagger engine and redesigned upper wing. The Fury, too, was refined into a Mark II version. By the time all these aircraft had been built in the 1920s and 1930s, not far short of 3,000 models had been produced, an overwhelming total for the days of comparative peace. In addition, different variants were produced for other air forces, and Hawker was in business in a big way. So ubiquitous was the Hawker Hart that hardly an airfield could be visited in the UK during the 1930s at which at least one such Hawker aircraft was not present.

Despite all the advances in military aviation which are implied in the spreading of the RAF's wings as outlined in these pages, it is probably not realised these days that in 1930 nearly all the RAF's flying was done in fair weather and by day, the exception being the night bombers (which in any case usually needed a moon for their operation). In fact, one of the biggest causes of accidents in those days was the sudden deterioration of weather conditions so that pilots were forced to fly in cloud when they had little or no ability to do so. But this was shortly to be remedied; the Central Flying School, by then stationed at Wittering, near Stamford, had learnt of developments being carried out by the French Farman company at Toussous-le-Noble in blind flying. Accordingly, one of their instructors, a Flight Lieutenant 'Pat' Johnson, who had some knowledge of the French language, was posted to the Farman course and began to fly solely on instruments, having a metal cover bolted over his cockpit so that he could not see out. Not only did he acquire the rudiments of elementary instrument-flying, but he also was able to examine the equipment. He returned to the CFS ready to initiate similar instruction in the RAF. The transition was enormous because pilots had, from the beginning, been taught to fly 'by the seat of their pants', in other words that feel and sensation were the main elements assisting the pilot's vision. This theory was soon found to be utterly faulty in a non-vision situation, for the rapidly disorientated sensations inevitably led to a loss of control. So the CFS had to begin teaching the average service pilot to disregard his previous training and to believe implicitly in what his instruments were telling him.

'Father of the RAF' retires

Avro 504Ns were rigged up with folding hoods over the rear cockpits and a special flight at Wittering formed for this task. So proficient did Johnson become that he would demonstrate a complete flight, solo, under the hood, comprising a take-off, aerobatics, and glide approach to 200 ft (61 m) before landing. This flight began activities in 1931, with the aim of converting all the service's pilots into instrument-flying pilots, and the task was completed in two years. Henceforward instrument flying was taught as part of the pilot's normal course and thus the RAF moved out of the realm of fine-weather-only operation.

On 31 December 1929 the RAF said goodbye to its first Chief of the Air Staff, Hugh Trenchard, the man who more than any other had created the service out of the vision he had before him when appointed to the task in 1918. He departed from the post with the minimum of fuss, as befitted a man

At the same time as the Hart, Hawker also produced possibly the most beautiful fighter of all time, the Fury. It was also the fastest aircraft in squadron service for several years and served at Tangmere with Nos 1 and 43 Squadrons (shown here) and at Hawkinge with No. 25 Squadron.

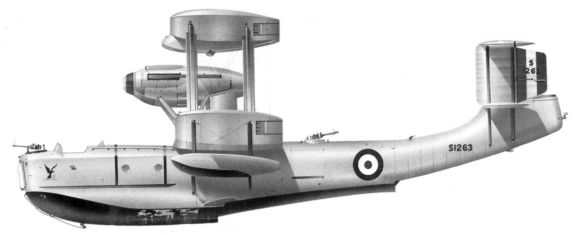

S1263 was one of four Blackburn Iris IIIs received by No. 209 Squadron at Mount Batten in 1930. Along with S1593, the aircraft was re-engined with Rolls-Royce Buzzards, to become an Iris V.

who had eschewed the limelight all his life, and thereafter continued to fight the RAF's parliamentary battles in the House of Lords. Into the seat of Chief of Air Staff came Sir John Salmond, Trenchard's most trusty of lieutenants. Salmond's tenure was not long, and before the decade of peace was over his place had been taken by Sir Edward Ellington. With him in the chair, the war clouds began to hover around the Royal Air Force.

Fascism rises

All during the 1920s the defence philosophies in the UK had planned for hostility from France; the enmity of centuries, little alleviated by the alliance of World War I, died hard in the hearts of Englishmen and, with a Germany shattered and torn by inner dissensions no real threat could be seen from any other quarter than Britain's traditional enemy. So the planning for future attacks were against the enemy across the Channel (no bad scheme, as it later turned out). However, with the beginning of the 1930s two new and sinister developments came into the open. First of these was the rising star of totalitarianism in Italy, in the form of one Mussolini whose bombast was stirring that lethargic nation into developmental activity. The other was the awareness that, despite appearances of peace and openness in the new Germany, there were in fact secret preparations, in flagrant violation of the Treaty of Versailles, to build up a new armed might, and in particular to build an air force at least equal to that of France. But such was the mood of heady peace in Britain that, as it arose from the misery of the Depression, few if any people were willing to listen to the scaremongering of those who professed to know the truth about the bellicosity of Italy and Germany. It is just the same now, 40 years later, with few Britons giving more

than a passing thought to the militaristic and imperialistic expansion of Soviet armed might: so in those early 1930s the latest gramophone record, sports car or fashion show were the things that really mattered.

So it was not until 1934 that the climate was such that Parliament would even listen to ideas of expanding the armed services. The economic crisis, coupled with the Disarmament Conference, had meant that the front-line squadrons of the RAF numbered only 42 out of the 52 which had been legislated for in 1923. Already the Germans' secret air force was two-thirds this strength and was expanding rapidly, whereas the RAF was at a standstill. The government of the day, in July 1934, introduced an Expansion Programme for the RAF which would now take it up to 75 squadrons as soon as possible and to 128 squadrons in five years. Truly the decade of peace was drawing to a close. That this was not before time became quickly apparent in the following year, when Italian imperialism set off on its uncertain course. Ethiopia was invaded in 1935 by Italian troops, and the Regia Aeronautica began a bombing and transport campaign which facilitated the bloody take-over within eight months. Because there was no air opposition the world learnt little about aerial combat and effectiveness in the 1930s; what it did learn, to its horror, was that the weapon of aerial bombardment was used by the aggressors against unarmed peasants in their villages to create unnecessary bloodshed and, even more horrible, that the Italians experimented with poison gas against these unarmed civilians. So, to the popular idea that bombing from the air was the terror of all terrors were added horrific news photographs to fuel the flames that 'the bomber will always get through' and that 'there is no defence against air attack' – two popular theories of the day which, to

During the Abyssinian crisis the four-engined Short Singapore IIIs of No. 203 Squadron at Basra were pressed into service to keep an eye open for Italian shipping in the Red Sea area. K4577 is here about to leave the water at Basra.

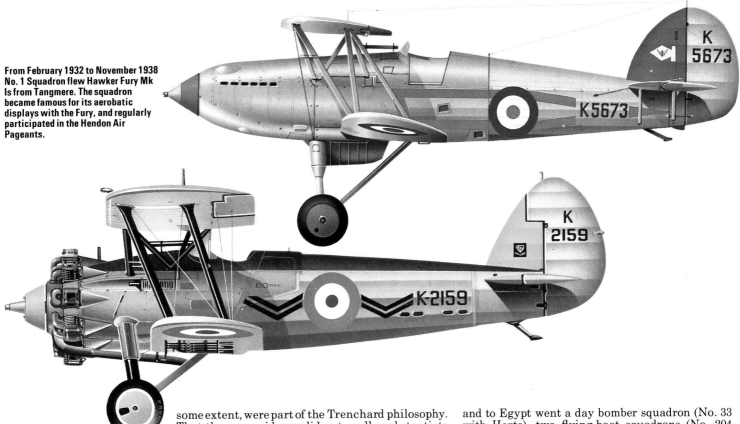

From February 1932 to November 1938 No. 1 Squadron flew Hawker Fury Mk Is from Tangmere. The squadron became famous for its aerobatic displays with the Fury, and regularly participated in the Hendon Air Pageants.

Above: Another participant of the Hendon Air Pageants in the 1930s was the Bristol Bulldogs of No. 17 Squadron. These flew from Upavon until 1934 when the squadron moved to Kenley.

The Hendon Displays had become an annual event by the 1930s, when most of the RAF was on display. Here a flight of No. 3 Squadron's Bulldogs lands at Hendon during the 1936 display, with other Bulldogs of No. 17 Squadron, together with the Furies of No. 1 Squadron and Demons of No. 23 Squadron, arrayed in the Service Park.

some extent, were part of the Trenchard philosophy. That the new evidence did not really substantiate these views (as a result of the total lack of air opposition) was not propounded with the same fervour.

But these activities in Ethiopia were taking place very near to British Somaliland and other major spheres of British influence in the Middle East – what then was the British reaction? On the air side, 12 RAF squadrons were moved out to the area – a fighter squadron to the Sudan (No. 3 with Bulldogs), a light bomber squadron (No. 12 with Harts), a two-seat fighter squadron (No. 41 with Demons) and a flying-boat squadron (No. 203 with Singapores) to Aden, a torpedo-bomber squadron (No. 22 with Vildebeests), and two two-seat fighter squadrons (Nos 23 and 65 with Demons) to Malta,

and to Egypt went a day bomber squadron (No. 33 with Harts), two flying-boat squadrons (No. 204 with Scapas and No. 230 with Singapores) and a two-seat fighter squadron (No. 29 with Demons) whilst another such (No. 64 with Demons) was formed in Egypt. At the same time the FAA units aboard carriers went along with the naval dispositions. In the event no action was needed, for Britain opted to exercise ineffectual sanctions against Italy, and the annexation was over without any other power taking action. The forces were withdrawn, with the exception of one Hawker Hart squadron which stayed in Egypt. Britain had revealed its unpreparedness (and unwillingness) to fight and the country had begun to see the shape of things to come – if indeed it would take heed of the writing in the sky.

The Race Against Time

Whilst Mussolini had undoubtedly been the first of the 1930s' aggressors to move into action, he was not the most ominous as far as Britain was concerned. Although banned from building its own air force, Germany had steadily gone ahead during the late 1920s and early 1930s with the building up of an air-minded nation and the exploitation of sporting and transport aviation in such a way as to mass a thinly-disguised corps of proficient air and ground crew together with large quantities of aircraft. Under the cloak of the German airline, Lufthansa, a secret air force was built up to plans drawn up in 1927, and when Hitler came to power the whole process received a tremendous boost – it moved from second to top gear. Hermann Goering was given charge of Lufthansa and, with Erhard Milch and Ernst Udet as his aides, the clandestine military air force grew to the position where it could scarcely remain a secret. It was this growth to power in Germany, rather than Mussolini's African escapades, which had provoked the 1934 expansion scheme for the RAF, but this was only the start. Incredibly, even at this time there was almost a preponderance of voices in the country to express surprise that the armed forces should be expanded to face such a threat, and those who produced realistic figures of what the Germans were up to were branded by the media of the day as warmongers.

A worrying aspect, apart from the growth of the Luftwaffe, was the rate of that growth. Starting from scratch, the Luftwaffe had initially had a long way to go; that by 1935 it was aiming for parity with the front-line strength of the home-based RAF was bad enough, but Hitler's aim was quickly to reach parity with the French air force. Until this point Britain had maintained that it would keep a superiority over any other air force in Europe; already by the autumn of 1934 the Lord President had modified British intentions to state that 'we would not accept a position of inferiority', thus admitting a policy of parity; and as events turned out, the acceleration of the Luftwaffe could not even be contained in terms of parity as the 1930s drew on.

But it was not just a question of numbers. True, the aircraft factories of the United Kingdom had by no means been working at full capacity and

1935 saw the entry into service of the Gloster Gauntlet fighter, the most advanced of its day. This type came in with the expansion schemes and was produced in greater numbers than any fighter since World War I. The blue-and-white checks show these aircraft to be from No. 19 Squadron, the first Gauntlet unit.

Two types widely used in the 1930s for training purposes were the Hawker Tomtit (right, with blind flying hood over the rear cockpit) and the Avro Tutor (below).

would welcome further orders, but it was seen by the Air Staff as essential that the aircraft produced should themselves be more advanced, for it was of little value to the RAF to fill its expanding squadrons with aircraft so obsolete that when combat came they would all be easy meat for the enemy. In fact, this was exactly what the French air force did under this same spur of rapid expansion – a vital factor in the failure of the French air force in 1940.

The biplane legacy

The principal obstacle to the advancement of the service's aircraft was the old rule, first instituted before World War I, that monoplanes were structurally dangerous and were therefore not to be procured for His Majesty's airmen. This meant that up until the early 1930s almost all the RAF's fixed-wing aircraft were biplanes, and the service was finding that some of the new civil monoplanes could show a clean pair of heels to any aircraft that the service put up alongside them. In terms of fighter defence this was a most disquieting state of affairs for, as was shortly to be seen in Germany, there was little potential difference between an airliner and a bomber, and the situation had to be faced that Bristol Bulldogs, Armstrong Whitworth Siskins and even Hawker Furies would be of little use against such aircraft. This problem of the inadequacy of the current fighter breed had already arisen several years before with the issue by the Air Ministry of Specification F.7/30 requiring submissions for a new fighter of greater speed, ceiling, climb, manoeuvrability and firepower. The designs that flowed in were mostly biplanes, although Supermarine produced a gull-winged monoplane with a trousered landing gear arrangement and a performance not substantially better than that of the biplanes. No aircraft was ordered from this design competition, although the Gloster

The new RAF Expansion Schemes meant a need for much greater flying training and soon there were as many as 10 flying training schools. Standard service trainer was the Hawker Hart (T), one of the many versions of the basic Hawker Hart, in this case having dual controls.

The Handley Page Heyford was the last of the RAF's biplane bombers. K4023 served at Boscombe Down in 1935 with No. 10 Squadron.

entry was developed into the Gladiator which entered RAF service in 1937 and became its last biplane fighter. To some extent it fulfilled the requirements of F.7/30 even in doubling up the firepower, from two to four machine-guns. But long before the Gladiator entered service it was seen that this was but a stop-gap, and that something much more radical was required.

Fortunately, British aircraft companies of the period were private companies, not simply working to RAF specifications, and two companies set about building what they believed to be the aircraft needed. Sydney Camm, chief designer of Hawkers at Kingston, was working on a Fury Monoplane design; and R. J. Mitchell of Supermarine, drawing on his experience with the Schneider Trophy monoplanes and his disappointments with the performance of the F.7/30 monoplane, was working to find another monoplane answer.

At the same time Rolls-Royce, which then was not a nationalised company but one of the proudest independent concerns in the country, was itself building a private venture engine, building on the success of the Kestrel and learning from the

mistakes of the Goshawk which had been the engine used in the F.7/30 designs. The new engine turned out to be a most significant advance, and in 1935 was ready for both Hawker and Supermarine prototypes.

One other factor was taking place which coincidentally had much bearing on the two aircraft. Not only was development necessary in aircraft but in armament as well, and the Armament Research Division of the Air Ministry was working to arrange the adaptation of the outstandingly successful Colt 0.3-in (7.62-mm) machine-gun for application to the RAF, and this eventually

The RAF in the Middle East came very much on the alert in 1935 during the invasion of Abyssinia by Italy. The Fairey Gordon, here seen flying over the Nablus Hills (Palestine) from the base at Ramleh, was one of the basic types serving on general-purpose duties in that area.

Vickers Vildebeests were used by Nos 36 (here) and 100 Squadrons in Singapore in 1941–2.

The Saro London entered service in 1936 for maritime patrol. No. 240 Squadron flew the London until June 1940, fitted with long-range tanks behind the cockpit.

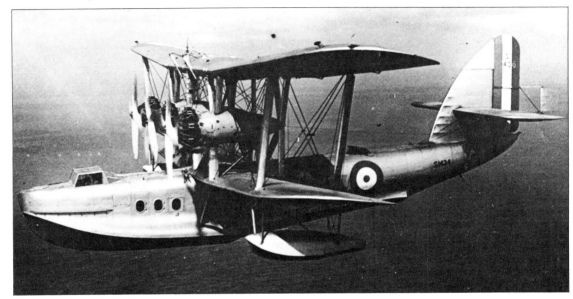

The flying-boat continued to play its part in the RAF's maritime reconnaissance activities and many different types came into service. The Short Rangoon served principally with No. 203 Squadron in the Persian Gulf in the early 1930s.

The first monoplane to be ordered in any numbers, the Avro Anson entered service with No. 48 Squadron at Manston in 1936. It served on coastal duties at the beginning of World War II, subsequently serving in thousands as a trainer and communications aircraft into the late 1960s.

emerged in 1934 as the Browning 0.303-in (7.7-mm) machine-gun.

As all this work was going on, the Operational Requirements Branch of the Air Ministry issued a specification for a new fighter with, at the insistence of a Squadron Leader Ralph Sorley, a battery of six or eight 0.303-in (7.7-mm) machine-guns. From all these strands grew the prototype Hurricane and Spitfire; the monoplane was now universally accepted for the RAF. Of course, others were also on the stocks, but it would be some time before the military skies of Britain saw anything but biplanes.

In those days in the mid-1930s there were many public-spirited people who could see more clearly than the politicians the need for awakening the British public to the needs of the air. None was more so geared than the Air League of the British Empire, and one of its more successful projects for the Royal Air Force was the institution of Empire Air Days. The first of these took place on 24 May 1934, and they really constituted miniature Hendon Pageants, local RAF stations opening to the public and showing all the facets of service life, together with a modest flying display. Proceeds went to the RAF Benevolent Fund. These Empire Air Days were a great success and grew annually until World War II put a stop to them; they became a prototype for the post-war Battle of Britain Displays.

Order of battle

On the eve of this expansion, what was the Royal Air Force's order of battle? It was still constituted in the same formal Areas as in the 1920s. The main operational side of the UK RAF came under the umbrella of the Air Defence of Great Britain, its AOC being Air Marshal Sir Robert Brooke-Popham (known to all as 'Brookham'); it comprised the Western Area with the Heavy Bomber Squadrons, all eight of them (of which three were Special Reserve squadrons) equipped with Vickers Virginias except for Nos 10 and 99 Squadrons which had just re-equipped with the new Handley Page Heyford; Central Area with 11 squadrons of single-engined bombers (Hawker Harts, Westland Wallaces and Fairey Gordons) and No. 101 Squadron with the twin-engined, aerobatic Boulton & Paul Sidestrand medium bomber; Fighting Area with 14 single-engined fighter squadrons (Bristol Bulldogs, Hawker Demons, Hawker Furies and the first squadron [No. 19] of Gloster Gauntlets); and No. 1 Air Defence Group covering the Auxiliary Air Force (seven bomber squadrons with Harts and Westland Wapitis, and one fighter squadron with Demons). Inland Area was its own command and included No. 22 Group (five army co-operation squadrons with Hawker Audaxes) and No. 23 Group which administered the flying training schools. Coastal Area, under Air Vice Marshal A. M. Longmore, looked after one torpedo-bombing squadron and four flying-boat squadrons (of which No. 210 was re-equipped with the new Short Singapore III four-engined flying-boat) and administered

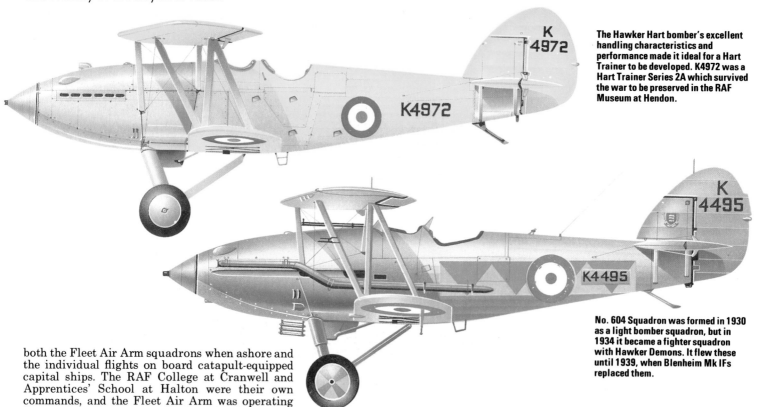

The Hawker Hart bomber's excellent handling characteristics and performance made it ideal for a Hart Trainer to be developed. K4972 was a Hart Trainer Series 2A which survived the war to be preserved in the RAF Museum at Hendon.

No. 604 Squadron was formed in 1930 as a light bomber squadron, but in 1934 it became a fighter squadron with Hawker Demons. It flew these until 1939, when Blenheim Mk IFs replaced them.

both the Fleet Air Arm squadrons when ashore and the individual flights on board catapult-equipped capital ships. The RAF College at Cranwell and Apprentices' School at Halton were their own commands, and the Fleet Air Arm was operating five carriers (*Courageous*, *Glorious*, *Eagle*, *Furious* and *Hermes*).

Overseas was the Royal Air Force, Middle East controlling the units in Egypt, under Air Vice Marshal C. L. N. Newall, namely three bomber squadrons with Fairey IIIFs and Fairey Gordons, one army co-operation squadron with Armstrong Whitworth Atlases, one bomber-transport squadron with Vickers Victorias and a Flying Training School; Transjordan and Palestine Command, under Air Commodore R. E. C. Peirse, had two bomber squadrons with Gordons; British Forces in Iraq under Air Vice Marshal C. S. Burnett had three bomber squadrons with Hardy, Wapiti and Vickers Vincent aircraft, a bomber-transport squadron with Victorias and a flying-boat squadron

with Short Rangoons; RAF India under Air Marshal Sir John Steel was a bigger command with four army co-operation squadrons with Wapitis, four bomber squadrons with Wapitis and Harts and a Bomber Transport Flight; RAF Mediterranean, under Air Commodore C. E. H. Rathbone, was based in Malta and had one flying-boat squadron and administered Fleet Air Arm units and carriers in the Mediterranean; Aden Command, under Group Captain C. F. A. Portal, had a bomber squadron with Vickers Vincents; and at the other end of the world was RAF Far East, under Group Captain Sydney W. Smith, with a flying-boat squadron of Singapores and two torpedo-bomber squadrons with Hawker Horsleys and Vickers Vildebeests

One monoplane entering service in 1937 was the single-engined Vickers Wellesley bomber, which served mainly in the Middle East. These nine are from No. 45 Squadron.

The RAF's first bomber to have powered gun turrets was the Boulton Paul Overstrand. No. 101 Squadron was the only squadron to fly the type, operating from Bicester from 1935 to 1938.

Below: The bomber transport aircraft was still a feature of the RAF in the Middle East during the 1930s. The Vernon had been replaced by the Victoria, and this had been re-engined and become the Valentia. These stalwarts served with Nos 70 and 216 Squadrons right up to and during the early stages of World War II, then continuing in service with No. 31 Squadron in India until eventually replaced by the Douglas Dakota. Heliopolis is the town under this low-flying Valentia of No. 216 Squadron in 1936.

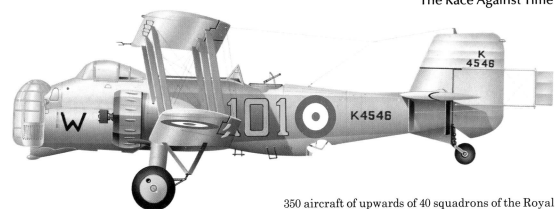

Below: In the UK the final biplane fighter entered service in 1937. It was the Gloster Gladiator, serving first with No. 3 Squadron at Kenley (illustrated) and No. 72 Squadron at Church Fenton. The occasion here was a display to Dominion representatives.

(all at Singapore) and responsibility for Fleet Air Arm units in the Far East.

1935 was very much the cardinal point of the RAF's expansion. What may be considered as the setting of the sun on the RAF of the peacetime era took place at the RAF Stations Mildenhall and Duxford on 6 July 1935, when H.M. King George V held a Silver Jubilee Review of his Royal Air Force:

350 aircraft of upwards of 40 squadrons of the Royal Air Force were drawn up at Mildenhall, where at 11.30 a.m. His Majesty arrived and began a slow drive around the five miles of aircraft, drawn up in semi-circular rows, taking three-quarters of an hour. The king was then driven to Duxford and joined by Queen Elizabeth: between 2.30 and 3 p.m. all the squadrons at Mildenhall flew past, in squadron formation, at half-minute intervals, the whole constituting an impressive ceremony and, in retrospect, a fitting climax to the first stage of the Royal Air Force's growth since 1918.

1935 also saw taking to the air the first prototypes of the new generation of monoplanes, the generation which was to form the bulk of the later expansion schemes and to bear the brunt of the air war when it came. First was the Avro Anson on 24 March: this was a military conversion of the Avro Type 652 twin-engined airliner, of which two examples had been built for Imperial Airways, and it became the standard shipping reconnaissance aircraft in the service. On 19 June a ponderous single-engined monoplane climbed out of the airfield in the middle of Brooklands racing track: this was the Vickers Wellesley, using the new geodetic method of construction, and it became a medium bomber in the service soon afterwards, though it was chiefly important as the predecessor of the Wellington. On 6 November, also at Brooklands, first flew the most important of them all, the first prototype Hawker Hurricane.

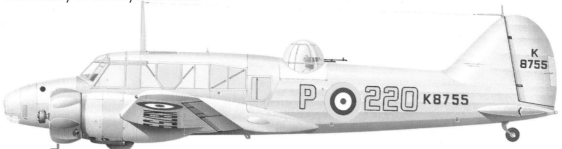

In that same month, as described in the previous chapter, the RAF made its overseas deployments to counter Mussolini's Ethiopian venture, and the year ended with a faint but perceptible quickening of the national pulse as sterner things loomed ahead for those who cared to look and to think. What was not known, even to them, was that already one of the most significant developments, for aerial warfare had begun under the aegis of the Air Ministry. One of the most disquieting matters as air performance advanced was that the detection of approaching aircraft was becoming increasingly difficult. Much reliance had been placed hitherto on audio-detection methods (the anti-aircraft batteries had their sound locators), but these could not cope with increased aircraft speeds and in any case could only detect over a limited range. Incredible as it may seem, the new idea came from the science fiction of the day, which was preoccupied with death rays. This basic idea led the Air Ministry, through the Aeronautical Research Committee under Sir Henry Tizard, to approach a scientist to find out to what possible use some sort of electro-magnetic energy ray could be put in the air defence field. This scientist, Robert Watson Watt, evolved a simple demonstration to show that such an emission would not be able to destroy or harm an incoming aircraft but would be able to detect its presence and to give some idea of height and bearing. The significance of this was not lost on the ARC and from then on the rush was on to make a practical radar system and get it into operational array.

Expansion

Such expansion as was envisaged (and increased in scope as the next few years showed the need for further growth) involved a vast move forward in every part of the Royal Air Force. And it was largely as a result of the foresight and planning of Trenchard and his lieutenants, and their insistence at the beginning to build small but build well, that the service of 1934–5 provided a sound basis upon which to build a vast new superstructure. The target, which in 1935 had been a total of 1,512 first-line aircraft in service by March 1937, was raised in 1936 to be 1,736 aircraft by March 1939, plus increases overseas and a much greater emphasis on reserves. All this had to be accommodated on service stations so a vast building programme was started. This increased the number of airfields

alone from 52 to 138 in the United Kingdom within four years, and similar big leaps forward were necessary in every sphere of RAF activity.

But of course it was the advance in aircraft that was of the utmost importance, for the *raison d'être* of any air force is to fly aircraft into battle. In this respect the expansion very wisely took two steps forward; the first was to increase the numbers of aircraft already in or about to come into production so that the mushrooming organisation and large numbers of new crews would have aircraft to fly and obtain experience in; the second was to develop as quickly as possible the advanced types which would be war-winners when conflict came, as most of those in the know were convinced it would.

Apart from training types, at the end of 1935 the following types were in production. On the fighter side the Gloster Gauntlet had just entered service; it was the fastest and most suitable aircraft for immediate capitalisation, so 204 were ordered for the newly-forming squadrons. It was quickly followed by the Gladiator, entering service in 1937 as the RAF's last biplane fighter. These two types had to suffice until the new monoplane fighters

With the formation of Bomber Command, many new squadrons were formed. Before they could be equipped with modern aircraft they were issued with Hawker Hinds, another development of the Hart. This No. 98 Squadron observer is showing a finer point of his Lewis gun to the ground crew before the pilot climbs into the front seat.

The Fairey Battle light bomber soon replaced many of the Hawker Hinds in bomber service, but by the outbreak of World War II was obsolescent. These No. 88 Squadron Battles are about to take off from Boscombe Down in 1939.

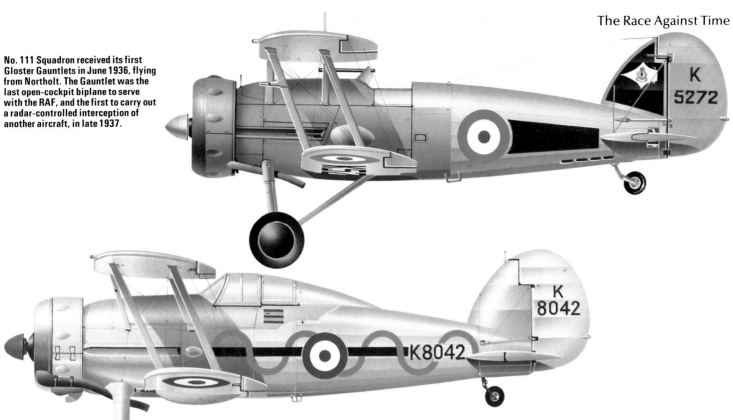

No. 111 Squadron received its first Gloster Gauntlets in June 1936, flying from Northolt. The Gauntlet was the last open-cockpit biplane to serve with the RAF, and the first to carry out a radar-controlled interception of another aircraft, in late 1937.

The Gloster Gladiator represented the height of biplane fighter design. No. 87 Squadron flew Gladiators from Debden for a year before Hurricanes became available in larger numbers.

Below right: 1937 was the year in which many of the wartime types of aircraft first entered RAF service. The first Armstrong Whitworth Whitley Mk Is joined No. 10 Squadron at Dishforth and were seen at the final Hendon Display in that year.

Below: An interim bomber which came into brief service at the end of the 1930s was the Handley Page Harrow, seen here with No. 115 Squadron at Marham. It was too slow for operations in the European theatre, and by the outbreak of war had been relegated to transport and experimental duties.

could come into service. The bomber picture was more obscure. As regards light bombers, Hawker had just produced the Hind, a developed edition of the Hart, and this was rushed into service in quantity, rather like the Gauntlet, as interim equipment of the new squadrons until a new monoplane light bomber, the Fairey Battle, could be put into the air and into service. Medium bombers in 1935 comprised but one squadron of Boulton Paul Overstrand biplanes, which were slow but immensely agile, and the decision was taken to go straight for two medium bombers, one single-engined interim aircraft, the Vickers Wellesley, and for the more distant future the twin-engined Bristol Blenheim. In the heavy bomber field the Handley Page Heyford was in full production and was maintained as such whilst monoplane bombers were developed. One of these, the Fairey Hendon, had been around for a long time and one squadron was bought immediately. For the interim a new bomber, the Handley Page Harrow, was ordered; this was the result of a competition to replace the existing bomber-transports in the Middle East, but so great was the immediate British need that the Harrow was ordered for home bomber squadrons until newer bombers could be produced. In the long term the RAF settled on no fewer than three types of heavy bomber: the Armstrong Whitworth Whitley, the Handley Page Hampden and the Vickers Wellington, all of which would come into service in four years. For maritime reconnaissance the Avro Anson had already been ordered, beginning a 17-year production run; longer-range reconnaissance was in the hands of the flying-boats, of which the Short Singapore III was already in production, with two other biplanes, the Saro London and the

Supermarine Stranraer, on the point of production. These three boats took the brunt of the coastal expansion until that supreme flying-boat, the Short Sunderland, made its presence felt in 1938. For army co-operation more Audaxes were ordered and a new variant, the Hawker Hector, followed until a new monoplane, the Westland Lysander, could come into service. Rather out in the cold in all this was the Fleet Air Arm, although the Supermarine Walrus amphibian and that most ubiquitous of all FAA aircraft, the Fairey Swordfish, were ushered into service in this period, while a dive-bomber, the Blackburn Skua, and a naval version of the Gladiator were developed.

To cope with this very considerable expansion, the structure of the RAF in the UK was reorganised on to the basis which has been familiar up until very recently, when with the substantial reduction of the RAF in the past decade the RAF's structure has become almost a monolith. The Royal Air Force in 1936 was divided into Commands which operated according to function. Bomber Command was formed under Air Marshal Sir John Steel, Fighter Command under Air Marshal Sir Hugh Dowding, Coastal Command under Air Marshal Sir Arthur Longmore, and Training Command under Air Marshal Sir Charles Burnett. These Commands in turn administered various Groups which operated on a regional basis, the Groups administering Stations and the Stations their resident squadrons or other units. So the scene was set, with the whole reorganisation process being given a new geographical bearing. Until now the likeliest enemy had been considered to be France, and so the Bomber Force had been centred in the South Midlands and Salisbury Plain area with the

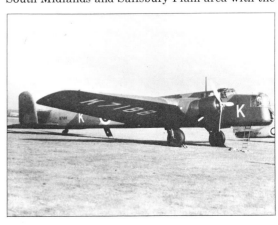

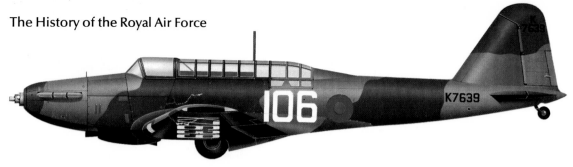

Left : To cope with the great influx of short-service commission pilots and to build up a reserve for wartime, over 30 elementary and reserve flying training schools were established throughout the country, often at civil flying fields. During the week they trained regular pilots and at weekends the reservists. Hart variants were the schools' staple service type, this Hart Special belonging to No. 5 E & RFTS at the London Air Park at Hanworth.

Far left : The Fleet Air Arm was still under the aegis of the RAF through the early 1930s, and it was during this time that carrier developments included the fitting of arrester wires and the entry into service of the Fairey Swordfish. The spirit of the era is captured in this photograph of the flypast, by Swordfish, during the 1937 Royal Naval review at Spithead with the Royal Yacht *Victoria and Albert* in view with HMS *Nelson* beyond.

fighter stations around London and in the south of England. Now, with Germany the obvious combatant, the bomber force was built up in East Anglia, Lincolnshire and the Midlands, and fighter bases were opened up along the length of the East Coast.

The monoplane arrives

The first monoplane to enter RAF service in any numbers joined No. 48 Squadron at Manston on the tip of Kent in March, 1936. This was the Avro Anson, destined for patrol of the sea routes around the British Isles and incidentally to be the navigation trainer for the new aircrew beginning to flow into the service. Manston became the focal point of both these ventures with the Anson, later Anson squadrons forming at Bircham Newton in Norfolk to patrol the North Sea.

The problem of manning all these new squadrons and providing enough crews for the service was no easy task. To cover this eventuality the RAF

Volunteer Reserve was created, drawing upon a new field of entrant. Instead of looking for university material this organisation drew on mainly grammar school boys who would join and receive non-commissioned rank, the idea being to produce 800 pilots a year. To do this new flying schools were set up near the main centres of population and their purpose was two-fold. Called Elementary & Reserve Schools, they took over all the elementary pilot training for the Royal Air Force on weekdays and at the weekends provided the same facility for the Volunteer Reservists. So successful was this organisation that in three years 5,000 men were trained as part of the RAFVR.

In that same year, 1936, there occurred a European development which sharpened the realisation that war was on its way. General Francisco Franco y Bahamonde moved into Spain from Morocco with his Fascist supporters and began a three-year civil war which he was eventually to win. Three European nations rushed ostensibly to aid one

The Bristol Blenheim Mk I bomber was the most workmanlike of the medium bomber aircraft entering service in 1937, and was soon in service in great numbers at home and overseas. No. 30 Squadron put up this squadron formation over the Shatt-el-Arab from the huge RAF base at Habbaniyah in Iraq.

As with the fighters, the bombers turned to monoplane configuration and the Handley Page H.P. 54 Harrow represented an early example of this. No. 214 Squadron flew this Harrow from Feltwell in 1939.

Product of the same specification as the Harrow, the Armstrong Whitworth Whitley proved more successful and remained in Bomber and Coastal Commands for several years through the war. K7207 was a Whitley Mk I of No. 78 Squadron at Dishforth in 1937.

Several 'firsts' were accomplished by No. 111 Squadron at Northolt when, in 1937, it received the RAF's first Hawker Hurricanes: it was the first squadron with monoplane, retractable landing gear fighters, the first with eight-gun fighters, and the first with aircraft having a top speed of over 300 mph (480 km/h).

side or the other: Soviet Russia supported the republican (Communist) government, while Italy and Germany supported Franco. All three, but most of all Germany, saw this as an opportunity to try out their forces and, particularly, equipment in a local war with little expense or risk to themselves. So it was over Spain that Italy and Germany developed their aircraft in readiness for the world conflict ahead, finding out just how their types operated in practice; at least, the Germans learnt from it and developed new tactics and new ideas, while the Italians and Russians were too inflexible to learn very much at all and concentrated on using the Spanish Civil War as a conflict in which to 'blood' personnel and equipment. So it was that Western observers could see the fruits of Germany's rearmament plans in action nearby, and what they saw added to the fears for a general European war, particularly when such types as the Dornier Do 17, Heinkel He 111 and Messerschmitt Bf 109 appeared on the scene.

In those days the doctrine that 'the bomber will always get through' was very much in vogue, so it became a period of extraordinary inventiveness when people came up with all sorts of ideas first to stem the bomber tide and then to beat it. Many of these ideas filtered through to the research estab-

lishments, notably the Royal Aircraft Establishment at Farnborough where a rapid expansion was taking place. With the great advance in aircraft, retractable landing gear, flaps, constant-speed propellers and many other new and more technically intricate devices, the RAE had to expand to cope with the flood of developmental work required of it. Much hard slogging went on behind its closed doors and many fruitful (and fruitless) ideas were explored. One idea, not specifically developed at the RAE, which came to fruition during this period was the rebirth of the barrage balloon first seen in World War I. Evolving out of the kite balloons of World War I, which had been used for artillery observation purposes, the barrage balloon was a similar beast which was moored, in company with many others, to form a barrage around and in front of important targets. The idea was that the balloons and their cables would form such a hazard to low-flying enemy aircraft that the aircraft would be forced to fly high, where their bombing accuracy would be impaired and where they would become better targets for anti-aircraft fire and defending fighters. Balloon squadrons were formed, originally under the Auxiliary Air Force, but this expanded in November 1938 into a separate Balloon Command, to provide barrages around the

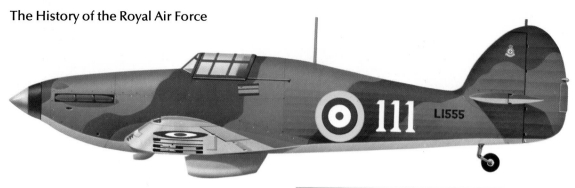

Based at Northolt, No. 111 Squadron's Hurricanes initially carried the squadron number, but with the war approaching this practice was stopped. This aircraft, flown by the squadron's CO, Squadron Leader J. W. Gillan, flew from Edinburgh to Northolt at 408 mph (656 km/h) on 10 February 1938.

major British cities and particular high-priority targets.

By 1937 the expansion of the Royal Air Force was fully under way, and the entry into service of several new aircraft types took place that year. In January 1937 Fighter Command was strengthened by the Gloster Gladiator, the first deliveries going to No. 3 Squadron at Kenley south of Croydon and No. 72 Squadron at Church Fenton near Leeds. In that same month the new medium bomber, the Bristol Blenheim, joined Bomber Command with No. 114 Squadron at Wyton in Huntingdonshire. (The first aircraft to arrive actually turned upside down on landing and was wrecked: so new were things like retractable landing gear and variable-pitch propellers that at first many unnecessary accidents took place.) In March 1937 the Fairey Battle, the new light bomber, joined Nos 52 and 63 Squadrons at Upwood, and the Armstrong Whitworth Whitley heavy bomber joined No. 10 Squadron at Dishforth in Yorkshire. April saw the Handley Page Harrow interim heavy bomber join No. 214 Squadron at Feltwell in Norfolk and the Vickers Wellesley join No. 76 Squadron at Finningley in Yorkshire. Then, at the close of the year, came one of the most significant arrivals, when the first Hawker Hurricane alighted at Northolt to become part of No. 111 Squadron, which became the first unit in the world to operate an eight-gun monoplane fighter.

The Hurricane was followed six months later by its fellow, the Supermarine Spitfire, which joined No. 19 Squadron at Duxford, Cambridgeshire in June 1938. By now Germany's intentions were quite clear as she had already seized Austria, and Czechoslovakia was under threat. British factories, including many 'shadow' factories which had been set up throughout the country and were run by car manufacturers, could not produce faster than they were doing, so orders were placed in the USA during 1938 for 200 North American Harvard single-engined trainers and 200 Lockheed Hudson general reconnaissance aircraft. The latter was a modified version of the Lockheed 14 airliner, which was already showing its speed on the routes of British Airways and was modified by putting a

bomb bay under the fuselage, a gun turret forward of the tail and twin Brownings in the top of the nose. The Harvards soon arrived at Spittlegate near Grantham in Lincolnshire at the local flying training school, and immediately caused a public outcry as a result of the noise made by their propellers which, having no reduction gearing, rotated their tips at supersonic speed. Despite the grumblings Harvards continued to train RAF aircrew well into the 1950s.

In August 1938 Europe marched to the brink of war over Czechoslovakia. The RAF brought its emergency routine into play and moved all its

The Supermarine Spitfire, culmination of the line developed from the Schneider Trophy seaplanes, entered service with No. 19 Squadron at Duxford in 1938, the finest fighter of its era.

After its long series of biplane flying-boats, the RAF received the doyen of all flying-boats with the introduction into service of the Short Sunderland Mk I seen here flying over the Channel with No. 210 Squadron.

K7718 was a Vickers Wellesley of No. 76 Squadron based at Finningley in 1937. The Wellesley was largely obsolete by the start of hostilities, but played a small part in the Middle East.

During the winter of 1938–9, Bicester was the home for this Blenheim Mk I of No. 90 Squadron. The outer yellow roundel has been painted over in the interests of camouflage.

For army co-operation the old biplanes had been replaced by the Westland Lysander monoplane, at first with No. 16 Squadron at Old Sarum where the commanding officer, Squadron Leader G. P. Charles, briefs his pilots before a sortie. Little did the pilots realize that within a year they would be thrown into the Blitzkrieg in France and the Lysander found to be totally inadequate in such a type of warfare.

Vickers produced the best bomber aircraft available to the RAF at the beginning of World War II, and the only one which was both in production and operational at the beginning and end of World War II. This was the Wellington, which entered service first with No. 9 Squadron.

squadrons to war stations, though realising that if war came at this moment the race against time had been lost. The prime minister, Neville Chamberlain, flew to Munich in September, where he proved no match for the bargaining and duplicity of Hitler. Chamberlain came away having convinced himself, but few other people, that he had bought off war for the decades ahead. Not fooled, the Air Staff were nevertheless relieved that the prime minister had bought precious time, even if

it was at the expense of the unfortunate Czechs. Time was now of the essence and, having learnt over the years to work miracles in a short time, the Royal Air Force now made the best use of every minute. No one knew how much longer was available before the holocaust began.

By January 1939 RAF first-line units comprised 135 squadrons compared with the 134 planned for March 1939 way back in 1936. The last of the new types of aircraft, the Vickers Wellington bomber, had entered service, and the new types were flowing into service in heartening numbers. Detailed preparations were going ahead for war, with air-raid precautions being taken seriously by service and civilians alike; RAF stations were camouflaged so as to cut down the ease with which they could become targets. RAF aircraft had been increasingly camouflaged since 1937 and, from the time of Munich onwards, squadron identity markings were either removed altogether or confined to small badges, the squadron identity being shown, to those in the know, by a two-letter code system, carried on the fuselage sides. This system became the standard used by British and American forces in the European theatre throughout World War II.

Only one aspect of the expansion had been left

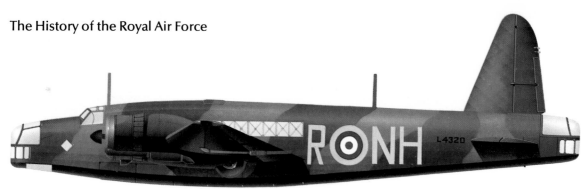

A Vickers Wellington Mk I during the summer of 1939. Soon this type would be spearheading the early bombing attacks on Germany.

out. In the RAF's scramble to ensure that it could fight its air battles satisfactorily, the Fleet Air Arm, which was supposed to provide the Royal Navy with its flying requirements, had received scant attention and, to the anger of their Lordships at the Admiralty, was obviously not going to receive fair treatment for the conflict ahead. In this climate they renewed their earlier battle to regain 'Navy control over the Navy's aeroplanes'. A new Parliamentary Committee was set up which, in practice, consisted solely of Sir Thomas Inskip, who promptly returned the Fleet Air Arm lock, stock and barrel to the Admiralty. Thus the chapter of naval involvement by the RAF ended, a period in which many of the major developments in carrier flying had been successfully brought into service and, at ship level, much worthwhile co-operation had been achieved. But with war only two years away the Royal Air Force would have enough on its hands without bringing the Fleet Air Arm up to date, and it was the right decision, even if taken at the 11th hour, for the Royal Navy itself. How the Admiralty responded to the difficult situation in which they had been put forms no part of this story now. But the Fleet Air Arm, in the war ahead, fought valiantly and well in the air alongside the RAF in many campaigns, despite the animosity which had all along existed in the higher echelons.

In the more peaceful days of its infant existence the RAF had shown a penchant for pushing ahead to the frontiers of flying development, and not a few world records had fallen to RAF aircraft. Even in the rush towards war the service still had time to break new records, spurred on by the need to develop to the limit for operational purposes. At the RAE Farnborough a couple of RAF test pilots had been using an experimental monoplane built

by the Bristol Aeroplane Company for developing pressure suits for use at high-altitude. In 1936 Squadron Leader F. R. D. Swain took this Bristol 138A up to 49,944 ft (15223 m) at Farnborough, breaking the world height record; nine months later Flight Lieutenant M. J. Adam lifted it to 53,937 ft (16440 m). In 1938 two Vickers Wellesley monoplanes, belonging to the Long Range Develop-

Blenheim Mk IFs of No. 29 Squadron exercise at Debden a few days before war breaks out.

Exercises in 1939: at Biggin Hill a Hurricane of No. 32 Squadron prepares for refuelling after a night sortie.

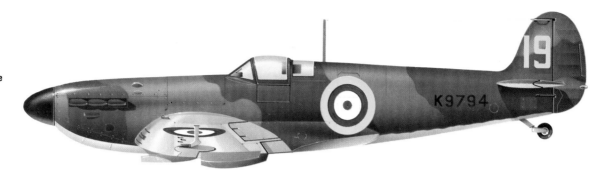

By the outbreak of war only nine squadrons had equipped with the Spitfire Mk I, of which No. 19 was the first. It was destined to become the most important Allied fighter and to continue in service long after the war's end.

In 1939 a display was held at Northolt for MPs to see the new RAF. Here is part of the line-up, with Spitfires from No. 74 Squadron (Hornchurch), Gladiators, a Gauntlet from No. 17 Squadron (Kenley) Hampdens from No. 144 Squadron (Hemswell), Whitleys from No. 58 Squadron (Linton-on-Ouse), Wellingtons from No. 38 Squadron (Marham), Blenheim Mk IVs and Battles. During this event a new secret aircraft, the Westland Whirlwind, flew over at high speed.

ment Flight of the RAF, extended the world distance record to 7,162 miles (11526 km) by flying nonstop from Ismailia in Egypt to Darwin in Australia in 48 hours. These were just the tip of the iceberg: for every development which hit the headlines, the scientists were beavering away to advance the art and science of flying so as to give the RAF the edge over any opponent in the approaching war. Nowhere was this so marked and yet so successfully secret as in the development of radar (known then as RDF, or radio-direction-finding). By September 1939 some 20 RDF stations had been set up around the coasts of the UK, able to detect aircraft at medium heights up to 100 miles (161 km) away – and a solution to the low-flying aircraft problem was under active development. A means had been found to identify hostile from friendly aircraft by means of a device called IFF (identification: friend or foe) which has since been developed into a normal civil aviation identity system. And the whole radar chain had been incorporated into Fighter Command's control system so that the information gleaned could be fed to the controllers with virtually no delay.

In June 1939 another development emerged, not a scientific one this time but one which added to the efficiency and the morale of RAF personnel. This was the formation of the Women's Auxiliary Air Force (whose members inevitably became 'WAAFs'), young women who were recruited to take over many of the routine duties hitherto performed by men, freeing the men for more warlike activities; the WAAFs, too, took on other duties more suitable to women and in the war years ahead exhibited much heroism and bravery when under bombing and fire. By the outbreak of war this fledgling branch of the service numbered 8,000, so keen were the young women of the day to 'do their bit' for the nation.

By June 1939, however, it was clear that Hitler's next round of acquisitiveness was beginning. His greedy eyes were upon Poland, against whom he was busy engineering an incident over Danzig. With British-French co-operation much closer now, it was decided that this time there could be no shilly-shallying – this would be the showdown: either Hitler would climb down or there would be war. So it transpired that on 3 September 1939, at 11 a.m., Neville Chamberlain announced that Britain was at war.

World War II: Britain at Bay

When Prime Minister Chamberlain's ultimatum to Germany expired on 3 September 1939, World War II found the home-based Royal Air Force established with a strength of 55 bomber squadrons (equipped with Bristol Blenheim IVs, Vickers Wellington Is and IAs, Armstrong Whitworth Whitley IIIs and IVs and Handley Page Hampdens), 35 fighter squadrons (with Hawker Hurricanes, Supermarine Spitfires and Gloster Gladiators), seven army co-operation squadrons (with Westland Lysanders), 11 general reconnaissance squadrons (10 flying Avro Ansons and one with Lockheed Hudsons), six flying-boat squadrons (with Short Sunderlands, Saro Londons and Supermarine Stranraers) and two torpedo-bomber squadrons (flying Vickers Vildebeests).

Spearhead of the service, Bomber Command, represented the manifestation of the Trenchard doctrine – the means of imposing the nation's will upon an enemy – yet as a result of the Chamberlain government's reluctance to drop bombs on enemy territory and appear to be guilty of invoking the horrors of modern warfare on a civilian population, the operational bomber squadrons were reduced to a first-line strength of 33 and the remainder relegated to a reserve status to provide operational training and make good wastage.

The unit establishment of the 116 squadrons totalled 1,466 aircraft, of which roughly 1,000 could be regarded as fairly modern, but the remainder (the biplanes, Ansons and Whitley IIIs) were in urgent need of replacement.

Committing the Air Component and Advanced Air Striking Force (AASF) to France for support of the British Expeditionary Force (BEF), with their complement of 10 Fairey Battle squadrons, five of Lysanders, four of Blenheims, four of Hurricanes and two of Gladiators, thus reduced the first-line strength from 94 (after allowing for the downgrading of the bomber units) to 69 home-based squadrons. If this force appeared puny compared with the Luftwaffe, each of whose three full-strength and autonomous Luftflotten (air fleets) was equipped with modern aircraft, it should be recalled that every pilot and aircrew member of the RAF and Auxiliary Air Force (AAF) had been peacetime trained within a structure whose rapid expansion in the late 1930s had yet to provide the necessary stream of newly-trained airmen. Few members of the RAFVR were yet joining the first-line squadrons, while modern aircraft were only just beginning to complete their initial combat clearance.

Early home-based operations

Against this background of depleted air strength at home and limitations imposed on the bomber force, early operations by the British and German air forces in the West were almost entirely confined to air attacks on the opposing maritime forces (apart from an extraordinarily naive 'campaign' of leaflet-dropping over German cities by the RAF's

When war was declared the Spitfire was in the minority in Fighter Command squadrons, only 10 being thus equipped (Nos 19, 41, 54, 65, 66, 72, 74, 602, 603 and 611, the last three being Auxiliaries). Seen here are six Spitfire Mk Is of No. 19 Squadron in green/earth camouflage with red/blue roundels and the code letters 'WZ' (concealing the squadron identity). This was changed to 'QV' on the outbreak of war.

K9013 was one of the last Tiger-engined Whitley Mk IIIs to be built. By the outbreak of war it was with No. 166 Squadron at Leconfield. The squadron moved to Abingdon in September 1939 to join with No. 97 Squadron as a training unit which in April 1940 became No. 10 Operational Training Unit, whose markings K9013 carries.

Just about to land at Driffield is a Whitley Mk V of No. 102 Squadron during the Phoney War. The Whitley was distinguishable by its huge, thick wings and nose-down attitude in flight. No. 102 Squadron was one of the No. 4 Group squadrons based in Yorkshire, which flew many freezing sorties during the first winter of the war dropping leaflets all over Germany.

achieved superficial damage to the *Emden* and *Admiral Scheer*, the destruction of a U-boat, a trawler and 10 enemy fighters, yet cost Bomber Command the loss of 43 aircraft and well over 100 aircrew. The bitter lesson, which was allowed to overshadow future strategic planning for years to come, was that unescorted daylight attacks by relatively slow bombers (however well they might be armed) was suicidal in the face of an organised force of forewarned interceptors.

Although attempted on a much smaller scale by the Luftwaffe, daylight attacks on the Royal Navy in its home ports were launched during the first months of the war. Most such raids were intercepted by home-based Spitfires, and half a dozen raiders were shot down. The principal activity by the Luftwaffe over the North Sea was a concerted effort to seal the British East Coast ports with air- and sea-sown magnetic mines, a campaign undertaken almost entirely at night by aircraft allocated to the Kriegsmarine. Not only was the RAF impotent in meeting this threat, but the enemy weapon came close to achieving its object and certainly severely disrupted the movement of coastal shipping off the East Coast.

The Norwegian campaign

The winter of 1939–40 was accompanied by early and prolonged fog, frost and snow which effectively restricted air operations over most of North-Western Europe, bringing atrocious conditions to the ill-prepared airfields of France and also reducing the flying effort, largely confined to training, in Britain. With little air activity over the Siegfried and Maginot Lines, there existed a feeling of lethargy which was particularly evident among the British land and air forces. This was the period of the 'Phoney War'.

The same lethargy had not existed elsewhere in Europe, however, and the tragic conclusion of the Polish campaign had been followed by the Soviet Union's attack on Finland, whose extraordinary determination and ability to resist invasion won worldwide admiration. Several Western powers sent military aid to the Finns, and early in 1940 the British government laid plans to send a squadron

night bombers which achieved little more than providing some navigation experience).

From the first day of the war reconnaissance flights by the RAF to locate German warships were quickly followed by a series of daylight 'reconnaissance in force' attacks on ships in the approaches to German North Sea bases, formations of unescorted Blenheims and Wellingtons being involved in a number of courageous but largely ineffective strikes.

These flights involved return distances of about 500 miles (800 km), often in poor weather and without any navigational aids, were invariably spotted on radar by the Germans, who ordered up intercepting fighters (usually from JG 1) and alerted their flak defences. (Radar, already an established fact within the British home air defence system, remained quite unsuspected as being in use operationally by the Germans for some months after the outbreak of war.) Wholly untrained in attacks on warships at sea, the RAF crews pressed home their assaults with great gallantry but suffered crippling losses. Moreover their 500-lb (227-kg) bombs proved entirely useless against the armoured targets. These attacks, which lasted until mid-December 1939 before being abandoned, and involved 861 bomber sorties and a mere 61 tons of bombs,

A scene typical at many East Anglian airfields early in the war shows this Wellington Mk IA standing on its dispersal miles from the hangars and about to be loaded with its nightly dose of bombs.

of Gladiators (No. 263) to Finland.

The Winter War in Finland ended, however, on 13 March 1940 before No. 263 Squadron could be embarked, but on 9 April the German attack on Denmark and Norway descended, thereby pre-empting British plans by a few hours to seal the northern iron-ore port of Narvik with mines. As the now-familiar Blitzkrieg deluged upon southern Norway, the British set in train preparations to embark an expeditionary force to fight alongside their new allies and with it, embarked in the carrier *Glorious*, No. 263 (Fighter) Squadron – still to some extent equipped and prepared for Arctic operations.

The establishment of powerful German forces in southern Norway (and the complete subjugation of Denmark in a single day) forced the decision to land the British force in central Norway, to prevent a northwards advance by the enemy. But this was an area particularly sparsely provided with air-fields, and it transpired that the RAF Gladiators were left with no alternative but to operate from the frozen Lake Lesjaskog, a feat made possible by snow-clearing efforts of 200 civilians led by an RAF officer, Squadron Leader W. Whitney Straight. No sooner had the 18 Gladiators landed on 24 April (after a hazardous flight from *Glorious* from which the pilots had made their first-ever deck take-off) than the Germans started bombing the ice runway. The attacks continued the following day and despite engine-starting difficulties following a freezing Arctic night and a chronic lack of tools and spares, the pilots did all they could to maintain cover over the ground forces. By mid-day 10 of the Gladiators had been put out of action on the lake while the runway was fast becoming unusable. By 26 April only one Gladiator remained serviceable and fuel for this was exhausted. Leaving the twisted, burned-out hulks of their aircraft littering the melting ice, the pilots of No. 263 Squadron arrived back in Scapa Flow on 1 May.

Such was the distance of central Norway from British bases that it had proved impossible for Bomber Command to give effective support to the Norwegians, and to give cover for the Allied forces now being disembarked far to the north at the port of Narvik (in an attempt to deny its use by the Germans) it was decided to send a Hurricane squadron (No. 46) as well as returning No. 263 with a new complement of Gladiators. Once more *Glorious* set sail for Norway and between 21 and 28 May the two squadrons became established on a landing ground at Bardufoss, 50 miles (80 km) from

Narvik, once again thanks to the efforts by an RAF officer, Wing Commander R. L. R. Atcherley, to coerce the local population into snow clearance.

In spite of all the difficulties inherent in such primitive operating conditions, the RAF pilots gave effective protection to the ground forces at Narvik, destroying a number of German bombers which, owing to the distances involved in their flights, were operating without fighter escort. However, as the German forces, with growing strength in the air and capable of overland reinforcement, advanced remorselessly northwards towards Narvik, the futility of maintaining a military force, dependent on exposed sea communications and only limited air cover, dawned upon the British command and on 1 June, covered by the Hurricanes and Gladiators of Nos 46 and 263 Squadrons, the evacuation of British forces from northern Norway was ordered. At midnight on 7 June the last Hurricanes took off to land on HMS *Glorious*, following a call for volunteers among the pilots to save their valuable fighters. The following afternoon, as if to underline the naked-ness of the whole Norwegian venture, *Glorious* was intercepted by the German warships *Scharnhorst* and *Gneisenau* and within two hours the carrier had disappeared beneath the Arctic wastes, taking with her all but two of the RAF pilots and all their precious fighters.

Thus ended the first of the RAF's wartime exploits, engendered entirely by a hopeless tactical situation, aggravated by inadequate planning and unsuitable aircraft, but garnished by tremendous courage and splendid adaptability. Alas, this was

Because of the terrain, there was little the RAF could do to help the Norwegians in their plight but send No. 263 Squadron, with Gladiators, to the frozen Lake Lesjakog in April 1940 to assist with fighter defence. But after five days fighting all the squadron's aircraft were destroyed or unserviceable, and the personnel returned to the UK to re-equip.

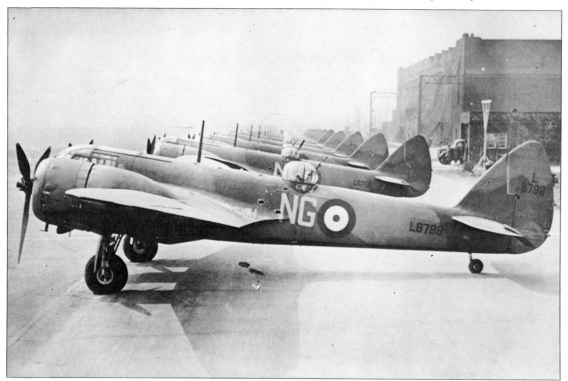

As war had approached the RAF realised that it had little to offer in terms of long-range or night-flying fighter aircraft so many of the Blenheim Mk Is still coming off the production lines were modified into fighters by fitting to their bellies a four-Browning pack firing under the nose. These aircraft were issued to several of the AAF squadrons as well as regular units. Here No. 604 (County of Middlesex) Squadron is lined up on the apron at Northolt in early 1940. The squadron went on to become one of the leading night-fighter units in the UK.

Because Dowding did not want to lose too many modern squadrons in France, his contribution to the Air Component of the BEF included two squadrons of Gloster Gladiators (Nos 607 and 615). N2304 had transferred to No. 615 Squadron from No. 605, and fought in the campaign as marked here. It was one of the few Gladiators to survive and return to the UK, subsequently serving with No. 16 (Army (Co-operation) Squadron.

The RAF had sent to France (in September 1939) its Advanced Air Striking Force for action against the advancing German armies. The strike element in this force consisted principally of squadrons of Fairey Battles such as No. 218 Squadron, here on formation practice over France in February 1940. Most of the Battle squadrons were wiped out within a few days of the Blitzkrieg's start on 10 May.

Maginot Line. As such a thrust would be levelled directly at the sector in which the BEF was deployed, the Luftwaffe anticipated a head-on confrontation with the RAF, and none of its previous experience suggested that it would find it daunting.

Since the first weeks of the war, the air elements of the RAF in France had been marginally strengthened, although little urgency had been apparent. The two Gladiator squadrons were scheduled to be re-equipped with Hurricanes, and most of the Hurricanes previously fitted with fabric-covered wings and with wooden propellers had given place to newer versions with metal wings and variable-pitch propellers. Perhaps one of the truly ironic features of the perceptible reinforcement process had been the deployment of a tactical reconnaissance unit (a photographic flight comprising a camera-equipped Spitfire and a Hudson) in France to provide warning of a German land attack. When such warning was afforded some 24 hours in advance, on 9 May, it was ignored by both British and French commands, who seemed simply to disregard the portents of massed enemy armour immediately behind the German frontier.

As it was, when the first German air attacks fell upon the Netherlands and Belgium at dawn on 10 May, and the BEF was ordered forward into the latter country to cover the enemy thrusts, the RAF's task was virtually confined to providing air cover over the battlefield. Moreover the French, whose own air force was pathetically deficient in modern bombers, forbade the RAF to carry out bombing raids on German territory for fear of provoking reprisals on French towns. The Luftwaffe required no invitation.

The only air assistance available to the Dutch, who faced widespread airborne troop assaults on key bridges, airfields, and road and rail key points, came from far-off British-based squadrons of Blenheims. Because of a lack of tactical communication these operated on an *ad hoc* basis, and any minor success they achieved was entirely

but a foretaste of events that now unfolded with terrifying ferocity upon the nations which had so reluctantly faced up to the reality of Germany's ambitions throughout the previous seven years of continuing political aggrandizement.

Collapse in the West

The defeat of Denmark and Norway had involved the employment of the equivalent of a single Luftflotte of the German air force with the temporary use of additional transport aircraft in the campaign's early stages. Meanwhile the Wehrmacht had been putting the final touches to its preparations for all-out attack in the West, an attack that would engulf the Low Countries in all the horrors of Blitzkrieg as a means of penetrating the unfortified northern flank of the supposedly impenetrable

The Bristol Blenheim Mk IV was the other light bomber serving in France. N6227 of No. 139 Squadron is being serviced in France, probably at Plivot, before the action started in 1940.

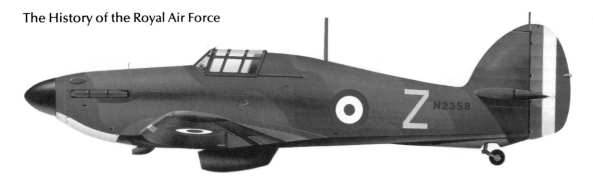

Two squadrons (Nos 1 and 73) of Hurricane Mk Is served with the AASF in France. Because they would be flying with French air force machines and their outline resembled that of the Dewoitine D.520 of the French, the Hurricanes were painted with rudder stripes. N2358 had come to No. 73 Squadron from No. 43 Squadron at Tangmere. It served as aircraft 'Z' of the squadron but was withdrawn and sent to the Finnish air force in February 1940 before seeing action.

fortuitous. For instance, an attack by six Blenheim fighters of No. 600 (City of London) Squadron, AAF, on Waalhaven, newly captured by the Germans, cost all but one of the RAF aircraft.

Likewise in Belgium, with whom neither Britain nor France had negotiated any detailed plan to meet a German attack save that of a tacit understanding that Allied troops would swing forward after such an attack had been launched, the initial assault by German airborne forces met little resistance (other than near Fort Eben Emael), with the result that vital crossing points on the natural waterway barriers were quickly taken. By the end of that first day much of the Dutch and Belgian air forces lay scattered and burned on the ground, and the British and French air forces had between them suffered the loss of almost 100 aircraft, a high proportion caught unawares on their airfields. By contrast, the Luftwaffe reported the loss of no fewer than 304 aircraft destroyed, 267 aircrew killed and 340 missing. But whereas the Allied losses represented a substantial proportion of the available air strength on the continental mainland, those of the Luftwaffe were made good almost immediately.

The next day, as the pattern of enemy intentions became clear in Belgium, the French appealed to Air Marshal A. S. Barratt, commanding the RAF in France, to attack German columns moving towards the Luxembourg border. Eight Battles of Nos 88 and 218 (Bomber) Squadrons were sent out; only one returned. The next day nine Blenheims of No. 139 (Bomber) Squadron attacked an enemy column near Maastricht but ran into an entire Gruppe of Messerschmitt Bf 109Es which shot down all but two of their number. The same day almost every Blenheim of No. 114 (Bomber) Squadron was destroyed in an enemy attack on its airfield.

It fell to five Battles of No. 12 (Bomber) Squadron to attempt to destroy the road bridges over the Albert Canal at Vroenhoven and Veldwezelt which

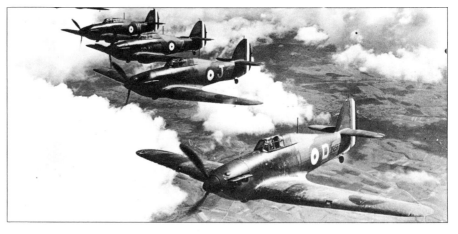

had been taken intact by the Germans and over which enemy columns were now pouring. Manned exclusively by volunteers, the Battles carried out low-level attacks in the face of murderous ground fire; all five aircraft were shot down, although the Veldwezelt bridge was hit. The leader of this attack, Flying Officer D. E. Garland, and his observer, Sergeant T. Gray, were posthumously awarded the Victoria Cross, the first to be won by members of the Royal Air Force for 22 years.

The catalogue of tragedies continued unchecked throughout the first week. Twenty-four Blenheims attacked the bridge in Maastricht itself, losing 10 of their number and without damaging the target. Within three days the RAF bomber squadrons had lost 63 aircraft out of the 135 originally available. On the evening of 14 May all remaining Battles and Blenheims were thrown into an attack on enemy forces massing at Sedan; of the 71 aircraft which took off, 40 failed to return. No other enterprise of the same scale undertaken by the RAF ever suffered a comparable sacrifice.

Two distinct RAF formations went to France in 1939, in the form of the Advanced Air Striking Force, which was an independent air force of its own, and the Air Component of the BEF, a basically army co-operating organisation. Both formations had two squadrons of Hurricanes as their main fighter defence, those seen here being from No. 73 Squadron of the AASF, the squadron which produced the first press-acclaimed 'fighter boy' in the person of 'Cobber' Kain.

The two BEF Air Component Hurricane squadrons were Nos 85 and 87 Squadrons, which moved across from Debden. Based at Lille/Seclin, No. 87 Squadron here provides a 'scramble' for the benefit of the press. It is interesting to note that only three of the aircraft had three-blade variable-pitch propellers at this time (February 1940) and that the aircraft still carried the squadron badge in an arrow-head on the fin, although this had been forbidden six months before.

The Westland Lysander Mk II was the standard army co-operation aircraft used by the RAF in the Air Component of the BEF, Nos 2, 4, 13, 26 and (eventually) 16 Squadrons serving there. The Lysander was a sitting target for German aircraft and many were destroyed. L4767 served with No. 13 Squadron throughout the campaign, survived to return to the UK where it continued on various duties, and was finally shipped out for service with the Indian Air Force until July 1944.

Far right: The winter of 1939–40 was very severe, and the squadrons in France had great difficulty keeping their aircraft flying. Some basic agricultural work appears to be needed at Mons-en-Chaussée to get this No. 13 Squadron Lysander Mk II unearthed.

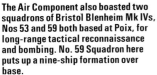

The Air Component also boasted two squadrons of Bristol Blenheim Mk IVs, Nos 53 and 59 both based at Poix, for long-range tactical reconnaissance and bombing. No. 59 Squadron here puts up a nine-ship formation over base.

Henceforth, with scarcely any bombers left to fly offensive sorties, the task of the RAF fighters in France was confined to battlefield cover, a task made infinitely more difficult by the swift retreat of the ground forces, and thus by an absence of raid warning. Occasionally formations of Hurricanes were fortunate to catch enemy bombers without escort and meted out harsh treatment.

Despite impassioned protests by Air Chief Marshal Sir Hugh Dowding, the commander-in-chief of Fighter Command, and responsible for home fighter defence, the German attack on 10 May had resulted in the despatch of four further Hurricane squadrons (Nos 3, 79, 501 and 504) to France, joining the four already deployed (Nos 1, 73, 85 and 87) and the Gladiator squadrons (Nos 607 and 615) which were at that very moment re-equipping with Hurricanes.

According to contemporary records, the Auxiliary Air Force pilots of No. 501 (County of Gloucester) Squadron, for instance, destroyed 18 German aircraft for the loss of two pilots in the first two days. But losses among these squadrons soon began to increase alarmingly and on 13 May 32 Hurri-

canes and pilots were sent to France as replacements before Dowding could persuade the Cabinet to call a halt to further inevitable wastage of his vital resources.

By 17 May losses among the Hurricanes caused the surviving pilots to amalgamate, thereby effectively creating three full squadrons. Such was the rate of retreat through Belgium and the Pas-de-Calais that as the BEF was isolated, following Guderian's Panzer thrust to Abbeville, the remains of the Hurricane squadrons in the north were evacuated from France, while those further south made their way westwards to evacuation ports such as Cherbourg, Brest and St Nazaire. At Merville, however, lack of fuel to evacuate the aircraft resulted in the deliberate destruction of 18 brand-new Hurricanes to prevent their falling into enemy hands.

The Dunkirk evacuation

With the departure of mainland-based fighter squadrons from the Pas-de-Calais, all air cover for the BEF, now making a desperate fighting withdrawal towards the port of Dunkirk, had to be provided by aircraft flying from airfields in Kent and Sussex. By 21 May the only aircraft left in the Pas-de-Calais were a few Lysanders of No. 4 (Army Co-operation) Squadron. The cost of supporting the French nation had been a total of 323 RAF aircraft up to the point at which the BEF started its historic evacuation from Dunkirk. More significant was the loss of Hurricanes, of which 195 had already been lost out of 261 deployed, and of which 120 had been destroyed to prevent them falling into enemy hands.

From 22 May an average of 200 fighter sorties was flown each day from England over northern France, doing everything possible to prevent the Luftwaffe from interfering with the withdrawal to Dunkirk. Inevitably Dowding's carefully husbanded Spitfire squadrons now entered the battle over France.

A new headquarters was created at Hawkinge in Kent to administer air operations over France and, apart from co-ordinating the fighter sorties, this also ordered up tactical night bombing sorties by the surviving Battles and liaison with the British Army by Lysanders (as well as some obsolete Hawker Hector biplanes).

On 26 May Operation 'Dynamo', the evacuation itself, started in earnest. From the outset some bitter criticism was levelled at the RAF by the shell-shocked and exhausted troops who seldom witnessed the air battles fought by the fighter pilots

The Fairey Battle was the mainstay of the Advanced Air Striking Force of the RAF in France, equipping Nos 12, 15, 40, 88, 103, 105, 142, 150, 218 and 226 Squadrons. Few returned intact as they were called upon to fly sacrificial attacks against the German armies. K9353 was typical: it was originally issued to No. 218 Squadron at Boscombe Down early in 1939, and went to France with the squadron in September as aircraft 'J'. It went missing during the fighting on 13 May 1940.

against approaching German bombers. The fact was that many attacks were beaten off before reaching the port and its crowded environs. On the other hand many other raids broke through to deluge bombs on the docks, beaches and streets of Dunkirk, reducing much of the town to rubble.

Dowding, and more particularly Air Vice Marshal Keith Park, commanding the vital No. 11 Group, Fighter Command, in south east England, were constrained to balance the need to protect the BEF's evacuation from the German air onslaught with the risk of permanent losses to Britain's metropolitan defences. Operating at fairly long distances from their home bases and without the benefit of accurate radar warning (British coastal CH radar could 'see' over the Pas-de-Calais but not clearly below about 10,000 ft/3050 m). Notwithstanding these difficulties, the Hurricane and Spitfire squadrons provided a remarkable degree of cover over the evacuation during the hours of daylight between 26 May and 3 June, when some 340,000 Allied troops were brought off by the armada of 'small ships'.

In the course of the hectic battles over Dunkirk one squadron (No. 264) of the new two-seat Boulton Paul Defiant fighters was involved for a short time and, although thought to have inflicted numerous casualties on enemy bomber formations at the time (since shown to have been exaggerated), the unwieldy turret and the tactics it imposed showed the aircraft to be unsuited for daylight air combat.

During the nine days of the great evacuation RAF fighter pilots flew a total of 2,739 sorties in the immediate area of Dunkirk; a total of 166 German aircraft are now said to have been destroyed at a cost of 131 RAF aircraft, of which 44 pilots were saved. In addition, 171 reconnaissance and 651 bombing sorties were flown by the RAF.

The importance of these losses lay not solely in their numbers but in the fact that they represented the professional hard core of Fighter Command. Some 87 pilots killed or taken prisoner represented the loss of an equivalent of five squadrons; moreover, a high proportion of the pilots lost were

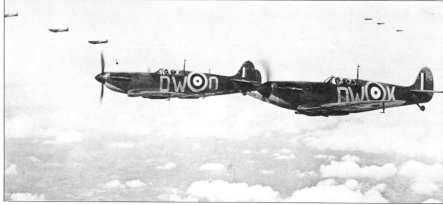

squadron or flight commanders – just the men on whom so much would have depended in the coming months.

The Battle of France, which continued until mid-June as isolated units continued to struggle back to other evacuation ports, cost the RAF a total of 959 aircraft, 477 of them fighters. The Air Component and AASF had lost 508 aircraft, Bomber Command 166, Fighter Command 219 and Coastal Command 66. To these must be added more than 50 fighters lost in Norway. How critical these losses were, particularly in fighters, was to be realised all too clearly in the approaching crisis.

Early home-based operations

Defeat in France and Norway left Britain without any foothold on the mainland of northern Europe. Moreover, as the German forces consolidated their positions in the newly-conquered territories, Britain now faced an enemy entrenched from the North Cape to the Spanish border. Three hostile air fleets were deployed against her, awaiting the word to launch an all-out attack to destroy the remains of Fighter Command as a necessary preliminary to a cross-Channel invasion by the Wehrmacht.

It was the fighting over Dunkirk that drew Spitfires into action for more than catching the odd raider over England. Day after day all the squadrons in the south east corner of England would send formations of fighters like this of No. 610 Squadron's Spitfire Mk Is (operating from Gravesend) over the Dunkirk beaches to try to establish air superiority and so enable the troops to escape.

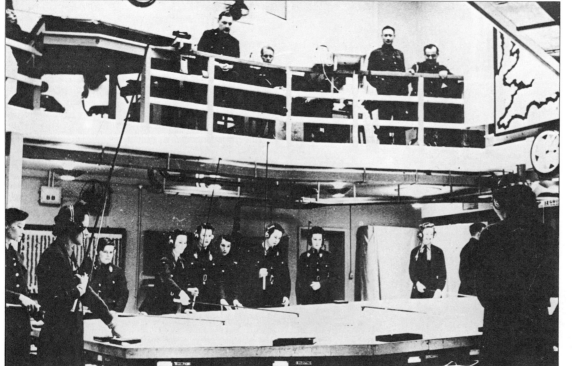

With the onset of the Battle of Britain, the key places in South East England were the Fighter Command operations rooms. In the middle of the floor the big table contained a map, stylized to show the various sectors and with large movable 'pieces' to denote the various forces, hostile and friendly. These were moved by the plotters (WAAFs with headphones and croupier's rakes) enabling the progress of the battle to be followed pictorially. The controllers sat in the gallery and in front of them had availability and readiness states of their various airfields. Information came in from the radar stations, Royal Observer Corps, airfields and the airborne fighters themselves, and from this welter of information the controllers directed the battle accordingly.

The Boulton Paul Defiant Mk I (see also picture, far right) worked on the principle that, information, aircraft with power-operated turrets would be a formidable force to break up enemy squadrons. No. 264 Squadron was formed to put this concept into practice, and N1535 joined the squadron in June 1940. The squadron had already been in action over Dunkirk: where the Germans thought the aircraft were Hurricanes and attacked from behind all was well, but when the Defiant formation was broken up and general combat took place the Defiant, with its heavy turret and no forward-firing armament, was a sitting duck. No. 264 Squadron was off day operations until 24 August, when in action again it destroyed three Ju 88s but lost three Defiants, including N1535.

Right: After fighting furiously with the AASF in France, No. 1 Squadron returned to the UK, re-equipped with factory-fresh Hurricane Mk Is and started in on the Battle of Britain, flying from Northolt, Hawkinge, Tangmere, Manston, North Weald and Heathrow before retiring on 9 September 1940 to Wittering, where this photograph was taken. It clearly shows the blast pens which were constructed to minimize the effects of a bomb falling on the dispersal area. The pilot climbing into P3395 is Flying Officer A. V. Clowes, DFM who painted the bee on the nose and added a stripe for every victory.

The place is Hawkinge airfield, the date is the 15 August 1940: two Hurricane Mk Is of No. 501 Squadron scramble to intercept yet another raid.

Whether the means (the airmen and aircraft of the Luftwaffe) of achieving this victory were adequate remained to be seen. Apart from some misgivings about the Spitfire, now seen to be at least a match for the best German fighters, recent experience in France and Norway showed the Luftwaffe to be capable of soundly defeating the RAF, or so thought the German High Command. Moreover, exaggerated victory claims by German airmen suggested that Fighter Command had already been fatally weakened.

Had the Luftwaffe been able to open its all-out assault on Britain immediately after Dunkirk there is little doubt that Fighter Command would have been crushed within four or five weeks.

Dowding however, ever mindful of the approaching battle, quickly re-arranged his order of battle, sending the mauled squadrons north to rest and remuster aircraft and pilots, and moving fresh units south to take their place. Fighter Command's organisation was based upon the Group-Area responsibility, each Group being divided into Sectors and each Sector possessing a number of principal and 'forward' airfields or landing grounds. At the beginning of the Battle of Britain there were two Groups (No. 11 in the south and No. 12 in the north), later increased by subdivision to four. The sectors were identified by their famous airfields, such as Biggin Hill, Tangmere, Hornchurch and so on. Operations rooms were located at Fighter Command HQ, the Group HQs and at the sector airfields, and into these flowed simultaneously-prepared information from the coastal radar stations, Observer Corps and neighbouring groups and sectors. By means of an efficient telephone network between these operations rooms and the pilots in their dispersals, squadrons could be ordered off the ground to meet enemy threats

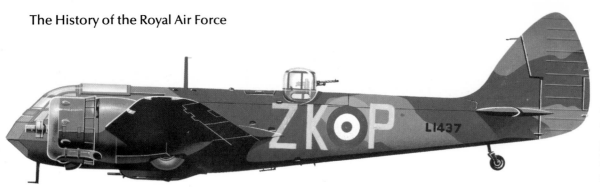

reported only two or three minutes previously. The
system had been developed over three years and
was already known to function very efficiently.

What gave rise to the greatest anxiety was
Fighter Command's poor strength. Long ago it had
been generally recognised that a minimum of 52
fighter squadrons was required to defend the
British Isles against a German air force based in
Germany. In June 1940 Fighter Command could
field no more than 32 fully operational, combat-
ready fighter squadrons against a German air force
poised just the other side of the English Channel,
with further components based in Scandinavia
and capable of raiding Scotland and northern
England. Moreover, of those 32 squadrons, four
were equipped with obsolescent Blenheims, one
with obsolete Gladiators and two with the suspect
Defiant.

In the event it transpired that the Luftwaffe
needed time to prepare its attack on Britain and to
make good its recent losses. Nor, when the preliminary skirmishing opened at the beginning of
July, were the operational aims fully appreciated
by the German air fleet commanders. To begin
with, coastal shipping and lesser-defended coastal
targets were selected as a means of forcing Fighter
Command into maintaining wasteful and vulnerable standing patrols. July proved a worrying time
for Dowding, however: as the air activity increased,
he saw his pilots engaging in unnecessary combat
without achieving a worthwhile victory ratio –
generally estimated to be at least four to one in
favour of the RAF. Even allowing for some exaggeration by his pilots, it seemed likely that they
were doing only little better than breaking even.
Moreover the coastal convoys off the British south
and east coasts suffered fairly heavily in the July
attacks, with the result that the Admiralty was
forced to reduce the movement of shipping and
went so far as to move some destroyers away from
the Channel. Such achievements must have
augured well for the planners of the forthcoming

invasion.

After this month-long skirmishing phase of the
Battle of Britain, the main assault opened on 8
August. On that day Fighter Command deployed
16 Hurricane squadrons (203 serviceable aircraft),
10 Spitfire squadrons (110 serviceable aircraft) and
four Blenheim night-fighter squadrons (32 serviceable aircraft) in the south (now divided between
No. 11 Group in south east England, commanded
by Park, and No. 10 Group in south west England,
commanded by Air Vice-Marshal Sir Christopher
Quintin Brand); and 14 Hurricane squadrons (148
serviceable aircraft), nine Spitfire squadrons (94
serviceable aircraft), three Blenheim squadrons
(28 serviceable aircraft), two Defiant squadrons (23
serviceable aircraft), and two Fleet Air Arm
squadrons of Fairey Fulmars and Gladiators (16
serviceable aircraft) in the north (now divided
between No. 12 Group covering the Midlands and
East Anglia, commanded by Air Vice Marshal
Trafford Leigh-Mallory, and No. 13 Group covering
the north of England and Scotland, commanded by
Air Vice-Marshal Richard Saul). In all there was a

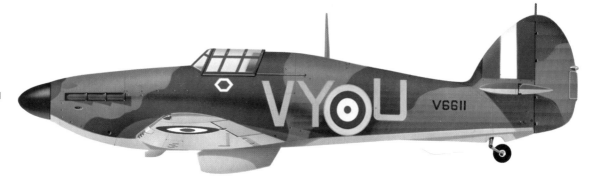

Hurricane Mk I V6611 was built at Hucclecote by the Gloster Aircraft Co., and joined No. 85 Squadron towards the end of the Battle. Like all other No. 85 Squadron machines it carried the white hexagon marking, here seen below the cockpit.

Above: This succession of camera-gun shots shows what happened to one Messerschmitt Bf 110 in the Battle of Britain. As the tracers whistle over and into it the starboard engine is smoking steadily and a burst on the port one helps to force it on its downward way.

Above right: Hawkinge became too close to the front line during the Battle of Britain for fighters to be based there permanently, so it was used as an advanced landing ground where squadrons would re-fuel and re-arm before the next operation. Here No. 610 Squadron has dropped in; its Spitfires are silent, ready and waiting as the pilots relax, some chatting together and others stretched out on the grass, all thinking about what they will be facing next.

Right: The airfields of South East England were the Luftwaffe's main targets in the Battle of Britain and received many heavy, damaging raids. This remarkable picture, taken presumably from an attacking Dornier Do 17Z, shows Kenley under attack, with a Spitfire (possibly of No. 66 Squadron) in one of the blast pens and a small bomb bursting just beyond.

grand total of 654 aircraft.

Opposing Fighter Command were 35 German bomber Gruppen, nine of dive-bombers, seven of heavy fighters and 22 of single-seat fighters. Assuming an average strength of 27 aircraft serviceable on each of the Gruppen (a fairly representative figure), this gives a total Luftwaffe strength on this day of 1,971 aircraft, including 594 of the Messerschmitt Bf 109E fighters.

The attacks which opened on 8 August gave Dowding no immediate indication that the Germans had shifted their aim as the principal target remained a Channel convoy. Only the scale of attack showed a significant increase in tempo. The first strike against the convoy was launched by about 60 Junkers Ju 87 dive-bombers escorted by 50 fighters, and was intercepted by about 30 Hurricanes and Spitfires of Nos 145, 257 and 609 Squadrons; seven German and two RAF aircraft were shot down, but four merchant ships in the convoy were sunk. Another sharp attack followed soon after mid-day and the same afternoon the remains of the convoy were struck by 82 Ju 87s escorted by 68 fighters, these again being intercepted by the fighters of Nos 43, 145 and 152 Squadrons; 12 German and four RAF aircraft were shot down. In these and a number of other combats over the Channel total losses for the day amounted to 26 German and 18 RAF aircraft (of the latter three pilots were saved, one severely wounded).

This pattern of combat continued for three days on a reduced scale until on 11 August heavy fighting again flared up over the Channel and the Thames estuary. Once again coastal convoys were the principal targets, but less reliance was placed on the Ju 87 by the Luftwaffe and more on such bombers as the Dornier Do 17 and Junkers Ju 88. Moreover a dangerous new tactic emerged, that of flying 'free chases' (*freie Jagd*) by roving Staffeln of Bf 109Es to catch RAF fighters returning to their airfields short of fuel and ammunition after combat. No fewer than 30 Hurricanes and Spitfires were

lost, while German records show that Luftwaffe losses amounted to 12 bombers and 24 fighters.

Very heavy fighting continued on the following day and on the 13th the pattern of attacks changed radically with a switch to land targets, in particular to the fighter airfields and coastal radar stations in the south. The operations in fact represented an abortive opening of Reichsmarschall Goering's all-out preparation for Operation *Seelöwe* (Sealion), the invasion of Britain. Codenamed *Unternehmen Adlerangriff* (Operation 'Attack of the Eagles'), the Luftwaffe's operations on 13 August proved a fiasco. As a result of bad weather some of the raiding formations failed to contact their escorts, and owing to a breakdown in communications the raids were not recalled. Considerable damage was however done to RAF installations and other targets in south east England.

The main attack was launched (and indeed the heaviest fighting of the entire battle took place) on 15 August when the Scandinavian-based air fleet (Luftflotte 5) joined the fray with a number of raids

over north east England as heavy attacks continued against airfields in the South. In a mistaken belief that all Fighter Command's resources had been concentrated in the south, the Germans sought to turn the British flank in the north, only to find 'resting' squadrons of Spitfires and Hurricanes awaiting them. Such were the casualties inflicted that Luftflotte 5 did not contribute any further significant daylight attacks during the Battle of Britain. In the south, however, further heavy damage was suffered on eight airfields. This day's fighting cost the Luftwaffe 75 aircraft destroyed and 15 severely damaged, compared with a loss of 30 RAF fighters in the air and 24 other aircraft on the ground; 16 of the RAF pilots were saved – most of them wounded – and two landed in France to be taken prisoner.

Nicolson's VC

Frantic fighting continued in the south on 16 August, and it was during a raid in the Southampton area that an RAF Hurricane pilot won the only Victoria Cross ever awarded to a member of Fighter Command. Flight Lieutenant J. B. Nicolson, a flight commander on No. 249 (Fighter) Squadron, was leading a section when it was attacked by Bf 110s. Despite his aircraft being set ablaze, Nicolson remained in the cockpit long enough to bring his gunsight to bear on one of the enemy fighters and shoot it down. Baling out with severe burns, the unfortunate pilot was shot at by Home Guard soldiers as he neared the ground on his parachute. Nevertheless Nicolson survived his ordeal and after a long spell in hospital returned to operations – only to lose his life in the Far East later in the war.

Culmination of this stage of the Battle of Britain was reached on 18 August, the day on which was achieved 'the defeat of the Stuka', the Ju 87. For 11 days the dive-bomber had been flown against ships, radar stations, airfields and dockyards in the south but, despite close fighter escort, had suffered heavy casualties at the hands of RAF fighters. In those 11 days 61 Ju 87s had been destroyed and 47 badly damaged and, as this aircraft was required to support the coming invasion, it was now virtually withdrawn from large-scale raids. In truth the Luftwaffe was taking stock of all the fighting since 8 August; it had suffered very heavy losses while, contrary to all expectations, the British fighter defences seemed, if anything, stronger than ever.

Certainly Dowding's pilots seemed to be holding their own. Tactics (once the old peacetime forma-

Enemy aircraft which had crash-landed in any sort of fair condition were soon pounced upon, as is this Ju 88, to be dismantled and sent to Farnborough for examination. Not only were new devices and equipment discovered, but the RAE built up a flying circus of Luftwaffe types for comparison purposes.

tion attacks had been discarded in favour of sections and combat pairs) were a match for those of the enemy. The radar chain remained largely intact, and none of the vital sector airfields had been destroyed, though many had been badly damaged.

A much more dangerous phase opened on 24 August, the aim of the German air force now being to destroy Fighter Command in the air as well as to destroy all fighter stations south of the Thames. Although large bomber formations with Bf 110 fighter escort continued to be flown by the Luftwaffe, the Bf 109E was now relieved of most of its escort duties and almost exclusively committed to the 'free chase'. At once British fighter casualties increased alarmingly. Particularly bitter air battles were fought on 26, 30 and 31 August, and on 2, 4 and 5 September. Although none of the sector airfields received crippling damage, many of their installations were destroyed.

In the fortnight up to 7 September, however, the

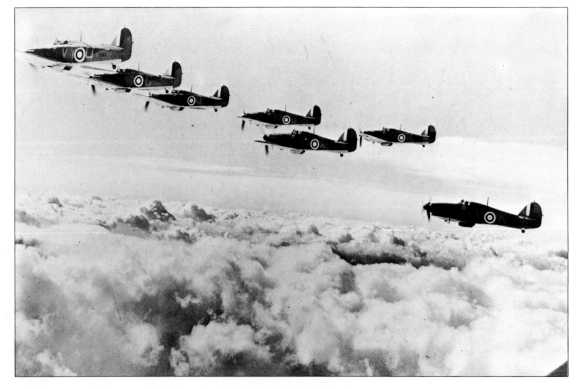

High above the autumn clouds flies No. 85 Squadron, under the leadership of Squadron Leader Peter Townsend. Having fought in France and then the Battle of Britain, it is here flying from Leconfield in Yorkshire, to which it had moved for rest and recuperation.

In the autumn of 1940 there appeared on the scene a potent and heavy new fighter, the Bristol Beaufighter Mk IF. The first few in service, with Nos 25 and 219 Squadrons, wore day-fighter camouflage but soon they were soot-black all over for the night defence of Britain. R2069 was one of the first to join No. 25 Squadron at North Weald. It subsequently served in the night-fighting role with Nos 68 and 256 Squadrons, surviving until a crash in March 1944 whilst with No. 51 OTU.

For Londoners the Battle of Britain was an unforgettable sight, a moving display of aerial strategy worked out in white condensation trails against the deep blue sky of 1940's summer.

The winter of 1940–1 brought a let-up for the day-fighter squadrons. Many of the squadrons by this time had become 'Gift' squadrons, with all their aircraft paid for by the donor. One such was No. 257 (Burma) Squadron, spending the winter at Coltishall under the leadership of Squadron Leader Bob Stanford Tuck.

RAF lost no fewer than 266 fighters in combat, or roughly one squadron every day. While the aircraft factories struggled to keep pace with their production of new aeroplanes, the main cause for concern was the alarming losses among pilots, added to which was the fact that many of the veterans were beginning to suffer the effects of the mounting strain of combat. For example, a Spitfire squadron in the south was being led by a newly-commissioned pilot officer, having lost its commanding officer, both flight commanders and six other pilots in five days (moreover this young pilot, despite being wounded, continued to lead the squadron for

three weeks, destroying 12 enemy aircraft before finally being shot down and very badly burned; his reward was a DFC). Volunteer pilots were sought from other RAF commands as well as from the Fleet Air Arm, and reluctantly Dowding chose to downgrade some of the hardest-hit squadrons to provide replacements to bolster those now being sent south. It is certain that had the tempo of fighting continued beyond 7 September, Fighter Command as a fighting force would have ceased to exist within three weeks.

7 September

Incredibly, the German High Command chose this very moment to shift its aim. Frustrated by the RAF's inexplicable capacity to put up a defence, and poorly served by his Intelligence branch, Goering now determined to strike at the British civilian population, beginning with a shattering attack on London itself. In the late afternoon of 7 September two huge formations of aircraft flew across Kent making for the capital's great sprawling dock area. Quickly realising that his sorely wounded airfields were no longer threatened, Dowding ordered every available fighter within 60 miles (95 km) to the Thames estuary, and at about 6 o'clock that evening one of history's greatest air battles raged in the area of the Isle of Sheppey when about 300 RAF fighters fought 900 German fighters and bombers. Both sides suffered severely, but the Luftwaffe broke through to London where it set large areas of the humble East End on fire – a blaze that could be seen for 100 miles (160 km) and attracted further bombers throughout the night like moths to a flame. To add to this trauma in the south east, a warning of imminent invasion flashed throughout the counties of Kent, Sussex and Surrey that night – mercifully false as it proved.

The Battle of Britain represented the first major setback for Germany in the war; that being so, the

During the war a tremendous number of individuals and organisations subscribed money to pay for aircraft, which were duly named. The Royal Observer Corps provided two Spitfire Mk IIAs, the first being P7666. It was issued to No. 41 Squadron at Hornchurch late in 1940 where it was flown by Squadron Leader D. O. Finlay, DFC. When the squadron left Hornchurch in February the aircraft transferred to No. 54 Squadron, with which it flew on Channel sweeps until going missing on 20 April 1941.

events of 7 September represented the turning point of the battle. From that moment on the Luftwaffe became embroiled in an ennervating campaign of night attacks against a nebulous target (sprawling conurbations) with the equally nebulous purpose of undermining the morale of the nation. This campaign was to become known as the Blitz, of which more will be told in due course.

Luftwaffe losses mount

The switch to attacks on London also marked a new stage in the daylight Battle of Britain for, although night attacks now increased, the daylight attacks continued to run their course. The three great day raids on London of 15 September brought about such heavy losses by the Luftwaffe that they marked the climax of German efforts to destroy the RAF in the air. Indeed, RAF claims to have destroyed 187 enemy aircraft (subsequently corrected to 60) resulted in this day being commemorated as Battle of Britain Day. It was at this moment that, frustrated by continuing excuses for heavy losses in the air by Goering, Hitler decided to abandon his plans to invade Britain, at any rate until after the coming winter was over.

Nevertheless the Luftwaffe continued to launch heavy daylight raids, particularly against aircraft factories in the south west, until the end of September when a new phase opened in which small numbers of high-flying, bomb-carrying Messerschmitts ranged over southern England. These proved difficult for Fighter Command to intercept, only the Spitfire possessing an adequate performance to reach the incoming raiders. For the Germans it was a misconceived and fruitless exercise as no attempt could be made to hit specific targets, and only succeeded in keeping Fighter Command – now quickly recovering its energy and strength – alert.

At the end of October, what Churchillian oratory had pronounced to be the Battle of Britain came to a close; and Churchill had been right in his appellation, for this had been a battle for survival, and a battle to ward off invasion. The German aims had been frustrated, and the invasion plans set aside. To the Germans the view nevertheless persisted that the battle had not been lost – after all, their bomber force not only remained in being, but was mounting a devastating night assault which would continue unabated for six months to come. Yet for Britain the corner had been turned; her air force stood undefeated and was becoming stronger daily. The scourge of Europe's skies for the past year had been thwarted, and the evidence of this lay in England's fields.

The long summer months of 1940 had wrought great changes in the RAF. Gone was the atmosphere of cavalier bravado that characterised the peacetime service, and with it many of the men on whom a splendid tradition had already been built. New names were on the lips of the public: men like Bob Stanford Tuck, Douglas Bader, 'Ginger' Lacey, Johnnie Kent, Colin Gray and Peter Townsend, to name but some of the immortal 'Few', the 3,000 men who had flown the Hurricanes and Spitfires day in and day out. Some 500 pilots had fallen, their places taken by newly-trained youngsters, while new squadrons had come into being – including two manned by Free Poles, two by Free Czechs and one by Canadians. Another, No. 71 (Fighter) Squadron, the first of the famous Eagle Squadrons manned by American volunteers, was just too late

The Hurricane was also pressed into night-fighting, so desperate was the need to knock down the German night raiders. Here is an all-black Hurricane of No. 85 Squadron about to start up for patrol.

The Blenheim Mk IF made a valiant attempt, in 1940–1, to provide a night-fighting service until the Beaufighter was in service, and it achieved a modest success. Thereafter the Blenheims were used as radar trainers for the oncoming Beaufighter crews. This aircraft (K7159) started life as a bomber with No. 61 Squadron, being converted to a fighter in 1939 and serving briefly with No. 222 Squadron when it formed, moving on to No. 145 Squadron at Croydon early in 1940. Thereafter it flew with Nos 5, 54 and 51 OTUs (the markings YX:N show it in No. 54 OTU service), then to No. 12 (PA)AFU, with whom it crashed on 6 May 1943.

to see combat during the battle, although several of its members had fought alongside British Commonwealth pilots on other squadrons.

The aircraft factories, continuing to function day and night, had kept pace with losses, and new versions of the Hurricane (the Mk IIA) and Spitfire (the Mk II) began appearing by the end of the battle. The Defiant had been redeployed as a night-fighter and already the old Blenheim I night-fighters were being replaced by the new and deadly Beaufighters.

The Blitz

If there was one area in which Fighter Command was sadly ill-equipped at the time of the Battle of Britain, it was in night defence. Blenheim fighters had equipped five squadrons (Nos 23, 25, 29, 600 and 604) during the summer of 1940, squadrons that had roamed aimlessly about the night skies with few targets and scarcely a single successful interception. Recourse had been sought in the night-time use of Hurricanes and Spitfires with only marginally better success and, although the Spitfire proved to be quite unsuitable for the job, the Hurricane showed itself to be fairly effective – being relatively simple to land at night. As already mentioned, the Defiant, having proved virtually useless as a day fighter, was transferred to the night fighting role, which it performed with much better results.

Moreover the CH (Chain, Home) radar chain, which had proved so vital in the day battles, together with the Observer Corps network, was quite inadequate at night, being incapable of bringing the night-fighter within visual range of its target. A great improvement was made with the arrival in service of the CHL (Chain, Home, Low) radar, and later CHEL (Chain, Home, Extra Low), together with its associated plan position indicators.

Since early 1939, however, No. 25 (Fighter) Squadron's Blenheims had been flying with the first rudimentary airborne radar sets, and trials had been laboriously progressing to evolve night interception procedures. First success by a night-flying, radar-equipped Blenheim (actually belonging to the semi-experimental Fighter Interception Unit, or FIU, based at Tangmere) had been achieved late in July when Flying Officer G. Ashfield located and shot down a Do 17 over the Channel. Indeed this was the world's first such success for airborne radar.

Towards the end of the Battle of Britain the first Bristol Beaufighters were appearing in service, destined to replace the Blenheim. By the end of October about a dozen of these powerful twin-engine aircraft, equipped with AI (Airborne Interception) Mk IV, had reached the night-fighter squadrons. By this time the German night Blitz was in full swing.

Although isolated night raids had been carried out by the Luftwaffe throughout the Battle of Britain, usually by single aircraft, they had been of little more than nuisance value to the enemy. With the devastating raid on London's dockland of 7 September a new campaign opened: every single night until 14 November the German bombers visited the capital in varying strength – a consistency of single-target air attack never again equalled, although of course RAF Bomber Command's later offensive against Germany was infinitely more destructive. By the end of October Goering had deployed 1,150 bombers (He 111s, Ju 88s and Do 17s) for the night offensive, in addition to about 120 bombers still available for daylight operations. Apart from a few Hurricanes, the RAF's night defences amounted to a nightly average strength of about 50 Blenheims, about 20 Defiants and single-figure totals of Beaufighters. As priority was given to the ground defences (guns and balloons) over London itself, such few successes that were achieved by the night-fighters were gained over the coast and open countryside.

More often than not the German bombers flew

Early in 1941 the Hurricane Mk IIC came into service with the RAF, the service's first aircraft operational with four 20-mm cannon. Many of them were used on the Channel sweeps and bomber escorts over France, but some went to the night-fighter Hurricane squadrons, as did BE500, shown here flying with No. 87 Squadron in mid-1941; No. 87 was responsible for night defence in the West Country at the time.

A lesser-known version of the Beaufighter night-fighter was the Mk IIF, fitted with two Rolls-Royce Merlin XXs. T3046 was one such, joining No. 307 (Polish) Squadron, in whose markings it is shown, towards the end of 1941 at Exeter. In the following year it transferred to No. 96 Squadron with whom it crashed, at Cranage, on 6 September 1942.

in over the Kent and Sussex coast, their approach reported by the radar stations. The night-fighters would have been flying patrols and unless the bombers were spotted in searchlight beams as they crossed the coast a long overland stern chase would follow.

Early in November the Luftwaffe also flew further afield, raiding Merseyside and Birmingham with moderately heavy forces, but now beginning to suffer perceptible losses as the British crews struggled to master the vagaries of their radar. Moreover the discovery of a German radio navigation aid, codenamed *Knickebein* (literally, Crooked Leg), by the British and its successful jamming, led to a loss of confidence in the equipment and also to a scattering of the bombing forces; this tended to assist the night-fighters, often searching areas in which no raid was being carried out.

The first real breakthrough occurred with the discovery that a German pathfinder unit, Kampfgruppe 100, was employing a new radio device, *X-Gerät*, which consisted essentially of a radio beam directed at the target, along which the pathfinders flew until they reached other intersecting beams indicating approach to the target and bomb release point. This equipment was in use on the night of 14/15 November when 437 German bombers devastated the centre of Coventry.

End of the Blitz

It was quickly discovered that not only could the *X-Gerät* beams be jammed or 'bent' (thereby diverting the raid from its intended target) but, provided the beam could be located soon enough, also that night-fighters could patrol it and catch incoming bombers. One of the first successful Beaufighter crews, Squadron Leader John Cunningham and Sergeant C. F. Rawnsley of No. 604 (County of Middlesex) Squadron, destroyed a Ju 88 on 20 November. (One of the RAF's most successful night-fighter pilots, John Cunningham became one of Britain's best known post-war test pilots, particularly in such famous aircraft as the de Havilland Comet.)

While it never proved possible to beat off raids on a particular target (nor were later RAF night raids ever beaten back), it was obviously possible to inflict such heavy losses in successive attacks that the enemy would come to regard their continuation as being too costly. But such an achievement lay in the future. Birmingham, Southampton, Liverpool, Bristol and Plymouth followed the fate of Coventry during November, and in December Manchester and Sheffield suffered heavy raids. At the end of the month the City of London was subjected to a particularly vicious incendiary attack which left many historic buildings gutted.

The New Year found Fighter Command desperately modernising its equipment both on the ground and in the air. Specialised fighter-control radar stations, or Ground Controlled Interception (GCI) stations, were coming into service employing the Type 7 metric radar and PPI (plan position indicator) display, although to begin with the four stations could each handle one night-fighter only. In January only three enemy raiders were destroyed by fighters, compared with 12 by the ground defences. In February the figures were four and eight respectively. In March, however, by which time five Beaufighter squadrons were fully equipped and operational together with eight Hurricane and Defiant squadrons exclusively allocated to night fighting, and 11 GCIs were available, the night-fighters destroyed 22 raiders, the guns 17.

As the German night Blitz continued unabated,

with 61 raids by more than 50 aircraft each on London, Birmingham, Coventry, Nottingham, Portsmouth, Plymouth, Bristol, Swansea, Merseyside, Belfast and Clydeside between mid-February and 12 May, in addition to constant minelaying, so Fighter Command took an increasing toll. In April the night-fighters shot down 48 bombers, the ground defences 39; but in May, which saw an end of the Blitz on the 12th, the night-fighters destroyed no fewer than 96 German aircraft, the ground defences 42. German records show that about 60 further aircraft either crashed at their home bases after combat or were otherwise severely damaged during those first 12 May nights.

An end to the Blitz was called by Goering, not simply on account of the losses being incurred (at 3.5 per cent of sorties flown such losses could be sustained, but only just). It soon became clear that Germany needed its bombers elsewhere: Hitler's attack on the Soviet Union was less than six weeks away.

Radar proved decisive in countering the night Blitz, as it had been in the daylight battles of the previous summer. In parallel with the operational use of radar to defeat the enemy in combat were numerous other electronic developments being undertaken, as will in due course be shown.

'Leaning forward into France'

Victory in the Battle of Britain was followed by considerable rearrangement of Fighter Command's hierarchy. At the top the architect of British victory, Air Chief Marshal Sir Hugh Dowding (long overdue for retirement from the service in any case, though many felt inadequately honoured for his prodigious achievement) was succeeded by Air Marshal Sir William Sholto Douglas, while Dowding's chief lieutenant, Keith Park, was replaced by Trafford Leigh-Mallory in command of No. 11 Group. During the battle there had existed some acrimony between Park and Leigh-Mallory over the use of fighter wings in combat; the latter, who had gained some support at Air Staff level for his wing advocacy, was considered ripe for command at the 'sharp end' of Britain's fighter forces; time and again throughout the war (and ever since), his unorthodox use of fighters was called into question. By the same

The Defiant Mk I had had a brief and inglorious record as a day fighter but it found some success in 1941 as a night-fighter as its style of operation was more suited to swanning around looking for unsuspecting targets. No. 264 Squadron, which had been adopted by the Madras Presidency, served at Biggin Hill and West Malling before moving to Colerne where this picture was taken in September 1941. This particular gift Defiant has five kill markings beneath the cockpit.

Some of the Douglas Boston Mk Is and Mk IIs which came to Britain in 1940 were retained in their bomber configuration, with the addition of forward-firing guns and issued to No. 23 Squadron at Ford. BD112 was one such and was used for intruder sorties over the northern French airfields in the spring of 1941.

In 1941 the Bristol Beaufighter Mk IF came into its own in the night-fighter battle and, equipped with AI radar, began to make inroads into the night bombing raids in which up till then the Germans had had it all their own way. This formation of three is from No. 600 Squadron and shows where the censor has clumsily tried to delete the radar aerials from the noses of the aircraft and has, in fact, drawn attention to them.

being sent to North Africa.

At the outset the limited RAF offensive was confined to two types of operation, both intended to disrupt enemy activities along the French coast and to attract the Luftwaffe into the sky where it could be fought and, hopefully, defeated. The first were 'Rhubarbs', simple offensive sweeps flown by small numbers of fighters (often at no more than single squadron strength, somewhat reminiscent of the German 'free chase' tactics of the previous year). Sometimes they carried out active low-level attacks on docks, railways or airfields, but more often than not they simply trailed their coats, hoping to catch enemy aircraft unawares. The other operations were 'Circuses', usually involving a small number of Blenheim IVs of Bomber Command escorted by several squadrons of fighters.

By January 1941 Fighter Command had grown to eight Groups (Nos 9, 10, 11, 12, 13 and 14 Fighter Groups, No. 60 Signals Group and No. 81 Training Group), comprising 72 squadrons. Their equipment was still dominated by Hurricanes (the Mk I, Mk IIA and Mk IIB, and soon to be joined by the four-cannon Mk IIC), but also included Spitfire IIs (and early in 1941 the excellent Mk V), as well as Defiant, Blenheim and Beaufighter night-fighters. There had been little change in German equipment, and the Luftwaffe early in 1941 still depended on the Bf 109E for air defence, although this was being eclipsed by the new Spitfires. The balance would soon be redressed by the arrival of the Bf 109F, and henceforward superiority in the air over the Channel would swing to and fro as the Spitfire V, Focke-Wulf Fw 190A and Spitfire IX came into service.

As the scale of these daylight operations increased in 1941 by such famous formations as the Biggin Hill, Kenley and Hornchurch Wings (now commanded and led by famous Battle of Britain

criteria, Park unquestionably achieved better results.

With no apparent attempt by the enemy to renew serious daylight attacks after October 1940 (apart from an ill-judged attempt by the Italian Regia Aeronautica to despatch some fighters and bombers, which were very roughly treated by RAF Hurricanes, against the south east in mid-November), Sholto Douglas obtained Air Staff approval to initiate a limited daylight offensive against targets in northern France. His Intelligence disclosed that the Germans were preparing to move some of the *Jagdverbände* (fighter formations) away from the west, and it was his intention to tie down as many of these forces as possible by committing the Luftwaffe to defensive operations. Better they should be kept in France than, perhaps,

The other major contributor to the night war was the Douglas Havoc. This was a night-fighter conversion of the American Boston bomber, which was big enough to house a formidable armament together with radar equipment in its nose. This is a Havoc Mk I of No. 85 Squadron taxiing out, probably at Debden, in early 1941.

Supermarine Spitfire

W3185 was a standard production Vickers-Supermarine Spitfire Mk VA and was issued to RAF Tangmere in 1941. Here it became the mount of the Tangmere Wing Leader, Wing Commander Douglas Bader. The illustration shows the Wing Commander's pennant just by the cockpit, with the initials 'D:B' signifying Bader. From 1941 onwards wing leaders were allowed to use their initials on their personal aircraft in place of the normal squadron identity letters. It was in this aircraft that Wing Commander Bader was lost over France on 9 August 1941; the tail was knocked off W3185 and it is presumed that a collision with a German fighter had done this. Bader baled out and was a POW for the rest of the war.

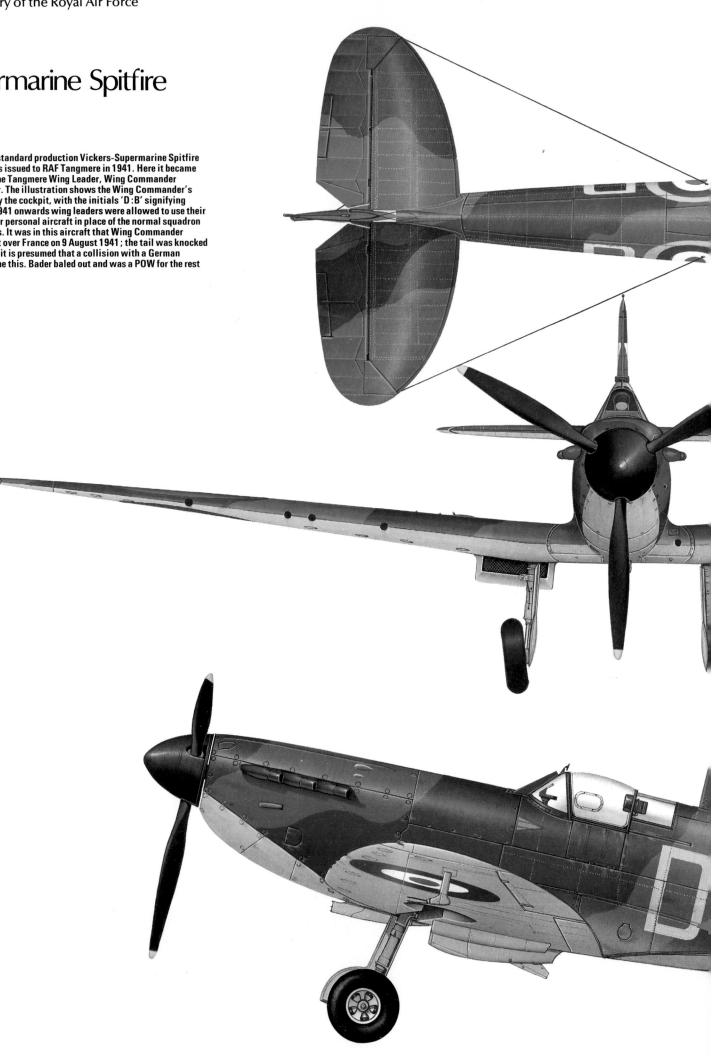

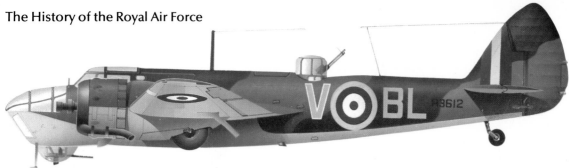

Until the advent of American medium bombers, the Bristol Blenheim Mk IV bore the brunt of the daylight offensive. R3612 is typical, having been delivered at first to the PDU at Heston in the spring of 1940 but soon transferring to No. 40 Squadron at Wyton, from where it flew operationally until being shot down over Ostend on 9 September 1940.

Far left: High over England flies yet another version of the Hurricane to see service – the Mk IIB fighter-bomber. Slung beneath the wings are two 250-lb (113-kg) bombs. Several fighter squadrons converted to this role in 1941 and were used for low-level bombing attacks on targets in northern France. This aircraft is from No. 402 RCAF Squadron, one of the foremost in the early use of this version. They were forerunners of the later Typhoon raids.

veterans), Bomber Command was also undergoing transformation. Since the ill-fated raids of 1939 the heavy bombers were now fully committed to night operations, as will be told in due course, while the Battle light bomber had been withdrawn from operational use in 1940. Mainstay of Bomber Command's daylight bombing force was still the Blenheim IV, with which 11 squadrons (Nos 18, 21, 82, 88, 101, 105, 107, 110, 114, 139 and 226) were equipped during 1941. Although these squadrons occasionally joined the night offensive on short-range missions, their main task was to participate in daylight 'Circuses'. But because of their small bombload (1,000 lb/454 kg carried internally), they did little significant damage. In October that year No. 88 (Bomber) Squadron was the first to take delivery of the Douglas Boston III, a greatly improved aircraft able to carry 2,000 lb (907 kg) of bombs.

Notwithstanding the previous remarks about the heavy bomber force, a small number of daylight raids was carried out by heavy bombers, particularly the big Short Stirlings of No. 7 (Bomber) Squadron, which had started accepting the Stirling towards the end of the Battle of Britain. These raids, carried out by two or three aircraft at a time, each aircraft carrying about 8,000 lb (3629 kg) of bombs, were however short-range missions escorted and covered by large Spitfire formations.

Another short-lived daylight bombing venture was that carried out by the Boeing Fortress Is of No. 90 (Bomber) Squadron during the summer of 1941. On the premise that by flying at 30,000 ft (9145 m) and relying on heavy defensive armament they could operate without fighter escort, it was thought that these aeroplanes would succeed where the Wellingtons had failed in 1939. Against American advice, which was that such operations should be carried out by large compact formations to give mutual defence, the RAF Fortresses flew in small numbers – sometimes even singly – and suffered accordingly. Moreover, difficulties with the bombsight and freezing up of the guns, as well as a fatal blind spot at the rear of the aircraft, resulted once more in prohibitive losses. So after attacks had been launched against Bremen, Brest, Emden, Kiel, Oslo, Rotterdam and Wilhelmshaven, the venture was abandoned and the surviving Fortresses sent to the Middle East.

Turning briefly from the build-up of the RAF's offensive over northern Europe, it is convenient here to mention another enterprise which in 1941 made demands on Fighter Command at home. At dawn on 22 June Germany launched its great assault on the Soviet Union, and during the follow-

ing weeks it became clear that the Russian forces were suffering massive losses in men, matériel and territory. Although far from politically sympathetic towards Communist ideals, Churchill at once pledged support for the Red Air Force with a promise of all aircraft that could be spared.

In August two Hurricane II squadrons, Nos 81 and 134, were assembled and despatched (under the command of Wing Commander H. N. G. Ramsbottom-Isherwood) by sea to Vaenga and Arkhangel'sk in the far north of Russia to assist in the defence of Soviet communications and installations. With Finland's re-entry into the war, now on the Axis side, accompanied by the arrival of German aircraft on her soil, the job of the RAF squadrons was considered vital to protect the northern ports for the arrival of the famous PQ convoys, now being sailed at frequent intervals.

Not only did the RAF Hurricane pilots succeed in destroying a fair number of German aircraft while operating in very difficult conditions, but also undertook the training of Russian pilots. The personnel returned home after six weeks, leaving their Hurricanes behind – the first of no fewer than 2,952 such aircraft to be supplied to the Soviet Union during the war.

Returning to northern Europe and the Channel in particular, a new turn of events occurred with the arrival of the first Focke-Wulf Fw 190As at Le Bourget. It was on 27 September that the RAF first became painfully aware that the Germans possessed a fighter which had more than an edge

The brunt of the daylight bombing offensive on northern France and the Low Countries in 1941 was being borne by the Blenheim Mk IV squadrons, either unescorted at ultra-low level or with fighter escort. Seen from the camera of a compatriot, this Blenheim Mk IV of No. 226 Squadron is over French fields in the autumn and provides testimony to the effectiveness of the camouflage scheme.

No. 7 Squadron was the first operational four-engine bomber unit in the RAF, with Short Stirling Mk Is including N6003, originally delivered in the scheme shown (N6003 joined the squadron in January 1941) but soon repainted with black up the side of the fuselage. It was used operationally by No. 7 Squadron until December, when it went on the training circuit with No. 26 Conversion Flight and then No. 1651 (Heavy) Conversion Unit.

By 1941 the four-engine bombers were tried on some daylight raids on the German battlecruiser base at Brest. This photograph was taken during one such raid in June or July 1941, showing a No. 15 Squadron Stirling.

With the onslaught by Germany on Russia the latter appealed to Britain for help. There was precious little that could be done, but the RAF did despatch No. 151 Wing, comprising Nos 81 and 134 Squadrons, to Russia with Hawker Hurricane Mk IIBs.

over the Spitfire V, now in service with 26 squadrons and scheduled to join 13 others.

By then the *Jagdverbände* in France had been reduced to two Geschwäder (the others having been moved to the Balkans, North Africa and the Eastern Front), of which JG 26 'Schlageter', commanded by the brilliant Oberstleutnant Adolf Galland, was soon equipped with the new Fw 190A. During the winter of 1941–2 the balance of air superiority swung firmly in favour of the Luftwaffe, reaching crisis point with the escape of the German warships *Scharnhorst*, *Gneisenau* and *Prinz Eugen* up the Channel on 12 February 1942. On that dismal

occasion, with both British and German air forces fully committed to battle, the superiority of the Fw 190 was never more keenly recognised by the RAF whose fighters, bombers and torpedo-bombers suffered heavy losses as the German ships made for the relative safety of their home ports.

Another aspect of the British offensive across the Channel was the support of resistance movements in enemy-occupied territories. During the dark days of 1940 it was as much as Britain could do to arm her own ground forces, and to begin with, in August that year, a single Flight, No. 419 (later 1419), was formed with Lysanders whose task it was to carry agents into France, supply them with weapons and explosives and, occasionally, to fly them back. Much of the work of these agents (of the Special Operations Executive, or SOE) was concerned with making preparations for the growing spate of amphibious Commando raids on the enemy coast. In August 1941 No. 1419 Flight was enlarged to become No. 138 (Special Duty) Squadron, and in February 1942 this was joined by a second Special Duty squadron, No. 161, formed out of a nucleus provided by the King's Flight, commanded by Wing Commander E. H. Fielden. These squadrons flew a number of different aircraft (Lysanders, Whitleys, Halifaxes and a Hudson) to maintain contact with the agents and resistance groups, a hazardous job which increased in tempo and importance as the day of eventual return to the Continent by Allied armies approached. Much of the work of these squadrons remains secret to this day owing to the sensitivity of foreign politics. Some measure of the importance of the flights may

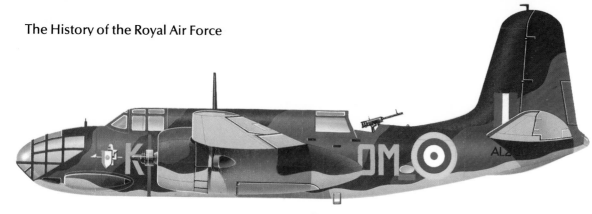

AL296 was a Douglas Boston Mk III which joined No. 107 Squadron at Great Massingham on 14 January 1942 and served with the squadron until 2 March 1943 except for a short spell on No. 226 Squadron in August. It flew 19 operations before being despatched to North Africa for further service there.

be judged from the increasing scale of successful sorties flown by the two squadrons: 22 in 1941, 93 in 1942, 615 in 1943 and 2,995 in 1944.

Indeed, motivation of almost all cross-Channel operations from 1941 onwards lay in the belief that the only means of achieving final victory over Germany was by means of full-scale invasion of France, followed by an overland advance to Berlin, a task that seemed less daunting after Germany had been committed to war in the Mediterranean and in the East, not to mention the USA's entry into the war at the end of 1941. It was thus that the large-scale amphibious landing (euphemistically referred to as a 'reconnaissance in force') was carried out at Dieppe on 19 August 1942.

Apart from all the tactical risks attendant on any enterprise of this size, this was an occasion fraught with all manner of unknowns for the RAF. To begin with, it was hoped to be able to determine the parameters for air support of a large-scale amphibious landing for future reference. Implicit in the success of this support was an assumption of superiority over the deadly Focke-Wulf Fw 190A, now known also to be an impressive fighter-bomber that could seriously threaten the whole operation. For this purpose the RAF had accelerated final deliveries of two new aircraft, the Spitfire IX with Merlin 61 engine and the Hawker Typhoon with Napier Sabre engine. Both aircraft had performances marginally better than that of the Fw 190A-1.

In the event, despite delays and postponement of the landings, neither of these aircraft was fully ready for operational service, only one wing of Typhoon IBs and one of Spitfire IXs being included in the order of battle. Neither was committed to combat correctly, and it was learned too late that new in-service versions of the Fw 190 eclipsed these latest RAF fighters. The result was that the brunt of the fighting continued to be borne by the out-

classed Spitfire VB.

Leigh-Mallory had at his disposal 56 fighter squadrons (Hurricanes, Spitfires and Typhoons), four squadrons of North American Mustang army co-operation fighters, and five squadrons of Bostons and Blenheims from No. 2 Bomber Group. American B-17 Fortresses of the USAAF flew their first raid in Europe with a diversionary attack on a target near Rouen, while radio-countermeasures Defiants flew a jamming sortie to confuse enemy radar and radio communications.

Unfortunately Leigh-Mallory's Intelligence underestimated not only the available strength of enemy fighter forces but also the skill with which the Dornier Do 217 force would be used. The Luftwaffe could field 150 of the type, whose crews were well trained in shipping strikes.

As air operations built up during the day of the landings it became painfully clear that the choice of confined beaches had been mistaken, for not only were the assault forces pinned down and

The next big advance in the daylight cross-Channel offensive was the advent of the Douglas Boston. Earlier versions had come to Britain in 1940 and turned into night-fighters; the Boston Mk III was sufficiently advanced to be ordered in quantity, and the type began to replace the Blenheims in No. 2 Group, Bomber Command in October 1941. The first squadron was No. 88 based at Swanton Morley and its aircraft are seen here wave-hopping over the Channel to keep below the German radar.

Another import from America was the North American Mustang. The early Mk I went into service with Army Cooperation Command for fighter-reconnaissance duties, replacing the unsatisfactory Tomahawk which had already replaced the outmoded Lysander. With the Mustang Mk I the FR Squadrons, such as No. 2 shown here, were able to become operational across the Channel once more, flying low-level reconnaissances and 'Rhubarbs'.

Westland Whirlwind Mk Is were only in operation with two squadrons, No. 137 and No. 263, the latter flying them from July 1940 until December 1943. P6969 was the fourth production aircraft and joined No. 263 Squadron at Grangemouth in July 1940. It flew operationally with the squadron until going missing on 8 February 1941.

The standard fighter for Channel sweeps and bomber escorts in 1941 and the early part of 1942 was the Supermarine Spitfire Mk VB with two 20-mm cannon and four 0.303-in (7.7-mm) guns. This formation is from No. 81 Squadron, back from Russia and flying as part of the Hornchurch Wing in July 1942.

eventually brought off with great difficulty, but the RAF was unable to provide adequate close support so that numerous enemy aircraft succeeded in penetrating the massive air umbrella. Instead of a resounding victory for Fighter Command, the Dieppe operation cost the RAF the loss of 106 aircraft of which six were Typhoons (none of whose squadrons had fired their guns), while 44 other aircraft were severely damaged. German records show that 48 Luftwaffe aircraft were lost, of which only 10 were Fw 190s.

On the credit side, one of the best features of the RAF's operations was the successful integration of squadrons flown by 'Free' pilots: apart from the hard core of British line squadrons, the three Eagle Squadrons (Nos 71, 121 and 133) flown by American volunteers, five Polish squadrons (Nos 302, 303, 306, 308 and 317), two Czech squadrons (Nos 310 and 312), two Norwegian squadrons (Nos 331 and 332), a Free French squadron (No. 340) and a Belgian squadron (No. 350), all flew combat

sorties, fully integrated in the order of battle.

For all the blunders and disappointments of the Dieppe operation, it must be said that there was no better means available to learn the lessons necessary to put into effect a full-scale invasion landing when the time came. In the air the most important of these was the vital need for meticulous planning and preparation. Nothing should be undertaken 'at the last minute', no new aircraft introduced without months of combat experience, and detailed Intelligence appreciation of enemy resources obtained. Such preparations as these would occupy almost two more years before the ultimate invasion of Europe could be undertaken.

Defending the base

While Air Marshal Sir William Sholto Douglas strove to carry the war to the enemy with the slowly improving fighters and fighter-bombers at his disposal in 1941–2, he continued to face the threat of enemy air attack on Britain, although after the end of the night Blitz in mid-May 1941 this danger re-appeared once more by day. From the early days he was concerned for the safety of his airfields in the south of England, for these were the bases from which the cross-Channel operations were flown, added to which were the numerous airfields further afield which accommodated the growing might of Bomber Command and the vital squadrons of Coastal Command struggling to protect the ocean approaches to British ports from the depredations of enemy aircraft and submarines in the Battle of the Atlantic. To these responsibilities was added in 1942 the defence of airfields being occupied by the men and aircraft of the USAAF.

Mercifully the Luftwaffe made few attempts to attack Britain in daylight at this time of stretched defence resources. Instead it remained content to husband its fighters, the two Jagdgeschwader of Bf 109Fs and Fw 190As, for protection of its French

Close-up of a Spitfire Mk VB of No. 303 (Polish) Squadron. This was the Polish squadron which acquitted itself well in the Battle of Britain and formed an integral part of the Northolt Wing during 1941 and 1942 on cross-Channel operations. Note the Polish national insignia behind the propeller, the squadron badge behind Donald Duck by the cockpit.

The Boulton Paul Defiant NF.Mk II was flown by No. 151 Squadron in the night fighter role from Wittering until mid-1942, when the much more effective Mosquito arrived.

bases, and refrained from use of bombers by day.

It was not until shortly after the ill-fated Dieppe operation that a new threat appeared. On 31 October 1942 about 30 Fw 190A-3/U1s, each carrying a single 1,102-lb (500-kg) bomb, attacked Canterbury, Kent, in daylight, causing heavy damage. The Germans had accumulated about 100 such bomb-carrying fighters (in Schnellkampfgeschwader 10) and these now embarked on a series of so-called tip-and-run raids on towns and ports in southern England. Carried out at very low level, they evaded radar cover until almost at the coast and thereby proved difficult to counter. Indeed Leigh-Mallory, who took over Fighter Command from Sholto Douglas on 28 November 1942, deployed no fewer than 22 fighter squadrons (including the first, No. 41, to be equipped with the new Rolls-Royce Griffon-powered Spitfire XII, designed for low-level operations) to counter these attacks, but was unable to prevent vicious attacks on Ashford, Dungeness, Eastbourne, Hastings and Rye, while others reached the outskirts of London and as far north as Chelmsford, Essex, on 14 April 1943.

Dismissed in contemporary reports as of no more than nuisance attacks, they nevertheless caused widespread damage to factories and railways, not to mention consternation at the demonstrated vulnerability of the British Isles during those years of massive build-up for the invasion of Europe.

Bomber Command's offensive

Returning to the early months of the war, the initial attempts to employ RAF bombers in daylight attacks on German warships, with their attendant losses, have been described. Moreover, the British government's reluctance to attack centres of civilian population was accompanied by an extraordinary series of leaflet-dropping sorties over German cities, principally using the obsolescent Whitley bombers during the first winter of the war.

It was not until the German attack in the west was launched in May 1940 that grudging approval was given to carry out bombing raids over the

Ruhr, it being emphasised that such attacks should be confined to military targets.

Air Marshal Sir Edgar Ludlow-Hewitt, Commander-in-Chief of Bomber Command, had been succeeded by Air Marshal Sir Charles Portal on 3 April 1940, and it was he who was responsible for Bomber Command's activities during the Battle of France and Battle of Britain. As a result of the extreme peril in which Britain found herself during 1940, there was little that RAF bombers could do of a far-reaching or strategic nature, so most of the available effort was applied against the growing concentrations of invasion craft being assembled in the Channel ports; these were relatively simple targets requiring little navigational skill and were poorly defended by enemy fighters. (German nightfighter defences had been even more neglected than those of the RAF. Only in mid-1940 were the first night-fighter units, NJG 1 and NJG 2, formed.)

However, a number of successful bombing raids were carried out further afield against Luftwaffe air bases, particularly at Leeuwarden on 1 August, at Haamstede on 7 August, at Vlissingen on 18 August, and at Tromsö in Norway on 26 August, in which about 30 enemy aircraft were destroyed, and a well-executed attack on Eindhoven on 10

Although the four-engine bombers were making their impact in 1941, the mainstay of Bomber Command's night offensive was still the Wellington, flying in Mks I, II and III versions. Taxiing out at Mildenhall one moonlight night is Wellington Mk IC OJ:W of No. 149 Squadron.

The Lincolnshire bomber airfields had begun the war with the Handley Page Hampden, for this was the standard equipment of No. 5 Group. It was not often possible to obtain a group photograph, as a result of operational exigencies; however, here are most of No. 50 Squadron's aircrew, grouped around two Hampdens at Waddington.

The Handley Page Hampden Mk I served No. 5 Group Bomber Command from September 1939 until the Avro Manchester (followed by the Lancaster) replaced it during 1941–2. AE202 served with No. 44 Squadron at Waddington in 1940–1.

September when 10 He 111 bombers were destroyed.

Two other attacks at this time were especially significant. To some extent stung to retaliation for the offensive being waged against London in September, the Air Staff authorised attacks on the German capital, albeit still insisting that only specific targets, such as power stations, should be attacked. Accordingly on the night of 23/24 September 119 Wellingtons, Whitleys and Hampdens took off to fly to Berlin. Of these, 84 reached their target and bombed: 22 Germans lost their lives on the ground, and three RAF bombers failed to return.

The other raid worth recording here was, by the standards of the time, an even more extraordinary feat of endurance and skill. During the night of 13/14 August 36 Whitleys flew 1,500 miles (2400 km) to attack Italian aircraft factories at Milan and Turin. With only four 250-lb (113-kg) bombs apiece, these old Whitleys achieved far more by propaganda effect than by material damage, for it was this (and a similar raid on 2/3 September) that stung Mussolini into persuading Hitler to allow his Regia Aeronautica to participate in the air attacks on Britain (resulting in the Italian attacks of November, already mentioned). The Italians had, after all, been led to believe that the UK, far from possessing a bomber force, had already been defeated in the air.

Roughly one-fifth of Bomber Command's effort was, during the latter half of 1940, devoted to attacks on Germany's oil industry as it was realised that, with substantial dependence on synthetic fuel processing, this industry was of

paramount importance, particularly to the Luftwaffe. Unfortunately the RAF in 1940 possessed few effective post-raid reconnaissance resources, and it was only after some months of a slowly-increasing bombing campaign that realisation dawned on the Air Staff that an alarmingly small proportion of the RAF bomber crews were even finding their targets, let alone hitting and damaging them.

These early attacks serve to illustrate how ill-prepared the RAF was to impose the nation's will upon a determined and ruthless enemy. Total war, epitomised by dictators in such flagrant bombing raids as those at Guernica during the Spanish Civil War, and on Warsaw and Rotterdam in World War II (although not yet critically assessed in their tactical significance), had not been allowed to cloud the issues of national survival as understood by peacetime politicians. Yet steps had been taken in peacetime to strengthen Bomber Command, and the first fruits of these were reaped at the height of the Battle of Britain with the first deliveries of the four-engine Short Stirling heavy bomber to No. 7 (Bomber) Squadron at Leeming in August. These were not ready for operations until 10/11 February 1941, when three aircraft took part in a night raid on oil-storage tanks at Rotterdam.

Second of the RAF's four-engine heavy bombers to enter service was the Merlin-powered Handley Page Halifax, which joined No. 35 (Bomber) Squadron, newly formed at Leeming, on 23 November 1940. The squadron's first operational mission was flown on the night of 10/11 March 1941, when six aircraft took off to bomb the docks at Le Havre,

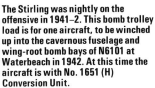

The Stirling was nightly on the offensive in 1941–2. This bomb trolley load is for one aircraft, to be winched up into the cavernous fuselage and wing-root bomb bays of N6101 at Waterbeach in 1942. At this time the aircraft is with No. 1651 (H) Conversion Unit.

The Wellington Mk IC was still the mainstay of Bomber Command through 1941, R1349 joining No. 301 Squadron at Swinderby. No. 301 was a squadron formed with Polish personnel and flew Wellingtons on the bomber offensive until 1943. This particular aircraft transferred to No. 12 OTU later was lost on a mission to Bremen on 26 June 1942.

but was marred when an RAF night-fighter shot down one of the bombers over Surrey. Another heavy bomber to join the RAF at the same time as the Halifax was the twin-Vulture engined Avro Manchester, which was first delivered to No. 207 (Bomber) Squadron at Waddington, also in November 1940; Manchesters were first flown on operations on 24/25 February 1941, when six aircraft took part in a raid on German warships in Brest harbour.

Growing numbers of these three heavy bombers provided new power for Bomber Command, which was still in 1941 largely dependent on the Wellington, Whitley and Hampden, although as a result of its inadequate gun defences the last was gradually transferred to other duties from mid-1941.

As the new aircraft were entering service, so Bomber Command's weapons were increasing in size and destructive power. At the outbreak of war the principal bombs in use were the 500-lb (227-kg) general-purpose weapon, of which the Wellington for instance could carry nine; and the 1,000-lb (454-kg) bomb, of which the Whitley could carry six. The first 2,000-lb (907-kg) semi-armour piercing bomb was dropped by a Coastal Command Beaufort on 7 May 1940, but quickly joined the bombers' armoury, the first being dropped by a Hampden of No. 83 (Bomber) Squadron flown by Flying Officer Guy Gibson against the *Scharnhorst* at Kiel on the night of 1/2 July; unfortunately the release mechanism proved faulty and the bomb fell off late and landed in the centre of the town.

First of the famous heavy bombs was the 4,000-lb (1814-kg) weapon, of which two were first dropped by two specially-modified Merlin-powered Wellington IIs of Nos 9 and 149 Squadrons over Emden on the night of 31 March/1 April 1941.

Meanwhile Portal had left Bomber Command on his appointment as Chief of the Air Staff (a post he was to occupy with great distinction until the end of the war), his place being taken on 5 October 1940 by Air Marshal Sir Richard Peirse.

By the end of May 1941, the month that had brought an end to the German Blitz on Britain, Bomber Command was embarked on a night offensive over Europe that would last to the end of the war. Already in one month 19 raids of over 50 bombers had been launched; indeed, one (on the

night of 8/9 May over Hamburg and Bremen) had been undertaken by over 300 bombers, and the 4,000-lb (1814-kg) bomb was in frequent use.

The next stage of Bomber Command's offensive was, however, to be beset by difficulty and uncertainty. As the Blenheim light bombers stepped up their daylight attacks and 'Circuses' with some success (during a famous low-level daylight raid by 15 Blenheims of Nos 105 and 107 Squadrons on Bremen, a long-range attack for such aircraft, Wing Commander H. I. Edwards, who led the raid and sustained severe wounds, won the Victoria Cross for his gallantry), delays in deliveries of, and operational problems with the new heavy bombers were now experienced. To begin with, the Stirling proved to be unable to operate at its intended altitude with anything like a full bombload, while the Rolls-Royce Vulture engines in the Manchester were proving thoroughly unreliable in service. Added to these difficulties were the German night defences, which had undergone considerable strengthening since the previous year and now comprised some seven Gruppen of fairly effective fighter adaptations of the Do 17 and Ju 88. Heavy losses to these defences during the autumn of 1941 resulted in the calling for a temporary reduction in RAF bomber activity at the end of the year, to

In 1941 the RAF acquired from the USAAC some Boeing B-17C Flying Fortresses and formed No. 90 Squadron at Polebrook. They soon began daylight raids at high-altitude over the continent, but were generally unsuitable for the European theatre and were soon withdrawn, after some losses, and eventually employed by Coastal Command. One of the squadron's aircraft is here seen taking off on an early raid.

The Handley Page Halifax Mk I followed the Short Stirling to be the second four-engine bomber in Bomber Command service. No. 76 Squadron was the second to fly the Halifax operationally. Aircraft 'L' (L9530) had first flown with No. 35 Squadron and went on to fly with No. 76 Squadron until August 1941, when it went missing. At the time this photograph was taken, L9530 had flown four missions.

Coincidentally with the Stirling entering service, the new twin-engine Avro Manchester joined No. 207 Squadron at Waddington in November 1940. L7316 was one of these early machines. The Manchester was plagued with engine problems, and by 1942 was ready for withdrawal. L7316 went missing on a raid to Bremen on 31 August 1941.

allow a build-up of strength.

Although it was not yet fully realised just how lacking in navigational skill the bomber crews were, or how little damage had yet been done to their targets, new aids were being prepared to assist them. Already a rudimentary radio aid, known as Gee, had been used successfully in a trial by the Wellingtons of No. 115 (Bomber) Squadron during a raid on Mönchen Gladbach on 11/12 August, and this equipment was being introduced throughout the Command; and in December an early blind-bombing device known as Trinity (a rudimentary form of the later highly-efficient Oboe equipment) was employed by No. 109 (Bomber) Squadron in attempts to bomb the *Scharnhorst* and *Gneisenau* in Brest harbour.

More significant was the first appearance in service of Bomber Command's most devastating and successful aircraft weapon of the war: the immortal Avro Lancaster bomber, of which the first three production examples arrived on No. 44 (Bomber) Squadron at Waddington on Christmas Eve, 1941. Contrary to general belief, the Lancaster was not conceived to overcome problems with the Vulture-powered Manchester. It had indeed originally appeared in prototype form as the Manchester III in January 1941 simply to employ Merlin engines, whose massive quantity production was by then an established fact. When troubles arose with the Vulture the initial service trials on the two Lancaster prototypes were well advanced and the first production aircraft nearing completion by the manufacturers.

It was at this watershed in the fortunes of Bomber Command that on 22 February 1942 Air Chief Marshal Sir Arthur Harris was appointed to succeed Sir Richard Peirse, and forthwith a new dynamic motivation became apparent throughout the command. When Harris arrived, more than two-thirds of the night bomber force still comprised Wellingtons, Whitleys and Hampdens; a year later the Lancaster, Halifax and Stirling had assumed this proportion. Moreover, during that year the Blenheim finally gave place to the Boston, Ventura and, most important of all, the superlative

de Havilland Mosquito.

The Mosquito (for all its unarmed, unescorted bombing connotations) represented the marriage of brilliant design technology with courageous tactical adaptation, for it was from the privately-sponsored commercial enterprise of the de Havilland company in conceiving a fast twin-Merlin bomber/reconnaissance aeroplane constructed largely of 'non-strategic' materials (for the Mosquito was almost entirely built of wood) that the aircraft was progressively developed as a bomber, fighter-bomber, night-fighter and intruder, photo-reconnaissance aircraft, as well as performing numerous other combat roles.

Thousand-bomber raid

As if to emphasise the auspicious appointment of its new commander, Bomber Command carried out a number of brilliant and significant attacks during the early months of 1942. Within a week of Harris's appointment Whitleys of No. 51 (Bomber) Squadron dropped paratroops on the French coast at Bruneval to dismantle and capture a German early warning *Würzburg* radar; on 8/9 March Gee equipment entered general use by large numbers of bomber aircraft during an attack on Essen. Two nights later Lancasters of No. 44 (Bomber) Squadron carried out their first bombing raid in another attack on the same target. On 10/11 April the first 8,000-lb (3629-kg) bomb was dropped by a Halifax II of No. 76 (Bomber) Squadron – yet again on Essen. On 17 April 20 Lancasters from Nos 44 and 97 Squadrons carried out a brilliant long-range, low-level daylight raid on the MAN factory at Augsburg (seven Lancasters were shot down on this raid, and its leader, Squadron Leader J. D. Nettleton of No. 44 (Bomber) Squadron, was awarded the Victoria Cross). And as if to underline the growing might of Bomber Command, Harris unleashed the first 1,000-bomber raid on Cologne (Operation 'Millenium') on the night of 30/31 May. Of the 1,046 aircraft despatched, 40 failed to return. Within four hours of this historic raid, No. 105 (Bomber) Squadron was flying the first Mosquito raid in a dawn attack on the stricken city.

All through 1941 the Handley Page Hampden soldiered on in No. 5 Group, augmented by a squadron (No. 455) of Australians of which this is one aircraft. The following year this squadron transferred to Coastal Command for anti-shipping strikes.

The War in the Middle East

For all the vital roles assumed by the fledgling RAF during the 1920s in the Middle East, and indeed the importance of this work to the very survival of the service in the face of jealous bickering by the nation's two senior armed forces' ministries, the strength of the RAF in that theatre was never adequate to protect British interests in the event of war with another European power. Numerically, it is true, the RAF had never been stronger than it was when Italy entered the war on 10 June 1940, but the 300-odd first-line aircraft in 29 squadrons were dispersed over an area of some four and a half million square miles. Moreover only 18 of these squadrons were equipped with fairly modern (at best obsolescent) aircraft: Bristol Blenheims, Short Sunderlands, Westland Lysanders and Gloster Gladiators; the remainder comprised a heterogeneous collection of outdated types such as Hawker Audaxes, Fairey Battles, Bristol Bombays, Gloster Gauntlets, Hawker Hardys, Hawker Harts, Hawker Hartebeests, Junkers Ju 86s (of the South African Air Force), Saro Londons, Vickers Valentias, Vickers Vincents and Vickers Wellesleys.

Although the Italians could muster no more than about 500 aircraft of fairly modern vintage in North and East Africa, their superiority lay in the potentially simple reinforcement by upwards of 1,200 aircraft from their bases in Sicily and Italy.

Principal responsibility of the RAF's commander-in-chief, Air Chief Marshal Sir Arthur Longmore, in Cairo was the protection of the sea route through the Red Sea and Mediterranean. It was through this landlocked sea that vital shipping carrying men and matériel to Britain from the Far East sailed if it was to avoid the time-consuming route around the Cape of Good Hope. Italy's entry into the war posed an immediate threat to this route not only because of that country's geographical position in the Mediterranean, but also because of her military deployments in Cyrenaica and East Africa.

'Cyrenaica': the early struggle

By invading France on 10 June Italy was putting herself at an immediate disadvantage in the Mediterranean, being weaker at sea than the combined British and French fleets, and so risking, at least theoretically, an attack in Tripolitania from Tunisia. With the signing of the Franco-Axis armistice, however, and the neutralizing of the French fleet at Oran, the balance of strength promptly shifted in Italy's favour.

At once Italian forces began a ponderous build up in Cyrenaica, an attack through Egypt towards the Suez Canal being their obvious intention. As British and Commonwealth forces prepared to withstand this attack some distance behind the border (for the coastal railway to bring up men and

When war came to the Middle East these Westland Lysanders of No. 208 Squadron, seen over the Suez Canal early in 1939, were quickly in action supporting the army in the Western Desert but were outclassed when the Luftwaffe later joined in the fray.

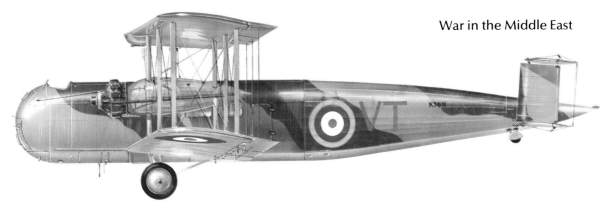

When war started the bomber force in the Middle East was vested in two squadrons of Vickers Valentias, biplanes that doubled up as troop transports. K3611 shown here served with No. 216 Squadron and was used on night bombing raids in 1940 before being relegated to the transport duties. It later moved to India and served with No. 31 Squadron there until a crash-landing in Persia in August 1941.

supplies stopped some way short of the frontier), the RAF, commanded in the Western Desert by that famous veteran, Air Commodore Raymond Collishaw, set about a courageous but necessarily limited campaign of ground support, reconnaissance and, when only occasionally demanded, active combat with the Regia Aeronautica. With only three squadrons of Gladiator fighters (Nos 33, 80 and 112), a Lysander squadron (No. 208), four Blenheim squadrons (Nos 30, 55, 113 and 211) and one of Bombays (No. 216), the RAF had to equate its attempt to dominate the front line with avoidance of unnecessary losses. The Italian supply ports of Tobruk and Bardia came in for naval and air bombardment, but despite occasional outstanding successes (as for instance that on 17 August when Gladiators, covering Admiral Sir Andrew Cunningham's fleet, shot down eight Savoia-Marchetti SM.79 bombers without loss), the real achievement of the RAF in Egypt was the establishment of a defensive mentality among the Italians. An example of Collishaw's ingenuity was afforded by his use of the only Hurricane in the Middle East (a very old aircraft that had been sent out to Khartoum before the war for tropical trials) which was switched rapidly between his landing grounds to provide an exaggerated picture of British fighter strength for Italian reconnaissance aircraft.

Reinforcement

Clearly the vulnerability of British strategic interests in the Middle East demanded swift reinforcement, not least of the RAF. Unfortunately such were the distances involved that only the longest-range aircraft (Vickers Wellingtons, Blenheims and Lockheed Hudsons) could make the journey by air, via Gibraltar and Malta (although a small number of Hurricanes succeeded in making the hazardous, if exciting journey after clandestine landings in France and North Africa before reaching Malta in June).

An alternative reinforcement route was there-

The Hawker Hurricane Mk I became the universal fighter in the Middle East from late 1940 onwards, replacing the Gloster Gladiator in the Desert and in Malta. The first Hurricanes to replace *Faith, Hope* and *Charity* (the three most famous Malta Gladiators) were these aircraft of No. 261 Squadron at Hal Far.

fore selected, involving a sea voyage to Takoradi in the Gold Coast where the aircraft were disembarked, re-assembled and made ready for the long flight across Africa. This journey, involving a flight of more than 3,500 miles (5630 km) over rugged, inhospitable terrain, followed the route flown by Imperial Airways before the war and pioneered by Squadron Leader A. Coningham, using the old landing strips along the way. (On 30 July 1941 Air Vice Marshal A. Coningham was appointed to command the RAF, Western Desert).

'Faith, Hope and Charity'

Under the direction of Group Captain H. K. Thorold at Takoradi, the first group of Hurricanes was assembled and despatched along the route on 19 September, together with a guiding Blenheim; seven days later they arrived in the Canal Zone, the first of a regular flow of reinforcements to be sent to the Middle East over this route during the next two years.

The mention above of Malta as a stepping stone on the direct reinforcement air route to the Middle East also provides emphasis for the strategic importance of this tiny island lying in the Central Mediterranean athwart the Italian sea and air lines of communication between Sicily and North Africa.

Despite peacetime proposals to deploy four RAF squadrons on the four newly-built bases on Malta for the protection of the naval base at Valletta, when war came none of the squadrons had arrived. As war loomed with Italy the senior RAF officer on Malta, Air Commodore F. H. M. Maynard, cast around for suitable aircraft with which to provide some measure of air defence and gained sanction to assemble some Sea Gladiators which were held in crates as spares for the Fleet Air Arm. (One of these aeroplanes was lost almost immediately and three of the remainder were later dubbed *Faith, Hope* and *Charity*: for many years a legend existed that only three Sea Gladiators were assembled but this has since been positively discounted.) For the first fortnight of the war with Italy the Sea Gladiators constituted the sole air defence of the island until the arrival of some Hurricanes on their way to North Africa, which were promptly detained by Maynard.

This tiny band of fighters soon proved capable of so discouraging the Italians (who had some 200 aircraft available in Sicily) from pressing home their attacks on the island (and eventually forced them to confine their raids to the hours of darkness) that it was decided to increase the deployment of aircraft on Malta, and when 12 further Hurricanes flew from the carrier HMS *Argus* to the island on 2 August three Martin Maryland reconnaissance aircraft were sent out from Britain to form No. 431 Flight, followed by 16 Wellington bombers which became No. 148 (Bomber) Squadron.

It was the exploits of one of the Marylands that led to the famous attack on the Italian fleet in Taranto harbour on 11 November, flown by a young man newly arrived from Britain, Pilot Officer Adrian Warburton (Warburton was to become a living legend in the Mediterranean, and particularly on Malta, for his prodigious feats of reconnaissance; by the time of his death on 12 April 1944 he was a wing commander with two DSOs, three DFCs and the American DFC). In his Maryland Warburton obtained such detailed information of the enemy fleet by flying round the inside of the

With the fall of France in 1940 the RAF took over the French order for Martin 167 reconnaissance bombers, known in RAF service as the Maryland. AR707 was one of the Marylands serving on Malta with No. 431 Flight.

harbour that the photographs taken enabled the crews of 21 Swordfish torpedo aircraft from HMS *Illustrious* to launch an audacious attack on the enemy port, sinking one battleship, and severely damaging two others, a heavy cruiser and a destroyer. At a stroke the balance of naval superiority swung back in favour of the British.

Desert successes

Meanwhile in the Western Desert the Italian forces under Marshal Rodolfo Graziani continued their build-up as the British ground forces strengthened their defences, covered by Collishaw's squadrons, now in turn being reinforced from home. It should incidentally be remembered that such reinforcements could be ill-afforded, for the Battle of Britain was at its height. Moreover the process was being slowed by demands from London that Longmore send a number of squadrons to Greece (to assist in the defence of that country against the Italian attack from Albania, as will be told below).

Nevertheless by the end of November the RAF supporting the army in the Western Desert now included two squadrons of Wellingtons (Nos 37 and 38) and the veteran of France and the Battle of Britain, No. 73 (Fighter) Squadron with Hurricanes. Three Blenheim squadrons (Nos 11, 39 and 45) had been assembled and a new Hurricane squadron (No. 274) was now available.

After checking the Italians' first hesitant advance (and realising that enemy pressure in Greece might well further deplete his forces in due course) General Sir Archibald Wavell opened his attack first on 9 December after widespread raids had been flown against enemy airfields by the Wellingtons and Blenheims. By now the Bombays had been largely withdrawn from bombing duties (although several such aircraft were flown to and fro over the front line at night to drown the noise of Wavell's tanks moving up for their surprise dawn attack).

In the almost total absence of the Regia Aeronautica from the skies over the land battle, the

Hurricanes were relieved of their patrol duties and given the task of attacking the Italian army, which by the 11th was in headlong retreat westwards. As the desert-based air force pounded the ports whose names (Bardia, Tobruk, Derna and Benghazi) were to become so familiar in the years to come, Wellingtons from Malta struck at Tripoli as well as the merchant ships bringing fuel and reinforcements across the Mediterranean. As the triumphant advance continued across the wastes of Cyrenaica, the squadrons of Hurricanes, Lysanders and Blenheims (many of whose pilots were flying four or more sorties each day) strove hard to keep pace, often landing after a combat sortie at a more advanced strip than that from which they had set out. The ground crews worked miracles of ingenuity in the frequent dust storms to keep aircraft serviceable as the engines began to show considerable wear and tear from constant encroachment of the desert sands, while their motor transport did its best to maintain the essential flow of spares, as well as of the vital bombs and ammunition.

By 22 January Tobruk had fallen after the advance had covered 100 miles (160 km); a week

One of the famous Sea Gladiators, later called *Faith*, starts up on Malta during its gallant defence of the island against the Italian air force. They were crewed by RAF personnel (this aircraft by Sergeant J. W. Robertson) and held out until Hurricanes arrived, eventually becoming No. 261 Squadron.

Starting in 1940 two squadrons of Wellingtons (Nos 37 and 38) went to the Middle East to take up the bombing offensive against the Italians. The Wellington was found ideal and more squadrons were formed, serving right through to the end of the North African campaign in 1943. This is a Mk IC showing why air-cooled engines were advantageous with all the dust flying about.

Typical of the Short Sunderland Mk Is serving in the Mediterranean is N9029, which joined No. 230 Squadron in the Far East at the beginning of World War II, moving to the Mediterranean in May 1940 and flying continuously in the eastern Mediterranean area until New Year's Day 1943, when it crashed in the Mediterranean.

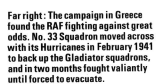

Far right: The campaign in Greece found the RAF fighting against great odds. No. 33 Squadron moved across with its Hurricanes in February 1941 to back up the Gladiator squadrons, and in two months fought valiantly until forced to evacuate.

later Mechili was reached; and on 8 February El Agheila, 130 miles (210 km) beyond Benghazi, fell to the British. The whole of Cyrenaica was effectively in British hands: 130,000 Italians had been made prisoner, 400 tanks and more than 1,200 guns had been taken in the 60-day, 600-mile (1000-km) advance. The Commonwealth air forces, never more than 200 aircraft strong, had destroyed or captured 400 of the enemy for a loss of 76 aircrew killed, wounded or missing, and 41 aircraft.

Nothing can detract from Wavell's brilliant generalship in this, one of the most remarkable of all British victories, yet it could not have been attained without the untiring efforts of the RAF (and SAAF), testimony of whose success lay scattered on roads and airfields across the breadth of Cyrenaica.

The loss of Greece and Crete

The worst forebodings of Wavell and Longmore were now to be fully realised. At the moment of triumph in the Western Desert Germany, becoming restless at her partner's repeated failures during the past six months, decided to take a hand in the Mediterranean theatre. At once a small but powerful element, X Fliegerkorps of the Luftwaffe, descended on Sicily to assist in the elimination of Malta, and units of the Wehrmacht (soon to become the famous Afrika Korps) started to disembark in Tripoli. Of more immediate danger, however, Germany invaded Yugoslavia and Greece.

As long ago as 28 October 1940 Italy, anxious to assert her influence in the Balkans, attacked Greece from its newly-acquired base of Albania. At once Longmore was ordered to send squadrons to assist Britain's newest ally. No. 30 Squadron, with a mixed complement of Blenheim fighters and bombers, was first to go, for the defence of Athens; by the end of November two more Blenheim squadrons (Nos 84 and 211) and No. 80 Squadron with Gladiators had followed. Soon afterwards, No. 112 Squadron took its Gladiators to Greece and handed them over to the Royal Hellenic Air Force before starting to re-equip with Hurricanes.

Despite appalling weather conditions, as winter settled over northern Greece and quickly reduced

the scattered airfields to quagmire, these squadrons had soon established superiority over the Regia Aeronautica, frequently discouraging the small formations of enemy aircraft from interfering with the activities of the Greek army in its successful resistance to invasion. For instance, the pilots of No. 80 Squadron's Gladiators had by the end of the year claimed the destruction of 40 Italian aircraft for the loss of six. Although now known to have been a small exaggeration (the Italians claimed to have destroyed more than 180 RAF aircraft – three times the total number in Greece), the fact remained that the Gladiators enjoyed undisputed superiority in the skies over the Pindus mountains. Further afield the indefatigable Wellington crews, based on Malta, kept up frequent attacks on south Italian ports through which supplies flowed to the enemy in Greece.

The situation in the Balkans underwent radical change during those winter months with the arrival of 20 German divisions in Romania, deployed there ostensibly to counter any British threat of attack from eastern Greece on the oilfields on which Germany depended so vitally. By early 1941 plans for Hitler's assault on Russia were well advanced and it was decided to ensure the safety of his southern flank by ending once and for all the British presence in the Balkans. On 1 March the German army entered Bulgaria, and Longmore was ordered to send further units to Greece, these comprising Nos 11 and 113 Squadrons with Blenheims, No. 33 Squadron with Hurricanes and No. 208 Squadron with Lysanders and Hurricanes. On the previous day the RAF fighters in Greece had administered a comprehensive thrashing to the Regia Aeronautica when 28 Hurricanes and Gladiators shot down 27 Italian aircraft without loss in full view of the Greek and Italian armies near Tepeleni.

On 6 April the Axis powers descended in unison upon Yugoslavia and Greece: 27 German divisions, with a further 23 provided by Italy, Hungary and Bulgaria, supported by some 1,200 aircraft of Luftflotte 4, attacked along a 400-mile (645-km) front. Opposing them were 24 Yugoslav divisions (almost all dependent on mule- and ox-drawn transport), six Greek divisions (little better equipped) and about three British.

Employing the now familiar ruthless Blitzkrieg tactics, the Wehrmacht cut swiftly through Yugoslavia and eastern Macedonia despite all the British air forces (commanded in Greece by Air Vice Marshal J. H. D'Albiac) could do. One hun-

The Sunderlands of Nos 228 and 230 Squadrons were vital in the eastern Mediterranean, tracing the whereabouts of the Italian fleet and submarines. With the Greek campaign they also were roped in for transport duties and played a great part in the evacuations of Greece and Crete, in which area this No. 230 Squadron aircraft (N9029) is seen.

The Bristol Blenheim Mk I was the basic bomber in the 1940–1 Middle East campaigns. L1381 had joined No. 84 Squadron at Shaibah in Iraq before the war, moved to Egypt and served in the early Desert campaign and moved to Greece in November 1940, where it soon transferred to No. 113 Squadron and went missing on a raid on 7 December 1940.

dred RAF bombing sorties were flown by Blenheims against enemy communications targets, including the railway marshalling yards at Sofia, before the first bomber was lost in action. Two visiting detachments of Wellingtons joined in attacks on enemy columns advancing towards the Vardar river.

Bad weather now intervened for 48 hours, and although this prevented the Luftwaffe from interfering, it also allowed the German columns to press ahead unmolested from the air; within four days the whole of western Thrace and eastern Macedonia had been lost, while in central Macedonia a defensive line was hurriedly established between Florina and Salonika.

Retreat from Greece

As the skies cleared once more on the 12th, German air attacks now broke with the utmost fury, not only on the ground forces struggling to extract their small quantities of armour from the mud of the mountain tracks but also on the airfields. At Niamata every Blenheim of No. 113 Squadron was destroyed or damaged by Messerschmitt Bf 109s. At Larissa two Hurricanes were shot down as they were taking off. On the 14th an entire formation of six Blenheims was shot down in an attack on the Monastir Gap, through which the Germans were pouring. By the following day D'Albiac reported to Longmore that only 46 RAF aircraft remained airworthy (apart from the visiting Wellingtons). As a general collapse now seemed imminent, the Wellingtons were withdrawn to Egypt whence they could still take a hand, and the remaining British and Greek aircraft divided between Paramithia in the west and the airfields covering Athens in the south.

Unfortunately this was the very moment when almost every surviving aircraft of the Royal Yugoslav air force chose to land at Paramithia, provoking a violent attack by the Luftwaffe which destroyed all 44. The next day a Greek Gladiator squadron was annihilated on the same airfield.

By 19 April all D'Albiac's surviving aircraft had been concentrated around Athens. At dawn the following day a Staffel of Messerschmitt Bf 110s attacked the airfield at Menidi, destroying almost all the surviving Blenheim force in Greece. The climax came the same afternoon when about 100 Junkers Ju 88s with Bf 109s and Bf 110s as escort carried out an attack on the Piraeus. Only 15 Hurricanes of Nos 33 and 80 Squadrons remained serviceable and these took off to intercept. About 14 of the enemy raiders were shot down against the loss of five Hurricanes, but among the latter was the aircraft flown by a young South African, Squadron Leader M. T. St. J. Pattle, commander of No. 33 Squadron. 'Pat' Pattle had enjoyed a brief but brilliant combat career, almost all of which was on Gladiators. Rising from pilot officer to squadron commander in only two years, he shot down more than 40 enemy aircraft (mostly Italian) in less than nine months to become the RAF's highest-scoring fighter pilot of World War II.

On 23 April the Greek army laid down its arms, and it was already the RAF's final duty to cover attempts to evacuate the surviving British ground forces, a duty faithfully performed by the last 18 Hurricanes of Nos 33, 80 and 208 Squadrons until the afternoon of the 22nd when a Gruppe of Bf 110s caught them refuelling in an olive grove near Argos and destroyed 13. Meanwhile many parties of officers and civilians, among them King Peter of

Yugoslavia and King George of Greece, were being evacuated by Sunderlands of Nos 228 and 230 Squadrons, and the Lockheed Lodestars and Bombays of No. 267 (Communications) Squadron. Two impressed BOAC flying boats, the Short C-class boats *Coorong* and *Cambria*, made 13 return flights between Cairo and Crete, between them bringing back 469 British troops evacuated from Greece.

On 24 April the last five Hurricanes (plus two newly-arrived replacements) finally left Greece and landed on Crete.

British losses in Greece during the six months of RAF involvement amounted to almost 200 aircraft, of which 151 were lost in the final three weeks after German invasion (87 of these being damaged on the ground and abandoned where they lay). Luftflotte 4 reported the loss of 164 aircraft.

If the events in Greece had been unfortunate (albeit inevitable once the German attack was launched) those on Crete were more so, for it was assumed that capture of the island would be forestalled by the Royal Navy.

While the Germans paused for three weeks to consolidate their forces in Greece, attempts were made to sustain the British garrison in Crete. Indeed, until the Germans themselves descended on Greece, no RAF squadrons had been permanently based on the island, and only two airfields (at Suda Bay and Heraklion) and two landing strips (at Retimo and Pediada-Kastelli) existed in an island roughly 150 miles (240 km) long and only 70 miles (112 km) from the Greek mainland. Upon these were dispersed the remnants of the three fighter squadrons from Greece (Nos 33, 80 and 112) plus an equally battered Fleet Air Arm squadron of Fairey Fulmars and Sea Gladiators. In command of these 24 fighters was Group Captain G. R. Beamish. Facing him across the water were 650 combat aircraft, 700 transports and 80 gliders. The Crete garrison amounted to 28,000 exhausted and ill-provisioned troops.

Significance of the enemy transport aircraft and gliders became all too apparent on 20 May when the first waves of some 15,000 airborne troops descended by glider and parachute around the island's airfields. By then – after constant attacks by the

Just about to emplane in a Blenheim Mk I for a sortie over the Western Desert in 1940 is this crew of No. 113 Squadron, probably at Maaten Bagush. Note that the aircrew are carrying tin helmets, presumably as protection from shrapnel on low-level attacks.

In the Persian Gulf No. 203 Squadron had maintained a long-range maritime reconnaissance role with Short Singapore Mk IIIs from September 1935, K6907 joining the squadron early in 1936. It remained in service until March 1940 when the squadron became a land-based unit with Blenheims.

Luftwaffe for more than a week – the resident fighter force had dwindled to four Hurricanes and three Gladiators, this despite the arrival of a daily quota of two Hurricanes as replacements from Egypt. Indeed, realising that the survivors faced profitless extinction, Beamish obtained permission for them to be evacuated from the island, and they were in the act of flying back to Cairo as the first German transports were taking off from their bases in Greece.

Now shorn of all air support, the fate of the British ground forces in Crete was sealed, and despite extraordinary heroism by the defenders it was decided to evacuate as many as possible. In this the Royal Navy made great sacrifices, equally bereft of air cover, and many valuable ships were sunk by enemy air attack.

The shortlived campaign in Crete cost the Germans 220 aircraft (of which roughly half were Junkers Ju 52/3m transports), excluding the gliders, while the RAF lost 38 aircraft and approximately half the 600 ground personnel on the island. The Royal Navy lost three cruisers and six destroyers sunk, and a battleship, aircraft-carrier, six cruisers and eight destroyers damaged – all by enemy air attack – greater losses than in any action at sea since Jutland.

Setback and victory in East Africa

There has already been passing reference to the Italian presence in East Africa and the potential threat it represented to the sea route through the Red Sea. In military terms this threat was posed by no fewer than 200,000 Italian and colonial troops, 150 aircraft, a flotilla of destroyers and a small number of submarines distributed throughout Abyssinia, Eritrea and Italian Somaliland, the naval vessels being based at Massawa.

In opposition Wavell had at his disposal some 19,000 troops and about 200 aircraft; as elsewhere, however, the number of aircraft belied their vintage for, apart from a small number of Blenheims and three squadrons (Nos 14, 47 and 223) of Wellesleys, the aircraft comprised the familiar assortment of Gladiator, Gauntlet, Vincent, Hardy, Hartebeest and Hart biplanes.

Obviously emboldened by their huge superiority on the ground, the Italians seized the initiative at the outbreak of war and as early as August 1940 moved against French Somaliland (whose resistance lasted no more than a few hours) and British Somaliland, from which all British forces were safely evacuated under air cover provided by the Gladiators of No. 94 Squadron based at Aden. A small incursion into Kenya was also made near Moyale.

Seeing that apart from the limited threat posed by the Italian air and naval forces, nothing could be gained by seriously resisting these advances, Wavell ordered his ground forces to disengage temporarily while his air forces slowly eroded the enemy's strength in the air, for few (if any) reinforcements could reach the Italians from home. This task was admirably achieved by the Wellesleys (despite spirited combat on occasion with Fiat CR.32 and CR.42 fighters) which carried out

The Eritrean campaign was one of the backwaters of the Middle East campaign but it was there that the Vickers Wellesleys made a significant contribution on long-range bombing raids. This No. 47 Squadron aircraft is seen over Eritrea on one such raid.

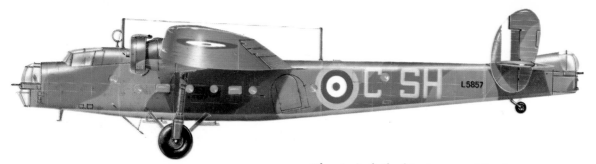

L5857 was the last of 50 Bristol Bombay Mk Is built, and flew out to join No. 216 Squadron in the summer of 1940. It served its entire career with the squadron, being finally destroyed in an air raid on Kufra on 25 September 1942.

numerous highly successful long-range raids. For example, on 18 August five aircraft of No. 223 Squadron set out from Perim Island in the Gulf of Aden to raid the airfield at Addis Ababa, where they destroyed four SM.79s and three hangars. In northern Eritrea No. 14 Squadron's Wellesleys had on the first day of the war bombed the oil tank farm at Massawa, sending up in flames 780 tons of vital fuel.

Occasionally the Regia Aeronautica put in an appearance, as for example occurred on 16 October when a heavily escorted SM.79 carried out an excellent attack on Gedaref which destroyed eight Wellesleys of No. 47 Squadron and two ancient Vincents. A single Italian bomber made almost nightly sorties over Aden for about a fortnight, inexplicably dropping its bombs some miles out to sea. It was at about this time that a Gladiator, Vincent and Blenheim surprised a brand-new Italian submarine on the surface off Aden and forced it to surrender; it was later towed into the port.

Italians finally beaten

However, throughout the winter months the British and Commonwealth forces gradually shifted their balance, bringing pressure to bear on the Italians at carefully selected points. In January an attack by two South African divisions from the Sudan, heavily supported by air cover, swept into Eritrea, capturing Keren, Massawa and Asmara within six weeks. In the south, covered by squadrons of the SAAF, a force of three divisions advanced from Kenya into Italian Somaliland and Ethiopia, taking Mogadishu (where the burnt-out remains of 25 Italian aircraft were found on the ground) on 25 February. Finally, after softening-up attacks by Aden-based Gladiators and Blenheims, a seaborne landing was made at Berbera on 16 March. On 6 April (the day on which Germany opened its attack on the Balkans) British troops entered Addis Ababa. The Italian presence in East Africa had been eliminated, thereby releasing valuable forces for use elsewhere in Wavell's hard-pressed theatre.

The Axis foiled in Iraq and Syria

As a result of treaty obligations, Britain had for some years maintained a limited military commitment to Iraq, a commitment that had in the mid-1930s brought about the construction of a large and elaborate air base at Habbaniyah, some 50 miles (80 km) west of Baghdad. By 1941 this base, which incorporated the RAF HQ complex for British forces in Iraq as well as an aerodrome, an Air Depot and two large repair shops, accommodated over 10,000 men, of whom 1,200 were RAF personnel and the remainder native levies. Although no operational flying units were based at Habbaniyah, No. 4 Flying Training School, located there, possessed about 70 Audax and Airspeed Oxford training aircraft.

On 2 April 1941 the Iraqi regent, Abdulla Illah, sought sanctuary at Habbaniyah, fearing an Axis-inspired coup d'état by an influential political opponent, Raschid Ali. The coup duly took place the following day and, in the face of mounting hostility, the British took immediate steps to protect their interests in the area. During that month troop reinforcements were flown to Shaibah by No. 31 Squadron, and some 230 members of British families were evacuated by lorry from Baghdad to Habbaniyah.

Recognising that the big RAF base represented the key to British interests in their country, the Iraqis now moved a force of some 9,000 men with about 30 pieces of artillery to Habbaniyah, and by 30 April this small army was installed around the perimeter of the base.

Meanwhile the workshop personnel had been hard at work equipping the Audaxes and Oxfords to carry bombs, the former being able to lift two 250-lb (113-kg) and the latter eight 20-lb (9-kg) weapons. In addition a few Gladiators of No. 94 (Fighter) Squadron, newly released from Aden, were flown over from Egypt, and 10 Wellingtons of No. 70 (Bomber) Squadron transferred to Shaibah, to be followed by some from No. 37 Squadron.

Spurred by a characteristic message ('If you have to strike, strike hard') from Churchill him-

In 1941 the Bristol Blenheim Mk IV became the ubiquitous workhorse in the Middle East, serving as a straight bomber, reconnaissance aircraft, shipping strike aircraft and long-range fighter into 1942. Seen over featureless desert is Z5960 of No. 14 Squadron.

Typical of the many Vickers Wellingtons which served in the Middle East is this Mk IA (L7779) of No. 37 Squadron. This aircraft returned from the Middle East after its first tour and continued on training duties with Nos 15 OTU and 1446 Flight until November 1944.

self, the Oxfords and Audaxes now went into action against the investing Iraqis, the procedure adopted being to start their take-off behind the hangars, out of sight of the enemy gunners, rolling out through the station gates and on to the runway before fire could be brought to bear upon them.

The events that now ensued, for all their perilous undertones, were charged with that high comedy which only the British soldier, sailor and airman seem able to appreciate in adversity. Amid the bursting shells and a torrent of machine-gun fire, the Oxfords and Audaxes (joined now by some decrepit Fairey Gordons) continued for four days to bomb the Iraqi forces, assisted by the Wellingtons from Shaibah; from time to time the armoured cars of No. 1 Company, RAF, dashed out to draw the fire as aged Douglas DC-2s and Valentias of No. 31 (Transport) Squadron flew in to pick up and evacuate the British women and children to Shaibah.

Although to begin with the fighting died down during darkness, on the night of 4/5 May the Audaxes and Oxfords continued to bomb by moonlight and the light of their own landing lamps. After a further day of incessant air attack (in which some Blenheims from Egypt joined) the Iraqis, whose own supply line had been cut by the bombing of the bridge over the Euphrates at Felluja, realised that they faced greater perils than those of the RAF and, during the night of 5/6 May, packed their tents and melted away into the desert.

As a British column set out in pursuit under the protection of No. 94 Squadron's Gladiators, and eventually reinstated the Regent in Baghdad, more ominous events took place elsewhere in Iraq: during the course of reconnaissance flights by two long-range Hurricanes flying from Habbaniyah, it had been discovered that a number of Luftwaffe aircraft (Heinkel He 111s and Messerschmitt Bf 110s) had arrived at Mosul, and in due course some of these, together with aircraft of the Regia Aeronautica, put in some attacks on the British base.

German threat collapses

While it was not yet known whether this foreshadowed an active campaign by the Axis to endanger British oil interests in the Middle East or was simply a token gesture to support Raschid Ali's insurrection, it gave rise to some alarm in Cairo, where the British command recognised a possibly serious threat to the northern flank of the whole theatre. However, after the abortive conclusion of the Habbaniyah adventure by the Iraqis, and the premature loss of a number of German aircraft (one of which was shot down by the rifles of some ill-informed tribesmen as it brought the senior German officer to confer with Raschid Ali at Baghdad), the insurrection collapsed and German involvement in the area evaporated.

As events in Iraq were approaching a satisfactory conclusion, signs were detected that the Vichy-inspired element at large in Syria was showing active strategic sympathy for the Axis cause. A circumstantial report to the Foreign Office in London on 8 May mentioned German aircraft landing to refuel at Damascus, a fact confirmed on the 14th during a reconnaissance flight by a No. 203 Squadron Blenheim.

Although by now the Iraqi revolt had ended, and it seemed likely that the enemy air traffic through Syria was engaged in evacuating German personnel and equipment from northern Iraq, it was

The Bristol Bombay had succeeded the Vickers Valentia as the Middle East's bomber transport aircraft. It took part in bombing raids along the North African coast, flew transport runs to Greece, Crete and back, trained SAS paratroopers (as here) and became ambulance aircraft flying up and down the desert well into 1943. Principal exponent of the Bombay was No. 216 Squadron.

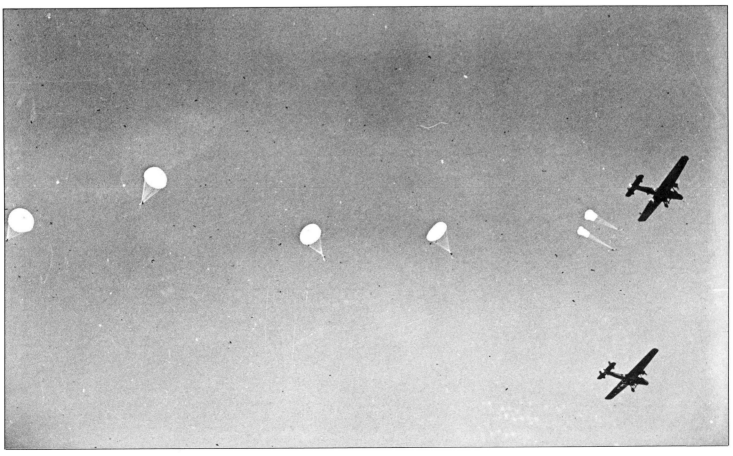

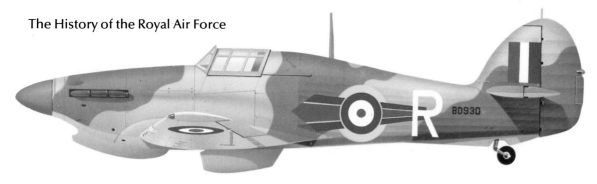

The Hawker Hurricane Mk II took over from the Mk I in the Desert for 1941 and 1942, and served throughout on ground attack and air defence. BD930 is a Mk IIB, shown in service with No. 73 Squadron early in 1942, and is interesting in showing that No. 73 and other desert fighter squadrons carried pre-war fighter insignia.

realised that in Syria a potential threat still existed within striking distance of Cairo and the Suez Canal, if the Germans and Italians wished to avail themselves of Syrian bases.

Preoccupation with Crete, East Africa, Iraq and Cyrenaica delayed military moves against Syria until 8 June, for it was recognised that only physical occupation of the country would dispel the German threat. On that date, supported by No. 80 Squadron (Hurricane fighters), No. 208 Squadron (reconnaissance Hurricanes), No. 3 Squadron of the Royal Australian Air Force (Curtiss Tomahawks), a flight of Gladiators, Nos 11 and 84 Squadrons (Blenheims) and two Fleet Air Arm Squadrons (Fulmars), and a cruiser squadron in coastal waters, two divisions of Commonwealth and Free French troops advanced into Syria from Iraq and Palestine.

Although early progress on the ground was swift, the Vichy French air force, which numbered about 100 aircraft, flying Morane Saulnier M.S.406s and Dewoitine D.520s, offered spirited resistance, while their Martin 167As strove to interfere with the advancing columns. Indeed in one day seven Fulmars were shot down, prompting urgent calls to the RAF to provide air defence over the cruisers. Added to the RAF's problems was recurring trouble with the Tomahawks being experienced by the Australians.

However, as the advance began to lose momentum towards the end of June, Air Marshal A. W. Tedder (who had recently assumed command from Longmore in the Middle East) was able to switch two further squadrons, Nos 45 and 260, from other fronts to Syria, and now increased pressure was brought to bear on the Vichy airfields; even when the French air commander, General Jeannequin, was forced to fall back on his northern airfield at Aleppo, he learned to his cost that even here his few remaining aircraft were not safe from the depredations of the RAF's long-range Hurricane fighters.

On 12 July General Henri Dentz, the Vichy French commander-in-chief, sought a ceasefire, and two days later a formal armistice was signed.

The Western Desert again

Returning again to the critical situation in North Africa in February 1941, the limit of Wavell's advance was reached at El Agheila when constant erosion of his hard-won strength on the ground and in the air by the demands of other fronts brought his forces to a standstill. Already the British in Africa were aware that the Germans had arrived in the theatre for, starting on 10 January, Malta and convoys approaching the island had come under heavy attack by X Fliegerkorps which had arrived in Sicily with some 200 fighters, long-range bombers, dive-bombers and reconnaissance aircraft. Principal target for much of the ensuing month was the aircraft-carrier HMS *Illustrious*, which was repeatedly hit and had to be withdrawn from the theatre for extensive repairs. In a matter of two weeks the Malta Hurricanes and ground defences accounted for about 30 German and Italian aircraft (and Wellingtons attacking Sicily destroyed nine more), for the cost of a dozen RAF aircraft.

Early in February the German 5th Light Division and other units, commanded by Generalleutnant Erwin Rommel, arrived in Tripoli, and on the 18th Hitler named the forces under Rommel's command the Deutsches Afrika Korps. Simultaneously authority was given to move elements of X Fliegerkorps

across the Mediterranean, now accompanied by two Gruppen of Bf 109E fighters fresh from the Channel Coast. All at once the RAF's hard-won air superiority disappeared.

Although RAF reconnaissance pilots had reported increased enemy activity in the Sirte area (where the German forces were being concentrated), their warnings went unheeded. By the end of March German armoured units had forced the British out of El Agheila; within three days Wavell's depleted desert army was in full retreat, pursued by three armoured or motorized divisions (only one of them German). Over the retreating army a few Tomahawks of No. 3 (RAAF) Squadron and a single flight of No. 73 Squadron's Hurricanes were all the fighters now left in Cyrenaica. Pressure on Malta had forced the withdrawal of the Wellingtons from the island, and these now joined the battle in the desert, although night raids in these circumstances could be of little value.

Air power gradually expands

Fully committed to support operations on other fronts, there was effectively nothing that Longmore (and later Tedder) could do to relieve the pressure from the air, such was the dominance assumed by the Luftwaffe. Whereas the Gladiators and Hurricanes had more than held their own in combat with the Regia Aeronautica, the 50-odd Bf 109Es proved to be one of the deciding factors of the whole battle; indeed the Hurricane, on which so much had hitherto depended, was now encumbered by an unwieldy desert air filter over its carburettor intake and proved to be at least 50 mph (80 km/h) slower than its German opponent, while the American Tomahawk was still being plagued by a spate of aggravating 'teething' troubles.

As the retreating army scrambled all the way back to its starting point on the Egyptian border, and frantically dug its heels in on that line, Tedder took stock of his resources and made impassioned pleas for increased reinforcements from home. Leaving the Hurricanes of Nos 6 and 73 Squadrons to operate within the perimeter of besieged Tobruk, he retired the remains of Nos 3 (RAAF), 45 and 55 Squadrons into Egypt. In July Operation 'Battleaxe', an attempt to relieve Tobruk, failed.

While the newly-named 8th Army settled down

In 1942 the Wellington bombing force in the Middle East was reinforced by detachments from Halifax squadrons in Britain. These aircraft were eventually combined into a new No. 462 Squadron, manned by the RAAF. This No. 462 Squadron aircraft had originally come out with a No. 10 Squadron detachment.

The Curtiss Tomahawk found its metier in the battles back and fro across the Western Desert in 1941, before being replaced by Kittyhawks in 1942. AK401 served during this period with No. 250 Squadron.

to a period of intense training, Tedder reorganised and strengthened his command. No. 257 Wing was enlarged to become No. 205 Group, comprising all long-range bombers (five squadrons of Wellingtons) in the Canal Zone, but most important was the promotion of No. 204 Group to become Air HQ, Western Desert, later to become the famous Desert Air Force, and in this capacity to administer all fighter, light bomber and reconnaissance squadrons based in the desert, now transformed into fully mobile wings and squadrons.

Many factors combined to transform Tedder's command from the poor relation of a year previously to a powerful air force in its own right. From Longmore's 29 squadrons it slowly grew an up-to-date command of 110 squadrons, now including 13 of the USAAF, 17 of the SAAF, eight of the RAAF, six of the Fleet Air Arm and two Greek squadrons. Although there were still the equivalent of 19 squadrons of Hurricane fighters and fighter-bombers, the first Supermarine Spitfire Vs had arrived: the type equipped six squadrons and was being delivered to four others, while the much improved Curtiss Kittyhawk was quickly replacing the Tomahawk. Moreover the first four-engine heavy bombers (Handley Page Halifaxes, Consolidated Liberators and Boeing Fortresses) were serving with 11 squadrons (six of them American). Many other aspects of reorganisation were undertaken, not least in the ambit of tactical support, an area in which the RAF had been particularly poorly informed as a result of some 20 years of inter-service jealousies and wrangling. And it must be to Tedder and the new army commander, General Sir Claude Auchinleck, that the credit for impetus in this transformation should be given. Communications

between air and ground forces were greatly improved; mobile warning radar posts and increased mobile gun defences were introduced to protect the forward landing strips; and most important of all, the headquarters of the army and air forces in the field were henceforth invariably located in close company so that commanders and their staffs could act in concert in all tactical conditions. At the same time, under the guidance of expert service specialists sent out from home, all the other essentials of an efficient air force underwent detailed scrutiny and expansion – including operational and technical training, aircraft maintenance, modification and repair, photographic reconnaissance, processing and interpretation.

Operation 'Crusader'

Despite constant pressure and Churchillian impatience, Auchinleck was not ready to take the initiative in the desert until 18 November 1941; the aim of his Operation 'Crusader' was not unnaturally to destroy all Axis forces in North Africa. During the past two months the desert air force had ranged far and wide in its efforts to prevent the build-up of Rommel's army – against a number of minor operations elsewhere.

Night after night the ports of Tripoli and Benghazi came under attack from the British long-range bombers based in Egypt and Malta. Further afield the Italian home ports were visited by aircraft of the Fleet Air Arm and by British-based heavy bombers. In the desert itself the new Martin Baltimores flew numerous sorties against enemy troop concentrations and supply depots. Temporary deployment of X Fliegerkorps units to the Dodecanese islands was followed by sporadic

The Curtiss Tomahawk had proved a failure in Britain but in the Desert it formed a valuable low-level fighter alongside the Hurricanes. The first unit to receive the type, in July 1941, was No. 112 Squadron which assumed shark's mouth markings retained for the rest of its career.

Curtiss Kittyhawk

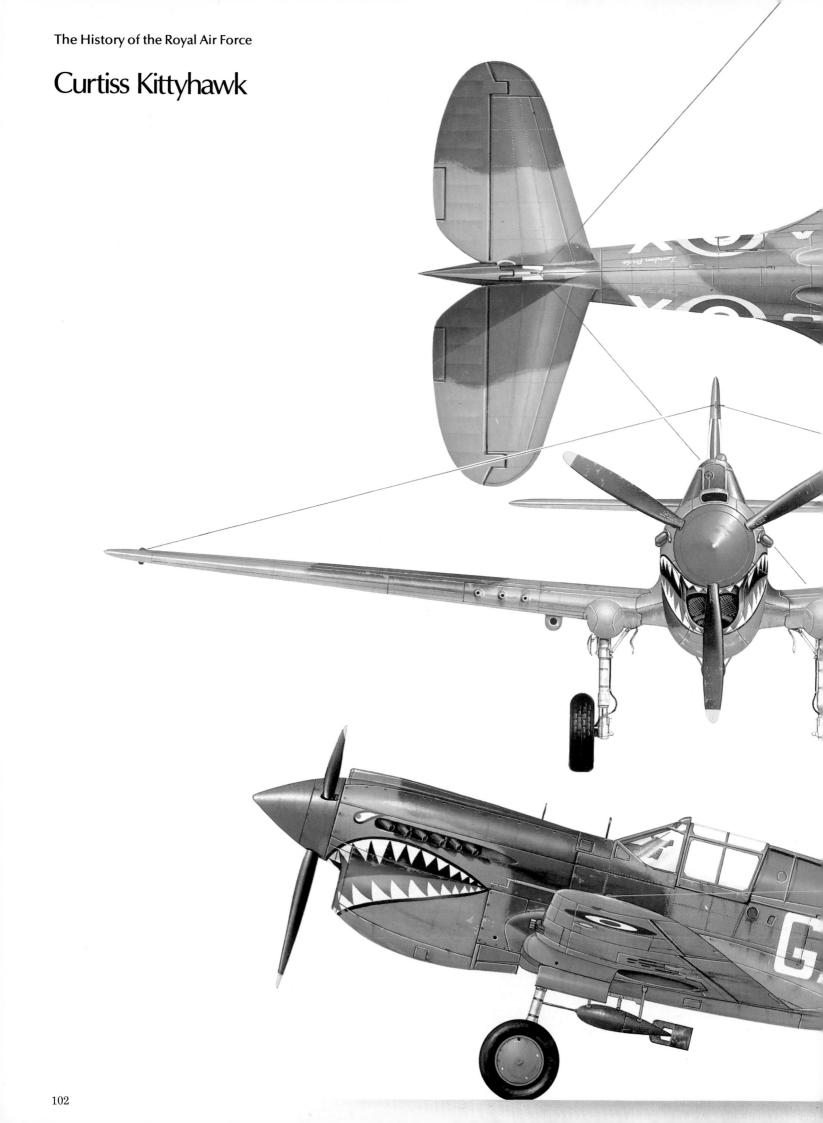

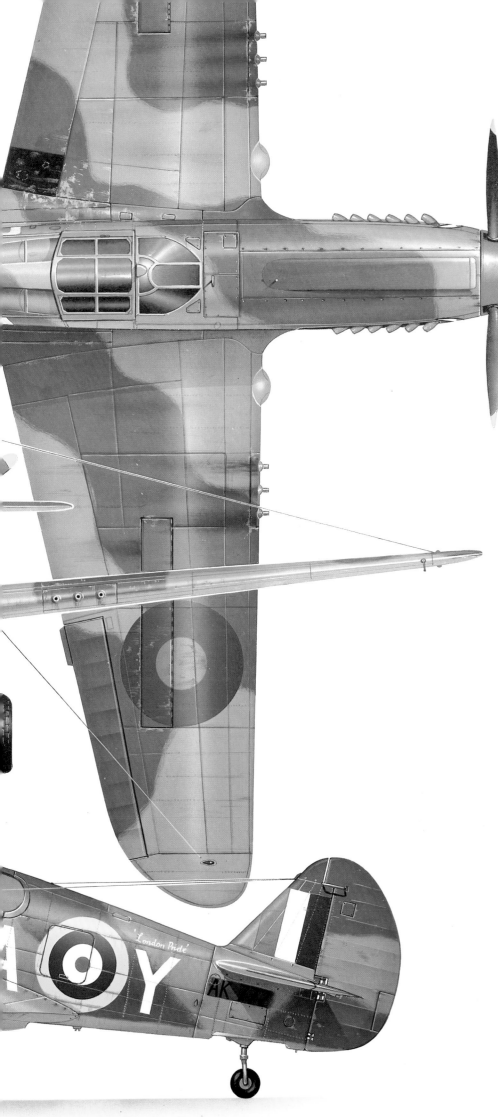

The Curtiss Kittyhawk found its metier with the Desert Air Force in 1942–3 and served to great effect in the battles winging back and forth across the desert wastes as a fighter and fighter-bomber. Shown here is AK772, a Mk I, which served with one of the most famous DAF squadrons, No. 112, from March to May 1942. This squadron early on adopted the 'shark's mouth' insignia on the noses of its aircraft, and this was perpetuated right up to its last aircraft type, the North American Sabre. AK772 began its short service with No. 112 Squadron as 'GA:A', changing later to 'GA:Y'. Its subsequent history is not known.

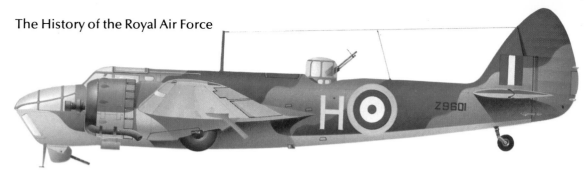

The Bristol Blenheim Mk IV served the Desert Air Force well into 1942. Z9601 was serving with No. 55 Squadron at Fuka early that year.

enemy raiding of the Canal Zone, but Hurricane night-fighters quickly discouraged these.

When 'Crusader' eventually opened, Tedder's 700 aircraft in 49 operational squadrons in Egypt and Malta were opposed by 436 enemy aircraft in Cyrenaica, 186 in Tripolitania, 776 in the various enemy-held Mediterranean islands and more than 600 in Italy and the Balkans. It was therefore vital to achieve air superiority over the ground battle before the enemy could bring up air reinforcements from further afield.

As the attack opened on 18 November the air force went into action all along the 50-mile (80-km) front as Bristol Beaufighters of No. 272 Squadron shot up concentrations of Italian transport and airfields and Hurricane fighter-bombers of Nos 33 and 213 Squadrons strafed troops assembling in the rear. Unless obscured by the frequent dust storms in the desert, scarcely any movement by the enemy ground forces escaped attention from the medium bombers and fighter-bombers. For several days the ground battle raged with neither side making significant gains, but as British and South African pilots in their Hurricanes, Tomahawks and Kittyhawks broke up attacks by enemy dive-bombers, a measure of air superiority was gained by the RAF. Tobruk was relieved, only to be isolated again on the 28th, although the enemy armour seemed to be moving back to a new line just to the west of the port. When Rommel suddenly tried to enclose the British forces by two rapidly moving armoured pincers, one along the coast and the other about 30 miles (50 km) inland, both were spotted from the air and eventually beaten back by the ground forces.

On 16 December the Axis forces, fighting on a line based at Gazala but now almost without adequate air support, were heavily beaten but managed to escape, first to Benghazi and then to the south. As the Eighth Army moved up in pursuit, the full evidence of the Allied air forces' attacks during the past three months was now exposed; on the dozen or so enemy airfields between the Egyptian

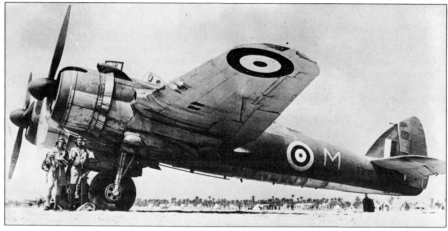

border and Benghazi the remains of no fewer than 458 German and Italian aircraft, roughly half of them German, were found crippled, burnt and abandoned, and many others were lying abandoned where they had been shot down in the desert.

Once more the Allied forces reached El Agheila, as Auchinleck strove desperately to strengthen his positions by moving reinforcements along the 1,000-mile (1610-km) route from Cairo. Once more, however, the demands of other theatres (the Japanese had struck in the Far East) forestalled British efforts to make the final advance to dislodge the Axis from North Africa.

Alamein: the turning-point to fortune

Sensing that the Allies faced considerable difficulties in sustaining their forward forces in Libya, the Germans now opened a savage onslaught by land, sea and air throughout the Mediterranean. Luftflotte 2 was moved from the Russian front in November 1941 to Italy and Sicily, and with it came Generalfeldmarschall Albert Kesselring, who now assumed command of II Fliegerkorps in Sicily,

The advent of the Bristol Beaufighter Mk I in the Middle East added a strong dimension to offensive capabilities. With its four 20-mm cannon and six 0.303-in (7.7-mm) machine-guns it provided a potent ground-attack aircraft over land and sea at long-range. This Mk IC belonged to No. 272 Squadron, which arrived at Abu Sueir in the Canal Zone in May 1941 and rapidly built up an enviable reputation in the Western Desert.

Early in 1942 Nos 92 and 145 Squadrons set out for the Canal Zone, a significant move because they brought the first Spitfires to the area. Two Mk VCs are seen here at a Canal Zone airfield.

The first Beaufighter Mk ICs to go to the Middle East were part of No. 252 Squadron which arrived there via Malta and Heraklion in May 1941. T4767 was one of these aircraft, and is shown carrying the code letters BT, which were dropped before the year was out.

In 1942 the Blenheim was augmented in the Desert by the Douglas Boston, and this played a significant part in the final sweeping of the Axis out of Africa, and then on to Sicily and Italy. The Desert Air Force Boston squadrons were predominantly SAAF units.

X Fliegerkorps in Greece and Crete, and the forces of Fliegerführer Afrika in Libya. During December over 400 enemy sorties were flown against Malta, but in the first week of January this increased to 500, virtually all being directed against the island's airfields. On the 5th a No. 69 Squadron Maryland from Malta spotted nine heavily protected supply ships entering Tripoli harbour, yet because of bad weather and atrocious conditions on their airfields the Malta-based Wellingtons could do nothing to stop them. In mid-February an entire Allied convoy sailing to the island was sunk by air attack.

Covered by bad weather on 21 January Rommel struck the Eighth Army while the RAF was unable to operate from its flooded airfield at Antelat, where a number of fighters had to be destroyed as the enemy forces approached. A temporary stand was made at Msus, where a lull in the storms allowed RAF fighters and fighter-bombers to take heavy toll of thin-skinned enemy vehicles on the 26th, but gradually enemy air pressure increased with well-escorted dive-bombers striking the 8th Army's armoured units, which now began to suffer the stringencies of over-extended supply lines. Benghazi was lost once more and a line of defence was established between Gazala and Bir Hakeim. Principally on account of the heavy toll taken of his motorised and armoured vehicles from the air, Rommel was content to pause for a moment before this line to gather his strength for the final push into Egypt.

Meanwhile the enemy made a renewed attempt to eliminate Malta. In February 1,000 tons of bombs were dropped and an average of 50 aircraft struck the island every day. On 20 March 143 aircraft . . . on the 21st 218 . . . the next day 112. By now the first 15 Spitfires had arrived to bolster the defences, but by the evening of the 23rd the air officer commanding, Air Vice-Marshal H. P. Lloyd, could report only five Hurricanes and Spitfires airworthy.

April proved to be the climax of the enemy assault on Malta. Twice during the month the number of enemy sorties rose above 300 in a single day; seldom, despite a few reinforcements, were more than half a dozen fighters available to meet the raids. Yet Valletta, despite its shattered buildings, still functioned as a port and naval base. On the 16th the island was awarded the George Cross for its continuing heroism. On the 20th 47 Spitfire Vs were flown in from the American carrier USS *Wasp*; at last Lloyd possessed fighters capable of matching Kesselring's Bf 109Fs. The following day a reconnaissance pilot reported seeing preparations being made in Sicily for the assembly of gliders. Was this the prelude to a second Crete?

The turning point arrived on 9 May when 62 further Spitfires arrived from the USS *Wasp*, and the following day the fast minelayer HMS *Welshman* succeeded in reaching Malta with several weeks' supply of ammunition. Having already lost more than 60 aircraft in six weeks, Kesselring realised there was little point in continuing the assault, at least for the time being, let alone attempting invasion. In any case, under cover of the previous weeks' bombardment, considerable quantities of supplies and reinforcements had been carried across to the Axis forces in North Africa.

That month Rommel launched his attack on the Gazala-Bir Hakeim line and, despite heroic resis-

The key to Malta's defence was to get as many Spitfires there as possible. BR344 was one of the Mk VCs which flew off USS *Wasp* in April 1942 to join the squadrons on the island. It is seen in its temporary ferry markings.

tance by the French at the latter, well supported by the newly-arrived anti-tank Hurricane IIDs of No. 6 Squadron, the Deutsches Afrika Korps succeeded in turning the 8th Army's position. As the British army raced back to the last defensible line in front of the Canal Zone, at Alamein, two convoys were sailed to Malta from opposite ends of the Mediterranean. For much of the voyage the ships from Alexandria were protected by the desert-based squadrons of the RAF, yet this convoy was forced to retire as the Italian fleet approached. The convoy from Gibraltar sailed on unprotected in the air save by its own carrier-based aircraft and those flying from Malta itself.

In the fierce attacks on these convoys the Bristol Beauforts of No. 217 Squadron hit and crippled the Italian cruiser *Trento*, which was finished off by one of Malta's submarines. Beaufighters of No. 235 Squadron were also based on Malta for the purpose of flying long-range patrols over the convoy and it was the result of their protection and that of the island's Spitfires that just two merchant ships eventually sailed through to Malta. Indeed, such was the scale of enemy air attacks that the cost of getting these two ships through was the loss of a cruiser, five destroyers, two minesweepers, six merchant ships and more than 20 aircraft.

Numerical superiority

By the beginning of August the 8th Army was dug in on the Alamein line, and for the next two months both sides set about a further desperate bid to build up supplies. Five further merchantmen reached Malta safely, prompting the return of cruisers, destroyers and submarines to the island, and these so threatened the enemy's direct shipping route between Sicily and North Africa that much of the Italian traffic chose to follow a huge detour to the east, sailing south from Greece, thereby bringing it within range of aircraft based in the Canal Zone. According to German records 35 per cent of the shipping despatched to North Africa in August failed to arrive; between 27 August and 4 September nine supply ships were sunk, six of them by aircraft, and three of them were tankers. Rommel reported that he was now desperately short of fuel.

Accordingly Kesselring now launched on Malta a final attack which lasted from 10 until 19 October. This assault, involving some 2,500 sorties, cost the Luftwaffe 46 aircraft and the Italians 39; the RAF lost 30 Spitfires. Realising that precious little damage had been done and that Malta's offensive capabilities had not been seriously impaired, Kesselring called a halt to the attack. The air commander on Malta at this time was Keith Park.

In the Western Desert and Palestine, on the eve of the great battle of Alamein, Tedder could field 1,200 serviceable first-line aircraft; the Axis powers had 690 aircraft in Africa, but of these only about half were serviceable.

As General Bernard Montgomery, the new 8th Army commander, launched his great attack, preceded by a massive gun barrage, Tedder's aircraft went into well-rehearsed action. It is not proposed here to describe the land battle in any detail save to say that the essence of Montgomery's tactics was to persuade the enemy that the main attack would be launched in the south of the line, but in fact to deliver it in the north. The tasks of the RAF were to prevent enemy aircraft from penetrating the deception, to prevent enemy air support of his forward forces, and to give complete air

support for Montgomery's infantry and armour in their main assault. While paths were being cleared through enemy minefields, the Wellingtons of Nos 37, 40, 70, 104, 108 and 148 Squadrons maintained a continuous bombardment of enemy artillery as Hurricane IIC night-fighters attacked troop concentrations and thin-skinned transport and Hurricane IID 'tank-busters' of No. 6 (Fighter) Squadron and No. 7 (SAAF) Squadron attacked enemy armour. This pattern was continued for three days and nights, the daylight raids being joined by the Bostons, Baltimores and Mitchells, principally of the South African Air Force. And when the Luftwaffe attempted to interfere by launching dive-bombing attacks, RAF fighters were there to intercept, often forcing the enemy aircraft to jettison their bombs on their own troops.

The final phase of Montgomery's attack, Operation 'Supercharge', began on the night of 1/2 November and was accompanied by a peak effort by the Hurricanes and Wellingtons. As the enemy broke and sought to disengage, Tedder unleashed all his tactical support squadrons, the anti-tank fighters and light bombers in particular achieving great damage among enemy vehicles: 30,000 enemy troops and vast quantities of war matériel fell into the 8th Army's hands.

The rout would have been even greater had not bad weather intervened and virtually grounded the RAF on 6 November, thereby allowing many enemy units, both air and ground, to escape. On the 13th Tobruk was captured for the last time, and on the 19th British fighters reached Martuba in time to cover a convoy which at last broke the siege of Malta.

In Operation 'Chocolate' two Hurricane squadrons (Nos 213 and 238) were sent to an abandoned enemy airfield far in advance of our troops, landed and refuelled, and then took off again to attack the enemy from his rear.

This time the desert army and air force scarcely paused at El Agheila, but swept on to Tripoli, which the Eighth Army entered on 23 January 1943 as the Desert Air Force landed at Castel Benito airfield.

The Battle for Malta raged through 1941 and 1942 and one of the greatest needs was for fighter aircraft. Aircraft-carriers were pressed into the task of sailing as near as they dared to Malta, from where Hurricanes and Spitfires flew off to the beleaguered island. Even US Navy carriers took part, and in April 1942 the USS *Wasp* took a squadron of Spitfires in this way.

Right: One of the success stories that came out of the desperate Malta fighting was the exploits of No. 39 Squadron with its Bristol Beauforts. Flying out from Luqa airfield, its aircraft used bombs and torpedoes with great effect against enemy convoys in 1942 and 1943.

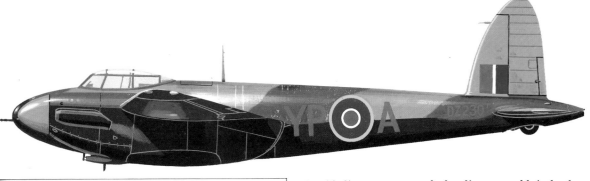

No. 23 Squadron had pioneered intruder operations from Ford over the northern French airfields from 1940 onwards with great success. Re-equipping with de Havilland Mosquito NF. Mk IIs in July 1942, it took these to Malta at the end of the year and began to take a satisfying toll of enemy aircraft, flying over Sicilian and Italian airfields at night. DZ230 was one of the Mk IIs which the squadron took to Luqa in December 1942.

Most aircraft survived only for a short while on Malta. This Short Sunderland Mk I was caught in one of the many air raids.

'Torch': the great pincers close

The Anglo-American landings in Morocco and Algeria, which took place as the Battle of Alamein was reaching its climax early in November 1942, were only one of a number of 'Second Front' ventures considered by the Allied war leaders. In deferring to British advocacy of the North African landings (rather than an invasion of France immediately, which the Americans favoured), President Roosevelt came to accept that by committing large Axis forces to the defence of the Mediterranean such landings would indeed assist the Soviet Union whose campaign with Germany, particularly around the city of Stalingrad, was about to reach its critical turning point. In due course, following the meeting of the Western war leaders at Casablanca, it was agreed that, while an American (General Dwight D. Eisenhower) would assume supreme command in North Africa, the majority of his senior subordinate commanders would be British.

The objects of the landings were twofold: the first was of course to speed the end of Axis operations in North Africa, thereby opening the way to launching an invasion of the European mainland; the second, hopefully by attracting Vichy France to join forces with the Allies, to secure the French fleet and thereby restore Allied naval supremacy in the Mediterranean. In the event progress towards Tunis was considerably slower than hoped, with the result that the Germans were able heavily to reinforce their army and air force across the Sicilian narrows. Moreover, although the French did eventually condescend to throw in their lot with the Allies, their fleet decided to scuttle itself at Toulon.

Three main areas of landings were chosen: those by the Americans were launched direct from America on to the Moroccan coast; those that concern this narrative, being supported by the RAF, were at Oran and Algiers on the Algerian coast on 8 November. Air support was provided by squadrons which had flown from Britain to Gibral-

tar, or were shipped out to Gibraltar where their aircraft were assembled. To accommodate the 600 aircraft that would eventually support the landings and the subsequent operations on the African mainland, the landing strip at Gibraltar was enlarged from 980 by 75 yards (896 by 69 m) to 1,400 by 100 yards (1280 by 91 m) by extending the runway some 400 yards (366 m) into the sea, while the ordered erection of aircraft and accommodation of aircrews was effected under the command of Air Vice-Marshal J. M. Robb.

Such was the efficiency and secrecy with which all these preparations were completed that when in due course German reconnaissance aircraft reported the presence of the invasion convoys as they sailed along the Algerian coast, the enemy assumed them to be reinforcing Malta. As darkness fell on the night of 7/8 November the invasion force altered course towards the landing points. Air support for the landings, which started at dawn, was provided by Fleet Air Arm aircraft from the fleet carriers HMS *Formidable*, *Victorious*, *Furious* and *Argus*, and the escort carriers HMS *Biter* and *Dasher*, which between them carried 35 Grumman Martlets, seven Fulmars, 30 Sea Hurricanes and (for the first time in action) 45 Supermarine Seafires, in addition to 35 Fairey Albacore and nine Fairey Swordfish torpedo bombers. Another escort carrier, HMS *Avenger*, was torpedoed by a submarine and blew up.

Although this naval air support continued for several days, the airfields at Maison Blanche and Blida near Algiers were captured quickly and on the first day the Hurricanes of No. 43 (Fighter) Squadron were flown in from Gibraltar, soon to be followed by Nos 81 and 242 Squadrons in time to intercept and rout an attack by Ju 88s. The Germans had indeed reacted swiftly elsewhere, and Allied reconnaissance disclosed that within 48 hours of the landings at least 115 Axis aircraft had arrived at El Aouina, near Tunis.

The next landing was at Bone, on the 12th, where 26 American Douglas C-47s, escorted by No. 43

Squadron, dropped paratroops to capture the port and airfield.

For all its initial successes, Operation 'Torch' soon slowed down. The linking up with Montgomery's Eighth Army was delayed for many weeks not only by the stiffening resistance of the Axis forces but by bad weather which severely reduced activity both on the ground and in the air. Nevertheless the latter did not prevent the steady build-up of British and American air forces throughout December and January, Nos 142 and 150 Squadrons with Wellingtons, No. 111 (Fighter) Squadron with Spitfires and No. 255 Squadron with Beaufighters being sent out from Britain.

These aircraft, and many others both British and American, kept up attacks on the enemy forces whenever the weather allowed, albeit against stiffening opposition by the Luftwaffe. For instance on 4 December No. 18 Squadron, flying Bristol Bisleys, was ordered to bomb the enemy landing ground at Chouigui; nine aircraft set course but failed to rendezvous with their Spitfire escort. Near the target the bombers were set on by a Gruppe of Bf 109Fs; all nine Bisleys were shot down. The squadron commander, Wing Commander H. G. Malcolm, was posthumously awarded the Victoria Cross for his gallantry in leading this attack.

The enemy driven out

The final phase of the Tunisian campaign began at the end of March 1943 with the 8th Army's breakthrough of the Mareth Line, brilliantly supported by the tactical squadrons of the Western Desert Air Force, now commanded by Air Vice-Marshal H. Broadhurst (Command of the Desert Air Force had passed to Broadhurst with Air Chief Marshal Sir Arthur Tedder's appointment to command the Mediterranean Air Command on 17 February 1943; Air Chief Marshal Sir William Sholto Douglas had taken the latter's place at Middle East Command.) While the bulk of the Allied armour carried out a wide flanking move-

As soon as the situation in Malta became more tolerable, the RAF sent in Beaufighter units both for night-fighting and for long-range strike duties. One such is taxiing out from its dispersal at Luqa.

Many squadrons – RAF, RAAF and SAAF – of the Desert Air Force used the Curtiss Tomahawk. AK578 is a Mk I which served with No. 112 Squadron RAF in the mid-1942 period of fighting in the Western Desert.

ment to the south of Mareth, three squadrons of Kittyhawk fighter-bombers attacked the enemy anti-tank gun screen and two Hurricane IID squadrons swept down at any sign of movement by enemy armour. On 8 April patrols of the Eighth Army and those of the American II Corps at last linked up east of Gafsa in southern Tunisia.

During the following week the enemy-held airfields at Mezzouna, La Fauconnerie, Sfax, El Djem, Kairouan and Sousse all fell to the armies advancing north through Tunisia, and by 1 May the Axis forces had been violently contained in an area about 100 by 50 miles (160 by 80 km) in the extreme north of the country. There now followed a fortnight in which the full might of the Western Desert Air Force, the North West African Tactical Air Force, and the squadrons now based on Malta, was thrown against the enemy. From 22 April until the end of the month tactical support fighters and fighter-bombers flew a daily average of more than 1,000 sorties; on the night of 4/5 May Wellingtons and Bisleys attacked transport concentrations around Tunis. On the 5th Fortresses joined Mitchells, Bostons, Wellingtons and Bisleys in attacks on enemy shipping trying desperately to bring supplies into the enemy pocket, and on the following day, behind a carpet of bombs rained down from the skies, the infantry moved forward. By the afternoon the Allied armour had torn the enemy defence line apart, and by the end of a day on which the Northwest African Air Forces had flown 2,154 sorties, the Allied armies were moving on Tunis.

Meanwhile as the Germans began an attempt to extricate their army by sea, the Luftwaffe tried to fly large quantities of fuel to the beleaguered forces in the huge Messerschmitt Me 323 transports. Alas for the enemy, these were spotted by RAF Kittyhawk pilots who needed no second bidding to descend upon the hapless monsters and send them crashing into the sea.

On 7 May, as the Americans occupied Bizerta, the British 7th Armoured Division rolled into Tunis. On 13 May the final capitulation of Axis forces in North Africa was accepted, after a quarter of a million Germans and Italians had been killed or captured. In his final Order of the Day Tedder addressed his forces as follows:

All Ranks of the Allied Air Forces
By magnificent team work between nationalities, commands, units, officers and men from Teheran to Takoradi, from Morocco to the Indian Ocean, you have, together with your comrades on land and sea, thrown the enemy out of Africa. You have shown the world the unity and strength of air power. A grand job, well finished. We face our next job with the knowledge that we have thrashed the enemy, and the determination to thrash him again.

Casablanca

The 'Torch' landings were only two months past when Churchill, Roosevelt and their chiefs-of-staff met in conference at Casablanca in French Morocco, their task being to decide on the future conduct of war against Germany and Italy in the West, a war that, until invasion of the European mainland

Hawker had developed the Mk IID version of the Hurricane with two 40-mm cannon under the wings and, in the hands of No. 6 Squadron, this variant was highly effective as a tank-busting device in the final offensive in North Africa.

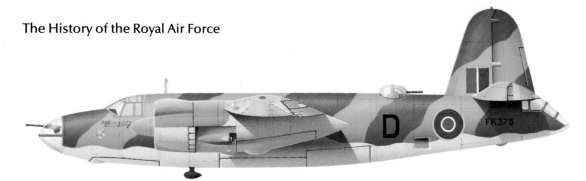

The Martin Marauder Mk I came into RAF service in August 1942 with No. 14 Squadron; FK375 was one of their aircraft. It flew bombing operations at first, transferring to minelaying and shipping reconnaissance missions later.

could be launched, would be limited almost exclusively to air operations. It should be remembered that by December 1942 the American air forces had only been actively engaged in operations over Europe for some five months (apart from the three American volunteer Eagle Squadrons with the RAF).

It had, moreover, to be decided formally whether to eliminate the European Axis nations first or, as might have been favoured by the Americans, to concentrate upon Japan. The latter had, after all, swept through the Pacific and South East Asia, inflicting heavy losses upon the Americans. A compromise was reached whereby America would retain the bulk of her navy in the Pacific to prevent Japan from consolidating her gains, while continuing to build up her air forces in Britain and North Africa for an all-out assault in Europe.

As was well known and mutually accepted by the time of the Casablanca conference, the British Air Staff was wholly committed to the strategic use of Bomber Command by night, whereas American policy for some six years had centred around the use of heavily-armed, high-flying four-engine bombers, the first of which was the B-17 Fortress, now being joined in service by the Consolidated B-24 Liberator. Both were excellent aircraft but neither could lift the same warloads as the British Handley Page Halifaxes and Avro Lancasters over similar distances. Additionally, the continuous process of build-up in RAF Bomber Command, and the shift to heavier bombs and bombers that had taken place over the past 18 months, meant that for some time to come a greater proportion of the strategic air offensive would continue to be undertaken by the RAF.

Ploesti

Next to be decided was the priority of targets. The geographical separation of the two great Allies by thousands of miles of ocean rendered the build up and sustaining of huge Allied forces in Britain and North Africa critically vulnerable to enemy air and submarine attack, so the German U-boat bases, particularly those on the French Atlantic coast, and the submarine manufacturing industry were given high priority for attack. The principal German source of natural oil, the Ploesti field in Romania, was far beyond the range of British-based bombers but, now that North Africa had been cleared of enemy forces, American long-range bombers might be able to reach this target

from Egypt or Libya.

This type of target did not find favour with the outspoken Air Marshal Harris, commanding RAF Bomber Command, whose instincts and long experience stoutly supported the use of strategic bombers against the enemy industrial concentrations and large areas of dense population. These, he felt were more relevant to the capabilities of large formations of heavy bombers flying at night. Nevertheless his instructions from the Air Staff were at once sufficiently forthright and equivocal to allow of broad interpretation: 'Your primary objective will be the progressive destruction and dislocation of the German military, industrial and economic system, and the undermining of the morale of the German people to a point where their capacity for armed resistance is fatally weakened.'

It was Air Chief Marshal Sir Charles Portal who at Casablanca argued the merits of more imminent operations, pointing out the strategic value of an invasion of Sicily and Italy, before any large-scale operation to invade northern France. (Large-scale landings in the Mediterranean and northern Europe simultaneously were ruled out because of a chronic shortage of landing craft, and this argument effectively ended any thought of an invasion of France until 1944).

Operation 'Torch' had used the Supermarine Spitfire VC as its standard fighter, and many squadrons operated in the air battles over Algeria and Tunisia. These aircraft all had the undernose air filter for sand and dusty conditions, as seen here on JG871.

Below left: One of the most successful American bombers to enter the fighting in 1942 was the Martin Baltimore, used exclusively in the Middle East. It served in two roles, as a medium day-bomber and for anti-shipping reconnaissance. Shown here is the Mk II version over the Western Desert.

Below: One of the more daring actions at the time of the Alamein breakout was to position two Hurricane squadrons, Nos 213 and 238, on a desert landing ground far behind the enemy lines, where they were entirely supplied by air transport in the form of the Hudsons of No. 117 Squadron. Both types are shown here as a No. 213 Squadron Hurricane taxis out for operations beside the Hudson.

The North American Mustang Mk I entered RAF service in Army Cooperation Command in 1942, the first successful tactical reconnaissance type the command received. The Mustangs served on a widespread basis in northern Europe, No. 225 Squadron being one of the units involved; it was the only unit to take this type to North Africa for Operation 'Torch'. The aircraft shown is of this period in the squadron's operations.

Another American type which came on the Middle East scene in the summer of 1942 was the Martin Marauder. Initially in service with No. 14 Squadron (shown here) it later was used by No. 39 Squadron.

Portal pointed out that only by attacking Italy, and thereby perhaps persuading that country to defect from the Axis, would there become available suitable air bases from which Allied bombers could carry out attacks on those parts of the German aircraft industry which lay buried deep inside Europe (particularly in Austria). Furthermore any attacks on Romania by American aircraft based in North Africa would involve only small warloads owing to the distances involved, whereas operations from Italian bases would permit almost twice the weight of bombs to be dropped.

Finally, and apart from agreement in principle that the task of the American strategic bombing force should be to aim to complement a 'round the clock' offensive against Germany and enemy-occupied territories with the RAF, it was decided to launch a crushing attack, first upon the Ruhr's heavy armament industries, and later upon the German capital. Apart from the hoped-for damage to many essential war factories and an undermining of enemy morale, it was expected that the Luftwaffe would be forced to withdraw many of its units from all other fronts (not least from the Eastern Front, thereby directly assisting the Russians) to counter the threat at home. Portal quoted his Intelligence estimates of 4,200 first-line German aircraft, of which 2,500 were likely to be serviceable, plus about 1,500 in reserve. Surviving German records are not complete, but by extrapolating known units and their strengths one is faced by a considerable discrepancy, the figure subsequently arrived at being about 6,000 first-line aircraft, of which almost 4,000 were serviceable, plus some 1,500 in reserve. It is known, however, that what would have constituted second-line aircraft in the RAF were being used operationally in the East.

As well as for strike, the Beaufighter was used for night defence. This Beaufighter Mk VIF warming up its engines has an early AI installation in its nose.

Coastal Command

Such was the diversity of tasks undertaken and the very special hazards faced by RAF Coastal Command during the war, not to mention the decisive nature of their mastering, that the command merits particular and detailed study. Although the command's primary task at the beginning of the war (and always) had been to safeguard the nation's sea lanes, its equipment was far from adequate to do so simultaneously in all parts of the world, so that not unnaturally the main burden was shouldered by the Royal Navy and its attendant Fleet Air Arm. Indeed, so paltry was the command's equipment when war broke out that its main area of responsibility was almost entirely confined to that implied by its title. Gradually however, as the strategic changes followed the course of war and technical progress came to the assistance of the hard-pressed command, so its capabilities increased a hundredfold, so that by 1945 it was indeed able to sustain prodigious feats of operation over much of the world's great expanses of ocean.

Nor were the command's duties confined to passive defence, and the war was not many months old before its airmen were in action against targets off the enemy coast and, as told in due course, assumed the main responsibility for long-range photographic reconnaissance.

Be that as it may, the principal enemy of the command was, at the beginning of the war as it was at the very end, the enemy submarine. This was the one weapon that could have brought Britain to her knees – and nearly did.

The narrow seas

Germany went to war relatively ill-equipped to pursue a decisive submarine campaign against Britain, although short-range boats chalked up a number of outstanding but isolated successes in the early months. Instead the German navy relied more upon its commerce raiders (the so-called pocket battleships, which were in effect little more than long-range heavy cruisers), and it was against these that much of the RAF's attention was directed, particularly by Bomber Command.

Coastal Command's home-based order of battle comprised 19 squadrons, of which 11 flew Avro Ansons, three Short Sunderlands, two Supermarine Stranraers, two Vickers Vildebeests and one Saro London (Ansons: Nos 48, 206, 217, 220, 224, 233, 269, 500, 502, 608 and 612 Squadrons; Sunderlands: Nos 204, 210 and 228 Squadrons; Stranraers: Nos 209 and 228 Squadrons; Vildebeests: Nos 22 and 42 Squadrons; and Londons: No. 240 Squadron), although two of the Anson squadrons were converting to the Lockheed Hudson. The Ansons were hopelessly outdated, yet it was such an aircraft of

The supreme aircraft of Coastal Command throughout World War II was the Short Sunderland. It was in service in its Mk I form when the war started, and still in production as the GR. Mk 5 when it closed. To help with the Atlantic patrolling the RAF sent over its No. 10 Squadron to fly alongside the RAF from Mount Batten in Plymouth, where this Mk I is taxiing out.

The Avro Anson Mk I K8754 had joined No. 206 Squadron at Bircham Newton in 1937 and served with it on North Sea patrols until 1940, being replaced by Hudsons. K8754 went to No. 1 OTU where it crashed on 29 August 1940.

The Stranraers of No. 240 Squadron initially flew out of Pembroke Dock but then moved to Stranraer, where they served until replaced by Catalinas in March of 1941. Cruising at 105 mph (169 km/h), the Stranraer had an endurance of 9½ hours.

No. 500 (Ulster) Squadron, flying from Detling, that made the first attack of the war on an enemy submarine on 5 September 1939, albeit without success.

The Sunderland was a magnificent flying-boat, being a military adaptation of the commercial Empire-class aircraft, and, in later versions, remained in service with the RAF until long after the war. It possessed long endurance, that vital attribute for ocean patrol, being able to remain aloft for more than 12 hours. The Vildebeest, on the other hand, was an anachronism, surviving in RAF service owing to delivery delays with the Bristol Beaufort torpedo bomber.

With such equipment the command was able to perform little more than routine coastal patrolling, although the flying-boats gave valuable air cover to the deep sea convoys approaching from the west, and this situation persisted well into 1940, by which time Hudsons were arriving in greater numbers.

An example of the fine work being done by the Sunderlands was afforded when the *Kensington Court* was sunk by a U-boat 100 miles (160 km) off Land's End; in response to the ship's SOS, two Sunderlands alighted and rescued the entire crew within a hour of the attack.

However, the weapons at the command's disposal were singularly ineffective. The Anson carried only 100-lb (45-kg) bombs, which were harmless to a submarine even if a direct hit was obtained, while the 250-lb (113-kg) bomb carried by the flying-boats inflicted worthwhile damage only if it exploded within 6 ft (2 m) of the enemy's pressure hull. Moreover, only when the Hudson arrived did the command possess a bomb distributor capable of delivering a properly spaced stick of bombs. Such immunity from damage was confirmed early in the war when two British submarines returned home undamaged, their captains reporting that they had been attacked by 'friendly' aircraft.

Fortunately the enemy was not yet ready with large numbers of submarines (only about a dozen being at sea at the outbreak of war). Instead the Germans pinned their faith on the magnetic mine for domination of the North Sea, and it was to counter this menace that Coastal Command operated half a dozen specially-equipped Wellingtons, known as DWI ('Directional Wireless Installation', a deliberately confusing title) aircraft, fitted with a great hoop containing a magnetic coil activated by an auxiliary engine. These Wellingtons started operations around the British coasts in January 1940, flying as low as 25 ft (7.6 m) over suspected waters to explode the mines; in seven months these aircraft exploded 15 per cent of all magnetic mines swept or detonated.

As early as October 1939 British coastal convoys plying the East Coast came under sporadic air attack, and to provide a measure of protection four 'trade cover' squadrons of Bristol Blenheim fighters were formed. So long as no major air attack developed over the British Isles these squadrons

When war was declared, the Avro Anson formed the mainstay of Coastal Command. This Anson Mk I of No. 48 Squadron at Hooton Park is seen over a convoy out of Liverpool.

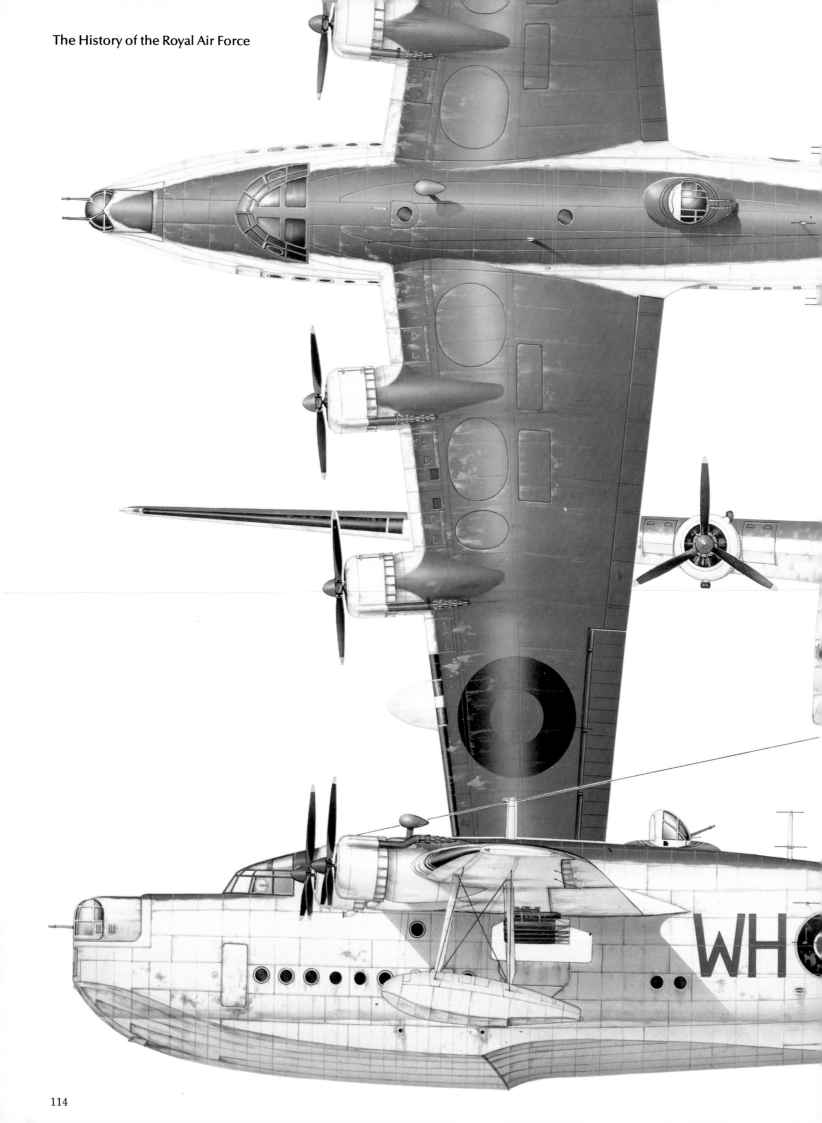

Short Sunderland

The Short Sunderland Mk III was the numerically greatest version of this flying-boat in the RAF. NJ188 was one of a number built by the Blackburn Aircraft Co. Ltd at Dumbarton. It was issued to No. 330 (Norwegian) Squadron of the Royal Air Force and flew with this Squadron, composed of Norwegian personnel who escaped and served in the RAF, until 1945 as 'WH:C', the markings in which it is shown. It was then re-engined as a GR.Mk 5 but did not go into RAF service as such and eventually was again converted, this time to a civil Sandringham airliner serving with BOAC as G-AHZF and subsequently with QANTAS Empire Airways as VH-EBY.

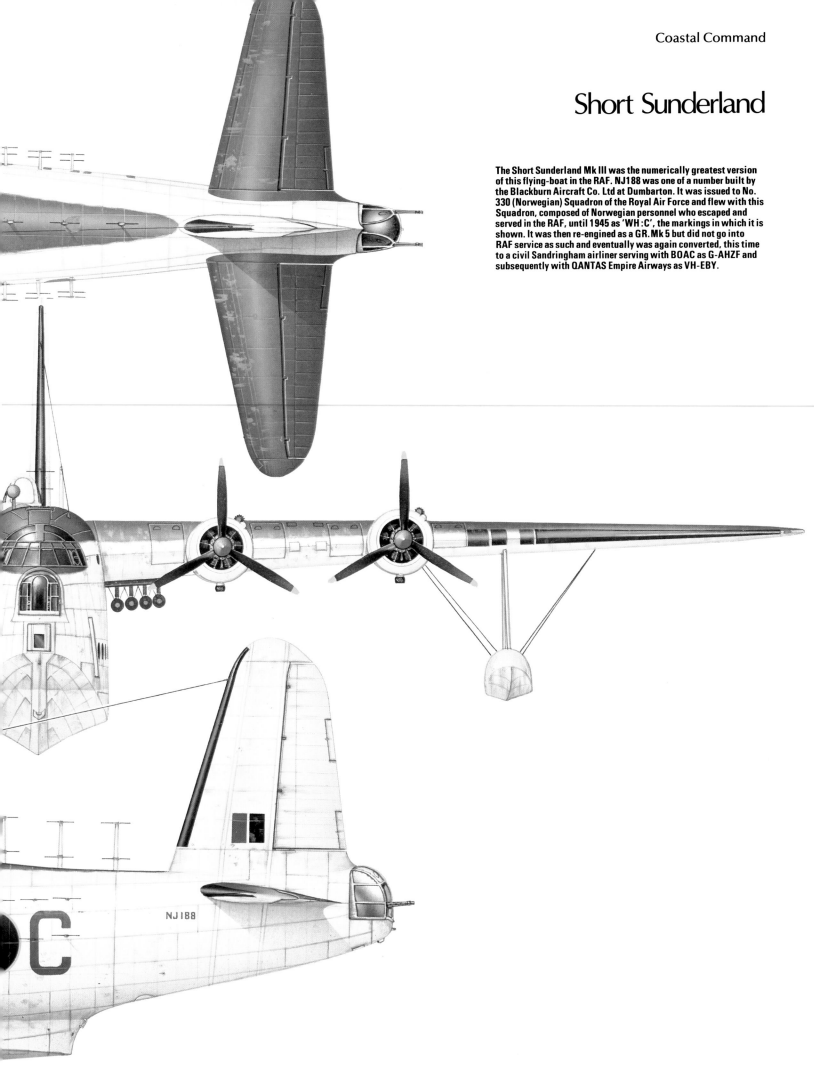

NJ188

Supermarine Stranraer of No. 240 Squadron, based at Stranraer. These slow flying-boats flew maritime reconnaissance over the seas near to the Scottish coast; not having the range to cover too far out into the Atlantic.

continued to operate wholly with Coastal Command, flying constant and tedious patrols over the crawling convoys. But when the Battle of Britain opened with its attacks on coastal shipping the Blenheim units came under temporary control of Fighter Command until it was painfully realised that the Blenheim was of little value in daylight air combat against enemy single-seat fighters, at which juncture the squadrons returned to convoy protection well outside the range of the Messerschmitt Bf 109s. Gradually, however, the Blenheims extended their operations further afield to include patrols along the Danish and Norwegian coasts, joining Hudsons already performing this task. As the summer of 1940 ended and autumn set in, casualties suffered during these long flights rose steadily both from the attention of the Bf 109s based in Norway and from the severe weather conditions.

A more positive role had however already begun for Coastal Command in April 1940 with the job of minelaying, the first such sortie being carried out by Bristol Beauforts of No. 22 (Torpedo) Squadron (the first to receive these aircraft) on the night of 15/16 April. The following month, as remarked above, a Beaufort dropped the RAF's first 2,000-lb (907-kg) bomb.

By the end of 1940 the military situation in Europe had entirely changed. Enemy naval forces (particularly U-boats) and long-range maritime aircraft were, or could be, deployed from the north of Norway to the south of France; Italy had entered the war, and enemy naval and air forces were at large in the Mediterranean and Indian Ocean. More important, however, was the considerable build-up of the German submarine fleet, now operating well out into the Atlantic, to some extent forced thither by the growing strength and

efficiency of Coastal Command at short range.

Leaving aside for the time being the submarine war and remaining with the command's operations around the coasts of Europe, much of the command's activity in the Channel had been devoted to anti-invasion patrolling and air mining of the invasion ports, while in the far north constant patrols had been flown in an effort to keep watch and report on the movement of German surface raiders, of which the most active were the *Scharnhorst* and *Gneisenau*. Unfortunately these great battle-cruisers on several occasions managed to elude the air patrols under cover of bad weather, and during a cruise on which they destroyed 115,622 tons of shipping orders were given from Berlin for them to be sailed into Brest on 22 March

The Bristol Beaufort had been designed specifically as a torpedo-bomber and entered Coastal Command service just after the outbreak of war. With torpedo and bomb it attacked enemy shipping around Britain and then later in the war was even more effective in the Middle East. Here a dummy torpedo is being loaded for practice purposes on a No. 86 Squadron aircraft.

At the beginning of the war Bristol Blenheim Mk IVs were drafted into Coastal Command squadrons for long-range fighter duties. In fact, they became shipping attack aircraft with high casualties. This is one of No. 248 Squadron's aircraft in 1940.

The Bristol Beaufort Mk I entered RAF service with No. 22 Squadron in November 1939, No. 22 operating within the command's bounds until February 1942.

1941. The presence of these powerful ships caused considerable concern at the British Admiralty which asked that Handley Page Halifaxes, then joining Bomber Command, should be diverted to Coastal Command for, amongst other tasks, attacks on enemy ports. This plan was instantly vetoed by Air Marshal Harris (then still Deputy Chief of the Air Staff), but instead Bomber Command itself embarked on heavy attacks on the Atlantic ports. It failed to inflict any significant damage on the enemy warships.

War against the battleships

It was at dawn on 6 April that Beauforts of No. 22 Squadron attempted to penetrate Brest's harbour. Only one aircraft, flown at low level by Flying Officer Kenneth Campbell, succeeded; catching sight of the *Gneisenau* in the inner harbour, this courageous pilot flew through an intense barrage of gunfire from three flakships as well as from the battle-cruiser herself and launched his torpedo from 500 yards (460 m). Although the aircraft was shot down and the crew perished, Campbell's torpedo struck the *Gneisenau*'s stern, causing severe damage which was still under repair eight months later. Campbell was posthumously awarded the Victoria Cross, on the evidence of testimony provided by the enemy.

As part of a grand design to launch several powerful capital ships into the Atlantic simultaneously, the Germans next sailed their latest and most powerful vessel, the battleship *Bismarck*, north through the Kattegat, intending to break through the Denmark Straits in company with the new heavy cruiser *Prinz Eugen*. The two ships were spotted near Bergen by a photographic Super-

marine Spitfire of Coastal Command on 21 May.

Although naval forces succeeded in shadowing the enemy for much of the following days, contact was lost and only re-established far out in the Atlantic by a Consolidated Catalina of No. 209 Squadron, one of the first of these American flying-boats to join Coastal Command and flown by Pilot Officer D. A. Briggs from Castle Archdale in Northern Ireland. He was soon relieved by a Catalina of No. 240 Squadron until warships of the Royal Navy could close and bring the *Bismarck* to decisive action. The *Prinz Eugen* escaped destruction and joined the *Scharnhorst* and *Gneisenau* in Brest.

The final episode in this saga of enemy commerce raiders was less auspicious for Coastal Command. Despite repeated attempts by Bomber Command to put an end to the threat in Brest harbour during 1941, photographic evidence gained early in 1942 suggested that preparations were being made for the enemy ships to break out. Radar-equipped Hudsons of Coastal Command were sent out each night from bases in Cornwall to patrol the western end of the English Channel to detect and report any attempt by the German warships to sail up the Channel. On the vital night, 11/12 February, the two Hudsons failed in this task (the radar of the first aircraft going unserviceable at the critical moment and the replacement Hudson being unable to reach its patrol line in time). The result was that the warships had sailed two-thirds of the length of the Channel before they were fortuitously spotted by pilots of Fighter Command.

Despite elaborate plans to meet this contingency, which required Coastal Command Beauforts to converge on bases in the south east of England from the north and west, bad weather and poor ground organisation so delayed their arrival that

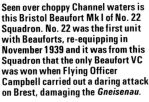

Seen over choppy Channel waters is this Bristol Beaufort Mk I of No. 22 Squadron. No. 22 was the first unit with Beauforts, re-equipping in November 1939 and it was from this Squadron that the only Beaufort VC was won when Flying Officer Campbell carried out a daring attack on Brest, damaging the *Gneisenau*.

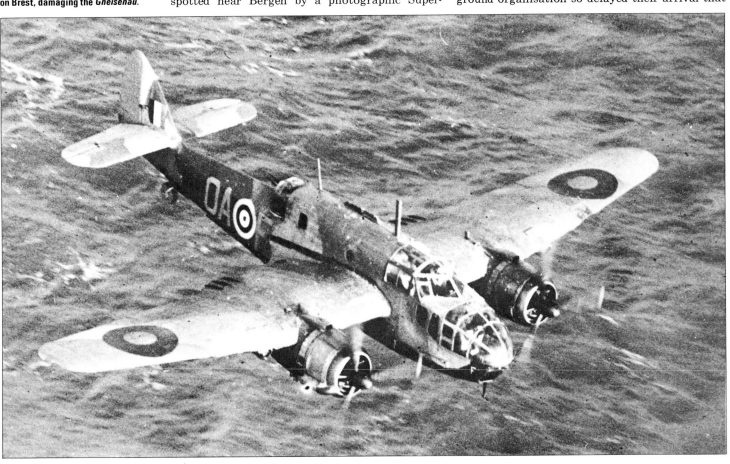

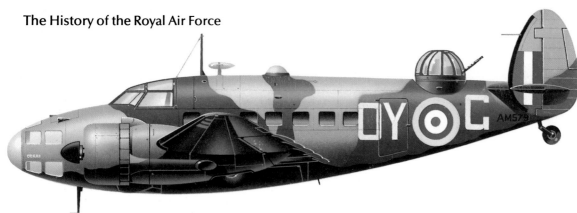

From 1939 until 1944 the Lockheed
Hudson was the standard Coastal
Command landplane and was used by
many squadrons. AM579 served with
No. 48 Squadron from Scottish bases
over the North Atlantic in 1941 and
1942.

the enemy squadron sailed through the Dover
Straits unharmed. It was not until after the loss of
six Fleet Air Arm Fairey Swordfish torpedo bombers
led by Lieutenant Commander Eugene Esmonde
(who was awarded the Victoria Cross posthumously
for his leadership and supreme gallantry) that the
first five Beauforts of No. 217 Squadron went into
the attack, but this and subsequent torpedo attacks
off the Belgian coast failed to damage the enemy
ships. In the event the *Scharnhorst* was partially
crippled, not from direct air attack but by mines
sown previously from the air.

Despite this setback, which inevitably aroused
bitter recrimination throughout the RAF and
Royal Navy, Coastal Command was moving ahead
in its campaign against enemy shipping in coastal
waters. Throughout the first 22 months of the war,
under the leadership of Air Chief Marshal Sir
Frederick Bowhill, the command had expanded to a
home-based force of 34 squadrons for the most part
equipped with modern aircraft. Handley Page
Hampdens and Beauforts provided the main tor-
pedo-launching element, while Sunderlands and
Catalinas equipped the flying-boat squadrons;
Hudsons had entirely replaced the old Ansons in
the general reconnaissance role, many of the latter
now giving yeoman service in the air/sea rescue
task alongside Supermarine Walrus and Westland
Lysander aircraft. Other aircraft, such as the Blackburn Botha and Saro Lerwick, had not proved
successful and did not assume significant roles
within the command.

Under Bowhill's successor, Air Chief Marshal

Sir Philip Joubert de la Ferté, a new and powerful
element was added to the command. The Hampden's
conversion to the torpedo-carrying role proved of
only limited success as a result of the type's poor
defensive armament and sluggish handling under
load, and it was Joubert himself who put forward a
proposal to adapt the excellent Bristol Beaufighter
to perform this task. In September 1942 the idea of
operating anti-shipping strike wings was accepted
and two months later the first such wing, comprising a Beaufighter fighter squadron (No. 143), a
Beaufighter fighter-bomber squadron (No. 236) and
a torpedo-carrying Beaufighter squadron (No. 254),
assembled at North Coates in Lincolnshire. After
an abortive start the same month, resulting from
inadequate training and bad weather, the wing
eventually began operations against enemy shipping in April 1943. The tactics involved careful integration of attacks by the fighters and bombers to
distract the enemy (whose escort often included
fighter aircraft) as the torpedo pilots selected and
attacked their targets. Apart from the growing
losses now inflicted, the strike wings, whose operations continued to mount right up to the end of
the war, forced the Germans to deploy quite dis-
proportionate defences for their shipping: valuable
fighter aircraft, escort and flak ships, and personnel that were desperately needed elsewhere.

In February 1943, when Joubert handed over to
Air Marshal Sir John Slessor, Coastal Command
in the United Kingdom possessed 51 operational
squadrons, including eight with Sunderlands,
three with Catalinas, five with Consolidated

Seen in their natural element are these
Lockheed Hudson Mk Is of No. 269
Squadron in 1940. The Hudson
quickly replaced the Anson as the
standard short-range maritime
reconnaissance and shipping attack
aircraft. No. 269 Squadron was later
based in Iceland.

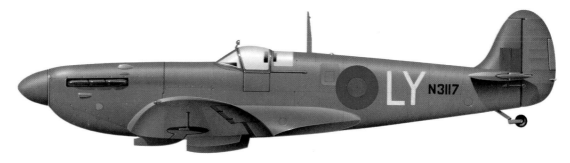

The original photo-reconnaissance Spitfires were Mk Is modified for photographic work. N3117 was one such which went to No. 2 Camouflage Unit (the odd name given to the Photo Development Unit to put the enemy off the track), then the PRU. It was converted to a Spitfire PR. Mk V in 1941 and served with No. 1 PRU until going missing in December 1941.

The Beaufighter Mk IC joined Coastal Command in December 1940 to replace the Blenheim. No. 252 was the first squadron, whose R2153 is seen here at Chivenor in April 1941. This squadron was soon moved out to Egypt but more squadrons followed and revolutionised the shipping strike scene.

Liberators (three of these American), and eight with Beaufighters. Many of the other squadrons were engaged in vital duties which it is now necessary to examine.

Intelligence in camera: photographic reconnaissance

At the beginning of the war, the RAF's ability to gather Intelligence by photographic reconnaissance was almost non-existent. For the British Army's purposes tactical reconnaissance over the battlefield was undertaken by observers using hand-held cameras in the rear cockpit of the 'army co-operation' Lysanders. For reconnaissance at longer range, ad hoc photography by bomber crews was all that was undertaken and this proved almost wholly useless, particularly when Bomber Command abandoned its daylight raiding at the end of 1939.

Nevertheless a tiny group of dedicated men led by Sidney Cotton, had been pursuing clandestine

operations over northern Europe using a converted Lockheed 12A to obtain photographs of German ports, albeit with little more than grudging approbation by the Air Ministry. However, the high quality of the material being gathered led to the mobilisation of this venture within the RAF as Cotton himself was commissioned as a wing commander. In due course his plea for the use of an unarmed Spitfire to perform reconnaissance flights was accepted and his unit, referred to as the Photographic Development Unit (PDU), was regularised at Heston on the outskirts of London. Before the German attack in the West, the Spitfire and Lockheed were detached to France where, as already mentioned, the unit's warning of German preparations for the great attack went unheeded. Meanwhile, further Spitfires were being delivered to Heston and from April 1940 onwards these high-flying aircraft, flown by volunteer pilots of considerable experience, carried out reconnaissance sorties over enemy-held territory from Norway to France, and even over Italy and the Mediterranean, gathering the information so vital to Britain during the summer of 1940 now that she possessed no foot-hold on the continent.

Inter-command squabbling and jealousies had already ended Cotton's buccaneering venture; the very idea of an 'outsider' being given preferential delivery of Spitfires was anathema to the commanders-in-chief, each of whom deemed that his command had special priorities in the choice of reconnaissance targets. On 16 June 1940 the PDU was incorporated into Coastal Command, and shortly afterwards re-titled the Photographic Reconnaissance Unit (PRU); command passed to Cotton's former assistant, Wing Commander G. Tuttle, and Cotton himself was relieved of his duties and given an OBE. The energy and leadership of this outstanding man, at a time of national peril, had however created the basis on which the science of efficient air photography would grow in the RAF during the next six years.

By midway through the Battle of Britain the task of covering 2,000 miles (3220 km) of enemy

The fast expanding photo-reconnaissance force came under the aegis of Coastal Command in June 1940. Its Spitfires roamed far and high over enemy territory from its main base at Benson. This pressurised Spitfire Mk IV of No. 140 Squadron is about to start on a sortie from Benson in the autumn of 1941.

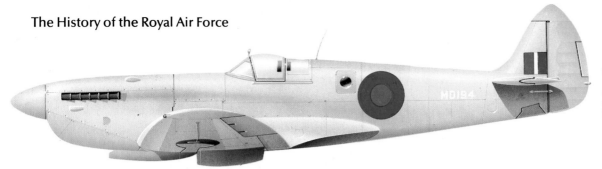

MD 194 was a Spitfire PR. Mk X flown by Nos 541 and 542 Squadrons from RAF Benson in 1945. This aircraft had a pressurised cockpit and a deeper cowling. The oblique camera window is clearly visible.

coastline was undertaken by just 11 Spitfires (eight PR.IBs and three PR.ICs) and three PR Hudsons. Already the task of flying the unarmed single-seaters was seen to demand the very highest qualities of stamina and skill from their pilots, who not only had to navigate with extreme accuracy over very long distances but had to overcome all the discomfort of long periods of breathing oxygen in the freezing cold of high altitude without the benefit of a pressure cabin, and of ennervating loneliness – and in the knowledge that their only defence against enemy fighters lay in the speed of their Spitfires. Overriding all other considerations, they knew that, without the safe return of clear photographs of their target, their sortie was useless. These men, on whom the spotlight of combat glamour never shone, were amongst the very best in the service.

The PRU moves east

The amalgamation of the PRU into Coastal Command failed to satisfy Bomber Command for, while it was recognised that information about enemy naval and mercantile targets was of prime importance to the Royal Navy as well as Coastal Command itself, the bomber authorities insisted that the selection of raid targets, not to mention the importance of raid damage assessment, was dependent upon photographic Intelligence. At the same time, the entry of Italy into the war demanded more extensive photographic cover of the Mediterranean than could be covered by long range flights from Britain (or the flight of Martin Marylands on Malta, previously mentioned), so in 1941 the RAF's photo reconnaissance arm was enlarged, No. 1 PRU being based at Benson in Oxfordshire, No. 2 PRU located at various bases to cover the eastern Mediterranean and No. 3 PRU based at Oakington for the exclusive use of Bomber Command. (Later No. 4 PRU was established at Gibraltar before the 'Torch' landings, and No. 5 PRU was formed in India during 1942.)

At the same time the Photographic Interpretation Unit (PIU) was established at Medmenham (not far distant from Benson) where the raw Intelligence was formulated.

Among the most important tasks undertaken by the PR Spitfires in 1941 was to maintain photo cover of Brest where the German battle-cruisers were sheltering, but in the longer term Coastal Command needed to build up its knowledge of the enemy's submarine building capacity and, following the introduction into service of the F8 camera with 14-in (35-cm) and 20-in (50.8-cm) lenses, a succession of large-scale photographs of Kiel, Bremen and the other German submarine yards was brought back to Benson, a stream of vital information that continued up to the end of the war. In due course British Intelligence was able to forecast accurately the strength of Admiral Karl Dönitz's submarine resources some six months in advance.

Meanwhile the early Spitfire PR.Is were being joined by the PR.IV, the first Spitfire specially designed for long-range reconnaissance. Various combinations of cameras could be fitted, in addition to enlarged fuel tanks which bestowed a normal range of 1,800 miles (2900 km), sufficient to reach Danzig in the Baltic from Benson. The first sorties by Spitfire PR.IVs were flown to such distant targets as Stettin, Swinemünde, Copenhagen and Genoa (the latter involving a flight of 7 hours 10 minutes). By the end of 1941 the first de Havilland Mosquitoes were being delivered to Benson, a welcome addition to the PRU if only to relieve its

pilots of the burden of navigation and the pervading loneliness of their work. The Mosquitoes' main task in those early days was to cover Norway and keep watch on German air and naval activities after the commencement of sailings by the North Cape convoys to Russia. These aircraft were in turn replaced by Mosquito PR.IVs which had a normal range of 2,350 miles (3780 km) and could reach Narvik, although to achieve complete cover of the North Cape route some PR Spitfires were detached to Vaenga in North Russia itself, later to be joined by Mosquitoes.

By 1943 scarcely any part of Europe lay beyond the range of Coastal or Bomber Command photographic aircraft based either in Britain or the Middle East. Principal equipment remained the Spitfire (the PR.XI) and the Mosquito (the PR.IX): the former, with a maximum speed of 422 mph (679 km/h) and a range of about 2,000 miles (3220 km) was flown by 14 squadrons, while the latter, with a speed of 425 mph (684 km/h) and a range of 2,450 miles (3940 km) equipped three squadrons at home, one in the Middle East and eventually one in the Far East.

The Battle of the Atlantic

Thus far, Coastal Command's responsibilities and achievements over Europe and home waters have been described, with only scant mention of operations over the vast expanse of ocean that separated Britain from the Commonwealth and from her vital sources of supply of oil, food, military equipment and munitions. Moreover, long before the United States of America entered the war, great quantities of these supplies were shipped by that nation to Britain in her hour of need.

As already explained, Germany possessed only relatively small submarine forces with which to threaten these supplies during the early months of the war, enemy preference being sharply divided between the use of surface raiders (capital ships and other heavy naval units, as well as converted merchantmen) and of the U-boat.

Moreover, the aircraft and weapons at Coastal Command's disposal were, as already explained, unable to combat enemy submarines; such successes as were achieved were the result of enemy boats being surprised on the surface.

In the mid-war years the Mosquito joined the Spitfire for longer-range photo-reconnaissance missions. LR412 is a Mk IX of No. 540 Squadron in 1943.

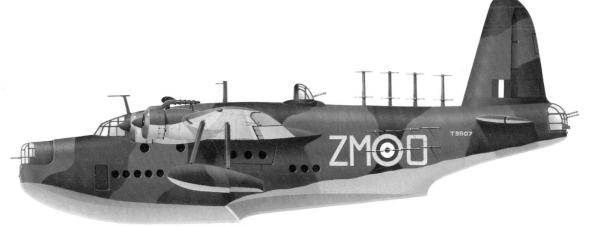

The Short Sunderland was the ubiquitous flying-boat of World War II. T9087 was a Mk II, with the early ASV aerials. It joined No. 201 Squadron at the end of 1941 and remained with the squadron until early 1944.

During 1940, however, with the gradual updating of the command's aircraft and a perceptible improvement in the rate of submarine sinkings (resulting mainly from increased air and naval escort of convoys) the U-boats moved farther out into the Atlantic for their main activities, a move made possible not only by boats of greater range but by the enemy's capture of the French Atlantic ports.

Indeed the occupation of France and Norway by Germany brought about a profound transformation of the war at sea, the first manifestation of which was an immediate increase in the sinkings of British ships in the Western Approaches not only by U-boats but by German long-range maritime aircraft, such as the Focke-Wulf Fw 200, based in western France with a patrol range of 2,000 miles (3220 km). To meet this threat Bowhill in June 1940 possessed just 34 Sunderlands, the only aircraft able to operate beyond 500 miles (800 km) from the coasts of Britain. The failure of the Saro Lerwick flying-boat, intended to complement the Sunderland in large numbers owing to a supposed high rate of production which was not realised, was a serious blow to the command as an accelerated build-up of Catalina deliveries from the USA was found impossible to negotiate at short notice.

But new equipment and weapons were being introduced during the latter half of 1940: air-dropped depth charges had large replaced the old anti-submarine bombs, while night-flying Hudsons were being fitted with early versions of the air-to-surface vessel radar (ASV). The latter, which underwent constant development during the war, was originally able to detect a fully-surfaced submarine at a maximum range of only 3 miles (5 km), yet at least discouraged U-boat captains from shadowing convoys at night while running surfaced, a tactic they had practised with impunity in mid-1940.

The spread of U-boat activity into mid-Atlantic not only placed these operations beyond the range of British-based patrol aircraft but also of the Fw 200s based in France, so that the enemy submarines, in order to locate and shadow the convoys without the air assistance previously afforded, were obliged to spend much more time surfaced. In an effort to increase the area of ocean covered by British air patrols, a squadron of Hudsons and one of Sunderlands were despatched to Iceland in January 1941, and these were followed shortly by a 'free' Norwegian squadron, No. 330, flying Northrop N3P-B floatplanes.

The U-boat threat

However, despite the withdrawal of some Blenheims from Bomber Command to take over short-range coastal reconnaissance duties, thereby relieving Hudsons for long-range patrol duties, sinkings by U-boats climbed alarmingly during early 1941, in March and April 1,176,000 tons of Allied shipping being sent to the bottom by enemy air and sea action. Such losses, if maintained, would inevitably have crushed Britain's ability to continue the war, and Winston Churchill was moved in his Battle of the Atlantic directive of 6 March to order the RAF to concentrate on objectives associated with this battle.

Gradually the presence of RAF aircraft flying from Iceland, Scotland and Northern Ireland forced the new long-range U-boats, now coming into service, to move farther south to the west coast of Africa; here they gathered a rich harvest of targets until once more frustrated by Coastal Command Sunderlands and Hudsons sent to operate from around Freetown, Sierra Leone. It was also at this

Convoy escort was one of the staple tasks of the coastal squadrons. Usually it involved hours of boring flying in cold and cramped conditions – only occasionally were the crews rewarded with a sighting of a U-boat.

The full answer to closing the reconnaissance gap in the Atlantic came with the advent in Coastal Command of the Consolidated Liberator. The first unit was No. 120 Squadron which re-equipped with Mk Is at Nutt's Corner in June 1941. AM926 was one of its early aircraft and was one of the squadron's aircraft to be fitted with a four-cannon tray under the fuselage for attacks on surfaced U-boats.

Far left: To bridge the gap in the middle of the Atlantic, Coastal Command set up base in Iceland during 1940, but this was originally served by detachments from flying-boat squadrons. In April 1941 No. 269 Squadron set up permanent base there for mid-Atlantic patrols. One of its aircraft was a Hudson, T9465, a gift to the RAF from the Lockheed employees at the Vega plant. After serving in Iceland with No. 269 Squadron it returned to England where it served on spy-dropping duties from Tempsford until mid-1943.

time that the new long-range, heavily armed Beaufighter entered service, and this soon gained a mastery of the Fw 200s flying from Brest over the Western Approaches.

By the time Bowhill handed over command to Sir Philip Joubert in June 1941 more than half of all Coastal Command aircraft had been equipped with ASV radar. In July and August the monthly shipping losses had fallen to 125,000 tons, and the immediate threat by the U-boat appeared to have been overcome.

The two major events that now occurred, Germany's attack on Russia in June 1941 and the USA's entry into the war the following December, were to bring about fundamental changes in the scope of the Battle of the Atlantic: the first on account of the sailings of large convoys from Iceland to North Russia (following Churchill's undertaking to give Stalin all possible assistance in his fight against Hitler), and the second as a consequence of the inevitable increase in Allied shipping (both mercantile and naval) to be protected in the Atlantic.

Fortunately for Coastal Command, the North Cape convoys were routed too far beyond the range of its aircraft for the command to be called on for ocean patrol, other than over and near the assembly areas off Iceland, and such air protection given in due course to these convoys during their hazardous voyage was provided by aircraft of the Fleet Air Arm operating from escort carriers.

The USA's alignment with Britain against Hitler had already assumed active form before her declaration of war with the escorting of shipping as far as Iceland on its way to Britain, but her formal entry into the war posed an immediate problem that Coastal Command was powerless to meet. No effective steps had been taken to introduce the convoy system off the American coast, nor was the US Navy adequately equipped to provide immediate long-range air cover over the Atlantic from bases in the USA.

In the meantime the German navy had been far from idle during the second half of 1941. In March, when Allied shipping losses had been increasing so

alarmingly, there were but 30 U-boats at sea, with 34 more working up in the Baltic; by December that year, when shipping losses reached 486,000 tons, the number of operational boats had increased to 86 with a further 92 working up. Of these, 27 U-boats had been sent to the Mediterranean and 18 had succeeded in making the passage; in November the battleship HMS *Barham* and the carrier HMS *Ark Royal* were sunk by U-boats, and this lent urgency to the strengthening of Coastal Command forces at Gibraltar. A new group was formed under Air Commodore S. P. Simpson with a squadron of Catalinas (No. 202) and one of Hudsons (No. 233), plus a Swordfish squadron of the Fleet Air Arm (No. 812).

Within a month of the USA's declaration of war Admiral Dönitz had ordered his six largest U-boats to North American waters where, in three weeks, they sank 40 ships totalling 230,000 tons; immediately afterwards he sent every available boat to the same area and to that off Central America, using a system of refuelling from other submarines at sea. In May alone, 109 ships (including 30 tankers) totalling 531,000 tons were sunk off the American coast.

As if to emphasise the contrast afforded between the growing efficiency of RAF Coastal Command on the eastern side of the Atlantic and the lack of air cover in the west, it is worth recording that while this enormous slaughter of shipping was being inflicted off the American coasts only nine ships were lost in five months in waters covered by Coastal Command.

No matter how quickly the US Navy and USAAF could take steps to organise efficient over-sea cover to combat the German submarine menace (and such expedients as re-deploying bomber squadrons as anti-submarine units were quickly adopted), there still existed an enormous gap some 2,000 miles (3220 km) wide in mid-Atlantic over which no shore-based aircraft could operate.

As the American remedies began to achieve results, the enemy submarines moved back into this gap and started to use the wolf-pack tactic, that of attacking in large numbers, having been assembled for action by other boats shadowing the convoys.

Leigh lights and new radar

Apart from using the very long range (VLR) Liberator I, which had an operational range of 2,400 miles (3860 km) but of which Coastal Command had only five in August 1942 with No. 120 Squadron, Joubert could do little to combat the U-boats operating in the 'gap', and therefore now turned his attention to the submarine transit areas, the area between Norway and Iceland through which new boats had to pass into the Atlantic, and the Bay of Biscay. While the former was fully covered by patrolling Hudsons, Sunderlands and Catalinas, the latter presented problems for a number of reasons. Following capture by the Germans of a Hudson with ASV radar, the U-boats were now being fitted with equipment designed to pick up ASV Mk II 1.5-m wavelength transmissions, enabling them to submerge as Coastal Command aircraft approached. Coupled with increased use of escorting aircraft (principally Junkers Ju 88s), this gave the U-boats much improved immunity from air attack as they set sail from the French ports to their hunting grounds.

Joubert's response to these problems was to introduce 10-cm ASV Mk III in Coastal Command aircraft (starting with the Liberators) and to fit airborne searchlights to such aircraft as the Catalina and Vickers Wellington, the latter now beginning to be phased out of Bomber Command. The Leigh Light, a 24-in (61-cm) searchlight de-

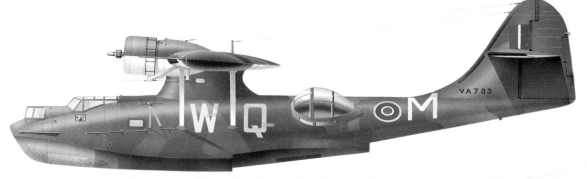

In 1941 the American Consolidated Catalina supplemented the Sunderland over the Atlantic. VA703 was a Mk IIA, part of a batch built for the RCAF and transferred to the RAF. It joined No. 209 Squadron at Pembroke Dock early in 1942 and went with the squadron to East Africa, serving until running ashore in a gale on Madagascar on 14 July 1943.

veloped by a Coastal Command officer, Squadron Leader H. de V. Leigh, was first used in the Wellingtons of No. 172 Squadron, and in conjunction with their ASV was first employed operationally on the night of 4/5 June 1942, one of the four patrolling aircraft illuminating and damaging a surfaced U-boat which was finished off three days later by a Halifax of No. 10 Squadron.

Although successes with the new equipment (which also included depth charges filled with Torpex, which was about a third more destructive than the old Amatol) were slow to accelerate, the pressure now being applied to the U-boats forced them to remain submerged for much longer periods, thereby severely reducing their patrol endurance.

Nevertheless, the wolf-pack tactics paid heavy dividends, and from August to October 1942 a monthly average of 500,000 tons of shipping was sunk, while new U-boats were being produced more than twice as fast as others were being sunk (mostly in the Bay of Biscay). It was in an effort to overcome the sinkings in transit that Dönitz asked for the Luftwaffe's new Heinkel He 177 long-range aircraft to be made available to cover the Bay of Biscay; the request was refused, but instead more Ju 88s (as well as a Gruppe of Fw 190 fighters) were deployed in the west of France, resulting in a sharp increase in air combat losses on both sides.

While sinkings continued at an alarming rate in the Atlantic 'gap', another Allied operation in the Atlantic was mounted with extraordinary success, largely owing to the strengthening of Coastal Command, particularly at Gibraltar. This was Operation 'Torch', the Allied landings in Morocco and Algeria in November 1942. The British landings alone involved the sailing of 14 slow-moving convoys from Britain, and the Admiralty had forecast

that these might attract as many as 70 enemy submarines. To counter the threat three further squadrons (No. 210 with Catalinas, and Nos 500 and 608 with Hudsons) were sent to Gibraltar, whose airfield was specially enlarged, as already related. At home, additional Coastal Command squadrons were based at St Eval and Chivenor for convoy escort. These squadrons included a Canadian Halifax squadron (No. 405) borrowed from Bomber Command and eight USAAF B-24 Liberators. Other RAF bombers laid mines off the Biscay ports.

Air cover holds out

These precautions, as well as a fortuitous but temporary switch by the U-boats against sea traffic off the west coast of Africa (well south of the American 'Torch' operations), resulted in only two German submarines being detected crossing the invasion convoys' path across the Bay of Biscay; both were sunk by Coastal Command Liberators of No. 224 Squadron. Not a single ship was lost.

By the eve of the landings Dönitz had summoned every U-boat within reach of the invasion areas, but still the air cover proved wholly effective. By the time the assault phase of 'Torch' was complete, the Gibraltar-based Coastal Command squadrons (joined by the second Leigh Light Wellington squadron, No. 179) had flown 8,656 hours on support patrols, during which they made 142 U-boat sightings, attacked 83, damaged 23 and sank three (sharing a fourth with the Fleet Air Arm); their losses were 17 aircraft, of which several were shot down by British and American forces.

The next tactic adopted by the German submarines was to remain surfaced when attacked from the air and to fight it out with their enhanced anti-aircraft armament. Though this caused a

One of the first squadrons to use the Catalina was No. 240, whose AM269 is seen here in 1941. The Catalina had a longer endurance than the Sunderland but could not carry such a heavy warload.

The Vickers Wellington GR. Mk XIV was the final version of the Wellington used by Coastal Command, serving from 1943 until replaced after the war. NC178 was a Mk XIV issued to No. 304 (Polish) Squadron in 1944.

number of losses among Coastal Command aircraft, it did not appreciably slow the mounting rate of U-boat sinkings being achieved early in 1943. Convoys were now being met far out in the Atlantic, and by the middle of that year the 'gap' south of Greenland had narrowed to about 500 miles (800 km) – still almost three days sailing by the slowest convoys.

Yet it was at the Casablanca Conference of early 1943 that stock was taken of the German submarine's potential threat to the build-up of Allied forces needed to launch an invasion of Europe, both in the Mediterranean and in northern France. At the time Joubert relinquished Coastal Command to Air Marshal Sir John Slessor, its strength had increased to 66 squadrons, including those based in Iceland and at Gibraltar (but not those in the Middle and Far East). They were now at full stretch, matching and countermatching the enemy submarines at sea; they were not, however, equipped to strike them while still under construction.

Largely as the result of Coastal Command's photographic cover of enemy submarine yards in Germany, it was estimated that Dönitz was receiving some 20 new boats each month, yet total monthly sinkings of U-boats had averaged fewer than seven since 1941. Accordingly, and in spite of protestations by Air Marshal Harris, an all-out bombing offensive against the U-boat industry was affirmed at Casablanca. It was with this industry foremost in mind that the devastating attacks by Bomber Command against such targets as Bremen, Hamburg, Kiel, Lübeck, Rostock, Augsburg and Flens-

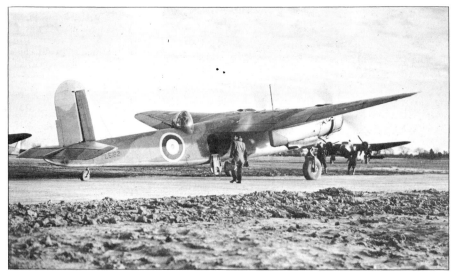

burg (where about 80 per cent of the manufacturers were located) were launched during the last two years of the war.

Another outcome of Casablanca was the proposal to create a joint Anglo-American organisation to standardise anti-submarine policies, procedures and tactics. Although such an organisation had thus far achieved considerable objectives in Britain during the past two years as the Anti-U-boat Sub-Committee of the War Cabinet, chaired as it was by

The Blackburn Botha was operationally unsuitable and was withdrawn, being used only for training duties.

Five different version of maritime reconnaissance Vickers Wellington were produced, the final one being the GR. Mk XIV, shown here in service with No. 304 (Polish) Squadron.

When the U-boat assault was at its height, it was necessary to find, very quickly, aircraft which could patrol the Bay of Biscay and attack enemy submarines using the French Atlantic bases. At first Armstrong Whitworth Whitley squadrons were detached from Bomber Command, but soon several squadrons were re-equipped with Whitleys in Coastal Command. These aircraft were fitted with ASV equipment and then a special version, the GR. Mk VII, was produced for these squadrons. Z9190 was one such which served with No. 502 Squadron from St Eval in late 1942.

Long oversea reconnaissance was provided for Coastal Command by the Consolidated Liberator. This is a Mk III of No. 59 Squadron in 1943.

This Sunderland Mk V of No. 201 Squadron flew the last operational Coastal Command patrol from Castle Archdale in Northern Ireland.

Churchill himself, the new two-nation body never achieved the hoped-for efficiency. To begin with, faced with the enormous task of gaining the initiatives at sea in the Pacific, the Americans felt that that theatre must have prior claim on their fleet carriers, while such long-range aircraft as the B-24 Liberator (which, given sufficient numbers, would have imposed an immediate and decisive influence on the Battle of the Atlantic) were largely denied to the maritime forces fighting the German submarine arm. Moreover, the successful British tactical philosophy of concentrating strength at points of stress, which had been so outstandingly successful in support of 'Torch', seemed to meet with constant opposition from the Americans, who were anxious to distribute the available forces (both naval and air) around the entire Atlantic seaboard. A degree of compromise was gained through the outstanding tact of Slessor, but the fact remained that about 70 per cent of all operational USAAF and US Navy anti-submarine patrol squadrons were never called upon to attack an enemy submarine in the Atlantic. Through constant deployment of Coastal Command squadrons to areas in which U-boats were likely to threaten, scarcely a single squadron failed to make at least one anti-submarine attack. Indeed, not only were the Americans determined to avoid a repetition of the appalling slaughters of January 1942 off their own coasts, but clearly regarded the Battle of the Atlantic as subordinate to the campaigns against Japan. Both sentiments were obviously understandable and entirely justified.

By mid-1943 convoy traffic across the Atlantic followed two main routes: shipping from the USA and Canada to Britain sailed through the waters south of Greenland and Iceland, where almost continuous air cover could be provided; and American convoys from the USA to North Africa travelled on a more southerly route where the 'gap' was still

Boeing Fortress Mk IIA FL459 was one of the many B-17Es allotted to the RAF Coastal Command. Arriving in Britain in late summer 1942, it joined No. 220 Squadron as aircraft 'J' and went out to the Azores with the squadron, serving there until December 1944, when it returned to Britain. In March 1945 it joined No. 519 Squadron at Wick for meteorological reconnaissance duties, transferring to No. 251 Squadron in Iceland in July, serving there until December 1945.

more than 1,000 miles (1,610 km) wide. To provide cover for these southern convoys the Americans moved their two Liberator squadrons (the 4th and 19th of the USAAF) from Britain to Morocco, thereby considerably weakening Slessor's campaign against enemy submarines sailing through the Bay of Biscay. With full agreement of the two nations' chiefs of staff, Slessor asked for six long-range Liberator squadrons to be provided from the American units on the western side of the Atlantic, but the most he ever received was three, and then only after the Battle of the Bay had been won.

Meanwhile the Battle of the Atlantic continued to be fought with fluctuating fortune for Axis and Allies. A month after Slessor took over Coastal Command, two convoys (HX229 and SC122, eastbound on the North Atlantic route) were subjected to four days of concerted U-boat attack, of which 68 hours were spent beyond the reach of shore-based aircraft: 20 ships were sunk in atrocious weather which not only prevented many of their crews being rescued from the sea but severely interrupted air patrols when eventually the convoys reached the protection of Liberators, Fortresses and Sunderlands. In the course of attacks by RAF aircraft, one U-boat was sunk and two others damaged. Indeed, at this stage in the Battle of the Atlantic for every enemy submarine sunk 45,000 tons of shipping was being lost.

This period was nevertheless the twilight of the U-boats' fortunes. Following prodigious feats of organisation and effort, the majority of Coastal Command's aircraft had by the summer of 1943 been equipped with centimetric ASV, while their depth charges, now set to explode at 25 ft (7.5 m) below the surface with improved pistols, were proving far more lethal. In May no fewer than 41 U-boats were sunk, six being destroyed in one night, while on another occasion a convoy sailed right through a large pack of enemy submarines without loss. German statistics for this period reveal that of all U-boats lost 35 per cent were destroyed by aircraft while in transit to their operational areas, a further 20 per cent succumbed to air attack while in the vicinity of their target convoys and 19 per cent to combined air/sea attack. The remaining 26 per cent of losses were attributable to action by naval surface forces alone. It must be emphasised, however, that many of the submarine sinkings were achieved by carrierborne aircraft of the Fleet Air Arm and US Navy.

The final phase

Faced with such losses, Dönitz shifted his boats away from the areas that were so dominated by Allied aircraft. In June 1943 only two U-boats were sunk by aircraft.

The next stage embarked on by Slessor was to perfect the process of collaboration between anti-submarine aircraft and surface hunting groups, an expedient made possible by the Admiralty in July 1943 with the assembly of the sloops *Kite, Starling, Wild Goose, Woodpecker* and *Wren* under the greatest submarine hunter of all, Captain F. J. Walker, DSO and three Bars, RN. By now two Coastal Command squadrons, Nos 206 and 220 were operating from the Azores under the command of Air Commodore G. R. Bromet, and within weeks this force was creating havoc among the U-boats in the Atlantic. On 30th July elements of this force sank all three of a group of U-boats in transit through the Bay, and a Sunderland of No. 461 Squadron destroyed a fourth. During the next

three days, four more submarines were sunk.

To such losses the Germans not unnaturally reacted swiftly. The Junkers Ju 88s were reinforced and joined by a Gruppe of Messerschmitt Bf 110 night-fighters drawn from Italy to Brest. The Luftwaffe also brought up a Staffel of bombers armed with the new Henschel Hs 293A glider bombs, and with these sank or badly damaged three naval vessels.

The fourth and final stage of the war against the U-boat started in the autumn of 1943, when the submarine captains abandoned their fighting-back tactics and reverted to moving submerged by day, surfacing for only brief spells under darkness to recharge their batteries. Nevertheless the RAF's ASV Mk III radar continued to operate without discovery of its wavelength by the Germans for much of 1943, until eventually a Bomber Command Halifax fell into enemy hands with its radar intact; by the time its significance had been associated with Coastal Command's search radar in September, the discovery was largely superfluous for in that month the German submarines were being equipped with a relatively simple device which enabled them to run submerged as they charged their batteries. This was the *Schnorkel* tube which, when raised from the submerged boat, allowed air to be drawn into the boat, which could therefore run its diesel engines, which exhausted through an adjacent tube. Another innovation introduced by the enemy submarines was the acoustic torpedo, whose sensor detected the target's propeller noise and caused the torpedo to steer towards it.

In Germany the repeated bombing attacks on the submarine yards had severely damaged the construction facilities and resulted in the introduction of prefabricated U-boats, the large Type XXI with 23 torpedoes and a range of 11,185 miles (18000 km), and the much smaller Type XXIII which carried only two torpedoes and a crew of 14. Dönitz also now reverted to pack tactics, positioning groups of

The RAF received various batches of Boeing B-17E and B-17F Flying Fortresses in 1942 at the same time as they were entering USAAF service. Because of their characteristics the RAF did not put them into service with Bomber Command but gave them to Coastal Command, where they flew alongside Liberators for a while. In 1943 the majority of them were put into Nos 206 and 220 Squadrons and sent to the Azores, where they fulfilled an important role covering the mid and south Atlantic.

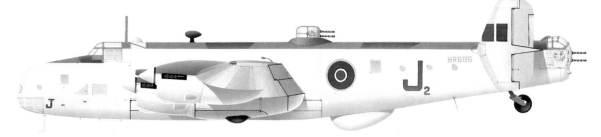

Another bomber aircraft which served in small numbers in Coastal Command was the Handley Page Halifax. HR686 was built as a GR. Mk II and delivered early in 1943 serving as 'J2' of No. 502 Squadron at Holmesley South and then St David's. It flew on until 3 October 1944, when it failed to return from a patrol.

The magnificent Mosquito found its metier in many roles. One of the least known but most effective was to supplement the Beaufighter in shipping strikes, with bomb and rocket, in Coastal Command.

At Banff in Scotland armourers load rockets under the wings of a Mosquito FB. Mk VI of No. 143 Squadron in preparation for a shipping strike against German shipping off the Norwegian coast early in 1945.

up to 20 boats in a line across the likely path of Allied Atlantic convoys.

The autumn of 1943 was punctuated by a number of vicious convoy battles as the Germans staged heavy pack attacks. However, despite significant losses among merchantmen and escort vessels alike, the almost continuous presence of Liberators over the convoys resulted in much higher numbers of submarine sinkings than had been achieved during the previous phase of pack attacks. For instance, in an attack on a convoy sailing south of Iceland early in October, 12 U-boats were sunk, seven of them by Liberators, Hudsons and Sunder-

lands of Coastal Command, one by a Sunderland of the RCAF, one by the USAAF, and three by the naval escort. A measure of the success now being gained in the fight to overcome the submarine menace may be gained from the fact that the monthly average loss of merchant ships in 1942 of 520,000 tons had fallen to about 130,000 tons by the end of 1943.

On 20 January 1944 Slessor, who was appointed Deputy Allied Air Commander in the Mediterranean, gave up Coastal Command to Air Chief Marshal Sir William Sholto Douglas. At this stage there were at sea about 60 U-boats, while Coastal Command possessed some 430 operational aircraft at home (now including rocket-equipped Mosquitoes, and indeed some Mosquitoes with 6-pdr (57-mm) guns for anti-submarine attack). The task confronting the new commander-in-chief was to prevent the enemy submarines from penetrating into the English Channel from their Biscay bases and interfering with the forthcoming Normandy invasion. The Germans could draw on 70 further submarines if those in the Baltic and Norwegian waters could be sailed through the North Sea. Such a force would represent a very serious threat if it could be brought to bear.

As Dönitz recalled his boats to their French bases from the Atlantic in anticipation of the Allied invasion, Sholto Douglas moved his Gibraltar-based Leigh Light squadrons back to Britain to start continuous night patrols over the western approaches to the Channel. Once more the submarine war had come back to the narrow seas, and to all intents the Battle of the Atlantic had been won.

The Invasion of the European Mainland

In 1942 the nadir of Allied fortunes was reached: the Wehrmacht had surged far into the Soviet Union; Rommel's Afrika Korps was within striking distance of the Suez Canal; the Battle of the Atlantic had brought disastrous losses to the merchant and naval fleets of Britain and the United States; and Japan had conquered Burma, Malaya, the East Indies and the Philippines.

Yet in Europe and North Africa the turning point was close at hand. In particular the Allied air forces were gaining strength on all sides as the immense resources of the United States were harnessed and brought to bear. It was however fully recognised that only by the Western Allies' fighting return to the continental mainland of Europe could the Axis be forced into unconditional surrender and, despite constant demands by Russia for an Allies invasion of Europe to relieve the desperate situation on the Eastern Front, such an operation was likely to be far beyond the resources available to Britain and America for many months to come.

Instead the Allies had to remain content with efforts to strike at Germany with the only means yet within their grasp, the continuation and gradual strengthening of the bombing offensive against Germany and enemy-occupied territories. The year 1942 had witnessed profound changes in the nature of RAF Bomber Command's operations, particularly after the appointment of Sir Arthur Harris as its commander-in-chief. Two magnificent weapons, the Avro Lancaster and de Havilland Mosquito, had become established in service, while the haphazard and wasteful bombing efforts of earlier months had been arrested and new techniques introduced.

Alongside Bomber Command, the Americans were beginning to take their place in the daylight skies over Europe so that the complementary efforts of the day and night offensives were beginning to impose a noticeable strain, one that eventually

Born out of the failure of the twin-engine Avro Manchester, the Lancaster became a fine bomber. First aircraft entered service in the last few days of 1941 but it was in 1942 that the type began to make its mark. Seen over the plains of Lincolnshire are three Lancaster Mk Is of No. 207 Squadron flying from Bottesford in the spring of 1942.

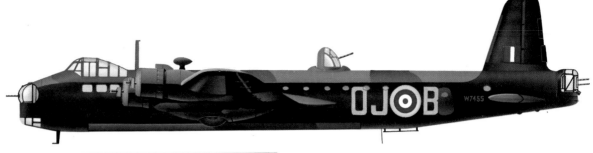

The Short Stirling Mk I flew predominantly with No. 3 Group, Bomber Command, from 1940 until 1943. W7455 is typical: it was delivered to No. 149 Squadron at Mildenhall early in 1941; as 'OJ:B' it served with the squadron, transferring later to No. 15 Squadron and then No. 214 Squadron. Transferring to training duties with No. 1657 (H)CU it was shot down over Britain on 7 September 1943 by a German intruder.

The Short Stirling continued to be developed and used in the mid-war years, the Mk III being the next version into service. This Mk III is landing at Short Bros airfield at Rochester, where many of the Stirlings were built.

came close to overwhelming Germany's air defences. As Allied air bases in the Mediterranean became available, so these defences could be taxed from north and south simultaneously.

This growing onslaught from the air by day and night, from north and south, by British and American bombers was the essential task of the Allies in their preparations for invasion of the European mainland. Indeed, until that invasion could be mounted, the bomber remained the only weapon that could be brought to bear against the German nation and its will to continue the war. It is as well to remember this when reading the post-war criticisms of the Allied bombing offensive by arm-chair strategists.

Bomber Command's offensive

The first year of Harris's command was significant for two major advances in the striking power of the bomber force. To begin with, the replacement of the first generation of wartime bombers was essential if worthwhile bombloads were to be

carried into the heart of Germany, and only the Handley Page Halifax and Lancaster proved capable of doing so. Bomber squadron Armstrong Whitworth Whitleys made their last raid in April, the Bristol Blenheims in August and the Handley Page Hampdens in September. Unfortunately the Avro Manchester proved to be a failure (as a result of its unreliable Vulture engines), and also had to be withdrawn in June, a setback which severely retarded the bomber force's build-up. Because of the Short Stirling's disappointing performance, Harris had thus to depend on the Lancaster and Halifax, even though the Vickers Wellington continued to give yeoman service.

Secondly, the unpalatable discovery (as the result of much improved photographic reconnaissance facilities) that the early night bombing raids had inflicted very little damage, as a consequence of poor navigation and inaccurate aiming, focussed attention on the pressing need to introduce efficient navigation and bombing aids, as well as to improve operational tactics.

Already the short-range Gee navigation aid had been introduced, and it was hoped that this would remain free of enemy jamming for at least six months while improved equipment could be brought into service.

The first raid in which Gee was widely used was launched by 235 bombers against the Renault factory near Paris on 3/4 March 1942. This was a relatively short-range attack which was designed, by concentrating the bombers in time and space, to saturate the defences. Considerable damage was caused and this encouraged Harris to return to the Ruhr (just within Gee range) using similar tactics. On 8/9 March 211 bombers took off to attack the great industrial city of Essen; unfortunately Gee only sufficed to bring the raiding force to the general target area, where the pervading industrial haze obscured the flares dropped by the leading aircraft, and the bombing was very scattered. The vital Krupps complex escaped almost unscathed.

The most destructive raid of this period was, however, carried out well beyond the range of Gee.

The de Havilland Mosquito proved revolutionary in several fields, not least in Bomber Command which at first used the Mk IV. Two squadrons (Nos 105 and 139) were formed at Marham, and flew low-level daylight raids with great elan and precision. This line-up at Marham shows No. 139 Squadron, with No. 105 Squadron aircraft near the hangars.

The Handley Page Halifax Mk I originally was underarmed and had control problems. L9530 entered service with No. 35 Squadron early in 1941 and then transferred to No. 76 Squadron as 'MP:L' until being shot down near Bremen on 13 August 1941 whilst on a Berlin raid.

On the night of 28/29 March 234 bombers, about half of them carrying only incendiary bombs, set out in bright moonlight to attack the old Hanseatic port of Lübeck, whose buildings were constructed largely of timber; widespread damage was caused by fire and much of the older part of the town was razed. Another Baltic port, Rostock, was successfully attacked on 23/24 April (causing, according to German records, over 100,000 inhabitants to be evacuated).

Mention has already been made of the next three milestones in Harris's growing offensive: the daylight attack on Augsburg of 17 April, the first '1,000-bomber' raid on Cologne and the first operation by Mosquito bombers (the two last during the night of 30/31 May). Bomber Command attempted to follow up the Cologne raid by '1,000-bomber' raids on Essen on 1/2 June and on Bremen on 25/26 June, and although British losses remained below five per cent it was decided that, despite their propaganda value, such raids could not be sustained owing to the disruption caused in assembling such a force (some 25 per cent being drawn from Coastal and Army Co-operation Commands as well as from training units); in any case, the latter raid was the last occasion on which the Manchester was used operationally.

Pathfinder force

In August Bomber Command sanctioned a major new bombing procedure, the use of 'pathfinder' aircraft, with the creation of a special force composed of experienced bomber crews under the command of Group Captain D. C. T. Bennett, an Australian and himself an experienced commercial pilot. Soon afterwards restyled No. 8 Group, the Pathfinder Force was equipped with Wellingtons, Stirlings, Halifaxes, Mosquitoes and Lancasters, the job of whose crews it was to fly ahead of the main bombing force (itself now concentrated into a carefully designed bomber stream) marking the route to the objective and the aiming point with specially-coloured target marker bombs. The new force flew its first operational mission in a raid on the U-boat facilities at Flensburg on 18/19 August. The following month a raid on Düsseldorf was the first occasion on which the Pathfinders dropped the 2,800-lb (1270-kg) 'Pink Pansy' target marker.

Among the growing number of spectacular raids being flown by Bomber Command, one in particular stands out: this was a dusk attack on 17 October by 86 Lancasters of Nos 9, 44, 49, 50, 57, 61, 97, 106 and 207 Squadrons against the Schneider factory at Le Creusot (appropriately codenamed Operation 'Robinson'). The medium and light bombers had also been increasingly active during the year, superbly executed daylight attacks by No. 105 Squadron's Mosquitoes on the Gestapo headquarters in Oslo on 25 September, and by 93 Douglas Bostons, Lockheed Venturas and Mosquitoes on the Philips radio works at Eindhoven on 6 December setting new standards in pinpoint accuracy.

The year 1943 opened with the first American heavy bomber attacks on Germany when Boeing B-17s and Consolidated B-24s of the USAAF attacked Emden and Wilhelmshaven in daylight on 27th January. Three days later Mosquitoes of Nos 105 and 139 Squadrons carried out the RAF's first daylight raids on Berlin. The same night Pathfinder Halifaxes and Stirlings used a new navigation/bombing aid, codenamed H2S, in a raid on Hamburg; this centimetric radar was self-contained within the aircraft and 'painted' a crude picture of the ground below the bomber on a radar display so

that such prominent features as rivers, coastlines and large towns could be distinguished. Hamburg was accordingly chosen as the first such target for its ease of identification. In due course H2S radar enabled bombers to carry out their attacks when the ground was wholly obscured by cloud.

Meanwhile another piece of equipment was being introduced into Bomber Command Mosquitoes at the beginning of 1943. This was Oboe, an exceptionally accurate navigation/bombing aid which employed a ground distance-measuring station; it could, however, be used by only a very small number of aircraft simultaneously, and was therefore employed by specialist pinpoint or pathfinding bombers. It was first used by No. 109 Squadron in a raid on Lutterade before the end of 1942 and became more readily available early in the following year.

By March Harris was ready to launch the first of his great concerted bombing campaigns, later defined as battles (Battle of Berlin etc). At the beginning of that month Bomber Command possessed 18 squadrons of Lancasters (321 aircraft), 11 of Halifaxes (220 aircraft) and seven of Stirlings (141 aircraft); the medium bomber force comprised 15 squadrons of Wellingtons (265 aircraft), three of Venturas (54 aircraft) and two of North American Mitchells (38 aircraft); and the light bomber force was made up of three Boston (33 aircraft) and three Mosquito (57 aircraft) squadrons. Of this force of 1,129 aircraft, the greatest weight of attack (10 Main Force Lancaster squadrons) was concentrated in No. 5 Group, deployed on the airfields at Waddington, Syerston, Woodhall Spa, Langar, Bottesford, Fiskerton, Skellingthorpe and Scampton.

In order to improve the bombing accuracy of Bomber Command raids, the Pathfinder Force was formed from experienced crews throughout the Command. Their task was to go in ahead of the main force and drop coloured markers accurately on the target so that the Main Force could bomb on the markers.

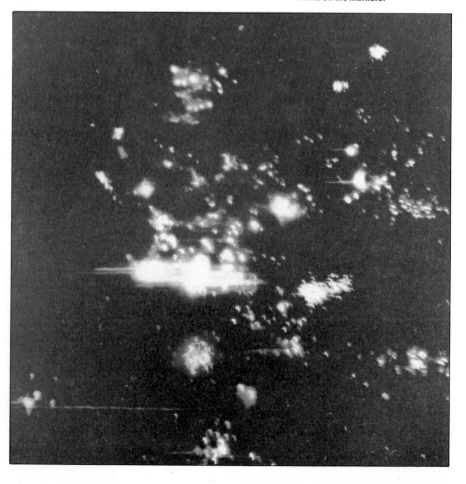

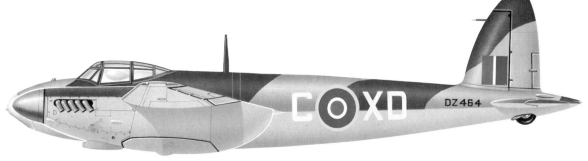

The de Havilland Mosquito Mk IV was the first version to enter Bomber Command service in November 1941. DZ464 joined the second squadron to be formed, No. 139, at Marham nearly a year later and served on their low-level raids from then on.

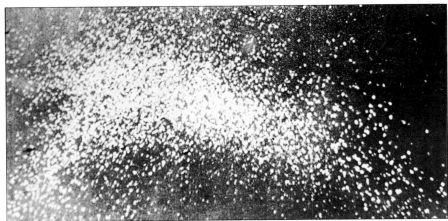

As the German radar became more effective Bomber Command found a simple jamming device in 'Window'' small metallic foil strips dropped in thousands to form a dense metal cloud, completely jamming the screens. This daylight drop of 'Window' reveals its effect.

A scene repeated hundreds of times all over eastern Britain nearly every night from 1942 until Victory in Europe: the Lancaster is on the runway threshold, a green light is flashed from the runway caravan, the four Merlins are opened up fully and the heavily-laden aircraft disappears into the night sky to be replaced by the next one in the stream.

The Battle of the Ruhr opened on the night of 5/6 March 1943 with an attack by 442 aircraft on Essen, full use being made of Gee, H2S and Oboe. Following eight Oboe-equipped Mosquitoes, which dropped yellow target flares along the line of approach and red target indicators in the centre of the Krupps works, 22 Pathfinders added more flares according to a highly accurate time schedule. With a high proportion of incendiaries, and high explosive bombs fitted with delayed-action and anti-handling fuses, the Main Force Lancasters, Halifaxes, Stirlings and Wellingtons completed their attack within 20 minutes. The planned raid was accomplished with little hitch, although 14 aircraft were lost to enemy action. The damage caused in this single raid, including devastation in the Krupps complex, was far greater than all previous raids on Essen combined. The natural defence provided by hitherto impenetrable haze over the target had been overcome.

Three further raids were launched against Essen on 12/13 March, 3/4 April and 30 April/1 May by an average of about 350 aircraft each, and by the time the last fire had been extinguished some 700 acres of the city had been gutted.

As the Battle of the Ruhr continued with particularly heavy raids against Duisburg on 26/27 April and 12/13 May, and against Düsseldorf on 25/26 May and 11/12 June (the latter by no fewer than 693 aircraft), another memorable 'set piece' attack was carried out by just 19 Lancasters on 16/17 May. This was the famous dams raid, carried out by night at very low level by No. 617 Squadron led by Wing Commander G. P. Gibson. Specially created for this attack on the Möhne, Eder, Sorpe, Lister and Schwelme dams, which controlled the level of the River Ruhr and provided hydro-electric power for much of the area, the squadron was crewed by men handpicked by Gibson himself. After undergoing intensive training beforehand and employing large mines, purpose-designed by Dr B. N. Wallis of Vickers, the Lancaster crews succeeded in breaching two of the five dams. Eight of the attacking aircraft were lost. (Gibson had been the first pilot to drop an 8,000-lb (3629-kg) bomb over Italy, having flown to Turin from Britain on 28/29 December 1942. He survived the dams raid, for which he was awarded the Victoria Cross; at the time of his death during a raid a little over a year later he had also been awarded two DSOs and two DFCs.)

Before embarking on his next great battle, Harris sent Bomber Command on its first 'shuttle-bombing'

Avro Lancaster

R5868 was an Avro Lancaster B.Mk I, built by Metropolitan Vickers and delivered to Avro for final assembly in early 1942. It was delivered to No. 83 Squadron at Scampton and served with this unit as 'Q-Queenie', going with the squadron to Wyton when it transferred from No. 5 Group to No. 8 (Pathfinder) Group. After service with No. 83 Squadron it transferred back to No. 5 Group and joined No. 467 Squadron at Waddington. This latter squadron was composed of Australian aircrew, and R5868 flew successfully with this unit until the war ended, by which time it had flown 144 operations (recorded on the side of the fuselage below the pilot's cockpit). This aircraft has been preserved as a historical exhibit in the Bomber Command Museum at Hendon.

The History of the Royal Air Force

The Avro Lancasters used to breach the Ruhr dams by No. 617 Squadron were modified as shown. This aircraft (ED912/G) was modified straight from the production line at Chadderton, joining No. 617 Squadron at Scampton on 3 May 1943. Twelve days later it flew on the raid captained by Pilot Officer L. G. Knight and was the aircraft which breached the Eder dam. It remained with the squadron until December 1943, when it was sent to an MU and did not serve again during the war, being scrapped in 1946.

attack on 20/21 June. In Operation 'Bellicose' heavy bombers, ordered off against Friedrichshafen, went on to land in Algeria, returning three nights later and attacking Spezia before landing back in Britain. It was following a subsequent shuttle raid against Turin on 12 August that one of the most richly-deserved Victoria Crosses was awarded to a Stirling pilot; his aircraft severely crippled by a night-fighter, Flight Sergeant Arthur Aaron DFM managed to reach a North African airfield despite appalling wounds which included a smashed jaw and bullets in a lung and an arm. This gallant pilot died before learning of his supreme award.

The Battle of Hamburg was characterised by exceptionally heavy 'round-the-clock' bombing both by RAF and USAAF bombers, and opened on 24/25 July with a devastating attack on this, the second largest city of the Reich, by 740 bombers which dropped 2,396 tons of bombs. Employed for the first time on a large scale was a new device: clouds of metallized strips of paper dropped by the raiders and codenamed 'Window'. Cut to the wavelength of German defence radar, these strips provided an indication of vast numbers of attacking aircraft and so confused the defences that only 12 bombers were lost. On 25 July 68 American bombers carried out a short daylight attack on the dock area

of the city, to be followed on the next day by a raid by 53 B-17s on Hamburg's Neuhof power station.

On the night of 27/28 July 739 RAF bombers dropped 2,917 tons of bombs and on the 29/30 July 726 aircraft delivered 2,382 tons. A final attack on 2/3 August, carried out in poor weather, brought a further 1,426 tons of bombs. By the end of this final attack the city's districts of Altona, Barmbeck, Borgfelde, Eimsbüttel, Hammerbrook, Hoheluft, Hohenfelde and Wilhelmsburg lay devastated. Such had been the intensity of fire in the city that a massive firestorm had been created which, by generating tremendous wind forces, had kept the fire fed, so allowing it to consume vast areas. The city's emergency services had been overwhelmed, with the result that 6,000 acres (2430 hectares) were no more than smouldering rubble; 61 per cent of the whole of Hamburg was destroyed; 41,800 persons were killed outright while many of the 37,439 grievously injured died subsequently.

The cost to Bomber Command of the Battle of Hamburg was 87 aircraft lost to enemy action, with 39 others written off on return to their bases. Some 606 aircrew were killed or posted missing.

The loss of 30 aircraft in the last and smallest of the four RAF raids on Hamburg was a reflection of Germany's swiftly growing night defences. At that time the Luftwaffe had some 550 night-fighter

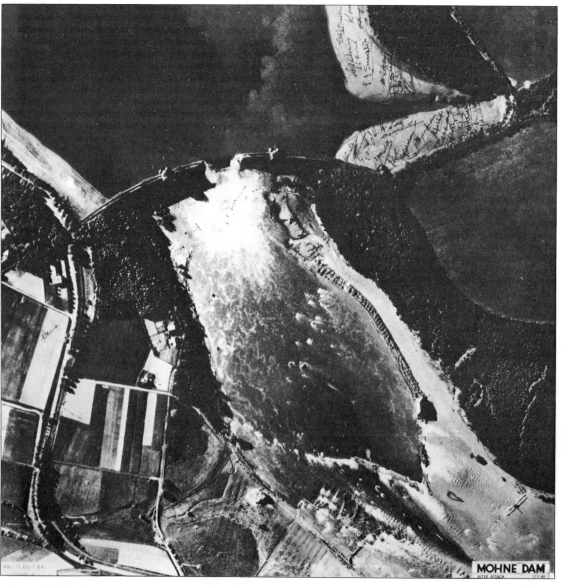

MOHNE DAM

Most spectacular of all the wartime raids was the attack by the specially formed No. 617 Squadron on the Ruhr dams. This photograph of the Mohne dam, taken by a photo-reconnaissance aircraft on the morning after the raid, shows water still pouring through the breach.

134

The low-level Mosquito squadrons of Bomber Command re-equipped with the developed Mk IX version and transferred to Pathfinder and night low-level raiding. LR508 was one such which served with No. 105 Squadron in 1943.

Back at Scampton the No. 617 Squadron crews which survived the dams raid relax in the mess. Wing Commander Guy Gibson, the squadron commander and leader of the raid, is sitting on the floor, third from the right, with a champagne glass in his hand.

crews, the majority of them flying the Messerschmitt Bf 110 and Junkers Ju 88C, both aircraft of relatively sluggish performance, yet quite capable of overhauling the heavily-laden British bombers. Now equipped with fairly efficient airborne radar, they only required that the ground controllers direct them towards the bomber stream, having been ordered off the ground at the first indication of RAF bomber activity over Britain. Except for the early occasions of the use of Window, which certainly confused the defences, the heavily-armed German night-fighters began to take a heavy toll of British bombers; in due course some of the Luftwaffe's *Experten* (aces) were each to down six or more bombers in single nights.

As an expedient to overcome a repetition of the devastation of the night attacks on Hamburg, the Luftwaffe adopted the use of day fighters at night during the autumn of 1943, their pilots simply being ordered towards the target where they could distinguish the raiders silhouetted against the glare of the fires below; codenamed *wilde Sau* (Wild Boar) tactics, together with those employing a commentary on the bombers' progress broadcast to night-fighters (known as *zahme Sau*, or Tame Boar), this represented the means by which the German defences were to destroy 1,047 RAF bombers during the seven months following the Battle of Hamburg.

With two victories behind him, Harris now approached his third major battle, the Battle of Berlin – a city which he believed could be laid to ruins, given some help by the Americans, by the end of March 1944, a devastated German capital that could well persuade the German people to surrender without the need to invade Europe.

Berlin was a very different target from Hamburg or the Ruhr, however. It was located well inland and was thus less distinguishable on the bombers' H2S screens; it was well beyond the range of Oboe and Gee, and the Luftwaffe could be expected to defend it with every day and night fighter available. The answer apparently lay in the efficiency of Bennett's Pathfinders and, not unnaturally, the success of each Berlin raid was directly proportional to the quality of route and target marking by the Pathfinders. In an effort to overcome the Luftwaffe's Tame Boar tactics, a number of innovations were adopted by Bomber Command, such as jamming of enemy broadcast transmitters and the constant relaying of spurious broadcasts to the German pilots, while the use of Window continued as a means of confusing the ground radar.

Berlin attacked in earnest

The first three major raids on Berlin, launched at the end of August 1943 by some 600 bombers, caused widespread damage and prompted the authorities to evacuate a million women and children from the city. But the bombing was not concentrated and relatively few bombs fell within 1 mile (1.6 km) of the aiming point. Losing about 150 aircraft, of which 125 fell to the German defences, Harris paused before resuming the attack. Instead he launched heavy raids on Mannheim, Kassel and Düsseldorf; the raid of 3/4 November on the last-named target was the occasion of the first successful use of a new device known as GH. This could be regarded as 'Oboe in reverse', in that the transmitter pulses came from the aircraft itself, so that any number of bombers could use the equipment simultaneously; in the Düsseldorf raid it was estimated that roughly half the bombs fell within 880 yards (805 m) of the aiming point.

The attack on Berlin resumed in earnest in mid-November and continued until the end of March 1944, by which time 16 heavy raids had been launched. The heaviest attack, on 15/16 February, involved an attack by 806 aircraft which dropped 2,642 tons of bombs and severely damaged a large number of important factories. Not all the Berlin raids were successful, as that on 24/25 March (the last of the series) showed. Almost the entire load of bombs fell more than three miles (4.8 km) from the aiming point, an error caused by poorly estimated wind strength and direction by the Pathfinders; moreover, the same mistaken estimates brought the bombers home over the heavily defended Ruhr whose guns and fighters caused many of the night's loss of 73 four-engine bombers.

Despite the prognostications of Harris, Berlin was not flattened, and Germany did not surrender in 1944. To many a historian the Battle of Berlin was a battle lost. If evidence of the Luftwaffe's ability to counter Bomber Command's efforts were needed, it was emphatically provided during the famous Nuremberg raid of 30/31 March.

Contrary to widely held opinions, the Nuremberg raid did not fail because of any lapse in security providing the enemy with warning of the target. It failed for three main reasons: the most important was the decision of Harris to go ahead with the raid even after preliminary weather reconnaissance suggested diminishing cloud cover, rendering the raid a suicidal venture so deep

Graphically illustrating a low-level Mosquito attack is this camera gun shot of an attack on Limoges.

Many revisions were made to the Handley Page Halifax during its service. Ultimate version of the Merlin-engined aircraft was the B. Mk II Series 1A, of which LW223 was one. Built by English Electric at Preston, it joined No. 78 Squadron at Breighton in August 1943. It served as 'EY:E' until November 1943, after which it is presumed damaged beyond repair.

inside Germany with a bright moon; second was inaccurate wind measurement by the Pathfinders' specialist crews, which allowed the Main Force to stray off track and over enemy night-fighter assembly points; and last, largely as a result of this error, was poor (if not downright inept) target marking, which led a large number of bombers to attack the wrong towns. The result was that out of 782 Lancasters and Halifaxes despatched on that night, 108 were lost, of which 95 are reckoned to have fallen to the enemy defences. A very high proportion of the bombers never hit Nuremberg at all, but more likely towns such as Schweinfurt. Compared with the loss of 545 RAF aircrew killed, 69 German civilians died in Nuremberg and 11 Luftwaffe aircrew were killed in the 10 night-fighters shot down.

Perhaps the greatest shock to Bomber Command on this night was the ease with which the enemy night-fighters (not, on this occasion, the Wild Boar day fighters) destroyed 79 aircraft. Given ideal night flying conditions, which rendered use of jamming tactics largely ineffective in any case, the Bf 110s inflicted heavy losses by stalking the bombers from behind and below, using their *schräge Musik* (shrill music, or jazz) upward-firing cannon with deadly effect from the bombers' blind spot. This weapon remained almost unsuspected for many months; indeed many of the Lancasters had had their ventral guns removed.

One further outstanding, major area attack was carried out on 24/25 April by Bomber Command, this time on Munich deep in the Reich. Intended to test an alternative method of marking the target and controlling the bombing, after the failure at Nuremberg, this attack was led by a Mosquito flown by Wing Commander G. L. Cheshire, then commanding No. 617 Squadron. Despite being subjected to intense flak for much of the flight to the target, Cheshire dived to 700 ft (210 m) over Munich to release his marker flares and then continued to circle the target at low level throughout the raid as he directed the Main Force crews by radio. (Promoted to group captain, Cheshire was awarded the Victoria Cross after this raid, although the citation made it clear that the Munich raid was the culmination of no fewer than four operational tours of duty, during the last of which he personally led every attack to some of the most heavily-defended targets in Europe. Unquestionably the outstanding bomber pilot of all time, his other gallantry awards included three DSOs and a DFC.)

Defeat or Pyrrhic victory, the Battle of Berlin and the attack on Nuremberg on 30/31 March 1944 marked the end, for the time being at least, of British area attacks on German cities. Instead, and for some months, Bomber Command was directed almost exclusively against targets whose destruction would have a direct effect upon the coming

The Handley Page Halifax eventually emerged from its problems and difficulties with the revision of the vertical tail surfaces and the installation of Bristol Hercules engines, giving it a better performance than the Lancaster in some respects. This version was the Mk III and is seen here in service with No. 462 Squadron (RAAF), one of the many Halifax squadrons in Nos 4 and 6 Groups in 1944.

Sixty-nine Boeing B-17Gs joined the RAF as Fortress Mk IIIs, and these were considerably modified with electronic equipment for spoofing and jamming duties with No. 100 Group. KJ109 joined No. 214 Squadron as 'BU:B' in December 1944, and served on these duties until April 1945 when it transferred to No. 1699 Flight for two months before finally joining No. 223 Squadron at Oulton as '6G:F' for service from June to August 1945.

invasion of Europe, a diversion that was prolonged by a campaign against the flying bomb industry and launching sites.

Invasion of Sicily and Italy

The invasion of Europe from the Mediterranean was undertaken as a precept of British rather than American strategy. Acknowledging that some form of 'Second Front' must be launched in the West in 1943 to provide some relief for the Russians, the Allied Chiefs of Staff eventually accepted that the build-up of forces in North Africa had provided the means to attack what Churchill favoured as Europe's 'soft underbelly', whereas preparations for a cross-Channel invasion of France could not be confidently undertaken until 1944. A suspicion that direct attack upon metropolitan Italy might bring about that nation's defection from the Axis proved wholly justified.

In preparation for the invasion of Sicily the whole might of the Allied strategic bomber force, now assembled in North Africa, was thrown against the island as well as the Italian mainland. Now commanded by Air Chief Marshal Sir Arthur Tedder, Mediterranean Air Command in July 1943

included the Northwest African Tactical and Strategic Air Forces, Troop Carrier Command, Coastal Air Force, the US 9th Air Force as well as components further afield in the Middle East and East Africa. This command embraced a total of 306 squadrons, of which 145 were American, 17 South African, seven of the Royal Australian Air Force, six of the Fleet Air Arm, four of the Royal Canadian Air Force, three Greek, two French, one Dutch, and the remaining 121 RAF. The strategic bomber force comprised 16 American B-17 squadrons, 20 American B-24 squadrons, three RAF and RAAF Halifax squadrons and 11 RAF and RCAF Wellington squadrons. The medium bomber force included 32 American squadrons of North American B-25 Mitchells, Marauders and Bostons, while 119 fighter squadrons flew Supermarine Spitfires, Bristol Beaufighters, Mosquitoes, North American Mustangs, Hawker Hurricanes, Curtiss Kittyhawks, Curtiss Warhawks, Lockheed Lightnings and Bell Airacobras. The transport force comprised 29 American Douglas C-47 squadrons and three RAF squadrons flying Halifaxes, Douglas Dakotas and Armstrong Whitworth Albemarles.

Against this force of more than 2,500 first-line aircraft were ranged some 1,850 German and

In 1944 the Main Force bomber streams were formidable collections of heavy bombers. In the summer these vast fleets of four-engine bombers would set out before nightfall, filling the evening sky.

Italian aircraft based in Italy, Sicily and Sardinia, of which about 1,000 were combat ready. However, many of the experienced Luftwaffe and Regia Aeronautica aircrew had been killed or captured in the final Tunisian campaign, and their replacement at this stage of the war was extremely difficult; moreover the precipitate withdrawal to Sicily had deprived many units of essential spares and equipment.

Invasion preparations

As the Allied forces made ready to sail against Sicily, troop-carrying gliders (British 25-seat Airspeed Horsas and American 15-seat Waco CG-4A Hadrians) were towed out from Britain or assembled in North Africa. As a preliminary to the landings, the Allied air forces set about attacks on enemy airfields and landing grounds to such good effect that on the date of the landings themselves there was scarcely any concerted opposition by the Axis air forces.

The invasion of Sicily was the first occasion on which the Allies employed a large-scale drop of airborne forces: the operation involved the delivery of 127 Hadrians and 10 Horsas towed by 100 C-47s of the US Troop Carrier Command, aided by 28 Albemarles and seven Halifaxes of the RAF's Nos 296 and 297 Squadrons. Their target was the Ponte Grande near Syracuse, but as a result of high winds and inadequate night flying training among the American towing and glider pilots, 69 of the gliders fell in the sea and 56 landed more than eight miles (13 km) from the target. Only 12 gliders, all of them Horsas towed by the RAF, landed (under cover of Hurricane IIC night-fighters of No. 73 Squadron) within reach of the bridge which was duly captured by eight officers and 65 other ranks. Elsewhere paratroops of the US 82nd Airborne Division had been scattered over 150 square miles (390 km²) between Licata and Gela in the south of the island.

Meanwhile at dawn on 10 July the seaborne assault was launched as planned under air cover provided by RAF Spitfires and US Warhawks and North American A-36s. At Pachino No. 3201 RAF Servicing Commando Unit went ashore immediately behind the assault waves to make ready an emergency landing strip (used the following day by a Spitfire of No. 72 Squadron which had run out of fuel). During the first night an RAF Ground Controlled Interception (GCI) unit was put ashore and this quickly came into operation to control the Beaufighter night-fighters of No. 108 Squadron flying from Malta, and No. 23 Squadron's Mosquito intruders. Within three days the Allied armies had established a sizeable bridgehead and five Spitfire squadrons were operating from Comiso, some 12 miles (19 km) inland.

On the night of 13/14 July, undeterred by the earlier fiasco, the Allies made a second airborne attack, this time 107 aircraft and 17 Horsas carrying the British 1st Airborne Brigade of the 1st Airborne Division to the Primo Sole bridge near Catania. Some 13 gliders landed in their assigned area and their troops once again succeeded in capturing their objective, but unfortunately the troop-carrying aircraft arrived over the Allied invasion fleet just as it was being attacked by German Ju 88s, with the result that 10 Dakotas, three Albemarles and a Halifax were shot down by the guns of the Royal Navy. About 80 per cent of the airborne forces were either shot down or, having lost their way, returned to bases in North Africa.

As the Allies continued to make progress, overrunning more than three-quarters of the island by the end of the month, all elements of their air forces were maintaining constant pressure against the enemy, not only in the immediate vicinity of the land battle but much further afield. The Wellingtons of No. 205 Group were particularly active, attacking the airfields at Capodichino and Pomigliano near Naples on 14/15 July, and Naples itself on the 17th. The Wellingtons of No. 36 Squadron, Northwest African Coastal Air Force, ranged over the western Mediterranean, sinking or severely damaging 10 enemy ships in a week.

Flying from Malta the Mosquito NF. Mk IIs and FB. Mk VIs of No. 23 Squadron maintained intruder patrols over the enemy airfields on Sicily and Italy to great effect.

Designated A-36A Invader, this attack version of the Mustang was evaluated by the RAF with underwing racks (not shown) and dive-brakes. Only one aircraft was evaluated and was not ordered.

Spitfire wings were instrumental in providing fighter cover for the invasion of Sicily and then, from Sicily, for the move on into Italy. By now it was common practice for wing leaders to carry their initials on their aircraft, 'IR:G' denoting Wing Commander I. R. 'Widge' Gleed, in company with two of No. 601 Squadron's Spitfire Mk VCs.

German resistance stiffened in the north eastern part of Sicily towards the end of the month as preparations were made to withdraw as much matériel and troops as possible in the inevitable evacuation from the island. In order to provide some measure of mobility for the ground forces, the Luftwaffe attempted to airlift supplies of fuel to the island in Junkers Ju 52/3m aircraft, using an improvised landing strip near Milazzo, which itself was under constant air attack by Allied fighter-bombers. On 25 July a formation of 31 Junkers, escorted by eight Bf 109Fs, was caught by 33 Spitfire VCs of Nos 81, 152, 154, 232 and 242 Squadrons; within 10 minutes 21 Ju 52s and four Bf 109s had been shot down for the loss of two Spitfires.

The final phase of the Sicilian campaign was marked by bitter fighting as one by one the last towns and ports remaining in enemy hands fell to the Allied armies amid the storm of land and air bombardment. As the port of Messina was virtually reduced to rubble, the Luftwaffe made one final but successful raid on the main American supply port of Palermo, this putting the dock facilities out of action, destroying large quantities of fuel and blowing up an ammunition train; seven Ju 88s and Dornier Do 217s were shot down. On 16 August Messina itself fell and the following day the last enemy resistance in Sicily ended. By dint of well-organised defence measures the Germans succeeded in recovering fairly substantial forces across the narrow straits to the Italian mainland; nevertheless the defence of Sicily had cost the enemy 32,000 men killed or wounded and 162,000 prisoners. Some 1,800 aircraft had been captured or destroyed (more than half of them German, the remainder Italian), for the loss of 400 Allied aircraft, excluding about 150 gliders, many of which were salvaged.

As the battle in Sicily neared its inevitable conclusion, the Allies stepped up their efforts to induce the Italian nation to surrender. On 25 July Mussolini was deposed and a military government under Marshal Badoglio established. Milan and Turin were subjected to heavy night attacks on 7/8, 12/13, 14/15 and 15/16 August by Bomber Command flying shuttle raids from Britain using path-finding techniques and H2S. As clandestine negotiations continued between Eisenhower and Badoglio for the surrender of Italian forces, emphasis was provided for the Allied arguments by heavy and continuous attacks by Tedder's aircraft on Italian airfields and rail centres, a total of 3,529 sorties being flown during the last fortnight of August against these targets alone. Moreover, Italian coastal shipping had come to a standstill following the destruction in its ports caused by the raids of the coastal air forces.

On 3 September the British 5th Division and Canadian 1st Division of the 8th Army landed on the toe of Italy near Reggio di Calabria, and on the next day at Bagnara, making good an advance of about 20 miles (32 km) each day during the first week against stiffening German resistance.

On 8 September Badoglio finally announced

By 1943 the Mediterranean Allied Coastal Air Force had plenty of Beaufighter TF.Mk Xs, which it used to attack enemy shipping and coastal installations with torpedo, bomb and rocket throughout the length of the Mediterranean.

Curtiss developed the Kittyhawk and in 1943/4 the Mk III found service with the Desert Air Force squadrons as fighter-bombers. FX561 served with No. 112 Squadron.

Italy's unconditional surrender, but even as he did so a large seaborne invasion fleet was approaching the coast at Salerno only 40 miles (64 km) south east of Naples. At dawn the next day, under air cover provided by long-range Lightnings, Mustangs, Seafires and Spitfires (the latter with drop tanks), the British X Corps and the American VI Corps assaulted the beaches. Opposition from the Luftwaffe was very sparse to begin with, such had been the scale of attacks on its airfields prior to the landings, although II/KG 100 flying Dornier Do 217s from the south of France and some Ju 88s attacked the Italian fleet on its way from Taranto and Spezia to Malta to surrender, sinking the battleship *Roma*. Until the Allied covering fighters could operate from the beach-head they were flying at extreme range from airfields in Sicily, so their patrol time was severely limited, and it was during the early stages of the landings that Do 217s carrying Hs 293A glider-bombs and heavy PC1400FX armour-piercing bombs attacked the invasion fleet off Salerno and badly damaged HMS *Warspite*, putting her out of action for six months.

The first landing strip was completed at Paestrum on the second day and on 12 September was occupied by 26 Seafires of the Fleet Air Arm and three Spitfire squadrons from No. 324 Wing of the RAF. By 12 September, however, German resistance by three divisions made the Allies' situation extremely perilous, and there were periods during the next three days when the RAF fighters had to abandon their use of the Paestrum strip when it came under enemy gunfire. But on 16 September elements of Montgomery's 8th Army, fighting their way north from their beach-heads on the toe of Italy, reached Vallo di Lucania and joined forces with American patrols breaking out from the area around Salerno.

By the end of the year the Allied armies had overrun the whole of southern Italy and occupied a line from the mouth of the Garigliano river in the west to Ortona on the east; the numerous Italian airfields now in Allied hands had been repaired by British and American field construction engineers and were in regular use by RAF and USAAF squadrons flying aircraft ranging from fighters to heavy bombers.

Greek setback

Elsewhere in the Mediterranean, however, Allied operations did not go according to plan. By occupying the Greek islands and their numerous airfields in the Aegean Sea it was hoped to open an invasion of Greece, thereby threatening the entire southern flank of the German eastern front, apart from considerably shortening the distance to be flown by Allied aircraft in attacks on the Balkans. It had been hoped to occupy the large island of Rhodes first, but when the Italian nation surrendered the Germans on Rhodes reacted with prompt efficiency, quickly reinforcing their garrison. It was therefore decided to take the islands of Kos, Leros and Samos, and, following a raid by 38 Liberators which temporarily rendered the airfields on Rhodes unserviceable, Spitfires of No. 7 Squadron, SAAF, landed at Antimachia airfield on Kos, followed by 120 paratroops dropped by Dakotas of No. 267 Squadron, and on 14 September the island was captured; the same day Leros also fell, followed two days later by Samos.

As Spitfires flew air cover over the islands, anti-aircraft units of the RAF Regiment were flown in, but on 17 September the Germans counterattacked in force with raids by Ju 88s which damaged the Dakotas with fragmentation bombs. During the following week the Luftwaffe brought up some 350 aircraft (Ju 88s, Heinkel He 111s, Bf 109s and Ju 87s) to the Aegean area, despite constant raids on Greece, Crete and Rhodes by Liberators, Halifaxes, Wellingtons and Hudsons. In the last week of September the Luftwaffe launched heavy attacks on Kos which could not be beaten off by No. 7

Right: Later in 1944 the Consolidated Liberator Mk VI supplemented the Wellingtons on the Mediterranean bombing force. This graphic shot shows a Liberator taking part in a raid, with bombs bursting on the harbour, a previously sunken ship and smoke trailing from the port inner engine of the Liberator.

Left: With the fall of Sicily the Desert Air Force squadrons were quick to base themselves on the island and from there begin the offensive against the Italian mainland. At Lentini No. 601 Squadron groundcrews work on one of the Spitfire Mk VCs or grab a 'cuppa' from the mobile canteen whilst another aircraft takes off on a sortie.

Squadron's Spitfires, even after reinforcement by No. 74 Squadron. On 3 October, employing the old familiar Blitzkrieg tactics, the Germans landed a well-equipped force of about 1,500 men on Kos under cover of air attacks by two Gruppen of Ju 87s, and within 48 hours the island had been lost.

Despite all assistance that Mediterranean Air Command could spare to assist the Aegean campaign (including a group of American B-25s armed with 75-mm guns which succeeded in destroying a number of landing craft off Kos), Leros fell to the Germans on 16 October and Samos on 22 November. The cost to the Allied air forces of this little-known, short-lived venture, was 115 aircraft; the Allies were attempting to accomplish too much too soon.

Winter slows the Allies

The campaign in Italy, which had got off to a promising start, soon slowed down as the winter of 1943-4 approached, not only restricting the movement of the Allies on the ground but transforming many of the forward airfields into acres of mud. Moreover it was soon made abundantly clear to the Allied commanders that in order to hasten the build-up of forces for the invasion of France from Britain, those in the Mediterranean (so laboriously assembled over the years) were to make sizeable contributions, both among the ground and air forces. However distasteful this might have appeared to the commanders (among whom Eisenhower, Tedder, Montgomery, Patton and others were to leave the theatre in any case), the containment of powerful German forces in Italy was at least preferable to their release for combat elsewhere.

Indeed as the front stabilised in Italy, the Luftwaffe's build-up was evidenced by increasing attacks on the Allied lines of communications. For example on the night of 2/3 December an attack by Ju 88s, covered by the dropping of the German equivalent of Window to confuse the RAF's GCIs in the area, on the port of Bari destroyed 14 Allied merchantmen, including an ammunition ship which blew up with such violence that the bulk fuel line took three weeks to repair; over 1,000 soldiers and seamen were killed or wounded, and 34,000 tons of military supplies destroyed.

In an attempt to break the deadlock, the Allies launched yet another seaborne landing behind the enemy lines, this time at Anzio on 22 January 1944. Instead of persuading the Germans to pull back their front line, however, the Anzio beach-head was successfully contained, together with some 50,000

troops who had to be constantly supplied by sea and air, and provided with air cover. And so the situation remained unchanged until 1 May.

Believing that the keystone of the main German line of defence lay at Cassino, a small town overlooked by an ancient monastery which the Allies thought was bound to be occupied by enemy forces, General Alexander, now commanding the British and Americans in Italy, ordered the monastery to be heavily bombed. Accordingly on 15 February 135 B-17s, 47 B-25s and 40 B-26s of the USAAF dropped 493 tons of bombs, reducing the target to rubble. In fact the Germans had not occupied the monastery before the air attack, but now they remedied the situation to such effect that a determined assault by the New Zealanders and the 4th Indian Division failed to dislodge them.

Exactly one month later an even heavier air attack on Cassino town by 11 groups of Strategic Air Force heavy bombers and five groups of Tactical Air Force medium bombers dropped 1,107 tons of high explosive, utterly destroying every building. As the assaulting infantry went in, covered by 200 USAAF P-38s and 74 RAF Spitfires, the German garrison of hardened paratroops emerged from their shelters to dispute every mound of debris. Not until 18 May, when the area had been outflanked, were the remains of Monte Cassino finally cleared of the enemy.

Meanwhile, in an effort to isolate the battle area, the Mediterranean Air Forces had embarked on Operation 'Strangle', an all-out offensive against the enemy's lines of supply in Italy. In March Allied aircraft dropped 19,460 tons of bombs on targets such as the marshalling yards at Bolzano, Mestre, Milan, Turin and Verona, and these operations would probably been decisive had not frequent spells of bad weather interrupted the raids and allowed running repairs to be made to allow essential supplies through.

Spring offensive

The Allied spring offensive in Italy started on 11 May, and on 4 June, two days before the Normandy D-Day, the Allies drove into Rome, and for two months thereafter advanced northwards towards the next fortified line between a point just south of Spezia in the west and Pesaro in the east, known as the Gothic Line. Resistance in the air was almost non-existent, all Junkers Ju 88s having been withdrawn from Italy to northern Europe at the time of the Normandy landings, so that by the end of June General Ritter von Pohl,

The Allies learnt their lesson about airborne forces from the Germans in the Mediterranean with the fall of Greece and Crete. When they returned they used the same methods – paratroopers are dropping into a DZ near Athens from RAF Dakotas.

Behind every front-line unit there are very many organisations which provide logistics support and see that the operational squadrons do not run out of equipment. Here in North Africa Spitfires and Hurricanes are being assembled after repair or shipment from Britain before being flown across to the operational squadrons.

commanding the Luftwaffe in Italy, could dispose but 120 serviceable aircraft; during the operations to capture the island of Elba on 19 June, only two Bf 109s put in an appearance and both were shot down by patrolling Spitfires. Throughout all the continuing attacks against communications targets in northern Italy scarcely any met with opposition in the air, and by September all the rail routes between the Po valley and Florence had been cut in several places.

Despite the constant drain on Alexander's forces in the Mediterranean, the Allies were able to launch a new overwhelming offensive with their invasion of southern France on 15 August, an operation which (benefitting from the lessons already learned in Sicily, and at Salerno and Anzio) was crowned by immediate and decisive success.

Preparations for these landings had started on 29 April with an attack by 488 heavy bombers on Toulon, while shuttle day and night raids between Britain and the Mediterranean by British and American bombers had severely damaged all important road and rail centres south of Lyons; in three months the Allied air forces dropped about 12,500 tons of bombs in this area alone. Opposing the landings themselves the Luftwaffe in the south and south west of France could field about 220 aircraft, of which 150 were long-range bombers and 45 were fighters; the Mediterranean Air Forces on the other hand could call on at least 5,000 aircraft.

As a preliminary to the assault, all the coastal batteries and radar stations were attacked on the eve of the landings, and during the night of 14/15 August 400 aircraft dropped about 7,000 paratroops, who were followed by 407 gliders with 2,000 troops, 221 jeeps and 213 guns with all the necessary fuel, ammunition and stores to sustain them. Owing to the distance of the landings from Allied airfields, initial air cover was provided by naval fighters flying from five British and two American carriers until the first strips could be made ready ashore.

The net closes

At sea German U-boats made sporadic attempts to attack the numerous Allied convoys in the Mediterranean, despite the fast dwindling number of ports still available to them; during 1944 they sank one destroyer and two merchantmen, a paltry effort that was a tribute to the efforts of the Coastal Air Forces which provided constant and far-ranging anti-submarine patrols; during the year these forces destroyed 14 Ju 88s and sank four U-boats; on 19 August two U-boats were scuttled at Toulon, and a third soon after; three were scuttled off the Turkish coast on 10 September and nine days later the last to be sunk in the Mediterranean went to the bottom.

Ashore in France the US 7th Army, which had landed east of Marseilles in mid-August, made its way swiftly north and eventually joined up on 12 September with elements of General Patton's US 3rd Army moving down from Normandy. In Italy, severely depleted by demands elsewhere, the British 8th Army and US 5th Army made slow progress until a month before the end of hostilities in Europe; during that month German resistance collapsed, allowing the Americans to capture Turin on 30 April 1945 and the British to reach Venice on 1 May.

In narrating the final chapter of events in the Mediterranean it only remains to describe the campaigns in the Adriatic and Balkans, which nevertheless made substantial demands upon the Allied air forces.

After the precipitate departure of British forces from Greece in 1941, the Germans found themselves confronted by a rapidly growing army of partisans in Yugoslavia, an army which Britain quickly realised as being a significant thorn in the Axis side and worthwhile supporting with whatever means could be made available. It was not until May 1942 that such means could be found, and during that month supply-dropping sorties started being flown by four Liberators of No. 108 Squadron based in far-off Egypt. This scale of operations con-

The Spitfire Mk IX represented a stopgap development to get the two-speed, two-stage Merlin 60 into a basic Mk V airframe. It was built in large numbers and is exemplified here by two aircraft on patrol over Italy.

tinued until March 1943 when the Liberators and 14 Halifaxes, which had then become available, were formed into No. 148 Squadron, thereby providing the nucleus of a small Special Operations Air Force, which in turn became the Balkan Air Force in June 1944.

It was not until the Allies were firmly established on the mainland of Europe in 1943 that direct air support for the Yugoslav Partisan Army could be furnished, and late that year units of the Allied Tactical and Coastal Air Forces started operating over the Adriatic and Yugoslavia, their aims being to prevent any build-up of Axis forces which might threaten the Allies' eastern flank in Italy and to keep open the sea routes for supplies to the partisans. After the Italian surrender the Germans reacted quickly and occupied most of the islands off the Yugoslav coast, though with considerable losses inflicted by RAF, SAAF and RAAF Kittyhawks of the Desert Air Force.

Support for Tito

To provide the direct support of Marshal Tito's partisans a new formation, No. 334 Special Operations Wing, was established at Brindisi with No. 148 Squadron, No. 624 Squadron (flying Halifaxes, and later Stirlings), the American 62nd Troop Carrier Group with 50 C-47s and about 36 CANT Z.1007s and Savoia-Marchetti SM.82s of the Italian Co-Belligerent Air Force.

During the last week in May 1944 the Germans launched a determined attack on Tito's headquarters at Drvar in central Yugoslavia, but although Tito and his staff were forced to take refuge in the surrounding hills, swift action by the Allied air forces, which flew more than 1,000 sorties against the enemy, brought the attack to a standstill. Two days later Tito was flown out to confer with Air Marshal Slessor at Bari while the American C-47s evacuated 118 wounded partisans from a landing strip at Kupresko Polje. Slessor was able to tell Tito that at that moment the Balkan Air Force was being formed with squadrons of Spitfires, Hurricanes, Mustangs, Beaufighters, Ly-

sanders, Halifaxes, Baltimores, Dakotas, Liberators and Macchi C.202s. For his part, Tito asked for three services from the Allies: the wresting of air superiority over Yugoslavia from the Luftwaffe, an increase in the close air support for the partisans, and the evacuation of all wounded partisans from his country (owing to a deplorable absence of medical services in the field); in meeting the last request, no fewer than 11,000 wounded were flown to RAF hospitals in Italy.

As a means of effecting the other objects the Allies infiltrated a number of ground reporting units into the enemy-held off-shore islands to relay requests for air operations, and in July attacks were stepped up against the enemy's coastal supply lines between Zagreb and Skopje, 262 railway locomotives being destroyed or badly damaged in 27 days, for the most part by Spitfire and Mustang fighter-bombers. In mid-July another German offensive against the partisans' II Corps in Montenegro was launched and, although it was temporarily halted by a Yugoslav counterattack supported by Spitfires and Mustangs, the enemy regrouped and attacked again in mid-August. At the critical moment, when all seemed lost, Romania and

The potent, long-range Mustang Mk IV joined the Desert Air Force in 1945, almost at the end of hostilities. The shark's mouth on this aircraft, together with the code letters 'GA', denote an aircraft of No. 112 Squadron.

The RAF diverted much effort in 1944–5 to assisting the partisans in Yugoslavia. Without this help there is little doubt that Tito's forces would have had less success. Prominent were the strikes with bomb and rocket by the Beaufighter squadrons. In this attack one of the Beaufighters can be seen at low level just above the billowing smoke.

The Martin Marauder continued to serve with the Desert Air Force on daylight bombing missions through 1944, mainly in the hands of the SAAF squadrons.

flying from Italy, the Germans started assembling a fleet of some 170 Junkers Ju 52/3m, Dornier Do 24, Heinkel He 111, Junkers Ju 290 and Messerschmitt Me 323 transports at and around Athens. With these the Luftwaffe sought to evacuate Wehrmacht forces from the area by night, but lost about 46 aircraft either to the guns of Allied night-fighters or in raids by the US 15th Air Force.

Liberation of Greece

One by one the Greek islands were captured, some by glider forces and paratroops but all under air cover provided by aircraft of the Balkan Air Force. On the Greek mainland the airfield at Araxos was seized by a force which included No. 2908 Squadron of the RAF Regiment. The liberation of Greece was completed in October 1944 only to be followed by a bloody civil war in which the RAF was frequently called upon to support the forces fighting ELAS (left-wing partisans). In particular, rocket-firing Beaufighters of No. 39 Squadron were in constant action against road vehicles and partisan-held buildings until 12 January 1945, when a ceasefire was agreed.

The Axis presence in Yugoslavia took longer to banish. By the end of 1944 the Balkan Air Force had flown 22,317 sorties across the Adriatic, involving 63,170 flying hours. In the New Year, harried by Tito's partisan army with support from Spitfires and rocket-firing Hurricanes, now flying from bases in Greece, the German forces attempted to retreat northwards from Sarajevo while enemy shipping in Fiume harbour was attacked by rockets from Beaufighters. During the first three months of 1945 the long-range Liberators, Halifaxes and Wellingtons dropped 31,000 tons of bombs on transport and communications targets in western Hungary, northern Yugoslavia, Austria and Bavaria, thereby supporting not only the Allied forces in Italy and Yugoslavia but also the Russian armies approaching from the east. To these activities were added the evacuation by air of more than 2,000 homeless Yugoslav refugees from the battle areas, as requested by Tito. On 1 May some 25 enemy vessels surrendered to rocket-firing Hurricanes of the RAF, and one week later, with the enemy's withdrawal from Slavonia, the Balkan Air Force flew its last operational sorties.

'Overlord': the Normandy invasion

In northern Europe, the decisive and long-awaited invasion of Normandy by the Allies was launched at dawn on 6 June 1944. For two years preparations had been under way for this the greatest amphibious military undertaking in history, involving the assembly in Britain of literally millions of soldiers, sailors and airmen, and immense quantities of war matériel.

Apart from the massed ranks of strategic bombing forces in RAF Bomber Command and the US 8th Air Force, and squadrons of RAF Coastal Command (whose activities hitherto have already been narrated), the air forces directly supporting the Normandy operation, the Allied Expeditionary Air Force (AEAF), were commanded by Air Chief Marshal Sir Trafford Leigh-Mallory; under General Dwight D. Eisenhower, the Supreme Commander Allied Expeditionary Forces, Air Chief Marshal Sir Arthur Tedder had been appointed Deputy Supreme Allied Commander.

The RAF elements of the AEAF comprised 61 squadrons of Spitfires, 21 of Typhoons, 12 of Mustangs, four of Seafires, two of Hawker Tempests and two of Hurricanes; 22 of Mosquitoes, four of Mitchells, two of Bostons, two of Beaufighters and one of Wellingtons; five of Dakotas, four of Armstrong Whitworth Albemarles, four of Stirlings and two of Halifaxes; in addition two air/sea rescue squadrons flew Spitfires, Vickers Warwicks and Supermarine Walruses. Alongside these 150 RAF squadrons flew 165 of the USAAF, comprising 39 squadrons of P-47s, 13 of P-38s, 10 of P-51s and three of P-61/P-70s; 33 of B-26s, 12 of A-20s and 55 of C-47s.

Although offensive operations by strategic and

Bulgaria defected from the Axis, thereby effectively isolating German forces in Greece. German attention was now diverted to the safety and evacuation of this force, immediately relieving the pressure on the Yugoslav partisans.

Meanwhile one of the war's most distasteful episodes was being enacted to the north. On 1 August 1944 Polish partisans in Warsaw rose against the Germans, confident that assistance would be provided by the advancing Russians; instead the Russian armies were halted short of the city while the Poles under General Bor-Komarowski were subjected to a devastating onslaught by the brutal elements of the SS and Gestapo. In response to impassioned calls by Bor-Komarowski for assistance from the Western Allies, and following a few successful sorties to Warsaw from the Mediterranean by No. 1586 (Polish) Special Duty Flight on 8 and 9 August, it was agreed to divert two Liberator squadrons, No. 31 (SAAF) and No. 178, from the invasion of southern France to join No. 148 in Italy to drop supplies to the Poles. These operations were fraught with hazard, as a result of quickly increased German night-fighter operations and flak, and after 17 Liberators and Halifaxes had been lost out of 93 despatched in five nights the missions were suspended; sorties by No. 1586 Flight were allowed to continue, and by the end of September, when the Polish uprising was finally crushed, 14 further Liberators had been lost.

Other operations over Poland by No. 334 Wing of the RAF at this time merit passing mention: flying from Italy, No. 267 Squadron's Dakotas made a number of hazardous flights to land in Poland behind the enemy lines to bring out agents and members of the Polish resistance; on one occasion vital components of the German V-2 rocket, which had been collected by patriots, were flown out by No. 267 Squadron for urgent despatch to Britain.

By September 1944 the scene was set for the assault on the enemy occupation forces in Greece and the Aegean Islands. With escape routes through Romania and Bulgaria now denied them, only the railway north from Skopje to Zagreb remained. As this now came under renewed attack by the Yugoslav partisans as well as RAF bombers

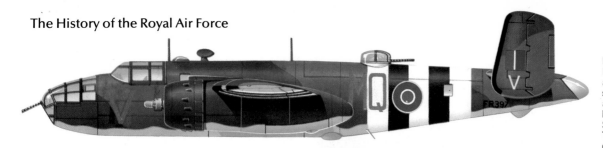

Four squadrons of North American Mitchell Mk IIs were involved in the assault on Europe. FR397 was one such, serving with No. 226 Squadron at Hartford Bridge Flats (Blackbushe). It later served on No. 2 Group Support Unit until a belly-landing at Thorpe Abbots on 23 March 1945 ended its career.

tactical aircraft had been flown across the Channel continuously since 1941 (including the combined operation at Dieppe in August 1942, which had provided such costly but vital lessons for the Allies), the main preparatory operations started in March 1944 with devastating raids by British and American heavy bombers on road, river and rail targets in France and Belgium, consolidated in the 'Transportation Plan' ratified by Tedder on 15 April. During the two months up to D-Day more than 42,000 tons of bombs were dropped by Bomber Command on 33 railway centres in Belgium and France; in the same period the USAAF delivered 11,648 tons on 23 such targets. Indeed, so successful was the Transportation Plan that after the Allied landings had taken place scarcely any enemy reinforcements could be brought into action without lengthy detours and delays, a factor which proved crucial during the vital consolidation of the invasion beach-heads.

As photographic reconnaissance aircraft roamed the enemy coast, bringing back important information of beach obstacles and defences (some 120,000 photographic prints were processed by an RAF Mobile Photographic Unit for issue to British and American army commanders before D-Day), Allied light and medium bombers attacked all manner of military targets on the Continent, including head-quarters, radar stations, equipment and ammunition dumps, and so on. Outstanding among these attacks were the controversial raid by 19 Mosquitoes of Nos. 21, 464 (RAAF) and 487 (RNZAF) Squadrons on Amiens jail on 18 February 1944 (the leader of this famous raid, Group Captain P. C. Pickard, was shot down and killed) to allow the escape of French partisans being held captive, and on 11 April by six Mosquitoes of No. 613 Squadron on the Kunstzaal Kleizkamp, a building in The Hague which housed population records being used by the Gestapo.

In the final month before the landings 40 enemy airfields within fighter range of the assault area, and 59 bomber bases further afield were heavily attacked (principally by American fighters, fighter-

bombers and bombers) while US 9th Air Force aircraft attacked bridges over the Meuse and Seine, 18 out of 24 being destroyed, as well as selected bridges over the Loire, Meuse, Moselle and Escaut; many hundreds of locomotives were destroyed, with the result that scarcely any movement by rail traffic over a considerable area of France and the Low Countries was possible. During the last seven days the radar station at Dieppe-Caudecôte was put out of action by 18 rocket-firing Typhoons of Nos 198 and 609 Squadrons; on 4 June 23 Spitfires of Nos 441, 442 and 443 Squadrons, RCAF, with 500-lb (227-kg) bombs, destroyed the radar installation at Cap d'Antifer, and on the eve of the landings themselves rocket Typhoons of Nos 174, 175 and 245 Squadrons put the radar station near the Cap de la Hague out of action. Other radio centres, vital to the enemy's air defences, were destroyed or severely damaged by RAF Bomber Command.

To give positive identification of Allied aircraft during the assault on the Continent, all aircraft were painted with black and white stripes on the eve of D-Day. This applied to all aircraft crossing the Channel including this Mosquito PR.Mk XVI of No. 540 Squadron which went to Berlin on D-Day.

The Douglas Boston continued in service with No. 2 Group light bomber squadrons and were heavily involved in the attack on Europe. This aircraft is attacking shipping at St Malo.

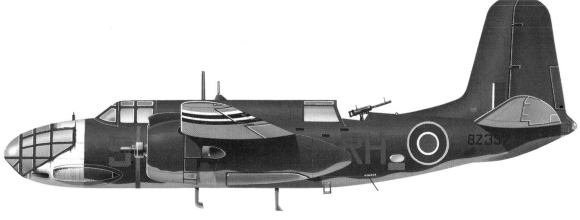

The Douglas Boston complemented the Mitchell and served until the war was over. BZ357 was a Mk IIIA serving with No. 88 Squadron, also at Hartford Bridge Flats at D-Day. This aircraft is equipped with pipes under the fuselage for laying smoke-screens.

Deprived of almost its entire radar cover over the Channel and northern France, the Germans were taken wholly by surprise when 13,000 men of the US 82nd and 101st Airborne Divisions dropped from the night sky over the base of the Cotentin peninsula; alas for this operation, only about a quarter of the forces dropped in or near the correct landing zones and around 60 per cent of their rquipment fell wide. On the eastern flank of the landings, entrusted to British and Commonwealth forces, the advanced guard of the British 3rd Parachute Brigade was dropped accurately from the Albemarles of Nos 295 and 570 Squadrons, but the main body of the brigade, carried in Dakotas of Nos 48, 233, 271, 512 and 575 Squadrons fared worse, two-thirds of its strength being scattered over a wide area. In the operations by the RAF's Nos 38 and 46 Transport Groups, 264 aircraft and 98 glider combinations (including the new General Aircraft Hamilcar heavy assault glider) carried 4,310 paratroops, 493 gliderborne troops, 17 guns, 44 jeeps and 55 motorcycles; their losses were seven aircraft and 22 gliders.

If the pre-landing destruction of the enemy's radar had concealed the real airborne landings, the deliberate leaving intact of German coastal radar in the Pas de Calais was designed to allow the enemy to watch the approach of a supposed in-

vasion fleet across the Channel; this was in fact an elaborate decoy being flown by 16 Lancasters of No. 617 Squadron led by Group Captain G. L. Cheshire, VC. By flying a slowly advancing series of orbits, and by dropping Window at carefully prescribed intervals, the aircraft provided radar indications of a fleet of ships advancing towards the French coast. A similar 'spoof invasion' was flown by Stirlings of No. 218 Squadron off Boulogne as bombers of Nos 138, 149 and 161 Squadrons dropped dummy paratroops further afield to create confusion, and other Bomber Command aircraft set up a veritable barrage of radio and radar jamming. As the real invasion armada approached the Normandy beaches, 1,136 heavy bombers of Bomber Command unloaded 5,267 tons of bombs on 10 of the principal heavy coastal gun batteries in the landing area itself.

The first step

While the first waves of American and British assault troops went ashore from their landing craft, the skies filled with the first of 171 squadrons of support aircraft, some laying smoke screens over the enemy positions, some attacking with guns, bombs and rockets, and others flying guard against interference by the Luftwaffe. In the event it is estimated that the German air force was un-

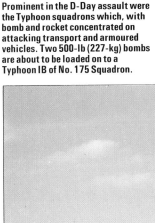

Prominent in the D-Day assault were the Typhoon squadrons which, with bomb and rocket concentrated on attacking transport and armoured vehicles. Two 500-Ib (227-kg) bombs are about to be loaded on to a Typhoon IB of No. 175 Squadron.

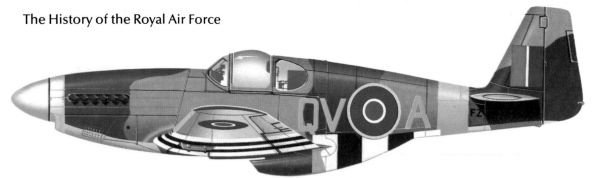

The Merlin-engined Mustang Mk III was in service in numbers in 1944 and was most effective as a long-range escort fighter to the daylight bombing raids which supported the 'Second Front'. The first RAF squadron with them was No. 19 and it took them to a base in France only 19 days after D-Day.

able to mount more than 140 sorties during the whole of D-Day; four Junkers Ju 88s and one Focke-Wulf Fw 190 were shot down. By the end of the day the Allied air forces had flown 14,674 sorties, from which 113 aircraft had been lost. Among the great force of men and weapons landed on 6 June were a number of RAF Base Defence Sector Control Units and Mobile GCIs, whose task was to control night-fighters over the invasion area. As the day drew to a close, 256 glider combinations bearing reinforcements to the British 6th Airborne Division passed over the beaches; 246 of them landed in their assigned zones. At sea, the Royal Navy, supported by the Fleet Air Arm and assisted by RAF Coastal Command, had sealed the invasion corridor so effectively that hardly any interference by enemy surface craft was possible.

The days following the assault landings were spent building up the forces ashore as the Germans attempted to bring up their armoured formations. In the air, reaction by the Luftwaffe was slow to materialise and some 175 German bombers, unable to make any serious penetration of the Allied fighter cover over the beach-head, resorted to minelaying and caused some casualties among the invasion fleet, while such fighters as had escaped the destruction of their airfields attempted to cover the reinforcements struggling to Normandy. Two RAF Construction Units, Nos 3207 and 3209, came ashore to create an airfield at Ste Croix-sur-Mer and this was completed on D + 4, the first emergency strip having been ready for use on the day after the landings. In due course no fewer than 30 airstrips and airfields were built in the British zone and 50 in the American sector. On 10 June three squadrons (Nos 441, 442 and 443) were flying their Spitfires from the lodgement area itself; within three weeks 31 squadrons were flying from French soil.

As before D-Day, air-attack setpieces were mounted. On 10 June 61 Mitchells of Nos 98, 180,

226 and 320 (Dutch) Squadrons of the RAF, flying at medium altitude, bombed the headquarters of Panzer Group West as 40 Typhoons of Nos 181, 182, 245 and 247 Squadrons went in with rockets; among the large number of German officers killed was its chief of staff, General von Dawans. On 17 July Field Marshal Erwin Rommel narrowly escaped death when his staff car overturned during an attack by No. 602 Squadron's Spitfires. On 30 July five No. 2 Group Mosquitoes attacked a U-boat crew rest centre in a chateau on the River Aulne, killing or wounding many of the 400 men within. On 2 August Mosquitoes of No. 305 (Polish) Squadron attacked and destroyed a German school for saboteurs at Poitiers.

So chaotic did these and countless other attacks render the enemy communications in France that

Sweeping over the Hampshire countryside, these Mosquito FB. Mk VIs were on the strength of No. 487 (RNZAF) Squadron shortly before D-Day.

The unguided rocket, unleashed from under the wings of 2nd TAF Typhoons, wrought havoc with the enemy rail transport on the continent, in this case near Soltau in Germany.

Bristol Beaufighter TF.Mk Xs of Coastal Command scoured the north European coastline, attacking shipping with bomb, rocket and torpedo, amongst them NE237 of No. 455 (RAAF) Squadron.

Right: Developed from the Typhoon, the Tempest Mk V arrived in south east England just in time for the assault on Europe but the squadrons were initially diverted to tackle the V-1 'buzz-bombs' flocking over Kent and on to London. Led by Wing Commander Roland Beamont, whose Tempest carried the letters 'R:B', these aircraft, among the fastest in the RAF, were the most successful in downing V-1s.

Far right: The course of the battle over the bridgehead was faithfully recorded by the photo-reconnaissance Spitfire PR.Mk XI's squadrons at Benson.

the Germans resorted to attempts to sustain Cherbourg by U-boats; four boats loaded with ammunition sailed, but the port was captured before they arrived. Elsewhere U-boats made determined bids to attack the flow of Allied shipping crossing the Channel to Normandy; in the four days following D-Day Coastal Command pilots attacked 18 enemy submarines which stayed on the surface to fight it out. Eight U-boats were sunk – two in one night by a Liberator of No. 224 Squadron. The command lost 26 aircraft. In the course of the anti-submarine operations of this period, two Victoria Crosses were awarded: the first, awarded posthumously to Flight Lieutenant D. E. Hornell, RCAF, of No. 162 Squadron, was for his sinking of a U-boat on 24

June, and the second was awarded to Flying Officer J. A. Cruickshank of No. 210 Squadron who, though severely wounded, sank a U-boat on 17 July.

The next phase in the Battle of Normandy brought about widely differing uses of air power. As the fighting on the American right flank remained fluid and progress was made across the Cotentin peninsula, the British left flank was pinned down by robust resistance by the Germans around the town of Caen. RAF Bomber Command, which had been blasting away at enemy communications centres well behind the enemy lines (dropping 23,500 tons of bombs on such targets as Amiens, Arras, Cambrai, Douai, St Pol and Poitiers) was

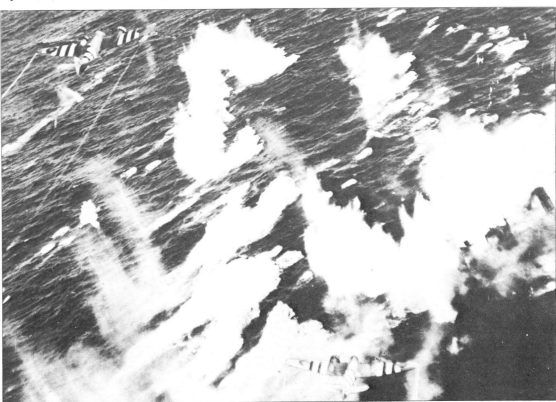

The Beaufighters of Coastal Command concentrated in June 1944 in attacking any coastal shipping, like this trawler off the Friesian Islands, which dared to operate along the Dutch and Belgian coasts.

The Lancaster was the largest single element in Bomber Command, replacing the Stirlings of No. 3 Group in 1944. This group's aircraft were fitted with GH blind-bombing radar for bomber leaders and this was denoted by the bars on the fin, shown on this No. 514 Squadron aircraft flying from Waterbeach in 1944. This aircraft (NG118) later served with No. 1653 (H)CU, eventually crashing after the war in October 1945.

now called upon to support the immediate ground battle, a course of action strongly advocated by Leigh-Mallory but one which found less favour with Harris. Nevertheless, on 7 July 457 heavy bombers dropped 2,363 tons of bombs on and around Caen as a prelude to an infantry assault by the British 3rd and Canadian 3rd Divisions. As had already been demonstrated at Monte Cassino, however, the massive cratering caused by the bombs prevented the Allied armour from penetrating into Caen, and a second heavy raid, this time by 1,570 heavy bombers and 349 medium bombers of the RAF and US 8th Air Force, which dropped 7,700 tons of bombs, was launched against Colombelles, a suburb of Caen – yet still no breakthrough was effected.

The reason was as unfortunate as it was inevitable. On two early occasions some of the Allied bombs had fallen among the leading units of the attacking troops, causing the bomb line to be advanced considerably so as to avoid a repetition of such errors. This allowed the enemy time to recover from the air bombardment before the attacking troops arrived, picking their way through the vast piles of rubble. Nevertheless, after some 16,000 further tons of bombs had been cast down to saturate the area, it was perhaps inevitable that enemy casualties would eventually so weaken the defences that a breakthrough would be possible, and in due course the Canadians were able to make ground south from Caen towards Falaise.

In the west the British 2nd Army and the US 1st and 3rd Armies were sweeping south from the Cotentin peninsula and, after a German counterattack had been repulsed at Mortain on 7 August with considerable assistance from RAF rocketfiring Typhoons, these forces were closing around the remnants of 16 enemy divisions. On 9 August Le Mans fell to the Americans, and four days later Hitler ordered the German 7th Army to fall back behind the Seine. Renewed attempts by the enemy to maintain an escape 'gap' near Falaise were largely frustrated on the 16th as every available fighter and fighter-bomber of the 2nd Tactical Air Force was sent into the battle against the enemy

forces desperately trying to disengage. This indeed was the rocket-firing Typhoons' killing ground: nothing that moved was safe and by the end of the month the 7th Army had simply ceased to exist as a fighting organisation. On the 25th Paris was surrendered by General von Choltitz to the French under General Leclerq as the Allies established numerous crossings over the Seine. Frantically the Luftwaffe tried to cover the German army's retreat, which quickly turned to rout. On 23 August No. 83 Group Spitfires shot down 16 Fw 190s and Bf 109s, and two days later Allied aircraft destroyed 36 enemy aircraft on the ground and 51 in the air. On 30 August the British 2nd Army occupied Amiens, crossing the Belgian frontier three days later. As already recounted, General Patton's American forces linked up with those moving up from the South of France on 12 September.

Up-to-the-minute reconnaissance photos of the battle were obtained by the Allison-engined Mustang Mk Is.

Taxiing out, possibly at Hartford Bridge, are Boston Mk IIIAs equipped with smoke-laying pipes to cover the Allied landings.

Mosquito night-fighters served with Bomber Command in 1944–5, being part of No. 100 Group, tasked with dealing with the enemy's defences. Mosquitoes flew with the bomber streams, attacking German night-fighters. One such was this Mk XIX (MM650) serving with No. 157 Squadron from Swannington.

Thus far, in 11 weeks' fighting, the Germans had lost half a million men in dead, wounded and prisoners. The Luftwaffe, whose reserves of fully trained airmen were dwindling as fast as those of fuel and equipment, had lost more than 460 aircraft in France alone. Those losses were to prove fatal in the final nine months of the defence of the Reich. It is scarcely surprising, therefore, that Hitler had seized upon weapons he believed could achieve results where Goering's Luftwaffe had clearly failed. These were the V-1 flying bomb and V-2 long-range ballistic missile.

Terror weapons: the last resort

Development of the Fieseler Fi 103 pilotless flying bomb originated in 1939, when the German air ministry initiated work on a small pulse-jet by the Argus company, and in 1942 ordered a winged bomb to be produced, sustained in flight by this powerplant. Originally the weapon was intended to be air-launched, and in December that year Gerhard Fieseler, flying a Focke-Wulf Fw 200, dropped an unpowered version of the bomb over Peenemünde on the Baltic coast. In due course it was decided to ground-launch the weapon from ramps, and it was the sighting of early bombs and test ramps at Peenemünde on British reconnaissance photographs brought back to Benson in 1943 that provided British Intelligence with the first evidence of the bomb's existence, although earlier documents which had fallen into British hands had sown the seeds of suspicion.

Aware that enemy weapon development was centred at Peenemünde, Harris ordered a heavy raid against this target on 17/18 August 1943, 597 aircraft dropping 1,937 tons of bombs. Despite the loss of 40 aircraft, Bomber Command created widespread damage to the ground installations as well

as killing about 600 persons, among them a number of key weapon scientists and engineers. At much the same time a number of mysterious buildings and installations, similar to those seen at Peenemünde, had been sighted in France and Belgium, and these were accordingly attacked in daylight by bombers of the US 8th Air Force. Factories at Friedrichshafen, Ludwigshafen, Oppau and Leuna, suspected of producing components for the new weapons, were also attacked by B-17s and B-24s, although little serious damage was subsequently found to have been caused.

Thus far, British Intelligence had been somewhat confused by reports of both 'rockets' and 'flying bombs', but when a Fi 103 landed in Denmark and its details were secretly smuggled to London, a clearer picture emerged. Meanwhile reports emanating from French Resistance units indicated that concrete installations (known as 'ski sites') were being constructed in northern France, and when these were photographed from the air it was found that their axes lay on a line with London, confirming the view that their purpose was for launching weapons at the British capital. The Spitfires of No. 541 (Photographic Reconnaissance) Squadron now systematically covered the entire coast of northern France from the Brest peninsula to the Pas-de-Calais to a depth inland of 40 miles (64 km), and by the end of November 1943 a total of 80 sites had been discovered; by the end of a further month eight more sites had been commenced.

Under the codename 'Crossbow', preparations were now made to counter the new threat. B-26s of the US 9th Air Force were joined by the heavy bombers of RAF Bomber Command and of the US 8th Air Force, and later by the Mosquitoes, Spitfires and Mustangs of the 2nd Tactical Air Force; by the end of 1943 5,266 tons of bombs had fallen on the 'ski sites'.

As the number of sites identified continued to increase early in 1944 so the Allied attacks intensified; by the end of May 103 out of 140 sites attacked had been destroyed. (Some interesting statistics emerged from these raids: when attacked by the American B-17s each site required an average of 165 tons of bombs to achieve its destruction; when attacked by RAF Mosquitoes only 40 tons of bombs were needed.)

To overcome the Allies' obvious success in obliterating their launching sites, the Germans in April 1944 started siting pre-fabricated ramps which proved much more difficult to locate and destroy, and by 12 June (when the first flying bombs were launched) such ramps had increased faster than it had proved possible to eliminate them. So determined were the Germans to defend the launching sites that flak defences were progressively strengthened in their vicinity to such an extent that the sites became among the most heartily disliked of all Bomber Command's targets. Six days after the Normandy landings had started the Germans were ready to open the flying bomb campaign.

By then, however, the British had evolved some idea of what to expect. To meet the onslaught a plan, Operation 'Overlord Diver', was put into effect on 13 June. In this, 11 fighter squadrons of No. 11 Group were ordered to fly standing patrols over three specific lines, over mid-Channel westwards from Cap Gris Nez for 70 miles (112 km), over the south coast of England between Dover and Newhaven, and on a line parallel to this about 20 miles (32 km) inland. Between the latter patrol

Logistics were a huge problem for the back-up forces. This rocket armoury serving No. 175 Squadron, probably at Le Fresney Camille, was doing lively business in June and July 1944.

The high-altitude Spitfire Mk VIIs of No. 131 Squadron were used in 1944 to escort the daylight bombing raids of Bomber Command over France. MD111 was one of the aircraft used by the squadron from Culmhead.

line and a line between Rochester and Leatherhead lay an area of about 2,100 square miles (5600 km²) in which anti-aircraft guns and rockets had exclusive freedom to fire; on the southern outskirts of London itself were deployed some 480 barrage balloons.

The flying bomb attack was slow to achieve a significant rate of launching. Nevertheless during the 24 hours following midnight of 15/16 June 151 of these unpleasant weapons were reported by the defences and 73 reached London. 14 were destroyed by ground fire and seven by the fighters.

As further attempts to destroy the pests at source continued with raids on the launching sites, it was soon realised that the defence measures so far adopted were unsatisfactory. The introduction of the VT fuse in 40-mm Bofors ammunition clearly gave the guns a much better chance of destroying the bombs as they crossed the Kent and Sussex coasts, so in July the entire defence organisation was altered. The number of anti-aircraft guns was increased from 380 to 916 and all were moved to the coast, and the number of balloons south of London was increased to 1,000. The fighters were now given free rein overland between the coast and the capital, aided by an improved procedure of bomb reporting adopted by the Royal Observer Corps.

Flying bomb defence

The Fi 103, or V-1 flying bomb as it was more commonly known, was a relatively small aircraft with a speed of around 400 mph (640 km/h), although many of them flew somewhat slower owing to poorly adjusted fuel supply. The bomb approached its target at heights of around 2,950 ft (900 m). It was therefore a fairly difficult target for the light anti-aircraft guns, but equally it required a fast traverse by the larger calibre weapons. Its high speed rendered it immune from many of the Allied fighters and, apart from the Spitfire XIV, Mustang III and Mosquito, two new aircraft were introduced into combat service in time to take a hand in the defence. The first was the Gloster Meteor jet fighter, of which the first examples reached No. 616 Squadron in 1944, and the other was the Hawker Tempest V. In the event the early Meteors proved only just fast enough to catch the V-1, but the Tempest achieved outstanding results, the highest number of bomb 'victories' being obtained by the Tempest-equipped Nos 3 and 486 (RNZAF) Squadrons, with 258 and 223 bombs destroyed respectively. The highest individual score, 61 bombs shot down, was gained by Squadron Leader Joseph Berry, DFC and two Bars, of No. 501 Squadron flying Spitfire IXs and later Tempests. It is also worth mentioning in passing that the RAF Regiment manned 168 40-mm Bofors and 416 20-mm Hispano guns among the defences against the flying-bomb. At the height of the attacks the RAF deployed 21 fighter squadrons (six of them night-fighters), the gun defences numbered 592 heavy weapons and 922 light, as well as 600 rocket barrels, plus 2,016 barrage balloons.

In September 1944, as the Allied armies in France reached and overran the launching sites, there occurred a lull in the attacks and it was immediately thought that the danger had passed. However, at early light on 16 September seven bombs crossed the Essex coast from the east, and two fell in London. It was soon discovered that the Luftwaffe was now launching the bombs from Heinkel He 111 aircraft over the North Sea. Flying

from their bases at Aalhorn, Varelbusch and Zwischenahn, the enemy aircraft were approaching at low level before climbing shortly before reaching the coast to release their single weapons. While the established defences took an increasing toll of these air-launched bombs, the Mosquito night-fighters of No. 25 Squadron, commanded by Wing-Commander L. J. C. Mitchell, went for the launching bombers, destroying five.

By December the Luftwaffe was using about 100 He 111s to launch flying bombs, usually attacking London but ringing the changes occasionally with bombs aimed at targets as widely separated as Manchester, Norwich and Southampton. Another short phase began early in March 1945, using ramps in the Netherlands, but the great majority of the bombs reported by coastal defences were destroyed without their causing any significant damage. The last bomb of all to fall on Britain (others also fell in Antwerp) was shot down near Sittingbourne on 29 March. Between June 1944 and March 1945 some 1,847 flying bombs were destroyed by aircraft of the Air Defence of Great Britain, 1,866 were shot down by Anti-Aircraft Command, 232 had struck balloon cables, and 12 were shot down by the Royal Navy. (More than 30,000 Fi 103s were produced, of which roughly 20,000 were launched against targets in the UK, France and Belgium.)

A very different weapon – and a harbinger of another era of warfare – was the A4, or V-2 (*Vergeltungswaffe 2*, or Retaliation Weapon No. 2) long-range ballistic rocket, whose offensive started against Paris on 5 September 1944 and against London three days later. In the face of this weapon there existed no defence other than destruction at source, its arrival on target being signalled by a shattering explosion, followed rather than preceded by the sound of its approach. The British were once more not wholly unprepared for this new weapon as its existence had been reported at Peenemünde. As the result of information gained through the Polish underground movement, already mentioned, and from a rocket which accidentally landed in Sweden during tests, its size and range had been estimated (albeit considerably exaggerated).

Right: Hot in pursuit of a V-1 over Kent is a Tempest Mk V. This type was the most successful in combating this menace.

Equipped with 'Airborne Cigar' and carrying an extra German-speaking crew member, the Lancasters of No. 101 Squadron from Ludford Magna passed misinformation to the attacking German fighter crews. In this case blind bombing on a daylight raid is 'B' of the squadron.

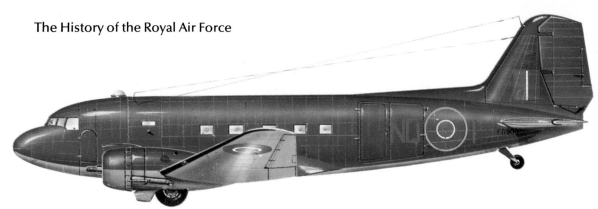

The Douglas Dakota entered RAF service in 1943 and by 1944 had become a ubiquitous transport at home and overseas. It flew as a glider-tug, paratrooper and line transport. This Mk III flew with No. 24 Squadron.

Reconnaissance cover of all suspected launching pads was undertaken by PR Spitfires during July and August 1944, and it was originally thought that four such sites, at Mimoyecques, Siracourt, Watten and Wizernes, had been located. Heavy raids by Allied bombers, occasionally using the new 22,000-lb (9990-kg) 'Grand Slam' bombs, were mounted and considerable damage caused, but in the event it was later discovered that only the sites at Watten and Wizernes were involved in the V-2 campaign. (The site at Mimoyecques was intended to discharge salvoes of 6-in/15.24-cm shells from 50 barrels sunk in concrete and aimed at London. This weapon was not used, partly owing to difficulties in stabilising the missiles in flight and partly to the damage caused by the bombing.)

Fighters and fighter-bombers of the RAF flew about 900 sorties over the Low Countries in mid-September in efforts to discover the launching pads but with very little success. The only defensive step thought possible was to detect the rockets (using No. 105 Mobile Air Reporting Unit located at Malines in Belgium) as they rose vertically from the pads and flash a warning to London where it was intended to fire salvoes of shells in the path of the rocket in the hope of exploding it in mid-air; it was soon realised, however, that for the sake of a single attack disproportionately large parts of the country would have to be alerted and therefore largely paralysed. In any case during the week after 25 September Norwich again joined the list of targets and no significant anti-aircraft defences existed so far north.

As much in desperation as for propaganda purposes, the 2nd Tactical Air Force flew 10,000 sorties between 15 October and 25 November over the Netherlands, attacking every conceivable transport target in the hope of disrupting supplies to the rocket sites, but it has remained unknown to what extent these attacks had any bearing on the rate of launchings; certainly the drizzle of rockets continued over south east England until well into 1945.

The last V-2 rocket fell in England at Orpington

on 27 March; it was the 1,115th to arrive in a campaign that had killed 2,855 people and seriously injured 6,268 others, the vast majority of them civilians. Compared with respective figures of 6,139 and 17,239 for the V-1 flying bomb, the long-range rocket was a costly and wasteful weapon, yet one which, in other circumstances, could have wrought a profound effect on the course of the war, bearing in mind the impotence of the Allies significantly to reduce the firing rate other than by overrunning the firing points themselves.

Victory in Europe: climax and final curtain

By October 1944 the scene was set for the final assault on the Reich homeland, with the Western Allies advancing to a line from Belgium to Switzerland and the Russians already at the gates of Warsaw. Yet many bitter battles and unpleasant surprises remained in store.

The RAF, though to some extent pre-occupied with efforts to combat the V-1 and V-2 weapons, was deployed to support the Allied armies in their advance to the German frontiers. In their rear a number of Channel ports had been bypassed by the British and Canadian forces in their swift uprush after the German collapse at Falaise. The first of

When the Allied forces spread across France into Belgium and the Netherlands the Dakotas kept up a bus service with supplies, a line-up here awaiting unloading.

Training for the assault on D-Day is this Stirling Mk IV, towing off a Horsa glider from one of the airborne forces bases in southern England.

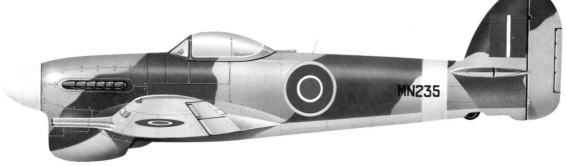

Designed as an interceptor, the Hawker Typhoon soon found its niche in the ground attack role. It was most notable for rocket attacks on trains, but proved rugged and devastating in all duties.

In 1944 Britain's first jet fighter entered service with No. 616 Squadron. The Meteor was at first turned to combating the V-1 but later moved to the Continent to deal with the Messerschmitt Me 262A. Wing leader was Wing Commander H. J. Wilson (his aircraft was coded 'HJ :W') who later went on to break the world speed record with a Meteor F.Mk 4 after the war.

these, Le Havre, which had seemed likely to hold out for many weeks, surrendered after Bomber Command had dropped 9,500 tons of bombs in seven daylight raids between 5 and 11 September; Boulogne surrendered on 23 September after similar treatment; and Calais followed a week later.

Meanwhile, in a bold effort to accelerate the collapse of German forces in the Low Countries and thereby weaken the northern flank of the Ruhr, whose encirclement by the British and Canadians in the north and the Americans in the south was part of the strategy for the assault on Germany, a large-scale airborne operation in the Netherlands was carried out in September. On the 17th, aircraft of the RAF's Nos 38 and 46 Groups towed the gliderborne element of the British 1st Airborne Division to Arnhem in the Netherlands to capture the key Rhine bridge, as the American 82nd and 101st Airborne Divisions secured bridges over the Maas at Grave and over the Waal at Nijmegen.

Despite being loaned C-47s by the US Troop Carrier Command, RAF Transport Command was unable to transport the entire British division in one lift, and the ultimate failure of this operation must be largely attributable to this lack of aircraft. As it was, Transport Command employed two squadrons of Albemarles, two of Halifaxes, six of Stirlings and six of Dakotas.

Following the marking of the landing zone by paratroops dropped from 12 Stirlings, 285 Horsas and Hamilcars were released over Arnhem, 35 others having been lost en route. In addition, 1,113 bombers and 1,240 fighters supported and protected the landings. Unfortunately British Intelligence had been unaware that German ground forces in the Arnhem area were particularly strong, and these reacted swiftly, effectively containing the British forces. The all-important second lift, which should have arrived at dawn on the 18th, was delayed for six hours by bad weather in England, as was the first re-supply mission by 33 Stirlings which nevertheless dropped most of their containers in the correct position.

On the third day the aircraft bringing the Polish Parachute Brigade Group failed to meet its fighter escort and suffered heavy losses, while a supply mission by Nos 38 and 46 Groups met heavy flak which destroyed 13 aircraft and damaged 97 others. The final tragedy of the day occurred when the survivors of this supply mission dropped their loads in an area still held by the Germans: the supplies were dropped accurately, but a radio message changing the dropping zone had been so distorted by jamming that it was not understood; furthermore, by the time a new dropping zone had been signalled and an accurate drop made by 33 Stirlings, this too had been captured by the Germans.

On this day the pilot of a No. 271 Squadron Dakota, Flight Lieutenant D. S. A. Lord, was awarded a posthumous Victoria Cross. Carrying a load of supply containers, his aircraft was hit by flak and an engine set on fire; knowing how sorely needed were his supplies, he stayed with the air-

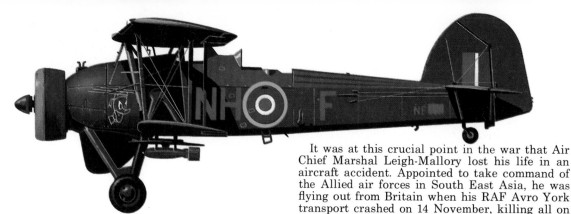

One of the strangest types serving with the RAF for the assault on Europe were the ex-Royal Navy Swordfish Mk IIIs of No. 119 Squadron, flying from Knocke/Le Zoute from January to May 1945 for night attacks on E-boats, R-boats and midget submarines.

craft stream, although losing height rapidly and becoming a target for many enemy guns, and eventually dropped his containers accurately; and then after ordering his crew to bale out, he remained at his controls to enable them to do so but himself died in his aircraft when it crashed soon afterwards.

After six days of desperate fighting at Arnhem, the surviving British troops were overwhelmed and either surrendered or made such escape as they could. The cost of this adventure had been very heavy, including 57 British and 18 American transport aircraft shot down or crashed, and 327 damaged by flak and fighters; moreover, despite every effort made to sustain the ground forces, only about seven per cent of all supplies dropped could be recovered by the beleaguered division.

Last-ditch weapon

Meanwhile as the American forces clung to their bridge objectives elsewhere, the Germans launched another weapon, the *Mistel* (mistletoe) composite aircraft, against these key targets (as far as is known, only one such weapon fell in Britain: it was aimed at but failed to hit an ammunition dump in north Kent in October 1944.) Employing a manned single-seat fighter perched atop a bomber packed with explosives which was released as it neared its target, the new weapons were launched against the Nijmegen bridge on 26 and 27 September but achieved little worthwhile damage. The RAF Spitfires of No. 83 Group, assigned to protect the Americans, succeeded in destroying 18 enemy aircraft in these operations.

Elsewhere in the Netherlands the heavily-defended island of Walcheren was still firmly occupied by enemy forces who, commanding the entrances to the Scheldt, prevented the Allies from enjoying the benefits of the great port of Antwerp which had fallen largely intact on 4 September. Walcheren itself lay almost entirely below sea level, but was ringed by huge sea defences on which were mounted numerous heavy coastal guns. On 3 October 247 Lancasters and Mosquitoes, led by No. 617 Squadron carrying 12,000-lb (5443-kg) 'Tallboy' bombs, attacked a number of points in the sea defences and breached them, causing the sea to pour inland around Westkapelle. Further attacks were carried out during the month, breaching the sea dykes near Flushing, and severely damaging the 25-cm (9.8-in) coastal guns near Domburg. By 30 October Bomber Command had flown 10 major raids to Walcheren, dropping nearly 9,000 tons of bombs, assisted by the 2nd Tactical Air Force whose bomb- and rocket-carrying Typhoons, Tempests and Spitfires flew about 10,000 sorties and discharged 11,637 rockets and 1,500 tons of bombs for the loss of 57 aircraft and 31 pilots. The island was eventually assaulted on 1 November, the Royal Marine Commandos' landing craft being closely supported by the rocket-firing Typhoons of No. 183 Squadron. In the subsequent actions to clear Walcheren and South Beveland, numerous units of the RAF Regiment fought alongside the infantry of the Allied armies: No. 2816 Squadron fought on Walcheren and was later joined by No. 2757 Squadron on the Leopold Canal until eventually relieved by Nos. 2717 and 2777 Squadrons. Another squadron (No. 2726) fought with the Irish Guards. By the end of 1944 elements of the RAF Regiment on the Continent consisted of 21 rifle squadrons, 19 anti-aircraft squadrons and six armoured squadrons.

It was at this crucial point in the war that Air Chief Marshal Leigh-Mallory lost his life in an aircraft accident. Appointed to take command of the Allied air forces in South East Asia, he was flying out from Britain when his RAF Avro York transport crashed on 14 November, killing all on board. In Europe Eisenhower had taken personal command of all Allied forces, handing over supreme command of the Allied air forces to Tedder.

Meanwhile the close-support aircraft of the 2nd Tactical Air Force were embarking on a new phase of 'interdiction' strikes, their aim being to halt all movement of forces between Germany and the Low Countries, either for evacuation or reinforcement purposes. Tactics employed featured the use of rocket-firing Typhoons to bring enemy trains to a standstill, either by direct attack on the locomotives or on the permanent way, leaving the remaining destruction of the train to Mosquito and Mitchell bombers which could attack at leisure; during October and November some 1,500 such attacks were carried out by the fighters, in which 80 locomotives were destroyed and over 300 damaged.

In a set-piece attack by 30 Typhoons of Nos 193, 197, 257, 263 and 266 Squadrons (led by Group Captain D. E. Gillan, DSO and two Bars, DFC and Bar, AFC), an important building in Dordrecht was demolished on 24 October; at the moment of the raid a meeting of high-ranking German officers was being held. Two generals, 17 senior staff officers and 55 other senior officers (all of the German 15th Army) were killed. A week later on 31 October 25 Mosquito VIs of Nos 21, 464 (RAAF) and 487 (RNZAF) Squadrons (led by Wing Commander R. W. Reynolds) attacked and destroyed the Gestapo headquarters at Aarhus in Denmark.

November and December were marked by exceptionally bad weather, however, and this severely restricted Allied air operations by the 2nd Tactical Air Force and reduced many of its makeshift landing grounds to acres of mud which frequently defied every effort by the Field Construction Units

For many years Barnes Wallis had worked on theories about bombs that would be big enough to penetrate the earth and form an 'earthquake' effect. The first production example was the 12,000-lb 'Tallboy' used by Nos 9 and 617 Squadrons on various targets such as bridges, tunnels and *Tirpitz*.

No. 171 Squadron was formed at North Creake in September 1944 in No. 100 Bomber Support Group. Handley Page Halifax MZ971 was part of its original equipment and served with the Squadron until it disbanded in July 1945. The squadron's task was to jam enemy radar by dropping 'Window' and using other devices and tactics.

to overcome with steel matting. However, operating as they were from well-constructed runways in Britain, the heavy aircraft of Bomber Command were not so constrained, and it was at this moment that the strategic bombing forces returned to attack the industries that had originally been defined at Casablanca early in 1943, chief of which was considered to be Germany's shrinking oil industry, particularly the synthetic oil plants, now that her natural supplies from Romania had been lost.

Moreover, Germany had been divested of her vital chain of early warning radar stations, so the task of achieving the necessary pinpoint accuracy by large numbers of heavy bombers attacking by night (many of them now equipped with the GH radio aid in any case) was greatly eased. Accordingly on 14 October 1,063 aircraft of Bomber Command attacked Duisburg in daylight, losing only 15 of their number. The same night 1,005 returned to the city to drop 4,547 tons of bombs on the still-blazing target. Under cover of Window and elaborate diversionary raids on Brunswick, Hamburg and Mannheim, the aircraft destined for Duisburg on this cloudless night approached the German frontier flying at low level over France before climbing up to attack their target. Only after the bombing

had been in progress for some minutes were the German fighter controllers aware of the target, with the result that only one bomber was lost.

This night raid on Duisburg has been singled out for particular mention to illustrate the efficiency with which Bomber Command was now able to operate. The command now possessed sufficient numbers of bombers to launch heavy diversionary attacks to support Main Force raids elsewhere (while 1,005 aircraft were attacking Duisburg, Brunswick was being raided by 233 heavy bombers, a force which two years previously would have represented a major attack). On 25 October 199 Halifaxes, 32 Lancasters and 12 Mosquitoes bombed a synthetic oil plant near Homburg in daylight – without loss; on 1 November the raid was repeated. On two occasions in that month the Wanne Eickel oil plant was heavily attacked, on the night of the 11/12 November the Dortmund oil plant received 1,127 tons of bombs, and on 21/22 November simultaneous heavy raids were sent against the synthetic oil plants at Castrup Rauxel and Sterkrade. But the heaviest raid of this period was flown by 955 bombers against the Krupps works in Essen on 23/24 October, when 4,538 tons of bombs were dropped: incendiary bombs set fire to the giant coal slag heaps near the factory and these were still

Most of Bomber Command became involved in the assault on Europe, even the Yorkshire-based Halifaxes of No. 4 Group. On D-Day itself the Halifaxes of No. 578 Squadron from Burn bombed Hazebrouck.

PD133 was taken off the Manchester production line of Avros and modified into a B.Mk I (Special) in order to carry 'Grand Slam' bombs. It joined No. 617 Squadron at Woodhall Spa in March 1945 and was used on several raids. After the war it went to Lindholme, thence to an MU and was eventually scrapped in May 1947.

smouldering two years later! In November Bomber Command flew no fewer than 15,008 sorties, dropping an astonishing total of 52,845 tons of bombs on oil, U-boat and other priority targets.

Although bad weather had little effect on the ground conditions at British bomber bases, the pervading fogs would have considerably reduced the scale of the above operations had it not been for an ingenious contrivance which had been introduced to assist bomber pilots returning in bad visibility. This was FIDO (Fog Investigation and Dispersal Operations), and it consisted of rows of petrol burners installed beside the runways, which, when ignited, raised the ambient temperature and thereby dispersed the fog sufficiently to allow aircraft to land. Emergency installations were laid down at Fiskerton, Graveley, Carnaby, Woodbridge and Manston, and a measure of their value may be judged from the fact that 1,200 'FIDO landings' were made at Woodbridge alone. (The Woodbridge FIDO runway was inadvertently used to good effect by the enemy on 13 July 1944, when a Luftwaffe Ju 88 landed with the latest German radar aboard; its pilot, who was prevented from destroying the aircraft and its priceless secrets, had thought he was over the Netherlands.)

One of the war's outstanding pinpoint raids was carried out by 31 Lancasters of Nos 9 and 617 Squadrons, carrying 12,000-lb (5443-kg) bombs, on 12 November; led by Wing Commander J. B. Tait, they flew from Lossiemouth in Scotland to Tromsö Fjord in Norway where they successfully hit and sank the mighty battleship *Tirpitz*.

In December the Bomber Command attacks continued unabated, 15,333 sorties being flown against such diverse targets as the Urft and Schwammenauel dams, an enemy troop concentration at St Vith, railway marshalling yards at Rheydt, railway workshops at Opladen, the Polish port of Gdynia, oil plants at Merseburg/Leuna and Scholven-Buer, and a chemical works at Ludwigshafen; losses of 135 aircraft represented less than one per cent of the forces despatched.

It was the bad weather of December that gave

cover for Field Marshal Gerd von Rundstedt's offensive in the Ardennes by 24 infantry and armoured divisions against the Americans in the St Vith/Bastogne area on the 16th. In little over a week, during which the air forces of both sides were prevented from joining the battle, the Germans overran an area of about 1,800 square miles (4700 km²), but on Christmas Eve the weather cleared and British and American heavy bombers were called in to attack enemy troop and armour concentrations as the Allied tactical aircraft ranged over Luftwaffe airfields to prevent enemy air interference over the battlefield. By the end of the year the German offensive had been broken and the deep salient towards Brussels forced back.

The absence of the Luftwaffe over the battlefield was partly explained at first light on New Year's Day, when the German air force staged its last, forlorn though spectacular attack in an attempt to destroy the 2nd Tactical Air Force, which was known to be heavily congested on its airfields. For some weeks preparations had been under way to

From the 'Tallboy' Barnes Wallis developed the 22,000-lb 'Grand Slam' The first of these was dropped by this No. 617 Squadron Lancaster B.Mk I (Special) on the Bielefeld viaduct on 14 March 1945.

In February 1945 the Gloster Meteor F.Mk IIIs of No. 616 Squadron, the first British jet fighter squadron, moved to Melsbroek and began ground-attack missions until the end of March.

On D-Day there were three squadrons of Hawker Tempest Mk Vs, Nos 3, 56 and 486. NV706 joined No. 486 (RNZAF) Squadron before D-Day and served with the squadron throughout its service.

assemble the largest possible number of fighters, fighter-bombers and bombers, together with as many pilots and aircrews as could be spared from other pressing tasks then facing the Luftwaffe. Almost 900 such aircraft took off from their air-fields in Germany and carried out simultaneous attacks on Allied bases over a wide area of France and the Low Countries. Some RAF and American fighters were already in the air and these attempted to catch the raiders, but on the whole the Allies were caught by surprise, and the majority of enemy aircraft that were shot down were accounted for by the light anti-aircraft guns round the airfield perimeters. Considerable damage was done to airfield installations and transport, while one Canadian Typhoon squadron was all but wiped out, together with some 28 RAF Dakotas, 41 American C-47s, 32 Lockheed P-38s and North American P-51s; total Allied losses among aircraft of all types amounted to 224, including 144 in the British and Canadian sector alone.

Whereas the Allied losses could be, and were, made good (the number of combat sorties flown in the week following the attack exceeded those of the previous seven days), those of the Luftwaffe could not and, in the event, proved catastrophic. German records show that 194 aircraft were lost to all causes, but it was the loss of just over 200 aircrew that deprived Germany of a major element of its crucial air defence reserves; for example, almost the entire staff of flying instructors of a key day fighter school was lost in this ill-advised venture.

As the Luftwaffe struggled to eke out its dwind-ling fuel reserves, priority being afforded to those squadrons defending the Reich against the day and night raids of the RAF and USAAF, Bomber Command pursued its own devastating offensive against the German oil industry, assisted now by H2S Mk III radar which provided greatly improved ground definition. In February 1945 62,339 tons of bombs were dropped on this industry alone, which by March was virtually at a standstill.

Dresden controversy

Yet it was over Dresden that two raids evoked bitter controversy that has not abated in the years since the war. The two raids, both on the night of 13/14 February by a total of 773 Lancasters, were carried out in accordance with a plan to assist the Russian forces by attacking centres of transport and munitions, and the fact that the town was packed with refugees from the Eastern Front was considered superfluous in the general conduct of the war at this stage. By the same criterion it was, moreover, no more than unfortunate that Dresden was one of the most beautiful old towns in Europe, and the combination of 2,659 tons of explosive and incendiary bombs not only destroyed the important rail centre and seat of government, but virtually erased the town from the map and killed somewhere between 30,000 and 50,000 people according to various estimates.

The assault on Germany on the ground moved to its conclusion, preceded by Operation 'Clarion', an air operation of extraordinary concept which opened on 22 February and lasted for 24 hours; it involved operations by almost 9,000 aircraft flying

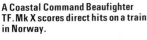

A Coastal Command Beaufighter TF. Mk X scores direct hits on a train in Norway.

The Consolidated Liberator Mk VI was used predominantly by the RAF for Coastal Command duties but a small number joined Bomber Command, being specially equipped to fly jamming and countermeasures missions with No. 223 Squadron from Oulton between August 1944 and the end of the war. TS520 was one such.

from bases in England, France, Belgium, the Netherlands and Italy against every imaginable transport target, from the humble signal box and level crossing to major marshalling yards, over a quarter of a million square miles of Germany. This was the first of a series of major air operations carried out as a preliminary to the crossing of the Rhine, scheduled for 24 March. As that date approached, the job of eliminating all opposition by the Luftwaffe was entrusted to the 70 squadrons of Spitfires, Typhoons, Tempests, Mustangs and Mosquitoes of Nos 83 and 84 Groups.

To lift the 6th British Airborne Division across the river Nos 38 and 46 Groups provided 440 aircraft and gliders, and the 52nd Wing of the US IX Troop Carrier Command supplied 243 aircraft for the British and Polish paratroops. Bomber Command contributed heavy attacks on Essen and Dortmund as medium bombers of the 2nd Tactical Air Force attacked the rail centres at Rheine, Borken, Dorsten and Dülmen. On 14 March No. 617 Squadron dropped 22,000-lb (9979-kg) and 12,000-lb (5443-kg) bombs on the Bielefeld viaduct linking the Ruhr with central Germany, collapsing two of its spans.

Apart from a concentration of enemy anti-aircraft guns near the dropping zone, which had escaped detection and which were still being eliminated as the airborne landings were taking place, the crossing of the Rhine by the British 2nd Army was accomplished with scarcely a hitch and at unexpectedly low cost. In the final surge across Germany, so fast were the squadrons of the 2nd Tactical Air Force advancing from airfield to air-

field (and so scarce was fuel in Germany) that its aircraft were wholly dependent upon petrol, oil and ammunition brought from England by the 280 transport aircraft of Nos 38 and 46 Groups, these Halifaxes, Stirlings and Dakotas returning home with newly-released prisoners of war and wounded soldiers. During April alone the two groups brought home to Britain 27,277 ex-POWs and evacuated 5,986 casualties.

The Elbe, whose crossing had been planned along similar lines to those of the Rhine, proved to be little obstacle and, following the quick fall of

Over the winter of 1944–5 the wings of 2nd TAF had encountered all kinds of weather from mud to snow and fog. In these conditions the Germans made a tremendous effort, on New Year's Day, to attack all 2nd TAF airfields.

On 23 March 1945 the Lancasters of No. 617 Squadron dropped the first 'Grand Slam' bombs on the Bielefeld viaduct. They fell into the ground and caused such tremors that much of the viaduct collapsed.

The most potent Spitfire to enter service during hostilities was the F. Mk 21 which joined No. 91 Squadron at Manston in January 1945. It was mainly used on armed reconnaissances along the Dutch coast. LA224 was part of the squadron's initial equipment.

The squadrons of Bomber Command, which lately had been devastating north Germany, now turned their hands to a different and more amiable task – that of flying home hundreds of prisoners-of-war freed by the end of hostilities.

At the end of the fighting in Europe, victory flypasts were the order of the day. This formation of three dozen Typhoons, forming one of 2nd TAF's wings, is typical.

Bremen, such a scale of operations was unnecessary, being effected by the troops of VIII Corps on 29 April with very little opposition, and none in the air. Apart from a small number of isolated instances (30 Luftwaffe fighters were shot down by the RAF on 30 April), the German air force was virtually incapable of taking to the air, as much beaten in combat as grounded through its shortage of fuel and shattered runways.

It was discovered with some surprise at the end of the war that more than 4,000 brand new aircraft were still awaiting delivery to the Luftwaffe from the factories: the chronic shortage of fuel had prevented their ever leaving the ground. Moreover, it was in other spheres that this lack of fuel had been keenly felt. Though a steady stream of young Germans had come forward to offer themselves for flying duties with their air force throughout the final year of the war (usually in preference to service with the army on the Eastern Front) there existed insufficient fuel to provide their training. Indeed, there had been a slow but steady trickle of aircrew members from the Luftwaffe to the army as unit after unit was disbanded when their combat roles were rendered superfluous by events in Europe. Had the Luftwaffe remained an effective force in being, capable of seriously contesting the Allies' air superiority (which inevitably and irrevocably moved to air supremacy) over Europe in the last year of the war, a stalemate might well have arisen, on the ground, at sea and in the air.

This was the measure of success achieved by Harris' Bomber Command, as well as by the heavy bombers of the USAAF, a policy of all-out attack on the enemy nation, the furtherance of the age-old Trenchard doctrine centred on the strategic bomber.

If the Allied air forces had made a decisive contribution to victory in Europe, which amounted to nothing less than unconditional surrender by the German nation, there was another contribution differing only in scale, so far as the RAF was concerned) to victory over Japan. It is that service's part in the Far Eastern war that now remains to be described.

The War in the Far East

If the British were poorly prepared for war in the Middle East in 1940, the situation in the Far East 18 months later was nothing short of disastrous. Years of parsimony, lack of interest and ignorance had left vast areas destitute of protection even after Japan's emergence as an aggressor power. As the war in Europe and the Middle East made ever-increasing demands for men and materials from the dominions and colonies of the Far East (the supply of which represented desperately vulnerable life-lines) so realisation dawned that in the event of Japan's entry into the war, defence of Allied interests in the whole theatre must come to be centred upon maritime power. Keystone of this power was the great port of Singapore at the southern tip of Malaya.

Commander-in-Chief, Far East, an area which for operational purposes included Hong Kong, Borneo, Malaya, Burma, Ceylon and the Indian Ocean as far as Durban and Mombasa in Africa, was Air Chief Marshal Sir Robert Brooke-Popham, his command extending over all army and air forces in the area. On strict instructions from London, the basis of his policy, in view of his lack of strength, was the avoidance of any provocation of Japan.

To add to Brooke-Popham's difficulties there existed in the Far East an almost total lack of military intelligence, brought about by age-old jealousies between the three services (both British and dominion), so that not only were the Allied forces under strict orders to avoid any provocative contact with the Japanese but were also hopelessly ignorant of the degree of Japanese presence in South East Asia, particularly in the South China Sea, if indeed war should come.

The fall of Singapore and the East Indies

For the defence of Malaya and Singapore early in December 1941 there were just 174 first-line aircraft, of which 54 were Bristol Blenheim Is, 29 Lockheed Hudsons, 23 Vickers Vildebeests, three Consolidated Catalinas and 65 Brewster Buffaloes. These equipped Nos 27, 34, 36, 60, 62, 100, 205 and 243 Squadrons of the RAF, Nos 1, 8, 21 and 453 Squadrons of the RAAF, and No. 488 Squadron of the RNZAF. Seven of these squadrons were based at the four stations on Singapore island and the other six distributed among the airfields of central and northern Malaya. Some 80 serviceable aircraft were held in reserve as replacements.

In the absence of a British aircraft-carrier in the

The principal bomber at the beginning of the Far East fighting was the Bristol Blenheim Mk I, which served with four squadrons, among them No. 60, whose L4911 is seen here in India shortly before the outbreak of war. No. 60 was the sole Blenheim squadron on the Burma front when war broke out.

In the scramble to buy as many aircraft as possible after the beginning of hostilities, Brewster Buffaloes were bought from the USA. Because their performance was too poor for the European theatre they were sent to the Far East, where also they were found to be pretty useless. AN210 was one issued to No. 453 Squadron, RAAF (based in Singapore Island), which fought briefly in the disastrous campaign.

theatre, and with the arrival of the warships *Prince of Wales* and *Repulse* at Singapore, No. 453 Squadron, flying Buffaloes at Sembawang, Singapore, was detailed for fleet defence.

Following a carefully orchestrated display of strength off southern Siam by the Japanese (in an effort to provoke the British into some hostile act) at the beginning of December, Brooke-Popham started patrols by his Hudsons and Catalinas over the South China Sea, and in due course enemy invasion convoys were spotted some 300 miles (480 km) off the Malayan coast, so that when eventually the first Japanese landings at Kota Bharu took place on 8 December some preparations had been made to meet the threat.

Japanese forces assembled for the invasion of French Indo-China, Malaya and the Dutch East Indies included 700 Imperial Army air force aircraft of the 3rd Hikoshidan (air division), and 413 naval aircraft of the 22nd and 23rd Koku Sentai (air flotillas) of the 11th Air Fleet. Among the formidable aircraft of the Japanese air forces were the Mitsubishi A6M2 Zero-Sen naval fighters (codenamed 'Zeke' by the Allies), the Mitsubishi Ki-21 heavy bomber (codenamed 'Sally') and the Kawasaki Ki-48 medium bomber (codenamed 'Lily').

The landings at Kota Bharu effectively drew almost all the RAF resources to northern Malaya, with unsuccessful attacks in bad weather by the Blenheims, Hudsons and Vildebeests on the Japanese fleet. The initial landings were, however, largely a feint to cover the main assault on Singora in Siam, following which the government of that country promptly surrendered. At the same time Singapore itself was suffering the first of many air raids by unescorted Japanese bombers which were scarcely reached by the defending Buffaloes.

The following day the Japanese landed in strength at Kota Bharu and within 12 hours the surviving Vildebeests and Hudsons had been withdrawn from the nearby airfield to Kuantan 180 miles (290 km) to the south. Elsewhere Japanese air attacks on the airfields at Sungei Patani, Penang, Alor Star and Butterworth had destroyed 60 aircraft by use of fragmentation bombs; No. 62 Squadron lost all but two of its Blenheims, and No. 27 all but four. The guns of No. 21 Squadron's Buffaloes had proved defective. During one of the few counterattacks by RAF Blenheims on 9 December, for which only one aircraft was able to leave the ground at Butterworth, the pilot, Squadron Leader A. S. K. Scarf of No. 62 Squadron, pressed home his attack on Singora despite being mortally wounded by enemy fighters; he managed to regain Malayan territory before crashlanding, thereby saving the lives of his crew. His posthumous award of the Victoria Cross was the first of the war in the Far East.

Meanwhile the battleship *Prince of Wales* and battle-cruiser *Repulse* were at sea off the east coast of Malaya investigating reports of the approach by further Japanese invasion convoys. Operating far beyond the range of the Singapore-based Buffalo squadron assigned for their protection, they were spotted by Japanese forces on the 10th and came under attack by 61 torpedo-bombers and 27 bombers of the 22nd Koku Sentai. Both were sunk after sustaining numerous torpedo strikes. Only as the escorting destroyers sought to rescue survivors was No. 453 Squadron able to reach the scene of tragedy, having flown north from Singapore via Kuantan.

In accordance with a pre-arranged plan negotiated with the Dutch, 22 Martin Marylands and nine Buffaloes of the Netherlands East Indies Army Air Corps arrived in Malaya on 9 December,

In Singapore, to combat the main threat of seaborne assault, were two squadrons of outmoded Vickers Vildebeest biplane torpedo-bombers, Nos 36 and 100. Incredibly, they fought valiantly, even managing to sink the odd ship and despite heavy losses No. 36 Squadron, one of whose 'Vildeys' is seen here at practice, continued to fight from Sumatra until all aircraft were lost.

but hardly any further reinforcements were able to reach Singapore for three further weeks. In the meantime, under diminishing air cover, the British army stumbled southwards through the Malayan jungle as one after the other the RAF airfields were overrun.

With no air cover allotted for defence, Hong Kong and Borneo fell to the Japanese on 25 and 26 December respectively, and Brooke-Popham was replaced by Lieutenant General Sir Henry Roydes Pownall as commander-in-chief.

On 3 January 1942 51 Hawker Hurricane Is and IIs in crates arrived at Singapore, together with a couple of dozen pilots from the Middle East. The fighters were hurriedly assembled and on the 10th flew for the first time in defence of the port. Ten days later 27 unescorted Japanese bombers attempted to attack Singapore but lost eight of their number to the Hurricanes. The following day came retribution; the bombers returned with escorting Zero fighters whose pilots shot down five Hurricanes without loss. The RAF fighters, originally destined for the desert skies of the Middle East, were still equipped with tropical air filters, so that their top speed of around 300 mph (483 km/h) was still some 30 mph (48 km/h) less than that of the formidable Zero fighter. Unfortunately Supermarine Spitfires, which might have redressed the balance, were still in such short supply that none could be spared for the Far East.

To add to the troubles of Singapore's air defences, the radar station at Mersing had to be dismantled to prevent it falling into Japanese hands, so that from mid-January onwards no more than 20 minutes' warning of an approaching raid was available; such short notice was barely adequate to allow the defending fighters to reach the height of the attackers. On 15 January General Sir Archibald Wavell assumed supreme command of the forces in the Far East.

On 26 January the Japanese landed in strength at Endau just 100 miles (160 km) to the north of Singapore, effectively preventing any further likelihood of a defence of the Malayan peninsula, and in less than five days the Japanese army had reached the end of the causeway joining Singapore to the mainland. Thereafter the airfields at Tengah, Sembawang and Seletar were subjected to constant artillery fire at a range of no more than 2,000 yards (1830 m).

The final air defence of Singapore was entrusted to the pilots of eight Hurricanes, six Buffaloes and three Fairey Swordfish (the last intended for

gunnery spotting). Already it had been decided to evacuate the island, and for 14 days this tiny force continued to provide what cover it could as the evacuation got under way. On 8 February Japanese forces landed on Singapore island itself and one week later the supposedly impregnable fortress, guarded by huge coastal guns, surrendered; it had been outflanked, not by an assault from the sea, but by an army approaching overland and supported by a vastly superior air force. In little over two months the entire balance of power in the Far East had swung heavily in favour of Japan.

The invasion of Malaya and capture of Singapore were but components of the broader Japanese strategy of southward aggression, on the one hand to secure the southern flank of an invasion of Burma, and on the other to provide a base from which to secure the Philippines and Dutch East Indies.

Sumatra

Long before the final surrender of Singapore Japanese aircraft had been attacking ports and airfields in the huge island of Sumatra, which lies parallel to the Malayan peninsula, but also extends 600 miles (970 km) farther south of Singapore. For three weeks aircraft of the Imperial Army air

Making a show of strength over Singapore Island before the Japanese attack are the Brewster Buffaloes of No. 243 Squadron, RAF.

Another radial-engined aircraft which was pressed into fighting in the Far East was the Curtiss Mohawk. These were taken over from a French order which lapsed when France fell in 1940. Two squadrons in India were thus equipped, Nos 5 and 155, and they served in 1942–3 over Burma, principally on escort duties, until replaced by Hurricanes. This line-up shows aircraft of No. 155 Squadron just after they received their Mohawks.

L8609 was a Bristol Blenheim Mk I built by Rootes and issued at first to the RAF base at Habbaniyah in Iraq. It then passed on to No. 60 Squadron in India, in whose markings it is shown and with whom it fought in the Burma campaign in 1942.

force had been based no more than 70 miles (110 km) from the Sumatran coast. Few airfields existed for use by the Allied air forces, with the result that following the evacuation of the survivors from Malaya, the two best airfields became dangerously congested. These airfields, known as P I and P II, were situated near Palembang in the south of the island, and it was to them that all aircraft reinforcements were ordered. On 26 January 28 Hurricane IIs reached P I from HMS *Indomitable*.

By 13 February, the day on which a Japanese invasion convoy was sighted approaching southern Sumatra, the Allied air forces on the island consisted of some 60 Blenheims and Hudsons of Nos 27, 62, 84 and 211 Squadrons of the RAF, and Nos 1 and 8 Squadrons of the RAAF, as well as about 46 Hurricanes and Buffaloes formed into No. 226 Group under Air Commodore S. F. Vincent. Among the pilots freshly arrived from Britain were those of No. 605 (County of Warwick) Squadron of the Auxiliary Air Force, most of whom had yet to fire their guns in anger.

Despite spirited attacks by the RAF bombers, which sank or badly damaged six Japanese troopships, the seaborne invasion of Sumatra opened on 14 February, accompanied by a paratroop attack on P I, an attack which was vainly opposed by the station commander, Wing Commander H. J. Maguire, with 20 men. The loss of P I resulted in concentration of all aircraft at P II, a secretly constructed airfield of whose existence the Japanese were as yet unaware.

The following day the RAF fighters and bombers launched a continuous series of attacks on the invasion force and succeeded in sinking numerous landing craft, eventually bringing all movement by the enemy to a halt. The Hurricanes also caught a number of Zero fighters on the ground on Banka island, refuelling after having flown off a Japanese carrier, and destroyed about nine. Such achievements demonstrated all too plainly what might have been gained had the peacetime governments provided adequate resources with which to protect their interests in the theatre.

As it was, while the Dutch set about the syste-

matic destruction of all their military installations and equipment to prevent them from falling into enemy hands, the RAF's resources quickly dwindled. The decision was taken to evacuate all Allied forces to Java, a 600-mile long (970-km) island to the south east, and separated from Sumatra by the 30-mile wide (50-km) Sundra Strait. In the panic to leave, orders were given at the embarkation port of Oesthaven to leave behind all transport and equipment, including almost all Hurricane spares and replacement Merlin engines. (As if to underline the premature nature of the evacuation, a party of volunteers from No. 605 Squadron returned to Oesthaven by sea two days later and recovered as much RAF equipment as their ship could carry.)

By 18 February all Allied air forces had left Sumatra and were operating as best they could from the airfields at Semplak, Tjililitan, Andir, Kalidjati and Tjilitjap in western Java. On that day 18 Hurricanes, 12 Hudsons and six Blenheims were all that remained of the RAF and RAAF, apart from the Vildebeests of No. 36 Squadron; the following day five of the Blenheims attacked Japanese shipping at Palembang and set a 10,000-ton transport ablaze. Two days later the Japanese attacked Semplak with 60 escorted bombers and destroyed almost all the surviving Hudsons and three Blenheims.

On 26 February a strongly protected Japanese invasion fleet was sighted in the Strait of Macassar moving towards Java, and following a gallant but vain attempt by the Allied squadron under Rear Admiral Karel Dorman to destroy it (a battle in which the entire Dutch force was lost), the surviving British and American air forces in the theatre were sent in to attack. The RAF contribution comprised the surviving Vildebeests of No. 36 Squadron whose commanding officer, Squadron Leader J. T. Wilkins, who had flown his outdated aircraft continuously since the first Japanese attacks in Malaya, was shot down and killed. (Only two Vildebeests survived, and these were lost a few days later in Sumatra while trying to make their way to Burma.)

Deprived of almost all air cover, the situation of

Two of the three Catalinas of No. 205 Squadron fly along the Malayan coast just before the outbreak of war. After considerable operations before the fall of Singapore, No. 205 Squadron retreated to Ceylon and used its Catalinas over the Indian Ocean until July 1945.

the Allies in Java was never less than critical. The invasion fleet attacked by the Vildebeests proved to be only one of three making for the north coast of the island, and on 1 March these discharged their troops at Batavia, Eretanwetan and Rembang. One by one the airfields were overrun until only Tjilitjap remained from which the Hurricanes of Nos 232 (newly arrived from Britain) and 605 Squadrons continued to oppose the landings. The outcome was inevitable; after a week of fighting (odds against the RAF and RAAF were frequently more than 20:1) the forces in Java which could not contrive to make their way south to Australia laid down their arms in surrender. Almost every fighter was flown until destroyed. A third Hurricane squadron, No. 242, had arrived in Java only to be ordered to combine with the remnants of Nos 232 and 605, but in the end all surviving members and pilots were taken prisoner. A measure of the bestial treatment by the Japanese of their captives during the following three years may be gained by the fact that, of the estimated 14,700 men of the Royal Air Force, Royal Australian Air Force and Royal New Zealand Air Force who fell into Japanese hands in Malaya, Sumatra, Java and later Burma between December 1941 and April 1942, only 3,462 were found alive at the end of the war in 1945.

The loss of Burma

Burma extends south from the foothills of the Himalayas to the neck of the Malayan peninsula, and occupies an area of some 260,000 square miles (673400 km²). Flowing southwards from the Chin, Naga and Shan hills are the great Irrawaddy, Chindwin, Sittang and Salween rivers, between which rise endless mountain and hill ranges, densely carpeted with steamy jungle. Only in the extreme south and along the west coast bordering the Bay of Bengal do plains exist, so that any invading army must perforce advance from south to north (or vice versa) along the river valleys.

Through the great city port of Rangoon had flowed the vital stream of Western aid to China in its five-year fight against Japan, supplies which were carried by the single railway and few well-built roads north to Mandalay and up the Irrawaddy to Lashio where in lorries they joined the winding Burma Road to Kunming, the Chinese terminus.

Realising the strategic importance of Burma itself as a natural barrier against any Japanese threat to the great Indian sub-continent, the British had created a line of defence in the south east along the Salween river, the easternmost of the great rivers, and constructed seven landing grounds in its support; further south landing strips had been hacked out of the jungle at Moulmein, Tavoy, Mergui and Victoria Point, and at Myitkyina in the far north. These preparations were not matched by the presence of modern aircraft, however, and in December 1941 no more than 16 Buffaloes of No. 67 (Fighter) Squadron and 21 Curtiss P-40s of the American Volunteer Group were available, the latter at Kunming in China. There was moreover but one obsolete radar warning unit in the whole of Burma, located east of Rangoon.

To overwhelm this tiny force, the Imperial Army air force assembled 400 fighters and bombers of the 3rd Hikoshidan, and on 23 December 80 bombers escorted by 30 fighters carried out a raid on the crowded and virtually unprotected city of Rangoon; their fragmentation bombs killed 2,000 Burmese and injured more than 6,000 others. Two days later, as the Christian community celebrated Christmas, the bombers returned, this time killing over 5,000 and injuring 16,000. The effect was immediate panic as 100,000 civilians fled north, to be joined by more than half a million others in a bid to gain the assumed safety of India. In due course, after leaving a quarter million dead from cholera, malaria, fatigue and starvation by the wayside, 400,000 disease-ridden survivors reached their goal, having trudged 1,000 miles (1600 km) of stinking jungle. Such was the grisly backcloth to

the enervating campaign that was now to be fought as the Japanese prepared to invade the country.

The Rangoon raid of 25 December cost the Japanese around 20 aircraft, which fell to the guns of the P-40s and Buffaloes. Immediate reinforcements flown to the area included 20 Blenheims of No. 113 (Bomber) Squadron flown direct from the Middle East, and 30 Hurricane Is (these being handed over to No. 67 Squadron). All RAF units were absorbed into a single Group, No. 221, commanded by Air Vice Marshal D. F. Stevenson. Almost as soon as they arrived in south east Burma, the Blenheims were sent out to attack the Japanese base at Bangkok, where they succeeded in destroying about 60 enemy aircraft on the ground, thereby depriving the enemy of total air supremacy. Unfortunately this hurriedly prepared raid, coming on top of a long haul from the Middle East, took its toll of the Blenheims, which had now to be sent north to Lashio for major overhaul which occupied a fortnight.

To the accompaniment of vain attempts to recover air supremacy by repeated use of fighter attacks on the airstrips in the south, the Japanese opened their ground offensive against Burma in mid-January, but with seldom more than a dozen Hurricanes and Buffaloes available at any one time the Commonwealth forces were obliged to give ground and on 19 January Mergui and Tavoy were abandoned, followed 11 days later by Moulmein. Deprived of landing facilities, the RAF was now unable to cover the 600 miles (965 km) of narrow Burmese territory to the south east of Rangoon, and this area was given up to the invaders. More serious was the consequent outflanking of the Salween defence line, now 'enfiladed' from the south.

Meanwhile a Hurricane squadron (No. 17) arrived from Britain together with the vanguard of a Blenheim squadron (No. 45) from the Middle East. Soon deprived of the use of Mingaladon airfield, on the northern outskirts of Rangoon itself, Stevenson realised that no further air defence of the capital was possible and ordered his remaining aircraft (three Buffaloes, 20 Hurricane Is and four P-40s) to be flown to Zigon, a hastily cleared dirt strip 100 miles (160 km) to the north.

On 7 March Rangoon was evacuated and the army struggled north along the valley of the Irrawaddy, closely pursued by the Japanese. By now most of the serviceable aircraft remaining, including those of Nos 17 and 45 Squadrons, were concentrated at Magwe in central Burma as 'Burwing', and at Akyab on the west coast as 'Akwing', the latter comprising No. 67 Squadron with Hurricanes and No. 139 Squadron with Hudsons.

Reconnaissance showed that Japanese aircraft were now using Mingaladon, and on 21 March 10

Such was the shortage of aircraft for the Far East campaign that Hawker Audaxes, including these aircraft of No. 28 Squadron, were withdrawn from policing the North West Frontier of India and used for coastal patrols around Calcutta, and also for a nominal fighter defence of the city.

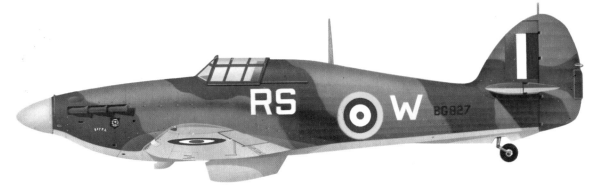

In February 1942 No. 30 Squadron was withdrawn from the Western Desert fighting and embarked on HMS *Indomitable*, landing at Ratmalana (Ceylon) in March 1942. It flew Hurricanes, BG827 amongst them, at first in the defence of Ceylon and then later in the campaign in Burma.

Hurricanes and nine Blenheims of Burwing attacked the airfield and scored their final victory of the campaign, destroying 16 aircraft on the ground and 11 in the air. In revenge 230 Japanese fighters and bombers delivered a series of devastating raids on Magwe, putting paid to all but six Blenheims and 11 Hurricanes, none of which were left in a fit state to fight, however. Following these attacks the Japanese next struck at Akyab, destroying seven Hurricanes and an ancient Vickers Valentia transport. The sole radar warning unit (tediously brought from Rangoon) had been calibrated to cover the south east, but the raiders had approached their targets from the north east.

The final stages of the defeat in Burma were as shortlived as they were dismal. Convinced that nothing could now stem the Japanese advance through Burma, Stevenson was forced to withdraw all but a handful of combat-ready aircraft north to prepare a defence of Calcutta, which would soon fall within range of Japanese bombers. Zigon was abandoned, and Prome fell on 1 April. The surviving pilots and aircraft of Burwing flew to Calcutta in the middle of the month, leaving their groundcrews to make their way back as best they could. Using the 150 lorries still left to them, 344 officers and men collected as much equipment as they could (including the radar warning unit) and set off to Lashio, and eventually arrived at Chungtu in China where, under the name Rafchin,

they spent a year assisting the Chinese by servicing aircraft, training groundcrews and instructing their hosts in operation of the venerable radar unit. The Hudsons in which it was intended to evacuate them never arrived.

Mandalay was evacuated on 30 April, Lashio having fallen the previous day, and a week later Akyab fell to a seaborne assault, the same day that Japanese forces entered Myitkyina in the north. All that could be done was to attempt to alleviate the suffering of the wounded, military and civilian, and the Douglas Dakotas of No. 31 (Transport) Squadron and the American 2nd Troop Carrier Squadron carried 8,616 men, women and children to safety from Magwe, Shwebo and Myitkyina. Token air cover was provided by a small number of Curtiss Mohawks flown at extreme range by No. 5 (Fighter) Squadron from Dinjin 200 miles (320 km) north west of Myitkyina. Among the last to be brought out of Myitkyina was Burma's Governor, Sir Reginald Dorman-Smith, taken out by air in a Hudson sent from India.

As the Japanese advance into northern Burma was slowed and eventually halted by the bursting of the monsoon, the first Burmese campaign ended in May 1942. Meanwhile the Japanese had not neglected to attend to matters in the Bay of Bengal. Air defence over this area had been undertaken by Westland Wapiti and Hawker Audax aircraft of the Indian Air Force Volunteer Reserve (manned

The Hawker Hurricane became the universal operational aircraft in India and on the Burma front. It served as a fighter, bomber escort, ground-attack aircraft, tactical reconnaissance machine, photo-reconnaissance aircraft and bomber. Servicing is taking place on this Hurricane Mk IIB, a tyre being changed and the top engine cowling being removed. This picture shows clearly the tropical filter under the nose of the Hurricane, which enabled it to fly in dusty conditions but cut down its performance.

To assist the RAAF to defend the Australian mainland from a possible Japanese invasion, No. 54 Squadron, a veteran of the Battle of Britain, moved out to Darwin where it set up base in September 1942. LZ846 was one of its Spitfire Mk VCs with which it flew in defence of the mainland and also shot down about a dozen aircraft during Japanese raids there.

by a group of European and Indian businessmen) and was in due course joined by six Hudsons of No. 62 Squadron of the RAF based at Port Blair in the Andaman Islands, reinforced by a flight of Westland Lysanders in February 1942. Until these islands were occupied by the Japanese on 23 March these aircraft had provided protection for Allied shipping in the Bay of Bengal before being withdrawn to Calcutta.

It was known, moreover, that a substantial Japanese naval force was at large in the vicinity of Rangoon, having escorted a convoy of reinforcements thither on 6 April; a number of long-range flying-boats arrived in the Andamans to provide reconnaissance for the fleet, but these were skilfully attacked by the Hudsons of No. 139 Squadron which, despite a formidable screen of defending Zeroes, managed to destroy five and damage 14 as they lay at their moorings.

The loss of Burma gave rise to fears that the Japanese might attempt to invade Ceylon or even India from the sea, and preparations were hurriedly undertaken to strengthen the air defences of Ceylon, where the Royal Navy had established its principal base facilities following the loss of Singapore. No. 222 Group was established at Colombo with two squadrons, No. 273 with Vildebeests and No. 205 with Catalinas, based at Koggala with mooring and fuelling facilities in the Cocos Islands, Christmas Island, the Maldives, the Seychelles and Mauritius. Airfields were constructed at Ratmalana and China Bay in Ceylon, and Hurricane Is and IIs of Nos 30 and 261 (Fighter) Squadrons were brought in by HMS *Indomitable* from the Middle East, being joined later in March 1942 by No. 11 Squadron (with Blenheims) and No. 413 Squadron, RCAF (with Catalinas).

It was a pilot of a No. 413 Squadron Catalina (Squadron Leader L. J. Birchall) who first radioed a sighting of the elusive Japanese fleet 350 miles (560 km) south east of Ceylon on 4 April, but he was never seen or heard of again. The warning proved vital for it confirmed the likelihood of an attack on Ceylon. All naval and merchant ships in the area were ordered to sail and disperse, and at dawn the following day the Japanese struck with 50 Aichi D3A 'Val' dive-bombers escorted by a similar number of Zeroes. Waiting for them were 36 RAF Hurricanes and six Fleet Air Arm Fairey Fulmars. Some 90 minutes later the raid was over; little damage had been done, but 23 Japanese aircraft had been shot down for the loss of 15 Hurricanes and four Fulmars. Elsewhere, however, 36 Japanese Nakajima B5N 'Kates' bombed and sank the cruisers HMS *Cornwall* and *Dorsetshire*.

Three days later 60 Japanese bombers, escorted by Zeroes, attacked the naval base at Trincomalee; their approach was spotted on newly-installed radar and they were met by 17 Hurricanes of No. 261 Squadron and six Fulmars, which shot down 21 of the enemy for the loss of eight Hurricanes and three Fulmars; nine other raiders were destroyed by ground fire. Considerable damage was caused in the naval base, and shortly afterwards the carrier HMS *Hermes*, whose Fulmars were busy defending Trincomalee, was sunk from the air. Unopposed air attacks had also been carried out by Japanese naval aircraft against Coconada and Vizagapatam on the eastern coast of India itself.

Little had been possible to counter the dangerous threat posed by the presence of Vice Admiral Chuichi Nagumo's fleet in the Indian Ocean. The main units of the British fleet were refuelling at Addu Atoll, 700 miles (1130 km) to the south west of Ceylon, and in the first nine days of April the Japanese ships and aircraft had sunk 13 merchant ships, a carrier, two cruisers and two destroyers. True, the Blenheims of No. 11 (Bomber) Squadron launched an attack on the Japanese carrier *Akagi* on the 9th, shooting down four Zeroes but losing five of their own number.

The opposition by the RAF and Fleet Air Arm had nevertheless proved decisive. The Japanese fleet had not suffered the loss of or damage to a single ship, yet the carrierborne air force had been sufficiently depleted to oblige Nagumo to order three of his five carriers home to Japan to replenish crews and aircraft. (Post-war interrogation of Japanese personnel disclosed that among the naval aircrews lost during April 1942 were some of the most experienced veterans of the Imperial Navy.)

There is little doubt that the absence of those three carriers at the Battle of the Coral Sea, fought the following month, was a vital element in deciding the American victory.

The danger to India, 1942-3

When the monsoon rains arrived in 1942, the Japanese Army had all but completed its occupation of Burma, with only a slender area in the extreme north still theoretically held by the British. For months RAF squadrons awaited the expected air attacks on Calcutta, the teeming capital of Bengal, as plans to create a realistic air defence of eastern India matured. Under the administrative command of Air Vice-Marshal A. C. Collier, five groups were established, including No. 222 at Colombo (already mentioned); No. 221 Group, originally based at Rangoon, was re-formed at Calcutta for all bombing and reconnaissance duties; No. 224 was formed to carry out all fighter operations in Bengal and Assam; No. 225 combined all air operations in the south, west, north west and north east India; No. 226 administered all replacements, reinforcements, maintenance and repairs; and No. 227, based at Lahore, was a training group.

The next priority was to increase the number of

In 1943 the ultimate version of the Blenheim, the Mk VA, was used by the bomber squadrons raiding the Japanese in Burma. Setting out on one such raid, with an escort of Hurricanes, is this Blenheim Mk VA, believed to be from No. 11 Squadron.

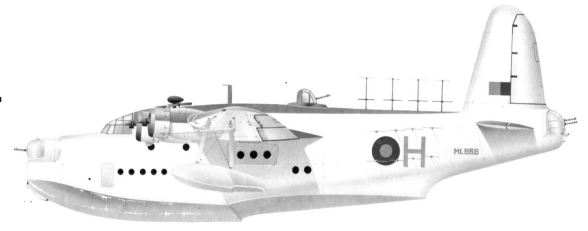

The Short Sunderland joined the Catalina in the Indian Ocean in 1943 and flew maritime patrols. ML868 flew with No. 230 Squadron throughout its service, operating from bases in Ceylon, India and East Africa during 1944 and 1945.

operational squadrons in the theatre, for in March 1942 there had been only five; the preliminary target was 64, but this was increased to 83 by the end of the year. By June there were 26 squadrons, including three with Blenheim IV light bombers (Nos 11, 34 and 110), 12 with Hurricane IIB and IIC fighters and fighter-bombers (Nos 17, 30, 67, 79, 135, 136, 146, 258, 261, 273, 607 and 615), and one (No. 45) with Vultee Vengeance dive-bombers; in addition the small Indian Air Force, comprising six Hurricane squadrons and two of Vengeances, was joining the order of battle. Total serviceable aircraft numbered 401 aircraft, of which almost 100 were held as reserves; more than half the total were Hurricanes.

Another urgent task was to construct a large number of airfields in India (each capable of accommodating two squadrons), for in mid-1942 only 16 existed in an 80,000-square mile (207200-km²) area in the north east, and few of these were adequately drained. In March that year a programme was adopted to construct no fewer than 215 two-runway airfields; within 18 months 275 airfields had been completed, of which 140 possessed two runways, 64 one, and 71 were 'fair-weather' strips. This extraordinary feat of labour and administration is all the more astounding when one recalls that, following a breakdown in negotiations between Sir Stafford Cripps and the Indian Congress Party involving home rule for India, a half-hearted, passive form of rebellion against the British Raj existed in 1942.

Key to Lord Wavell's operations against the Japanese between mid-1942 and mid-1943 was the policy of attack being the best form of defence. By reason of the still small resources at his disposal, such offensive operations as he could perform were of strictly limited nature. His first effort, known as the First Arakan Campaign, was fought between December 1942 and May 1943, its object being to recapture the key airfield at Akyab and clear the Japanese from the Mayu peninsula on the Burmese coast. The land operation failed principally because

the Japanese were quicker to reinforce their forces than the British. Nevertheless the RAF provided excellent support, on the one hand with strafing attacks on enemy-held villages, roads and waterways, and on the other with air supply by Dakotas of the forward troops. During the closing stages of the campaign the Japanese attempted a heavy raid on the important airfield at Chittagong, but were turned back by defending Hurricanes. (One was flown by Wing Commander, later Group Captain, F. R. Carey: Frank Carey had until recently commanded No. 135 Squadron but despite promotion, continued to fly operational sorties. He was one of the highest-scoring RAF pilots in the Far East and was officially credited with 28 air victories during the war.)

While the First Arakan Campaign was in progress another remarkable operation was being carried out in the Burmese interior. Led by Brigadier Orde Wingate, seven columns of jungle-trained troops, known as Chindits, set out from Imphal with orders to create confusion and alarm far behind the Japanese front. Success or failure depended wholly on the sustaining of these columns from the air, a task given to the Dakota crews of Nos 31 and 194 Squadrons. Often flying low over the dense jungle-clad hills and valleys at night, these pilots were almost entirely without radio aids and were briefed to watch for the flares lit on the ground to mark their dropping points. The Chindits slogged 1,000 miles (1600 km) through northern Burma, destroying roads, railways and bridges before the 1943 monsoon arrived in June, effectively preventing further operations on the entire front.

By then, however, the air force had grown to 53 squadrons, of which 39 were fully operational, including 17 fighter, seven bomber, nine general reconnaissance, one photo reconnaissance, two transport and three IAF squadrons on the north west frontier. Hurricanes continued to arrive in India in ever-increasing quantities and these replaced the ageing Blenheims on the light bomber

Without the Dakota the war in the Far East could not have been so successfully accomplished. The squadrons in India flew the air routes to cover the vast distances for bringing up supplies and then spent many hours operationally dropping supplies to the troops in the jungle and the chindits miles behind the Japanese lines.

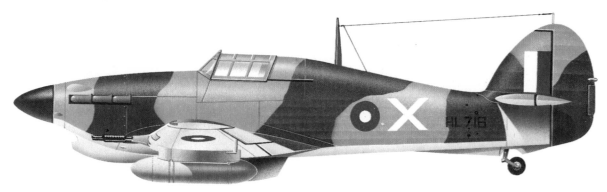

The ubiquitous operational RAF aircraft throughout 1943, 1944 and into 1945 was the Hawker Hurricane, the Mk IIC predominating in the latter stages with its four 20-mm cannon armament and long-range tanks.

squadrons (Nos 11, 34, 42, 60 and 113). In October 1943, the first Spitfire Mk Vs arrived and were issued to Nos 136, 607 and 615 Squadrons.

At the end of the year South East Asia Command came into being, a unified command embracing all British Commonwealth and American forces under the supreme leadership of Admiral the Lord Louis Mountbatten. Commanding the air forces was Air Marshal Sir Richard Peirse, his deputy being Major General George Stratemeyer of the USAAF; the air forces comprised the RAF in India, and the US 10th Air Force, and was further divided into a Tactical Air Force under Air Marshal Sir John Baldwin, a Strategic Air Force commanded by Brigadier General Howard Davidson, USAAF, and Troop Carrier Command under Brigadier General D. Old, USAAF.

When SEAC was created its air force comprised 48 RAF and 17 American squadrons with a total of 1,105 aircraft, of which some 900 were of modern vintage; a further 640 second-line and reserve aircraft were also on charge in India; modern replacements were arriving in the theatre at a rate of about 200 every month from Britain, America and Australia. Against the Allies were ranged about 750 Japanese aircraft, of which half were modern fighters, bombers and reconnaissance aircraft deployed in Burma with the remainder in Malaya, Sumatra and Indo-China.

The reconquest of Burma

Like Wavell before him, Mountbatten decided to engage in a number of limited offensive campaigns in northern Burma before the major undertaking of rooting out the Japanese from the whole country, a task realised as still being beyond the capabilities of his resources.

Once more, as preparations went ahead for a second attempt to capture Akyab, the RAF air defences in and around Calcutta were put to the test as the Japanese resumed their attacks. Now however, with Spitfires among the defending squadrons, the raiders suffered heavily: for example, a force of 60 aircraft which attacked shipping off the Arakan coast on 31 December 1943 lost 12 to the Spitfires of No. 136 Squadron.

In due course the enemy introduced heavy fighter escorts, but the balance was redressed with the arrival of Nos 81 and 152 Squadrons with the excellent Spitfire VIII whose performance and maximum speed of 419 mph (675 km/h) was markedly superior to that of the Japanese Nakajima Ki-44 'Tojo' fighter.

The Second Arakan Campaign opened in November 1943 as units of XV Corps set out down the Mayu peninsula; once more they were sustained by the Dakotas of No. 62 Squadron, while Consolidated Liberators, North American Mitchells, Bristol Beaufighters, Hurricanes and Vickers Wellingtons maintained constant attacks on Japanese reinforcements being hurried to the area, many attacks being launched as far afield as Rangoon and Bangkok.

As Maungdaw fell to XV Corps on 9 January 1944, a second thrust was launched southwards in eastern Arakan by the 81st West African Division towards Kyauktaw, an enterprise also wholly dependent on supplies delivered by air. Once more the Japanese reacted vigorously and by superhuman efforts managed to contain the coastal

advance at Sinzweya, where the 7th Indian Division was encircled, despite the seaborne landing of the 5th Indian Division at Maungdaw. The situation remained critical throughout February and victory for the Japanese seemed imminent as the Allied transport squadrons (temporarily assisted by Curtiss C-46s diverted from operations over the 'Hump' to China) mounted a tremendous effort to fly supplies to the beleaguered force; in 26 days over 2,100 tons of food and ammunition were airdropped for the loss of only one Dakota thanks to the air cover provided by RAF Spitfires and Hurricanes.

Fortunately at the height of the crisis in the Arakan the Japanese commander, Lieutenant General Hanaya, chose this moment to open his major offensive in the north, aimed at an invasion of India, thereby relieving the pressures in the Mayu peninsula. Thus, unlike the campaign of a year earlier, although Akyab remained uncaptured XV Corps was able to consolidate the gains made, retaining its hold on Maungdaw. The victory at Sinzweya, a victory of survival made possible only by Peirse's all-out supply achievement, was regarded as the first decisive victory of the Burma campaign.

Hanaya's plan was to split the British front by attacking westwards to capture Chittagong, thereby isolating the forces in the Arakan; a month later the Japanese were to attack and capture the bases at Imphal and Dimapur and sever the lines of communication through Assam. In preparing these plans, however, the Japanese general overlooked one vital factor: that air superiority had been firmly wrested by the Allies.

The survival of the predominantly Indian and West African forces in the Arakan effectively preempted the Japanese plan to attack towards Chittagong, and RAF reconnaissance disclosed enemy preparations for a major attack along the Chindwin river towards the main base at Imphal. The attack by two Japanese divisions opened on 8 March, and for many days the situation was serious. The 17th Indian Division was ordered to with-

It was in 1944 that the build-up in forces in India and re-equipment with more modern aircraft presaged the ability to strike back at the Japanese. Amongst the most successful of the aircraft was the Spitfire Mk VIII, which equipped many of the fighter squadrons, such as No. 152, which had moved out east from the Mediterranean theatre. The squadron was distinctive in painting its leaping panther badge around the roundel. The squadron's commander, Squadron Leader G. Kerr, DFC shows what the well-dressed RAF pilot wore for operations in the steamy atmosphere of Burma.

Another purchase from the USA which found its way to the Far East was the Vultee Vengeance dive-bomber. It equipped four RAF squadrons and was used for all forms of bombing on the Burma Front until replaced both by Hurricanes and Mosquitoes.

draw from Tiddim, but delayed doing so for five days during which it was cut off when the Japanese cut the Tiddim-Imphal road. When it was found that insufficient aircraft were available to evacuate the division by air, Mounbatten once more requested aircraft from the China supply route, not to evacuate the Tiddim forces but to support them by lifting the 5th Indian Division from the Arakan to Imphal, a task in which No. 194 Squadron also participated. Such a bold stroke almost certainly saved the situation at Imphal and involved 758 sorties and the delivery of 3,056 men, their weapons, ground transport, ammunition and supplies.

The gateway to India was thus guarded by the 5th, 17th and 20th Indian Divisions in the Imphal area (by April invested by the Japanese 15th and 33rd Divisions) and the 33rd Indian Division which marched from Dimapur to Kohima only to be surrounded there by the Japanese 31st Division. In addition to the constant flow of air supplies brought up by the British and American Dakotas, four Hurricane fighter-bomber squadrons and four of Vengeance dive-bombers flew repeated sorties against the enemy, covering the lumbering Dakotas and bombing Japanese transport and armour as it strove to reach the battle areas. Some measure of the scale of task undertaken by the air forces may be judged by the fact that no fewer than 150,000 Allied soldiers were in contact with the enemy in the Imphal-Kohima area, and the nearest railhead was 138 miles (222 km) distant; 400 tons of supplies had to be air-dropped daily into a valley totally dominated by enemy guns.

Meanwhile a Second Chindit Expedition was being mounted in northern Burma in concert with other long-range thrusts by ground forces. Their purpose was to sever the main supply routes feeding the Japanese forces opposing Lieutenant General Stilwell's American-Chinese columns advancing south from Ledo. One and a half brigades were airlifted in Dakotas and gliders and set down on a landing strip previously cleared in the jungle 60 miles (96 km) south west of Myitkyina between

5 and 11 March; half a brigade was lifted to a strip 80 miles farther south (130 km), and two other brigades to a strip close to the Rangoon-Myitkyina railway. In six days 9,052 men, 175 ponies, 1,183 mules and over half a million pounds of stores were carried from India to places 150 miles (240 km) behind the Japanese lines in Burma. Not one Dakota, and only nine gliders, were lost. Another unique feature of the campaign lay in the evacuation of the wounded, for which helicopters (American-operated Sikorsky Hoverflies) were employed for the first time, while Short Sunderland flying-boats alighted on the Indawgyi Lake to remove 537 casualties.

Battle of the 40 Hairpin Bends

It had been hoped to capture Myitkyina at the outset, for this would have effectively sealed the fate of enemy forces in the north, but the Japanese contrived to withstand all assaults for more than two months, albeit suffering casualties since estimated at more than 20,000 in dead and wounded. However, the efforts of the long-range penetration columns which continued throughout April, May and June 1944, contributed no less to the final defeat of the Japanese 15th Army than the direct clash of arms in the north.

In the malaria-infested Kabaw Valley was fought what came to be known as the Battle of the 40 Hairpin Bends; having first destroyed the bridges over every chaung (stream) and river, the Hurricane fighter-bombers sprayed the whole length of road with DDT before the Allied troops went in to the attack. By 22 June the road between Imphal and Dimapur had been re-opened by the British 2nd Division.

The whole nature of the war in Burma had undergone complete change. As captured enemy soldiers complained of disease, starvation, shortage of weapons and ammunition and absence of air cover, the Allied army was now highly organised, well supplied and enjoyed almost total air protection. The stage was now set for the re-conquest of

The RAF and USAAF combined in India to provide a massive airlift support to all the forces in the area. Both C-47 Dakotas and C-46 Commandos were used both tactically and on the 'Hump' route, flying supplies over the mountains into China.

The Republic Thunderbolt became the long-range escort and strike fighter for the RAF in 1944, extending the range of such operations considerably. This Mk II (HD247) served with No. 79 Squadron during 1945.

Burma.

In July that year Peirse had at his disposal 64 RAF, SAAF, RCAF and IAF squadrons, and 26 of the USAAF. Of these, 34 fighter and fighter-bomber squadrons flew Hurricanes (the Hawker Hurricane remained numerically the most widely used aircraft in the Far East; at this time it equipped Nos 5, 11, 20, 28, 34, 42, 60 and 113 Squadrons of the RAF, and Nos 1, 4, 6 and 9 Squadrons of the Indian Air Force), Spitfires, Beaufighters, Curtiss Warhawks, North American Mustangs, Lockheed Lightnings and Republic Thunderbolts; 23 bomber squadrons flew Liberators, Wellingtons, Lockheed Venturas, Mitchells and Vengeances; 12 transport squadrons flew Dakotas and Hudsons; 11 maritime reconnaissance squadrons flew Catalinas and Sunderlands; five photo-reconnaissance squadrons flew Spitfires, de Havilland Mosquitoes, Mitchells, Lightnings, Warhawks and Liberators; and two torpedo-bomber squadrons flew Bristol Beauforts and Beaufighters. In addition there were two special duties squadrons (Nos 357 and 628) flying Hudsons, Lysanders, Liberators and Catalinas, and an air-sea rescue squadron (No. 292) flying Vickers Warwicks.

Instead of abandoning all air and land operations during the monsoon season, as had occurred in the two previous years, Mountbatten and Peirse determined to keep up the pressure on the Japanese, this despite the fact that in the rains of 1944 175 in (444.5 cm) fell in northern Burma and 500 in (1270 cm) in Assam.

But before describing the final campaign in Burma it is convenient here to give passing mention to a minor event in the RAF's participation in the Far Eastern war.

Following the inexorable Japanese advance through the East Indies in 1942, fears were expressed for the safety of Australia itself. As political wrangling centred around demands for the return home of Australian forces for the defence of their homeland, No. 54 (Fighter) Squadron was despatched with Spitfire Mk Vs from Britain in June

1942, arriving at Richmond, NSW, in September. By early 1943 the squadron was based at Darwin in time to intercept Japanese raids against the Australian mainland, destroying about a dozen enemy aircraft in the first three months.

Two other squadrons (Nos 548 and 549) were formed at the end of 1943 and were given Australian-built Spitfire Mk VIIIs early in 1944; these were found to include faulty materials which suffered severe corrosion, so that little operational flying was undertaken when the squadrons arrived at Darwin. No. 54, also re-equipped with Spitfire Mk VIIIs in April 1944, fared better and eventually took the offensive with ground-attack sorties against Tepa and other targets in southern Indonesia until the final summer of the war.

As further modernisation of RAF squadrons continued during the latter half of 1944 (Thunderbolts replaced some of the Hurricanes, Vengeances gave way to Mosquitoes, and Liberators replaced Wellingtons), so the senior air commands underwent change. It had been intended that Peirse should hand over to Leigh-Mallory in November, but when the latter was killed in an air crash on his way out from Britain, command passed temporarily to Air Marshal Sir Guy Garrod and eventually, on 23 February 1945, to that magnificent commander Air Marshal Sir Keith Park (who had headed the vital No. 11 Group during the Battle of Britain and was the air officer commanding RAF Malta in the island's perilous days of 1942–3; before his appointment in the Far East he had been Air Officer Commanding-in-Chief in the Middle East).

By August the Allied ground forces were ready with preparations to assault the line of the Chindwin river as Wellingtons and Mitchells sowed mines to prevent movement by Japanese river traffic, and Beaufighters sought out enemy road and rail transport moving through the steaming jungles; and all the while the ubiquitous Dakota droned overhead, bringing up ammunition, food and mail to the forward troops. Tiddim was cap-

Far left: Towards the end of the war the Hurricane was carrying eight unguided rockets under its wings and, operating from forward strips in Burma, had great success on the Mandalay front.

Left: Setting out from its base in Ceylon for a lonely patrol over the Indian Ocean is this Sunderland Mk III of No. 230 Squadron. The 'goalpost' radar aerials are clearly visible above the fuselage as well as others on the fuselage side and under the wingtips.

KH224 was a Consolidated Liberator Mk VI which served over Burma with No. 356 Squadron in 1945. The Far East bomber squadrons of the RAF used different pattern markings on the rudders to denote the different units, No. 356's being this white cross.

Far right: Towards the end of the war the standard RAF bomber in the Far East was the Consolidated Liberator Mk VI. With its long range it was able to strike far behind the Japanese lines at supply dumps and enemy installations. This aircraft, from No. 356 Squadron, is dropping 12 1,000-lb (454-kg) bombs on a target amidst the hilly jungle typical of the Burmese/Malayan frontier.

tured on 19 October; Fort White followed on 9 November and Kalemyo on the 14th. The Chindwin was crossed at Kalewa, Mawlaik and Sittaung. The Japanese had been driven from the mountains into the plains, where Lieutenant General W. J. Slim's armour could be used to the full under a veritable umbrella of air power as the rains abated.

The campaign that followed was one which, so far as the air force was concerned, involved operations not only in the immediate vicinity of the land battle, which itself occupied a front of over 180 miles (290 km), but as far south as Bangkok and Rangoon, and even Malaya, and into the Indian Ocean. Now that the superb long-range Mustang fighter was available, fighter sweeps could be mounted against Bangkok, where 31 Japanese aircraft were destroyed in a single raid 780 miles (1250 km) from the nearest Allied base; in European terms this was equivalent to a flight from Britain to Vienna, but almost entirely over featureless terrain and in conditions of treacherous tropical weather.

The bombers, of which the bulk were now Liberators which could reach the Malay peninsula with a round trip of 2,800 miles (4500 km), were tasked with four main duties: to prevent enemy reinforcements from moving along the 5,000 miles (8000 km) of railways in Burma (in particular the infamous Bangkok-Moulmein line which had been built by Allied prisoners of war at a cost of 24,000 lives) with attacks on junctions and bridges; to attack reinforcements moving into Burma with raids on the main ports as well as on the shipping itself; to destroy concentrations of enemy stores and munitions; and to saturate areas of the battlefield itself with bombs at the behest of the ground forces. One squadron of Liberators was employed to lay mines in enemy waters.

As the remaining Hurricanes undertook bombing, rocket-firing and anti-tank duties, Spitfires, Warhawks and Thunderbolts ranged the skies to keep watch against any attempt by the Japanese to interfere with the land battle; but the enemy air force had been reduced to a doubtful strength of no more than 200 of all aircraft types in the theatre, and appearances by this small force were rare.

Further afield the photo-reconnaissance squadrons not only paid frequent visits to Rangoon, Bangkok, Sumatra, Singapore and Java, but also completed a photo survey of the whole of Burma. The Mosquito, on which much of the long-distance work depended, surprisingly proved something of a disappointment, its wooden construction and bonding glues being found to decompose in the clammy heat of the jungle tropics.

At sea the flying-boat and other coastal squadrons ranged far and wide over the Bay of Bengal and Indian Ocean, an area twice as great as that of the North Atlantic. True, they never sank a Japanese submarine in this area, but closer to the enemy-held coast of Burma they disposed of countless small Japanese craft slinking between river mouths, and by February 1945 the coastal Beaufighters had accounted for 700 such vessels. Postwar Japanese records indicate that more than 40,000 casualties were suffered from air attacks during the final Burma campaigns.

And all the time an army of 300,000 men was supplied and sustained by the Dakotas of the Combat Cargo Task Force, formed in October 1944 under Brigadier General Frederick W. Evans, USAAF; this force at no time comprised more than nine RAF and eight USAAF squadrons.

The reconquest of Burma opened on three fronts, in the north west by forces commanded by General Stilwell (soon to be recalled to Washington after disagreements with Generalissimo Chiang Kai-shek), in the centre by the 14th Army driving south towards Mandalay and eventually Rangoon, and on the west coast by XV Corps. On 2 January 1945 the town of Akyab, which had for so long defied capture, fell to XV Corps without a shot, although when six Japanese aircraft appeared on the scene shortly afterwards five were shot down by patrolling Spitfires. Three weeks later, preceded by a smokescreen laid by Hurricanes and covered by Thunderbolts, Mitchells and Spitfires, a successful amphibious assault was made on Ramree Island, 70 miles (112 km) south of Akyab.

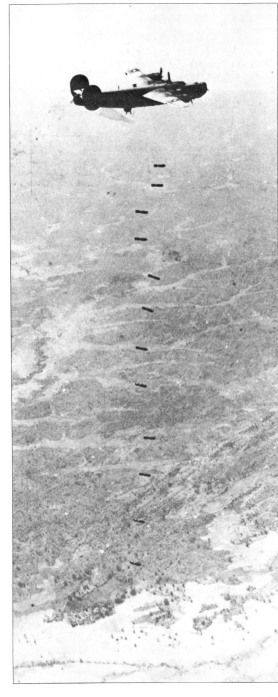

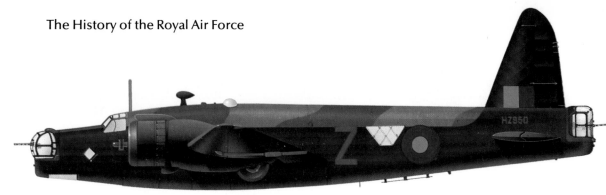

Before the advent of the Liberator the bomber offensive had valiantly been maintained by two squadrons of Vickers Wellingtons, Nos 99 and 215. This Wellington Mk X (HZ850) served with No. 99 Squadron during the Imphal fighting in 1944 and was used for bombing raids in this operation.

On the central front the 14th Army was across the Irrawaddy at Thabeikkyin and Singu, and by February was poised to bring the Japanese to main battle on the Shwebo plain near Mandalay. Already Hurricanes were operating from jungle strips only 8 miles (13 km) behind the forward troops, and proved the most effective of all aircraft with their pinpoint accuracy of attack on enemy bunkers and transport. Despite elaborate attempts to conceal their armour, the Japanese suffered the loss of almost all their tanks at Myinmu on 19 February when Hurricane pilots attacked a number of suspicious-looking objects, revealing the presence of the armoured vehicles. This action proved decisive in establishing a bridgehead over the Mu river and, despite desperate resistance by the Japanese, opened the way to Mandalay. In the battle for this, Burma's second city, the great Fort Dufferin was attacked by bomb- and rocket-carrying Thunderbolts, Hurricanes and Mitchells which blasted 26 breaches in the immensely thick earthen walls, employing the Master Bomber technique. On 21 March the city fell as Japanese resistance in the surrounding plains crumbled.

The race to the south was as much a race against the arrival of the monsoon as against a ruling by the American Chiefs of Staff to the effect that much of the Allied air transport strength would be withdrawn from Burma for deployment elsewhere by 1 June. If the port of Rangoon could be captured by that date, the dependence upon air supply would in any case be superfluous.

With such incentive for speedy victory in mind, the advance south by IV Corps from Meiktila started on 12 April and within three weeks had covered 250 miles (400 km), and when the airfield at Lewe fell to the advancing troops dismantled bulldozers were brought in by gliders to assist in the work of repairing the shattered railways; and when these had been repaired, 18 locomotives, also in transportable components, were brought up in Dakotas. Nothing to match this scale of supply by air has ever been achieved, before or since, in the history of warfare.

Rangoon eventually fell to a combined air and sea attack. On 1 May a battalion of Gurkha para-

troops was flown from Akyab and landed south of the port at Elephant Point, and on the following day a seaborne landing was made by the 26th Indian Division under heavy air cover. By the time it reached the city itself on the 3rd, the Japanese had fled. That day the monsoon broke!

The 14th Army was still some 30 miles (48 km) to the north, but it was but a matter of a week or two before the whole of central Burma was cleared of organised enemy resistance. A final desperate battle was fought early in July around Nyaungkashe at the mouth of the Sittang river, but once more the efforts of the Spitfire and Thunderbolt pilots, flying 'cab rank' patrols overhead, were largely instrumental in ensuring victory. Thereafter it remained for the Burmese guerrillas throughout the country, who had for many months been sustained by the aircraft (among them Lysanders) of the Special Duties Squadron, to winkle out the isolated pockets of fanatical Japanese troops. Between November 1944 and May 1945 these two squadrons had delivered 2,100 tons of supplies to the guerrillas and dropped a thousand agents.

Victory in Burma was complete by the end of July. It was a victory won by the 356,000 men of the Commonwealth armies wading and hacking their tortuous path through dense malarial vegetation, fighting a ferocious, often unseen enemy; yet

Known by the Japanese as 'Whispering Death', the quiet Bristol Beaufighter Mk Xs serving in the Far East were most effective as low-level strike aircraft with bombs and rockets, principally against the considerable river traffic on the jungle river arteries. With little room on the forward airstrips, this 'Beau' pilot has to land on a small strip edged on each side by aircraft dispersed and undergoing maintenance.

Seen with the aircraft it replaced (the Hawker Hurricane) these Thunderbolts taxi out on an airstrip in Burma. Eight 0.5-in (12.7-mm) machine-guns and long-range tanks enabled them to provide a fighter escort for bombing raids far into Japanese territory.

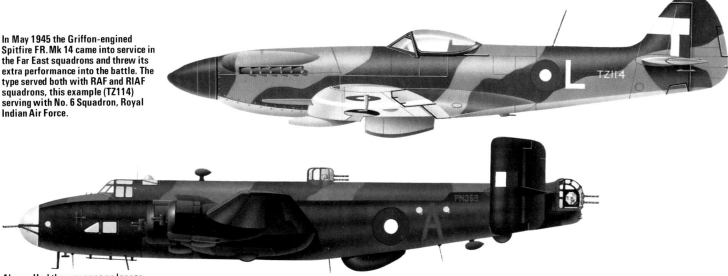

In May 1945 the Griffon-engined Spitfire FR. Mk 14 came into service in the Far East squadrons and threw its extra performance into the battle. The type served both with RAF and RIAF squadrons, this example (TZ114) serving with No. 6 Squadron, Royal Indian Air Force.

Above: Had the war gone on longer, the Handley Page Halifax would have served in the Far East in greater numbers. Precursor of such an influx was No. 1341 Flight, which served in India on transport support duties from February 1945 onwards. This Halifax Mk IIIA (PN369) was part of its equipment.

Right: Much of the ability to find the right enemy targets amongst the jungle-covered areas of Burma, Siam and Malaya was due to the excellent photo coverage provided by Nos 681 and 684 Squadrons, the former flying Spitfires and the latter Mosquitoes. This Mosquitoe PR. Mk XVI of No. 684 Squadron takes off on a mission in 1945.

The standard interceptor in the Far East during the closing stages of the war was the Spitfire Mk VIII, seen here with No. 607 Squadron. The pilots must have found the walk back to their huts as hazardous as the actual flights, so basic were the conditions on the airstrips during the monsoon period.

glimpsed overhead through the jungle canopy flew the victorious fighters, bombers and transports of the British and American air forces, whose pilots and crews had striven to achieve a skill in locating and destroying that enemy and his tools of war. No other victory in World War II had made such demands on an air force; nowhere else were the demands so desperate; and nowhere else were they so completely satisfied.

The Burma campaign of 1944–5 cost the Japanese some 180,000 casualties, the greater proportion of them killed – for that was the fighting nature of the enemy. The balance sheet of achievement was impressive indeed. In 15 months the RAF element of Eastern Air Command had dropped 36,000 tons of bombs, 900 enemy aircraft had been destroyed, and the transport aircraft had lifted 600,000 tons of supplies to the front.

By now of course the war against Germany was over. The full might of the Allied war machine was to be turned against Japan. As preparations went ahead to deliver final, horrific retribution against her cities, the Royal Air Force completed plans to despatch numerous wings and squadrons from Europe to the Far East, and preparations went ahead for the recapture of Malaya and Singapore. In the event all this proved to be unnecessary as first one, and then a second atomic bomb fell from the skies over Nippon scarcely a week after victory had been won in Burma.

On 14 August 1945 Japan accepted the Allied demand for unconditional surrender.

The Aftermath of War

One of the decisions on defence taken by the British government in the immediate post-war years was to become of paramount importance. In January 1947 the research needed to develop an atomic weapon was given official sanction and the necessary funds were made available. Opinion in favour of taking this step had been hardening among the government's inner circle of advisers throughout the previous 12 months, three main arguments being advanced.

First of these arguments was the notion that atomic weapons could provide a means of avoiding the long drawn-out campaigns which had been a prominent feature of the recent war; second, that as the United States was proceeding with its own atomic research and the Soviet Union would almost certainly possess atomic weapons within a matter of years, Britain too must develop them for if she did not, and if the new United Nations organisation failed to provide the security she needed, the consequences could be catastrophic; and third, that the best defence against nuclear attack was the deterrent effect of possessing the means to retaliate, or as Sir Winston Churchill restated the argument in a speech to the House of Commons in December 1954: 'Safety and even survival must be sought in deterrents rather than defence.'

Eight years earlier, however, atomic weapons and the aircraft needed to deliver them had been almost a decade away from squadron service, and the government had still to reach a final decision on the size and shape of Britain's armed forces in the meantime. That decision was taken a few months later in the autumn of 1947, when it was announced that defence expenditure was to be limited to some £600 million per year (a considerable sum at the time, and more than 6 per cent of Britain's gross national product) but much less than the services had hoped. Indeed, the RAF would now receive only £173 million for the year 1948–9, compared with £255 million for 1946–7 and £214 million for 1947–8.

Disappointing though these new restrictions might be, there was some consolation for the RAF in the government's declared policy. As the Defence Minister, A. V. Alexander, explained to the House of Commons in October 1947, the first priority was to fund the research needed to develop the weapons of the future; the second was 'to maintain the structure of the RAF and its initial striking power', a commitment which was renewed four months later in the 1948 Defence Statement. The Royal Navy, as protector of Britain's sea communications, came next in order of priority, with the Army following after the RN.

In the context of Britain's financial and industrial weakness in the aftermath of World War II

Right: With the war over, the RAF dwindled rapidly and the vast numbers of aircraft which had been in service and had rolled off the production lines were very surplus to requirements. Most of them were flown to Maintenance Units where they were stored in the open until they could be scrapped. High Ercall in Shropshire was one such MU and in this aerial photograph of the base there are 770 aircraft on the field. One airfield thus held more than the entire RAF of the 1980s.

Below: Within a few weeks of the end of the war with Japan, a victory flypast was organised over London. Prominently in the lead was Group Captain Douglas Bader back from POW camp and with a fine set of tin legs, who led in his personal Spitfire. He is seen here at North Weald with Air Chief Marshall Lord Dowding, former chief of Fighter Command.

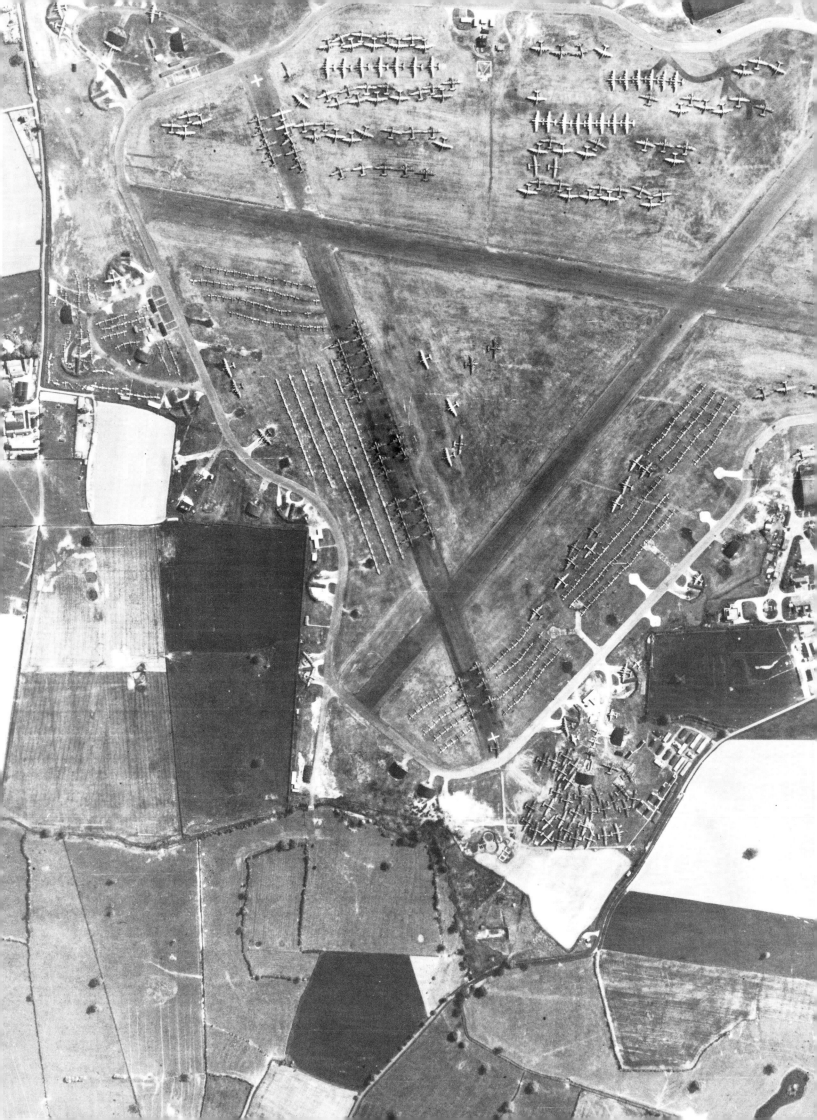

the decision to limit defence expenditure and establish these priorities was inevitable. What made it acceptable, even to the services, was the assumption, endorsed by the government, that a major war was unlikely in the five years to 1952, and hardly more likely in the following five years.

For the RAF, government policy inevitably meant a concentration on essentials: on developing the resources of Bomber and Fighter Commands, and to a lesser extent those of Coastal Command, to the detriment of other elements, particularly Transport Command. In contrast, the Air Staff had long proposed a broader base to the permanent peacetime air force. This was to include a sizeable transport element, one of whose roles would be to give substance to the concept of squadron mobility, now widely advocated as the best means of reducing the RAF's dependence on elaborate and expensive overseas bases. Even the memorandum accompanying the 1948–9 Air Estimates, the first to be issued after the government's decision on defence expenditure, acknowledged its importance but failed to offer the air transport backing needed to make it fully effective.

'Plan E'

The Air Staff plan for a broadly based air force had emerged from the detailed discussions begun four years earlier in September 1943. Over the intervening years a number of plans had been produced, but none had been given official sanction and none was based on any clear indication of what resources would be available and what responsibilities the post-war RAF would be expected to undertake. Plan E, however, which emerged in the summer of 1947 just before the government's pronouncement on defence expenditure, was believed by the Air Staff to be adequate for immediate needs, while at the same time providing the structure upon which the permanent peacetime air force could be built and from which it could expand when the necessary resources became available.

Plan E proposed a front-line target of 165 squadrons or about 1,500 aircraft, including 51 fighter squadrons (536 aircraft), 41 bomber squadrons (328 aircraft), 13 maritime squadrons (84 aircraft) and 42 transport squadrons (341 aircraft). Most of this front-line strength would be retained in the UK, but 24 squadrons would be based in Germany, 18 in the Middle East and a further 18 in the Far East. The plan also proposed a strategic reserve with a high inbuilt mobility factor which would enable it to reinforce overseas theatres at short notice should the need arise. For the moment this reserve was to consist of 12 squadrons: three short-range fighter (48 aircraft), four heavy bomber (32 aircraft) and five medium-range transport (40 aircraft). More squadrons might be added later.

When the Air Staff began to trim the Plan E target to meet the new limit on defence spending, the main victim was the transport force, which was to lose eight long-range, 96 medium-range and 24 airborne forces aircraft out of its planned front-line strength of 341 aircraft. In addition, the heavy bomber element was to be reduced by 16 aircraft, the maritime force was to lose all four of its strike squadrons, and the AOP element was to be cut from 112 aircraft to 35; only the fighter force was to survive virtually intact. It was also made clear that when additional resources became available in perhaps two or three years, they would be used to strengthen the fighter and bomber elements and not to restore the cuts in Transport Command and AOP.

Manpower problem

These were, in fact, particularly difficult years for the planners. Whatever they might propose and whatever the government might sanction, the size, shape and operational efficiency of the RAF would depend in large measure on the availability of trained manpower. The government's determination, however, to keep faith with the principle of demobilisation by age and length of service, as laid down by its predecessor, and so to provide the men and women needed to revitalise British industry, had produced a manpower crisis throughout the services.

The numbers released and the rate at which they left the services was one factor. As the Defence Statement published in February 1946 announced, the total strength of the armed forces was expected to fall from some 5,100,000 in May 1945 to 1,100,000 in December 1946, with a further 100,000 under training. In the event, the actual numbers in the services at the end of 1946 proved to be 1,427,000, but although the rate of release then began to fall sharply, the estimated strength of the armed forces was put at less than 1 million in March 1948 and at 716,000 a year later. The decline of RAF manpower was equally rapid. The maximum number of personnel permitted in the financial year 1946–7 was 760,000 including 142,000 on terminal leave; a year later that total had fallen to less than 375,000. Thereafter the decline was less dramatic, to 325,000 in 1948–9 and 255,000 in 1949–50. The actual num-

Not a few aircraft were still coming off the production lines immediately to be sold outside the service. This brand-new Halifax A. Mk IX had little service with the RAF before being sold to Aviation Traders at Southend and then on to the Egyptian Air Force.

The RAF itself began to shape itself for the peacetime future and work out new tactics and operational methods. Much of this was carried out at the Central Fighter Establishment at West Raynham, where wartime and post-war types rubbed shoulders in the process. This July 1946 photograph shows Spitfire F.Mk 21, Mosquito FB.Mk 6, NF.Mk 13, NF.Mk 30, NF.Mk 36, Firefly FR.Mk 1, NF.Mk 2, Meteor F.Mk 3, Tempest F.Mk 5 and Hornet F.Mk 1 aircraft on the airfield.

air force and its peacetime successor was expected to last another year, with stability and normal levels of efficiency beginning to return in 1949.

A further problem which affected all operational commands of the RAF was the provision of aircraft and other equipment. Many of the aircraft being operated by the RAF at the end of the war had been provided by the United States under the Lend-Lease Act of 1941. With the exception of the Douglas Dakota medium-range transports, all Lend-Lease aircraft were to be given up and replaced by British types. At the same time the government announced a very considerable reduction in the provision of new weapons and equipment, primarily to limit the burden on the national economy and assist industrial recovery, but also to avoid the accumulation of equipment which would quickly become obsolete as research produced new and more advanced weapons; inevitably a number of promising designs were lost in the process. The 1946 Defence Statement, however, had explained that existing stocks would be used whenever possible and modern replacements made available only to a limited degree. What those limited replacements would be was announced in the 1947 statement, which referred to the progressive rearmament of Fighter Command with the most modern types of jet fighter and of Transport Command with small numbers of British-designed and -built transport and airborne forces aircraft.

Consequently, in June 1948, when Britain was faced with crises simultaneously in Europe and the Far East, the RAF was considerably smaller than the target force proposed in Plan E or the revised version produced after the government's cuts in defence expenditure. At home the front-line force consisted of 80 squadrons with a further 20 squadrons in the Royal Auxiliary Air Force. Based overseas were 33 more full squadrons and six cadre squadrons.

Furthermore, shortages of manpower, equipment and spares were affecting all operational commands and causing a rise in unserviceability, a reduction in flying hours and an overall loss of efficiency. In addition, each command had its own particular problems. Fighter Command (25 squadrons and 207 aircraft, including AOP) had the advantage of being progressively rearmed with the best jet fighters then available, but its control and reporting system, although constantly updated, covered only the most vulnerable area of the United Kingdom. In Bomber Command (24 squadrons and 160 aircraft) the main weakness was the

bers, however, were substantially less: 225,000 in April 1949 and 202,000 in April 1950.

Rapid demobilisation

Unhappily, the problem was not simply one of numbers. While the defence statements of the immediate post-war years were stressing the need to keep a balance between the requirements of industry in helping to rebuild the national economy and those of the services in carrying out essential tasks in the aftermath of war, the memoranda accompanying the air estimates were explaining the consequences to the RAF of rapid demobilisation. In February 1947 the Air Ministry pointed out that while in normal times the flow of officers and airmen into and out of the air force was small compared with its overall size, since May 1945 a high proportion of wartime entrants had been released, the most experienced being the first to leave. Consequently, an abnormally large part of the RAF was engaged either in training or in the routine administrative work involved in the processes of demobilisation and reorganisation.

A year later, the 1948 memorandum acknowledged that the RAF was under severe strain, with a low average level of experience, frequent postings and a very considerable dilution of manpower. To make matters worse, demobilisation had combined with the very different periods of training required in the various RAF trades to produce not only an overall shortage of trained men, but also a lack of balance between the trades, which was seriously disorganising the work of many units. In all, the transition period between the wartime

The Tiger Force, that part of Bomber Command scheduled to go to the Far East, received the first of the Avro Lincolns, the Lancaster's successor. From No. 75 Squadron, a New Zealand unit in the RAF, this aircraft was soon re-absorbed by other home-based squadrons as were all the Tiger Force aircraft.

lack of aircraft with the radius of action needed to strike against targets as far afield as the USSR. For Coastal Command (11 squadrons and 87 aircraft, including the photographic reconnaissance and meteorological elements) the problem was to find replacement aircraft of adequate range and an anti-submarine weapon as effective as the American torpedo used during the war, the remaining stocks of which had been returned to the United States. Transport Command (20 squadrons and 160 aircraft, including the airborne forces element) had been given some priority in obtaining men and equipment in the first two years after the war while it was providing essential airline services in a world where normal communications had been severely disrupted; now, however, it was under threat of contraction and the replacements for its Avro Yorks and Dakotas were still to come. In Germany, the British Air Forces of Occupation had received a substantial number of de Havilland Vampires, but in the Middle and Far East the RAF had yet to be given any modern jet aircraft and was thus reliant on a front-line strength made up of Supermarine Spitfires, Hawker Tempests and Bristol Beaufighters.

Widening activities

However, for all its problems, the RAF in 1948 was hardly a 'shop window' air force, the description given to it somewhat despairingly by one member of the Air Council. Indeed, all its operational commands had been working to the limit of their resources, reorganising and retraining their front-line units. In addition, the RAF had been involved in many other activities: Coastal Command had continuing meteorological and survey commitments; Transport Command had established new trunk routes to the Middle and Far East; in Germany the RAF had shared in the problems of occupation; and in the Middle East it had had a role to play in the last stages of the British mandate in Palestine and the first rumblings of the political changes which were to transform the region in less than 20 years. In the Far East the RAF had helped in the evacuation of prisoners of war and internees, and in the course of doing so had joined the Army in fighting a long and bitter campaign in the Indonesian island of Java.

What mattered in the long term, however, was that there had begun to emerge a coherent entity which promised to be a solid basis for future expansion. To make this easier, it had been arranged that some of the squadrons which made up the RAF in the immediate post-war years should be given

two number plates while others existed for the moment only in cadre form. The command structure itself remained very much as it had been established before the war with functional commands at home and theatre commands abroad, the concept of an RAF composed largely of tactical air forces being rejected as better suited to wartime conditions. Instead, the three operational commands formed in 1936 (Bomber, Fighter and Coastal) were retained, together with Transport Command which had been formed only in 1943. In support were Maintenance, Flying Training and Technical Training Commands; Reserve Command was re-formed in May 1946 to train reserves of both flying and ground personnel; and in the communications field No. 90 Group was formed in April 1946 from the two wartime signals groups, Nos 26 and 60. Abroad, three theatre commands were firmly established, in Germany, the Mediterranean and Middle East, and the Far East; involvement in the Indian subcontinent ceased with independence.

Further, although there were many recruitment and training difficulties to come, the worst of the RAF's manpower problems belonged essentially to a period of transition, and had the compensating virtue of encouraging an examination of the ways and means by which manpower could be used more efficiently. For the future, other factors were no less important: developing and testing new tactical doctrines, an aspect stressed by the memorandum accompanying the air estimates of 1948-9; and taking the initial steps needed to produce the aircraft and other equipment which would ensure the effectiveness of the RAF well into the next decade and beyond. In this respect the immediate post-war years were a particularly successful period from which emerged not only the Vickers Valiant, Handley Page Victor and Avro Vulcan, but the English Electric Canberra, de Havilland Venom, Hawker Hunter and Avro Shackleton as well.

The potential, therefore, was considerable, and of growing importance as the assumption that no major war was likely within the next five or 10 years began to look increasingly insecure. Events in the Middle and Far East were alarming enough; of more immediate concern was the conduct of the Soviet Union towards occupied Germany and the overthrow of democratic governments in one East European country after another and their replacement by Communist regimes tied closely to Moscow. A trial of strength, therefore, was only to be expected; the form it would take and the West's ability to respond were less predictable.

Although production was severely cut down at the end of the war, development continued. The latest Spitfire in service at the war's close was the F. Mk 21. This was developed immediately into the F. Mk 22 and later into the F. Mk 24. Small numbers of all these variants were used in RAF service after the end of hostilities. In this formation two F. Mk 22s and an F. Mk 21 are seen flying from the Supermarine test airfield at High Post.

Airlift into Berlin

All lingering hopes that Europe would settle into a period of prolonged peace and stability after World War II were shattered on 24 June 1948 when the cumulative effects of the obstructive tactics being practised by the Soviet Union finally brought all surface communication between Berlin and the West to a halt in defiance of international agreements. These had provided for the division of Germany into four zones (British, American, Russian and French) and for the division of Berlin into four equivalent sectors; they also guaranteed certain lines of communication, surface and air, between the Western sectors of the city, across the Soviet zone of Germany and into the Western zones.

The rumblings of dissension between Russia and the Western Powers had begun many months before, and the Soviet Union had first given an indication of the action it might take early in 1948 when a train from Berlin to Bielefeld was delayed for 11 hours in the Soviet zone. In April the Russians threatened to search all rail shipments into Berlin, and the Americans responded by flying 327 tons of supplies into their sector in 12 days. For their part, the British Army of the Rhine and RAF Transport Command finalised a plan to airlift into Berlin all the supplies needed by the British garrison there (some 65 tons each day), two Douglas Dakota squadrons being earmarked for the task.

The cause for the growing dissension was a fundamental divergence of view between Russia and the West on the future of Germany. The West, prompted by memories of Versailles, had proposed that Germany should in time be helped back on to her feet to become a full member of the European community of nations. In Russian eyes, however, a resurgent and united Germany spelled yet another threat to national security; and a Western enclave such as Berlin, situated within the Soviet zone, appeared to represent a danger of another kind, a constant reminder to those living under Soviet administration that the West offered a very different way of life.

When surface communications between Berlin and the West ceased, and only the air routes remained open, the situation was fraught with danger. Neither side wanted open war, but with the West's position in Berlin indefensible from a strictly military viewpoint Russia had much to gain if the West failed to take effective action to keep their sectors of the city sustained; it could lead to the collapse of their authority in the city and perhaps later in the Western zones of Germany – leading to a fundamental change in the strategic balance of power in Europe.

Both the RAF and USAF were adequately prepared to mount a limited airlift sufficient to keep their Berlin garrisons supplied, and operations

Wunstorf became full of Dakotas from Britain as the Berlin Airlift began. From here supplies were flown in continuously to Gatow airfield in Berlin. An air traffic controller is signalling to the Dakota taxiing towards the tower by means of an Aldis light.

began immediately with RAF Dakotas and USAF Douglas C-47s, ferrying food and other necessities into the city. To go further and meet the needs of two million or more inhabitants of the Western sectors entirely by air was a very different matter: an airlift on such a scale had never been contemplated before and was widely believed to be unachievable.

Nevertheless within a day or so the decision was taken, after consultations in London and Washington, to mount a full-scale airlift, at least as a holding operation to gain time while negotiations with the Soviet Union proceeded. By 29 June the whole of RAF Transport Command's Dakota fleet had arrived at Wunstorf, one of the RAF bases in Germany and some 20 miles (32 km) north west of Hanover; it was reinforced later by aircrews from Australia, New Zealand and South Africa. The whole of the RAF's fleet of Avro Yorks followed on 1 July.

All of the RAF's front-line transport aircraft (64 Dakotas and 56 Yorks) were now in Germany. The Dakotas (Mks 3 and 4 aircraft) were part of No. 46 Group, and were normally based at Oakington (Nos 27, 30, 46 and 238 Squadrons) and at Waterbeach (Nos 18, 53, 62 and 77 Squadrons); the Yorks were on the strength of No. 47 Group, usually based at Abingdon (Nos 40, 51, 59 and 242 Squadrons) and at Lyneham (Nos 99, 206 and 511 Squadrons).

In addition Coastal Command despatched its two Short Sunderland flying-boat squadrons, Nos 201 and 230, with 10 aircraft, to operate between Hamburg and Havel lake in Berlin. The Sunderlands continued to fly until December and although the total tonnage they carried was small in relation to the total their appearance over Berlin proved to be an immense encouragement to the population. The three OCUs involved, No. 235 (with Sunderlands), No. 240 (with Dakotas) and No. 241 (with Yorks) also contributed aircraft and aircrews for varying periods. The United States Air Force meanwhile was mobilising every Douglas C-54 which could be spared from other duties and sending them to supplement the C-47s at the two bases in the American zone, Rhein/Main and Wiesbaden.

The coming weeks were to be vital: if the negotiations with the Russians were to have any chance of success it had to be demonstrated that the Western allies were acting decisively and in concert. Yet the sheer size of the task was daunting. Initial

Even the two Coastal Command flying-boat squadrons made use of the Havel lake in Berlin, flying in supplies from Hamburg. This aircraft came from No. 201 Squadron.

calculations suggested that at least 2,000 short tons of food, coal and other bare essentials would have to be flown into the city every 24 hours, a figure that was soon to be doubled, partly to stockpile supplies against the winter weather to come in the event that the airlift, now known to the RAF as Operation 'Plainfare', lasted months rather than weeks.

Early achievements were encouraging: on 20 July for example the RAF and the USAF together flew 2,250 tons into Berlin, and a week later a number of British civil aircraft joined the operation. The daily average for the combined tonnage brought into the city by the Western Allies rose steadily to 3,839 tons in August and over 4,600 tons in September and October. What many on both sides of the Atlantic had considered impossible was now being achieved.

The RAF contribution to these tonnages in the first weeks of the airlift was very considerable. At full stretch the Yorks, Dakotas and Sunder-

Operation 'Plainfare' planning was carried out in this Transport Command operations room. The wallmap shows the routes from Britain and the routes into Berlin from the bases in West Germany.

At the 'export' end of the corridor the Yorks are busy loading up to go into Berlin. In the background can be seen Lancastrians belonging to charter airlines which augmented Transport Command's efforts.

Gatow Airfield in Germany was operational day and night during the airlift. Yorks line up under the floodlights, having offloaded their cargoes, and wait either for backload or for clearance to fly back down the corridor for more loads.

context the York and Dakota were adequate aircraft, although soon due for replacement.

The Berlin Airlift made special demands. With only two airfields immediately available in the Western sectors, Gatow in the British and Tempelhof in the American, the only criteria were the number of landings made every 24 hours, and the tonnage carried by each aircraft. In this respect the American C-54 had considerable advantages as a highly reliable aircraft designed to carry a 10-ton payload and able to survive the strains of intensive flying, particularly taking off and landing with full loads several times every day, day in and day out. The RAF York was an 8/9-ton carrier and, as a result of the wartime priorities afforded to fighters and bombers, the only sizeable military transport aircraft Britain had been able to build since before the war. Being based on the wartime Lancaster bomber, although with an entirely new fuselage, it was best suited to long-distance route-flying and to much less frequent take-offs and landings than was demanded during the airlift. Maintenance of the Yorks therefore soon presented a considerable problem. The Dakotas, provided originally under the American Lend-Lease Act of 1941, were more robust and reliable in the intensive operations, but suffered the considerable disadvantage in being able to carry only 3/3½ tons, with the result that each landing by a Dakota brought in only about a third of the tonnage carried by the C-54. The American C-47s were indeed withdrawn for this very reason.

The RAF's problems with aircraft were compounded by the peculiar circumstances of the airlift. Not only were the Western allies restricted to two airports in Berlin (until a third, Tegel in the French zone, was added in November) but access to them from the Western zones of Germany was limited to three corridors, each 20 miles (32 km) wide, the northern being used by aircraft from bases in the British zone, the southern by aircraft

lands carried an average of over 1,100 tons a day between July and September, an achievement of great importance which helped to consolidate the position of the Western allies while the US Air Force in Germany was gathering its complement of C-54s to full strength.

The problem for the RAF, however, was that the rundown in the immediate post-war years had left its transport force without the resources to sustain so intense a level of operations. The task to which Transport Command was now primarily geared was route-flying on scheduled services to destinations in Europe, the Middle East and South East Asia, with strict limitations on flying hours (to conserve airframes) and the provision of aircrews. In that

from bases in the American zone, and the central by returning aircraft.

This limitation posed no significant problems in the early weeks of the airlift, but as the C-54 force grew and was able to operate intensively with an aircrew ratio double that of the RAF, it was agreed that a proportion of the American aircraft should be based in the British zone at Celle and Fassberg, which were considerably nearer to Berlin than Rhein/Main and Wiesbaden, and nearer even than Wunstorf whence the Yorks were operating, Lübeck where the Dakotas had moved, or Fuhlsbüttel, the base for British civil aircraft.

The airlift intensifies

The problem now was to organise the flow of several different types of aircraft along the northern corridor and into Gatow, the target being an average landing frequency of one aircraft every three minutes. The solution was the time block system, with height separation for different aircraft types to provide additional safety margins. The time block system divided the 24-hour day into six cycles of four hours; within those four hours each base was allotted a block of the precise times at which its aircraft were to pass over the Frohnau beacon, the point of entry into the Berlin air traffic control area. The C-54s took precedence with the first and largest block of times, followed by the Yorks, Dakotas and British civil aircraft.

Under the time block system the RAF was at a considerable disadvantage. A four-hour cycle was ideal for the C-54s, which could fly to and from Berlin comfortably in that time; but with their bases farther away, the Yorks and Dakotas needed longer, and could well miss their place in the next cycle in consequence. Furthermore it was the Yorks and Dakotas which carried awkward cargo requiring longer to load and unload, and carried back from Berlin passengers, in particular children and the sick, together with the manufactured

goods still being produced in the city for export. When bad weather caused aircraft to straggle along the corridors the Dakotas faced an additional hazard: as the smallest load-carriers they were likely to lose their place in the cycle to any larger aircraft returning late to base.

For all these reasons, serviceability, the time block system and the weather, the tonnage carried by the Yorks and Dakotas averaged only 700 tons a day in the last quarter of 1948, a result that had been foreseen at staff level. Modifications to the time block system were introduced to the RAF's advantage and when the two new Handley Page Hastings squadrons, Nos 47 and 297, began to operate from Schleswigland at the end of the year the situation started to improve. But the Hastings had a crosswind problem with which to contend, and was not permitted to take off and land when the crosswind component was above 23 mph (37 km/h).

The total tonnage being carried into Berlin was enough to meet immediate demands, however, and

Back at Wunstorf the base tried to keep operational whilst swamped with Transport Command aircraft. These two Spitfire FR.Mk 14Es of No. 2 Squadron take off for a sortie in between the Dakotas, Yorks and Hastings.

The scale of operation on the airlift was such that the crew briefings were of a size not seen since the Bomber Command raids during World War II.

During the dangerous early years of peace the RAF always kept a squadron of fighters at RAF Gatow, Berlin, as a deterrent. In this photograph Tempest Mk Vs of No. 33 Squadron maintain their presence in formation over the city.

accompanying fog was confined mainly to November.

Coal was in fact the main cargo carried into Berlin. Of the 2,325,809 short tons airlifted by Western aircraft between late June 1948 and early September 1949, 1,586,530 tons were coal; food, dehydrated where possible and the meat boned, made up 538,016 tons; and wet fuel, carried exclusively by British civil aircraft, 92,282 tons. Of the total tonnage, the RAF airlifted 394,509 tons or 17 per cent, and British civil aircraft 147,727 tons or 6.3 per cent.

The blockade of Berlin was lifted on 12 May 1949, but the airlift continued for almost another four months to build up a stockpile in case of any further interference with surface communications. What had been achieved was the defusing of a highly dangerous situation and, ironically, although American Boeing B-29 bombers were brought to Britain as a warning signal to the Soviet Union, the front line had been held throughout by the British and American transport forces and those who supported them on the ground, together with the service and civilian staffs needed to ensure that supplies were delivered to the airheads as required and distributed once they had arrived in Berlin. Ironically, too, the rundown of the RAF transport fleet, which had been planned in 1948 but was suspended during the airlift, began as soon as it was over. The emphasis was now to be on giving back to the RAF some of the teeth it had lost over the past four years.

The success of the airlift also marked a decisive stage in two separate but related developments, the establishment of the Federal Republic of Germany on 21 September 1949, and the signing on 4 April 1949 of the North Atlantic Treaty that was to come into effect on 24 August 1949. The Soviet Union now found itself in a Europe in which the whole Western position of solidarity had been immensely strengthened.

although dipping to 3,800 tons a day in November when many sorties were cancelled as a result of fog, rose again to 4,500 tons in December and 5,500 tons in January and February. The C-54 force was now at its peak of some 200 aircraft, and with steadily increasing contributions from the RAF and British civil aircraft daily average tonnages improved to 6,300 tons in March and almost 8,000 tons in April, the last full month of the main airlift.

There had been moments of anxiety at the turn of the year when bad weather could have upset what was still a delicate balance: 4,000 tons a day was then both the most that could be achieved and the minimum needed to sustain civilian morale. A long hard winter would have brought good flying weather but also a soaring demand for coal, which it would have been impossible to meet; as it was, the winter was milder than usual and the

The Post-war Bomber Force and Strategic Deterrent

By the summer of 1948 the front-line establishment of Bomber Command had been cut from 1,560 aircraft to no more than 160 and an actual strength of even less. In time, the decision taken in January 1947 to develop an atomic bomb would result in a massive increase in striking power, but for the immediate future there were obvious weaknesses in the force which was accepted to be a major element in Britain's defence policy. As it stood in June 1948, Bomber Command's front-line strength consisted of 48 Avro Lancasters, 96 Avro Lincolns and 16 de Havilland Mosquitoes, deployed in 24 cadre squadrons, each with establishments of six or eight aircraft.

But the sharp contraction of its front-line squadrons was not the sum of Bomber Command's difficulties. Along with other RAF Commands, it was

suffering from the effects of an acute shortage of trained manpower following demobilisation, and also of spares, two factors which combined with others to cause considerable serviceability problems, especially with the Lincoln when operating in tropical conditions. Notwithstanding these handicaps, the tasks facing Bomber Command in the late 1940s were daunting, training for its primary war roles with frequent 'Sunray' (the then-current exercise codename) detachments to Egypt where live bombing and fighter affiliation practice could be carried out in a reliable climate; and, in addition, aircraft had to be made available for overseas reinforcement, in particular to Malaya where the Emergency was as yet only in its opening phases.

During 1949 the remaining Lancaster squadrons

At the close of the war the Avro Lancaster was retained as the standard Bomber Command aircraft. Most of those in service were B.Mk 1 (FE)s which had been modified for operation in the Far East. They thus were painted in a white and black colour scheme. One typical squadron was No. 35 (stationed at Graveley) which in July 1946 set off across the Atlantic for a goodwill tour of the USA.

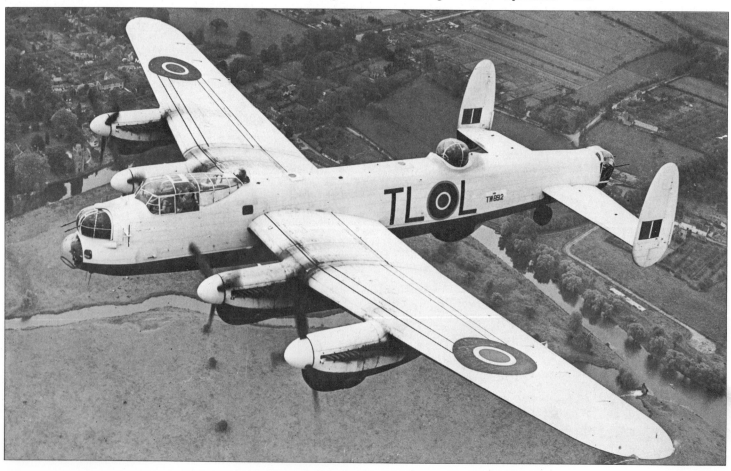

The Avro Lincoln arrived as the Lancaster's successor just as the war ended. No. 57 Squadron at East Kirkby, was one of the first to receive the type, intended for the Far East. RF385 had been built by Armstrong Whitworth at Baginton in about April 1945 and joined No. 57 Squadron in August. Its career was cut short on 20 February 1946 when it crashed near Barsby in Leicestershire.

The Lincoln served faithfully until the mid-1950s and was used overseas operationally as recorded elsewhere. RF445 was in service with No. 44 (Rhodesia) Squadron when this photograph was taken, and is obviously near the country of its squadron. No. 44 had been a 'gift' squadron during World War II and many Rhodesians had served, and died, in it.

were re-equipped with Lincolns, but the command's weakness persisted: it still possessed no aircraft with a radius of action adequate to operate against targets in the Soviet Union in the event of war. The only aircraft which might be available at short notice to meet this requirement was the American Boeing B-29 Superfortress.

The first phase of an expansion of Bomber Command therefore began with a British request to the United States to supply sufficient B-29s under the Mutual Defense Assistance Program to equip eight RAF squadrons. These aircraft, with their somewhat ambivalent reputation as atomic-bomb carriers, were already well known in Europe as a result of their visits to Britain and elsewhere in November 1946, and again two years later when 90 B-29s had been sent to Britain during the Berlin Airlift to bolster Western strength in the opening stages of the cold war.

The first squadron of Washingtons (as the B-29s were called in RAF service) was formed in June 1950, and by the autumn of 1951 all eight squadrons were in being with Nos 35, 90, 115 and 207 at Marham, Nos 15, 44/45 and 149 at Coningsby, and No. 57 at Waddington. At the end of that

year Bomber Command's front-line strength had increased to 205 aircraft, a figure which included 64 Washingtons, 90 Lincolns, seven photo-reconnaissance Lancasters and 16 Mosquitoes.

The Washingtons represented a much-needed boost to the RAF's striking power, their primary task being to attack targets in the Soviet Union in times of war. With a maximum bomb load of 20,000 lb (9072 kg), they were equipped with the Norden bomb sight, the US equivalent of H2S radar, a radio compass and a Loran set. In operation the Washingtons were popular and had a number of good features, providing a high level of crew comfort; they were pressurised to a cabin equivalent of 8,000 ft (2440 m) and the automatic pilot could be employed at all times except during take-off and landing; there was no difficulty in maintaining height on three engines and the tricycle landing gear rendered asymmetric landings easier. However the Washington suffered from the unreliability of reconditioned engines, and the shortage of spares was a result of priority being afforded to USAF B-29s operating in the Korean war.

Indeed, Bomber Command had raised objections to the purchase of the B-29s on the grounds that they would be extremely expensive to maintain and, as they required an eight-man crew (compared with six or seven in the Lincoln), would still further exacerbate the RAF's manpower problem. It was also said that they could not operate above 26,000 feet (7295 m) as the engines might blow up or catch fire when the required additional boost was applied. At a time of necessity these objections were overruled, however, and from 1951 until March 1954, when the last aircraft was returned to the United States, the Washington squadrons successfully performed a heavy programme of intensive training and exercise.

It was also during the period of the B-29's RAF service that Bomber Command investigated the possibility of introducing the four-jet North American B-45 into RAF squadron service, and a small number of aircrews did in fact undertake operational evaluation of the aircraft both in the USA

BOMBER COMMAND'S FRONT-LINE STRENGTH AT JUNE 1948

No. 1 Group

Squadron	Aircraft	Location
9, 12, 101, 617	Lincoln B.2	Binbrook
83, 97, 100	Lincoln B.2	Hemswell
50, 57, 61	Lincoln B.2	Waddington
109, 139	Mosquito B.35	Coningsby

No. 3 Group

Squadron	Aircraft	Location
35, 115, 149, 207	Lancaster B.1(FE)	Stradishall
7, 49, 148, 214	Lancaster B.1(FE)	Upwood
15, 44, 90, 138	Lincoln B.2	Wyton

To augment the aircraft in Bomber Command, and to bring them more into line with modern operating techniques until the Canberra came into service, the RAF acquired from the USAF a number of Boeing B-29A Superfortress aircraft which were known as the Washington B.Mk I in RAF service. They served at Marham and Coningsby from 1950 until 1954. This formation is from No. 115 Squadron (Marham) in 1950.

The Boeing B-29A was introduced into the RAF as a stopgap until the arrival of the Canberra. It served at both Marham and Coningsby from 1950 to 1954. WF443 joined No. 90 Squadron at Marham in 1950, in whose markings it is shown.

and Britain, several aircraft carrying RAF markings during the course of a series of politically sensitive operations while based in the United Kingdom.

Meanwhile the English Electric Canberras, that were to constitute the second phase of Bomber Command's post-war expansion and to provide the main strength of its front-line forces until the arrival of the V-bombers, had begun to enter squadron service in May 1951. Negotiations for a new bomber, ostensibly to supersede the classic wartime Mosquito, had opened in 1945, the original intention being to build an interim replacement for the Lancaster and Lincoln in the shape of a long-range high-flying bomber. A Canberra prototype did in fact fly as early as May 1949 but in the meantime plans had been changed, so that the end product was very different: a shorter-range but highly versatile aircraft whose war role was to provide close air support for NATO ground forces as a bomber, interdictor or reconnaissance aircraft.

With the RAF's small force of Lincolns and Washingtons becoming obsolete (at least compared to North American B-45s and Boeing B-47s), and relations with the Soviet Union becoming daily more tense, the necessity to have a large number of Canberras in squadron service was urgent, and a substantial production order was placed for the first light bomber version, the Canberra B.Mk 2. First to receive this version was No. 101 Squadron at Binbrook in May 1951, and by the end of the year the squadron was almost up to its established strength of 10 aircraft. Seven more squadrons were formed during 1952: Nos 9, 12, 50 and 617 (all former Lincoln squadrons) at Binbrook; Nos 109/105 and 139 Squadrons (previously with Mosquito B.Mk 35s) at Hemswell; and the first photographic-reconnaissance Canberra squadron, No. 540 (previously flying Mosquito PR.Mk 34As) at Benson.

By the spring of 1955 a total of 29 Canberra

squadrons had been established, 26 in the light bomber role (including four deployed in Germany as the result of a shortage of suitable airfields in the United Kingdom) and three in the photo-reconnaissance role. Bomber Command then possessed a total of 259 Canberra aircraft, including the first examples of the more powerful Canberra B.Mk 6 version with longer range. In addition plans had been laid to create four further photo-reconnaissance and four interdictor squadrons in Germany, equipped with other Canberra variants.

An early assessment had rated the Canberra as a very efficient tactical bomber with an effective radius of action of between 850 and 900 miles (1368 and 1448 km), carrying a 6,000-lb (2722-kg) bombload. Although valuable in the photo-reconnaissance role and in interdictor operations, the Canberra could not carry an atomic bomb or any single conventional bomb larger than 5,000 lb (2268 kg). Compared with the Lincoln it was well over twice as fast, pressurised, unarmed and highly manoeuvrable; it also possessed the valuable asset

North American B-45C Tornadoes were flown from Britain on clandestine missions. Although they were USAF aircraft flown by American crews, they carried RAF roundels and fin flashes (but no RAF or USAF serials). No political or operational explanations has ever been disclosed

The advent of the Canberra was the biggest step forward for Bomber Command since the arrival of the Blenheim in 1937. It brought new heights, new speeds and entirely new operating techniques. The first squadron to receive the English Electric Canberra B.Mk 2 was No. 101 Squadron at Binbrook in the spring of 1951. Its first aircraft are seen here on the airfield in company with one of the aircraft they were replacing, the Lincoln.

The English Electric Canberra B.Mk 2 was the first jet bomber in service with the RAF and first equipped the Binbrook Wing. WD995 was issued to No. 617 Squadron. All the Binbrook squadrons carried a different coloured lightning flash on the nose of the aircraft, No. 617's being dark blue edged in gold. This aircraft subsequently served in the Middle East with Nos 249 and 32 Squadrons until being lost in a collison with a Javelin on 26 October 1961.

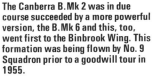

The Canberra B.Mk 2 was in due course succeeded by a more powerful version, the B.Mk 6 and this, too, went first to the Binbrook Wing. This formation was being flown by No. 9 Squadron prior to a goodwill tour in 1955.

of being crewed by a three- and later a two-man crew, compared with the Lincoln's seven. In squadron service it proved to be a generally docile aircraft with a low wing loading and a good power-to-weight ratio; situations did arise, however, when the pilot could lose control either through lack of experience, particularly during instrument flying, or because stick forces increased beyond the limits of human strength.

Nevertheless squadron life with the Canberra consisted of a busy and absorbing programme of continuation training and joint exercises with Fighter Command and Allied air forces, and of detachments overseas, notably to Malaya. As a result the Canberra proved to be the best imaginable training aircraft for the time when the RAF would receive its first V-bombers.

V-bombers arrive

The first of these, the Vickers Valiants for No. 138 Squadron, had arrived at Gaydon early in 1955 to mark the beginning of the third phase of Bomber Command's expansion, and to give it a strategic nuclear bombing capability. The Valiant's gestation process had been long, eight years since the British government's decision in January 1947 to develop a nuclear weapon, a period of intensive and highly secret research which resulted in three types of bomber coming into production, together with the Blue Danube plutonium bomb.

This was a period of extraordinary achievement, not only by the RAF (and Bomber Command in particular) but by the government administration and aircraft industry, comparable in many respects with the prodigious efforts that had achieved the expansion of Bomber Command's muscle during the war. For these were years of peace, albeit fragile, and abbreviated military expenditure; nevertheless three highly sophisticated bomber aircraft and their associated nuclear weapons systems were successfully developed during a period of accelerated advance by technology elsewhere in the world and after five years of national parsimony in research funding between 1945 and 1950.

The specification issued in December 1946 had suggested a turbojet-powered aeroplane capable of a speed of 600 mph (966 km/h) and a height above the target of 45,000 feet (13715 m); it was to have a five-man crew but no defensive armament. By the end of the following year a large-scale V-bomber procurement programme was under way with Handley Page contracted to proceed with what was to become the Victor, and Avro with the future Vulcan. As an insurance against undue development and production delays with these very advanced types, two prototypes of a more conventional aircraft, the Sperrin, were ordered from Shorts, but in the event this type was not needed for production. A fourth type was ordered from Vickers in 1948, at a time of mounting international tension (*vide* the Berlin Airlift crisis) and became the Valiant, the 'interim V-bomber' which was the last to be ordered and the first to enter squadron service.

In the course of development only one technical

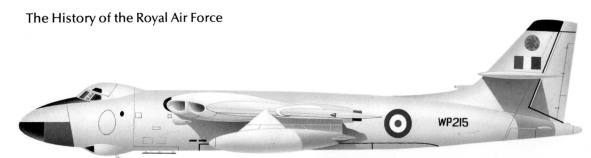

The Vickers Valiant B.Mk. 1 WP215 is shown here with the markings of No. 18 Squadron. It had joined No. 199 Squadron at Honington in February 1958 after serving with the original Valiant unit, No. 138 Squadron at Gaydon from May 1955. No. 199 Squadron was renumbered No. 18 Squadron in December 1958, and the Valiant remained in service with this unit until April 1963.

problem caused prolonged anxiety: the manner of escape in emergency at low level of the three rear crew members, only the pilot and co-pilot having ejector seats. A number of improvements were adopted, but the situation was never radically altered. Other difficulties proved more tractable, but in the event the lead time before the three aircraft entered service (10 years for the Victor, eight and a half years for the Vulcan and rather less than seven years for the Valiant) compared not too unfavourably with five years for the Hunter.

Nevertheless a second Valiant squadron (No. 543) was formed at Gaydon in 1955, and tasked with a strategic reconnaissance role. By the end of the year No. 138 Squadron had settled in at Wittering and No. 543 at Wyton. In little over a year the Valiant force was virtually complete, with one strategic reconnaissance squadron and seven bomber squadrons, two being based at Wittering (Nos 138 and 49), three at Marham (Nos 214, 207 and 148), two at Honington (Nos 7 and 90) and No. 543 at Wyton, for a total establishment of 57 bomber and nine strategic reconnaissance aircraft.

Vulcan enters service

The first Vulcan B.Mk 1 squadron, No. 83, was formed at Waddington a few months later in May 1957, and almost immediately two of its crews were sent to the United States to participate in the bombing competition organised by the USAF's Strategic Air Command. A second squadron, No. 101, previously the first of the Canberra squadrons, was formed in October 1957 and opened up the new V-bomber base at Finningley, and a third, No. 617 (the 'Dambusters'), re-formed at Scampton in May 1958.

Two Victor squadrons also formed in 1958, both at Cottesmore, No. 10 in April and No. 15 in September. By the end of that year, therefore, the V-force comprised 14 squadrons including No. 18, the electronic countermeasures squadron (formerly No. 199). As already remarked, much effort had gone into achieving this result. The bomb which the V-force carried was the Blue Danube, a free-

fall plutonium bomb developed for the RAF and tested in October 1952 in the Monte Bello Islands. During the years of research which went into its development the British scientists working on the project were effectively cut off from their former colleagues in the United States, an enforced isolation caused by the MacMahon Act passed by the US Congress in August 1946 and intended to secure an American monopoly in the atomic field until an effective measure of international control could be achieved.

Notwithstanding this handicap, the Monte Bello test, in which the British bomb was exploded aboard a Royal Navy frigate, HMS *Plym*, was entirely successful. But before the RAF could bring its first production bombs into service there remained a formidable amount of preparatory work to be undertaken at the Bomber Command Armament School at Wittering, including the writing of training manuals and the scheduling of training courses, the designing of suitable accommodation to house the bombs and the devising of servicing and security procedures. The first bomb was delivered in November 1953, well ahead of the first V-bombers. Each weapon possessed an ex-

The next big step in Bomber Command was the formation of the V-Force. The two main V-bombers were to be revolutionary designs, the Victor and the Vulcan, but to play safe a more conventional type was also ordered and this went into service first as the Vickers Valiant B.Mk 1.

The Avro Vulcan was the second type into service. Originally it came as the B.Mk 1 and Waddington was the base *(right)* for the first of these delta-winged bombers. No. 83 Squadron received the first operational aircraft in July 1957. But already Avro had designed a new wing and more powerful engines were installed to create the B.Mk 2 which followed into service in 1960. With the Vulcan was perfected the new immediate response method of having aircraft assembled on an operational readiness platform beside the runway with aircraft plugged into intercom, crews aboard, already to go at a moment's notice. This is demonstrated in this picture of four B.Mk 2s at readiness *(left)*.

XA897 was the ninth production Avro Vulcan B.Mk 1, and was delivered to Waddington in 1955 where it served with No. 230 OCU. In 1956 it flew on a tour to Australia and New Zealand, returning to the UK only to crash in bad weather at London Airport on 1 October 1956. The crash caused a furore, for the captain and second pilot were able to eject to safety but the rest of the crew, with no ejection seats, were killed. Despite this obvious anomaly Vulcans (and Victors too) are still flying today without such safety devices for the rear crew.

NUCLEAR V-FORCE AT END OF 1958

Squadron	Aircraft	Location
49, 138	Valiant B.1	Wittering
148, 207, 214	Valiant B.1	Marham
7, 90	Valiant B.1	Honington
543	Valiant B.1	Wyton
83	Vulcan B.1	Waddington
101	Vulcan B.1	Finningley
617	Vulcan B.1	Scampton
10, 15	Victor B.1	Cottesmore
18	Valiant B.1 and Canberra B.2	Finningley

The third V-bomber was the Victor with Handley Page's crescent wing. In many ways this was the most advanced of all the types and it entered service at Cottesmore with No. 10 Squadron in April 1958, XA922 being one of its aircraft. The Victor's production was curtailed very soon afterwards for political reasons: the government of the day had been trying to get all the aircraft manufacturing companies to merge into larger units, but Sir Frederick Handley Page held out and refused, so his order for V-bombers was cut.

plosive power at least equivalent to that of all the bombs dropped by Bomber Command during World War II.

Preparations for V-force operations also included the development of 10 Class One airfields at Finningley, Scampton, Waddington, Coningsby, Cottesmore, Wittering, Marham, Honington, Wyton and Gaydon. The runways were to be 9,000 ft (2745 m) long plus a 1,000 ft (305 m) overrun, and up to 200 ft (61 m) wide, as well as being capable of withstanding aircraft weights of 200,000 lb (90720 kg). In addition, taxiways and hardstandings for at least 16 aircraft per station were to be provided, together with all the other essential accoutrements such as lighting and landing aids, new air traffic control equipment, storage facilities for weapons and spares, aircraft handling and servicing equipment, and pipeline installations for the large quantities of fuel required.

The priority now was to turn this first generation of V-bombers into an efficient fighting force, first and foremost as a deterrent to Soviet aggression, but in war capable of delivering its bombloads in high-level operations with pinpoint accuracy. Training was therefore intensive in order to ensure a high degree of readiness and to achieve the skills needed to carry out the assigned tasks efficiently. In addition to its nuclear role, the V-force was to develop a conventional capability and be available for overseas reinforcement. Already Valiants had taken part in operational bombing tasks, dropping conventional bombs on Egyptian airfields during the Suez operation late in 1956.

During the following years the effectiveness of the V-bomber force was progressively improved. Dispersal airfields were developed to ensure that aircraft would not be destroyed at their home bases by a hostile pre-emptive strike; readiness procedures were upgraded; the British hydrogen bomb was tested and placed into production; a second generation of V-bombers with greatly improved performance entered service; and close co-operation was developing with the US Air Force, including the co-ordination of targeting plans and the stationing of Thor intermediate-range ballistic missiles (IRBM) in Britain.

V-force dispersal

When completed, the V-force dispersal plan gave it a high degree of immunity from a nuclear first strike, the airfields selected to supplement the 10 main bases being scattered throughout the British Isles. They included airfields in Fighter, Coastal, Transport and Flying Training Commands, and others belonging to the Royal Navy and the Ministry of Aviation besides some in Bomber Command itself; practice dispersals became a regular part of the V-force's training programme.

Equally vital was the rolling programme which Bomber Command introduced to improve the readiness states of its V-bombers. This was based on two categories of warning devised in 1957, and subsequently on the early warning station at Fylingdales which became operational in 1963; the strategic warning gave 24 hours' notice, during which 20 per cent of the force would be at readiness

within two hours, 40 per cent in four hours, 60 per cent in eight hours and 75 per cent within 24 hours. The tactical warning provided for aircraft to be at 15 minutes' readiness for up to a week, or 40 minutes' readiness for up to a month. These were expensive provisions because, to meet them, additional manpower was required to mount a two-shift, 18-hour working day.

In 1962 a further improvement was achieved when the Quick Reaction Alert (QRA) procedure was introduced in which one aircraft from each bomber squadron was permanently at 15 minutes' readiness. Closer integration was then possible with the Reflex forces of the US Strategic Air Command deployed in Britain. The QRA became increasingly significant as the threat grew of a missile attack on the V-bomber bases; it discouraged the Soviet Union from automatically assuming that the V-force was an easy target, while at the same time it reduced the damage that any such attack might inflict and ensured that retaliatory action could be launched within minutes.

Three-minute readiness

Three minutes was, in fact, the time said in 1959 to be available to the V-bombers to fly clear of any missiles and make their own response. Urgent steps were therefore taken to reduce reaction time below the four minutes at which it then stood. Operational readiness platforms (ORP) were built and a programme introduced to provide simultaneous engine starting; as a result the reaction time was cut to two minutes.

By then the British hydrogen bomb was in service. The decision to produce it had been taken in 1954 following similar decisions by the United States in 1952 and the Soviet Union a year later. After three years' research the results were put to the test in Operation 'Grapple' during May and June 1957. Christmas Island was used as the base

and a Valiant was tasked to drop a number of devices to detonate at 15,000 ft (4570 m) in the vicinity of Malden Island. The results were successful and one of the warhead designs was used in the production of Bomber Command's first megaton weapons, the Yellow Sun free-fall bombs delivered in the summer of 1958 on a limited-approval basis for use by the Vulcans operating from airfields in the United Kingdom.

The effectiveness of the V-force was also greatly improved by the introduction of a second generation of bombers, the Vulcan B.Mk 2s entering service in April 1961 and the Victor B.Mk 2s 10 months later. Some redesign work had been required to accommodate larger and more powerful engines as well as additional countermeasures equipment, but there had been many compensations: better take-off performance, especially at dispersal airfields where the runways were usually shorter than at the main bases; the radius of action substantially increased with the result that more targets in the Soviet Union now lay within range and indirect approaches became feasible; better chances of survival in the presence of surface-to-air missiles and enemy interceptors; maximum speeds improved to Mach 0.98 for the Vulcan and Mach 0.92 for the Victor; and increased operating heights over the target, a matter of particular importance so long as manned fighters remained the enemy's main defence.

An early plan to deploy 120 Vulcan B.Mk 2s and Victor B.Mk 2s was never fulfilled, but by September 1961 three squadrons (Nos 27, 83 and 617) were redeployed with Vulcan B.Mk 2s, and in the following year the upgraded force was completed with the re-equipping of Nos 9, 12 and 35 Squadrons with Vulcan B.Mk 2s, and Nos 100 and 139 Squadrons with Victor B.Mk 2s. By December 1962, therefore, Britain's nuclear deterrent force was deployed in 15 squadrons. In addition, the front-line force

The V-Force squadrons were proud of their ability to get airborne and on their way within seconds of the order to go. This graphic photograph taken at Scampton shows an operational take-off by four Vulcans: the first is climbing steeply away, the second is just off the runway and cleaning up, the third is accelerating down the runway and the fourth is hidden by the smoke of the first three as it taxis on to the threshold.

NUCLEAR DETERRENT FORCE AT DECEMBER 1962

Squadron	Aircraft	Location
9, 12, 35	Vulcan B.2	Coningsby
27, 83, 617	Vulcan B.1	Scampton
44, 50, 101	Vulcan B.1A	Waddington
100, 139	Victor B.1	Wittering
10, 15	Victor B.1	Cottesmore
55, 57	Victor B.1A	Honington

Readiness around the clock was part of the V-Force's task, particularly when it was the country's nuclear deterrent. This Scampton-based Vulcan B.Mk 2 has its Blue Steel stand-off missile installed and is at readiness.

included one Canberra tactical reconnaissance squadron and six Valiant squadrons: No. 543 in the strategic reconnaissance role; Nos 49, 148 and 207, now assigned to NATO as a tactical bombing force; and Nos 90 and 214, undertaking a task new to the RAF – that of inflight refuelling. The remaining Valiant squadrons had been disbanded.

Meanwhile the decision by the British government to produce the hydrogen bomb and the clear evidence that the V-force had become a viable independent strategic nuclear deterrent had encouraged the United States to begin discussions in 1957 on co-operation with Britain in the nuclear weapons field. In particular an integrated strike plan was introduced in 1958 to avoid duplication of targeting, and to co-ordinate V-force and Strategic Air Command tactics over flight paths, timing and electronic countermeasures.

Anglo-American co-operation

Furthermore, the United States agreed to supply tactical nuclear weapons for the Valiants assigned to NATO and for the Canberra interdictor squadrons in Germany, and to share with Britain the information which would in time lead to the introduction of a new type of megaton-range warhead, Red Snow, for the next generation of British free-fall hydrogen bombs, the Yellow Sun Mk 2s.

A further aspect of Anglo-American co-operation was the loan to Britain of 60 ground-launched Thor missiles to supplement the V-force. As an intermediate-range ballistic missile (IRBM) the Thor could deliver a megaton-range warhead a distance of 1,500 miles (2414 km), and was therefore well suited for deployment in Europe to counter Russian advances in missile technology, but of inadequate range to be discharged from bases in the United States against targets in the Soviet Union. After some months of negotiation the agreement reached in February 1958 provided for Thors to be manned and operated by RAF units, the warheads to be kept in American custody, and launching to take place only after a joint positive decision by both governments.

In line with the final deployment plan of 1960, 20 missile squadrons with five launch crews to each squadron were formed at dispersed sites, mainly in East Anglia, Lincolnshire and Yorkshire. Operationally and administratively they were part of the deterrent force under Bomber Command, wielding the equivalent destructive power of 60 V-bombers armed with megaton-yield bombs, but lacking their re-use, re-think and conventional warfare capabilities. For the 1,200 men in the Thor force, life involved living on isolated sites, a round-the-clock roster which included an RAF launch control officer working alongside a USAF authentication officer, and a regular programme of crew training and readiness exercises which included at least one count-down every day.

Test firings were carried out by RAF crews at Vandenberg Air Force Base in California, indicating that Thors were far more reliable than had at one time been rumoured, but in 1962 the United States decided to concentrate on strategic missiles and withdraw logistic support from the Thor squadrons in 1964. They were therefore phased out of service during 1963 and the missiles returned to the United States. In all, the Thor deployment had revealed a number of shortcomings. Reaction times could never be less than 15 minutes and, as static above-ground missiles, Thors were unlikely to survive a surprise nuclear attack and therefore could never be a satisfactory second-strike weapon; nor could they be part of a wholly independent contribution to the deterrent forces of the West.

By now Britain was facing a crisis over her deterrent. It had long been appreciated that what was needed in the face of the surface-to-air missiles (SAMs) which the Soviet Union was expected to deploy in the early 1960s was the means to make her deterrent as invulnerable to them as possible, thereby maintaining its effectiveness throughout the 1960s and beyond. There were two alternatives: a surface-to-surface medium-range missile, or an air-launched bomb which itself flew to the target.

An official requirement for the former had been issued in 1955 by the Air Staff: a ballistic missile to be fired from underground and with a range of up to 2,000 miles (3219 km), fulfilling the strategic bombardment role and complementing the manned bombers as a deterrent, and later replacing such bombers when developments in enemy ground defences rendered them obsolete. The resulting weapon, Blue Streak, was to enter service in the 1960s, superseding the Thors but profiting from experience gained in operating them.

Early experiments with guided bombs had produced the Blue Boar, but its operational limitations had proved so serious that it was abandoned in 1954 after five years' research. A requirement was then issued for a controlled bomb capable of being launched up to 100 miles (161 km) from the target, by day or night and in any weather; two years later a contract was awarded for what was to become the Blue Steel stand-off guided weapon. Both Blue Steel and Blue Streak were to have megaton warheads, prototypes of which had been tested during Operation 'Grapple' in May and June 1957, together with the warhead for the Yellow Sun free-fall bomb.

The problem with Blue Steel lay in its limited range, but when it came to planning a replacement matters began to go seriously wrong. Work began on the Mk 2 version with the range increased to 1,000 miles (1609 km), but early reports of a weapon which the United States was developing, the Skybolt air-launched ballistic missile, with a range and yield similar to those proposed for Blue Steel Mk 2, proved encouraging. As a result the British government decided to cancel Blue Streak and order Skybolt as the main British deterrent, at the same time abandoning work on Blue Steel Mk 2.

When Skybolt was also cancelled, Britain was offered submarine-launched Polaris missiles in compensation. The V-force was thereby left with

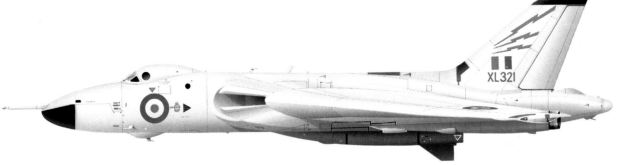

Avro Vulcan B.Mk 2 XL321 was modified for Blue Steel carriage before entry into service, and was allocated to No. 617 Squadron in whose markings it is shown. At this time it was the Wing Commander Flying's aircraft, as indicated by the pennant behind the squadron badge behind the fuselage roundel. The lightning flashes on the fin are drawn from the emblem on No. 617's badge. The aircraft subsequently served with No. 230 OCU at Finningley.

The Avro Vulcan B.Mk 2s belonging to the Scampton Wing had been modified to carry Blue Steel, as seen here. In 1963 it was decided to transfer the Vulcans to the low-level penetration role and the aircraft were camouflaged and trained in this new and more exacting type of flying.

operations. To make the latter possible it was necessary to modify Blue Steel so that it could be launched from below 1,000 ft (305 m); to develop the low-yield retarded lay-down bomb being designed for the naval Blackburn Buccaneer into a higher-yield version suitable for use by the V-force; and to strengthen the bombers' airframes originally intended for high-altitude operation. The most difficult problem was the modification of Blue Steel, the favoured solution being to give it a low-level launch with an up-and-over trajectory from an 'over the shoulder' delivery. The modified version became available in mid-1964 and the lay-down bomb, the WE 177, in September 1966.

Change to low-level operations

The operational profile of the V-force in the mid-1960s assumed training in low-level operations for all the Vulcan and Victor medium bomber squadrons. The B.Mk 1 aircraft would be armed with the second generation of free-fall megaton-yield weapons (the lighter Yellow Sun Mk 2 with Red Snow warhead, the product of American willingness to share the results of their own nuclear research). The B.Mk 2 aircraft would carry either the modified Blue Steel, or the new lay-down bomb, or Yellow Sun Mk 2. When dropping the latter the V-force would employ the pop-up technique, involving a climb from low level to release at a height of about 12,000 ft (3660 m).

The whole force was assigned to NATO from 1963 as part of the agreement under which the United States would provide Britain with Polaris missiles; the V-force would therefore be available to carry out attacks in accordance with NATO's nuclear strike plan, but would otherwise continue to meet national requirements, including the retention of its conventional bombing and overseas reinforcement capabilities.

Training in the low-level role began in 1963, when there were still 15 medium bomber squadrons. Contraction started in the following year, however, when two Victor B.Mk 1 squadrons, Nos 10 and 15, were disbanded; two more, Nos 55 and 57, converted to the tanker role in 1965 to replace Nos 90 and 214 Squadrons with Valiants. By the time

Blue Steel Mk 1 as its only stand-off weapon. Production delays and escalating costs added to the difficulties: with 1960 planned as the in-service date, Blue Steel would have had a useful life but, delayed to 1963–4 as it was, it became considerably less economic. To reduce its eventual cost, moreover, the number ordered was cut from 75 to 57.

Early trials of the new weapon at the Woomera range in Australia were not notably successful, but preparations went ahead in 1961 to bring it into service, including the decision to modify the aircraft of the three Vulcan B.Mk 2 squadrons at Scampton to carry it. As better reports came from Woomera in 1962 No. 617 Squadron began training, but it was not until the spring of 1963 that enough weapons were available for it to become fully operational in the Blue Steel role. Later that year the other two squadrons completed their training. The Victor B.Mk 2s of Nos 100 and 139 Squadrons at Wittering were also modified, and training of these two squadrons was completed in 1964. A total of 36 B.Mk 2 bombers was then equipped to carry Blue Steel: 24 Vulcans and 12 Victors.

To repair a situation in which there were no long-range stand-off weapons in prospect and to maintain its credibility as a deterrent, the V-force now modified its tactics from high- to low-level

Blue Steel was also fitted to the two Handley Page Victor B.Mk 2 squadrons at Wittering, Nos 100 and 139. This photograph emphasises the small ground-clearance in the Victor for this stand-off missile.

As well as carrying nuclear weapons, the Victor and Vulcans could be used in the conventional bombing role with 'iron' bombs as witness this graphic picture of a No. 15 Squadron Victor B.Mk 1A from Cottesmore dropping 35 such bombs.

conversion to the low-level role was complete in 1966, 11 medium bomber squadrons remained: three Yellow Sun Mk 2 squadrons at Waddington (Nos 44, 50 and 101), whose Vulcan B.Mk 1s were being replaced by B.Mk 2s; three WE 177 lay-down bomb squadrons at Cottesmore (Nos 9, 12 and 35) with Vulcan B.Mk 2s; and five Blue Steel squadrons, three with Vulcan B.Mk 2s (Nos 27, 83 and 617) at Scampton, and two with Victor B.Mk 2s (Nos 100 and 139) at Wittering.

TSR 2

The adoption of the low-level role by the V-force had in fact coincided with another philosophy favoured by the Air Staff since the late 1950s, that of low-level tactical strike by Bomber Command (employing tactical or enhanced-yield nuclear weapons) as a follow-up phase after the assumed destruction of the established V-force bases. A NATO thesis had foreshadowed the likelihood of secondary airfields in the west of France (then a full military component of NATO) surviving the initial nuclear attack, so that a requirement was voiced for a high-speed low-level strike bomber with short-field operating performance, and this potential successor to the existing V-bombers naturally attracted the attention of the RAF and British aircraft industry alike, resulting in the issue of General Operational Requirement (GOR) 339 and ultimately the ill-fated BAC TSR 2 (tactical strike reconnaissance) project.

Many professional careers were staked on this courageous concept, and indeed a very large proportion of the available defence funding was accordingly earmarked for its development between 1959 and 1964. But it was unfortunate that this phenomenally costly project was being pursued at a time when defence spending was suffering savage cutbacks and, it must be said, when the V-force itself was demonstrating considerable progress in survivability expedients. So it required only a fundamental shift in political attitudes towards defence to endanger the whole TSR 2 project.

Such a situation arose in 1964 with the election of a Labour administration, with the result that not only was TSR 2 summarily abandoned, but with it every advanced military aircraft project then being undertaken for the RAF. Whether or not the service could have supported the costs of introduc-

ing TSR 2 into squadron use, as well as of its very advanced support equipment and operating techniques, without scrapping the entire V-force prematurely has never been authoritatively confirmed. As it was, only one of the TSR 2 prototypes ever flew before the whole project was consigned to the scrapheap.

With the time approaching for the Polaris submarines to take over Britain's nuclear deterrent, the process of Bomber Command's contraction continued. No. 12 Squadron was disbanded in December 1967, followed by Nos 100 and 139 Squadrons in September and December 1968 respectively, and by No. 83 Squadron in August 1969. Two squadrons, Nos 9 and 35, were deployed to Akrotiri in Cyprus early in 1969 to replace the Canberras of the Near East Air Force Strike Wing.

Blue Steel was phased out of service between 1968 and 1970, the two squadrons concerned, Nos 27 and 617, changing to the free-fall role, with long-range maritime reconnaissance as an additional task. The QRA ceased on 30 June 1969. A year earlier Bomber Command had itself merged with Fighter Command to form Strike Command, eventually becoming No. 1 Group within that command, but responsibility for overseas reinforcement continued until 1971.

By the mid-1970s the Vulcan bombing force numbered six squadrons, No. 27 having disbanded and re-formed as a strategic maritime reconnais-

The RAF's decision to buy General Dynamics F-111 helped to seal the fate of the TSR2. XR219 was the only example to fly, and test pilot Beamont enthused over its flying qualities whilst the aviation industry marvelled at its technology.

The English Electric Canberra B.Mk 6, with 200 Series R. R. Avon engines, succeeded the B.Mk 2 in Bomber Command service, WJ756 being one such. It, too, served with the Binbrook Wing, at first with No. 101 Squadron and then with No. 9 Squadron, in whose markings it is shown.

The arrival of Vulcans and Victors into service enabled the first V-bomber, the Valiant, to be transferred to the flight-refuelling role. No. 214 Squadron at Binbrook in the spring of designated as the development unit for this task and XD870 was one of the aircraft, designated BK.Mk 1, used in this role. It is here seen refuelling another Valiant from the same squadron.

The Canberra B.Mk 6 remained in first-line bomber service with Bomber Command until 1961, but thereafter has served in many guises in the RAF and still serves today, although modified to other versions. This formation shows three aircraft of No. 12 Squadron, one of the last 'straight' Canberra bomber squadrons in the Command.

sance squadron, and Nos 9 and 35 Squadrons having returned from Akrotiri. All six units (Nos 35 and 617 Squadrons at Scampton, and Nos 9, 44, 50 and 101 Squadrons at Waddington) were operating in the tactical bombing role (much the same as had been intended for TSR 2) as part of NATO's strike force and were capable of delivering free-fall nuclear weapons or conventional bombs.

At the same time the V-force continued to carry out other important tasks, as it had done since the early days of the Valiants. When it became evident in 1957 that there would be a surplus of these first V-bombers two new tasks were proposed in addition to the strategic reconnaissance already being carried out by No. 543 Squadron: supplementing the Canberra squadrons in RAF Germany assigned to NATO for tactical bombing support, so compensating for recent reductions in the command's front-line strength; and the new role of inflight refuelling.

In the tactical support role the Valiants possessed the advantage over the Canberras of blind bombing aids independent of ground facilities; and while the Canberras could carry only one of the Mk 28 weapons which the United States was supplying under close supervision, the Valiants could carry two. The three Valiant squadrons involved (Nos 49, 148 and 207 with Marham as their base) were allotted NATO targets and maintained the normal V-force QRA capability with one aircraft available at all times. From 1962 they employed the same low-level tactics as the main force squadrons, together with a high-speed run known as the 'fast dash'.

Towards the end of 1964, however, the Valiants were found to be critically affected by metal fatigue and were finally grounded in January 1965. Plans to replace them with Vulcan B.Mk 1s in the tactical bomber role were eventually rejected on the grounds of expense and until July 1969, when the Vulcan B.Mk 2s were released from their strategic commitment, all that was available in the tactical bombing role was the Canberra interdictor force in RAF Germany.

Tanker/receiver modifications

In the matter of inflight refuelling, the grounding of the Valiants only hastened their replacement by Victor B.Mk 1s, a measure that had already been approved, so valuable had the tanker force proved itself to be. The gestation process had been lengthy, however, and it was not until the development of the probe and drogue system in 1949 (enabling bombers to be converted quickly into tankers and back again) that the RAF expressed serious interest. Five years later it was decided to make as many V-bombers as possible capable of the double tanker/receiver role, but as a result of financial and technical problems it was only in 1959 that permission was finally given to form a Valiant tanker force of two squadrons, Nos 90 and 214.

The advantages became clear as soon as the two squadrons began to train and operate with receiver aircraft. In particular the increased flexibility in

Avro Vulcan

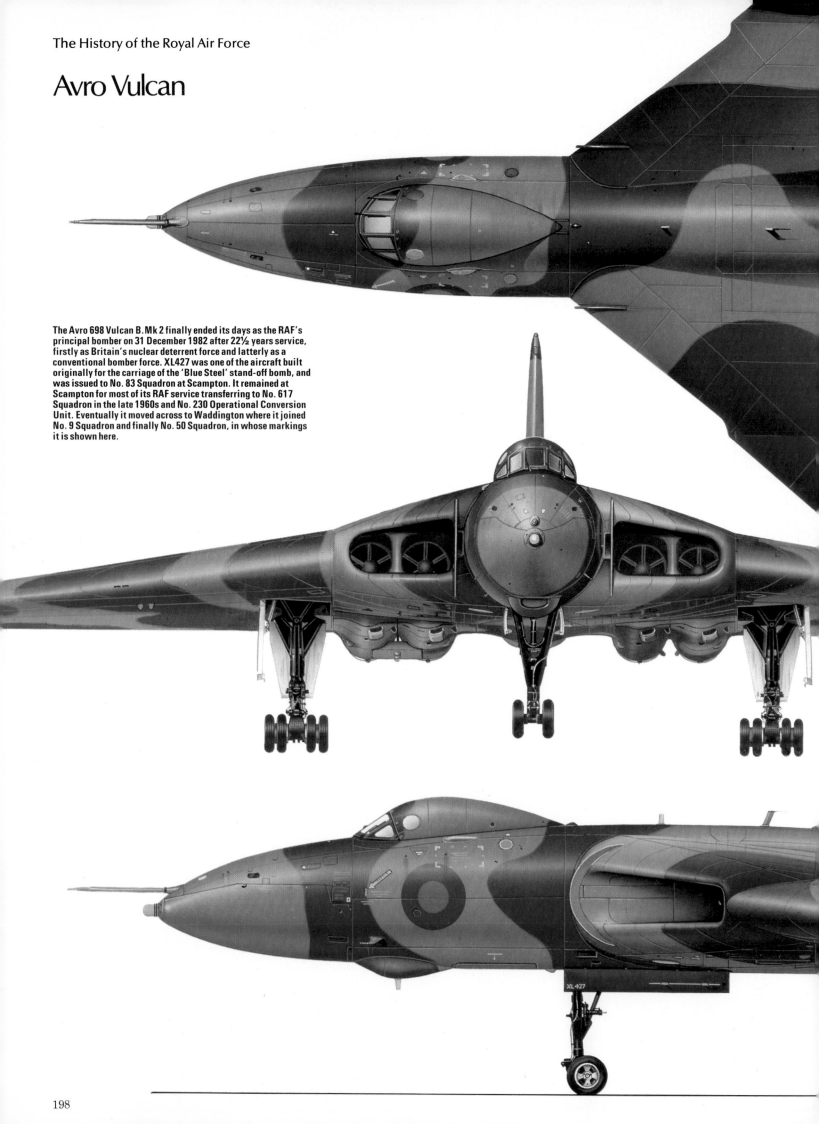

The Avro 698 Vulcan B. Mk 2 finally ended its days as the RAF's principal bomber on 31 December 1982 after 22½ years service, firstly as Britain's nuclear deterrent force and latterly as a conventional bomber force. XL427 was one of the aircraft built originally for the carriage of the 'Blue Steel' stand-off bomb, and was issued to No. 83 Squadron at Scampton. It remained at Scampton for most of its RAF service transferring to No. 617 Squadron in the late 1960s and No. 230 Operational Conversion Unit. Eventually it moved across to Waddington where it joined No. 9 Squadron and finally No. 50 Squadron, in whose markings it is shown here.

XL427

With the demise of the Valiant tankers the wing of Victor B.Mk 1As at Honington were converted into tanker aircraft. This aircraft (XH619) served at first as a bomber with No. 57 Squadron, then as a K.Mk 1A tanker subsequently with Nos 55 and 214 Squadrons.

mounting overseas reinforcements was apparent, especially in the case of fighter squadrons. Also, with inflight refuelling aircraft were better able to use the shorter runways commonly available overseas. A number of spectacular refuelling sorties were carried out by the Valiant tankers between 1961 and 1964, including the supporting of a Vulcan of No. 617 Squadron which flew non-stop from Scampton to Sydney in June 1961, taking on fuel four times in the course of a flight lasting 20 hours 3 minutes. Nine Valiant tankers were deployed for this operation, four at Tengah, two at Karachi and three at Akrotiri.

The formation of a third tanker squadron was approved in principle in 1962, but did not take place until after the force had been re-equipped with Victor B.Mk 1 two-point tankers. Nos 90 and 214 Squadrons were finally disbanded early in 1965, and the first Victor tanker squadron, No. 55, was fully operational in July, followed by No. 57 Squadron in December and by No. 214 Squadron in the summer of 1966. All were now based at Marham.

The Victor tankers began training with the V-bombers, an aspect of their work which continued until 1969, but otherwise they continued as before, refuelling aircraft as diverse as Armstrong Whitworth Argosy and Short Belfast freighters, Harrier close support aircraft, SEPECAT Jaguar and Hawker Siddeley Buccaneer strike aircraft, and McDonnell Douglas Phantom multi-role aircraft. Two of the last flew non-stop to Singapore in 14 hours 8 minutes in May 1970. No. 214 Squadron disbanded in 1977, and in the meantime Nos 55 and 57 Squadrons had re-equipped with Victor K.Mk 2 dedicated three-point tankers.

The growth in importance of the strategic reconnaissance role for the V-force had been considerable since the formation of No. 543 Squadron with Valiants in 1955. Re-equipped with Victor B.Mk 2s in 1965–6, the squadron could exploit the Victors' greater range in carrying out what was now to be its main task, high-level maritime reconnaissance to provide ocean surveillance for NATO's air and naval forces. The Victors had many uses in addition to mapping large areas of ocean quickly and in a limited number of sorties: they could record the damage wrought by hurricanes and earthquakes; reconnoitre peripheral areas of Eastern bloc territories; and contribute to the assessment of any situation which might lead to global war.

In May 1974 No. 543 Squadron was disbanded six months after No. 27 Squadron had re-formed at Scampton in the strategic and maritime reconnaissance role with Vulcan B.Mk 2s. At the same time No. 1 Group also had one squadron of Canberra reconnaissance aircraft, No. 39 Squadron at Wyton; a second Canberra squadron, No. 13, moved there from Malta in 1978.

Nine years earlier, the group had been given yet another commitment when No. 12 Squadron re-formed at Honington with Buccaneer S.Mk 2As as a maritime strike squadron, moving to Lossiemouth in 1980. A second Buccaneer squadron, No. 208 (for long a ground-attack squadron in the Middle East) was re-formed, also at Honington, in July 1974 in the overland strike and attack role.

In the mid-1960s the V-bombers went over to the low-level role, with their white aircraft camouflaged thus. Here two Vulcans from the Cottesmore Wing practise at low-level in 1965.

With the passing of the Wittering Victor wing, the aircraft were converted into tankers in the early 1970s and re-equipped Nos 55 and 57 Squadrons at Marham. This K.Mk 2 of No. 57 Squadron is seen refuelling two Jaguar GR.Mk 1s from No. 6 Squadron at Coltishall, emphasising the mobility that such a scheme permits the Royal Air Force.

Air Defence
of the British Isles

When the first-line strength of RAF Fighter Command started to expand once more towards the end of the 1940s, in the presence of clear indications that the Russian air force was already immensely powerful, the years of contraction which followed World War II had taken a heavy toll. Four of the eight fighter groups which had existed in May 1945 had disbanded within a year; moreover, No. 38 Group had been transferred to Transport Command and No. 60 had amalgamated with No. 26 to form No. 90 (Signals) Group. Only No. 11 Group at Uxbridge and No. 12 at Newton survived.

By the end of 1946 Fighter Command possessed no more than 192 front line aircraft in 18 day and six night fighter squadrons, all reduced to a cadre basis of eight aircraft per squadron without reserves. The mainstay of the day fighter force were the Gloster Meteor Mk 3s and Mk 4s and de Havilland Vampires, with four longer-range de Havilland Hornet squadrons in addition; the night force was equipped with de Havilland Mosquito NF.Mk 36s.

Both fighter groups were organised with two Sectors apiece: No. 11 Group's Metropolitan Sector at North Weald had four Meteor and two Mosquito squadrons, tasked with the day and night defence of London; its Southern Sector at Middle Wallop controlled six day fighter squadrons (three of Vampires, two of Meteors and one Supermarine

Spitfire squadron) and one Mosquito night-fighter squadron. No. 12 Group's Yorkshire Sector at Church Fenton had four Meteor, two Hornet and one Mosquito squadrons; its Eastern Sector at Horsham St Faith controlled two Hornet and two Mosquito squadrons. Included in No. 12 Group were the Central Fighter Establishment and most of the Command's other training establishments and units.

The vital Control and Reporting (C & R) System had also been reduced to a minimum, and by the end of 1946 was confined to covering an area extending coastwise from Flamborough Head to Portland Bill, and inland as far as a line joining Cape Wrath, Banbury and St Davids. The logic of these dispositions has often been questioned as no air threat from the continent could possibly exist, while any such threat from the Soviet Union exposed the north of Britain no less than the south; but those dispositions were regarded as no more than a basis on which any future expansion of the air defence system might be structured.

For the immediate post-war years, when no air attack was deemed likely, such a situation was regarded as acceptable. Indeed, the interim directive given to the commander-in-chief in November 1946 stated that his first priority would be research and experiment in air defence, and in this field the Central Fighter Establishment assumed an im-

The onset of peace found Fighter Command at an exciting stage, introducing jet fighters into its system. Foremost amongst these was the Gloster Meteor F. Mk 3, and one of the early peacetime bases to boast a Meteor wing was Horsham St Faith near Norwich. This photograph, taken in the late 1940s, shows the old wartime control tower and pre-war hangars still camouflaged, the pre-war designed petrol bowser moving along the line of Meteors whilst a foursome flies past for the benefit of the photographers.

At the end of the war the finest piston-engine fighter in Fighter Command was the North American Mustang F. Mk 4, but as these had been acquired under Lend-Lease terms they soon had to be replaced. No. 19 Squadron was flying them sufficiently long, however, to paint on their traditional blue/white check markings in addition to the code letters 'QV'. KM118 was part of the squadron when it was based at Molesworth in 1946.

The other type just entering service was de Havilland's Vampire F. Mk 1. No. 247 Squadron was the first one to receive the type at Chilbolton in March 1946, but it soon took the squadron to Odiham, where the first Vampire wing was formed. The F. Mk 1, with the high tail, was soon superseded by the later F. Mk 3 and FB. Mk 5 at Odiham.

Above right: Spitfires still had their part to play in air defence, especially the later Griffon-engined versions such as the F. Mk 21 which were issued to the newly re-formed Auxiliary Air Force squadrons, soon to be renamed the Royal Auxiliary Air Force. It is with No. 602 'City of Glasgow' Squadron at Abbotsinch that this Spitfire F. Mk 21 is serving.

Last of the piston-engine fighters to enter service with Fighter Command was the de Havilland Hornet, seen here in its F. Mk 3 version. It was established in four squadrons for long-range fighter duties and escort work as well as low-level strike for which it could carry four rockets under the wings. These particular aircraft belong to No. 41 Squadron, airborne from Church Fenton in 1950.

portant role: to achieve the highest possible interception rate, by day and night, and whatever the weather; to devise an efficient raid reporting and fighter control organisation; and to standardise all operating and training techniques so that, in an emergency, the BAFO fighter squadrons could be brought back quickly to reinforce Fighter Command. A lower priority was given to deploying the command's resources to provide, with the army's Anti-Aircraft Command, air defence for the largest area which could be defended effectively.

Nevertheless much was being done during those years of contraction to improve the command's efficiency in two vital areas: aircraft and the C & R System. By 1947 the RAF fighter squadrons were equipped with the best aircraft then being produced in Britain, but the establishment of the jet engine in service had meant that engine design had outstripped airframe design (at least in Britain) and was posing knock-on problems in weapon technology and the C & R System. The formation of the High Speed Flight at Tangmere in June 1946 had therefore a dual purpose: to improve on the record set up by Group Captain H. J. Wilson in a Meteor at Herne Bay in Kent in November 1945 at 606.25 mph (976 km/h), and to provide data for research into the characteristics and techniques of high-speed flight. (In the interests of post-war economies the Labour government had refused to sanction a full programme of manned high-speed

flight research, permitting instead a limited programme of flight by unmanned models whose value was soon shown to be almost worthless.)

The Meteor shows its paces

During the life of the High Speed Flight airframe capabilities were expected to be the limiting factor, but in eight attempts at Littlehampton, Sussex, in September 1946 the speed record was raised to 616 mph (991.76 km/h), or a Mach number of 0.80, after buffeting and vibration had made the aircraft all but uncontrollable. Some valuable information was gained, as well as a clear demonstration that the Meteor Mk 4 was at least 80 mph (129 km/h) faster than most of its contemporaries. What was not fully recognised was that the Meteor was effectively at the end of its performance development and was therefore on the threshold of obsolescence. And that was in 1946.

Furthermore, high speeds posed problems for the C & R System, and the rolling programme of upgrading, which had begun during the war, continued into the years of contraction. Precise interception had become practicable following the development of the GCI (ground-controlled interception), where the controller could work directly off the PPI (plan position indicator) and watch the exact relative positions of fighter and target, but the introduction of jet aircraft meant that no one station could by itself intercept fast and high-

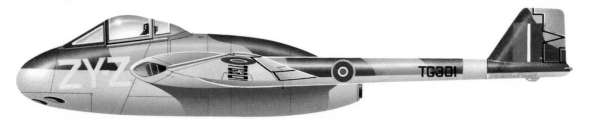

flying enemy aircraft. In 1946, therefore, trials were conducted with a new system in which data provided by radar and the Royal Observer Corps were co-ordinated at a selected master radar station (MRS), and by August that year it was clear that the new system was workable, although obviously vulnerable to saturation of control resources. Plans were then made to establish MRSs in each of Fighter Command's four sectors, at Sopley (Southern), Trimley Heath (Metropolitan), Neatishead (Eastern) and Patrington (Yorkshire).

The RAF tests its defences

As a result, when it was announced that jet fighter production was to be doubled, older fighter aircraft were to be reconditioned and the Royal Auxiliary Air Force was to be brought up to strength, Fighter Command possessed a better base on which to build than had existed two years earlier. Indeed the results of Exercise 'Dagger', which was held that month to test Britain's air defences were certainly encouraging; USAF Boeing B-29 Superfortress bombers were intercepted at 33,000 ft (10060 m), and Spitfires carried out attacks at 29,000 ft (8840 m). The interception rate, particularly before the raiders crossed the coast, proved satisfactory despite the use of radio counter-measures. The Auxiliary squadrons also gave good results.

The problem, however, lay in continuing man-power shortages, which compelled a 10-hour stand-down in the middle of the exercise, which in turn allowed unrealistic opportunities for equipment servicing and resting of personnel. Shortcomings spotlighted in the new C & R System led to further modifications which worked well in the two big air-defence exercises in 1949, 'Foil' and 'Bulldog', the first in which Britain's Western European allies also participated. (For many years these 'annual exercises' were major defence operations and were the only means of testing the nation's defence systems against current world tactics and technology, just as they had been during the years between the world wars; more recently their scale has diminished although their numbers have multiplied.)

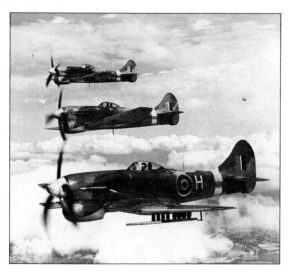

A new directive to Fighter Command's commander-in-chief, issued in April 1949, underlined the changes in priorities. The main task was now to defend the United Kingdom against air attack, and in the next two years a number of important steps were taken to achieve this. In July 1950 the command's readiness state was increased when day fighters were put on armed alert (codenamed 'Fabulous') to intercept any unidentified aircraft approaching British air space. By early 1951 the front-line day fighter strength had been doubled and all squadrons were equipped or equipping with jet aircraft, and by the end of the year a Canadian fighter wing, with North American F-86 Sabres, had arrived at North Luffenham.

Thus, in December 1951, Fighter Command possessed 25 front-line squadrons with a total establishment of 402 aircraft: 276 Meteor F.Mk 8s, 48 Vampire FB.Mk 5s, 36 Meteor NF.Mk 11s, 35 Vampire NF.Mk 10s and six Mosquito NF.Mk 36s.

In addition there were the RCAF Sabre wing and the 160 Meteors and Vampires of the Royal Auxiliary Air Force. The main elements of the training

FIGHTER COMMAND FRONT-LINE STRENGTH AT DECEMBER 1951

No. 11 Group

Southern Sector

Squadron	Aircraft	Location
1	Meteor F.8	Tangmere
29/22	Meteor NF.11	Tangmere
54. 247	Vampire FB.5	Odiham

Metropolitan Sector

Squadron	Aircraft	Location
25	Vampire NF.10	West Malling
41/253	Meteor F.8	Biggin Hill
56/87, 63	Meteor F.8	Waterbeach
64, 65	Meteor F.8	Duxford
72	Vampire FB.5	North Weald
85/145	Meteor NF.11	West Malling
257, 263	Meteor F.8	Wattisham

No. 12 Group

Northern Sector

Squadron	Aircraft	Location
19/152	Meteor F.8	Church Fenton
66/111	Meteor F.8	Linton-on-Ouse
92	Meteor F.8	Linton-on-Ouse
264/79	Meteor NF.11	Linton-on-Ouse

Eastern Sector

Squadron	Aircraft	Location
23	Vampire NF.10, Mosquito NF.36	Coltishall
74/34	Meteor F.8	Horsham St Faith
141/142	Meteor NF.11	Coltishall
245/266	Meteor	Horsham St Faith

Caledonian Sector

Squadron	Aircraft	Location
43/17, 222	Meteor F.8	Leuchars
151	Vampire NF.10	Leuchars

Most handsome version of the Hawker Tempest was the Centaurus-engined F. Mk 2 which first served in Fighter Command with Nos 54 and 247 Squadrons at Chilbolton in the summer of 1945. MW774 was a No. 54 Squadron aircraft.

De Havilland produced an ad hoc night-fighter by putting a Mosquito cockpit on to a Vampire and dubbing it the NF. Mk 10. This is from No. 23 Squadron at Coltishall in 1951.

By the early 1950s all the auxiliary squadrons had converted to jets, many receiving Vampires. This detachment of No. 601 (County of London) Squadron is in Malta in 1950. Note the squadron's red and black triangle markings on the booms of the Vampire F. Mk 3s and the winged sword on the nose.

organisation remained in No. 12 Group, namely the CFE at West Raynham, and the three operational conversion units (No. 226 at Stradishall, No. 228 at Leeming and No. 229 at Chivenor). A fifth sector, the Caledonian, had been formed in 1949 to control the squadrons in Scotland and Ulster.

A major problem of the early 1950s was that the RAF was flying no more than stopgap fighters with which to counter the growing power of Russia's formidable air force. All the British aircraft in service were certainly improvements on their predecessors, and the introduction of the de Havilland Venom NF.Mk 2 in 1953 provided a further minor improvement, but to match the Russian

Mikoyan-Gurevich MiG-15, whose capabilities had been amply demonstrated in Korea, a swept-wing fighter was long overdue. Two types, the Hawker Hunter and the Supermarine Swift, had been ordered off the drawing board in 1950 after years of vacillation by Ministry of Supply and Air Staff alike, but it would be some time before either could enter service. To fill the gap the Air Ministry negotiated to acquire the F-86 Sabre to be made available under the Mutual Defense Assistance Programme (MDAP). Deliveries began at the end of 1952, the aircraft being ferried across the Atlantic during the following 12 months by RAF pilots in Operation 'Bechers Brook'. The first squadrons to be equipped with this, the first RAF transsonic fighter, were Nos 3, 67 and 71 in Germany during the spring of 1953; two Fighter Command squadrons also received Sabres, No. 66 in December 1953 and No. 92 in February 1954.

In step with the strengthening of the command's front line forces was a programme to modernise the C & R System. New equipment was introduced to increase the range and height at which approaching aircraft could be detected, as well as a large measure of automation in the correlation and display of information, but all took time to develop, integrate and install. All that could be achieved for the time being was a series of stopgap measures, known as the Rotor Plan, put forward in 1950 and given first priority (even over aircraft production) in March 1951. The reliability of existing equipment, some of which had been installed as long ago as 1941 (for example, the old Type 7 radar), was to

The Gloster Meteor NF.Mk 14 was the last version of the Meteor to see service in the fighter role. WS775 was initially issued to No. 85 Squadron at West Malling in 1954 and carries here the squadron's black/red checks and the hexagon emblem on the fin.

be improved by making servicing simpler; overall cover was to be increased by duplicating radar stations; vulnerability reduced by building underground; and readiness improved by manning additional watches with regular personnel. The last expedient was achieved by re-mustering redundant aircrew members to the Control and Reporting branches of the service.

The shortage of trained regular manpower remained a problem, however, even when the first phase of the Rotor Plan had been largely implemented in 1954, as many radar stations were still being manned on a part-time basis. Further improvements soon followed, and by the time, early in 1956, that the new British Type 80 long-range radar came into service, enough personnel were available to mount a continuous watch at Neatishead in Norfolk. By then night-fighters had joined the quick reaction force, already provided by the day fighters, so that aircraft were always available at varying degrees of readiness to investigate unidentified aircraft approaching British air space. Also, as part of a programme to modernise the command's main fighter bases, operational readiness platforms (ORPs) were being built at the ends of main runways to enable fighters to be positioned for immediate take-off; reaction time was further improved by linking pilots at cockpit readiness directly with their controllers by 'tele-scramble'.

Improved types enter service

The most important step forward had come in 1954 with the introduction of the Hunter and Swift aircraft. As a result of accelerated development by their manufacturers, even while production was under way, problems arose at the time of their intended delivery to the service. Indeed, in the case of the Swift difficulties in introducing armament and a need to re-engine the design rendered the development so complex that what was in effect little more than a revamped research aircraft never reached an acceptable service version in its Mks 1 to 4 variants; the Swift came into service with No. 56 Squadron early in 1954 but was withdrawn 15 months later after a number of flying accidents. A modified version, the FR.Mk 5, was produced in 1955 and sent to Germany in the fighter-reconnaissance role, where it replaced the Meteor FR.Mk 9.

The Hunter, on the other hand, became the RAF's standard single-seat fighter and remained so until 1960, replacing the Meteor and Sabre; in the ground-attack role it remained in service with the RAF until well into the 1970s. With its single-point refuelling system and detachable Aden gun-pack, its turn-round time was reduced to only seven minutes between sorties, while its four 30-mm Aden guns delivered 10 times the weight of fire of the MiG-15. The Hunter F.Mk 4 and F.Mk 6 versions were significant improvements on the earlier F.Mk 1 and F.Mk 2 versions, the F.Mk 4 with its additional fuel and external weapon facilities, and the F.Mk 6 with its uprated Rolls-Royce Avon engine.

A third advanced fighter, the all-weather Gloster Javelin, entered service in 1956. The first twin-jet, delta-wing fighter in the world, it was designed to intercept bombers flying at high altitude and high subsonic speeds. In all 363 were produced; a late variant, the FAW.Mk 7, delivered in 1958, was the first of its type to carry the Firestreak air-to-air missile as standard armament.

World tension, sparked by the war in Korea, had highlighted the measure to which Britain's air force was falling behind, as well as its inadequate coverage of the surrounding air space. A sixth sector, the Western, became operational in January 1952, and at the same time No. 81 Fighter Group was re-formed to control Fighter Command's

The purchase of Canadair Sabres in 1953 was a panic measure to cope with the arrival of the MiG-15 as a possible opponent. Formation ferry flights brought the type across from Canada to equip the squadrons in Germany and two squadrons (Nos 66 and 92) in Britain. This photograph shows a batch of these aircraft after arrival on a ferry flight across the Atlantic.

Below left: As newer types entered regular service so Meteor F.Mk 8s became available for the RAuxAF. Two units were based at Bigging Hill, No. 600 (City of London) and No. 615 (County of Surrey) Squadrons. This eight-ship formation taken in 1965 is led by four from No. 600 Squadron and, nearer the camera, four from No. 615 Squadron.

Below: The standard night-fighter had become the Gloster Meteor NF.Mk 11, manufactured by Armstrong Whitworth at Baginton. First squadron to fly this type was No. 29 at Tangmere, who put up this impressive echelon formation in 1952.

Two squadrons of Canadair Sabre F.Mk 4s served with Fighter Command, both Nos 66 and 92 Squadrons being based at Linton-on-Ouse. XD727 served with No. 92 Squadron, as evidenced by the red/yellow checks, from 1954 to 1956.

The swift F.Mk 1 was intended to be the next generation of fighter after the Meteor, along with the Hunter. The type entered service with No. 56 Squadron at Waterbeach in 1954 but it had not been sufficiently developed by then and was found to have serious faults, particularly at altitude. No. 56 soon re-equipped with Hunters.

The Meteor night-fighter was developed with new radars and later equipment during the 1950s, the last version being the NF.Mk 14, seen here in formation of No. 25 Squadron from West Malling in 1954.

training units. Three years later No. 13 Group was re-established to control the Northern and Caledonian Sectors, while No. 11 Group retained the Southern and Metropolitan Sectors, and No. 12 became responsible for the Eastern and Western Sectors.

By the end of 1956 Fighter Command reached a peak strength of some 600 front-line aircraft in 35 squadrons: 16 Hunter and two Meteor day fighter squadrons, eight Meteor and eight Venom night-fighter squadrons, and the first of the Javelin all-weather fighter squadrons. The strength of the auxiliary fighter squadrons remained unaltered.

Despite the employment of home-based fighter squadrons (hurriedly sent to the Mediterranean) during the Suez operations at the end of 1956, that year's peak was followed by a steady decline in terms of both aircraft and squadrons. In the following six years up to December 1962 the total front-line establishment fell to 320 aircraft in 1958, to 272 in 1960 and to 140 in 1962, when the number of home-based squadrons had dropped to no more than 11. Furthermore, on the pretext of cost-saving, the Royal Auxiliary Air Force fighter squadrons were disbanded in 1957, together with No. 81 Group and two of its OCUs. Despite these savage reductions Fighter Command was still required to reinforce overseas theatres in times of emergency.

It has been suggested that against the ever-present background of economies in defence spending in peacetime, and of British and NATO strategies, contraction of Fighter Command was logical. With British thinking turning on the deterrent value of the V-bomber force, and NATO relying on the 'tripwire' philosophy, first priority would inevitably go to the defence of the bomber stations. What this priority dictated was not an extensive air defence organisation in the United Kingdom or Germany but a small, highly efficient manned force in which a new interceptor fighter, the English Electric Lightning, would progressively replace the Hunter, and air-to-air missiles replace

Hawker Hunter

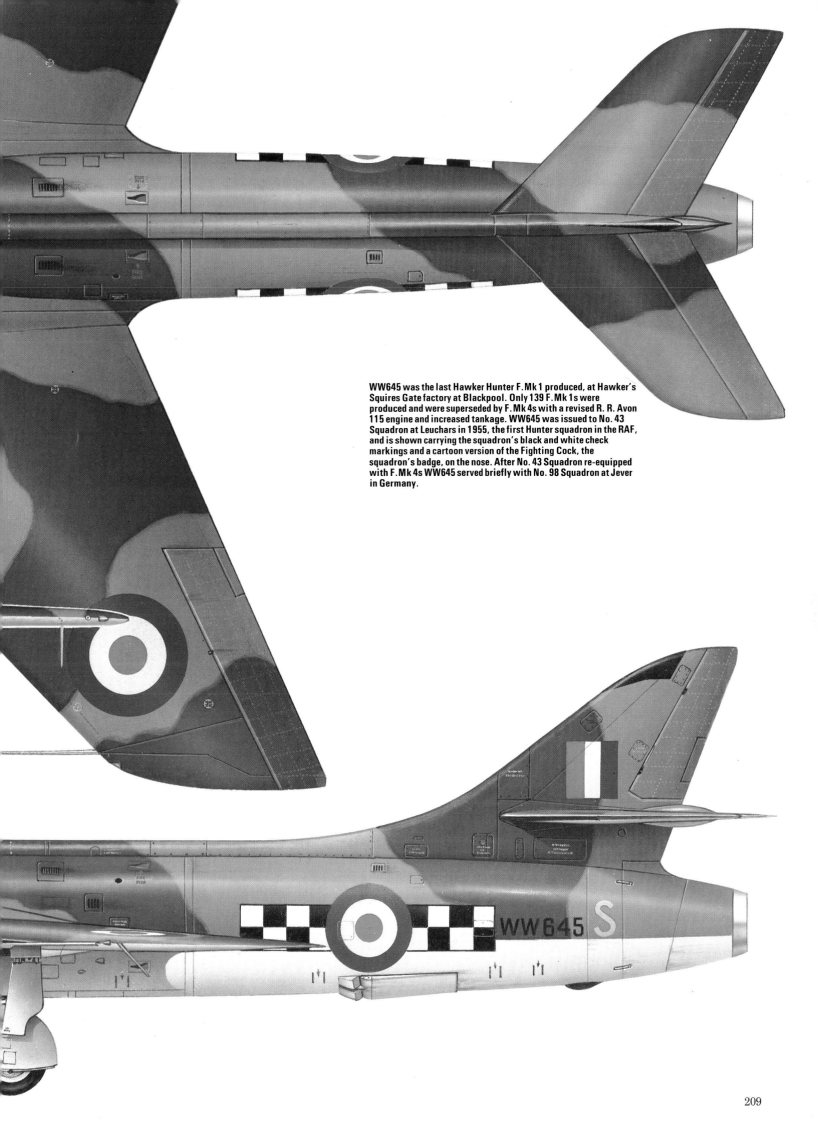

WW645 was the last Hawker Hunter F. Mk 1 produced, at Hawker's Squires Gate factory at Blackpool. Only 139 F. Mk 1s were produced and were superseded by F. Mk 4s with a revised R. R. Avon 115 engine and increased tankage. WW645 was issued to No. 43 Squadron at Leuchars in 1955, the first Hunter squadron in the RAF, and is shown carrying the squadron's black and white check markings and a cartoon version of the Fighting Cock, the squadron's badge, on the nose. After No. 43 Squadron re-equipped with F. Mk 4s WW645 served briefly with No. 98 Squadron at Jever in Germany.

WW645 S

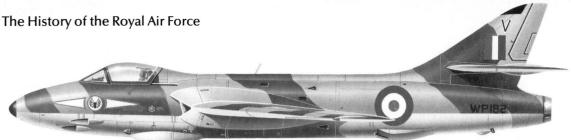

The Hawker Hunter Command came in several versions, two of which were powered by the Armstrong Siddeley Sapphire engine instead of the Rolls-Royce Avon. These were the F. Mk 2 and F. Mk 5. WP182 was one of the latter and entered service with No. 1 Squadron at Tangmere in 1955. By 1957 it had transferred to No. 34 Squadron, also at Tangmere, but the career of the F. Mk 5 came to an end when the Tangmere Wing was disbanded in 1958.

existing forms of armament. In time, so the authors of the 1957 White Paper on Defence believed, British air defence would depend entirely on surface-to-air missiles – once problems of range and proneness to radio countermeasures had been overcome. For the time being, the assumption was that the threat came from a combination of manned bombers and missiles. When in the early 1960s the conviction grew that the main danger was from surface-to-surface missiles, against which it was thought that no defence existed, a further reduction in the manned fighter force seemed the logical consequence, so that by 1965 it had dropped to no more than 60 aircraft, all Lightnings and Javelins, the level it was to remain for four years. By extreme good fortune no serious threats to overseas theatres brought demands for reinforcement from the home-based fighter squadrons.

Mach 2 fighter

For the moment, however, the manned fighter was to be retained and there were no plans to curtail production of the Lightning, due to come into service in 1960, or the air-to-air or surface-to-air missile programmes. The Lightning represented a considerable technological advance (bearing in mind government parsimony in research funding during the early 1950s), with its Mach 2 capability in level flight and a ceiling of over 60,000 ft (18290 m), well in excess of any previous RAF fighter; its highly sophisticated radar system locked on to the target and passed back the information needed to bring the pilot into firing range. Successive versions, produced between 1961 and 1966, improved the aircraft's range and performance with the introduction of a refuelling probe, overwing and ventral fuel tanks, and Avon 301 turbojets. Indeed by 1967 all Fighter Command

front-line aircraft were equipped with inflight-refuelling probes, and by the end of 1969 Lightnings were being flown to the Far East with only a single stop at Masirah, as part of the RAF's policy of maintaining a rapid reinforcement capability.

The de Havilland Firestreak infra-red homing air-to-air missiles, which had first entered service on the Javelin FAW. Mk 7 in 1958, embodied a solution to two problems posed by raiders approaching at high subsonic speed: the very short time available to intercept and the loss of manoeuvrability caused by the interceptor's own speed and height. With the radius of turn greatly increased at supersonic speed, interception had to be initiated outside human visibility distance and under radar control, with the result that the attack must be limited to one pass only. A highly lethal weapon was therefore essential, capable of homing on to the target from any angle. The Firestreak was

No. 66 Squadron at Linton-on-Ouse put up this Hunter F. Mk 4, followed by the CO's Sabre F. Mk 4 and finally the Sabre's predecessor, a Meteor F. Mk 8.

Right: The 1950s were the years when the fighter squadrons were vying with each other to put on squadron aerobatic teams. Doyen of all these was No. 111 Squadron at North Weald and later Wattisham, with Hunter F. Mk 6s.

With the advent of the Gloster Javelin, high-speed all-weather fighting proceeded a stage further. The first Javelin FAW. Mk 1s joined No. 46 Squadron at Odiham in March 1956 and soon after put up this formation for the Air Ministry photographer.

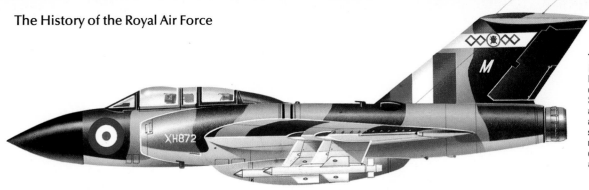

The Gloster Javelin was developed into various versions, the ultimate being the FAW.Mk 9. XH872 served originally as a FAW.Mk 7 with No. 23 Squadron but on being re-engined as an FAW.Mk 9 joined No. 64 Squadron at Duxford in whose markings it is seen. The squadron subsequently moved to Binbrook in 1962 and then out to Tengah in Singapore to augment No. 60 Squadron in 1965.

powered by a solid-fuel rocket and homed on to its target (usually the jet exhaust) by means of a heat-detecting cell. A later development, the Red Top, with a more powerful rocket motor and manoeuvrability, could be launched at greater ranges and approach its target from wider angles of attack. For some 10 years after World War II missiles retained their manufacturers' commercial names, such as Firestreak; thereafter their service code-names such as Red Top, Blue Steel etc, gained universal usage.

A further element in the defence of the V-bomber bases was the Bloodhound I surface-to-air guided missile, first introduced in July 1958. Over the following three years 352 were deployed in four missile wings, each with a Tactical Control Centre (TCC) to control its missile sites: No. 2 at Lindholme, the northern deterrent complex; No. 148 at North Coates covering the V-bomber bases at Scampton, Waddington and Coningsby, and the Thor squadron at Hemswell; No. 151 Wing at North Luffenham defending the bases farther south; and No. 24 at Watton defending those in East Anglia.

The Bloodhound I was designed to engage targets flying between 10,000 ft (3050 m) and 60,000 ft (18290 m) at 20 miles (32 km) range. It was powered by two Thor ramjets and had four short-burning rocket-boost motors to accelerate it to its cruising speed of Mach 2; its proximity fuse actuated a high explosive warhead. On the ground a complex sequence of events would follow identification of a potential target by the C & R System and a decision at the Master Radar Station to use guided weapons rather than manned fighters. The appropriate TCC would then be given the target's position, height, course and speed, and would allot it to a selected launching site, where the missile would be fired, to home on to the reflected radar response produced

Above: Second base to receive the Lightning was Wattisham, where the type went into service with No. 56 Squadron in 1961. This was the F.Mk 1A version with provision for inflight-refuelling. Armament was two Firestreak missiles.

Above left: The supersonic age really reached Fighter Command in June 1960, when No. 74 Squadron at Coltishall was re-equipped with the English Electric Lightning F.Mk 1. This squadron pioneered into service this formidable new fighter, eventually taking a later version to Singapore for Far East Air Force.

Right: Nine Javelins make an impressive picture in the afternoon sky, heralding the end of Fighter Command's profusion of squadrons. With the arrival of the Lightning the command was whittled down to only a few bases and squadrons.

The first surface-to-air missiles were introduced into Fighter Command in the form of Bristol Bloodhound Mk 1s sited at the V-bomber bases for point defence. Marham's battery is seen here with a Vickers Valiant BK.Mk 1 of No. 214 Squadron being towed past.

The strangest addition to Fighter Command in recent years has been the Avro Shackleton AEW. Mk 2. This aircraft has served with No. 8 Squadron at Lossiemouth since 1972 and has provided airborne early warning of approaching aircraft and limited fighter direction facilities to bring the Lightnings and Phantoms of No. 11 Group to find Soviet aircraft approaching from the east and north.

by a target illuminating radar at the site.

Within three years of the Bloodhound I missile system being completed, however, it fell victim to a further round of defence economies; the TCCs, which had been found susceptible to jamming, were closed in January 1963, and the squadrons, controlled meanwhile by the Master Radar Stations at Patrington and Bawdsey, were disbanded in June 1964. An improved missile, however, the Bloodhound II, which was air-transportable, entered service with No. 25 (SAM) Squadron (previously a famous night-fighter squadron) in 1964 mainly for overseas reinforcement, but available also to strengthen home defences when not serving elsewhere. The squadron moved to Germany in 1970 and a second squadron, No. 85, was re-formed for service in the United Kingdom.

Accent on early warning

Even without the Bloodhound I squadrons, the defence of the V-force bases provided by the Javelins and Lightnings remained for some years formidable. Their role, together with that of the C & R System, was clear: to provide the greatest possible warning of an air attack, and to deter or inhibit violations of British air space, including those by aircraft which might be intent on reconnaissance or jamming Britain's early warning system. To these ends their hand was strengthened by three further developments in the 1960s: the establishment of the Fylingdales early warning system in September 1963 to give warning of a ballistic missile attack in time for the V-bombers to disperse; the close links being forged between British and continental air defence organisations; and the growing sophistication of the C & R System itself.

The RAF had since 1952 benefited from early warning afforded by continental radars, and had ever since participated in joint air defence exercises; in September 1960 NATO approved a plan which provided an integrated air defence structure which at the same time safeguarded national interests. The United Kingdom was to form one of four air defence regions and, with some reservations, RAF squadrons were assigned to NATO, together with the missile squadrons and the C & R System. The Commander-in-Chief, Fighter Command, became Commander, United Kingdom Air Defence Region, responsible to SACEUR (Supreme Allied Commander, Europe) for the operation of all assigned air defence forces in Britain, and for co-ordinating air defence plans and operations with other NATO commanders. The reservations voiced by Britain concerned control over the size, composition and role of Fighter Command, and over its deployment, particularly the movement of squadrons for reinforcement overseas.

With so many changes taking place in the air defence organisation from the late 1950s onwards, the C & R System itself was necessarily constantly under review, being required to respond to new concepts and developments. With the contraction of the front-line force and the need for economy, the old Rotor Plan was succeeded by the Razor Plan, intended to streamline the system and make substantial savings in manpower, but at the same time to improve efficiency. By taking full advantage of the better equipment now available, the Type 80 long-range radar and the photographic display unit, which together gave a true picture of the air situation at any given moment, the new plan divided the United Kingdom into eight defence sectors. Each was under the control of a Master Radar Station and a Master Controller and, being autonomous under the general supervision of the Air Defence Operations Centre, was able to respond swiftly to any attack.

The first stage of the Razor Plan was completed in the summer of 1958 but the second stage, not to be completed before 1961, was overtaken by the need to develop a more sophisticated system, code-named Plan Ahead and designed to cope with supersonic aircraft and ballistic missiles. This new plan soon proved too costly and out of scale with a defence force soon to consist of no more than 60 aircraft. It was therefore succeeded by the Linesman/Mediator programme, agreed by the government in 1964, the year in which the new Labour administration virtually abandoned all pretence of supporting an indigenous aircraft industry capable of producing military aircraft on its own. The new programme had been conceived originally as a joint military and civil project but was later redefined with Linesman covering the air defence aspects and Mediator the civil aviation requirement, but with an integrated Master Control Centre at West Drayton catering for both.

Mach 2 import from America

Linesman had been evolved in the years when NATO's tripwire philosophy predominated, but with NATO thinking moving towards the concept of flexible response, and the appearance of a fast-growing number of Russian aircraft operating in sensitive areas, progressive modifications were

Eventually limited to one base at Binbrook, two Lightning squadrons (Nos 5 and 11) have flown from there since 1964, using the F. Mk 6 as their basic aircraft. This aircraft (XR747 originally served with No. 23 Squadron.

No. 23 Squadron received Phantom FGR.Mk 2s in 1975, initially based at Coningsby before moving to Wattisham. With their aircraft now painted in low-visibility grey, No. 23 is engaged in air defence of the Falkland Islands, flying from RAF Stanley.

introduced into the original programme and elsewhere in the air-defence organisation.

In particular, the increase in Russian air activity in the areas around the British Isles and out in the Atlantic gave proof that by the mid-1960s the Soviet Union was pursuing a deliberately expansionist policy, which clearly included the probing of defences and the gathering of intelligence.

As a result Britain's manned aircraft defences were increasingly engaged in intercepting and turning away intruders entering the United Kingdom Air Defence Region. The front line itself was strengthened by an increase in fighter aircraft to 70 in 1969 and 76 in 1975, and the addition of a squadron of early warning Avro Shackletons. As it had also become obvious that an attack could now come from any direction, radars were installed to cover the west and north west of the British Isles.

Following the abandoning in 1964 of the Hawker P.1154, a highly sophisticated V/STOL fighter for the RAF, a newcomer to the front line, the American McDonnell Phantom, was ordered and entered service in the FG.Mk 1 interceptor version with No. 43 (Fighter) Squadron in 1969. Five years later the FGR.Mk 2 tactical reconnaissance variant, superseded in Germany by the SEPECAT Jaguar, joined the air defence force in the United Kingdom to supplement the ageing Lightning. With a maximum speed of Mach 2.1 and capable of flying supersonically at tree-top height, the Phantom possessed a ceiling comparable with that of the Lightning but could fly farther without refuelling; the

armament provision was for four Sparrow air-to-air radar-guided missiles and four Sidewinder air-to-air infra-red missiles.

The Shackleton early warning aircraft joined the air defence organisation has adapted steadily of low-level attacks, a task which no ground-sited radar could do satisfactorily. But it soon became clear that the Shackleton could use its radar not only for early warning purposes, but also to control intercepting fighters in the event that the normal controlling authority was unable to see the incoming raiders, and guide strike aircraft operating below enemy radar cover thereby avoiding the risk of their own radars being detected.

Throughout the years of change the structure of the air defence organisation has adapted steadily to new circumstances, both military and economic. With the contraction of the front line force the number of fighter groups had been reduced to two in January 1961: No. 12 at Horsham St Faith and No. 13 (renumbered No. 11) at Oulton.In April 1963 the two groups were replaced by three sectors, No. 11 (Northern), No. 12 (East Anglia) and No. 13 (Scottish). Two years later the three sectors were disbanded to give Fighter Command direct control over all its resources, and in April 1968 the command itself merged with Bomber Command to form Strike Command, and became No. 11 Group within the new command, thereby perpetuating the most illustrious of all fighter groups in the RAF and the one that had played so vital a part in the Battle of Britain.

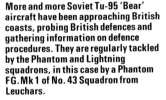

More and more Soviet Tu-95 'Bear' aircraft have been approaching British coasts, probing British defences and gathering information on defence procedures. They are regularly tackled by the Phantom and Lightning squadrons, in this case by a Phantom FG.Mk 1 of No. 43 Squadron from Leuchars.

The RAF's Maritime Commitment

The expansion and re-equipment of Coastal Command, which began in 1951, followed six years of retrenchment in which the forces under its control faced many obligations but possessed strictly limited resources with which to meet them. Its main function during that period, as the Air Ministry had outlined to the Commander-in-Chief, Sir Leonard Slatter, in September 1946 was to study and develop modern methods of achieving the prime objectives of a maritime air force: the defence of friendly shipping at sea against all forms of attack other than air attack, and the location and destruction of enemy surface and underwater craft.

Secondary responsibilities were the co-ordination and control of all air-sea rescue operations in the sea areas around the United Kingdom and Gibraltar, and operational and administrative control of the meteorological and home-based photographic reconnaissance squadrons, the latter being part of the Central Photographic Establishment, previously known as No. 106 (PR) Group. Furthermore, Coastal Command might be asked to provide aircraft and crews to assist in air transport operations in an emergency.

The command's resources had begun to contract immediately after the end of World War II in Europe, the intention then being to retain a small nucleus of maritime aircraft in the United Kingdom, while transferring a number of squadrons to the Far East for air-sea rescue and transport work in the war against Japan, handing over others to a rapidly-expanding Transport Command, and disbanding the remainder. With the surrender of Japan, the rundown began in earnest, as in other commands, so that by October 1946 Coastal Command had been reduced to two group headquarters, No. 18 at Pitreavie Castle and No. 19 at Plymouth, and the equivalent of two other groups in the form of RAF Northern Ireland at Aldergrove and the Central Photographic Establishment at Benson.

The command's front-line strength in October 1946 amounted to 50 aircraft in two squadrons of flying-boats, four land-based squadrons of general reconnaissance aircraft and two medium-range strike squadrons, each unit being established on a

Most of Coastal Command's land-based maritime squadrons were equipped with Lease-Lend Liberators at the end of World War II. As these were due for return to the USA, the Avro Lancaster was speedily converted to GR. Mk 3 configuration and supplied to the command. SW370 here is in service with No. 210 Squadron at St Eval circa 1951.

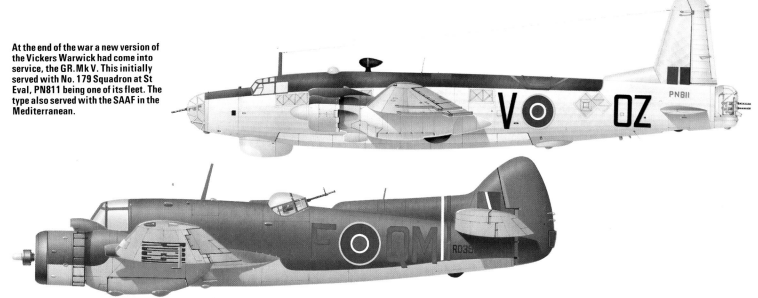

At the end of the war a new version of the Vickers Warwick had come into service, the GR.Mk V. This initially served with No. 179 Squadron at St Eval, PN811 being one of its fleet. The type also served with the SAAF in the Mediterranean.

A sizeable part of Coastal Command's strike force had consisted of Bristol Beaufighter TF.Mk 10s, of which RD351 is typical. It served with No. 254 Squadron in the North Coates Strike Wing. With the cessation of hostilities this force was cut down to one squadron, No. 254, which moved to Thorney Island and was renumbered No. 42 Squadron.

COASTAL COMMAND'S FRONT-LINE STRENGTH AT OCTOBER 1946

No. 18 Group
Squadron	Aircraft	Location
120, 203	Lancaster GR.3	Leuchars

No 19 Group
Squadron	Aircraft	Location
210, 224	Lancaster GR.3	St Eval
210, 230	Sunderland GR.5	Calshot
36	Mosquito FB.6	Thorney Island
42	Beaufighter TF.10	Thorney Island

cadre basis with no more than five aircraft on a flying-boat squadron, six on a land-based squadron and eight on a strike squadron, a strength that would permit rapid expansion if the need arose.

In addition Coastal Command controlled No. 202 Squadron (numbered No. 518 until October 1946) whose Handley Page Halifax Mk 6s flew meteorological reconnaissance sorties from Aldergrove and Gibraltar; and the de Havilland Mosquitoes, Supermarine Spitfires and Avro Lancasters of the two photo-reconnaissance squadrons, Nos 58 and 82 (numbered Nos 540 and 541 until October 1946).

As in the RAF as a whole, Coastal Command's immediate problem in the late 1940s was to balance commitments against limited resources. In common with other commands it had to suffer the dire consequences of the rapid rundown in 1945 and 1946, particularly in the loss of aircrew and skilled tradesmen. Consequently, although its front-line strength had been substantially reduced, it still did not have the manpower needed to produce the number of flying hours with which to meet its commitments. With priority afforded to meteorological flights and photographic survey work, the hours available for specialised training in maritime operations were strictly limited, a situation that could be accepted only because the risk of war in the immediate future was considered to be very small.

Despite its limited resources Coastal Command was still able to maintain an effective training organisation to match the demands made of maritime crews in terms of skills, patience and endurance throughout long over-water patrols. All operational conversion was concentrated at No. 236 Operational Conversion Unit (OCU) at Kinloss

in 1947; crews destined for a long-range general reconnaissance squadron were given a 16-week course there, including instruction in maritime reconnaissance, ship recognition, weaponry and the use of the latest (sic) search and detection equipment; flying-boat crews then went on to No. 235 OCU at Calshot for a four-week conversion course on Short Sunderlands, which was expanded in December 1949 to a full flying-boat operational conversion course. Crews for the strike squadrons attended a 12-week course on Bristol Beaufighters at Kinloss, but this was discontinued in October 1947 when all maritime strike squadrons were disbanded in the interests of economy and the task assumed by Bomber Command. Squadrons at home and overseas pursued a regular training programme, and there were a number of overseas training 'cruises', to some extent perpetuating the pre-war practice.

It also proved possible from August 1947 to send a number of Coastal Command Lancasters to Ein Shemer in Palestine to reinforce their counterparts in the Mediterranean; the task was to locate ships carrying illegal immigrants to Palestine. Indeed, most of the more colourful activity involving RAF maritime aircrews occurred overseas during those years, particularly in the Far East: the *Amethyst* incident of 1949, the Malayan Emergency and the Korean War.

Meteorological reconnaissance

First priority for Coastal Command, however, was afforded to the meteorological reconnaissance flights over the North Atlantic, a commitment that survived until 1964, the Halifaxes being replaced by Handley Page Hastings in 1950. Regular reports

The Vickers Warwick was another aircraft which had entered Coastal Command service during the war and had been used principally for air-sea rescue duties, although those stationed overseas had also doubled in the straight maritime reconnaissance role. Of such were the aircraft of No. 38 Squadron at Luqa (Malta), seen preparing for a sortie in August 1945. The version is an ASR.Mk 1.

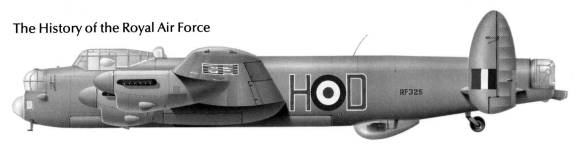

on frontal weather systems approaching the British Isles were important for forecasting conditions over the United Kingdom, Europe and the civil air routes across the Atlantic. The flights usually followed a triangular course, two legs being flown at some 1,500 ft (460 m) and a third at about 18,000 ft (5485 m). Measurements of temperature, wind, visibility and other atmospheric conditions were reported every 50 miles (80 km) and at pre-determined levels during the climb to and descent from altitude.

The sorties flown by the two photo-reconnaissance squadrons were designed to meet air survey requirements and to assist planning authorities in post-war reconstruction. In 1946 a survey of West Africa was started on behalf of the Colonial Office and by the time, four years later, that control of the Central Photographic Establishment was transferred to Bomber Command, photo-reconnaissance aircraft were operating over many parts of East and southern Africa.

In the longer term, Coastal Command's principal difficulties during the late 1940s concerned equipment. The elements of success in a maritime campaign had been unequivocally demonstrated in the Battle of the Atlantic: aircraft with adequate range for the tasks, efficient search and detection equipment, and effective weapons to destroy the target once detected. With the return of the war-time Consolidated Liberators, Boeing Fortresses and Consolidated Catalinas to the United States, and the retirement of the Vickers Warwicks and Vickers Wellingtons, the maritime force in the late 1940s came to depend on the Lancaster GR.Mk 3 and the Sunderland GR.Mk 5, the former being introduced as an interim general reconnaissance aircraft in 1946 and the latter having been in service in various versions since 1938.

The Lancaster had an endurance of 12 hours and a normal operating radius of action of some 950 miles (1529 km) with a warload of 7,000 lb (3175 kg), including 18 250-lb (113-kg) depth charges. In the search and shadowing role its endurance could be stretched to 16 hours and its normal operating radius to 1,300 miles (2092 km) by replacing the

depth charges with overload fuel tanks. The Sunderland, loaded with 16 250-lb (113-kg) depth charges, had an endurance of 11 hours and a normal operating radius of action of 625 miles (1006 km); without its depth charges its endurance in the search and shadowing mode were increased to almost 16 hours and its radius of action to 900 miles (1448 km). Both types of aircraft thus had a significantly shorter radius of action than the wartime very long-range Liberators and Catalinas.

Early equipment

Both the Lancaster and the Sunderland were equipped with the air-to-surface vessel (ASV) radar which at a normal operating height of 1,000 ft (305 m) could detect a schnorkelling submarine in a reasonable calm sea at about 5 miles (8 km), and a 10,000-ton vessel at between 25 and 30 miles (40 to 48 km). Both aircraft also carried sonobuoys, which had become available in the later stages of the war, but only in limited numbers; they were, however, to have a profound influence on the post-war development of anti-submarine warfare. When dropped into the sea, the early non-directional buoy could detect the sound of a submarine's

The Avro Shackleton MR.Mk 1 entered service first with No. 120 Squadron at Kinloss in April 1951. It had ASV radar under the nose and a mid-upper turret with two 20-mm cannon. WB854 served first with No. 224 Squadron in Gibraltar from April 1953 to September 1954 before joining No. 120 Squadron and eventually served in the Far East with No. 205 Squadron at Seletar (Singapore) from July 1958 to October 1962.

The new maritime reconnaissance aircraft for RAF service was the Avro Shackleton, a far-reaching development of the Lincoln. This quickly allowed the expansion of the command to cope with the rapidly-growing Soviet submarine threat.

COASTAL COMMAND'S FRONT-LINE STRENGTH AT JULY 1954

No. 18 Group

Squadron	Aircraft	Location
120	Shackleton MR.1, MR.2	Aldergrove
204, 240, 269	Shackleton MR.1, MR.2	Ballykelly
217	Neptune MR.1	Kinloss
202	Hastings Met.1	Aldergrove

No. 19 Group

Squadron	Aircraft	Location
42, 206, 220, 228	Shackleton MR.1, MR.2	St Eval
201, 230	Sunderland GR.5	Pembroke Dock
36, 203, 210	Neptune MR.1	Topcliffe

Air Headquarters, Gibraltar

Squadron	Aircraft	Location
224	Shackleton MR.1, MR.2	North Front

Until the Shackleton could come into service in sufficient numbers the arrival of some US Navy Neptunes in RAF service was welcome. The first squadron was No. 217, newly reformed at St Eval, and soon a wing was formed in 1953 at Topcliffe, to cover the northern seas. The Neptune MR.Mk 1 remained in service with three squadrons of the RAF until 1957.

turning propellers by means of a hydrophone and transmit it back to the aircraft; by comparing the signal strengths received from different buoys, whose relative positions were known, an operator in the aircraft could determine the submarine's course and speed. A more advanced type, the directional sonobuoy, not introduced until the early 1950s, could indicate the submarine's bearing from the buoy. For search and detection, therefore, Coastal Command was little better equipped in the late 1940s than it had been in wartime.

In weaponry however the same could not be said. The command's main weapon against an enemy submarine in the immediate post-war years was the depth charge. Its lethal range was only some 19 ft (5.8 m), and to stand a reasonable chance of success an attack had to be made within 30 seconds of the target submerging. More effective was the American torpedo or Mk XXIV mine, carried by some of the very long-range Liberators and designed to home on to a submarine making a noise, but the remaining stocks of these were returned to the United States after the war. The 600-lb (272-kg) anti-submarine bomb, which had been used occasionally in the war mainly against surfaced submarines, had also been withdrawn from use. As a

result, until a new homing torpedo became available in the 1950s, the command was in a considerably worse position than it had been in the latter phases of the war.

Replacements needed

Thus, when it became evident in 1950 that the Soviet Union was engaged in a rapid expansion of its naval forces and was conceivably preparing to have 1,000 submarines in service by the early 1950s, it was not simply a matter of increasing Coastal Command's front-line strength in concert with Britain's naval forces. What was required was a replacement for the Sunderland and Lancaster, with a better radius of action and a British version of the homing torpedo. Proposals for a new medium-range flying-boat came to nothing, although the Short Seaford (originally the Sunderland Mk IV) underwent operational trials with No. 201 Squadron in 1946 before being withdrawn as a victim of the defence cutback. Plans had also been laid as early as March 1946 for a new long-range maritime reconnaissance land-based aircraft based on the Avro Lincoln bomber and capable of operating in any part of the world with a 6,000-lb (2722-kg) weapon load and a normal operating radius of action of 1,725 miles (2776 km). In a revised specification the weapon load was reduced to 4,000 lb (1814 kg) and the radius of action agreed at 1,500 miles (2414 km). The resulting aircraft, the Avro Shackleton, was introduced into service in 1951 and soon settled down to become the RAF's maritime mainstay for the next two decades. It could carry a crew of 10, including two pilots, two navigators, an engineer and five signallers. Its introduction led to many changes in Coastal Command's infrastructure: runways, hardstandings and servicing areas had to be strengthened and training facilities extended.

Adequate numbers of Shackletons would not become available in the early 1950s to meet the command's increasing commitments and its new responsibilities within the NATO alliance. A stopgap was sought and found in the American Lockheed P2V-5 Neptune, of which 52 (sufficient to

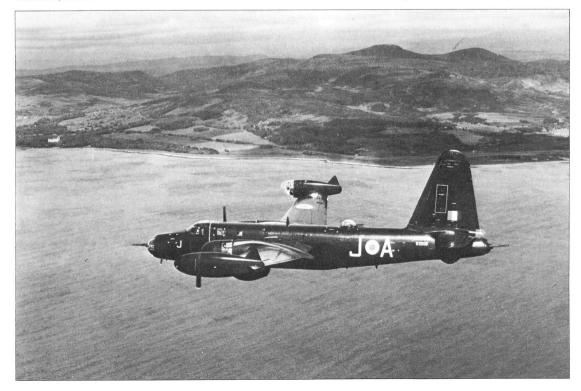

WR965 was a Shackleton MR.Mk 2 which entered service first with No. 37 Squadron in November 1954 at Malta, transferring to No. 38 Squadron there in July 1957 until March 1959. It then had Phase 1 modifications to its equipment and went to Gibraltar with No. 224 Squadron from March 1960 until August 1961, when it returned to Britain for Phase 2 modifications. With these it joined No. 203 Squadron at Ballykelly in April 1962, serving with that unit until March 1966. This period was followed by Phase 3 modifications and then a move to Singapore to serve with No. 205 Squadron from July 1967 until November 1968. In that month the aircraft returned to Britain and joined No. 204 Squadron at Ballykelly again until the squadron's disbandment in April. It then underwent a lengthy conversion to AEW.Mk 2 standard and joined No. 8 Squadron at Lossiemouth in 1972 where it has been serving ever since. This airframe certainly owes the taxpayer nothing at all!

equip four squadrons) were supplied by the United States under the Mutual Defence Assistance Program. With a radius of action of 1,275 miles (2052 km) and a weapon load of 2,700 lb (1225 kg), the Neptune was an effective aircraft whose real strength lay in its powerful APS 20 search and APS 31 attack radars, its search receiver (which intercepted radar transmissions from enemy vessels), and wing-mounted searchlight for night-time illumination of target. But an acute shortage of spares led to problems which had not been fully resolved when the Neptune started being withdrawn in August 1956 after only four years in service.

By July 1954 Coastal Command's expansion programme was complete. The command now possessed a front-line strength of nine Shackleton squadrons, four of Neptunes and two of Sunderlands in the maritime role, plus one Hastings squadron performing the meteorological reconnaissance task, in all comprising a force of 119 aircraft (eight on Shackleton and Neptune squadrons, and five on Sunderland and Hastings squadrons). Shackletons and Sunderlands were based on the western seaboard to cover the eastern Atlantic, and the Neptunes at Kinloss and Topcliffe to cover enemy submarines and surface ships using northern waters and the North Sea.

Shortly after the completion of its expansion programme, Coastal Command started to receive the Mk 30 homing torpedo which, with the introduction of the directional sonobuoy, gave its maritime aircraft much improved tracking and attack capabilities. There remained the problem of making the initial detection. Improvements in this area came with the introduction of a device (the 'sniffer') which could detect a submarine's diesel exhaust gases, and of a British airborne search receiver that brought the Shackleton up to the standard of the Neptune in this respect.

By 1955, therefore, Coastal Command had been largely transformed. Nor was it acting alone, as it was now part of the NATO alliance's forces. Its aircraft had been earmarked for SACLANT (the NATO Supreme Commander, Atlantic) since 1952, and its commander-in-chief commanded jointly with his British naval opposite number all NATO forces in the Eastern Atlantic, one of the two areas into which the Atlantic as a whole had been divided for operational purposes. Together the two commanders were to be responsible in time of war for maintaining the Atlantic lifeline, emphasis being placed upon convoy protection, anti-submarine measures and a highly mobile striking fleet; in peacetime they would concentrate on the development of new tactical concepts and devising the frequent joint exercises which were to weld the various air and naval forces involved into an effective fighting force.

Meanwhile Coastal Command was also engaged in numerous other activities around the world, which provided experience in the kind of instant deployment that might be required if a threat developed outside the NATO theatre. Overseas training flights continued: aircraft were sent to Malta for anti-submarine training, and maritime aircraft were often employed as transports, supporting the British North Greenland Expedition in 1951–4 for example, or ferrying supplies to the Ionian Islands after an earthquake. Later, between 1956 and 1958, Coastal Command aircraft provided search and rescue cover during the Monte Bello, Maralinga and Christmas Island tests of the British atomic weapons; they also carried out meteorological reconnaissance sorties during the tests and maintained ocean patrols to keep shipping from straying into the danger zones. The Shackleton was in fact proving to be a highly versatile aircraft with a very wide range of capabilities.

A new approach to a traditional task began late in 1955 with the formation at Thorney Island of No. 22 Squadron with six Westland Whirlwind helicopters for search and rescue work. Detachments were later provided at Martlesham Heath and Valley to cover the RAF training areas, and in due course most of the busier coastal waters around the United Kingdom came within the scope of the search and rescue helicopters.

The chill wind of contraction which started to blow through the RAF in the later 1950s was tempered to some extent for Coastal Command by

Above left: During the 1950s the Shackleton was progressively developed, the final maritime version being the MR.Mk 3 with tricycle landing gear and greatly increased weight. This version was probably over-developed and incurred problems which eventually required small underwing jet engines to give it added power. Seen off the rugged coast of Cornwall is this No. 220 Squadron MR.Mk 3.

Below left: The advent of the practical helicopter, in the form of the Bristol Sycamore and Westland Whirlwind, led to the re-forming of search and rescue elements of Coastal Command, with No. 22 Squadron flying Whirlwinds and No. 275 Squadron Sycamores. Practising off the Cornish coast is a Whirlwind HAR.Mk 2 of No. 22 Squadron based at St Mawgan in 1956.

Below: Farewell—a final flypast at Pembroke Dock, Milford Haven when the flying-boats finally left Coastal Command in 1957.

XF707 was a Shackleton MR. Mk 3 which first served with No. 201 Squadron at St Mawgan in February 1959. It is shown in the squadron markings. It left No. 201 in April 1962 for Phase 2 modifications and joined No. 201's sister squadron, No. 206 at St Mawgan in July 1963. With No. 206 Squadron until February 1965, it then went for Phase 3 modifications and joined No. 42 Squadron, also at St Mawgan, in January 1966, serving until August 1971 when it was delivered to Benson for use by the fire brigade and subsequently burned.

the government's acceptance of the thesis that Soviet naval expansion constituted a particular threat to Britain. All the same, the four Neptune squadrons were disbanded between August 1956 and March 1957, and the two Sunderland squadrons early in 1957. Thoughts of ordering the Short Seamew for the short-range anti-submarine reconnaissance role, and of using helicopters for inshore operations, were abandoned, and even the order for the Mk 3 version of the Shackleton (with tricycle landing gear and auxiliary wingtip fuel tanks) was reduced. The first squadrons to take delivery of the last, No. 220 in September 1957 and No. 206 in January 1958, were given only six aircraft instead of the previous establishment of eight. However, a programme of progressive improvement of the Shackleton's radar equipment was started, and the Mk XXI ASV radar was introduced together with a

new sonobuoy and improved tracking and navigation equipment.

The 1960s witnessed two fresh problems: the appearance of the nuclear submarine and the development by the Soviet navy of a greatly enhanced ocean-going capability. The qualities of the nuclear submarine (its greater underwater speed and its ability to travel vast distances without surfacing and to operate at much greater depths) rendered anti-submarine operations considerably more complex. Moreover, the rapid growth of the Soviet Union's ocean-going fleet, including nuclear submarines armed with intercontinental ballistic missiles, forced a shift of emphasis upon Coastal Command. As well as protecting convoys in the Western Approaches and the English Channel, and supporting NATO's strike fleet, it now had the additional task of maintaining an air screen to

Sea, cloud and sky: two Shackleton MR. Mk 2s in their element at sunset.

The Hawker Siddeley Nimrod MR. Mk 1 became the standard maritime reconnaissance aircraft in No. 18 Group, Strike Command from October 1970 onwards, equipping Nos 120, 201 and 206 Squadrons at Kinloss, No. 42 Squadron and No. 236 OCU at St Mawgan and No. 203 Squadron at Luqa in Malta. XV232 originally served with OCU, moving out to Malta with No. 203 Squadron in 1972 and serving there until the squadron disbanded in December 1977.

detect and monitor Russian ships and submarines moving down through the Norwegian Sea into the Atlantic.

To match this shift of emphasis, Coastal Command had by 1965 three of its eight Shackleton squadrons based at Ballykelly, three at Kinloss, one at St Mawgan and one in Gibraltar, all with six aircraft apiece. This deployment represented a movement of the centre of gravity from the south west towards the north and north west, now the main areas of Soviet activity.

The Shackletons were now beginning to show signs of their age and were kept in service throughout the 1960s only by a rolling programme of modernisation that included a steady improvement in their weapon capability, introduction of jet-assisted take-off and progressive updating of their radar, navigation and electronic countermeasures equipment.

Meanwhile the search for a Shackleton replacement had run into difficulties, resulting principally from enforced contraction of the British aircraft industry as well as the perennial demands for reductions in defence expenditure. Nevertheless the resulting Hawker Siddeley Nimrod, an extensively modified adaptation of the de Havilland Comet airliner, matched the demands of the original specification, namely a high transit speed to the patrol area some 1,000 miles (1609 km) from base, and the ability to remain on patrol for at least four hours carrying a substantial weapon load.

The new aeroplane was introduced into squadron service in the latter half of 1970 and early 1971. By then the maritime front-line strength had been reduced to no more than four squadrons, each with

six aircraft: Nos 120, 201 and 206 Squadrons at Kinloss and No. 42 at St Mawgan; some would consider this a logical extension of the previous deployment concept which sought to concentrate the greater weight of forces in the north, and it is generally accepted that the drastic reduction in numbers of aircraft was partly offset by the Nimrod's greatly improved operating capability. On the other hand the maritime task had meanwhile

In the 1970s the adoption of the Buccaneer S. Mk 2 by the RAF enabled the service to set aside one of its squadrons, No. 12, with the responsibilities of maritime strike.

Hawker Siddeley evolved the Nimrod MR. Mk 1 from the basic Comet airframe and fitted with many anti-submarine detection devices.

The yellow Westland Whirlwind HAR.Mk 10s have been a common sight around English, Cypriot and Singapore coasts since 1962. XP346 was a Whirlwind built from the start as an HAR.Mk 10 (others were converted from Mk 2s and Mk 4s) and served almost all its time with No. 22 Squadron at various detachments around Britain.

XH563, a Vulcan B.Mk 2(MRR) is seen plugged in and ready for start on one of Scampton's hardstandings in 1976.

This Wessex HC.Mk 2 is from the No. 22 Squadron detachment at Valley and is practising mountain rescue techniques over the Snowdon range.

increased in the mid-1970s by the need to afford protection to the growing number of offshore installations in the northern waters, and it remains to be seen how long the Nimrod can survive in service having regard to the effect of high utilisation upon its fatigue life.

No. 1 (Bomber) Group had been making a contribution to the maritime task since 1969, however, the Royal Navy having assumed responsibility for

the strategic nuclear deterrent. In October 1969 No. 12 Squadron re-formed at Honington with Blackburn Buccaneer S.Mk 2As for the maritime strike/attack task, moving to Lossiemouth with S.Mk 2Bs in 1980; fatigue problems with this aircraft in recent years have led to speculation about the continuing effectiveness of the Buccaneer in the role. Additional long-range maritime reconnaissance was provided by the Victor B.Mk 2s of No. 543 Squadron, also in No. 1 Group, until May 1974 when the task was assumed by the Vulcans of the newly re-formed No. 27 Squadron.

As well as the Nimrods, there were also in the maritime front-line force in December 1975 two search and rescue helicopter squadrons: No. 22 Squadron at Thorney Island with Whirlwinds (to which the Westland Wessex was added in 1976), and No. 202, formed at Leconfield in 1964 with Whirlwinds, to which Westland Sea Kings were added in 1978.

In terms of organisation Coastal Command, which originally formed under the title of Coastal Area in 1919, disappeared 50 years later in November 1969, being replaced by No. 18 Group, a component of the new Strike Command, while its former subordinate groups, Nos 18 and 19, became the Northern and Southern Maritime Air Regions respectively.

Distinctive in their brilliant yellow colour schemes, the Westland
Sea King HAR.Mk 3 helicopters of the Royal Air Force are the latest
SAR (search and rescue) machines for use around the UK's coasts
and mountainous regions. Replacing the Whirlwind HAR.Mk 10,
they entered service in early 1978, and the force of 16 were all in use
the following year. They have H.1400-1 engines and six-blade tail
rotors, flight crew of two plus air electronics/winch operator and
loadmaster/winchman, and navaids including radar, Doppler and
computer. All are nominally on the strength of No. 202 Squadron at
Lossiemouth, but are deployed in pairs around the country. There is
also a detachment to the Falklands, where the helicopters are in
grey colour scheme.

Westland Sea King

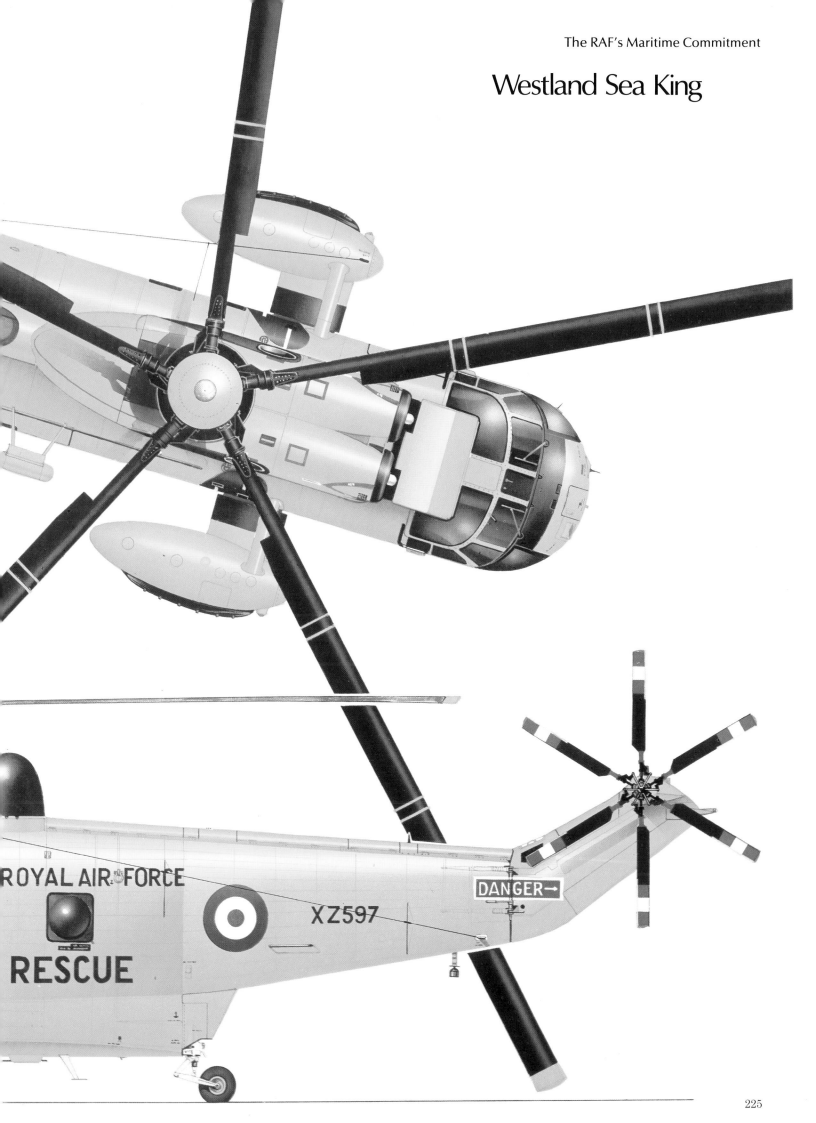

ROYAL AIR FORCE

XZ597

DANGER→

RESCUE

Swansong in the Far East

The abrupt end of World War II in the Far East in August 1945 brought about special problems for South East Asia Command (SEAC) and to its RAF component, Air Command South East Asia (ACSEA). In Europe, the Mediterranean and the Middle East there had been ample warning of impending victory, and time in which to prepare for the tasks ahead. In South East Asia the expectation was that war against Japan would last at least a further year or 18 months, so that preparations were in hand for a long and arduous campaign.

However, with the surrender of Japan the tasks facing SEAC changed abruptly but lost nothing of their urgency. Priority was afforded to the locating and repatriating the many thousands of Allied prisoners of war and internees known to be in camps scattered throughout the whole of South East Asia and living in appalling conditions of squalor and deprivation. Two other tasks were also to be undertaken: the rounding-up and dis-arming of several hundred thousand Japanese troops, and re-establishing civil administration in countries occupied by Japan since 1942. Simul-taneously, many British and Allied servicemen were themselves joining the demobilisation process already under way in Europe, while others,

who would remain with the colours, were preparing for a peacetime role yet to be decided.

To add to SEAC's problems, the area for which it was responsible had been increased immediately before the Japanese surrender from 1 million to $1\frac{1}{2}$ million square miles (2.59 million to 3.88 million km²), and now included Borneo, Java, Celebes and Indo-China south of the 16th parallel, as well as the territories previously allocated to it, namely India, Ceylon, Burma, Siam, Malaya and Sumatra.

SEAC's resources were substantial, as were those of ACSEA, which in August 1945 controlled 12 groups, 73 squadrons and a number of specialist flights. Considerable redeployment was essential to meet the new requirements, and by mid-October seven subordinate headquarters had been created to deal directly with the problems of particular regions. The first, in Burma, dated back to December 1944, and the others followed in September and October 1945 to serve Siam, French Indo-China, Malaya, Hong Kong, the Netherlands East Indies and Ceylon. In addition, at the end of 1945 ACSEA still controlled six subordinate formations in India; the two transport groups in the area, No. 229 at New Delhi and No. 232 at Rangoon, remained within Transport Command until the following March.

With the recapture of the lands previously under Japanese domination, old places took on an unfamiliar look. The famous RAF base at Seletar, Singapore was found to be a graveyard of Japanese navy aircraft.

In 1946 an RAF Spitfire squadron, No. 122, moved into Hong Kong for fighter defence of the base. Two young Chinese boys were officially adopted by the squadron.

There was much still to be done by the squadrons in the Far East, including the dropping of food and medical supplies to natives in the jungle. Liberators, operating from the Cocos Islands, carried canisters in the bomb bays to be dropped where they were needed.

In the task of locating and repatriating Allied prisoners of war and internees the RAF played an important role, first dropping leaflets (150 tons in three days) and then parachuting Red Cross relief teams into all known camps. But there were many others whose exact whereabouts were not known, and RAF aircraft were used to locate them: the Consolidated Liberators, whose crews were experienced in clandestine operations, were deployed for the more distant areas, while Republic Thunderbolts, Douglas Dakotas and Westland Lysanders operated where the search areas were closer to base. Despite the monsoon conditions, extensive areas of Malaya, Siam, French Indo-China and Sumatra had been covered by early September, and Dakotas and Liberators had dropped supplies and control teams to all the camps so far located. By the end of the month 53,700 prisoners and internees had been liberated; a month later the total had reached 71,000, and only in Java, where a tense political situation had developed, had Allied teams met with hostile reception.

At the same time progress was being made in resettling the territories seized by Japan three years previously. Burma was already largely reoccupied and acted as a base from which forces could move back into Siam and French Indo-China. Siam had been technically at war against the Allies, but after brief negotiation its king returned from exile and the RAF established a staging post at Bangkok to handle the Dakota flights needed to bring in troops and supplies. No. 909 Wing arrived

from Burma shortly afterwards (without its Thunderbolt aircraft) to establish an air headquarters. Two squadrons followed, No. 20 with Supermarine Spitfire F.Mk VIIIs and No. 211 with de Havilland Mosquito FB.Mk VIs, and a detachment of Mosquitoes from No. 684 (Photographic Reconnaissance) Squadron was also sent in to locate the more isolated internment camps and to update the existing photographic survey of the area.

The evacuation of prisoners of war and internees proceeded quickly, as did the rounding-up of Japanese troops, so that by December the situation had become sufficiently stable to allow the return of No. 20 Squadron to Burma, and No. 211 to disband. By January the RAF presence in Siam had been reduced to no more than 150 men.

Britain aids France

In French Indo-China, however, Britain faced a delicate political situation. The re-imposition of French colonial rule was expected to meet deep resentment and, as there were no French troops immediately available to undertake the task, the onus fell initially upon Britain. An advance party of SEAC personnel was flown into an airfield near Saigon on 9 September, followed during the next two weeks by a whole army division and its equipment, lifted in by ACSEA Dakotas in monsoon conditions as bad as any experienced during the Burma campaign. The RAF was once more represented by an air headquarters, supported by the Spitfires of No. 273 Squadron and the main body of No. 684 (Photographic Reconnaissance) Squadron.

The evacuation of prisoners of war and internees, and the disarming of Japanese forces, went ahead under SEAC control, and as French troops became available they were flown in by Dakotas together with their equipment and supplies. Before the build-up was complete, however, No. 273 Squadron became involved in providing offensive air support to a French garrison besieged by rebel forces, the French air force contingent which had recently arrived being still training in its borrowed Spitfires.

With the French able to assume control by January 1946, No. 273 Squadron was withdrawn at the end of the month, and the air headquarters was disbanded two weeks later, leaving only a small party behind in Saigon to handle aircraft in transit.

Of much greater importance to Britain in the longer term was the reoccupation of Malaya and

The British outpost of Hong Kong on the Chinese mainland was liberated after the Japanese war was ended, and the first RAF aircraft to move in to be based there was this Sunderland GR.Mk 5 of No. 209 Squadron which set up base at Kai Tak on 27 October 1945.

Singapore, which would become the main British base east of Aden once India had achieved independence; and, as elsewhere, there were very large numbers of prisoners of war and internees to be evacuated and Japanese troops to be disarmed. It was therefore decided to go ahead with the original plan of invasion which had provided for troops to be landed on the western beaches of Malaya, and a naval task force to be sent into Singapore, supported by RAF aircraft. Previously, stiff Japanese resistance had been expected; now, happily, there was none.

By chance the first British servicemen to arrive in Singapore were the crew of a No. 684 Squadron Mosquito which landed there on 31 August after one of its engines had failed. Six days later two Spitfire squadrons (Nos 152 and 155) and two Mosquito squadrons (Nos 84 and 110) arrived, having flown south from Penang, which had been occupied by Royal Marines on 3 September. Six Short Sunderlands of Nos 205 and 209 Squadrons reached Singapore on 10 September.

Evacuation of POWs

On the same day the advance headquarters of No. 224 Group arrived in Malaya and established itself at Kalang, where it was joined by two Spitfire squadrons, Nos 11 and 17; later four Thunderbolt squadrons (Nos 131, 258, 60 and 81) reached Port Swettenham, moving later to Kuala Lumpur. On 18 September the main body of No. 224 Group also arrived at Kuala Lumpur, and then deployed to Singapore, where it became AHQ Malaya.

Some 39,000 prisoners of war and internees were soon evacuated by air and sea, and the RAF, which had no immediate operational commitments (other than reconnaissance) in Malaya itself, settled down to develop Singapore as the main air force base in the Far East. The airfields were found to be in very poor state of repair; Tengah, which was in better shape than the others, became the home of Nos 152 and 155 Squadrons, thereby inaugurating a main RAF operational base. The other two Spitfire squadrons (Nos 11 and 17) together with three Mosquito squadrons (Nos 84, 89 and 110) settled into Seletar, although the runway there was hardly adequate for modern operational use and could not be satisfactorily extended. Kallang, the pre-war civil airport, and Changi (built by prisoner of war labour) were still proving unsatisfactory in use, even after pierced steel planking (PSP) had been

laid over the runways. Enough progress had however been made by November 1945 for ACSEA to move forward to Singapore; AHQ Malaya therefore returned to Kuala Lumpur.

Thus by the end of 1945 significant progress had been made in most of the territories under SEAC control. In addition to Siam, French Indo-China, Malaya and Singapore, Hong Kong too had been reoccupied at the beginning of September, and an air headquarters had been established there, supported by No. 132 Squadron with Spitfires which had arrived aboard HMS *Smiter*. Once again, ACSEA Dakotas had been used to fly in supplies and evacuate prisoners of war and internees, a task which was substantially reduced once Hong Kong port had been opened to shipping.

Only in the Netherlands East Indies had British forces become involved in bitter fighting, a situation that was to last well into 1946. As in French Indo-China, British involvement resulted from the absence of forces belonging to the colonial power concerned; the Netherlands had no troops available for the initial reoccupation of the territories and the liberation of the many internment camps scattered among the islands. The situation had been exacerbated by the creation of an independent Indonesian republic, sanctioned by the Japanese just before their own surrender to the Allies. In consequence, when SEAC teams arrived to repatriate the prisoners of war and internees, they were met with hostility both from the Indonesian government, which feared a resumption of Dutch

The Dakota squadrons came into their own in the Far East in the first year after the war, establishing regular routes in the region as well as flying against the terrorists in Malaya. One of their more pleasant tasks was to repatriated prisoners-of-war, collected here from Don Muang airport at Bangkok.

All the pre-war bases were reoccupied by the Far East Air Force, and the RAF squadrons found themselves carrying out many unusual tasks. This Dakota, from one of the transport squadrons at Kalang, Singapore, was rigged up as a chemical sprayer and sprayed the dock area of Singapore with DDT spray to combat the malarial mosquito.

Before the dropping of the atomic bomb on Japan, the RAF's Bomber Command had been mustering a sizeable bomber force within Bomber Command (Tiger Force) to take the bombing offensive to Japan. With the war over this force was cut down and retained as part of Bomber Command, but squadrons within it were rotated to Middle and Far East bases both for training purposes and to be there in case of fresh outbreaks of fighting as happened in Indonesia. Landing here at Kallang is one of these aircraft, a Lancaster B.Mk 1 (FE) of No. 7 Sqn from Upwood in Huntingdonshire.

colonial rule, and from extremist elements which were challenging the government's authority, and were even more bitterly opposed to any European intervention.

The camps had to be evacuated as quickly as possible, however, otherwise their occupants would be crippled by starvation and possibly used as hostages. An army division was sent to Java, the main trouble spot, at the end of September together with an air headquarters formed from No. 221 Group in Burma. No. 904 Wing followed with two Thunderbolt squadrons, Nos 60 and 81, and established itself at Kemajoran, the civil airport at Batavia, the Indonesian capital (now Djakarta).

Java

The Thunderbolts were soon reinforced by detachments of Mosquitoes from Nos 84, 47 and 110 Squadrons at Singapore, No. 47 Squadron aircraft being armed with rocket projectiles, and the remainder carrying bombs only. To these reinforcements were added the rest of No. 84 Squadron, the 24 Dakotas of No. 31 Squadron, a small detachment of Spitfires from No. 681 (Photographic Reconnaissance) Squadron, and a Bristol Beaufighter of No. 27 Squadron for jungle search and rescue work. With some additions from No. 321 (Dutch) Squadron of the RAF, the aircraft strength at Kemajoran rose to 110, far more than the airfield could conveniently handle.

It was clearly impossible with the troops available to reoccupy the whole of Java, an island some 600 miles (965 km) long but never more than 90 miles (145 km) wide. The strategy adopted was to establish three bridgeheads on the north coast, each with a port and an airfield, from which it was hoped to reach all known camps, using aircraft to evacuate any which were inaccessible to ground forces. Batavia was to serve as the operational base for western Java, Semarang for the central area and Surabaja for the east. Kemajoran was to act also as the main air force base on the island, not only for mounting operations in the western area but for supplying and reinforcing Semarang and Surabaja.

Even in western Java only Batavia itself was for the moment reasonably stable; outside the city

towards Bandung, where large internment camps were known to be, government authority barely existed. The only means of reaching the camps and bringing the internees back to Batavia was by Dakota or heavily escorted road convoys with Thunderbolt or Mosquito cover; as the latter method proved highly dangerous, much depended on the Dakotas of No. 31 Squadron which maintained an average of 28 sorties every day to Bandung throughout November and December. When road convoys were sent through, the escorting Thunderbolts and Mosquitoes were sometimes also used to strafe terrorist positions in and around Bandung.

At the other end of Java SEAC troops had begun to move into Surabaja at the end of October, their arrival coinciding with a demonstration flight by all available Thunderbolts, using long-range tanks on a round trip of more than 900 miles (1448 km) from Kemajoran with some 30 minutes over the town. The distances involved showed that if the ground forces were to receive adequate air support, aircraft would have to be based at Surabaja, and as the situation became more tense eight Thunderbolts of No. 60 Squadron and two Mosquitoes of No. 110 Squadron arrived at the airfield there. In three weeks of heavy fighting in and around the town, No. 31 Squadron's Dakotas flew in supplies and evacuated internees, and the Thunderbolts and Mosquitoes mounted attacks on the buildings occupied by the extremists. Dakotas, Thunderbolts and Mosquitoes alike were hit by anti-aircraft fire, but the ground forces eventually cleared the town, only to find that the opposition had moved inland.

Eventual triumph

In central Java the initial landing at Semarang on 19 October had been unopposed, but an ugly situation soon developed when troops moved south towards the camps where several thousand internees were known to be held. In danger of being surrounded and overwhelmed, the ground forces were kept supplied with food and ammunition by the Dakotas, and given close support by the Thunderbolts and Mosquitoes. After three weeks' fighting some 10,000 internees had been assembled in and around the town of Ambarawa, some 15 miles (24 km) south of Semarang, and by then it was clear that the fate of the many other internees, still held in camps farther south at Jogijakarta, would depend on using the Batavia government as a go-between in what would almost certainly be long drawn-out negotiations with the extremists. In the event the negotiations proved successful, but it was not until April 1946 that agreement was reached for aircraft to be sent to Surakarta to start ferrying the internees out. The first Dakotas arrived on 20 May, but as only two aircraft a day were allowed it was many weeks before the evacuation was complete.

Elsewhere the turning point had been reached in the early months of 1946, as the Dutch began taking over responsibility for the island. No. 31 Squadron remained at full stretch almost to the end, however, and in March concentrated air cover was still being given to convoys on the Batavia-

The Thunderbolt squadrons which had fought so well over Burma returned to action in 1946, when the Indonesian fighting flared up. Seen at Surabaya are No. 60 Squadron aircraft bombed up and taxiing out for strikes against the terrorists.

Bandung road in the face of a sudden upsurge in violence. With the arrival of the Dutch, a gradual withdrawal of RAF squadrons had begun, among the last to leave being Nos 31 and 60. The former had flown 11,000 sorties in just over a year in Java, and carried 127,000 passengers and 26,000 tons of freight. The air headquarters itself was disbanded in November.

Thus, after some 15 months, SEAC's main objectives had been achieved. The cost had been high: 350 army and 21 RAF personnel were killed in the first 10 weeks alone. Particularly tragic was the loss, on 23 November 1945, of a Dakota which forcelanded in a paddy field near Batavia. The occupants were seen to emerge uninjured, but when no trace could be found of them it came to light that they had been taken to the local jail, murdered and buried in a grave nearby, where their mutilated remains were later discovered. Two other aircraft were lost: a second Dakota, which crashed in inaccessible jungle while returning to Batavia from Bandung, and a Thunderbolt of No. 81 Squadron shot down by anti-aircraft fire near Ambarawa in central Java.

Return to peace

The withdrawal from Batavia marked a further stage in the return to peacetime conditions in South East Asia. SEAC itself disbanded in November 1946, and ACSEA was renamed Air Command Far East (ACFE), so becoming directly responsible to the Air Ministry in London. With three of its air headquarters disbanded (Siam, Indo-China and the Netherlands East Indies), it still controlled four others: Malaya, Hong Kong, Ceylon and Burma.

In the 15 months since the end of the war, the RAF presence in Burma had been progressively reduced, but the air headquarters continued to provide facilities for RAF aircraft in transit and for the British, Dutch and Australian civil airlines as they resumed services. The Dakota squadrons, reduced from nine to three (Nos 62, 96 and 267) by early 1946, had maintained an intensive level of flying, ferrying supplies to the army and the civil population (the hill tribes in particular being in urgent need of rice, their crops having been devastated by the war). Hostility to the British presence was increasing (fuelled by Aung San, the militant Communist in Burma) and with independence and a decision to leave the Commonwealth

imminent, the air headquarters was disbanded at the end of 1947.

In Ceylon, which only recently had been a large Sunderland and Liberator base supporting operations in the Indian Ocean, the RAF presence had also been considerably reduced. Superseded also as an important staging post when Singapore opened to four-engine aircraft, it accommodated no more than two squadrons at the beginning of 1947, No. 205 (Cadre) with Sunderlands, and No. 45 with Mosquitoes. Ceylon too became independent (as Sri Lanka) but, as it remained within the Commonwealth, the air headquarters was able to remain.

The greatest change of all had taken place in India. What had, by mid-1945, become a vast supply depot to support the war against Japan had been progressively run down since the autumn of that year. In the first months of peace, demobilisation had not proceeded as quickly as had been hoped, as a result of the world shortage of shipping, and the resulting frustration among servicemen had been demonstrated by strikes at a number of RAF stations. As more shipping became available, and as BOAC services started to operate, the pace quickened throughout 1946. In any case, with independence approaching (and Malaya and Singapore being progressively rehabilitated) India need no longer remain as a principal British base. The work of returning Lend-Lease aircraft to the United States, re-equipping RAF squadrons with British aircraft and closing down the many units involved (not to mention the enormous task of

With peace spreading in many parts of South East Asia but war flaring up in Korea, aircraft deployment continued on a grand scale. No. 132 Squadron, equipped with Spitfire F.Mk 14Es, embarked on HMS *Smiter* and went to Hong Kong.

The RAF's major contribution to communications and maritime reconnaissance in the peacetime Far East was made by the Short Sunderland squadrons (Nos 88, 205 and 209).

Auster AOP.Mk 6s were taken by sea to the Far East for the AOP squadrons working with the army.

dismantling the apparatus of two centuries of British military presence in the sub-continent went ahead in the face of growing manpower shortages. By August 1947, however, when India and Pakistan became independent, there remained only two RAF squadrons, Nos 10 and 31, whose Dakotas were based temporarily at Mauripur, Karachi; they too had been withdrawn by the end of the year.

By now the RAF's resources east of Aden were concentrated in Malaya and Singapore, with small elements in Ceylon and Hong Kong. AHQ Malaya controlled eight squadrons at the beginning of 1948, the main base being Changi with three Dakota squadrons (Nos 48, 52 and 110), one photo-reconnaissance Mosquito squadron (No. 81, formerly No. 684) and one Beaufighter light bomber squadron (No. 84). Tengah accommodated two Spitfire squadrons (Nos 28 and 60), and Seletar No. 209 (Cadre) Squadron with Sunderlands. No. 205 Squadron remained in Ceylon with No. 45, now equipped with Beaufighters. In Hong Kong the air headquarters controlled one squadron, No. 88 with Sunderlands.

Defence of colonial interests

Lend-Lease aircraft had been returned to the United States, and Beaufighters had largely replaced the Mosquitoes, whose wooden construction had proved unable to withstand the humidity of the Far East. Only on No. 81 Squadron were they retained, at considerable cost in manpower, because the specialised camera installation in the PR.Mk 34 version could not be fitted easily in any other aircraft.

In effect ACFE had now stabilised at roughly its intended peacetime strength of some 100 front-line aircraft, a sizeable reserve of aircraft and spares, and provision for major servicing to be carried out in the Far East. The airfield situation had also been rationalised. Kallang had been handed back for civilian use; Changi had been developed to handle four-engine aircraft; Tengah had been confirmed as the air-defence base, and Seletar, which could not be extended to meet the needs of modern land-based operational aircraft, was now the supply and maintenance base, providing facilities also for the Sunderland flying-boats while they remained in service.

The presence of British forces in the Far East was intended first and foremost as defence of

Britain's colonial territories and trading interests, and as a contribution to the overall stability in the area, with the RAF providing air defence and co-operating generally with the other two services. But any hope that British forces would possess a mainly deterrent role was quickly shattered by the events of the next three years: the start of the Malayan Emergency in 1948, the *Amethyst* incident in 1949, and the outbreak of the Korean War in 1950. Indeed, Britain's Far East forces were to be involved in fighting of one kind or another for most of the next 18 years.

'Amethyst' and Korea

The *Amethyst* incident in April 1949 was an indication of a new factor in Far Eastern affairs: the approaching victory of the Communists in China and their evident hostility towards the West. A Royal Navy frigate, HMS *Amethyst*, had been badly damaged by Communist gunfire and gone aground in the Yangtse river some 45 miles (72 km) below Nanking. A Sunderland of No. 88 Squadron landed alongside on 21 April, its pilot intending to transfer doctors and medical supplies, but it also soon came under fire and, with only one doctor and some of the supplies transferred, it was forced to take off. In a second attempt the next day, it again came under fire and, being damaged, took off once more. The same aircraft was again damaged on 23 April during an attempted reconnaissance and forced to withdraw. The frigate later managed to escape under its own steam.

In the Korean War the Sunderlands again had an important role to contribute. The country had been divided along the 38th parallel following World War II, Russia sponsoring the northern half and the United States the southern. As the Americans scaled down their forces in South Korea, the Russians encouraged the North Koreans to attack, hoping that a successful invasion would strengthen their own position in the Pacific and encourage anti-Western and pro-Communist elements in South East Asia. So began three years of bitter warfare in which Chinese Communist volunteers and then regulars quickly became involved.

The RAF's contribution was of necessity severely limited as the service was already heavily involved in Malaya, but aircraft of the three Sunderland squadrons (Nos 88, 205 and 209), not being fully engaged there, could be made available to help in Korea. Working in conjunction with United

It was the Sunderlands of the Far East Air Force which provided the RAF's participation in the Korean conflict. Detachments from the three squadrons were based at Iwakuni in Japan, from where they flew long oversea patrols on reconnaissance duties around the Korean coastline.

Nations naval forces and patrol aircraft of the US Navy, with which they shared a base at Iwakuni on the southern tip of Japan's Honshu island, they helped to maintain a total blockade of the Korean coastline, and made it impossible for enemy shipping to use any port in Korea without coming under heavy attack from aircraft called forward by the reconnaissance patrols. These operated round the clock and in all weathers (with winter temperatures often as low as minus 20 degrees Centigrade) and covered an area which extended from Vladivostok to the mouth of the Yangtse. In addition to searching for enemy shipping, the patrols provided weather information and screened the fleet while refuelling. Each of the three Sunderland squadrons spent a month at a time at Iwakuni and between them they flew over 1,600 sorties, totalling some 13,000 flying hours.

The RAF contributed in two other ways, by the loan of pilots (ostensibly experienced in tactical air operations, but in practice including a number of very inexperienced, recently trained young men) and by the provision of two Auster air observation flights. By 1953 17 pilots of the RAF were fighting in Korea, either with No. 77 Squadron of the Royal Australian Air Force (which had converted to Gloster Meteor F.Mk 8s in 1951 with RAF assistance), or with United States Air Force fighter squadrons. The RAF's experience in intruder tactics, especially at night, proved particularly valuable and a number of improvements were made in procedures, notably in target identification and in the control of close support operations.

Of the two Auster flights sent to Korea, with at most 10 aircraft between them, No. 1903 Flight was engaged in battlefield reconnaissance and artillery spotting, and No. 1913 in light liaison work. The Austers were flown by army pilots and serviced by a combination of RAF and army ground personnel, who faced increasingly formidable problems in keeping their light aircraft operational in Korean conditions. In all, nearly 3,000 sorties were flown; two Austers were shot down with the loss of their pilots.

The Malayan crisis

Malaya, however, was an equally tempting target for infiltration by Communist and other disruptive elements. For many years under British protection, the country was now the centre of Commonwealth influence and communications in

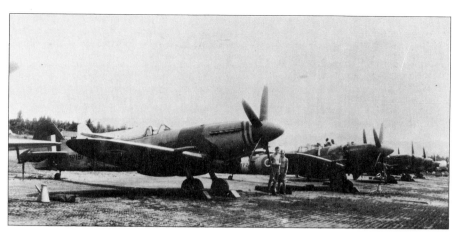

South East Asia and, as the world's largest producer of rubber and a major producer of tin, it was also of great economic value to Britain as a dollar-earner, a particularly important factor in the late 1940s. The loss of Malaya would be a serious setback for the West and could in the end lead to destabilisation of the whole of South East Asia from India to China, leaving it wide open to communist domination.

In Malaya itself, Communist activity dated back almost 30 years, but it was only after the Japanese invasion that the Malayan Communist Party began to achieve significant influence. It became the main centre of resistance to the Japanese, forming the nucleus of the Malayan People's Anti-Japanese Army (MPAJA), which by the end of the war numbered 4,000 guerrillas and 6,000 ancillaries. When the MPAJA was officially disbanded in December 1945 a number of guerrillas remained in the jungle to continue subversion under communist control.

Malaya was seemingly ideal territory for such disruption. Its leading communities, the Chinese and Malays, were about equal in number but very different in character, the former constituting the business element and retaining strong ties with China, and the latter being mainly of agricultural stock. Malaya was also well suited to guerrilla activity, with a central backbone of mountains rising to over 7,000 ft (2134 m) and a preponderance of jungle with an almost unbroken canopy of trees some 150 ft (46 m) high. The climate is generally

The Malayan Emergency involved the RAF in many years of anti-terrorist operations. It provided the last action for the Spitfire, with No. 60 Squadron using its Spitfire FR.Mk 18Es for rocket strikes against terrorist hideouts.

The Beaufighter, too, flew its twilight operations in Malaya with Nos 45 and 84 Squadrons. It had been nicknamed 'Whispering Death' by the Japanese, a reputation maintained in its attacks on terrorist camps and lines of communications. Groundcrew of No. 45 Squadron are here servicing the radar in the nose of a Beaufighter.

Supermarine Spitfire PR.Mk 19 operated by No. 81 Squadron, RAF, at Seletar, Singapore circa 1950. In the Malayan Emergency the Spitfires were engaged in photographing vast expanses of jungle for signs of terrorist activity.

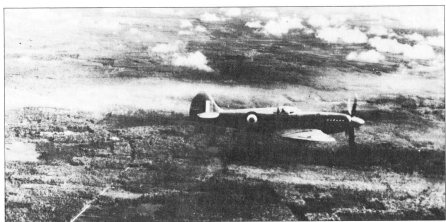

The very final operational sorties flown by the Spitfire fell to the PR.Mk 19s of No. 81 Squadron, based at Seletar. Photo-reconnaissance assumed an even greater importance in this kind of campaign where so much of the enemy's whereabouts were hidden in the jungle. The last Spitfire sortie was flown on 1 April 1954.

disagreeable by reason of unrelieved humidity, but from the operational viewpoint more important is the frequency of prolonged tropical storms accompanied by a rapid build-up of huge, dense clouds with violent turbulence, endangering aircraft of anything less than of robust construction. These storms tend to be localised, with excellent flying weather between them.

The guerrillas lacked one significant advantage, that of possessing a common border with a country which would permit a flow of supplies and reinforcements on a substantial scale. All outside assistance would have to arrive by sea, and this a combination of RAF aircraft and ships of the Royal Navy would be able to prevent.

The Malayan Communist Party had prepared a three-stage programme of subversion which it hoped would bring it ultimate control of the country. The first stage, starting in 1948, was to use murder and sabotage to bring terror and chaos to the rural areas; the next was to establish local administration in selected rural areas; and the

third was to declare a Communist republic. The whole process was expected to occupy two years. In the event it was to be 12 years before the state of emergency, declared by the Malayan government in June 1948 and corresponding with the Communists' first stage, could be brought to a successful conclusion.

Jungle support

The counter-strategy developed during those years was to harass the terrorists in their jungle hideouts, while cutting them off from their sources of supply (voluntary or otherwise) in the rural areas and the jungle. The administrative action needed to isolate the terrorists was to come later, and for the moment the counter-terrorist offensive, codenamed Operation 'Firedog', was mounted primarily by the ground forces supported by the RAF.

In operating in the jungle, the army required three types of support from the air force: reconnaissance, offensive air action and air transport support (including supply dropping, trooplift and casualty evacuation). Accordingly the operational task force which was created in Kuala Lumpur in July 1948 consisted of detachments of Spitfires from Nos 28 and 60 Squadrons, Beaufighters from No. 45 Squadron based in Ceylon, and Dakotas from No. 110 Squadron; the photographic-reconnaissance role was undertaken mainly by No. 81 Squadron which, at the beginning of the emergency was equipped with six Mosquitoes and two Spitfires. Because of their structural problems the Mosquitoes operated in the main from Tengah, but the Spitfires were often sent forward on detachment to handle the short-range tactical work.

No. 81 Squadron's contribution to the ultimate success of the anti-terrorist operations was twofold. To meet the demand for large-scale maps to replace the pre-war editions (now out of date and covering little more than the populated areas of

No. 81 Squadron also used Mosquito PR.Mk 34s extensively in the Malayan campaign right up to 15 December 1955, when RG314 flew Mosquito's final operation.

western Malaya) the Mosquitoes began a detailed survey of the whole country in collaboration with an army liaison team; from this were produced the tactical maps essential for the accurate planning and manoeuvring of jungle patrols, and the location of dropping zones and target areas. It was a formidable task which took four years to complete.

In addition the tactical reconnaissance sorties, carried out mainly by the Spitfires operating from Kuala Lumpur or Taiping (a civil airfield in northern Perak), were essential to the strike and transport aircraft, providing them with the visual and photographic information they needed in planning their own sorties. The problem was that flights below 15,000 ft (4570 m), in order to obtain large-scale photographs, could give the terrorists ample warning of an impending attack; the choice therefore had to be made in the early days between the risk of compromising the security of a ground or air attack, and of accepting the limitations of small-scale photographs.

Air strike

For the strike aircraft the problem was of locating the target in a terrain that was, by its nature, highly unfavourable to them. The strategy was to attack the terrorists in their jungle camps, mainly with rockets and cannon, and force them to split up into smaller groups. The terrorists provided only fleeting targets, however, and could disappear into another part of the jungle before aircraft could reach and attack them. The cab-rank principle, developed during World War II, was of little use because it was always necessary to establish the exact whereabouts of any troops or civilians in the area before an attack could be mounted. In addition, radio communications between aircraft and ground forces in the jungle were reduced to a quarter of normal efficiency, and the radio set then in use by the army was not only very heavy but needed a tree aerial, which took time to erect; moreover the control vehicles, which in different terrain could have helped solve the problem, were quite unable to penetrate the jungle.

In spite of these initial handicaps the pressure on the terrorists was maintained throughout the early years. Results were never conclusive, but the largest of the early strikes, mounted on 7 July 1949, by 26 Beaufighters, supplemented by Sunderlands, Spitfires and North American Harvards, did have a measure of success by driving a terrorist group into

the arms of waiting troops. Later, in December 1950, 98 sorties were flown against another terrorist gang (70 to 100 strong) which had taken refuge in inaccessible terrain. The force involved consisted mainly of Lincolns, Bristol Brigands, Spitfires and Hawker Tempests, but there was also one Sunderland sortie and three by Dakotas acting as airborne tactical headquarters. The results were encouraging: the gang was dispersed and driven back into a rubber estate where it was engaged by the army; 29 terrorists were killed, 10 were captured and five surrendered.

The main achievement of the air strike programme was to harass the terrorists, keeping them on the move, inhibiting their activities and making them increasingly aware that no camp, however inaccessible, was ultimately safe from air attack. It was a situation that became more and more difficult for them as the air strike techniques improved.

It was the theatre transport forces which provided the RAF's largest contribution to the anti-terrorist campaign. As operations got under way, a rota system was introduced so that the three Dakota squadrons (Nos 48, 52 and 110) and the Dakota element of the Far East Communications Squadron each spent six months at Kuala Lumpur dropping supplies (by parachute or free-fall) and lifting troops and freight into the forward airfields. Working with them later were the Dakotas of No. 41 Squadron, RNZAF (between September 1949 and November 1951), and of No. 38 Squadron, RAAF

With the advent of jet aircraft in RAF Germany, many piston-engine fighters were rejected as surplus and most suitable amongst these to replace the ageing Spitfires in Malaya were the air-cooled Centaurus-engined Tempest F.Mk2s. So No. 33 Squadron moved out from Germany and engaged in rocket strikes from Kuala Lumpur, where this photograph was taken.

The last Mosquitoes to see action were the PR.Mk 34s of No. 81 Squadron, flown over the Malayan jungle on reconnaissance sorties to locate terrorist hideouts.

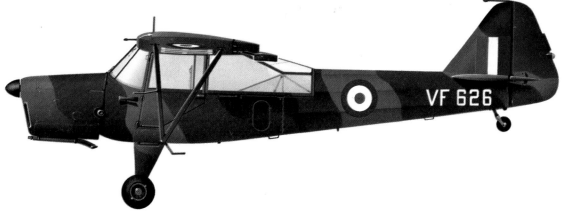

The Auster AOP.Mk 6 became the standard Air Observation Post aircraft in the RAF post-war. VF626 was one such, serving in the Malaysian campaign with No. 656 Squadron during the period 1950–55. No. 656 Squadron was based at Kuala Lumpur but had detachments all over the Far Eastern theatre.

The Malayan campaign was probably the classic example of an army being maintained by air, following on from the similar activities during the war in Burma. Some idea of the problems and scale of such flying is graphically displayed in this picture of a Dakota having identified a tiny dropping zone in the featureless jungle and two parachutes descending into it from the open door of the aircraft.

(from June 1950 until November 1952). Operating farther forward were the Austers of No. 656 Squadron, using whatever jungle airstrips were available.

Without air transport, the only means of maintaining forward troops would have been by road convoy, with all the attendant risks of ambush; and when road vehicles could go no further the supplies would have had to be carried by the ground forces themselves. As an inevitable result, operations would have been limited to holding a number of defended areas, and the terrorists would have been immune to attack while they remained some 5–10 miles (8–16 km) inside the jungle. With air transport the ground forces could penetrate as deep as they wished, and could stay in the jungle for weeks at a time.

The supply system in operation was simple, with the jungle patrols radioing their requests to army and police headquarters which passed them on to the Joint Operations Centre (JOC) at Kuala Lumpur for allocation to the Dakotas. Details were also sent to the army's air despatch company which packed the supplies into 200-lb (91-kg) packs, attached the parachutes and provided the personnel to act as despatchers in the aircraft. The parachutes soon became a significant addition to the cost of the operation, since with less than half of them returned, consumption rose to 18,000 a year at some £32 per parachute.

Locating the dropping zones (DZ) chosen by the patrol commanders proved as difficult as locating targets for air strikes. In terrain mostly covered by trees up to 200 ft (61 m) high, DZs could seldom meet the minimum normal requirements for size and visibility from the air. Most were only holes in the jungle canopy some 20 yards (18 m) across, and as their limited field of vision often left ground patrols with only a hazy idea of their own position, briefings to the pilot consisted of an estimated map reference, which frequently turned out to be inaccurate. The procedure was for the patrol to fire a smoke grenade as soon as the aircraft was heard approaching, thereby giving a general indication of the DZ, and for coloured smoke and cloth panels to be used to mark the aiming point. After dropping his load the pilot would await confirmation that the packs were recoverable and that a second drop was not required. Over 60,000 lb (27216 kg) of supplies were dropped in the first six months of the operation, but as the ground forces penetrated deeper into the jungle the rate of effort increased rapidly, and in later years over 500,000 lb (226800 kg) of supplies were being dropped each month.

For all this activity, the level of terrorist violence showed no sign of dropping. Indeed, the number of

VS584 was a Bristol Brigand B.Mk 1 of No. 84 Squadron, powered by two 2,470-hp (1842-kW) Bristol Centaurus engines giving a top speed of 358 mph (576 km/h).

recorded incidents rose from some 100 a month in 1949 to over 500 a month in 1951. Counter-terrorist operations increased in proportion, with nearly 3,300 offensive air strikes in the first eight months of 1951. In the course of these strikes 5,000 tons of bombs were dropped and 14,000 rockets fired; in addition there were over 6,500 transport sorties during the same period, with over 10,000 passengers and 1,700 tons of freight carried. Reconnaissance sorties totalled 2,200.

Victory however was still no nearer, and would not be achieved as long as much of the population lived in fear of the terrorists. Worst affected were the large numbers of Chinese squatters on whom the terrorists depended for food and information. Under a plan introduced by the first Director of Operations, Lieutenant General Sir Harold Briggs, about 500,000 of these squatters were moved from their isolated communities to new villages protected by a barbed-wire perimeter fence, within which they could be provided with land for cultivation, schools and other social amenities.

At the same time the Far East Air Force (FEAF), as ACFE had been renamed in June 1949, was being substantially strengthened by the arrival of many new aircraft types. Nos 45 and 84 Squadrons, which formed the light bomber element of FEAF's strike force, were re-equipped with Brigands in 1950. Almost immediately No. 45 Squadron suffered two fatal accidents, probably as a result of the premature detonation of incendiary ammunition; a few months later, in June 1951, fractures of the propeller hubs around the base of the blades caused three more fatal accidents, but even when the Brigands began to fly again in August after being grounded, they were plagued by hydraulic problems and by low serviceability. Finally, No. 45 Squadron was re-equipped with de Havilland Hornets in February 1952; No. 84 Squadron carried on with Brigands until it was disbanded in 1953 to re-form in the Middle East as a transport squadron.

Significant arrivals were the de Havilland

Vampire FB.Mk 5s which re-equipped No. 60 Squadron at Tengah and No. 28 in Hong Kong; the Vampire proved to be well suited to the Malayan environment, rugged and easy to maintain, yet with adequate performance and fire power for the theatre. The Tempests of No. 33 Squadron, which had arrived at Butterworth in August 1949, were another useful reinforcement (being fast, heavily-armed and reliable), but with only one Tempest squadron in the theatre it was found very expensive to provide the resources needed to maintain the aircraft, and they were soon replaced by Hornets. Additionally, the first of a number of detachments from home-based Avro Lincoln squadrons arrived in March 1950, and were joined by the Lincolns of No. 1 Squadron, RAAF. In the photographic reconnaissance role No. 81 Squadron's Mosquitoes continued to fly until they were replaced by Meteor PR.Mk 10s in October 1953.

In the transport field, Vickers Valettas started to replace Dakotas in 1951. Four years later the Bristol Freighters of No. 41 Squadron, RNZAF, arrived to augment the medium-range transport force. More significant in the long term was the

Designs which materialised too late for wartime operations found an operational role in the Malayan campaign. Successor to the Beaufighter was the Bristol Brigand B.Mk 1, which equipped both Nos 45 and 84 Squadrons during 1949. No. 84 Squadron had from the 1920s had a habit of carrying playing card motifs on their aircraft and this was revived on the Brigands, as can be seen on 'K', here making a rocket strike in the jungle.

Another post-war type which found its metier in Malaya was the de Havilland Hornet. This type replaced both Brigand and Tempest in 1952 and was ideal for the jungle task with a greater range than the Tempest and greater manoeuvrability than the Brigand. No. 45 Squadron (seen here) re-equipped with Hornets in January 1952 and used the type to good effect until the advent of Vampires in 1955.

No. 33 Squadron replaced its Tempests with de Havilland Hornets in April 1951, PX311 being one of its aircraft. Notice that this aircraft carries both the wartime squadron identity letters '5R' and the post-war squadron colour markings on each side of the roundel on the fuselage.

The first jet fighters to operate in the Far East were Vampire FB.Mk 5s, coming out to No. 60 Squadron at Tengah in December 1950. They were flown out, escorted over the jungle by No. 81 Squadron Mosquitoes as navigational 'mother ships'. Both types are seen here on the hard-standing at Tengah.

arrival in April 1950 of the RAF's first operational helicopters, the three Westland Dragonflies of the Casualty Evacuation Flight. Although grossly underpowered and untested in Malayan conditions, because the requirement was so urgent, they soon proved their worth and their pilots began to develop the operating procedures suited to the theatre. With a cruising speed of 70–75 mph (113–121 km/h) and an endurance of three hours with a full fuel load, the Dragonfly could carry two passengers or one casualty in a specially-constructed stretcher positioned athwartships. Being underpowered, it could lift vertically from a jungle clearing only when its fuel load was no more than enough for 30 minutes' flying at 70 mph (113 km/h). Nevertheless, by the end of 1950 29 casualties had been evacuated successfully, often with Austers guiding the Dragonfly pilots to their destinations; a further 42 casualties were evacuated during the next six months. The effect on morale was considerable as the risk diminished of a sick or wounded man being sent back on a long and uncomfortable journey through the jungle, and of men being spared to carry him. Three more

Dragonflies were added to the flight early in 1952, giving it a total strength of five (one having been lost without casualties in the previous October), and although the production rate was slow, Dragonfly establishment grew steadily to 12 by the end of 1952 and 18 in 1953 when the CEF was re-established as No. 194 Squadron.

Helicopter reinforcements

Although by then the versatility of the helicopter was widely appreciated (and even the Dragonfly was being used for the occasional trooplift) further development could only be achieved with the arrival of larger helicopters. First to reach Malaya, in January 1953, were the Sikorsky S-55s of No. 848 Naval Air Squadron, seconded from their NATO duties. The S-55 could carry five fully-armed soldiers in and out of large clearings, and four soldiers when the clearing was of 'Dragonfly standard'; alternatively it could lift three stretcher cases and two walking patients. Fifteen months later the first of FEAF's Bristol Sycamores joined No. 194 Squadron, providing a larger cabin, better performance and more positive handling characteristics; its serviceability rate was excellent apart from one fault, the cracking and swelling of the wooden members of the rotor blades, a fault that was still uncorrected in April 1959 when two fatal crashes (caused by the disintegration of the rotor blades) led to all the Sycamores being grounded.

In contrast, the Westland Whirlwinds, which arrived in September 1955 to form No. 155 Squadron, were initially disappointing. Although they were expected to be the RAF's first genuine troop-carrying helicopters, carrying 10 passengers, it was quickly discovered that in Malayan conditions they could only carry two. Notwithstanding these difficulties, sufficient Sycamores and Whirlwinds were available by 1956 to enable No. 848 Squadron to be returned to its NATO duties.

The fixed-wing element of the short-range transport force was likewise significantly improved in September 1953 when the first Scottish Aviation

Malaya became the testing ground, as far as the RAF was concerned, for the helicopter. In 1953 four Westland Dragonflies formed the complement of No. 194 Squadron and at once began to show their potential by enabling troops to be dropped at trouble spots within minutes and casualties to be lifted out with similar speed. These four aircraft were backed up by Whirlwinds of No. 848 Squadron of the Fleet Air Arm until more and better helicopters could be got out to the RAF.

Pioneers arrived to form No. 1311 Transport Flight, this in turn becoming part of the newly established No. 267 Squadron a few months later, with Hunting Pembrokes and Austers in its inventory, as well as Pioneers.

With these reinforcements, the RAF was able to offer the ground forces much improved support as they drove the terrorists further and further back into the jungle. An analysis of past strike operations had shown that rapid response to targets of opportunity was wasteful in the Malayan environment and that offensive sorties should be mainly confined to carefully co-ordinated large-scale operations, ordered through a combined operations room at GHQ Malaya District. It had also been shown that strafing with cannon and rocket fire was generally effective, but that bombing was worthwhile only when the bomber could remain over the target for three hours or more, dropping bombs at irregular intervals and using a mixture of instantaneous and delayed-action fuses, a practice that was known to possess an abrasive effect on the guerrillas' morale; hence the importance of the Lincolns, with their endurance of up to 11 hours, carrying a load of 14 1,000-lb (454-kg) bombs.

Target-marking

But there still remained the problem of locating and pinpointing the target without alerting the terrorists and giving them time to disperse. Numerous marking techniques were tried. Austers, for example, were used to drop phosphorus grenades, smoke and flares, but unless an air strike followed immediately the terrorists had time to take cover. More successful was the practice of positioning ground markers at a known distance and bearing from the target, allowing the strike aircraft to make timed runs from the datum point. Delayed action flares, which allowed the ground party setting them to escape a possible ambush, were used in daylight and searchlights, trained vertically, at night.

The intractability of the problem led to the wasteful practice of laying down the largest possible bomb pattern in order to cover the inevitable errors in target location, a procedure which also involved the close co-ordination of any air strike in which more than one aircraft was used; otherwise the terrorists would have dispersed before later aircraft arrived. No. 1 Squadron, RAAF, could after intensive practice operate up to five Lincolns in Vic formation on moonlit nights, and three on dark nights, laying down an exceptionally heavy, widespread and simultaneous pattern of 1,000 (454-kg) bombs.

During 1954 the RAF developed a new technique, using the Lincolns to mount the main attack while Hornets struck simultaneously at targets nearby, pinpointed for them by the Austers. In the course of several such operations between July and November that year 181 terrorist camps were destroyed, but the small number of terrorists killed or captured was an indication of the difficulties involved in bringing the campaign to a swift conclusion. Cumulatively, however, a number of important objectives was achieved by offensive action in addition to the destruction of camps: driving the terrorists into ambushes or terrain suitable for

ground operations, reducing their operational potential by breaking them up into smaller groups, and generally undermining their morale by continual harassment.

The role of the air transport forces had meanwhile become increasingly important as the number of troops operating in the jungle approached its peak in 1955. For the Valettas the main tasks were still supply-dropping, and routine trooplift and re-supply operations to forward airfields. Supply dropping in Malayan conditions remained as exacting as ever, but monthly averages rose to some 300 short tons in 1954 and 1955, with a high of over 400 tons in March 1955. Even more demanding for the aircrews was the task of dropping paratroops into the jungle, a hazardous form of operations used only when it was necessary to introduce troops into some of the remoter areas without alerting the terrorists. The obvious risk that the paratroops would be caught up in trees 200 ft (61 m) from the ground was largely overcome by the development of a special abseil gear consisting of 200 ft (61 m) of webbing carried in a bag attached to a special harness. A number of such paratroop operations was carried out in the early 1950s, but by 1955 the expanding helicopter force had proved itself capable of introducing larger numbers of less specialised troops, more quickly and with less risk of personal injury, and was itself dropping paratroops, although mainly in the course of casualty evacuation or jungle rescue.

Indeed, as the campaign progressed in the mid-1950s, helicopters and light aircraft were playing an increasingly prominent role, mainly in providing services between the forward airfields and the

Far left: To provide area bombing of terrorist hide-outs the RAF sent detachments from Bomber Command squadrons in Britain. This had the additional advantage of providing good operational training for the UK squadrons. No. 57 Squadron are seen unpacking from their Lincolns on arrival at Tengah.

With the great difficulty of pinpointing terrorist targets, area bombing of the jungle (a Lincoln's load goes down here) was the most effective way of destroying their camps and supply dumps.

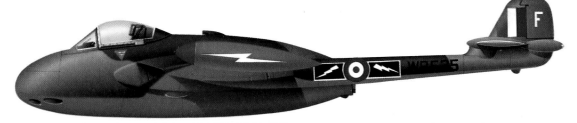

The de Havilland Venom replaced the Vampire with No. 60 Squadron but was not well-suited to jungle fighting. This FB.Mk 4 (WR525) displays the No. 60 Squadron black-and-silver lightning marking on the tail booms and sports red tiptanks and a red rudder, denoting A Flight.

With almost the capability of the helicopter, the Scottish Aviation Pioneer found a ready role in Malaya. The army had established a number of fortified installations in the jungle and, by building small airstrips there, regular air supply could be easily affected with the Pioneers of No. 267 Squadron.

One additional role undertaken by the RAF, and one that increased in importance as the anti-terrorist campaign gained momentum, was the use of aircraft to wage psychological warfare. Leaflet-dropping had begun in the first months of the emergency, and increased steadily through the years to a peak of 141 million leaflets dropped in 1955, the aircraft used being Dakotas, Austers and Valettas. Loud-hailing began in October 1952 and after an experimental period with Valettas, during which their engine noise was found too obtrusive, a voice flight of Dakotas and Austers was eventually formed in No. 267 Squadron.

Victory approaches

By early 1956, with the terrorists beginning to surrender in substantial numbers, the tide had clearly turned against them. A hard core was still left in the jungle, mainly in Johore and Perak, but being scattered in very small groups they offered an increasingly difficult target, and air strikes were mounted only when there were very convincing prospects of success. Activity therefore declined, although a formidable strike force remained in Malaya. Now largely re-equipped, it consisted of three de Havilland Venom squadrons (Nos 45 and 60 of the RAF, and No. 14 of the RNZAF), one Lincoln squadron (No. 1, RAAF), and the English Electric Canberras which had replaced the Lincolns in the detachments provided by Bomber Command. Re-equipment had brought its own problems. Compared to the Lincoln, the Canberra possessed relatively short endurance, particularly when flown at low level, and could not remain long over the target area. Venoms too were at a disadvantage in Malayan conditions compared with the Hornets, and jets generally created greater maintenance problems than the disappearing piston-engine aircraft.

There was no comparable decrease in the air transport activity, which continued at a high level until the end of 1958. Valettas, Austers and Pioneers, together with the helicopters, were fully occupied during the final years, but as more and more areas were freed from emergency restrictions the Valettas tended to carry fewer troops and to concentrate on freight.

By now, and in the interim before the Emergency officially ended in July 1960, the Far East Air Force was planning a gradual return to peacetime conditions in which all its energies could be devoted to its primary roles in South East Asia. As Malaya

many new airstrips being built. In addition to the 17 airfields which Valettas could use, 68 others had become available by 1955, all of them suitable for Pioneers and helicopters, and the great majority usable by Austers.

The great value of the tiny Auster lay in target marking and visual reconnaissance. But as a communications aircraft its use was limited, being able to carry only one passenger safely in Malayan conditions. The Pioneers, on the other hand, which had arrived in 1953, could carry up to four passengers and 600–800 lb (272–363 kg) of freight, and proved invaluable not only in maintaining communications between forward airstrips, but also in substituting for Valettas when only a limited carrying-capacity was needed. An additional role was found for them when police forts were built in the jungle to protect the aborigines, or Sakai, from intimidation by the terrorists. Initially the forts could be maintained only by helicopters or supply-dropping helicopters, but once airstrips had been built nearby the Pioneers could take over the task.

Meanwhile for the helicopters, trooplifting, reconnaissance and liaison flights had become well-established roles, supplementing casualty evacuation. Throughout 1955 and 1956 the monthly average of passengers carried was over 2,500, and of casualties evacuated, approaching 60.

Not all the aircraft designed for European war were successful when deployed in the Far East. In the mid-1950s the Canberra squadrons of Bomber Command took their turns with the rapidly diminishing Lincoln squadrons, but the Canberra could not effect the same area density with only half the bomb load and, with all the modern aids required for its operation, did not at first match up well to Malayan conditions of fighting. No. 101 Squadron from Binbrook was one of the early Canberra B.Mk 6 squadrons to go to Tengah.

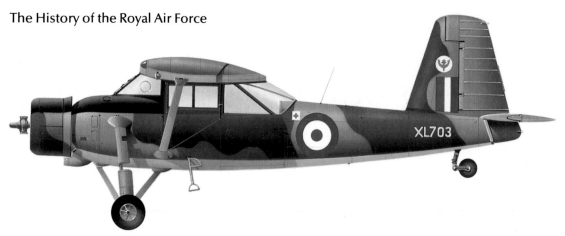

XL703 is one of the Scottish Aviation Pioneer CC.Mk 1s which went out to the Far East in 1954 and served with No. 267 Squadron until it was renumbered No. 209 Squadron in November 1958 (note the No. 209 Squadron badge on the fin).

had achieved independence in August 1957, AHQ Malaya reverted to its former title as No. 224 Group; it returned to Singapore when Kuala Lumpur was handed over to the newly-formed Royal Malayan Air Force in April 1959.

At the same time FEAF squadrons were being re-equipped for their peacetime roles. No. 45 Squadron exchanged its Venoms for Canberra B.Mk 2s in November 1957; two years later No. 60 Squadron was re-equipped for the night-fighter role with Meteor NF.Mk 14s, which were replaced by Gloster Javelin FAW.Mk 9s in July 1961. Two months later No. 20 Squadron re-formed at Tengah with Hawker Hunter FGA.Mk 9s. Canberra PR.Mk 7s began to replace the Meteors on No. 81 Squadron in January 1960, but it was to be more than a year before the process was finally completed.

The last of the Sunderlands were withdrawn from No. 205 Squadron in May 1959; these flying-boats had made a distinguished contribution to the Malayan campaign, maintaining coastal patrols and adding to the capabilities of the strike force as being the only aircraft able to carry the highly effective 20-lb (9.1-kg) anti-personnel bombs in sufficient quantities to justify their use. Over the years the Sunderland had proved a versatile aircraft in a theatre with large areas of open sea and, at the time, a shortage of modern airfields. Flying-boats had, however, become expensive to maintain, requiring their own special facilities, and the Sunderlands inevitably gave place to the more economical, land-based Avro Shackletons.

There were changes too in the transport force. On No. 48 Squadron the Valetta was withdrawn in May 1957 in favour of the Handley Page Hastings, which were joined two years later by a flight of Blackburn Beverleys; in October 1960 the Bever-

leys and their crews were used to re-form No. 34 Squadron. No. 110 Squadron disbanded in December 1957, re-forming later as a helicopter squadron. The only Valetta squadron then remaining was No. 52.

In the short-range transport role, No. 267 Squadron was re-numbered No. 209 with an establishment of single- and twin-engine Pioneers, together with elements of Pembrokes, Austers and Dakotas, all of which had been withdrawn by December 1959.

A problem had arisen with the helicopter force. The intention had been to retain only the Sycamore squadron in Malaya, but after two fatal accidents in April 1959 the whole force was grounded. Nos 155 and 194 Squadrons were disbanded two months later, and No. 110 Squadron was reformed with five Whirlwinds to complete the

The Dragonfly had done magnificent work with No. 194 Squadron in establishing techniques of jungle helicopter operation, but it had distinct operational limitations, especially in the hot and humid conditions prevailing in the jungle. The type was replaced in 1954 by Bristol Sycamore HR.Mk 14s, which had a marginal edge in performance over the Dragonfly.

FEAF SQUADRONS AT BEGINNING OF 1962: FULL PEACETIME ORDER

Controlled directly by FEAF

Squadron	Aircraft	Location
No. 48	Hastings C.Mk 1 and C.Mk 2	Changi
No. 205	Snackleton MR.Mk 2	Changi

Controlled by RAF Hong Kong

Squadron	Aircraft	Location
No. 28	Venom FB.Mk 4	Kai Tak

Controlled by No. 224 Group

Squadron	Aircraft	Location
No. 20	Hunter FGA.Mk 9	Tengah
No. 34	Beverley C.Mk 1	Seletar
No. 45	Canberra B.Mk 2	Tengah
No. 52	Valetta C.Mk 1	Butterworth
No. 60	Javelin FAW.Mk 9	Tengah
No. 81	Canberra PR.Mk 7	Tengah
No. 110	Sycamore HR.Mk 14	Butterworth
No. 209	Pioneer CC.Mk 1, plus Twin Pioneer CC.Mk 1 and CC.Mk 2	Seletar

The most successful helicopter in the Malayan jungle operations was the Westland Whirlwind, which came out to the RAF's No. 155 Squadron in September 1954.

Slowly the Far East Air Force was succumbing to the influx of jet aircraft. The Gloster Meteor PR.Mk 10 had taken over from Spitfires and Mosquitoes for photo-reconnaissance and these aircraft bore the brunt of the PR work from 1953 to the end of the decade. They flew their last sorties in 1963. Pre-flight inspection is in progress here; note the 'sunshade' erections to keep the cockpits from becoming blistered in the tropical sun.

Eventually, the jet replaced the piston-engine aircraft in the strike role, and FEAF's own strike squadron (No. 45) re-equipped with Canberras in 1957. They remained in service until 1970 when the squadron was disbanded. The version seen here is the B.Mk 15.

helicopters' trooplifting and casualty evacuation commitment in Malaya, and await the return of the Sycamores during 1960.

Accordingly, by the beginning of 1962, FEAF squadrons were in full peacetime order.

In addition the Royal Australian Air Force was providing one Canberra squadron (No. 2) and two CAC Sabre squadrons (Nos 3 and 77), all based at Butterworth, which was now under Australian command, and the Royal New Zealand Air Force a Canberra squadron (No. 75) at Tengah, and the Bristol Freighter squadron (No. 41) at Changi. It had also become standard practice to send small detachments of conventionally-armed V-bombers to Malaya for short periods, these replacing previous Canberra detachments.

Together the RAF and Commonwealth squadrons formed part of a Commonwealth strategic reserve, conceived as an element in the plan, developed during the 1950s, to broaden the basis on which the defence of South East Asia was built. The first stage had been completed in 1955 when the South East Asia Collective Defence Treaty Organization (SEATO) came into force. Comparable in

many ways with NATO in Europe and CENTO in the Middle East, SEATO was designed to protect South East Asia and the Western Pacific from communist aggression, and had five signatories in addition to Britain, Australia and New Zealand: France, Pakistan, the Philippines, Thailand and the United States of America. But although it had a headquarters in Bangkok, it had no command structure and no permanently assigned forces. All eight members, however, deployed substantial resources in the area, and Britain had a mutual defence and assistance agreement with Malaya, signed in October 1957. Furthermore, rapid reinforcement from the British Isles was becoming much simpler with the formation of Transport Command's new long-range squadrons, and the development of Gan as a main staging post. Moreover, No. 38 Group had been established as a tactical support force, and inflight refuelling was allowing modern fighters to reach the Far East without the need to use staging posts not under RAF control.

Flare-up in Borneo

Consequently, when a new emergency arose in South East Asia FEAF was in a strong position with well-equipped and well-trained forces already in the area, and reinforcements within reach. The new emergency began in December 1962 with minor rebellions in the British-protected sultanate of Brunei in northern Borneo, and in the adjoining Crown Colony of Sarawak, but it soon developed into a much larger conflict, similar in some respects to the Malayan campaign just ended, but in others very different.

The two terrains were alike; Borneo has the same vast expanses of mainly featureless jungle, with mountains rising to 13,000 ft (3960 m). As surface communications away from the coastal plain were by river or jungle track, air transport was once again an important element in the campaign. The climate was, if anything, worse: hotter and more humid, with torrential rain following the

build-up of immense formations of cumulo-nimbus cloud; but there were four or five hours of good flying weather each day between mid-morning and mid-afternoon, night operations being seldom practicable as locating an objective in the dark was virtually impossible. Navigation had its problems even in daylight as the maps available in 1962 were few and too small in scale to be of tactical use, and aircrews came to depend heavily on their growing knowledge of such local features as there were (ridges, rivers and valleys) and the use of timed runs on specific bearings.

The main difference between the Malayan and Borneo campaigns lay in the fact that soon after the initial rebellions in Brunei and Sarawak had been suppressed, Britain became involved, not in a worsening internal security situation, but in a confrontation with a foreign power, Indonesia, which shared a common border in Borneo with British colonial territories. In the south, and occupying by far the greater part of Borneo island, lay Kalimantan, Indonesian territory inherited from the Dutch; to the north were not only Sarawak and Brunei, but also a second Crown Colony, Sabah or North Borneo. Between the two parts of the island was an ill-defined frontier running for 1,000 miles (1609 km) through the featureless jungle.

It had been Britain's intention to incorporate her two Borneo territories in a Greater Malaysia which would include also Malaya and Singapore. Brunei, however, having no wish to share the wealth which she derived from her oilfield, declined to join the new state. Indonesian reaction to the British plan was immediate: not only was she reluctant to see the formation of a powerful new entity in her own sphere of influence, but she had also long nourished hopes of annexing the three northern Borneo territories, and so gaining control of the whole island.

All three territories had ready-made dissident factions, each with its own political leanings, anti-colonialist, anti-Malaysian, pro-Communist and pro-Indonesian. It was simple therefore for Indonesia to foster rebellion within the territories themselves and to persuade potential guerrillas to go to Kalimantan for training in infiltration and subversion. Thus, when the formation of the new Malaysia was officially proclaimed in September 1963, Indonesia was able to counter by infiltrating Kalimantan-trained guerrillas across the border, to be supported as the need arose by her own regular forces.

What had begun as an internal rebellion had become an international confrontation across a common frontier. Britain's task was not only to maintain internal security in the territories for which she was responsible, but also to protect the frontier with Kalimantan from incursions on the ground and in the air, and prevent infiltration into northern Borneo by sea. It was also necessary to provide for the security of Malaya, with which Britain had a defence treaty, and maintain the deterrent forces which would dissuade Indonesia from escalating confrontation into open conflict. At the same time, to ensure that she herself did nothing to escalate the situation and so antagonise world opinion, Britain had to forswear pre-emptive action against the Indonesian homeland.

As in Malaya, there was also a civil dimension: to ensure ultimate success it was necessary to retain the support of the civilian population, and what became known as the 'hearts and minds' campaign ran in tandem with activity on the ground and in the air, all mutually interdependent.

FEAF therefore had many roles to play, primarily in the provision of short- and medium-range transport forces, but also in reconnaissance and the creation of an air defence identification zone (ADIZ) along the frontier with Kalimantan. It had

For more intimate photo-reconnaissance No. 81 Squadron at Seletar received, alongside its Meteors, some Pembroke C(PR). Mk 1s for local PR duties, and the type served for two years in this role. No. 81 Squadron had, for some years, carried an 'ace of spades' on its aircraft and this was even carried on the Pembrokes.

In the Borneo conflict the RAF established base at Labuan, and this became a hub for all the flying, with transport aircraft bringing supplies in, Canberras and Javelins flying operational sorties and Twin Pioneers darting in and out to the jungle strips.

Scottish Aviation, who had produced the Pioneer, went on to produce a larger, twin-engined version, the Twin Pioneer. This joined No. 209 Squadron in March 1959 and served alongside the Pioneers for nine years, enabling bigger loads and more troops to be airlifted into tiny jungle airstrips.

The Sunderland flying-boat had finally retired from the RAF in 1959 and No. 205 Squadron, the FEAF maritime reconnaissance squadron, continued to provide oversea reconnaissance and anti-shipping tasks with Avro Shackletons until the end of the RAF in the Far East.

also to ensure the air defence of Malaya and Singapore, and provide the bomber forces which would deter further Indonesian action.

Instant response had been the key to bringing the rebellions in Brunei and Sarawak under control and restoring order. With only a few hours' warning of the uprisings on 8 December 1962, troops and their equipment began to leave Singapore for Borneo in the aircraft immediately available: Hastings, Pioneers, Valettas and Beverleys, together with a Transport Command Bristol Britannia that happened to be at Changi. By then most of Brunei state, except Brunei town itself, was in rebel hands. The first Beverley to arrive was able to land at Brunei civil airport, and this the Gurkhas immediately secured, thereby allowing following aircraft to bring in troops, vehicles and ordnance.

The Britannia meanwhile had made two trips to the RAF staging post at Labuan, the only airfield in northern Borneo able to accept it.

By 9 December the situation in Sarawak had been restored, but tension continued in Brunei. Reinforcements were flown in during the next few days by a transport force which now included Shackletons of No. 205 Squadron, a RNZAF Bristol Freighter and an RAAF Lockheed Hercules. Within a fortnight some 3,200 passengers, 113 vehicles, assorted guns and trailers, two Austers and 300 tons of freight had been flown in, with the heavier equipment following by sea. Troops and supplies were then moved on to their destinations by the Beverleys, Pioneers and Sycamores, as well as the Bristol Belvederes of No. 66 Squadron that had arrived in the Far East in May 1962; the Valettas also carried out a number of supply drops. Meanwhile Labuan, which had the advantage of being an offshore island and therefore secure from rebel action, was being developed as an operational base.

Militarily the first essential had been to isolate and mop up the main centres of revolt before the rebels could consolidate their position and receive support from the Indonesians. The main objectives for the British forces were therefore the oilfield at Seria and the airstrip at Anduki. Twin Pioneers of No. 209 Squadron reconnoitred both and, as landings were found to be feasible, a force of five Twin Pioneers, a Beverley and an Army Air Corps DHC Beaver was prepared. The Twin Pioneers landed on rough grass near the Seria oilfield and the troops on board quickly relieved the local police station. At Anduki the Beverley approached low along the coast to avoid detection, climbed over the trees at the last moment and braked hard on landing, using only a quarter of the runway. Two minutes later, with the troops disembarked, it executed a short-field take-off in the same direction, sustaining two hits in the course of the manoeuvre. As at Seria, the Anduki operation was completely successful and the airstrip was quickly

restored to government control.

In the course of other operations, the Shackletons of No. 205 Squadron carried out a number of shipping and coastal surveys, and No. 45 Squadron's Canberras made three reconnaissance sorties in the Brunei area. Mock attacks were mounted on the rebels by a Canberra and four of No. 20 Squadron's Hunters in attempts to dissuade the rebels from harming their European hostages, all of whom were eventually released unharmed.

In the lull that followed the suppression of the rebellions a number of cross-border raids took place, the frequency increasing noticeably after the formation of Malaysia in September 1963. There were relatively few places where infiltration was possible, however, and the nature of the terrain made it difficult for the guerrillas to vanish quickly into the interior after they had made the crossing. Once again No. 81 Squadron, now with Canberra PR.Mk 7s, played an important role by providing the photographs from which crossing points and jungle tracks could be clearly identified and up-to-date maps prepared.

To counter infiltration the security forces created a series of strong points near known crossing places, but as these could be maintained only by air the RAF's commitment in Borneo grew rapidly, with a consequent increase in the FEAF's transport force. In August 1963 two squadrons were re-formed: No. 215 Squadron with Armstrong Whitworth Argosies, and No. 103 Squadron with the greatly improved Mk 10 version of the Whirlwind, powered by Gnome turbine engines. By the end of September Whirlwind HAR.Mk 10s had replaced No. 110 Squadron's Sycamores in Borneo, and two months later No. 225 Squadron, also with the new Whirlwinds, arrived from Odiham. In March 1965 yet another Whirlwind squadron, No. 230, was deployed in Borneo, and later that year No. 66 Squadron was allotted the Belvederes which the disbanding of No. 26 Squadron at Aden had made available; in October No. 225 Squadron was disbanded, however, its aircraft being distributed between Nos 103 and 110 Squadrons.

As the campaign against guerrilla incursions increased in intensity, a well-defined pattern of air supply began to emerge. Forward air bases were established at Labuan and Kuching, in south western Sarawak, to receive the daily stream of urgent supplies brought in by the Hastings, Argosies, Beverleys and Bristol Freighters; heavy machinery and bulk supplies of food and ammunition arrived by sea. The next link in the supply

The ideal jet strike aircraft was the Hawker Hunter and this became the weapon wielded by No. 20 Squadron, in its FGA. Mk 9 version, from August 1961 onwards. With cannon, bombs and rockets it was able to provide a credible strike force during the Indonesian confrontation.

chain consisted of a number of airstrips hastily constructed in the interior and usable by Pioneers, the helicopters and sometimes even Beverleys and Valettas; the strips were often rough, short and with difficult approaches, but they were soon proving valuable both as focal points for air supply and as centres from which the ground forces could mount patrols.

The patrols themselves were maintained either by supply drops from Hastings, Beverleys and Valettas, or by the helicopter force. The versatility of the latter was now widely appreciated and, to save transit time from Labuan and Kuching, helicopters were based at the forward airstrips to undertake the growing number of tasks: supply of food and ammunition, casualty evacuation, troop-lifting and rotation, the last an operation that had to be carried out according to strict timetable as accommodation throughout Borneo was very limited. Where the helicopters could not land, supplies were winched down and passengers would climb down a knotted rope or use the abseil gear introduced in Malaya.

The Belvedere, which could lift heavy and awkward loads, had additional tasks to perform, particularly transporting the army's 105-mm howitzers. These were proving valuable weapons, but as there were too few of them in Borneo it was important to deceive the enemy into thinking that a

In Borneo the ubiquitous Whirlwind was the helicopter maid-of-all-work. The turbine-powered HC. Mk 10 provided a welcome advance in performance and safety. Further Whirlwinds came to FEAF from Britain with No. 230 Squadron and a detachment from No. 225 Squadron. They flew in all weathers including, as seen here, the monsoon season.

The Westland (Bristol) Belvedere HC. Mk 1 had an indifferent career in Britain, where it was regarded with disfavour. Eventually all the aircraft found their way to No. 66 Squadron in Seletar and for seven years from 1962 performed wonders of airlifting there and in Borneo. XG449 was the third Belvedere built and was used in Britain for development flying before going out to No. 66 Squadron in the Far East.

With the confrontation with Indonesia in 1965 it was more than ever necessary to have a viable air defence force and this role was performed by No. 60 Squadron, which had re-equipped with Gloster Javelin FAW. Mk 9s in 1961.

The Belvederes of No. 66 Squadron became known as 'Flying Longhouses' by the local population. Their contribution in Borneo was a significant one.

large number was available by using the simple bluff of moving them rapidly from site to site, one Belvedere carrying the gun, and a second the ammunition, equipment and crew. Another load which the Belvedere could handle was the anti-mortar radar detector which could trace a 3-in (76-mm) mortar bomb back to the base plate and allow reciprocal mortar fire to be opened up within seconds. The Belvederes could also lift an unserviceable Whirlwind and the cumbersome UPS 1 ground radar; to prevent the long, heavy case in which this was housed from upsetting the aircraft's stability, a light wood and fabric framework was built around it to form a six-sided symmetrical package which gyrated slowly and evenly under the Belvedere.

As the number of cross-border incursions increased, with more regular troops taking part, Indonesia began to escalate the conflict in other ways, mounting air incursions across the Kalimantan border and even sending raiding parties to infiltrate Malaya itself. Frequent violations of Malaysian air space led in February 1964 to the creation of an air defence identification zone (ADIZ), running the length of the border with Kalimantan. It was policed by eight Hunters of No. 20 Squadron and two Javelins of No. 60 Squadron, half of the force being based at Labuan and half at Kuching. The task of these aircraft was to escort supply-dropping aircraft and provide a permanent 24-hour all-weather defence system, with pilots authorised to engage and destroy any Indonesian aircraft violating the ADIZ. The problem was that any air incursion was so fleeting that Indonesian aircraft could be back across the border before the Hunters and Javelins arrived; consequently even the air attacks mounted in September 1965 against villages on the Malaysian side of the border were impossible to intercept. Nevertheless the presence of RAF fighter aircraft in Borneo clearly acted as a deterrent against incursions on a larger scale.

Indonesian raids into Malaya itself also posed problems. The first took place in August 1964, when

100 regular Indonesian troops went ashore at three different points on the west coast of Malaya. Two weeks later Indonesian paratroops were dropped in north central Johore, making it obvious that if a Hercules could penetrate so far, other Indonesian aircraft could do the same. Consequently, with Malayan and Singapore air space declared an ADIZ in September 1964, FEAF's air-defence squadrons were put on full alert; the Hunters meanwhile also engaged in a series of air strikes in support of the ground forces. By the end of September all but 10 of the paratroops had been eliminated; a month later all those that had landed from the sea had also been rounded up.

In the course of the next six months there were some 40 further landings, attempted landings and acts of sabotage. In an incident in December 1964 Hunters and Canberras were used to carry out real and simulated attacks on infiltrators, with Belvederes and Whirlwinds in support to lift troops and supplies.

In the meantime the air defence of Malaya had been considerably strengthened. HMS *Kent* was sent to the Malacca Strait in the air defence role; Fleet Air Arm Fairey Gannets, disembarked from HMS *Victorious*, joined RAF aircraft patrolling Malayan air space; and No. 60 Squadron was reinforced by No. 64 Squadron, also with Javelins, from the United Kingdom. Additionally No. 65 (SAM) Squadron, which had been engaged in tropical trials at Seletar, brought one of its missile sections to operational readiness.

In the end, although landings and attempted landings continued throughout 1965, no air attacks were mounted against Singapore airfields, and by the following year it was clear that the campaign both in Borneo and the Malayan peninsula was beginning to run out of steam. Throughout the years of confrontation the Indonesians had been faced with their own problems, but it was the success of Britain's carefully controlled response to Indonesian infiltration, combined with the deterrent value of FEAF's strike forces, including the V-bomber detachments, which staved off any major escalation.

The FEAF runs down

In the months which followed the formal ending of confrontation in August 1966, British forces in Borneo were progressively withdrawn, signalling in fact the beginning of a whole new era in British involvement in South East Asia. As the 1966 Defence Review had clearly stated, Britain could

no longer afford either to mount a major campaign virtually single-handed, or to keep a large permanent garrison overseas. She intended, however, to retain the capability to deploy substantial forces to the Far East should the need arise. The 1968 Defence White Paper went further and announced that all British forces would be withdrawn from Malaysia and the now-independent state of Singapore by the end of 1971, and that no more than a general reinforcement capability would be retained beyond that date.

A rapid rundown of FEAF's front line had in fact already begun. By early 1970 five transport squadrons (Nos 34, 52, 66, 209 and 215) had been disbanded, as well as four strike squadrons (Nos 20, 45, 60 and 64) and the photo-reconnaissance squadron, No. 81. No. 48 Squadron meanwhile had been re-equipped with the Hercules, and No. 74 Squadron had arrived with English Electric/BAC Lightning F.Mk 6s to fulfil the air defence role. In Hong Kong No. 28 Squadron, a Hunter unit, had been disbanded in December 1966, to be re-formed 15 months later with Whirlwind HAR.Mk 10s, which were well-suited for what was now to be the squadron's main task, that of countering smuggling and illegal immigration.

As a result of this contraction, FEAF by March 1970 controlled only five squadrons in Singapore, and one in Hong Kong. The rundown continued through 1971, with No. 110 Squadron disbanding

The V-bomber force was brought into the Indonesian conflict in a minor way, largely for training purposes. Victors from Cottesmore (No. 10 Squadron shown) were detached to Singapore and flew area bombing sorties against terrorist and Indonesian camps.

Right: Operations against terrorists also meant long, hard hours for groundcrews in the hot and humid conditions of South East Asia. This armourer is changing a gunpack for the four 30-mm Aden cannon of a No. 20 Squadron Hunter FGA.Mk 9. The insignia on the side of the aircraft comprises the squadron's official badge on a white disc, flanked by its colour insignia. The red, white and green bands indicate associations with Italy. The nosewheel door is red for A Flight and on it is the aircraft letter 'F' and 'XX' for No. 20 Squadron.

FEAF IN SINGAPORE AND HONG KONG AT MARCH 1970

Squadron	Aircraft	Location
No. 28	Whirlwind HAR.Mk 10	Kai Tak
No. 48	Hercules C.Mk 1	Changi
No. 74	Lightning F.Mk 6	Tengah
No. 103	Whirlwind HAR.Mk 10	Changi
No. 110	Whirlwind HAR.Mk 10	Changi
No. 205	Shackleton MR.Mk 2	Changi

Detachments of conventionally configured V-bombers were frequently sent to Malaysia from Britain. Here Victors of No. 57 Squadron (RAF Honington) are bombed up prior to a raid against Indonesian infiltrators.

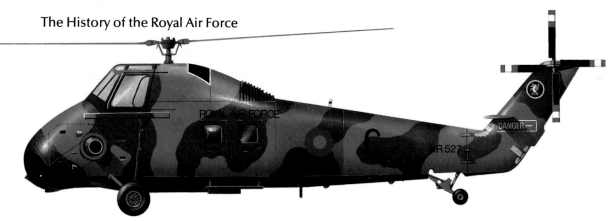

After the end of the Far East Air Force the only permanent squadron left in the area was No. 28 Squadron in Hong Kong. This was changed from a fighter unit to a helicopter squadron for tactical support and rescue duties. For the last decade it has flown the Westland Wessex HC.Mk 2 of which XR527 is one, becoming part of No. 28 Squadron's complement after serving at Odiham with No. 72 Squadron. The squadron badge is carried on a black disc on the fin.

in February, No. 74 Squadron in August and No. 205 Squadron in October; No. 48 re-deployed to Lyneham in September. FEAF itself closed down in October.

In its last years FEAF had controlled one final operation, which took place in the Mozambique channel at the western edge of the Indian Ocean. In one of the longest regular surveillance operations ever mounted by the RAF, a small number of Shackletons, operating from Majunga in Madagascar, kept watch for tankers heading for Beira, where oil could be offloaded and transported by pipeline to Rhodesia in defiance of British and United Nations sanctions. The area to be covered could be swept in a 10-hour sortie and, with three such sorties a week, an average of 250 contacts was made each month, one-third of which proved to be tankers. A Royal Navy frigate was on station in the southern approaches to the channel, ready to act on sightings reported by the Shackletons. Surveillance continued until March 1972, controlled in the last six months by No. 18 (Maritime) Group.

By then the British government's intention to withdraw completely from the Far East had undergone some small modification. The Supplementary Statement on Defence, published in October 1970, had proposed a small contribution by British forces to the defence of South East Asia in association with Australia, New Zealand, Malaysia and Singapore. The RAF element was to consist of permanent detachments of Whirlwind helicopters and Hawker Siddeley Nimrod long-range reconnaissance aircraft, reinforced by visiting units from the United Kingdom. These proposals took final shape in a five-power agreement, accompanied by a separate pact between Australia, New Zealand and the United Kingdom which created what became

No. 28 Squadron had become Hong Kong's resident RAF unit from 1957. Its last fixed-wing aircraft was the Hawker Hunter FGA.Mk 9, seen being refuelled and rearmed after a sortie from Kai Tak airfield.

known as the ANZUK force with its headquarters at Singapore.

Tengah then became the base of No. 103 Squadron with 11 Whirlwinds and No. 204 Squadron (Far East) Detachment with three Shackletons; the latter were replaced in January 1972 by a detachment of No. 206 Squadron with up to four Nimrod MR.Mk 1s. This situation was destined to be short-lived. The 1975 Defence White Paper announced the government's decision to withdraw the British contribution to ANZUK by April 1976. No. 103 Squadron was disbanded in July 1975 and the Nimrod detachment was withdrawn. Gan was closed down in March 1976 after 19 years of activation, during which it became one of the RAF's largest staging posts. As a result of these changes the only squadron remaining in the Far East was No. 28 at Kai Tak, Hong Kong, which had been re-equipped with Wessex HC.Mk 2s by August 1972.

With the end of the Indonesian confrontation there was little need for the Belvedere, so No. 66 Squadron put up this formation flypast on its disbandment at Seletar on 20 March 1969.

The Middle East and Mediterranean

Although much of its wartime structure had been cleared away by the end of 1947, the RAF in the Mediterranean and Middle East was still a considerable command operating in a theatre which stretched from Greece to Kenya, and from Malta to Iraq. In terms of front-line aircraft its resources were very slender, no more than 15 squadrons (two of them cadres), but there were still four air headquarters: Malta, with units also in North Africa; Levant, with units in Palestine and Cyprus; Iraq, with units in Bahrain and Sharjah in what were then the Trucial States; and East Africa, with units in Kenya and Somaliland. Additionally, No. 205 Group in the Canal Zone of Egypt had responsibilities there and in the Sudan, and British Forces Aden had responsibilities also in Oman. The last mentioned had long been an inter-service formation controlled by the RAF, which provided most of the facilities used by the other services.

Little more than 10 years later the situation was very different. After the withdrawal of British forces from Palestine and Egypt, and with a depart-

ure from Iraq imminent, the theatre was effectively divided into two, and in consequence two separate commands were now established. The Middle East Air Force (MEAF), as the RAF in the Mediterranean and Middle East had been known since June 1949, was based in Cyprus and controlled units there and in North Africa and, for the moment, Iraq; while British Forces Arabian Peninsula, the successor to British Forces Aden, was responsible for the RAF in Aden, the Persian Gulf and East Africa. Malta was at that time directly under Air Ministry control.

Ten years later again, British forces had been withdrawn from Aden and were temporarily established in Bahrain, where Air Forces Gulf controlled units there and at Sharjah. Cyprus, however, remained a substantial RAF base housing the Near East Air Force (NEAF), as MEAF had been renamed in March 1961; Malta was now under NEAF control. In the 1970s there were further withdrawals, from the Persian Gulf in 1971 and from Malta in 1979; and by 1975 the only front-line

Historically the Suez Canal had been a major reason for the presence of the RAF in Egypt. With most of Britain's oil supplies coming along this route its defence was vital. As this tanker sails north from the Great Bitter Lake it is buzzed by three Mosquito PR.Mk 34s of No. 13 Squadron.

squadron in Cyprus was No. 84 with Westland Whirlwinds.

Although the rising cost of defence had played its part in British withdrawal from the theatre, a major cause was the growth of nationalist feeling and the increasing incompatibility of old treaty and mandate arrangements, and colonial relationships, with the prevailing sentiment in the Middle East in the 1950s and 1960s. From the end of World War II Britain had been faced with dissidence of one kind or another in almost all the territories in which her forces were based, and yet the theatre was of outstanding strategic importance, as a source of oil for the West and as a centre of communications, including not only the Suez Canal but also vital air links to East and Southern Africa, and to India and the Far East. Consequently, it was assumed that instability in the area could have serious consequences for Britain and for the West.

Palestine

The first signs of unrest were spread widely across the theatre, in Kenya and the Ogaden region on the borders of Somaliland and Ethiopia, and in Aden and Oman. The first major operation, however, took place, as expected, in Palestine, which Britain was administering under a League of Nations mandate of the early 1920s and where much of the RAF's front-line force was then based. Here the cause of conflict was the irreconcilable hostility of the two Palestine communities, Arab and Jewish, to each other and to Britain's restrictions on Jewish immigration into the area, imposed by Britain with the intention of mitigating Arab hostility but having the effect of angering the Jewish population without reducing Arab determination to prevent Palestine being turned into a Jewish homeland. They also meant that RAF aircraft based there had to undertake one of the more melancholy tasks of the immediate post-war years, the search for illegal Jewish immigrants infiltrating into Palestine by sea. Likely ships would be identified from the air and the Royal Navy alerted to intercept and search them.

The RAF's resources at the end of 1946 for this and other tasks consisted of a flight of No. 38 Squadron with Avro Lancaster maritime reconnaissance aircraft; Nos 6, 32, 208 and 213 Squadrons with Hawker Hurricanes, Supermarine Spitfires and North American Mustangs; and No. 13 Squadron with photographic reconnaissance de Havilland Mosquitoes. In addition, No. 113 (formerly No. 620) Squadron, an airborne forces unit equipped with Handley Page Halifaxes, continued to exercise with the 6th Airborne Division, although on a very reduced scale; this task had previously been shared with No. 644 (later No. 47) Squadron until the latter returned to Britain in September 1946. In 1947 the maritime reconnaissance element was increased to two full squadrons, Nos 37 and 38,

with a total of 18 Lancasters, but as the prospects of peace became increasingly remote, No. 113 was sent home, and Nos 6, 13 and 213 were moved to the Canal Zone.

For the Lancasters the task of searching for illegal immigrants continued until Britain ended the mandate in May 1948; since the beginning of 1946 47 ships had been intercepted by the Royal Navy, almost always after location and shadowing by the RAF. In all, some 65,000 illegal immigrants were transferred to camps, mainly in Cyprus.

Meanwhile acts of terrorism within Palestine were occurring almost daily. In February 1946 Mount Carmel radar station, which controlled aircraft searching for ships carrying illegal immigrants, was blown up and a few days later 11 Halifaxes, seven Spitfires and two Avro Ansons were destroyed or seriously damaged in attacks on airfields at Qastina, Petah Tigya and Lydda. Five months later, in the most serious incident of all, the King David Hotel in Jerusalem was destroyed with over 200 British, Arabs and Jews killed. The RAF's main contribution to internal security necessarily came from the RAF Regiment, but aircraft too had a part to play: during a major search and cordon exercise at the end of June 1946, for example, Austers of No. 651 Squadron and Spitfires of No. 208 Squadron flew a number of tactical reconnaissance sorties in an operation which resulted in over 2,700 arrests and the confiscation of large quantities of illegal arms and ammunition.

But it was in the delicate process of withdrawing British forces from Palestine and the increasingly unstable situation there that aircraft proved to be of particular value. The policy was to support the Army whenever necessary with a show of force by unarmed fighters; but if it was essential to arm the

Within a short span after the end of World War II, two trouble spots blew up in the eastern Mediterranean: Cyprus and Palestine. The fighter force in the area consisted primarily of Spitfire FR.Mk 18E squadrons, of which No. 32 was based in Cyprus (Nicosia), where propeller changes seem to be the order of the day.

One of the immediate problems faced by the RAF was the steady stream of illegal Jewish immigrants sailing into Palestine. Based at Ein Shemer was No. 38 Squadron equipped with Lancasters for maritime reconnaissance, and to it fell the task of finding and identifying the immigrant ships. The squadron's GR.Mk 3s were supplemented by B.Mk 7s left over from the Tiger Force squadrons.

The Spitfire FR. Mk 18E was the definitive fighter in the Middle East in the late 1940s. TZ214 served with No. 32 Squadron in Cyprus in this period and carried the squadron's hunting horn emblem, code letters 'GZ' and a temporary blue and white check marking.

fighters they were to achieve their objectives without or with minimum casualties among the rioters. A number of such demonstration sorties were flown, and these were usually effective in dispersing the trouble-makers without casualties. Spitfires were also used for patrolling oil pipelines, and in April 1948 they were called upon to attack a guerrilla sniping post. The damage proved slight, but the post was evacuated.

Disturbance in Kenya

As part of the withdrawal of British forces from Palestine in May 1948, Nos 37 and 38 Squadrons were sent to Malta, and Nos 32 and 208 to Nicosia. The following years were scarcely peaceful, but it was not until the early 1950s that the RAF was again engaged in operations on any scale. These took place at opposite ends of the Middle East theatre, in Kenya and Oman, and demonstrated again how varied were the applications of air power, and how economical, with aircraft detachments brought in temporarily from outside the operational area to meet immediate demands.

In Kenya, Britain (as the colonial power) had been faced since 1948 with labour unrest among African workers, fostered by the Kikuyu tribe,

which was beginning to claim back the land which it had sold years before to European settlers. But it was only in 1952 that violence began in earnest. A state of emergency was declared in October, and Army reinforcements began to arrive at RAF Eastleigh, Nairobi, in Handley Page Hastings transports of Transport Command and in civil aircraft. The calls for local air support (reconnaissance, leaflet-dropping, communications and casualty evacuation flights) soon grew beyond the capacity of the small Eastleigh communications flight, and as there was also a need for accurate and discriminate offensive air action, the decision was taken to fit North American Harvards of the Rhodesian Air Training Group, which was then winding up, with forward-firing guns and racks for light bombs. So No. 1340 Flight was formed in March 1953, initially with four aircraft, and sent up to the airstrip at Mweiga to join the Police Reserve Air Wing which was already there. Mweiga was close to the two main operational areas, the Aberdare Forest region and the jungle country around Mount Kenya, where the Kikuyu had been forced to retreat under pressure from the Army and police, but from where they could still sally forth to raid farms and kill Africans and Europeans

Three Scottish Aviation Twin Pioneers of No. 21 Squadron formate for the cameraman. This squadron flew light transport and army support duties in Kenya until 1965, when it moved to Aden.

The Avro Lincoln B.Mk 2 made a much bigger contribution to post-war RAF operations than has been credited. RE299 was built by Avro at Manchester just after the war in Europe ended and at first went to Rolls-Royce at Hucknall for engine development flying. It then moved on to No. 7 Squadron and during the late 1940s and early 1950s served, in succession, with Nos 149, 49, 148 and 7 Squadrons before joining No. 214 Squadron in whose markings it is here shown and with which it operated over Kenya. It finally served with No. 49 Squadron for a second time and was eventually scrapped in 1957.

alike. But with the Mau Mau, as the terrorists now called themselves, confined to these two areas, air action could be used to good advantage.

The Police Wing proved particularly effective in reconnaissance as the pilots could use their intimate knowledge of the terrain to identify even the most difficult targets; and with their small and highly manoeuvrable Cessnas and Piper Tri-Pacers they could fly low into valleys and jungle clearings in spite of the restrictions placed upon lower-powered aircraft when operating in areas mostly above 7,000 ft (2135 m). For the RAF there were two main tasks: to use the Harvard flight, now with eight aircraft, to attack the targets identified by the Police Wing, and to drop supplies to search parties at pre-arranged dropping zones.

However intensive the Harvard effort might be (332 offensive sorties were flown in one month alone in 1953) it soon became clear that the 20-lb (9-kg) bomb, the largest the Harvard could carry, was not powerful enough to be effective in the jungle. Two Avro Lincolns from one of the Bomber Command 'Sun Ray' detachments sent to the Canal Zone for bombing practice were therefore diverted to Kenya and, as they proved highly successful, a permanent detachment of six Lincolns was established at Eastleigh, drawn from Bomber Command squadrons in turn. To ensure that the Lincoln effort was well directed, two Gloster Meteor PR.Mk 10s from No. 13 Squadron in the Canal Zone were also sent to Kenya, along with the necessary processing and interpretation facilities. At full strength, the RAF in Kenya also operated two Austers and one Hunting Pembroke for sky shouting, which proved effective later in the campaign, and a Bristol Sycamore which, after an experimental period adapting to operations at heights substantially above those so far achieved elsewhere, flew a total of 506 hours and evacuated 30 casualties.

Although confined strictly to areas where it was certain that only the Mau Mau remained, the bombing had proved so successful by the late summer of 1954 that it was given priority over ground operations during a four-month period in

preparation for land sweeps through the Aberdare Forest region and later in the Mount Kenya area. These tactics worked well and with more and more Mau Mau surrendering, the scale of RAF activity was progressively reduced. The last bombing sortie took place in June 1955; the Lincolns and Meteors then returned to their bases, and three months later No. 1340 Flight was disbanded.

Potential trouble

In Oman, with which Britain had signed a treaty of friendship in December 1951 to confirm close ties which went back more than 150 years, the RAF had very different tasks to perform. The seeds of conflict lay in a disputed boundary with Saudi

As in Malaya, so in Kenya during the Mau Mau troubles the Avro Lincoln bomber was found to be useful in bombing terrorist camps and supply dumps. Detachments came from each Bomber Command squadron in turn. RF555 was part of No. 61 Squadron's contribution, on detachment from Hemswell.

For fighter and ground attack duties in the late 1950s the RAF maintained No. 208 Squadron at Eastleigh, Nairobi, equipped with Hawker Hunter FGA.Mk 9s. This foursome is seen carrying out a formation loop with Mount Kilimanjaro as a backcloth.

The de Havilland Vampire, in its FB.Mk 5 and FB.Mk 9 versions, served as the standard fighter and ground-attack aircraft in the Middle East for the first half of the 1950s. WR211 is an FB.Mk 9 in service with No. 32 Squadron, whose blue and white insignia are carried on the tail booms.

The jack-of-all-trade fighter aircraft of the 1950s in the Middle East was the de Havilland Vampire FB.Mk 5. In Cyprus, Iraq and the Canal Zone the Vampire squadrons were involved in all the alarms and excursions of the period, and were sent on detachment wherever they were needed. This No. 6 Squadron FB.Mk 5 makes a veritable dust-storm as it taxis out at Mafraq in Jordan.

Arabia and in the long-standing inability of the sultans of Oman to exercise more than tenuous authority over the tribes living in the interior of the country. Matters first came to a head in August 1952 when a party of some 60 Saudis arrived at an Omani village near the Buraimi oasis; this lay on the Oman–Abu Dhabi border far from the Saudi frontier and was important not only for its abundant water supplies, but also as a crossroads giving access to central Oman, with its possible oil reserves, and the coast in an area of considerable strategic significance alongside the main oil tanker route to the West.

For the moment Britain did no more than arrange for a party of Trucial Oman Levies to go to the Abu Dhabi side of the oasis, and for a flight of de Havilland Vampire FB.Mk 5s from No. 6 Squadron at Habbaniyah to move to Sharjah on the Persian Gulf, from where it flew a number of low-level sorties over the oasis area. The Vampires, however, were not well suited to the task, as their endurance was too short and their low-slung jet efflux played havoc with the natural sand surface of the Sharjah runway. Consequently, when negotiations with the Saudis produced no results, there was instituted a blockade to prevent supplies reaching their detachment at the oasis. This could be done only by air as every caravan track within 200 miles had to be inspected at least once a week; sightings would then be reported to strategically placed detachments of Trucial Oman Levies or RAF armoured cars, which would intercept and interrogate. The problem, however, was to find suitable aircraft.

The blockade implemented

The blockade began in March 1953, using No. 6 Squadron's Vampires, plus Vickers Valettas and Ansons from the communications flights at Bahrain and Aden. Meteors from No. 208 Squadron in the Canal Zone were also tried, but their short endurance made it almost impossible to cover the blockade area with the few aircraft available. Lancaster GR.Mk 3s from Nos 37 and 38 Squadrons at Malta were then used for a time, based temporarily at Habbaniyah, but operating from Sharjah; they proved well suited to the task as four aircraft could manage almost all the 180 flying hours a month needed to maintain the blockade, but with NATO commitments to meet the Lancasters were returned to Malta in July. For a while Valettas and Ansons filled the gap with occasional help from the Lancaster PR.Mk 1s of No. 683 Squadron at Habbaniyah, but in September 1953 No. 1417 Flight was formed at Bahrain with five Ansons and one in reserve to maintain a reduced blockade. A disused airstrip at Tarif on the Trucial Oman coast west of Abu Dhabi was brought back

into commission and the Ansons were able to refuel there and stay overnight if necessary.

The blockade continued in conditions of severe discomfort until July 1954, when both sides agreed to withdraw their forces while arbitration took place. No satisfactory conclusion was reached, however, and when it became obvious that the Saudis were sending reinforcements to Buraimi, Britain decided to expel them. A small force of two Lincolns from No. 7 Squadron, Bomber Command, two Valettas, two Pembrokes and two Ansons from No. 1417 Flight assembled at Sharjah, with the de Havilland Venom FB.Mk 1s with which No. 6 Squadron had been re-equipped on call. On 26 October 1955 two parties of Trucial Oman Levies entered Buraimi while a Valetta and an Anson landed on the airstrip near by. The Saudis soon capitulated and were eventually flown back home; the Lincolns remained to patrol the frontier and proved so valuable that they were formed into No. 1426 Flight based at Bahrain.

The RAF resorts to attack

Saudi Arabia, however, was now beginning to exploit the hostility of the Omani tribes towards the Sultan by giving open support to their religious leader, the Imam Ghalib, and his brother Talib. But the sultan, encouraged by his success at Buraimi, decided to oust the Imam from his stronghold at Nizwa in central Oman, promised to provide Valettas to fly a squadron of Trucial Oman Levies from Sharjah to Nizwa if reinforcements were needed, and aircraft of No. 1417 Flight and No. 6 Squadron were also to be available. It was to be the beginning of a long campaign in the most difficult country.

Nizwa itself was soon occupied and aircraft of No. 1417 Flight were the first to land there on a roughly cleared strip, which later became a passable airfield. The Imam capitulated, but his brother Talib escaped into the mountains to found the Omani Liberation Army with Saudi help, returning to central Oman in June 1957. As his threat to the Sultan's authority was now becoming serious, Britain was reluctantly compelled to act and decided to use the offensive air weapon. With Avro Shackletons dropping leaflets 48 hours before, Venoms from Nos 8 and 249 Squadrons carried out rocket attacks on a number of strongholds thought to be occupied by Talib's men and made them uninhabitable; and any movement seen in the area believed to be occupied by the rebels was attacked by patrols of Venoms and Shackletons. Talib, however, escaped to the Jebel Akhdar, a mountainous area rising to 11,000 ft (3350 m) and honeycombed with steep tracks and wadis, which are impassable by any kind of vehicle.

The problem now was to dislodge him from the village of Saiq, which lies in a strong defensive position on a plateau dominating the southern approaches to the mountain. Two assaults failed, although supported by aircraft, and a campaign of harassment and attrition followed with a combination of air action and artillery fire. A daily barrage by two 5.5-in howitzers was closely co-ordinated with attacks by No. 37 Squadron's Shackletons based in Aden but operating from Masirah off the Omani coast, the main targets being water supplies and the irrigation system. Venoms from Sharjah maintained their harassing patrols, while Pembrokes dropped leaflets and broadcast to the inhabitants.

When no definite results were achieved, the British government finally agreed to an assault in which intensive air support would be given to the SAS troops who were to scale the mountain and lead the Sultan's forces on to the plateau. Shackle-

tons and Venoms began the long softening-up process in December 1958, and it was not until January 1959 that the actual assault took place. The Jebel Akhdar was taken without much difficulty and although Talib escaped, probably to Saudi Arabia, the rebellion was over, at least for the moment, and a programme of rehabilitation began. In the course of the long campaign the Shackletons of No. 37 Squadron had dropped some 1,560 tons of bombs, and the Venoms of No. 8 Squadron had flown 1,315 sorties and fired 3,500 rockets and 27,000 rounds of ammunition.

A reversal in Kenya or Oman could have had undesirable consequences in the longer term, but well before the end of the Omani campaign Britain's strategic position in the Middle East had begun to change dramatically. The withdrawal of her forces from Egypt to Cyprus, from where the Suez operation was mounted a few months later, was followed by further withdrawals from Iraq and Jordan, completed in 1958 and 1959. The consequence of these events had been foreseen (the development of an air barrier between the northern part of the Middle East theatre, based in Cyprus, and the southern, based in Aden) and steps were taken in April 1958 to establish two independent commands in the area: MEAF in Cyprus and British Forces Arabian Peninsula (BFAP) in Aden. The further threat which emerged in 1961 that Iraq might attempt to annex Kuwait at the head of the Persian Gulf was, however, successfully resisted.

Build-up in the Canal Zone

In Egypt, where this upheaval process had begun, hostility to the presence of British troops, permitted under the Anglo-Egyptian treaty of 1936, had grown steadily since the end of World War II. The removal of troops from the Nile delta to the Canal Zone in 1947 did nothing to diminish the hostility, and Britain finally agreed in July 1954 to remove all her troops within 20 months. The years between 1947 and 1954 had not been devoid of incident. In 1948 the fear of a Russian thrust down into the Levant to attack Egypt had prompted a review of air defences in the area which left no doubt that they were sadly inadequate. Months would be needed to build up radar and fighter control facilities to an acceptable standard, and of the six fighter squadrons in the theatre only two, Nos 6 and 213 with Hawker Tempests, were actually in the Canal Zone. Nos 32 and 208 with Spitfires were in Cyprus until the latter was moved to Egypt in January 1949; No. 39 with Tempests was in Khartoum and No. 73 with Vampires in Malta.

In 1948 too came the threat of Britain being brought into a war between the newly created state of Israel and her two Arab neighbours, Egypt and Jordan, with whom Britain also had treaty relationships. When the Israeli army crossed the Egyptian frontier at the end of the year and advanced into Egyptian territory, Britain did in fact become involved, although unintentionally. Four Spitfire FR.Mk 18s of No. 208 Squadron were despatched on a tactical reconnaissance mission to be carried out strictly within Egyptian territory; one was shot down by ground fire and three more by Israeli Spitfires, which could easily be confused with RAF aircraft as they were in British-type camouflage and had the same red airscrew spinners as No. 208 Squadron's aircraft. During a search for the missing Spitfires a further RAF aircraft, a Tempest of No. 213 Squadron, was shot down. In all,

one pilot was killed.

Two years later tension in the area was again growing and steps were taken to increase RAF strength in the Canal Zone: Nos 683 and 219 Squadrons were formed with Lancaster PR.Mk 1s and Mosquito NF.Mk 36s respectively, and No. 32 Squadron was brought from Nicosia. By the end of 1951 14 squadrons were deployed in the zone, giving a front-line strength of 152 aircraft.

Hostility grows

These 14 squadrons represented the bulk of MEAF's resources at the time, as there were only five other squadrons in the theatre: one in Aden (No. 8 with Bristol Brigand B.Mk 1s) and four in Malta (Nos 37 and 38 with Lancaster GR.Mk 3s and Nos 73 and 185 with Vampire FB.Mk 5s). Canal Zone squadrons were normally available for rapid deployment to other parts of the theatre, but as Egyptian hostility turned into a mass withdrawal of local labour, the ambushing, kidnapping and murder of British personnel, and sporadic attacks on Army and RAF installations it was the British forces in Egypt which needed temporary reinforcement.

The overall trend, however, over the next four years was away from the Canal Zone. Nos 6 and 683 Squadrons moved to Habbaniyah in 1952, No. 249 went to Amman in 1954, and with the withdrawal from Egypt in full swing in 1955 Nos 32 and 39 Squadrons moved to Malta and No. 70 Squadron to Nicosia. In the following year Nos 13, 84 (formerly No. 204), 114 and 208 Squadrons moved to Cyprus. Three squadrons (Nos 78, 213 and 219) had been disbanded in 1954, and No. 216 Squadron was transferred to Transport Command a year later. Meanwhile MEAF itself had been installed in Cyprus in December 1954, with No. 205 Group remaining in the Canal Zone until the following October.

By the spring of 1956 MEAF was fully established in Cyprus controlling two subordinate formations, RAF Levant at Nicosia (with responsibilities in Cyprus, Iraq, Jordan and Libya) and British Forces Aden at Steamer Point (with responsibilities extending to Kenya, Oman and the Trucial States). RAF Levant was then operating four Venom FB.Mk 1 and FB.Mk 4 squadrons (Nos 6, 32, 73 and 249); No. 13 Squadron with Meteor PR.Mk 10s

RAF DEPLOYMENT IN CANAL ZONE AT END OF 1951

Squadron	Aircraft	Location
No. 6	Vampire FB.Mk 5	Deversoir
No. 13	Mosquito PR.Mk 34	Kabrit
No. 32	Vampire FB.Mk 5	Shallufa
No. 39	Mosquito NF.Mk 36	Kabrit
Nos 70, 78, 114, 204 and 216	Valetta C.Mk 1	Fayid
No. 208	Meteor FR.Mk 9	Abu Sueir
No. 213	Vampire FB.Mk 5	Deversoir
No. 219	Mosquito NF.Mk 36	Kabrit
No. 249	Vampire FB.Mk 5	Deversoir
No. 683	Lancaster PR.Mk 1	Kabrit

The air defence of the Canal Zone assumed greater importance as potentially hostile neighbouring countries acquired their own air forces. The defence rested primarily on No. 39 Squadron which had soldiered on with Mosquito night-fighters until 1953, when it re-equipped with these Gloster Meteor NF.Mk 13s, subsequently being augmented by a second squadron, No. 219.

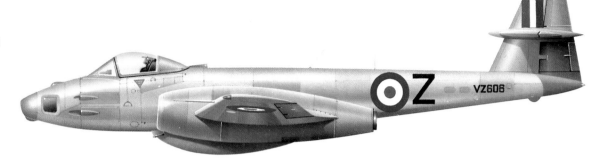

The principal squadron to use the Gloster Meteor FR.Mk 9 was No. 208 Squadron, to which VZ606 belonged in the mid-1950s.

Far right: The fighter reconnaissance requirements of the Middle East were in the hands of No. 208 Squadron in the early 1950s. Based at Abu Sueir, the squadron flew Gloster Meteor FR.Mk 9s from March 1951 until 1958, and flew this magnificent six-ship formation loop with the type soon after re-equipping.

and No. 208 Squadron with Meteor FR.Mk 9s; and three Valetta squadrons (Nos 70, 84 and 114). With British Forces Aden, renamed British Forces Arabian Peninsula in October 1956, were one Venom squadron (No. 8), one Scottish Aviation Pioneer squadron (No. 78) and No. 1426 Flight with Lincolns; also under Aden's control was No. 1417 Flight in Bahrain, with Pembroke aircraft. RAF Malta, for the moment directly under the control of the Air Ministry, operated three squadrons: Nos 37 and 38 with Shackleton MR.Mk 2s and No. 39 with Meteor NF.Mk 13s.

Guerrilla-hunting once more

Promising though Cyprus was as a base, Britain was once again faced with local hostility: the Greek Cypriot community there was demanding an end to the island's crown colony status, which it had been given in 1925, and union with Greece in its place, a prospect to which the Turkish minority in Cyprus was as deeply opposed as was Britain. Consequently, from April 1955 until February 1959 British forces were engaged in a struggle with Greek Cypriot, or EOKA, guerrillas and once again the RAF was closely involved in anti-terrorist activities. As arms were obviously being smuggled in by sea from the mainland, Shackletons from Nos 37 and 38 Squadrons mounted surveillance patrols from Malta, or from temporary detachments at El Adem in Libya and Nicosia, working in conjunction with the Royal Navy and radar installations on the island. In December 1955 an Internal Security Flight of Ansons was formed to counter the air drops of arms which the guerrillas were known to be receiving.

But it was in the light aircraft and helicopter field that the most striking advances were made. Before Field Marshal Sir John Harding took over as governor of Cyprus in October 1955, the Austers of Nos 1910 and 1915 Flights had been employed successfully on reconnaissance in conjunction with the Army's guerrilla-hunting drives through the island's mountainous hinterland, but the two Sycamores then in Cyprus were being under-used. Harding, however, appreciated the value of the helicopter in guerrilla warfare, and the number of Sycamores available was steadily increased until No. 284 Squadron was formed in October 1956 with nine aircraft. Between April 1956 and May 1957 the

Sycamores flew 2,561 sorties and carried over 3,400 troops and 200,000 lb (90720 kg) of equipment, giving the Army a high degree of mobility when operating in mountainous country and the vital element of surprise when searching villages suspected of harbouring guerrillas. Whirlwinds of the Joint Helicopter Unit were also involved in the later stages of the campaign along with a growing element of light fixed-wing aircraft, which included Pioneers (No. 230 Squadron) and de Havilland Chipmunks (No. 114 Squadron).

The Suez crisis

In the midst of these anti-terrorist operations, Cyprus was called upon to take part in Operation 'Musketeer', the landing of a joint British and French force in Egypt during the Suez crisis of 1956. The RAF's contribution was in three phases, shared with Royal Navy and French aircraft: neutralising the Egyptian air force; mounting air attacks against selected key points; and taking part with the Army in an airborne assault on Port Said. To meet these requirements a considerable redeployment of RAF resources was necessary. Nos 1 and 34 Squadrons with 24 Hawker Hunter F.Mk 5s arrived at Akrotiri from Tangmere; eight Meteor NF.Mk 13s of No. 39 Squadron moved to Nicosia from Malta, where they were replaced by No. 208 Squadron's Meteor FR.Mk 9s, which lacked the range to operate over Egypt effectively. Three squadrons of Venoms were made available

The Douglas Dakota, in the Middle East as elsewhere, was the universal RAF transport of the late 1940s and early 1950s, equipping the Middle East Transport Wing and flying the transport routes of the region. Even after the wing re-equipped with Valettas some Dakotas soldiered on in various parts of the command. These two served in Aden right into the 1960s.

One of the many Canberras which took part in the Suez bombing was WH667, a B.Mk 2 in service with No. 10 Squadron, Honington. Note the black-and-yellow 'Suez stripes' for identification purposes, the Honington wing badge on the fin and the No. 10 Squadron emblem on the tip tank.

at Akrotiri: No. 6, normally resident there; No. 8, the Aden squadron, which was brought from the Armament Practice Camp at Habbaniyah where it was on temporary detachment; and No. 249 which came from Amman; No. 73 Squadron, which had temporarily relieved No. 8 Squadron in Aden, remained there.

The biggest contingent was of English Electric Canberra and Vickers Valiant bombers from home bases. In all, 62 Canberra B.Mk 2s and B.Mk 6s arrived at Nicosia, from seven squadrons: Nos 10, 15, 18, 27, 44, 61 and 139, the last mentioned operating in the marker role. With Akrotiri and Nicosia full to capacity, a second bomber wing was established in Malta with four Canberra B.Mk 6 squadrons (Nos 9, 12, 101 and 109), with 29 aircraft, and four Valiant squadrons (Nos 138, 148, 207 and 214) with 24 aircraft.

The disadvantages of having the bomber wings in two widely separated locations were obvious. Not least was the risk of communications difficulties, but pressures on accommodation were extreme in a base which had only just begun to expand and which was already highly vulnerable to air attack (which in the event fortunately did not come) as the control and reporting system was inadequate in spite of last-minute efforts to improve it. Also, although the Hunters could match any opposition the Meteors were outdated. There were other problems: the Venoms were obsolescent and lacked the range to remain long over their target areas; the Valiant squadrons were just beginning an extensive training programme and many aircraft were not yet fitted with their proper navigation and bombing equipment, nor with visual bomb-sights; the Canberras were best suited to operating in the European environment with its extensive Gee chain system and had to rely during 'Musketeer' on dead reckoning navigation, monitored by visual pinpoints.

As it happened, the task force was given only 10 hours' final warning of the start of operations. After 11 photographic reconnaissance sorties, four by Canberras and seven by French air force Republic RF-84Fs, the first bombing attack was launched. The initial target was to have been the airfield at Cairo West, but at the last moment it was discovered that a party of Americans was assembling there before leaving Egypt and the target was hurriedly changed to Almaza, an airfield adjacent to Cairo International Airport. With little time for

The Suez crisis brought reinforcements to the Middle East from Britain, and these reinforcements brought a 'hot war' to Egypt. Canberra B.Mk 6s of No. 101 Squadron, temporarily based on Malta, bomb up for attack on Egypt in November 1956.

the crews to study the new target area, an error was made and the international airport was bombed instead of Almaza. In a second raid that evening the airfields at Almaza, Kabrit, Abu Sueir and Inchas were bombed.

On the following day attacks on Egyptian airfields continued, carried out on this occasion by Royal Navy carrierborne aircraft, French F-84s and RAF Venoms. In all, 386 sorties were flown, including 106 by the Venoms, which attacked Kasfareet, Abu Sueir, Fayid and Shallufa, where many enemy aircraft were destroyed on the ground. That night Canberras and Valiants attacked the airfields at Cairo West, Luxor, Fayid and Kasfareet. Virtually no opposition was encountered and the results convinced the Air Task Force's commander that the Egyptian air force had been neutralised and that the second phase of the operation should begin.

The bombing of airfields continued for another day while other aircraft began to attack second-phase targets, all military with the exception of Cairo Radio. This was attacked, with only moderate success, on the morning of 2 November by 20 Canberras, escorted by 12 French F-84s, in the first daylight raid to be carried out by the bomber wings. Later that day the three Venom squadrons flew 100

Troop reinforcements to the Middle East put such a strain on the RAF's transport force that Coastal Command Shackletons were brought into temporary use as somewhat uncomfortable troop transports.

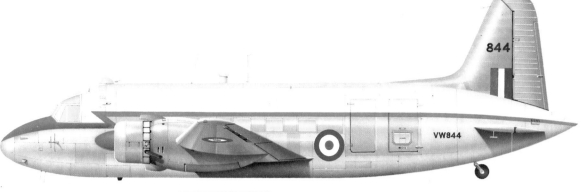

The Vickers Valetta C.Mk 1 took over from the Dakota as the equipment of the Middle East Transport Wing late in 1949. Each squadron was identified by the colour of the spinners and the fuselage cheat line. Thus VW844, with its green markings, belonged to No. 114 Squadron.

The Vickers Valiant, the first of the V-bombers, was just working up to operational efficiency in the RAF. With the Suez crisis a detachment of Valiants was sent to Malta from the Marham Wing and took part in some of the raids, although not particularly suited to what was basically a tactical conflict.

sorties against large concentrations of tanks and military vehicles at Huckstep Camp near Almaza, where they met considerable anti-aircraft fire; Canberras and Valiants returned there in the evening. Meanwhile Royal Navy aircraft were carrying out numerous sorties against other targets.

On 3 November the main weight of the attack shifted to roads and railways, including the Nefisha railway marshalling yards which were bombed by 22 Canberras from Nicosia, escorted by Hunters. Naval aircraft destroyed the Gamil bridge which carried the only road from Port Said to the Nile delta.

By 4 November the second phase of the operation was almost completed and, in preparation for the following day's airborne landings at Gamil, Venoms attacked AA guns at nearby Port Said, and Canberras and Valiants struck at radar and coastal gun installations. Early the following morning a force of 18 Valetta and 14 Hastings transports left Nicosia with 600 paratroops to begin the assault on Port Said with a series of drops on Gamil. Hunters carried out protective sweeps over the airfield there and Venoms strafed it immediately before the landings; no enemy aircraft appeared.

The paratroops landed accurately on a dropping

zone already marked with 1,000-lb (454-kg) target indicators by Canberras of Nos 18 and 139 Squadrons, a service which they also carried out for the French paratroops. More drops followed in the afternoon, but it was soon apparent that Egyptian resistance was too strong for Port Said to be taken by the paratroops alone, and that the reinforcements approaching by sea would meet stiff opposition.

The main landing

Bombing and the use of heavy naval guns were prohibited to avoid civilian casualties, but Venoms were sent to eliminate gun emplacements north of Port Said and these attacks, combined with strikes by Royal Navy aircraft and a naval bombardment, enabled the seaborne assault force to land without the casualties normally expected in an attack on a defended coast.

A novel feature of the landings was the decision to use six Sycamores and six Whirlwinds of the Joint Helicopter Unit (JHU) and 10 naval Whirlwinds to ferry No. 45 Marine Commando ashore. In the first two and a half hours 178 men and $12\frac{1}{2}$ tons of stores were landed on the chosen site, de Lesseps Square in Port Said, casualties being carried on the return trips.

Later the JHU Whirlwinds landed an advance party of No. 215 Wing at Gamil, where it was to open up the airfield to RAF traffic. Further men and equipment arrived in Valettas, including an RAF Regiment squadron which took over the defence of the airfield.

With a ceasefire called at midnight on 6 November, Operation 'Musketeer' was virtually over, but Gamil was kept open for transport aircraft bringing in supplies for Allied troops and was not finally handed over to an emergency United Nations force until 20 December. Only 18 months later, while MEAF was still building up its Cyprus base, it was faced with a worsening situation in Iraq. Following lengthy negotiations against a background of constant civil disturbance, agreement had been reached in May 1955 on the revision of the 1930 treaty which sanctioned the presence of British forces in the country. It was now agreed that the RAF stations at Habbaniyah and Shaibah should

Taking off for a raid on Egypt is this Hemswell Wing Canberra B.Mk 6 of No. 109 Squadron.

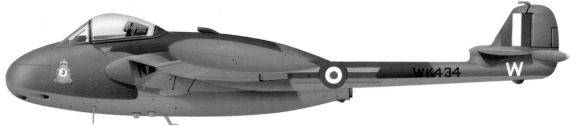

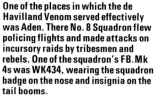

One of the places in which the de Havilland Venom served effectively was Aden. There No. 8 Squadron flew policing flights and made attacks on incursory raids by tribesmen and rebels. One of the squadron's FB.Mk 4s was WK434, wearing the squadron badge on the nose and insignia on the tail booms.

in May 1955; RAF Shaibah was disbanded in March 1956, although the air traffic control organisation remained in RAF hands; and No. 6 Squadron was sent to Akrotiri a month later. RAF Habbaniyah remained primarily as a staging post, but after the assassination of the Iraqi king in July 1958 and the installation of a revolutionary government, its activities were severely restricted and RAF aircraft were not allowed to use it. As the RAF was still providing facilities, but receiving nothing in return, the decision was taken to withdraw completely from Iraq: RAF Habbaniyah was disbanded in May 1959, so ending a connection which had lasted almost 40 years.

Withdrawal from Jordan

Meanwhile a somewhat similar situation had arisen in neighbouring Jordan, with which Britain had signed a new treaty in 1948. There had long been an RAF station in Amman, and in 1954 No. 249 Squadron arrived there with Vampire FB.Mk 9s, re-equipping with Venom FB.Mk 4s a year later. When No. 249 Squadron was moved to Cyprus for the Suez operation it was replaced by No. 32 Squadron with Venom FB.Mk 1s, but with growing hostility to the British presence it too was sent to Cyprus in January 1957. Two months later Britain's treaty with Jordan was rescinded and the remaining RAF elements were withdrawn in May.

Overflying was not prohibited over large parts of the Levant, including Israel, Jordan and Syria, and the position in Iraq was under growing threat. The British government did not entirely despair, however, and saw in the federation of Jordan and Iraq, formed in February 1958, a reconstitution of the old northern bulwark against instability in the area. Such hopes were dashed by the July revolution in Iraq, but in the month before Jordan had herself called for British help in the face of growing anarchy in neighbouring Lebanon, where a large body of opinion was violently opposed to the government's pro-Western stance, and of the danger that the anarchy in Lebanon would lead to a coup in Jordan itself. British and American reinforcements were promptly sent to the Mediter-

Far left: The de Havilland Venom replaced the Vampire in the Middle East squadrons in the mid-1950s. With a more powerful engine and new wing it had a performance edge on the old Vampire and served all over the command, taking part in the Suez campaign with rockets and bombs. No. 6 Squadron was the first to receive the type in the Middle East and is seen here flying over Jordan.

be handed over to Iraqi control, with the RAF continuing to provide certain facilities; that the two Venom squadrons at Habbaniyah, Nos 6 and 73, would be withdrawn within a year; that the two Habbaniyah maintenance units, Nos 104 and 115, would remain; and that the RAF would train the Iraqi air force.

Iraq had been of value to Britain as part of the latter's network of air communications to the Persian Gulf and the Far East, and as a base from which to counter any threat to her oil supplies arising from instability within the area or from overt Russian penetration. But now the situation was to change: No. 73 Squadron moved to Nicosia

Operations room for No. 208 Squadron at Amman in Jordan during 1958 was this tent, where sorties were planned for the Hunter F.Mk 6s on the strip in the background.

In 1958 a detachment of No. 208 Squadron, then equipped with Hunter F. Mk 6s and based at Nicosia, Cyprus, spent some time detached at Amman in Jordan, whence these two are scrambling.

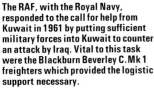

The RAF, with the Royal Navy, responded to the call for help from Kuwait in 1961 by putting sufficient military forces into Kuwait to counter an attack by Iraq. Vital to this task were the Blackburn Beverley C.Mk 1 freighters which provided the logistic support necessary.

ranean, including No. 66 Squadron's Hunters from the UK and No. 39 Squadron's Meteors from Malta. Both squadrons were based temporarily in Cyprus, reinforced later by the Hunters of Nos 43 and 54 Squadrons, and the Canberras of Nos 59 and 139 Squadrons, the Canberra B(I).Mk 8s of the former squadron from Geilenkirchen being considered better suited to the kind of operations envisaged than the Canberra B.Mk 2s of the Cyprus-based squadrons.

On 15 July US Marines landed in Lebanon, and two days later an RAF transport force of 16 Blackburn Beverleys, 23 Hastings and four Valettas, based either in Cyprus or the United Kingdom, began to airlift the 16th Parachute Brigade Group into Amman. Hunters provided a combat air patrol of two fighters during daylight over the northern part of the route; aircraft of HMS Eagle then took over. Six Hunters from No. 208 Squadron, based in Nicosia, were sent to Amman along with two Valettas for desert rescue and local transport work.

The expected coup in Jordan did not take place and the situation began to return to normal in August, but significantly one of the problems of the build-up, and later of the rundown, had been the severe restrictions placed by Israel on the over-flying of her territory by RAF aircraft, followed by a complete ban; and before the withdrawal began considerable pressure had to be brought before Syria permitted any overflying.

Overflying problems again affected operations in the area in 1961, when Iraq appeared to be challenging the independence of Kuwait, with which Britain had had a treaty relationship since

1899. When oil was discovered there, Britain became one of Kuwait's largest customers and the commitment, renewed in June 1961, to defend Kuwaiti independence became one of the main responsibilities of British forces in the Arabian peninsula.

Iraq reacted angrily to Britain's renewed commitment, claiming Kuwait as part of her own territory and moving troops south towards the border. The problem for Britain now was Kuwait's general inaccessibility, and as reinforcements could come only from Bahrain, Aden, Kenya, Cyprus or the United Kingdom, the contingency plan was necessarily based on receiving four days' warning of an attack. The bulk of the land forces were to be flown in from Cyprus and Kenya by Bristol Britannias and de Havilland Comets from Transport Command, supported by the Beverleys and Valettas based in the theatre. In addition, Aden was to provide its two squadrons of Hunters for air defence, while Canberras from Germany and Cyprus, and Shackletons from Aden, would be deployed in the interdiction role.

As precautionary measures, the Hunters of Nos 8 and 208 Squadrons moved up to Bahrain, from where they could just reach targets on the Kuwait-Iraq border with long-range tanks, and HMS Bulwark was ordered from Karachi. When on 30 June Kuwait asked formally for British assistance, the intention was to fly a parachute battalion directly into Kuwait from Cyprus and begin the lift of the follow-up force from Kenya; meanwhile No. 42 Royal Marine Commando would land from Bulwark and after securing Kuwait New Airfield would call in the Hunters from Bahrain.

These plans were thrown into confusion by the totally unexpected refusal of Turkey and the Sudan to allow RAF aircraft to overfly their countries. That both the parachute battalion and the follow-up force would be delayed seemed for the moment inevitable, with the result that the initial force would be inadequately supported. However, a change of heart on the part of both countries meant that Transport Command Britannias were still able to reach Aden in time to fly alternative reinforcements (in the shape of No. 45 Royal Marine Commando) on to Kuwait during the following day (1 July), to join No. 42 Commando and the two Hunter squadrons which had already arrived. Later on that day the parachute battalion began to arrive, but its build-up was slower than expected because Turkey was still prohibiting daytime flights.

The Scottish Aviation Twin Pioneer CC.Mk 1 found a useful niche in the Middle East as well as in the Far East. XM961 was one which served with No. 21 Squadron both in Kenya and in Aden between 1959 and 1967.

Weather conditions in Kuwait were appalling: intense heat, blowing sand and bad visibility. Another hazard was the absence of adequate radar facilities; HMS *Bulwark* (and later HMS *Victorious*) provided somewhat limited cover, but the RAF's own mobile radar was new in the theatre and its teething troubles were not overcome until the operation was virtually over.

By mid-July it had become obvious that Iraq did not intend to invade and British forces began to disperse, although one or other of the two Hunter squadrons was kept on stand-by in Bahrain. The overflying problem had caused temporary disruption to the planned build-up, but British treaty obligations had been met and any plans to invade Kuwait had been frustrated.

Indeed, by 1961 Britain's position throughout the region was looking rather stronger than it had done for some years past. Cyprus was now the base for a powerful strike force of four Canberra squadrons which formed the main British contribution to the Central Treaty Organization (CENTO), a defence alliance to which Turkey, Iran and Pakistan also belonged and whose objective was to counter any expansionist tendencies on the part of Russia from the north and the antagonism of Arab countries from the south. The reconnaissance needs of the area were being met by the two Malta-based squadrons, one with Shackletons and the other with Canberras.

Aden

Only in Aden did the future seem less than certain. The southern half of the old Middle East theatre had necessarily expanded after the withdrawal from Egypt had made the rapid reinforcement of Aden from the northern half very difficult. Kenya, which had become the base of part of the

Army's strategic reserve, was allotted two transport squadrons to support it, one with Beverleys and the other with Pioneers. They remained there until the East African territories gained their independence, after which No. 30 Squadron moved to Bahrain in October 1964 and No. 21 Squadron to Aden eight months later.

The RAF's strength in Aden had increased steadily from one squadron (No. 8) of Venom

Another aircraft which found plenty to do in the Aden Protectorate was the Westland Belvedere HC.Mk 1 helicopter. Flown by No. 26 Squadron, it made a great contribution to the effectiveness of the operations in the Radfan area.

Although there were Beverley squadrons in the Middle East, for the Kuwait and other crises they were reinforced by aircraft from the Abingdon Wing in England. One of these, a No. 53 Squadron aircraft, lands in a cloud of sand dust.

To reinforce Nos 8 and 208 Squadrons in the Aden and Arabian Gulf area, No. 43 Squadron moved out from Leuchars to Cyprus in 1961 and then on to Aden in 1963, forming part of the strike wing there until October, 1967. XE546 was one of the Hunter FGA.Mk 9s it took with it to the Middle East.

RAF STATION AT KHORMAKSAR, ADEN IN 1961

Squadron	Aircraft
Nos 8 and 208	Hunter FGA.Mk 9
No. 37	Shackleton MR.Mk 2
No. 78	Twin Pioneer CC.Mk 1
No. 84	Beverley C.Mk 1
No. 233	Valetta C.Mk 1

The unguided rocket, fired from under a Hunter's wings, was most effective in the fighting in the Radfan area.

FB.Mk 1s in 1955, and a communications and support squadron, to a substantial force of six squadrons and a front-line strength of 48 aircraft at the end of 1961, making the RAF station at Khormaksar one of the largest and most complex in the RAF at that time.

In addition, No. 152 Squadron was based in Bahrain with Pembrokes and Twin Pioneers, a presence which was augmented after the Kuwait crisis by detachments of Hunters, Beverleys and Canberras. By 1961 also there had been important changes in the command structure: British Forces Arabian Peninsula (BFAP) had become a unified command in October 1959 with Air Forces Arabian Peninsula (AFAP) as its air element. In March 1961 both were renamed, BFAP becoming Middle East Command (MEC) and AFAP turning into Air Forces Middle East (AFME).

Within a year the situation in Aden had begun to deteriorate. Civil disobedience, prompted by neighbouring Yemen, had been a recurring feature of life in the colony since the end of World War II, while a coup in Yemen in September 1962 led to a propaganda campaign against Britain and aircraft attacks on targets on the Aden side of the border. Reconnaissance indicated that arms were flowing into Yemen from Egypt and that a determined attempt was to be made to undermine British authority in the area. Subversion had easy targets both in Aden itself with its conglomeration of military establishments, and in the Radfan area to the north of Aden where the Dhala road running up towards the Yemen border was constantly under attack from dissident tribesmen who, with Yemeni support, attacked and looted caravans travelling along it.

Operation 'Nutcracker' was therefore launched in January 1964 to bring the situation under control. Once again the RAF played an important role, Hunters giving close support to the ground forces and helicopters undertaking troop-lifts and re-supply sorties. Troop-lifts were left more and more to Royal Navy Westland Wessex helicopters, while the Belvederes of No. 26 Squadron, which had arrived in Aden in March 1963, concentrated on positioning the Army's 105-mm artillery, often into the most precipitous firing positions and usually leaving them pointing in approximately the right direction.

The success achieved during the operation was short-lived, and the situation deteriorated rapidly again. A further operation into the Radfan was planned for May with support once again from a large RAF element, consisting of Hunters, Shackletons, Belvederes and Twin Pioneers, along with Royal Navy Wessex and aircraft of the Army Air Corps. As the rebels retreated they were attacked without respite by the Hunters and Shackletons, and air supply to the ground forces steadily increased, sometimes by parachute drop but more usually by helicopter. Finally on 10 June 1964 the last rebel vantage point, the Jebel Huriyah, a

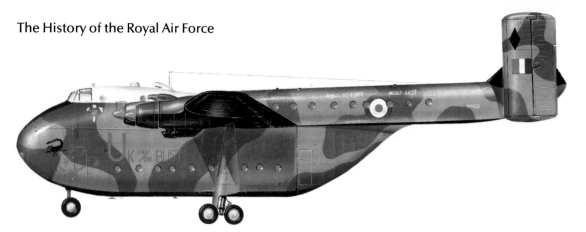

The Blackburn Beverley C.Mk 1 was the RAF's short-field, heavy-lift freighter and, as such, was most effective in the Middle East. The longest-lived squadron there was No. 84 Squadron, based successively at Khormaksar, Sharjah and Muharraq until October 1971. Its aircraft carried playing card markings; XM103 here also carried the squadron's scorpion emblem on the nose and some wag had painted on 'UK and/or Bust' prior to its final flight back to the UK.

5,500-ft (1675-m) peak, was captured after the Hunters had given very close support and the Shackletons, having completed their part in the softening-up process, had dropped flares behind the peak to silhouette the summit.

By then the British government had announced its intention to leave Aden by 1968, but the decision brought no respite. Terrorism in Aden itself increased sharply until in September 1965 three infantry battalions were needed for internal security. Helicopters were used to move troops quickly to the scene of any incident, and Twin Pioneers were employed on leaflet-dropping and reconnaissance. But in general the trend was to move aircraft away from the airfield at Khormaksar, which was an easy target for mortar fire. The Hunters were kept on detachment in the Gulf as often as possible; No. 26 Squadron was disbanded in November 1965 and its Belvederes sent to the Far East for the Borneo campaign, the gap in Aden being filled by the Wessex with which No. 78 Squadron had been re-equipped five months before. The Twin Pioneer presence was maintained, however, by the arrival of No. 21 Squadron from Kenya in June 1965.

Against the background of mounting tension (nearly 100 terrorist incidents a month at the end of 1966) the decision was taken to leave Aden during 1967 and build up British forces in Bahrain, where the RAF station had been renamed Muharraq in December 1963, and in Sharjah. The purpose, as always, was to protect British oil interests and, in particular, to meet her treaty obligations to Kuwait. The evacuation of families from Aden began in May, the Air Officer Commanding moved to Bahrain at the end of October, and the evacuation was completed by a massive seven-day airlift in late November, using the BAC (Vickers) VC10s, Shorts Belfasts, Lockheed Hercules and Britannias of Air Support Command.

The heat of the Radfan was no real problem to the Westland Wessex HC.Mk 2s of No. 78 Squadron, which flew tactical support missions with the army in the hills during the fighting there.

Last years in the Gulf

It had already been decided that the forces at the disposal of the new command in the area, Air Forces Gulf, replacing Air Forces Middle East, would consist of two fighter/ground-attack squadrons and two tactical transport squadrons. In the course of 1968 the pattern was established of basing the two Hunter squadrons (No. 8 with eight Hunter FGA.Mk 9s and four Hunter FR.Mk 10s and No. 208 with 12 Hunter FGA.Mk 9s) at Muharraq and the two transport squadrons, (No. 84 with six HS Andover C.Mk 1s and No. 78 with 10 Wessex HC.Mk 2s) at Sharjah.

The RAF's last years in the Gulf were quiet but not idle; Muharraq became a very busy staging post and the Gulf squadrons were kept occupied with an intensive training programme. But British policy now was to encourage the Gulf states to develop their own air forces and provide for their own defence, so allowing Britain to withdraw from the area by the end of 1971. The rundown began early that year, the last squadron to leave being No. 8; Sharjah closed on 14 December and Muharraq a day later.

With the main withdrawals from the Far East also complete, the principal air force presence overseas was now in Cyprus and Malta. MEAF itself had become the air force element of Middle East Command (MEC), the unified command

established in Cyprus in May 1960; both were renamed in March 1961, MEC becoming Near East Command (NEC) and MEAF becoming Near East Air Force (NEAF).

The squadron pattern in Cyprus had undergone a number of modifications since 1957, when MEAF's resources there had consisted of the four squadrons of the Canberra strike force (Nos 6, 32, 73 and 249) at Akrotiri with 32 aircraft; No. 13 with four Canberra PR.Mk 7s, also at Akrotiri; and three transport squadrons at Nicosia, (No. 70 with 10 Hastings C.Mk 1s/C.Mk 2s, No. 84 with 12 Valetta C.Mk 1s and No. 284 with 12 Sycamore HR.Mk 14s. In addition, a MEAF squadron (No. 208 with 16 Meteor

In Cyprus No. 103 Squadron had formed with Bristol Sycamore HR.Mk 14s in August 1959, using the type for two roles: support of the army in coping with the EOKA terrorists, and search-and-rescue around the coasts.

With unfriendly countries around the Mediterranean acquiring Soviet-supplied air forces the RAF established an important large base on Cyprus at Akrotiri. For defence of this base No. 56 Squadron moved out from Wattisham in 1967 with its English Electric Lightning F.Mk 3s.

FR.Mk 9s) was still detached to Malta.

The backbone of the Cyprus force was the Canberras until they were replaced by the 16 BAC (Avro/HS) Vulcan B.Mk 2s of Nos 9 and 35 Squadrons in 1969. The four Canberra squadrons had been sent to Akrotiri in 1957 in fulfilment of Britain's pledge to support what was then known as the Baghdad Pact but became the Central Treaty Organization (CENTO) in 1959 after one of the signatories, Iraq, had withdrawn. None of the other members (Turkey, Iran and Pakistan) had a bomber capability and the British contribution, along with No. 13 (PR) Squadron, was an essential element in achieving CENTO's main objectives, the maintenance of peace and stability in the area and the frustration of any Soviet ambitions (a new guise, in fact for long-standing Russian aims); the Canberra force acted also as a buttress to NATO's southern flank.

Final reduction in Middle East force

From 1959 the Canberra force had begun to be re-equipped with the more powerful B.Mk 6s, but until after 1961 it could operate only in the conventional bombing role, each aircraft having the capability to carry six 1,000-lb (454-kg) bombs. During 1962 and 1963 the four squadrons acquired even more sophisticated versions of the Canberra, the B.Mk 15 and B.Mk 16, which had been developed for overseas. They now constituted a highly versatile force which could operate as conventional or nuclear tactical bombers, or as ground-attack aircraft, equipped for a wide range of delivery roles: the low-altitude bombing system (LABS); pop-up delivery; medium-level and shallow dive-bombing; and rocket-firing. Two squadrons were equipped to fire an air-to-surface guided missile.

The Canberra training programme was intensive throughout the squadrons' 12 years of residence in Akrotiri and included bombing practice at the El Adem range in Libya and rocket-firing practice at Sharjah. They worked also with NATO forces, carrying out price sorties against NATO convoys and targets in Italy and Sicily, and co-operating with the Royal Navy and the United States 6th Fleet.

The two Vulcan squadrons which replaced the Canberras had a better night and all-weather capability, but could not operate in the ground-attack role. Two further Vulcan squadrons were declared to CENTO but remained in the UK to avoid the expense of providing additional facilities in Cyprus.

Of the other squadrons on the island, No. 13 moved away to Malta in September 1965, by which

time the transport element in NEAF had been reduced to one medium-range squadron (No. 70) re-equipped with Armstrong Whitworth Argosy C.Mk 1s in November 1967 and Hercules C.Mk 1s three years later. A helicopter unit remained in Cyprus throughout, equipped with Sycamores until 1963 and then with Whirlwind HAR.Mk 10s, and finally emerging as No. 84 Squadron in 1972.

For air defence, Cyprus had a resident fighter squadron, No. 208 with Hunter F.Mk 6s, briefly from November 1958 until March 1959, but from then until June 1961 it was a Fighter Command responsibility to provide for the air defence of the island and keep one squadron permanently deployed there. In June 1961, however, No. 43 Squadron with 16 Hunter FGA.Mk 9s arrived in Cyprus as the resident fighter unit, to be replaced in February 1963 by No. 29 Squadron with Gloster Javelin FAW.Mk 9s. In May 1967 No. 29 Squadron was relieved by No. 56 Squadron with BAC (English Electric) Lightning F.Mk 3s, which were replaced by F.Mk 6s in 1972. As in the United Kingdom area, the air-defence task became more and more to ward off Soviet-built aircraft intent on probing local air defences.

In January 1975, following a government decision to end the declaration of forces to CENTO and reduce numbers in Cyprus, Nos 56 and 70 Squadrons were withdrawn to the UK, together with the Vulcan force, to be replaced by smaller detachments of aircraft as occasion arose; only No. 84 Squadron's Whirlwinds remained in residence. NEAF itself was disbanded in April 1976 and AHQ Cyprus formed in its place within Strike Command. The two Malta squadrons were also to be withdrawn, No. 203 with BAe (HS) Nimrods disbanding in December 1977 and No. 13 with Canberras returning home in the following October; the last RAF units left Malta in 1979. Britain, however, retained sovereignty over her military bases in Cyprus and the RAF its airfield facilities to be reactivated as required.

Far right: As part of the CENTO Pact the Near East Air Force, established in Cyprus and Malta, was equipped with a bomber wing of Avro Vulcan B.Mk 2s when Nos 9 and 35 Squadrons moved to Akrotiri from Cottesmore in January 1969, providing a potent (nuclear) capability in the region.

The RAF in Germany

After four years of contraction, the Royal Air Force in Germany entered a period of expansion in 1950, prompted largely by the potentially explosive situation not only in Europe (evidenced by the events that led to the Berlin Airlift) but by the war in Korea which highlighted the deepening distrust between East and West blocs. Those four years had been a difficult period for the 2nd Tactical Air Force, renamed the British Air Forces of Occupation (BAFO) in July 1945. There had been a number of unfamiliar tasks to perform, in particular the dismantling of the German air force and co-operating with the ground forces in the routine chores of occupation. It had in addition to continue training in its basic roles as a tactical air force: air defence, ground attack in collaboration with the army, and tactical reconnaissance.

Furthermore, in common with other commands of the RAF, it had been faced with the inevitable problems resulting from rapid demobilisation and the loss of highly trained personnel. Unsettling too was the general uncertainty about the formation's future role, size and shape in the permanent post-war air force. If experience of the years following World War I was any criterion, the outlook seemed bleak indeed. One important difference now existed, however: a potentially hostile and immensely powerful nation deployed its forces not behind an established, fortified frontier, but beyond a politically demarcated line drawn on the map.

At the end of 1945 the BAFO was still a very sizeable command with four Group headquarters: No. 2, a mainly bomber group; Nos 83 and 84 with fighter, ground attack and reconnaissance roles; and No. 85 Group, primarily a support organisation controlling the technical and administrative units serving BAFO's 34 front-line squadrons.

Of these squadrons, 18 were purely RAF, four were provided by the Royal Canadian Air Force, and four by the Royal Australian Air Force; there were also four French, four Polish and two Belgian squadrons, all still serving in the RAF while awaiting disbanding and return home. Of the 18 RAF squadrons, six were to serve in Germany for many years, Nos 2, 3 and 4 being founder units of the Royal Flying Corps, and Nos 16, 26 and 98 being created during World War I. Between them they flew most of the aircraft types operating in Germany over the following 35 years, from the Supermarine Spitfire and de Havilland Mosquito of 1945 to the McDonnell Douglas Phantom, SEPECAT Jaguar, BAe Harrier and BAe Buccaneer of the 1970s.

It was to be 10 years before there were again as many squadrons based in Germany as there were

British Air Forces of Occupation started its existence with a fleet of wartime aeroplanes. Most potent amongst these was the Hawker Tempest F. Mk 5: at Fassberg this line-up of No. 33 Squadron was seen in August 1946. The Tempest squadrons rotated turn by turn at Gatow in Berlin to provide teeth for the British enclave there.

VS979 was a Gloster Meteor PR.Mk 10 built in 1951 and delivered in that year to No. 541 Squadron at Benson. It moved out to Bückeburg in June, serving there with the squadron until 1957, when it was struck off RAF charge.

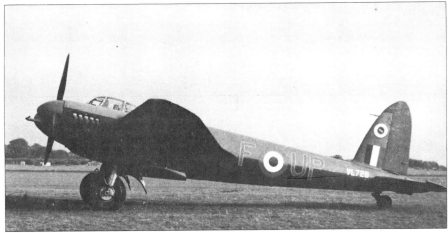

For a bomber force BAFO had wings of Mosquito FB.Mk 6s and B.Mk 16s. No. 4 Squadron was at first based at Gütersloh and, when this picture was taken in 1949, at Wahn, with Mosquito FB.Mk 6s. Note the re-appearance of the squadron emblem on the fin.

BAFO FRONT-LINE STRENGTH IN 1950 (AFTER SIGNATURE OF NORTH ATLANTIC TREATY-1949)

Squadron	Aircraft	Location
16, 93, 94	Vampire FB.5	Celle
14, 98, 112, 118	Vampire FB.5	Fassberg
2, 79	Meteor FR.9	Gütersloh
541	Meteor PR.10	Gütersloh
3, 67, 71	Vampire FB.5	Wahn
4, 11, 26	Vampire FB.5	Wunstorf

at the end of 1945. The rundown in BAFO was as dramatic as in other RAF commands such that with disbandments and the return of Allied squadrons to their home countries the number of squadrons in BAFO had fallen to 15 by the end of 1946 and to 10 a year later: five day fighter squadrons with Hawker Tempest Mk 2s and Mk 5s, four light bomber squadrons with Mosquitoes, and one fighter reconnaissance with Spitfires. The total establishment of the 10 squadrons was 131 aircraft.

During the same two years, three groups were disestablished (Nos 2, 83 and 84), and BAFO was left in direct control of its operational squadrons, while No. 85 Group, reduced to Wing status, provided support facilities.

Ten squadrons might well have been adequate for the occupation tasks had Europe succeeded in settling down to a period of sustained peace, but the circumstances which led to the Berlin Airlift and the accompanying 'cold war' soon became all too evident. BAFO's role in Germany had therefore to be re-assessed so that duties associated purely with occupying a defeated nation began to

take second place to the vital need to defend the border with the Russian zone against incursion by Communist bloc forces.

BAFO's 10 squadrons were moved forward to former Luftwaffe bases at Bückeburg, Fassberg, Celle, Gütersloh, Wunstorf and Detmold; and an Air Defence Zone, some 30 miles (48 km) deep, was established along the frontier and kept under constant surveillance. In addition, fighter patrols were mounted along the air corridors to Berlin to preserve the right of access and discourage interference by Soviet fighters, among which the jet Mikoyan-Gurevich MiG-15 was already prominent.

The signing of the North Atlantic Treaty in April 1949, and the establishment of the Federal Republic in the Western zones of Germany five months later, brought further changes, but the turning point for BAFO came in 1950 when expansion started in earnest. During the following year the command's front-line strength grew to 16 squadrons, 13 flying de Havilland Vampire Mk 5s in the day fighter and ground-attack roles, two in the fighter-reconnaissance role with Gloster Meteor Mk 9s, and one photographic-reconnaissance squadron with Meteor Mk 10s. No. 2 Group was re-formed to take operational control of BAFO squadrons, but No. 85 Wing, raised to Group status during the Berlin Airlift, was disbanded.

Simultaneously all 16 squadrons were assigned to the operational control of NATO's newly-established Supreme Allied Commander, Europe (SACEUR), and in September 1951, as if to emphasise the fact that Britain was no longer an occupying power, but would soon serve alongside Germany as a partner in the new military alliance, BAFO was renamed the 2nd Tactical Air Force (2TAF). Within a few months, in 1952, two Allied Tactical Air Forces were formed as part of the NATO structure in central Europe: the 2nd (2ATAF) operating to the north and the 4th (4ATAF) to the south, with the RAF assuming the leading role in the former and the USAF in the latter. Although 2TAF had a number of non-NATO responsibilities (in Berlin

Amongst the early jet aircraft to join BAFO were the reconnaissance Meteor PR.Mk 10s and FR.Mk 9s. The latter served with No. 2 Squadron at Bückeburg, when this pair are taking off for a tactical reconnaissance exercise.

The Gloster Meteor NF.Mk 11 was the RAF's mid-1950s night-fighter, serving in both Britain and Germany and, slightly modified as the NF.Mk 13, in the Middle East. WM293 served with No. 68 Squadron at Wahn in Germany and was the commanding officer's aircraft, as denoted by the nose pennant and the squadron insignia stripe up the fin.

for example), its commanders-in-chief also commanded 2ATAF, except for a brief period in the 1960s.

NATO's resources still remained inadequate, however, and an urgent expansion of 2TAF's front-line forces was set in train. By the end of 1952 the command had grown to 25 squadrons and a second group headquarters (No. 83) was established. The Vampires were replaced by de Havilland Venom FB.Mk 1s and by the Canadair Sabres provided under the Mutual Defense Assistance Program; in the night-fighter role 2TAF acquired Meteor NF.Mk 11s.

Additional airfields at Jever and Oldenburg were brought into service, but more significant was the solution of a long-standing problem: the vulnerability of a command whose aircraft were based entirely at forward airfields which could be overrun in the early hours of an advance by enemy ground forces. Forward bases would still be required, but by the time 2TAF had been fully re-equipped it would also have the use of a group of four new airfields which were being developed well to the west of the Rhine. Wildenrath was the first to come into service, followed by Geilenkirchen, Brüggen and Laarbruch. At the same time 2TAF's headquarters moved back from Bad Eilsen, less than 100 miles (160 km) from the East German border, to Rheindahlen, west of Düsseldorf.

In the course of the next two years No. 149 Squadron with English Electric Canberra B.Mk 2s was deployed to Germany and three more Canberra B.Mk 2 squadrons (Nos 102, 103 and 104) were formed there as a result of the shortage of airfields which now existed in the United Kingdom; these squadrons remained under the overall policy control of RAF Bomber Command, however, the intention being that their deployment should be brief, and in the event they were disbanded in 1956 at the very beginning of the rundown of the Canberra

light bomber force.

Re-equipment continued with 13 of 2TAF's squadrons receiving Hawker Hunter Mk 4s and Mk 6s, the last of the Sabres being withdrawn in the early summer of 1956. The first Gloster Javelins arrived in the autumn of the following year. Meanwhile 2TAF's own Canberra force was being built up. Four photo-reconnaissance squadrons (Nos 69, 31, 80 and 17) were formed in Germany between 1954 and 1956, with Canberra PR.Mk 3s and PR.Mk 7s, providing 2TAF with its medium-range reconnaissance capability until the Canberras were replaced by Phantom FGR.Mk 2s in the early 1970s.

A further four Canberra squadrons were formed in the newly-defined 'interdictor' role, and were at full strength by March 1958; these were Nos 16, 59 and 88 with Canberra B(I).Mk 8s, and No. 213 with B(I).Mk 6s. By then the command had undergone another rapid transformation with the number of its front-line squadrons slashed to 18, and its

The advent of the MiG-15 in 1950 in Soviet hands made the Meteors and Vampires of the RAF obsolete. Before new British supersonic fighters could be brought in service the RAF acquired from the USAF under the MDAP Canadair Sabre F.Mk 4s, and these were rushed into service at the new NATO base at Wildenrath in 1953.

One of the first RAF Squadrons to receive the Sabre at Wildenrath had been No. 3 Squadron. It retained the type until June 1956, when this photograph was taken on the occasion of the arrival of the squadron's first Hawker Hunter F.Mk 4s.

The Supermarine Swift equipped two squadrons in Germany, Nos 2 and 79. This FR.Mk 5, XD916, joined No. 2 Squadron in February 1956 and serving with the unit at Geilenkirchen and then Jever until December 1958 when it was returned to the UK and subsequently sold for scrap in 1960.

Right: For night-fighter defence of the RAF in Germany there were established two night-fighter wings, at Wahn and Ahlhorn, with four squadrons equipped with Meteor NF.Mk 11s.

Far right: The new ground-attack fighter to enter 2nd TAF service in 1953 was the de Havilland Venom FB.Mk 1. This foursome came from No. 11 Squadron at Wunstorf.

Below right: The Vickers-Supermarine Swift served in Germany with Nos 2 and 79 Squadrons from 1956 until 1960. WK303 here carries No. 79 Squadron's red arrowhead marking.

Below: In the photo-reconnaissance role, so vital in Germany, the English Electric Canberra PR.Mk 7 equipped Nos 17 (seen here), 31 and 80 Squadrons in 2nd TAF in the late 1950s and through the 1960s.

operational aircraft establishment cut from 500 to 224; its two group headquarters were disbanded later that year. The principal reasons for this drastic contraction were Britain's economic problems and the fundamental change in defence policies which followed the commissioning of the V-force; to offset the cost of defence changes foreshadowed in the 1957 White Paper on Defence, production of the Hunter was summarily halted for the RAF. Under the tripwire strategy then accepted by Britain and NATO, the role of 2TAF's fighter force would henceforth be to mount no more than a limited holding operation until the

inevitable resort to nuclear weapons.

Consequently nine Hunter squadrons were disbanded in 1957, together with six Venom squadrons, thereby making way for the four new Canberra interdictor squadrons, a reduction which SACEUR accepted on account of the superior firepower of the Canberras, soon to be augmented still further by the addition of American tactical nuclear weapons. In addition four bases east of the Rhine (Celle, Oldenburg, Wahn and Wunstorf) were given up.

At the end of the 1950s 2TAF, in its new guise, still represented a formidable force, with four day

With advances in the Warsaw Pact armoury, new aircraft were needed in RAF Germany. The Meteor night-fighters were replaced by Gloster Javelin FAW. Mk 5s, No. 11 Squadron (shown here) flying from Geilenkirchen in 1962.

and four all-weather/night-fighter squadrons, four interdictor squadrons, four medium-range photo-reconnaissance squadrons and two fighter reconnaissance squadrons. Much of its strength now lay in the quality of its aircraft, the Hunter and Javelin, and the two Canberra variants, but there had also been considerable improvements in the command's control and reporting system. Radar cover had been sparse during the 10 post-war years, relying as it did on obsolete equipment (largely patched up and deployed from other overseas

theatres), but early in 1955 the first fruits of a programme designed to improve the RAF's radar provision overseas reached Germany, and more followed later that year. In 1957 three Type 80 long-range radars (adaptations of those in the UK Rotor Plan) were installed to give 2TAF far better early warning and air control facilities, as well as to extend the United Kingdom's own early warning cover.

There followed a short period of relative stability in Germany, with only minor changes in the front-

The Hawker Hunter F. Mk 6 had become the standard fighter in the now depleted numbers of fighter/ground-attack squadrons. The blue diamonds on the fuselage show these aircraft to be from No. 14 Squadron at Gütersloh in 1961.

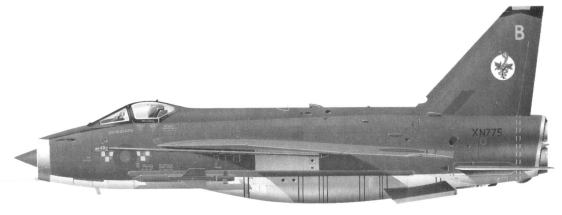

line forces, but in 1961, in the face of yet more financial problems at home, the number of fighter squadrons in the command (restyled RAF Germany from January 1959) was again reduced. The intention had been to disband the fighter force altogether by the end of 1960, but it was later decided to keep one Hunter F.Mk 6 and two Javelin FAW.Mk 5 squadrons for a further year, to be reinforced if necessary from Britain. By that time the command would have returned Jever to the German air force and would be operating from the four rear bases and from one forward base, Gütersloh.

Plans to withdraw the last of the fighter squadrons were cancelled, however, and the front-line force at the end of 1962 included what was to remain a long-term feature of RAF Germany: two fighter squadrons. Alongside them remained the Canberra interdictor and photo-reconnaissance squadrons, and the two fighter-reconnaissance squadrons whose Supermarine Swift FR.Mk 5s had been replaced by Hunter FR.Mk 10s. RAF Germany's total strength had now dropped to 142 aircraft.

The command had reached a plateau on which its front-line strength remained broadly stable at around 12 squadrons. The main changes in the middle 1960s were the addition in 1963 of No. 230 Squadron with Westland Whirlwind HC.Mk 10 helicopters, replaced in January 1965 by No. 18

Squadron with Westland Wessex HC.Mk 2s, both being based at Gütersloh to provide mobility and training for forward British Army units; and the arrival, also in 1965, of English Electric/BAC F.Mk 2s to replace the Javelins which were by now inferior to the all-weather fighters being flown by the Warsaw Pact air forces.

Busy years for the Lightning

For a time the two Lightning squadrons were based at different airfields, Geilenkirchen and Gütersloh, an unsatisfactory situation as the Lightnings could not operate to full advantage in the Berlin air corridors when based as far back as Geilenkirchen. With the latter handed over to the German air force in March 1968, however, it was decided to base the two squadrons together at Gütersloh. RAF Germany was thus reduced to only four airfields, but there were compensations for the new arrangement: the Canberras were concentrated on three neighbouring bases to the rear, and the interceptors were based well forward.

For the command these were very busy years. The two fighter squadrons were particularly stretched, maintaining a battle-readiness flight to intercept any unidentified radar tracks and to counter Soviet aircraft flying close to the border; in addition there were frequent air defence and ground support exercises, as well as detachments

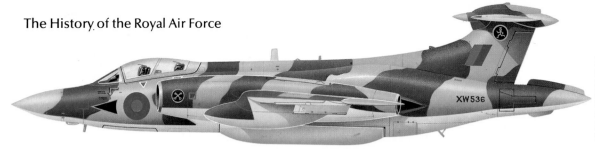

In the 1970s the RAF in Germany was almost totally re-equipped. The strike force was equipped with Hawker Siddeley Buccaneer S. Mk 2Bs, forming Nos 15 and 16 Squadrons at Laarbruch. No. 15 is shown in the photograph below whilst No. 16 is depicted by XW536 on the left.

to other NATO bases in Germany and elsewhere in Europe, and even to RAF bases in the Near and Far East.

The Canberra reconnaissance squadrons were fully engaged on long-range and high-altitude tasks well beyond the capabilities of their predecessors in the role. The Canberra B(I).Mk 6s and B(I).Mk 8s had been given a nuclear weapon-carrying capability in 1959 when the American Mk 7 nuclear weapons were made available under strict supervision by the United States Air Force. Until the Mk 7s were replaced in 1966 by the American Mk 43s with their retarded lay-down delivery, the priority role of the four interdictor squadrons was the delivery of the Mk 7s using the low-altitude bombing system (LABS); they also maintained a quick-reaction alert (QRA) with one aircraft and crew always available at 15-minutes' readiness. Between 1961 and 1964 they were supplemented in the tactical bombing role by three Marham-based Vickers Valiant squadrons, also armed with American nuclear weapons and assigned, as were the Canberras, to SACEUR; from July 1969 the home-based Avro Vulcan B.Mk 2s also became available in the same role. The Canberra B(I).Mk 6s and B(I).Mk 8s could also be converted rapidly to the ground attack role in which they employed air-to-ground gun firing and shallow dive-bombing techniques.

In addition to their crowded calendar of training commitments in Germany, the interdictor squadrons carried out overseas detachments, to Malaya for example in 1965 for operations against Indonesian infiltrators. There were also regular detachments to Cyprus for training in the ground-attack role and to Malta for LABS training on ranges in Libya and later in Sicily.

In the early 1970s the command's overall effectiveness was considerably improved by a number of expedients, namely the arrival of Phantom FGR.Mk 2s, which assumed the photo-reconnaissance role from the Canberras and combined it with a devastating ground-attack capability; introduction of the Harrier V/STOL aircraft and of the Buccaneer, the latter replacing the Canberra B(I). Mk 6s and B(I).Mk 8s in the interdictor role and providing a greater weapon-carrying capacity, higher performance and enhanced all-weather operating capability. In addition, No. 25 (SAM) Squadron was deployed to Germany equipped with

Right: From 1970 until 1977 the ground-attack role in Germany was carried out by squadrons of McDonnell Phantom FGR.Mk 2s. No. 31 Squadron was one of the squadrons in this force and is putting up this foursome.

Below: Probably the most significant aircraft to enter 2nd ATAF service was the Hawker Siddeley Harrier GR. Mk 1. This V/STOL aircraft has made possible the existence of a battlefield strike force which is entirely independent of airfields. Taxiing out for take-off on a German road is a Harrier GR. Mk 3 of No. 4 Squadron.

Each Harrier squadron has its own two-seater T. Mk 4 which doubles as an instrument trainer and as a fully operational machine. XZ146 joined No. 4 Squadron in 1981 and served with that squadron until crashing at Hohne on 29 April 1982.

RAF GERMANY'S FRONT-LINE STRENGTH AT EARLY 1972

Squadron	Aircraft	Location
14, 17, 31	Phantom FGR.2	Brüggen
19, 92	Lightning F.S, F.2A	Gütersloh
2	Phantom FGR.2	Laarbruch
15, 16	Buccaneer S.2B	Laarbruch
3, 4, 20	Harrier GR.1, GR.1A	Wildenrath
18	Wessex HC.2	Gütersloh

Bloodhound Mk 2 surface-to-air missiles to strengthen the defences of Brüggen, Laarbruch and Wildenrath; the low-level defence of these bases, and that of Gütersloh, became the responsibility of the Rapier squadrons of the RAF Regiment after the mid-1970s.

Moreover, the home-based V-bombers had become available to SACEUR as a tactical strike element when responsibility for the nuclear deterrent passed to the Royal Navy at the end of June 1969.

With re-equipment completed early in 1972, RAF Germany's front-line force consisted of four Phantom squadrons, including one in the reconnaissance role, three squadrons of Harriers, two of Buccaneers, two of Lightnings and one Wessex squadron.

Later in the 1970s there was a further re-assessment. Jaguars had become available to replace the Phantoms of Nos 14, 17 and 31 Squadrons in the strike-attack role, and a fourth Jaguar squadron was later added at Brüggen when No. 20 exchanged its Harriers for Jaguars. Also replaced were the Phantoms of No. 2 Squadron, which received a reconnaissance version of the Jaguar. Phantoms thus became available to assume the air defence

British Aerospace Harrier

The British Aerospace Harrier GR.Mk 3 is important to the RAF in Germany as its ability to operate from woodland clearings means it is less susceptible to air strikes. The example shown is an aircraft of No. 4 Squadron based at Gütersloh, which is NATO's most easterly airfield. Notable are the revised nose with a laser ranging and marked target seeker, absence of the bolt-on inflight-refuelling probe and longer-span ferry wingtips, and external stores including two rocket pods and a pair of underfuselage 30-mm Aden cannon. The aircraft is so versatile that it played a significant role alongside the Royal Navy Sea Harriers in the Falkland Islands campaign, flying with No. 1 Squadron from HMS *Hermes*.

XZ 131

M

task in Germany (as in the United Kingdom), and in 1977 they replaced the aged Lightnings of Nos 19 and 92 Squadrons and moved to Wildenrath. The Harriers of Nos 3 and 4 Squadrons, augmented by ex-No. 20 Squadron aircraft, were then able to move forward to the former Lightning base at Gütersloh where, with the Wessex helicopters of No. 18 Squadron, they were better placed to provide close support for the forward elements of the British Army of the Rhine. The Harriers, in particular, underwent a programme of progressive improvement, on the one hand in weapon carriage by fitting more powerful engines, and on the other with the inclusion of laser ranging and marked target seeking (LRMTS) and passive radar warning receiver (RWR) equipment.

Improvements to local defence

In line with other developments the RAF in Germany had steadily improved its infrastructure, its living accommodation, servicing procedures and the active and passive defence of its bases. One of the servicing problems was to strike a balance between the advantage (economy) and disadvantage (overdependence) of resorting to facilities in the United Kingdom. The need for mobility and instant response dictated a system of daily servicing localised on the squadron, and second-line servicing centralised on the station, with much of the major servicing carried out at home. For the Harrier, highly mobile procedures were developed and became a unique feature within NATO; this aircraft may well foreshadow a considerable shift away from dependence upon extensive fixed airfield facilities in the years to come, particularly viewed with embarrassment in the German environment of battlefield support.

In addition to the introduction of the Bloodhound 2 and Rapier units, a number of other measures were adopted to improve airfield defence, notably the construction of hardened concrete shelters for aircraft, operations centres and communications facilities, and the development of the type of

camouflage known as 'toning down', in which the more obvious features of an airfield were made to blend with the heavily wooded surroundings in which Laarbruch, Brüggen and Wildenrath were built.

Over the years the operational effectiveness of RAF Germany has been greatly enhanced by a number of other factors not readily quantifiable, such as the steadily improving association between the member air forces of NATO; the quality of the command's equipment and of its training and operating standards; and the development of new tactical concepts, a field in which the RAF has exercised a potent influence within 2ATAF. It is no longer necessarily relevant to compare the strength of the command in terms of numbers of aircraft with those of former years, such is the devastating power and efficiency of the single modern combat aircraft.

The Jaguar entered full-scale service in RAF Germany in 1976 and still equips five squadrons there. This formation depicts all the squadrons, the nearest aircraft being from No. 2 Squadron, the other machines being from Nos 14, 17, 20 and 31 Squadrons. All the latter are from the attack wing at Brüggen, whilst No. 2 is at Laarbruch and has a primary role as a reconnaissance squadron, carrying a special pod under the fuselage.

Standing at readiness outside its shelter at Brüggen is a Jaguar GR.Mk 1 of No. 20 Squadron.

Training and Support for the Post-war RAF

The end of hostilities in 1945 brought about widespread contraction of the RAF both in personnel and equipment, as well as closure of numerous operational, training and maintenance establishments at home and overseas. Such a state of affairs would have presented few administrative problems had the nature of operational responsibilities been capable of simple definition, yet the policing of a major nation in Europe and supervising her disarmament was to a large extent compromised by the enigmatic stance of the Soviet Union.

The administration of the RAF in the immediate post-war years had therefore to strike a balance between the controlled reduction in operational strength and the maintenance of essential services to ensure continuity in preparing for whatever the future might hold. For example, Maintenance Command, whose units had prepared and repaired aircraft of all sorts for operational use during the war, was now put to work to recover aircraft 'surplus to

requirements', and to salvage equipment and scrap materials for disposal to industry. Many types of wartime aircraft (particularly those supplied under Lend-Lease by the USA and which were to be returned across the Atlantic) were summarily declared obsolete, so that the task of assembling more than 10,000 aircraft was indeed formidable for a Command the bulk of whose personnel were due for immediate demobilisation.

In the two Training Commands, Flying and Technical, the rundown was even more drastic. The wartime flying training establishments had multiplied many times, and the demands had been met largely by the Empire and Commonwealth training schemes whose numerous facilities in Canada, Rhodesia and the United States had produced the essential flood of operational aircrews, but were dismantled during the last year of the war. No means had survived during the war to maintain training for Regular commissions in the

After the war the Empire Air Training Scheme soon ended and the RAF reorganised its British training machine with wartime aircraft. No. 7 FTS at Cottesmore was an all-through school with Tiger Moths and Harvard T. Mk 2Bs, here preparing for the next round of sorties.

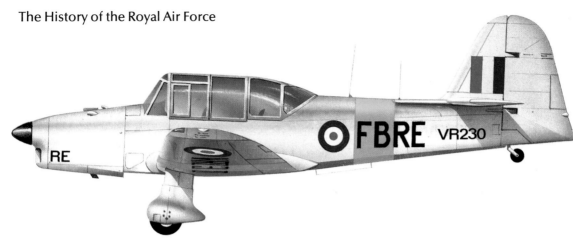

The Percival Prentice T.Mk 1 was the first attempt after World War II to provide an elementary and basic trainer for RAF pilot training. VR230 was built at Luton in 1948 and served with No. 3 FTS at Feltwell until the end of 1952.

RAF in either the flying or ground branches, the emphasis being on the Short Service commission. Those Regular officers whose commissions were granted before the war and who wished to remain in the service naturally continued to serve until normal retirement age; others, usually those with distinguished wartime records, were offered Regular commissions, though with much reduced seniority in order to fill the fast-emptying junior officer ranks.

Another feature of the post-war Royal Air Force was the retention of NCO-rank personnel (master aircrew, flight sergeants and sergeants) in the aircrew posts, a phenomenon that dated back to the very earliest years of the service. It soon became obvious that in due course the RAF would come to depend on a steady flow of young officers, professionally dedicated to a long Regular career in the service, and within two years the Royal Air Force College at Cranwell had reopened, initially for university graduates and soon afterwards for school leavers of 18 or 19 years of age, to provide the necessary junior officers and their basic flying training; a proportion of Cranwell entrants was also sought among other ranks of the service and among the young ground technical apprentices who had already successfully graduated from the School of Technical Training at Halton (the RAF's famous 'Brats' who had given such vital service the world over during the war). Cranwell also produced Regular officers for the Administrative Branch and for the RAF Regiment.

The standard flying training programme immediately after the war consisted of the de Havilland Tiger Moth/North American Harvard/Airspeed Oxford formula up to the Advance Flying School

The Harvard became the standard advanced trainer, serving into the 1950s; this foursome came from No. 3 Flying Training School at Feltwell.

(AFS), at which student pilots were first introduced to the training version of their operational aircraft, principally de Havilland Mosquito T.Mk 3s, Wellingtons and so on. In 1949 the Percival Prentice replaced the Tiger Moth and the Boulton Paul Balliol was partially adopted in place of the Harvard. The Gloster Meteor T.Mk 7 appeared in jet AFS from 1948 onwards, and for some years constituted the sole jet trainer in the RAF, serving

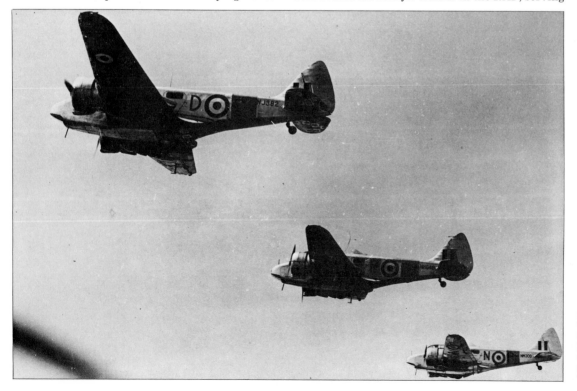

With the Korean crisis in the early 1950s the training structure was rapidly expanded, advanced flying training schools being established at redundant airfields rapidly brought back into use. Also brought out of storage were Airspeed Oxfords such as these serving with No. 9 AFTS in 1953.

To provide ancillary tasks such as target-towing many operational aircraft no longer needed in front-line service were brought into use. RD807 was produced as a Bristol Beaufighter TF.Mk 10 for Coastal Command but in the late 1940s was converted to a TT.Mk 10 serving with No. 34 Squadron at Horsham St Faith in 1949–50.

The first new trainer to enter service after the war was the Percival Prentice, a three-seater in which the third seat was expected to be occupied by an additional student observing the one under instruction. This system was found to be unworkable, so the aircraft served as a two-seater. These Prentices come from No. 3 FTS at Feltwell.

A new advanced trainer to replace the Harvard entered service in 1953. This was the Boulton Paul Balliol T.Mk 2, and No. 7 FTS at Cottesmore received the type. The Balliol, however, was overtaken by events because by then jets were entering the training system and advanced piston trainers were definitely yesterday's aircraft.

to train single- and twin-engine fighter pilots and, initially, English Electric Canberra pilots when that excellent bomber entered service. Mosquito T.Mk 3s and FB.Mk 6s continued to serve as trainers for night-fighter pilots on AFSs and OCUs, but the Vickers Wellington gave way to the Vickers Varsity at bomber AFSs and OCUs early in the 1950s.

A typical training syllabus in the early 1950s would thus comprise about 60 hours on ab initio trainer (the Prentice or Chipmunk, the latter also being used by the University Air Squadrons), between 60 and 100 hours on an advanced trainer (Harvard, Provost or Anson) at an AFS, and about 60 hours on an operational conversion trainer (such as the Meteor T.Mk 7, Mosquito T.Mk 3, FB.Mk 6 or PR.Mk 34, or Varsity) at an OCU. Operational training would continue during the first six months or so on the pilot's first squadron, the pilot becoming acquainted with operational procedures, 'all-

weather' flying and use of armament before becoming regarded as an operationally-ready pilot. Bad weather flying proficiency was instituted with the issue of 'Green Card' and 'Master Green' ratings to define a pilot's ability to fly in varying degrees of visibility conditions, and ratings were updated through a system of examinations by visiting instructors in Meteor T.Mk 7s.

The Prentice, which introduced side-by-side seating for student and instructor, was not considered entirely satisfactory in service, and it was not long before the Air Staff started considering the possibility of introducing an all-through jet training syllabus, foreshadowing the approach of an all-jet air force. This in turn resulted in an upgrading of the flying instructor training at the Central Flying School.

New basic trainers

The Boulton Paul Balliol, originally planned as a turboprop trainer at the advanced stage, came into service, re-engined with a Rolls-Royce Merlin, to replace the Harvard as the advanced trainer. It first went to No. 7 FTS at Cottesmore early in 1953, but was overtaken by events as the policy changed to making the advanced stage an all-jet stage in training, and so, soon afterwards, the aircraft (apart from a few retained at the RAF College, Cranwell) the Balliol went on to ancillary duties.

At the same time, in 1953, the Prentice started phasing out, being replaced by a much more suitable successor from the same stable, the Percival Provost, which turned out to be one of the finest piston trainers ever produced and was used for the elementary and early advanced stage until 1959 when RAF training went all-through jet.

By 1950, with the pattern of the post-war RAF emerging as a service committed to such aircraft as the Meteor and Vampire, and soon to receive the Canberra, the flying training processes had stabilised on the Flying Training School (FTS), the Advanced Flying School (AFS) and the Operational Conversion Unit (OCU), with successfully graduating Cranwell cadets (whose course at the College was of about 30 months' duration) joining the stream at the AFS stage. Other specialist establishments, such as the Empire Navigation School, Empire Test Pilots' School, Central Flying School (for the training of flying instructors) and the Central Fighter Establishment (for training of flight and squadron commanders, particularly on newly-introduced operational aircraft) found their place in the structure of the RAF.

Unfortunately serious weaknesses soon became apparent in the nature of the training provided at Cranwell, being particularly evident during the RAF's very limited participation in the Korean War of 1950–3. It had been intended that the Cranwell-trained junior officer would quickly provide the hard core of line pilots in the peacetime service. However, a high accident rate in the final stages of training and during the early months of squadron flying suggested that the training balance between flying and academic studies at Cranwell was far too diluted to prepare the young pilot for efficient operational duties. The valuable concentration of flying achieved by the NCO and Short Service officer pilots at FTSs (in a period of six months) was not matched by the training received in 30 months

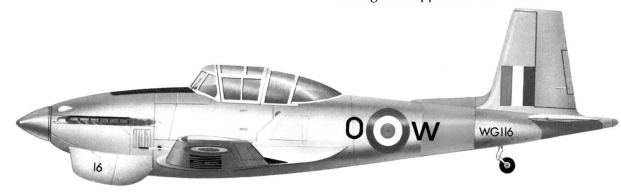

WG116 was one of the Boulton Paul Balliol T. Mk 2s issued to No. 7 FTS at Cottesmore in 1953 as the only FTS to use the type. This aircraft later served with No. 238 OCU for training radar operators.

As the war ended Bristol had produced a new family of heavy twins to replace the various marks of the Beaufighter. The Buckingham never entered service, the Brigand was used in the Middle and Far East operationally and the Buckmaster T. Mk 1 (seen here) served briefly with the Empire Flying School and the Home Command Communications Flight.

Vickers probably never realised, when they developed the Viking airliner into the Varsity general-purpose trainer, that it would serve in the training role for 30 years. It served as a pilot trainer, navigation trainer, trainer for all other aircrew grades and radar and radio calibration aircraft. These three, seen here at Merryfield, served in yet another role, going to Australia with No. 76 Squadron for sampling duties in the early atomic bomb tests.

at Cranwell, whose academic instruction could not adequately emphasise that the successful graduate would for many years be a line pilot primarily and an administrator secondarily. Only when he rose to flight or deputy flight commander on his squadron would his officer training really benefit him.

In due course, therefore, the status (but not the ultimate purpose) of Cranwell underwent change: it assumed more the role of post-graduate estab-

lishment, greater emphasis being placed on the FTS and OCU to provide the flying training. The NCO aircrew status disappeared with the phasing out of the Avro Lincoln bomber and the introduction of aircrew electronic specialists in the new V-force bombers.

The first modification to this structure was made in 1959 when the Hunting Percival Jet Provost basic trainer was introduced, powered by a single

de Havilland Vampire

Second of the RAF's two-seat jet trainers, the de Havilland D.H.115 Vampire T. Mk 11 entered service in 1952 and was used for the conversion of pilots to jet flying, for straight pilot training in the expansion days of the 1950s, and for many other training tasks within the RAF. The aircraft here, XD621, is shown in the markings of the Central Flying School with whom it served at Little Rissington, followed by a long spell at the Central Navigation and Control School at Shawbury where it provided fast jet flying for navigators and also was used to train Air Traffic Controllers.

KEEP OFF

KEEP OFF

KEEP
OFF

KEEP OFF

XD621

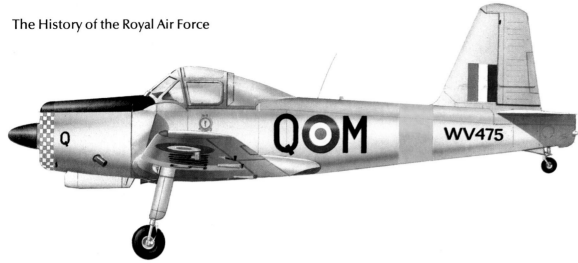

The Hunting-Percival Provost T.Mk 1 was the final piston-engine trainer in full-scale service in the training of RAF pilots. WV475 was part of the first batch built by Hunting and served with No. 6 FTS at Tern Hill from 1956 onwards.

With the Vampire being released from the front-line squadrons it was used (alongside the Vampire T.Mk 11) for solo flying. This foursome of FB.Mk 9s belonged to the RAF College, Cranwell as evidenced by the light blue band round the booms.

Viper turbojet, initiating the first all-jet syllabus with No. 2 FTS at Hullavington; subsequently the T.Mk 3A and T.Mk 5A versions entered service at other FTS and the RAF College, remaining the RAF's standard basic trainer ever since. At much the same time equipment at the Operational Con-

version Units was being upgraded with the introduction of modern aircraft little different from the latest front-line equipment. Single-seat Hawker Hunter F.Mk 6s and English Electric Lightnings, as well as Canberras, Vickers Valiants, Avro Shackletons and so on all started to equip the

For basic training the Prentice left much to be desired, but Percival followed it with the near perfect piston-engine trainer, the Provost T.Mk 1 which served in quantity with much success from 1953 onwards. This formation was used by the CFS at Little Rissington for its formation aerobatic team.

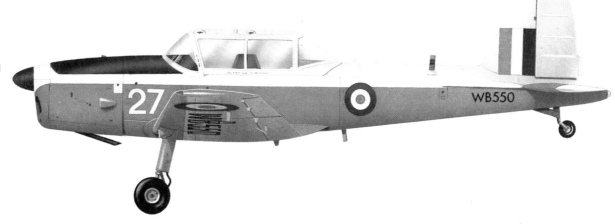

WB550 was the second Chipmunk T. Mk 10 built for the RAF. After being used for evaluation it served with the RAF College at Cranwell, the Central Flying School at Little Rissington and No. 2 FTS at Church Fenton, in whose markings it is seen here.

Above: The Handley Page Company had taken over Miles Aircraft when it got into financial difficulties in the late 1940s. The most useful product that could be produced first was the Marathon light airliner, and the RAF took 28 of these as navigation trainers in 1954. XA274 served with No. 1 ANS.

Above right: With the re-emergence of the RAF Volunteer Reserve many of the EFTSs, equipped with Tiger Moths, were turned into reserve flying schools. To replace the Tiger Moths the RAF acquired a large batch of DHC Chipmunk T. Mk 10s, some of which are still serving today with the Primary Flying Squadron and Air Experience Flights. This formation, flying along the Sussex Coast, came from No. 18 RFS at Fairoaks in 1951.

OCUs, and this phase was followed by the 'specialist aircraft' OCU, for Hawker Siddeley Harrier, Blackburn Buccaneer and SEPECAT Jaguar pilots, the OCUs being given a secondary squadron designation for emergency first-line deployment. The Balliol was withdrawn from the training syllabus after only limited service, to be replaced exclusively by the Jet Provost, while the Folland Gnat took over from the Meteor and Vampire trainers during the 1960s.

For many years an all-through jet flying training syllabus had been advocated, and was attained by the introduction of the Jet Provost, the young would-be fast-jet trainee commencing his instruction in this aircraft before moving on to the Gnat and Hunter (the latter for operational conversion). Aircrew training, other than for pilots, took place in the ubiquitous Vickers Varsity through the 1950s, 1960s and well into the 1970s with those navigators destined for fast jets adding to their

Not to be outdone by Gloster, de Havilland in 1950 produced a two-seater trainer, the Vampire T. Mk 11, and this originally served with the advanced flying schools, which later were combined with the FTSs. XD520 of No. 5 FTS is climbing out of Oakington.

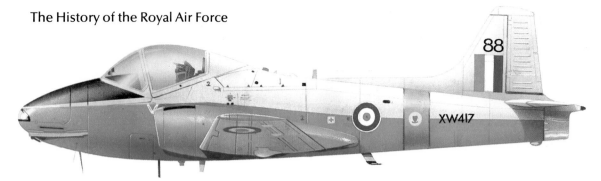

The Jet Provost was extensively redesigned in the 1960s and appeared as the T. Mk 5. This version is still in widespread service as the standard pilot trainer. XW417 served for many years with the RAF College, Cranwell, in whose markings it is shown here, subsequently transferring to No. 1 FTS.

experience on the Hawker Siddeley Dominie, a trainer version of the HS 125 executive jet.

Two important events had occurred during the 1950s: the ending of the two-year national service enrolment in the mid-decade and the disbanding of the flying squadrons of the Royal Auxiliary Air Force in May 1957 (on account of the cost and complexity of modern fighter aircraft, as well as the belief that the days of the manned fighter were already numbered). These posed new problems of recruitment and training in the RAF, already aggravated by the closure of the Basic Flying Training Schools and the civilian-staffed flying schools of the RAFVR, and it was at this stage that the more compact 21-month 'wings' course, involving all-through jet training (principally in the Jet Provost) came to realisation.

Amalgamation into one command

In due course the tasks of flying and technical training in the RAF were combined into a single Training Command, and this in turn came to be absorbed into Support Command, thereby effectively creating a compact two-command air force. Henceforth more than half the long-service pilot intake into the service would be through the universities and their associated air squadrons, where the aspiring pilot officers would complete some 70 hours of air experience in Scottish Aviation Bulldog trainers (which eventually replaced the Chipmunk).

The College of Air Warfare was established at Manby, with a satellite at Strubby. It had several tasks, amongst them providing refresher flying for pilots coming back from ground tours. For this they used Meteor F. Mk 8s, three of which are seen in this impeccable formation loop.

Below: Part of the Central Flying School in the early 1950s was the Handling Squadron, whose task was to fly each new type coming into service and write the Pilot's Notes for the type. The Handling Squadron put up this formation in 1951 led by a Shackleton MR. Mk 1 with a Vampire T. Mk 11 as no. 2 and Meteor T. Mk 7 as no. 3, followed by a Varsity T. Mk 1 with a Sabre F. Mk 4 as no. 2 and a Balliol T. Mk 2 as no. 3.

To replace the Chipmunk with the University Air Squadrons and for sundry other pilot training tasks the RAF acquired in the 1960s a large number of Scottish Aviation Bulldog T.Mk 1s. XX543 originally served with No. 2 FTS (as shown) but is now with the Yorkshire University Air Squadron.

This impeccable formation roll was flown by Vampire T.Mk 11s from No. 208 Advanced Flying School at Merryfield in 1953. The AFSs were formed at the time of the introduction of jet aircraft into the training scene to convert pilots from Harvards and Balliols on to fast jets.

Direct-entry cadets flew 15 hours in Bulldogs before moving to No. 1 Flying Training School at Linton-on-Ouse (later moved to Church Fenton) or Cranwell for 100 hours in Jet Provost T.Mk 3s. The university graduates also went to Cranwell for 75 hours in Jet Provost T.Mk 5As. Thereafter the two streams merged, the fast-jet pilots completing 60 further hours in Jet Provost T.Mk 5As before passing on to No. 4 FTS at Valley where they completed 70 hours in BAe Hawks (which replaced the Gnat at the end of the 1970s), followed by 50 hours in Hawks at the Tactical Weapons Unit at Brawdy. Multi-engine pilots followed their initial flying training on the Jet Provost with a course in the Handley Page/Scottish Aviation Jetstream (which replaced the Varsity) with No. 5 FTS, which moved from Leeming to Finningley in 1979. Helicopter pilots trained with No. 2 FTS at Shawbury on Westland Whirlwind HAR.Mk 10s. Shawbury also accommodated the Central Flying School's helicopter training element, its other elements being located at Cranwell (Jet Provosts), Leeming (Bulldogs) and Valley (Hawks). The non-pilot aircrew students (navigators and air electronic operators) were trained with No. 6 FTS at Finningley in the Dominie T.Mk 1. The famous Red Arrow formation aerobatic display team, with Folland Gnats and later BAe Hawks, has been for

After a pilot scheme with early Jet Provosts at Hullavington, the Jet Provost was ordered in large numbers late in the 1950s in the T.Mk 3 and T.Mk 4 versions, and the whole pilot training system was reorganised, pilots flying their whole training to 'wings' standard on the Jet Provost, with no piston experience. XN470 is a T.Mk 3 of the second batch produced by Hunting, and served with No. 1 FTS.

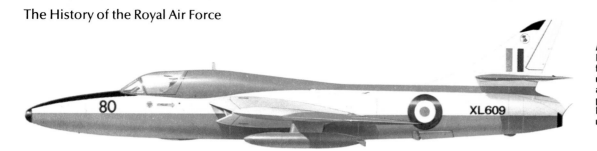

As the RAF went over largely to a low-level fast jet force in the 1970s, the fast jet FTS, No. 4 at Valley, was under pressure to process the pilots and the Gnat was no longer in production. So Hunter T.Mk 7s and F.Mk 6s were drafted in and served until the arrival of the Hawk.

many years an integral part of the Central Flying School. The Hawk itself, a high performance aircraft in its own right, has been afforded a secondary operational role, in line with the system of back-up squadron status in time of emergency.

The responsibility of the Maintenance Units has also undergone considerable change in the past 30 years, and with the steady increase in complexity of service equipment, particularly in such areas as electronics (which today include the immensely costly and sophisticated operational flying simulators installed at many RAF stations), so has the level of technical expertise advanced. The process of technical advance was first manifestly evident in the mid-1950s with the introduction of such aircraft as the Hunter, Canberra and Valiant, and it quickly became painfully apparent that facilities at RAF Maintenance Units were inadequate to cope with all repairs and modifications previously found to be within their capacity. A much closer relationship between manufacturer and service was therefore fostered, provisions being introduced by which a greater proportion of aircraft was returned to the manufacturer for repair, while the civilian contractors themselves provided working parties to undertake work on service establishments. An example of this was afforded by the substantial modification programme on the Hunter, which was largely undertaken by civilian technicians working at UK and German RAF stations; later, when it was decided to transfer the Hunter from the air defence role to ground support, almost the entire RAF inventory of Hunter F.Mk 6s (amounting to more than 100 aircraft) was returned to the manufacturers for rebuilding and strengthening for a service life far beyond the originally planned fatigue life. This enhanced association between service and contractor clearly eased the manpower burden on the service, always most keenly felt in peacetime by the ground tech-

nical trades of the RAF.

Notwithstanding this, the traditional tasks of the Maintenance Units, the storage of reserves and the introduction of minor service modifications and limited repairs, have remained for the most part unchanged, however, specific units being responsible for the handling of individual aircraft types or equipment.

One other element of support in the Royal Air Force is the RAF Regiment, although being an operational element it forms a separate entity and

After leaving the purely training types of aircraft, aircrew moved on to the operational conversion units to train on the type they would fly. In 1952 No. 231 OCU was formed at Bassingbourn and was equipped with a large number of Canberra B.Mk 2s, PR.Mk 3s and T.Mk 4s to train the vast numbers of crews for the expanding Canberra units. These are T.Mk 4s from Bassingbourn (seen top right corner) in the mid-1950s.

Right: In the early 1960s the Black Arrows and Blue Diamonds had been the formation teams representing the RAF, but they were operational squadrons and, with the adoption of the Lightning in place of the Hunter, the expense and feasibility of an operational squadron being the 'official' formation team was too difficult. So in 1964 No. 4 FTS put up a fine team, called the 'Yellowjacks', on their Gnat T.Mk 1s. In the following year these aircraft were transferred to the Central Flying School who initiated the 'Red Arrows' and established a reputation second to none on the international circuit. The Gnats continued to serve with the Red Arrows until 1979, when they were replaced by Hawk T.Mk 1s.

For many years the training of helicopter pilots was carried out by the rotary-wing detachment of the Central Flying School at Ternhill. As more and more pilots were needed No. 2 FTS was formed at this base, later transferring to Shawbury, flying Westland Whirlwind HAR.Mk 10s.

Entering service in the mid-1960s were 20 Hawker Siddeley Dominie T. Mk 1s. These were converted HS.125 executive jets, fitted up as navigational classrooms to train navigators at the speeds they would encounter operationally. They served originally with No. 1 ANS at Stradishall and at the College of Air Warfare at Manby, but latterly have all been concentrated at No. 6 FTS at Finningley.

is controlled by Strike Command's No. 38 Group. Its primary task has remained unchanged since World War II: defence of RAF stations and its equipment in the field. In the ground defence role it continues to constitute semi-mobile infantry, with self-supporting services characteristic of this ground force. In the air-defence role the regiment comprises six squadrons of surface-to-air missiles (replacing the traditional Bofors L40/70 guns which are retained as back-up weapons), these being deployed for the defence of the RAF's four active bases in Germany, and Leuchars and Lossie-mouth in the UK. Each squadron has eight fire units, and these are deployed on an ad hoc basis to accompany Harrier squadrons when they operate from dispersed sites. Replacement of the BAe Rapier low-level surface-to-air missile was announced in 1982, but in the meantime the Marconi DN181 Blindfire radar has been introduced to extend Rapier operation to all-weather, day-and-night conditions. A Territorial element of the RAF Regiment also exists for Reserve activity in the United Kingdom.

Just about to touch down at Valley is this Hunter T. Mk 7 of No. 4 FTS. The two-seat Hunter has been the classic jet trainer for 30 years and is still the only swept-wing fighter authorised for spinning training (this only to be done by the Empire Test Pilots School at Boscombe Down) although Hawks are now taking up the role.

Transport Command and Air Mobility

The expansion of Transport Command in the last years of World War II had been something of a phenomenon even by wartime standards. Formed in March 1943, it had grown in little more than two years from a handful of makeshift units to a formation controlling 12 groups, 17 wings and 40 fully operational squadrons with an establishment of nearly 1,200 aircraft. In addition another 20 squadrons and flights with a proposed establishment of 500 aircraft were in training for the final assault on Japan which the bombing of Hiroshima and Nagasaki made unnecessary. In the course of this rapid expansion Transport Command had been given one notable, if temporary, privilege enjoyed by no other home-based operational command: all overseas transport elements came directly under the control of Transport Command itself and not of the appropriate theatre formation, as did their bomber, fighter and maritime counterparts.

This situation, however, lasted only until March 1946, and by then Transport Command's claims to recognition as an essential part of the post-war air force, on an equal footing with the other functional commands, were beginning to be questioned, although still generally accepted by the Air Staff. In two respects the role of transport aircraft was well established. British airborne forces had played a spectacular part in the final stages of the war against Germany, and the Army was eager to keep alive the techniques of airborne warfare with the aid of the RAF. The value of theatre air transport also was generally accepted, having been demonstrated many times over since the early 1920s, when the RAF had pioneered its use in the Middle East, and its contribution to the success of the Burma campaign of 1944–5 was a very recent memory.

But circumstances had not allowed Transport Command the opportunity to prove the value of strategic air transport. Such an opportunity had seemed almost within its grasp in 1945, when plans were being made to airlift large numbers of troops from Britain to the Far East for the war against Japan. Indeed, the airlift had already begun on a small scale when the Japanese surrender put the whole operation into reverse and, while outgoing aircraft merely ferried replacement troops to India, home-coming aircraft brought back prisoners of war and large numbers of troops due for demobilisation. In all, over 90,000 personnel were carried on trooping operations to and from India between May 1945 and April 1946.

At the end of World War II the Douglas Dakota was retained in Transport Command service for some time, until new tactical transports could be developed. This particular aircraft is in use here with the Transport Command Development Unit for parachute trials.

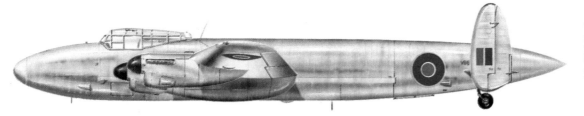

The Lancastrian was a transport development of the Lancaster primarily adopted by airlines after the war. However, the RAF procured 64 and used them for a short while on Transport Command routes.

Valuable operating experience had been gained in the course of those 12 months, and Transport Command was eager to establish regular scheduled services to the Middle and Far East to carry priority passengers and freight. The problems, however, were considerable. Doubts were expressed about the need for such services, and it was argued that when the time factor made it necessary for service personnel and freight to go by air rather than by sea, which was still the normal method of overseas deployment, commercial airlines should be used, and that the RAF should not be allowed to set up in opposition to them.

Predictably, a compromise was reached. It was agreed that Transport Command should maintain regular scheduled services to British bases overseas, as there would always be certain urgent service requirements which only RAF aircraft could meet; but the resources, particularly in terms of the number of aircrew to be made available to the command, fell well short of what it considered necessary for efficient operation.

Even with the strategic role given official recognition, Transport Command had many other problems to face. The post-war rundown of the RAF and the consequent loss of experienced air and ground crews, together with a general lack of facilities at the staging posts along the overseas routes, made it difficult to keep services running to schedule at least for the first year or two. Further, as the command was operating in peacetime conditions it had to achieve, and be seen to have achieved, a level of safety unsurpassed by any commercial airline. To this end it set up under No. 4 Group an intensive training programme to retrain aircrews to peacetime standards.

Lack of suitable aircraft

In the longer term the command's most pressing problem was the provision of aircraft to meet the needs of route, theatre and airborne forces operations, and it was in fact in the field of aircraft procurement that Transport Command was at its greatest disadvantage compared with other commands. In the haste to rearm in the late 1930s the RAF had necessarily concentrated on the production of fighters and bombers, a concentration which continued through the war years. Consequently, the only transport aircraft to be developed in Britain since the Bristol Bombay in the late 1930s was the Avro York which, although adapted from the Lancaster to save the long lead time needed to produce a completely new aircraft, still suffered many delays. When it finally came into full-scale RAF service in 1945 it was without the clearances needed for it to operate in the paratrooping role as had been intended.

For the war years Transport Command had relied on a mixture of converted bombers and the Douglas Dakotas supplied by the United States under Lend-Lease and a supplementary agreement made in May 1942. This allowed Britain to continue to concentrate on the manufacture of combat aircraft and provided for her transport aircraft requirements to be met from American resources. Over the following three years some 1,900 Dakotas were supplied to the RAF, and with the ending of Lend-Lease Britain arranged to buy 600 of them for $US 15,000 each and to lease a further 650.

All the same, steps had been taken well before the end of the war to find suitable successors to the York and Dakota and so build up an efficient transport fleet for the early post-war years. What finally emerged, however, after a number of attractive alternatives had been discarded in an increasingly difficult economic climate, were the Handley Page Hastings and Vickers Valetta. These were generally regarded even then as no more than stopgaps, valued as multirole aircraft, but failing to incorporate the best design concepts of the day.

While this new generation of aircraft was in process of production, however, Transport Command was undergoing a series of rapid transformations. It had first survived the convulsions of the post-war rundown to stabilise in late 1947 with a front-line establishment of 153 aircraft in 20

For the trunk routes of Transport Command was evolved the Avro York, a Lancaster with a boat-like fuselage. It had had a long gestation during the war, but blossomed into the command as soon as hostilities ceased.

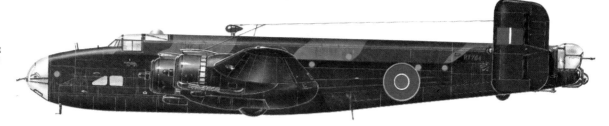

RT764 was a Handley Page Halifax A. Mk 7 which was produced at the end of 1945 and never entered RAF unit service, being scrapped four years later.

The Handley Page Halifax remained in service for a while after World War II as a transport, glider-tug and parachute dropping aircraft. LW385 had entered service with No. 190 Squadron as the European war ended, and was subsequently sent to the RAE at Farnborough.

squadrons: seven York squadrons based at Abingdon and Lyneham, eight Dakota squadrons at Waterbeach and Oakington, four Handley Page Halifax airborne forces squadrons at Fairford, and No. 24 (Commonwealth) Squadron flying from Bassingbourn on VIP and other special duties.

The command had also brought a good measure of stability into the operation of the scheduled services. For the Dakota squadrons the pattern of tasking had changed considerably since the end of the war in Europe, when for the first few months they had operated a basic air transport network across a continent where most forms of communication had been severely disrupted by military action. By early 1946, however, British European Airways was beginning to take over Transport Command's non-military commitments in the area, and by the end of the year the Dakotas were able to concentrate on providing regular passenger and freight services to meet the needs of the British Army of the Rhine and the British Air Forces of Occupation. A year later the destinations being regularly served included Bückeburg, Gütersloh, Wunstorf, Wahn and Berlin (Gatow), with an extension to Warsaw; an additional service staged through Istres and Malta to Castel Benito and El

Adem in Libya, while a detachment was maintained in Vienna for a time to carry official passengers and cargo to and from Budapest and the Balkan capitals, destinations not then served by BEA.

Meanwhile, the Yorks were engaged in operating a network of passenger and freight services to the Middle East, East Africa and Singapore. Initially, and until the British withdrawal from India, the main destinations had been Karachi, Delhi and Calcutta, staging through Malta or Castel Benito, Cairo and Shaibah in Iraq. A Singapore service, however, was introduced in April 1946 by way of Calcutta until the route was changed to go through Negombo in Ceylon. In the early days as many as 7,000 flying hours a month had been achieved and the use of slip crews had been common, although disputed by those who argued that the higher utilisation achieved was outweighed by passenger discomfort and servicing difficulties. However, with the growing shortage of manpower, which continued through 1947 and beyond, the use of slip crews was severely curtailed and the frequency of the various services was reduced in line, with a cut in flying hours to 4,000 a month.

Problems on the long routes

Reports written at the time stressed the hazards of route flying in the late 1940s and the problems faced by aircraft captains, who were responsible for the safety of their aircraft, crews and passengers on flights which in the case of the Singapore schedules of July 1946 lasted from 08.00 on the first day to 07.00 on the fourth with a night stop at Cairo and a long day stop at Karachi. Some improvements were noted over the months, particularly in servicing and catering, but black spots remained and the briefing and control facilities at staging posts were generally criticised. One particular hazard was noted: the long leg over the sea between Calcutta and Singapore, where no radio aids were available and navigation was carried out by 'dead reckoning with the aid of the drift sight'.

The transport squadrons were also involved in a

The Dakota replacement in Transport Command service was the Vickers Valetta C. Mk 1, which equipped the transport wings in the Middle and Far East and was used by one home-based squadron, No. 30, one of whose aircraft is here taking off from Northolt in the mid-1950s.

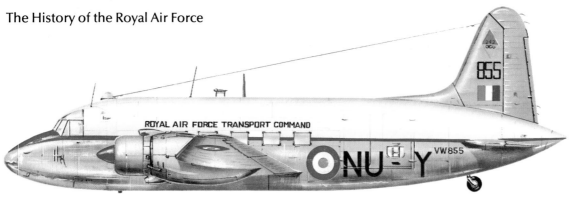

The Vickers Valetta C.Mk 1 entered RAF service in 1947 and replaced the Dakota as a medium-range troop and passenger transport. VW855 was built in 1949 and entered service with No. 30 Squadron a year later at Abingdon. It was soon transferred to No. 242 OCU at Dishforth, where it served training Valetta crews until 1957. It is shown carrying the OCU's code letters 'NU' and fin diamond.

number of additional activities, including routine and emergency trooplifts and the support of squadron moves. With the services to India withdrawn by early 1948 the command began to have York capacity to spare and, significantly, this was increasingly used to provide mobility for forces. Transport Command had also become involved in a tentative return to airborne forces training, an area in which, in spite of Army pressure, little had been done since the end of the war, mainly through lack of resources. The Halifaxes based in Palestine, and since the spring of 1946 under the control of the local theatre commander, had carried out joint exercises with the Army until their return home was completed in April 1947; and a full-scale airborne forces exercise, codenamed 'Longstop', was mounted in the autumn of that year. But with further cuts in the transport force imminent, following government limits on defence expenditure, the outlook for airborne forces training seemed bleak.

The next in the series of rapid transformations which affected Transport Command in the late 1940s, however, was not the result of defence cuts, but of the decision of the Soviet government to strangle all surface communications between the West and Berlin. The airlift which followed absorbed virtually the whole of the command's resources for a year or more, with the result that the scheduled services, painstakingly developed over the past two and a half years, were abandoned and not resumed until late 1949.

By then the promised reduction in the transport force had begun to take effect and by early 1951, at a time when other commands were beginning to expand, the transport force had assumed an entirely new, and very attenuated, shape with a total permitted establishment of only 50 aircraft.

All Transport Command's remaining groups had

been disbanded: No. 4 in February 1948, No. 46 in March 1950 having amalgamated with No. 47 four months earlier, and No. 38 in February 1951. Even the command itself was under threat for a time in the face of the suggestion that further economies could be made by transferring the remaining transport squadrons to Home Command.

Ironically, the contraction of the transport force coincided with the beginning of a period of intense activity. For the Valetta squadron the task, although much reduced in scale, remained broadly the same as in the days of the Dakota, combining routine services to British bases in Germany with VIP flights, trooplifts and the support of squadron moves. Similarly, the long-range squadrons were employing the increased passenger- and troop-carrying capacity of the Hastings on the trunk route network set up by the Yorks, while introducing a number of changes, notably bringing back the slip crew system to meet emergency require-

For some time after the York had been replaced in the Transport Command squadrons, this aircraft soldiered on as part of the Far East Communications Squadron at Singapore.

HOME-BASED TRANSPORT FORCE IN EARLY 1951

Squadron	Aircraft	Location
24	Hastings C.2, York C.1	Topcliffe
30	Valetta C.1, C.2	Abingdon
47	Hastings C.1	Topcliffe
53, 99, 511	Hastings C.1	Lyneham

For light communications duties the RAF acquired two types in the early post-war years, both types remaining in service for a long time. The first was a very updated version of the Avro Anson with a new fuselage and revised wing. This came in several versions, with detailed differences, the main communications version being the C.Mk 19. Seen at Odiham in the early 1960s is VV967, previously a T.Mk 21, converted to Mk 19 standard and used by No. 1 Group Communications Flight.

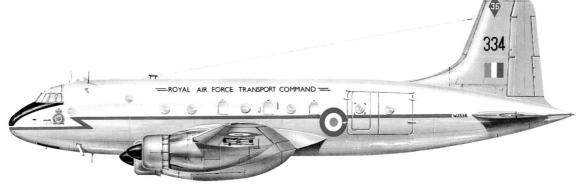

In Transport Command the Handley Page Hastings served in three versions, C.Mk 1, C.Mk 2 and C.Mk 4. WJ334 was a C.Mk 2 and is shown here in service with No. 36 Squadron based at Colerne. In the late 1950s and early 1960s all the transport squadrons had a coloured diamond on the fin for identity purposes, each squadron having a different colour, with the squadron number superimposed.

At Hatfield de Havilland produced a batch of its popular new Dove civil transport as the Devon C.Mk 1 for the RAF. This found immediate use as a VIP transport and is still serving today, with uprated engines as C.Mk 2s, with No. 207 Squadron at Northolt and with the RAE at Farnborough.

In 1949 the major new transport for RAF Transport Command entered service. This was the Handley Page Hastings C.Mk 1. It was soon to be seen flying down the trunk routes through to Singapore, and took part in all the major troop airlifts of the 1950s and early 1960s, remaining in service until 1967.

ments and adding two new destinations (Hong Kong and Australia) to the Far East route. The outbreak of the war in Korea in June 1950 added a further task and in September the Singapore service was extended to Japan, staging through Clark Field in the Philippines. This new route, used to fly in and support the British troops being sent to Korea to form part of the United Nations force there, was later replaced by a shuttle service between Singapore and Japan, operated by one crew on a four-week detachment.

Almost simultaneously, the political situation in Egypt began to deteriorate and the Hastings squadrons were at once involved in moving reinforcements from Cyprus and the UK to the Canal Zone and bringing service families back home. A slipping service to Fayid was introduced in November 1951 and, as an additional precaution, aircraft and crews were sent to Cyprus, Libya and Egypt on standby or to operate shuttle services in

the area, supplementing the theatre transport force. The emergency continued through much of 1952 and the slip service to Fayid remained a feature of Hastings activity until the British withdrawal from Egypt was completed some three years later.

'Sandbag' and medical supplies

With such strategic moves now well established as one of Transport Command's primary roles, two other tasks were growing in importance, along with a number of widely varying special flights and an increasing emphasis on casualty and medical evacuation. From the early 1950s transport support training, including paratrooping, heavy supply drops and joint exercises with the Army, particularly the 16th Independent Paratroop Brigade, began to account for a rising number of flying hours. Additionally, Hastings crews were called on for relief operations, including, for example, Operation 'Sandbag' in February 1953 to collect sandbags from Milan, Zürich and Oslo following the major flood disaster which affected the east coast of England and parts of the Netherlands. Later in that year medical supplies were flown to Greece after a volcanic eruption and further supplies were lifted to Cyprus following an earthquake.

Meanwhile, plans were being made to reinforce Transport Command with a new generation of aircraft to meet the requirements of what was now a rapidly changing world situation. By the early 1950s it was becoming increasingly obvious that Britain, as a power with worldwide colonial responsibilities and an interest in maintaining stability wherever it might be threatened, would more than ever need to deploy ground and air forces appropriate to the situation. It was also clear that speed of deployment would be an essen-

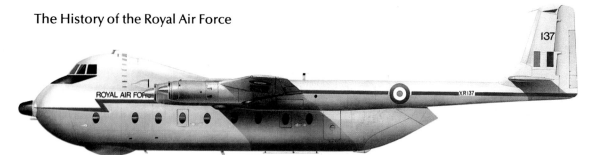

Hawker Siddeley Argosy XR137 was the 50th of 56 RAF Argosies, and served originally with No. 267 Squadron at Benson from 1963. It later moved to No. 242 OCU at Thorney Island on crew training duties before becoming an E. Mk 1 and serving until 1975 with No. 115 Squadron at Cottesmore in whose markings it is shown. It was sold in August 1975.

tial prerequisite of success. In an earlier age, Britain had maintained substantial forces in India and Egypt, near to potential troublespots, but following her withdrawal from both countries and in the face of clear evidence that large foreign bases were becoming unacceptable to host countries, as well as a growing drain on British foreign currency reserves, it was decided that reinforcements would now come mainly from a strategic reserve based in the UK.

Concurrently, two other influences were at work. The airlifting of troops was becoming a more widely accepted practice with the growth in the use of civil charter aircraft for routine troop movements and the discovery that air transport for personnel was, all factors considered, more economical than a long sea passage, although bulk freight would necessarily continue to go by ship. There were, however, strong objections to the use of civil aircraft in emergencies, a fact which underlined the need for a strategic air transport fleet operating under service conditions. As important was the decision, announced in the 1957 Defence Statement, that National Service was to be phased out in favour of a much smaller, but highly trained and highly mobile all-volunteer force. Mobility presumed the availability of strategic and tactical transport aircraft, particularly as the strategic reserve was to be based mainly in the UK, and a high level of training presumed the use of aircraft to work with the Army in practising modern battlefield techniques. Fortuitously, this trend towards the use of air transport coincided with the availability of aircraft with greatly improved capabilities and, as other RAF programmes were nearing completion, with the likelihood that the necessary resources would be released to purchase and operate them.

So began what was to become as dramatic an

expansion of resources as that which transformed Bomber, Fighter and Coastal Commands in the early 1950s, although spread over a much longer period. Between 1956 and 1969 the front-line establishment of Transport Command and its successor from 1967, Air Support Command, grew from 56 to 229 aircraft. The latter figure, however, included the 44 McDonnell Douglas Phantoms, BAe Harriers and Hawker Hunters, which formed the offensive support element of the recently reestablished No. 38 Group.

The expansion of the transport force took place in two phases. The first began in March 1956 with the almost simultaneous formation of No. 216 Squadron at Lyneham with de Havilland Comets and No. 47 Squadron at Abingdon with Blackburn Beverleys, events which marked the growing division between the strategic and tactical transport roles, hitherto combined by the Hastings

The Beverley C. Mk 1 entered service with the RAF in 1956 as a heavy-lift freighter designed for use from small airstrips. This particular Beverley was used at Boscombe Down for parachuting experiments.

When the de Havilland Comet came under a cloud in 1954 it was withdrawn from airline service. The company built a Mk 2 version which avoided the fatal flaw in the Mk 1 and a batch was built for the RAF. This batch was flown by No. 216 Squadron at Lyneham from June 1956 on urgent and VIP transport flights. Subsequently some C. Mk 4 aircraft were flown by No. 216 Squadron as well.

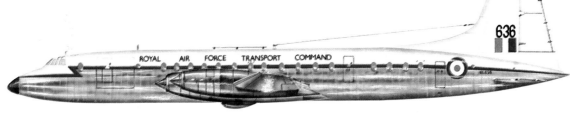

XL636 was a Bristol 253 Britannia C.Mk 1 built at Belfast in April 1959. Two months later it joined No. 99 Squadron at Lyneham and was named *Argo*. It served with No. 99 and 511 Squadrons from there and Brize Norton until December 1975.

The Hawker Siddeley Argosy C.Mk 1 was intended to replace the Hastings in RAF service. Initially it flew alongside the latter, but then replaced it and continued as the medium-range general-purpose transport aircraft from 1962 until 1971.

Two squadrons of Bristol Britannias were formed in 1959 for the RAF, and these provided splendid service until 1976, enabling large quantities of troops to be airlifted swiftly for long distances. The squadrons (Nos 99 and 511) were based at first at Lyneham and then (from 1970) at Brize Norton, and pooled their aircraft as on an airline.

squadrons. It was not, however, until three years later that the division widened still further with the introduction of Bristol Britannias to re-equip No. 99 Squadron from April 1959 and No. 511 Squadron from the following December; both squadrons were based at Lyneham alongside the Comets, forming by the end of 1960 a total strategic force of 33 aircraft (10 Comets and 23 Britannias).

As the Britannias came into service on the trunk routes, the Hastings concentrated more and more on tactical transport duties, joining the Beverleys of which there were now two squadrons. The second had been formed in January 1957 from one of the Hastings squadrons at Lyneham, No. 53, which then moved to Abingdon to join No. 47. The Valetta squadron, No. 30, had also been re-equipped with Beverleys, three months after No. 53, but was redeployed from Dishforth to Nairobi in

November 1959. By then the Hastings were concentrated at Colerne in three squadrons: No. 24, the only survivor of the original Hastings force; No. 36, re-numbered from No. 511 in September 1958; and No. 114 which had been formed in the following April to replace No. 99.

So by mid-1960 the tactical transport force consisted of five squadrons (two Beverley units with 16 aircraft and three Hastings units with 28 aircraft). In 1962 the Armstrong Whitworth Argosy came into service and two squadrons were formed in the UK, No. 114 (the former Hastings squadron) in January and No. 267 in November. Seven months later the two Beverley squadrons were amalgamated into one squadron, No. 47. As a result of these changes the number of squadrons in the tactical transport force remained unaltered at five, but the total aircraft establishment was increased to 58: 28 Hastings, 22 Argosies and eight Beverleys.

Meanwhile, a new element had been added to Transport Command's front-line strength: a short-range force consisting initially of the Scottish Aviation Pioneers, Bristol Sycamores and Westland Whirlwinds which had proved their worth during the Malayan emergency and which were now to undertake army co-operation duties in the UK. The first and only Pioneer squadron in Transport Command was No. 215, formed in April 1956 and renumbered No. 230 in September 1958. Scottish Aviation Twin Pioneers were added in March 1960, but both types were phased out towards the end of 1962 and replaced by Whirlwinds in preparation for the squadron's move to Germany at the beginning of the following year.

The first helicopter squadrons to serve in Transport Command were No. 225, formed in January 1960 for army co-operation duties and equipped initially with Sycamores and Whirlwinds, and No. 118, a Sycamore squadron transferred from Coastal

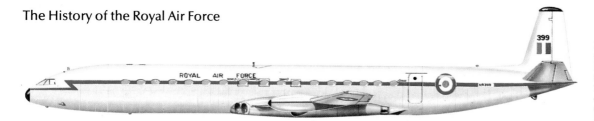

ROYAL AIR FORCE

XR399 was the last of the Comets to enter RAF service. A C.Mk 4, it joined No. 216 Squadron at Lyneham and served on the transport routes until the squadron was disbanded on 30 June 1975. It was then sold on the civil market and became G-BDIX with Dan-Air.

Command four months later, but retaining its internal security role until its disbandment in August 1962. Meanwhile, nine months before, a second army co-operation squadron, No. 72, had been formed at Odiham, where No. 225 was now based; it was equipped initially with Bristol Belvederes, but these were replaced by Westland Wessex helicopters in August 1964, when all available Belvederes were needed for service in Borneo. No. 72 Squadron became for a while the mainstay of the helicopter force in Transport Command, as No. 225, now equipped wholly with Whirlwinds, was detached to the Far East in November 1963, and a second Wessex squadron, No. 18, formed at Odiham in January 1964, remained there for only a year before moving to Germany to relieve No. 230, which was also destined for the Far East.

No. 38 Group

So at the end of 1965 the home-based transport force consisted of nine squadrons and 102 aircraft. With the tactical force building up towards this size, No. 38 Group re-formed at Upavon at the beginning of 1960 with responsibility for tactical transport operations and exercises, particularly liaison with the Army and the development of transport and airborne assault techniques. By mid-1961 the new group had moved to Odiham and assumed control of the Beverley and Hastings squadrons along with the short-range transport force, leaving Transport Command to continue operating the Comets and Britannias. Early in the following year a new dimension was added with the transfer from Fighter Command of two Hunter FGA.Mk 9 squadrons, Nos 1 and 54, so enabling the group to provide fighter reconnaissance and ground-attack support as well as tactical airlift.

For this expanding force the task was to extend the operating pattern established in the early 1950s. In route flying the radical changes pioneered by the Comet C.Mk 2s with their greater speed and range, when compared with the Hastings, were further developed by the Britannias and Comet C.Mk 4s; the latter, brought into service in 1962, had a passenger carrying capacity approaching

Two of the Lyneham Britannia wing's aircraft fly down the routes in the 1960s. XL657 was named *Adhara* and XM490 *Aldebaran*.

100, double that of the Comet C.Mk 2s, while the Britannias with an even greater load-carrying capacity (some 100 troops or 18 tons of freight) had a range more than 50 per cent greater than that of the first Comets. At the same time the opening of the Gan staging post in 1957, and the introduction of improved communications and navigation equipment further eased the problems of route flying.

But the operation of services to Cyprus, Aden, Bahrain, Singapore, Hong Kong and Australia, important in itself, was also preparation for another of the primary roles of the strategic transport force: the rapid deployment of the Army's strategic reserve in exercise or emergency, using slip crews as necessary. Turmoil in the Middle East in 1958, for example, kept the Comets and Britannias at full stretch lifting troops and equipment, a situation which was repeated during the reinforcement of Kuwait in 1961. Other tasks included the support of squadron moves, aeromedical services and, for the Comets particularly, VIP flights; in addition, once the Comet C.Mk 4s were fully operational, the Comet C.Mk 2s mounted

HOME-BASED TRANSPORT FORCE AT END OF 1965

Squadron	Aircraft	Location
99, 511	Britannia C.1, C.2	Lyneham
216	Comet C.2, C.4	Lyneham
24, 36	Hastings C.1, C.2	Colerne
47	Beverley C.1	Abingdon
114, 267	Argosy C.1	Benson
72	Wessex HC.2	Odiham

As part of No. 38 Group came the tactical transport units, and foremost amongst these were the battlefield helicopter squadrons. The application of turbine power to the Westland Whirlwind, resulting in the HAR.Mk 10 in 1962, upgraded the capabilities of this force. Seen here during an exercise on Salisbury Plain that year are Mk 10s of No. 225 Squadron from Odiham, lifting panniers of stores.

The Vickers VC.10 C.Mk 1 joined the RAF in July 1966, XR807 being the second aircraft of the batch. The VC.10 fleet has been operated by No. 10 Squadron at Brize Norton ever since. All the fleet is named after various RAF Victoria Cross awards, XR807 being *Donald Garland, VC & Thomas Gray, VC*.

Amongst the No. 38 Group force were the two squadrons of ground-attack Hunters at West Raynham, Nos 1 and 54. One of their duties was to supply a small fighter force at Gibraltar, where these two FGA.Mk 9s of No. 54 Squadron are keeping an eye on a Soviet warship entering the Mediterranean in 1969.

No. 216 Squadron's de Havilland Comet C.Mk 2s were augmented, in 1962, by five C.Mk 4s, and these proved suitable and popular on the routes.

routine trooplifts to and from Gibraltar, Malta, Cyprus and Libya. The bulk of routine trooping, however, was still being carried out by charter aircraft.

In parallel with the development of a rapid deployment capability by the strategic transport force, the tactical and short-range squadrons were engaged in practising and improving the techniques of tactical mobility with elements of the Army's strategic reserve. The introduction of the Beverleys and Argosies brought as radical a change to tactical concepts as did the Comets and Britannias to the pattern of strategic operations. The Beverley, with its high capacity (over 90 troops, 70 paratroops or 20 tons of freight) and an ability to operate from small airfields, was the first British aircraft to be designed specially to drop heavy equipment through rear loading doors; the Argosy, faster but of smaller capacity, and with a kneeling landing gear arrangement, also had a short take-off and landing capability and could operate from rough surfaces.

Training for the tactical squadrons ranged from practising the basic techniques of transport support, particularly paratroop and supply dropping, to a programme of field exercises. With the formation of No. 38 Group and of the two offensive support squadrons, these joint exercises with the Army became more frequent and sophisticated, the aim being to test the ability of British forces, operating increasingly in a NATO context, to respond to a threat wherever it might arise. During Exercise 'Starlight I', for example, in March 1960 the group's forces were used to deploy elements of the strategic reserve to Libya and maintain them in the field; six months later a similar exercise, code-named 'Holdfast', mounted a defence of the Jutland peninsula. In later exercises 2,000 troops and 40 tons of equipment were dropped in Cyprus; an airborne assault on Libya was mounted from Malta, with offensive support and air resupply provided by No. 38 Group in the subsequent land battle; and a further airborne assault took place in northern Greece with fighter reconnaissance and ground-attack support, and helicopters playing a part in a secondary landing.

The Hastings, Beverleys and Argosies were also used to supplement the airlift capacity provided by the strategic transport force, carrying personnel

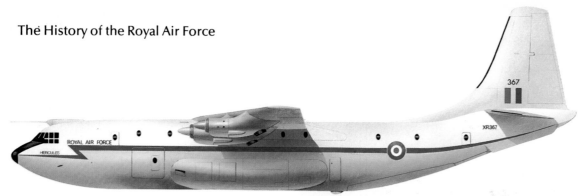

Shorts Belfast C.Mk 1 XR367 was the sixth of 10 aircraft built for the RAF and operated by No. 53 Squadron at Brize Norton from January 1966 to September 1976. This aircraft was named *Heracles,* and after the disbandment of the squadron was sold outside the service. It now flies with Heavylift Air Cargo as G-BFYU.

and equipment to and from exercises, and taking part in routine and emergency deployments, most notably the Middle East operations of 1958 and the reinforcement of Kuwait in 1961. Aircraft were also detached overseas to augment theatre transport forces and on numerous occasions gave assistance during disaster relief operations.

It was therefore against a background of day-to-day involvement in air transport operations combined with intensive air-mobility training that Transport Command received additional reinforcements. First to arrive were the Shorts Belfasts to form No. 53 Squadron at Brize Norton in November 1965 and the Vickers (BAC) VC10s for No. 10 Squadron, which formed eight months later, also at Brize Norton. The Comet squadron, however, was reduced to five Comet C.Mk 4s, the Comet C.Mk 2s being withdrawn in 1967.

The re-equipment of the tactical force began in September 1966 when No. 46 Squadron formed with Hawker Siddeley Andovers; based initially at Abingdon, it redeployed to Thorney Island in 1970. More significant was the gradual build-up of a Lockheed Hercules force to replace the command's Hastings, Beverleys and Argosies. The process began in August 1967, when the first of the two remaining Hastings squadrons, No. 36, moved to Lyneham to re-equip, followed in January 1968 by No. 24. Later in the year two former Beverley squadrons were re-established and equipped with Hercules: No. 47 in February and No. 30, which had recently disbanded in the Persian Gulf, in June; both squadrons were based at Fairford until they moved to Lyneham in 1971. By then a fifth Hercules squadron, No. 48, had arrived there, returning from

Queen of the skies: XV104, one of the RAF's fleet of 14 Vickers VC.10 C.Mk 1s flown by No. 10 Squadron at Brize Norton on the RAF's long-range transport needs world-wide since 1966.

service in the Far East; a sixth, No. 70, previously based in Cyprus, followed in February 1975. Meanwhile, the two Argosy squadrons had continued at Benson until, as a result of British withdrawal from her overseas bases, they began to be phased out five years earlier than had been intended, No. 267 being amalgamated with No. 114 in May 1970 and No. 114 itself being disbanded in October 1971. Reinforcement of the helicopter element consisted of the addition of two Westland Puma squadrons,

Entering service in January 1966 were the 10 Shorts Belfast C.Mk 1s which became the RAF's unique heavy-lift long-range freighters. They were capable of carrying many items of RAF equipment complete without dismantling (such as helicopters, missiles, etc.) and performed a vital role. The squadron was disbanded in September 1976, as one of the many defence cuts. Fortunately a civilian company, Heavylift Air Cargo, bought some of them and operated them so that when the RAF urgently needed them for the Falklands operation, they were able to charter from Heavylift.

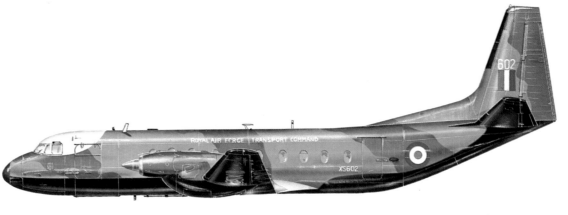

The Hawker Siddeley Andover C.Mk 1 came into RAF service in July 1966, 31 aircraft being built for short-range tactical transport duties with the ability to make landings and take-offs from unprepared strips. XS602 was first used by the Andover Conversion Unit at Abingdon, then joined the fleet of No. 46 Squadron until the squadron became victim to one of the frequent defence cuts and was disbanded on 31 August 1975.

The No. 38 Group strike units (Nos 6 and 54 Squadrons) moved to Coningsby in 1969 and re-equipped with McDonnell Phantom FGR. Mk 2s. One aircraft from No. 6 Squadron is seen here armed with Sparrow missiles and rocket pods.

NOS 38 AND 46 GROUPS IN EARLY SPRING 1975

No. 38 Group

Squadron	Aircraft	Location
1	Harrier GR.3	Wittering
6, 54	Jaguar GR.1	Coltishall
33, 230	Puma HC.1	Odiham
41	Phantom FGR.2	Coningsby
72	Wessex HC.2	Odiham
45, 58	Hunter FGA.9	Wittering

No. 46 Group

Squadron	Aircraft	Location
10	VC10 C.1	Brize Norton
24, 30, 36, 47, 48, 70	Hercules C.1	Lyneham
46	Andover C.1	Thorney Island
53	Belfast C.1	Brize Norton
99, 511	Britannia C.1, C.2	Lyneham
216	Comet C.4	Lyneham

Flight-refuelling had become one of the important functions of the RAF in the early 1960s to enable operational squadrons to be deployed world-wide. The task was originally carried out by Vickers Valiants, but these had to be withdrawn hurriedly in 1965 with spar trouble, and the Handley Page Victor was converted to take its place. In this picture a No. 54 Squadron Jaguar GR. Mk 1 from Coltishall is hooked up to a Victor K. Mk 2 of No. 57 Squadron.

No. 33 being established in June 1971 and No. 230, which exchanged its Whirlwind Mk 10s for Pumas in January 1972; both squadrons were based at Odiham with the Wessex squadron, No. 72. Also in No. 38 Group from January 1968 to August 1970, when it returned to Germany for a second tour, was No. 18 Squadron, also with the Wessex and based first at Acklington and later at Odiham.

In the meantime, the offensive support element

had been reinforced with the formation of a Harrier squadron, No. 1, in July 1969, and of two Phantom squadrons, No. 6 in May 1969 and No. 54 four months later, the Harriers being based at Wittering and the Phantoms at Coningsby; a third Phantom squadron, No. 41, was formed alongside the other two in April 1972. As a result of these changes the Hunters were reduced to a detachment at Wittering, but in time two new squadrons were formed there, No. 45 in August 1972 and No. 58 a year later, their main role being tactical training. A further change occurred in 1974 when Nos 6, 54 and subsequently 41 Squadrons were moved to Coltishall and rearmed with SEPECAT Jaguars.

While the various elements of the transport force were expanding and re-equipping, substantial changes in organisation were also taking place. Air Support Command, which had replaced Transport Command in August 1967, was itself absorbed by Strike Command in September 1972; at the same time No. 46 Group was re-formed to assume control of the strategic and tactical forces, while No. 38 Group retained the offensive support and helicopter elements. Taken together, the two groups controlled in the early spring of 1975 227 aircraft: 50 strategic transports, 65 tactical transports, 60 offensive support aircraft and 52 helicopters.

By 1975, however, massive changes had also taken place in the political sphere. In the years between 1967 and 1971 British forces were withdrawn from Aden, Libya, Bahrain and very largely

The Jaguar GR. Mk 1 succeeded the Phantom in the ground-attack role during 1975, and the UK-based Jaguars, belonging to the wing at Coltishall, are committed to mobile action. XX721 was one of the first to join No. 54 Squadron at Coltishall, and still serves with it. The squadron's rampant lion emblem and blue/yellow checks are seen on this aircraft.

In service with two RAF squadrons is the Aérospatiale/Westland Puma HC. Mk 1. XW229 joined No. 33 Squadron initially at Odiham but transferred later to No. 230 Squadron, going with that squadron to Gütersloh in 1981.

also from the Far East, where only residual elements remained. Inevitably these withdrawals were followed by corresponding changes in the long-range scheduled services provided by Air Support Command and, after 1972, by No. 46 Group; as a result, by the mid-1970s the main destinations still being served were Hong Kong, North America and the two Gulf stations, Salalah and Masirah.

But although the overseas scheduled services were being progressively curtailed, other commitments were still taking the transport force to many different parts of the world. For the Britannias, the major commitment of 1966 was ferrying oil from Kenya to Zambia, the result of Rhodesia's decision to cut off supplies and so to escalate the conflict with Britain which had begun with the Rhodesian declaration of unilateral independence in November 1965; in all, the Britannias flew over 10,000 hours in the course of a year-long operation. In 1967 another major operation was mounted, on this occasion to complete the evacuation of Aden, and four years later similar operations were needed to assist with the withdrawals from Bahrain and the Far East. In 1971 again, aircraft were engaged in evacuating British civilians during the war between India and Pakistan. At the same time, in response to a threat from Guatemala, troops and equipment were flown to British Honduras, the future Belize, in an operation which was to become a continuing trooping and resupply commitment, with Harriers and Puma helicopters also detached to support the ground forces. Other overseas tasks included the rotation of Gurkha troops between Hong Kong and Katmandu; a programme of long-range training flights; frequent involvement in relief operations in areas as far apart as Algiers, Bangladesh, Cambodia and Nepal; and in 1970 a major exercise, codenamed 'Bersatu Padu', in which most of the transport force was involved, the objective being to test Britain's ability to come to the aid of Malaysia and Singapore should they be threatened.

Commitment shifts to NATO

But while Britain was withdrawing from her overseas bases, her commitment to the defence of the NATO area steadily increased. As a result, the pattern of tasking which the transport force had developed before 1967 was progressively adapted to a European setting. A growing commitment was routine troop rotation within the NATO area, with flights to bases in Germany and to the Mediterranean stations (Gibraltar, Malta and Cyprus); from 1969 the transport force was also increasingly involved in supporting British forces in Northern Ireland. In addition, it lifted troops and equipment to and from exercises, including those mounted by the two mobile forces which had been set up to

provide rapid reinforcement of any area under threat and which it would support in time of war: the United Kingdom Mobile Force (UKMF) and NATO's Allied Command Europe Mobile Force (AMF), both with land and air contingents. Significantly, the offensive support and helicopter elements of No. 38 Group were now assigned or earmarked for assignment to one or other of these forces; the RAF's strategic and tactical transport elements, however, were not formally assigned to NATO until 1976.

Deployment exercises

Meanwhile, the Hercules aircraft were further developing the techniques of transport support, in particular day and night flying in large tactical formations, bad weather penetration, scatter procedures and fighter affiliation. For the Wessex and Puma helicopters there was a training programme which included not only the basic techniques of helicopter support, airlifting troops and stores, paratrooping and supply dropping, and transporting the Army's 105-mm howitzers and other external loads, but also rapid deployment exercises and navigation training flights across Europe.

Consequently, while many of the exercises mounted in support of NATO during these years were designed to deploy forces to areas under threat, the emphasis in others was primarily on airborne assault. The purpose of Exercise 'Arctic Express' in 1970, for example, was to test the deployment of the AMF to northern Norway under winter conditions. In contrast, 'Ruby Signet' in 1972 was the largest airborne assault exercise mounted since the end of World War II and in-

Below right: The only UK-based Harrier squadron, No. 1 Squadron at Wittering, is committed to a high degree of mobility. It is part of the ACE mobile force attached to NATO and in time of war would operate in northern Norway where these GR. Mk 3s are seen on exercise with temporary Arctic camouflage. The squadron has also provided a detachment for the forces in Belize and operated from HMS Hermes during the Falklands campaign.

In 1966 the functions of several RAF transport types were vested in the Lockheed Hercules, 66 of which were bought from the USA. At first two wings of these classic transports were established in Britain, together with No. 48 Squadron at Singapore and No. 70 Squadron in Cyprus. With the reduction of overseas bases the whole Hercules force has been concentrated in four squadrons at Lyneham, whence they operate world-wide.

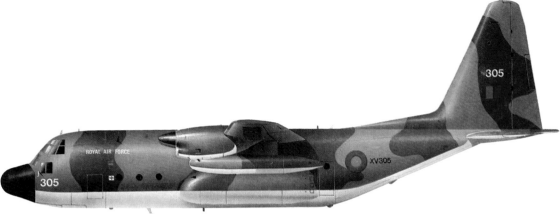

Thirty of the fleet of 66 Lockheed Hercules aircraft in the RAF have been and are being converted to C.Mk 3s by putting two extending 'plugs' into the fuselage, thus enabling longer freight loads and greater weights to be lifted. XV305 is one such C.Mk 3 and serves with the transport wing at Lyneham.

Two of No. 1 Squadron's Harrier GR.Mk 3s are seen operating over the jungle in Belize, Central America. A permanent unit, No. 1417 Flight, has now taken over the Harrier duties there, crews being detached to it from all the Harrier squadrons.

closures imminent, some reduction in the transport force had become a virtual certainty. The first steps were taken in 1975 when the Britannia and Comet squadrons were disbanded, along with one of the Hercules squadrons, No. 36, the Andover squadron and No. 46 Group itself. No. 38 Group then assumed control of all remaining forces. Further disbandments followed in 1976: the Belfast squadron, the Hunter wing at Wittering and a second Hercules squadron, No. 48. Later changes included the re-equipping of No. 41 Squadron with Jaguars and its redeployment to Coltishall, and the transfer of one of the Puma squadrons, No. 230, to RAF Germany in October 1980. So, by the end of that year the strength of the various elements now included in No. 38 Group had fallen to 145 aircraft.

For the force which remained, the tasks continued much as before. The loss of the Belfasts had deprived it of its heavy-lift capability and made the transporting of helicopters considerably more difficult. But the VC10s, with their cruising speed of over 500 mph (805 km/h) and range of some 3,700 miles (5955 km) carrying 150 passengers, plus the multi-role Hercules still provided substantial strategic and tactical mobility, as was demonstrated in the Agila operation of 1979–80 during which Britain's monitoring force was deployed to Rhodesia to oversee new elections and was subsequently maintained in the field by a force of Hercules and Pumas.

volved 33 Hercules flying in stream formation to drop two battalions of paratroops in Denmark; later assault exercises involved 36 aircraft flying at low level to dropping zones in Turkish Thrace and another 36 aircraft formation dropping elements of the UKMF in northern Germany.

However, with the withdrawal from overseas bases largely complete by 1975, and with further

RAF Operations in the Falkland Islands

Significant changes have been apparent in the structure and numerical strength of the RAF as Britain has transformed itself from a global power into a fully paid-up member of Europe. As possessions gained independence from the Crown and protectorates assumed responsibility for their own defence, so the RAF's overseas presence shrank to a mere shadow of its former self, and by the dawn of the present decade a flight of Harriers in Belize represented the total of RAF combat aircraft based outside Europe.

Not unnaturally, Britain's armed forces have been organised, trained and equipped to meet the threat of Soviet aggression, but when British soil was occupied by foreign troops in April 1982, the attack came from a completely unexpected direction and achieved the surprise normally only granted to generals in their wildest dreams. The enemy was not the USSR but Argentina, and the battlefield was 8,000 miles (12875 km) from London

in a 'little England' blasted by the harsh, damp winds of the South Atlantic.

The Falkland Islands and their dependent territories, though thoroughly British, remained as the dimly-remembered subjects of school geography lessons to the majority of those living in the United Kingdom until they were snatched by seaborne forces on 2 April. However, to the citizens of Argentina, 400 miles (645 km) away to the west, they are regarded as usurped territory which was to be liberated from the colonial occupiers at whatever cost, and fierce pride conveniently overlooked the fact that the islands had been British long before Argentina existed.

Credit for returning the islands to British rule goes in no small part to the soldiers and sailors of the South Atlantic Task Force, the first elements of which left Portsmouth on 5 April. BAe Sea Harriers and helicopters of the Fleet Air Arm were of incalculable value in offensive, defensive and

A mixture of Royal Navy Sea Harrier FRS.Mk 1s and Royal Air Force Harrier GR.Mk 3s grouped on the deck of HMS *Hermes*. The GR.Mk 3s provided much-needed support for the ground forces whilst the FRS.Mk 1s kept the Argentine air forces at bay.

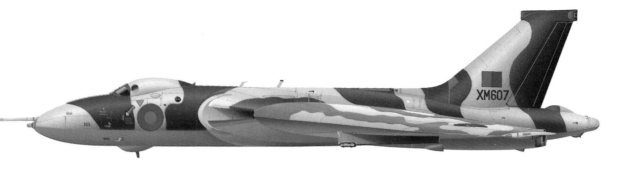

Avro Vulcan B.Mk 2 XM607 was built in 1963 as part of the batch of Vulcan bombers to be equipped with underwing Skybolt stand-off missiles. At the time of the Falklands campaign it was with No. 44 Squadron and was modified, using the wing points for the Skybolt, with two underwing pylons for carrying ECM jammers and missiles. Thus equipped, it flew three of the bombing missions on the Falklands, the first and the last being two of them.

At RAF Wittering, home of the Harriers, aircraft were quickly modified to carry two Sidewinder AAMs on the outer wing pylons for air combat. They were then taken by pilots of No. 1 Squadron, some by sea on *Atlantic Conveyor*, some flying with flight-refuelling to join HMS *Hermes* and operate, in the ground-attack role, in the fighting over the Falklands.

BAe Harriers, BAe Nimrods, Lockheed Hercules, BAe VC10s, BAe Victors and Westland Sea Kings augmented and sustained the Task Force's efforts, whilst at home the Ministry of Defence, the manufacturers and research establishments worked in unison and at unprecedented speed to modify aircraft for new roles and fitments.

April was a month of feverish behind-the-scenes activity as the RAF geared itself for the operations which lay ahead, whilst the diplomats at the United Nations and elsewhere attempted to find a peaceful solution. Mediation was of no avail, however, and at 04.46, Falklands time, on 1 May, a stick of 21 1,000-lb (454-kg) bombs rained down on Port Stanley airfield from a Vulcan B.Mk 2 to mark the start of a hard-fought campaign to oust the invader.

The planning and effort devoted to that Vulcan raid, and four successful sorties which followed, ranks as a major achievement in the annals of air warfare, not least because the entire Vulcan fleet was less than three months away from the scrapyard when its 25-year service career was hastily extended for participation in Operation 'Corporate'— the regaining of the Falklands. Running-down of the Vulcan force was put smartly into reverse, and ground crews at Waddington worked with speed to renovate the unused inflight-refuelling system and replace bomb-bay fittings with mounts suitable for conventional weapons.

Five Vulcans were prepared for use in the Falklands, additional modifications including a Carousel inertial navigation system, a home-made weapons pylon attached on wing strongpoints originally incorporated in the airframe for Skybolt missiles in the early 1960s, and an undersurface coat of dark sea grey paint for additional camouflage effect. A similar number of crews was given brief inflight-refuelling experience and practice in dropping 'iron' bombs, and on 29 April, two Vulcans deployed to Ascension Island to await orders for their first mission.

Ascension was a key element in Operation

support operations, the Royal Marines and Army Air Corps also adding their light helicopters to the Force once a landing had been made at San Carlos on 21 May. At sea, naval personnel endured the attacks of Argentine fighter-bombers and missiles, spending endless hours at action stations and servicing aircraft in all weathers, whilst on land the army pressed home its attack to ultimate victory, aided by prodigious feats of endurance on the part of each man and the clandestine SAS activities behind enemy lines.

The RAF contribution, though small in terms of numbers employed in the front line, was a significant aspect of the events which led to surrender of the Argentine forces on 14 June. Strike, surveillance, support and SAR missions by BAe Vulcans,

Sitting at dispersal on Wideawake Airfield, Ascension Island is a Victor K.Mk 2 of No. 57 Squadron, miles from its home base of Marham in Norfolk.

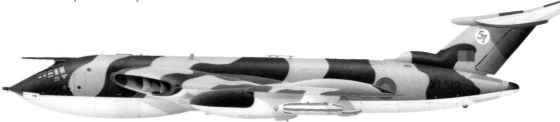

The Handley Page Victor K.Mk 2 was instrumental in making RAF operations to the Falklands feasible. Aircraft from both Nos 55 and 57 Squadrons (this aircraft is from the latter) were based at Wideawake Airfield, Ascension Island and flew many times their normal number of sorties to refuel Hercules, Vulcans, Harriers and Nimrods to enable them to fly the great ranges needed for operations.

'Corporate': it is a tiny island half-way to the Falklands, dominated by a US staging airfield bestowed with the unusual name of Wideawake. Normally handling an average of a little over one aircraft movement per day, the airfield saw no less than 400 in the same period at the height of Falklands-related activity, with up to 30 aircraft on the ground at any time. Without such a base, bombing, reconnaissance and transport flights on behalf of the Task Force would have been out of the question, not that they were an easy undertaking with this 'forward' base still some 3,900 miles (6275 km) from the target.

A little over an hour before midnight on 30 April, the two Vulcans (one of them a reserve) strenuously lifted off from Wideawake at 6,000 lb (2722 kg) above normal maximum weight, accompanied by their first wave of Victor K.Mk 2 tankers. Both carried conventional bombs and an AN/ALQ-101 ECM pod on the starboard wing pylon, but when the primary aircraft suffered a pressurisation failure early in the mission, the reserve aircraft (XM607, captained by Flight Lieutenant Martin Withers) proceeded with Operation 'Black Buck 1', the bombing of Port Stanley airfield.

Descending after its sixth airborne refuelling to a mere 250 ft (76 m) above the featureless ocean for the last 300 miles (480 km) the Vulcan then pulled up to 10,000 ft (3050 m) before dropping its bombs exactly on target, the first landing in the very centre of the runway and others damaging installations. After a further refuelling, the Vulcan landed at Wideawake more than 16 hours after its departure, establishing a world bombing sortie endurance record which is unlikely to be beaten.

That the Argentine ruling junta publicly denied that the raid had taken place is sufficient proof of the psychological effect which it had on the occupying force. Though transport aircraft were still able to make limited use of Port Stanley, if willing to run the risk of interception by Sea Harriers, the Argentinians were forced to redouble their defensive efforts and were dissuaded from basing high-performance jets on the islands, much to the relief of the Task Force.

Further Vulcan raids

Two similar raids were accomplished successfully by the same Vulcan on 4 May and 11 June, but different missions were also undertaken to blind the radar 'eyes' on the Falklands. For this, Vulcan B.Mk 2 XM597 was fitted with a pair of AGM-45A Shrike anti-radar missiles on each of its two wing pylons and extra fuel tanks in the bomb bay. The original intention of using Martels had been shelved when the USA agreed to supply Britain with the Shrike and numerous other items of equipment and supplies. Operating by night from Wideawake on 1 June, the aircraft was forced to loiter over the islands for some 45 minutes before acquiring and attacking a TPS-43 radar installation, although a less successful, but equally hazardous, mission on 3 June nearly ended in disaster when the inflight-refuelling probe broke during

Considerable modifications had to be made to the Hawker Siddeley Nimrods of No. 18 (Coastal) Group, Strike Command to enable them to fly maritime reconnaissance patrols over the South Atlantic. Most significant was the fitting of refuelling probes so that they could refuel from Victor tankers. Two such Nimrods are seen awaiting the next sortie on Ascension Island's Wideawake Airfield.

Harrier GR.Mk 3s of No. 1 Squadron from Wittering were speedily modified for service in the Falkland Islands campaign. Alterations to the radio and navigation fit were made but the major modification was to fit Sidewinder AAMs on the outer pylons.

Seen aboard HMS *Hermes* in the South Atlantic are three of No. 1 Squadron's Harrier GR.Mk 3s lined up for operation against ground targets in the Falklands. The nearest aircraft carries laser-guided bombs which were used to accurate effect in the last few days of the campaign. The other aircraft are one of *Hermes'* Sea Kings and five Sea Harriers of 809 Squadron of the Royal Navy.

contact with a Victor on the homeward leg, and the Vulcan made an emergency landing at Rio de Janeiro with just five minutes' fuel remaining in its tanks.

Refuelling the Vulcans on their epoch-making flights was merely one of the many tasks given to the Victor K.Mk 2s of Nos 55 and 57 Squadrons, which deployed more than half their 23 aircraft from Marham to Wideawake, the figure reaching 70 per cent at times. No fewer than 14 sorties by 10 tankers were required to place one Vulcan over the Falklands, the Victors refuelling each other as well as their 'customer' in order to locate one almost fully-laden supplier 300 miles (480 km) north of the Falklands on the outbound leg, and abeam Rio de Janeiro on the homeward sector.

Victors additionally refuelled Nimrods and Hercules, but had earlier turned their attentions briefly to reconnaissance, the first such sortie taking place on 20 April when a 14 hour 20 minute surveillance flight was made to the Falklands dependency of South Georgia (800 miles/1285 km farther out into the Atlantic) which had also been occupied. Both photographic and maritime radar reconnaissance flights were undertaken by specially modified Victors (using equipment taken from recently-retired Vulcan B.Mk 2MRRs in the latter instance) before probe-equipped Nimrods became available, the converted tankers performing useful

work in the pre- and post-attack surveillance role.

Some 3,000 hours in almost 600 sorties were flown by Ascension-based Victors during hostilities, whilst USAF Boeing KC-135As (modified with a 'hose and basket' at the ends of their booms) stood in at home for the absent refuellers from 18 May onwards. Additional capacity was provided by conversion of six Vulcans to K.Mk 2 standard and four Hercules to C.Mk 1Ks, the first of each version flying on 18 June and 8 June respectively, and neither seeing operational service. The Hercules were nevertheless dispatched to Ascension and Port Stanley for support of transport flights into the Falklands after hostilities had ended (a further two C.Mk 1Ks being added early in 1983), and the Vulcans were concentrated in No. 50 Squadron at Waddington to back up the UK-based refuelling force pending the introduction of VC10 tankers.

Several British aircraft received their baptism of fire in the Falklands war, but none achieved the acclaim so deservedly accorded to the Sea Harrier FRS.Mk 1 and the RAF's Harrier GR.Mk 3. The naval aircraft carried out the greater proportion of sorties (some 1,200 compared with 125) and destroyed 20 Argentine aircraft, plus three probables – including 16 and one probable with AIM-9L Sidewinder missiles, but the Harrier GR.Mk 3s undertook the bulk of the ground-attack work after their arrival, freeing more Sea Harriers for air-defence duties.

As the sole operational Harrier unit based in the UK, No. 1 Squadron at Wittering was automatically selected for service in the Falklands, and whilst its pilots practised carrier take-offs on the 'ski-jump' ramp at Yeovilton and engaged in mock combat with French Dassault Mirages and Dassault Super Etendards to simulate possible future engagements, aircraft were cleared to fire Sidewinders and Royal Navy 2-in (51-mm) rockets, and readied (as far as possible) for flying in the corroding salt air.

In a record-breaking 9 hour 15 minute endurance flight for the type, nine Harrier GR.Mk 3s were inflight-refuelled by Victors when they positioned at Ascension between 3 and 5 May, and three days later six embarked on the chartered container ship *Atlantic Conveyor* for the long journey south, leaving the remainder to provide defensive cover for Ascension Island in the event of an Argentine attack. A further five aircraft arrived at Wideawake in later delivery flights, and eventually all 14 were deployed to the Falklands (four of them too late to see action) after Phantoms were stationed there for air-defence duties on the vital staging-post.

RAF Harrier's first mission

The first six Harriers transferred to HMS *Hermes*, one of the two Task Force carriers, on 18–19 May, joining the already overcrowded complement of Sea Harriers and Sea Kings, and it was from here that they launched their first mission, a successful attack on a fuel dump at Fox Bay, on 20 May. Harrier GR.Mk 3s were at a disadvantage to their navalised brothers in several respects, not the least of which was the inability to align their inertial navigation system on a rolling deck. Although portable equipment was rapidly produced to alleviate the problem, the aid of Sea Harriers was enlisted to guide their RAF counterparts to a pre-arranged landfall, and thereafter, pilots used the 'Mk 1' navigation kit of eyeball, map and compass to find their targets.

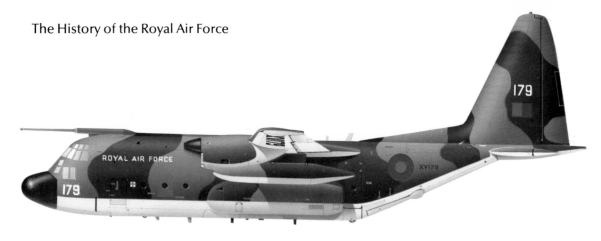

The Lockheed Hercules C.Mk 1 was the RAF's transport aircraft which did so much in making the Falkland Islands episode possible. Detached from the Lyneham wing, crews from Nos 24, 30, 47 and 70 Squadrons flew supply missions with airdrops to the troops, devised a method of picking-up messages akin to the old army co-operation days of the 1930s – and all this having learned to flight-refuel from Victor tankers until their own Hercules tankers were fitted out. These 22 aircraft still maintain the air bridge into Stanley Airfield two years after the war. XV179 was the second aircraft modified to C.Mk 1P standard.

Land-based operations considerably eased navigation difficulties when, early in June, Harrier GR.Mk 3s began flying from an 800-ft (244-m) aluminium planking airstrip at San Carlos, the scene of the initial British landing. The Harrier GR.Mk 3s, although hastily wired up for Sidewinders, did not fit these missiles to the wing pylons for operational sorties, but on the final two days of the conflict they made the first successful drops with laser-guided bombs, target designation being provided by troops on the ground.

Low-level support missions against heavily-defended targets resulted in the loss of three Harrier GR.Mk 3s to missiles and gunfire (on 21, 26 and 30 May) but all aircrew escaped, as did the pilot of a Harrier GR.Mk 3 which was seriously damaged in a landing accident on the San Carlos strip after an engine failure on 9 June. (In fact, the only RAF casualty of Operation 'Corporate' was a forward air controller lost in a helicopter crash at sea.)

It must also be noted that seven RAF pilots were flying with the Royal Navy's Sea Harrier force in the South Atlantic, and one of these, Flight Lieutenant Paul Barton of No. 801 Squadron, shot down the first Argentine aircraft of the conflict: a Mirage on 1 May. Harrier GR.Mk 3s also destroyed three Argentine helicopters: a Chinook and a Puma by gunfire near Mount Kent on 21 May, and a further Puma in a cluster-bomb (CBU) attack in the same area five days later.

One of the least publicised aspects of the Falklands war was the work of the Nimrod maritime reconnaissance aircraft which operated from Wideawake, flying in excess of 1,000 hours on patrol in almost 150 sorties. Nimrod MR.Mk 1s of No. 42 Squadron, normally based at St Mawgan, mounted regular patrols in support of the task force from the moment it left port, but on 12 April they were replaced by the Nimrod MR.Mk 2 versions from the Kinloss Wing (Nos 120, 201 and 206 Squadrons) with their more effective surveillance equipment, including Searchwater radar.

The requirement for Nimrods to penetrate farther south on surveillance, SAR and mail-dropping tasks prompted installation of an inflight-refuelling probe above the nose and a small ventral finlet to counterbalance aerodynamic effects. As with the numerous other modification programmes undertaken at the same time, this was accomplished at breathtaking speed (three weeks, compared with a peacetime schedule which would have taken up to two years) and the first refuelled sortie was flown from Ascension Island on 9 May. Thereafter, Nimrod MR.Mk 2Ps (for Probe) regularly flew sorties of up to 19 hours, their duties including patrol of the Falklands exclusion zone within easy reach of enemy fighters and co-ordination of the Vulcan raids. A total of 16 Nimrods received the inflight-refuelling modifications.

For the first time, Nimrods were fitted with wing pylons to carry four self-defence Sidewinders (rushed from the United States), offensive armament in the weapons bay including Harpoon anti-ship missiles (also US-supplied), Stingray torpedoes and conventional bombs for attacking targets of opportunity. It transpired, however, that none of these was used.

In its largest re-supply effort since the Berlin Airlift of 1948, the RAF called on the services of the Lyneham Transport Wing's Hercules C.Mk 1s and stretched C.Mk 3s (of Nos 24, 30, 47 and 70 Squadrons), the VC10s of Brize Norton's No. 10 Squadron, and civilian Boeing 707s and Shorts Belfasts (the

Captained by Squadron Leader Dickie Langworthy, the one surviving Chinook HC.Mk 1 (ZA718) of No. 18 Squadron was busily involved in the campaign. Here it is flying supplies ship to shore in San Carlos Water.

With the battle over, Stanley airstrip was quickly pressed into use by the RAF, even though it was less than the best. The daily Hercules from Ascension is seen landing on the runway edged by seven damaged Pucarás and a Bell 212 helicopter of the Argentine air force.

At first the anti-submarine and maritime reconnaissance role over the South Atlantic was flown by Nimrod MR.Mk 1s of No. 42 Squadron but, after modifications had been incorporated in certain MR.Mk 2s (to make them MR.Mk 2Ps) the task was taken over by No. 206 Squadron, one such an aircraft being XV239, here showing the nose probe, the ventral stabilising fin and the tailplane finlets.

Dispersed amongst the Victors on Wideawake airfield are three Harrier GR.Mk 3s of No. 1 Squadron, RAF. These provided airfield defence duties until replaced by Phantoms when they joined other members of the squadron aboard HMS *Hermes* for direct action over the Falklands.

last-mentioned, of course, being ex-RAF equipment). The initial detachment of eight Hercules arrived at Wideawake the day after the Argentine invasion, their first duties being forward-positioning of stores for the Task Force to collect on its journey southwards. Thereafter, a continuous stream of essential spares, mail and personnel was maintained by the hard-worked transports in the course of over 500 sorties (17,000 hours of flying, including 13,000 hours by the Hercules) up to the cease fire, carrying 7,000 tons of supplies, 5,500 passengers, nearly 100 vehicles and over 20 helicopters.

Parachute drops to the Task Force, and ultimately over the Falkland Islands, were made possible by addition of inflight-refuelling probes to the Hercules, and from 16 May onwards, the aircraft regularly flew sorties lasting some 26 hours, the record (thanks to a strong wind) being 28 hours 3 minutes. Speed incompatibilities with the Victor were overcome by the novel means of refuelling during a steep descent to allow the Hercules to pick up momentum, a distinctly 'hairy' procedure employed until the Hercules C.Mk 1K tankers became available. Sixteen Hercules converted to receive fuel in flight were designated C.Mk 1Ps, although when some added further fuel capacity in the hold to gain another 800–900 miles (1285–1450 km) of range, they were known as C.Mk 1P(LR)s.

With a hose unit protruding from the sealed rear ramp, plus a nose probe, the Hercules C.Mk 1K aircraft relieved the Victors at Ascension of their transport support flights, and even after Stanley airfield was reopened (the first Hercules touchingdown on 24 June) they were still much in demand. With no suitable diversion airfield near the Falklands, each Hercules flying to the islands had to be provided with tanker back-up in case bad weather forced it to return, and thus every trip was regarded as a nonstop round flight.

Newest of the RAF aircraft to be employed in Operation 'Corporate' was the Boeing Vertol Chinook HC.Mk 1 transport helicopter, five of which were deployed, including one retained at Ascension Island. The force, provided by No. 18 Squadron from Odiham, was quartered at a stroke when three Chinooks were lost in the Exocet missile attack on the container ship *Atlantic Conveyor*, but the solitary survivor performed invaluable work in supporting the advance of British troops to Port Stanley, on one occasion carrying 81 soldiers instead of its normal load of 30. With their personal and maintenance equipment lost, the Chinook air and ground crew used their ingenuity to keep the aircraft operational, the tally of 1,530 troops, 600 tons of cargo and 650 prisoners carried between 27 May and 23 June bearing ample witness to their success.

Ascension was also the base for a single RAF Sea King HAR.Mk 3 from 'B' Flight of No. 202 Squadron at Brawdy, this assisting with shore-to-ship transport of stores when not required for its primary role of SAR – such as the six-hour sortie

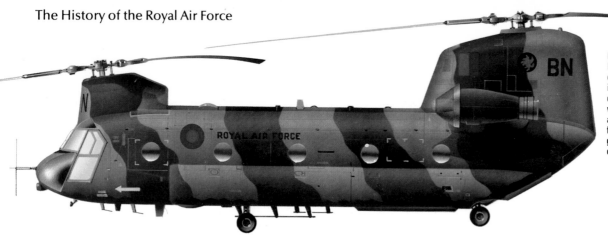

Four Boeing Vertol Chinook HC.Mk 1s of No. 18 Squadron were embarked on *Atlantic Conveyor* for duty in the Falklands. Three of these were destroyed when the *Atlantic Conveyor* was hit by Exocets, but the fourth was airborne. This aircraft, ZA718 'BN', flew magnificently in support of the ground troops through the remainder of the campaign.

to recover a seriously ill sailor from a Task Force vessel. Following the conflict, No. 202's 'C' Flight transferred from Coltishall to Port Stanley to maintain a permanent SAR detachment, its three helicopters exchanging their traditional bright yellow SAR finish for a coat of dark grey.

Many other RAF formations contributed to success in the South Atlantic, from the Rapier SAM-equipped No. 63 Squadron of the RAF Regiment, which deployed its missiles from Gütersloh, Germany, to protect the beach-head at San Carlos, through supply, bomb-disposal and communications branches to medical staff. VC10s and Hercules undertook 57 medevac flights between April and early August, carrying 738 patients, including 568 in 11 VC10 sorties from Montevideo in Uruguay.

The return of an uneasy peace to the Falklands saw British forces consolidating their garrison, one of the first priorities being extension of Port Stanley's runway from 4,100 to 6,000 ft (1250 to 1830 m) to allow operations by high-performance aircraft. This was accomplished by an army team laying aluminium matting, and the first of several No. 29 Squadron McDonnell Douglas Phantom FGR.Mk 2s touched down at RAF Stanley on 17 October to strengthen the islands' air defences in conjunction with the retained Harriers of No. 1 Squadron. Other changes included installation of the Sea King HAR.Mk 3; a detachment of five Chinooks of the newly-formed No. 7 Squadron as replacements for No. 18; and two of the initial four Hercules C.Mk 1K tankers to refuel incoming and

outgoing air traffic. SAM defences of the airfield were assumed by Rapiers of the Brüggen-based No. 37 Squadron, RAF Regiment, when No. 63 returned to Germany in September.

Numerous items of British military equipment saw operational service for the first time in 1982, and the lessons learned in the Falklands will undoubtedly improve their efficiency in any future combat. However, the modifications and changes of procedure which resulted from experiences in the South Atlantic are peripheral issues compared with the central lesson imparted by Operation 'Corporate': the efficiency of military operations is considerably improved when freed of the dead hand of bureaucracy.

During the Falklands war, the RAF collaborated closely with its civilian contractors to embody a multitude of modifications in aircraft. These were achieved in a fraction of the timescale expected in peacetime; usually at lower cost; and, most importantly of all, they worked. Application of these principles to new projects in future years could yield similar benefits for the RAF, for it has again been established that an unrealistic proportion of a programme's cost and duration is expended on attempting to achieve the last few percent of operational efficiency, without greater prospect of eventual success. A brilliant performance in the Falklands has strengthened the RAF's claim to the best combat equipment which Britain can provide; the lessons learned there indicate that this need not be the most costly, or the longest in the making.

Indicative of the winter conditions in the Falklands is this shot of a No. 1 Squadron Harrier GR.Mk 3 plugged in and ready to go from a strip on the Falklands. It is configured in the air defence role with two Sidewinder AAMs.

The RAF Today and Tomorrow

Throughout its distinguished history, the RAF has sought to maintain the highest standards both in personnel and equipment, its performance in peace and war bearing adequate testimony to its achievement of this ideal. Though standards are unchanged with the passage of time, both the men and aircraft serving today's RAF are, superficially at least, far removed from their counterparts in the early days.

For its size, the modern combat aircraft is undoubtedly the most sophisticated engine of war yet devised by man. Its conception in the forefront of many sciences demands equal technological expertise on the part of those who are to fly and maintain it in operational service, and whilst intelligence and initiative remain, as always, the prime prerequisite for wearing the light blue, the 1980s are, more than any other decade has been, the age of the scientific airman.

The immense cost of perfecting a new aircraft design, allied to the ever-quickening pace of avionics development, has also led to a new breed of aircraft in the air force of today. The time is now long past when an annual pilgrimage to Farnborough would be rewarded by first sight of one or more new aircraft types shortly to enter service. Now, prototypes are acquaintances of some standing long before their production successors are seen wearing squadron insignia. Once in service, the operational career of an aircraft is mapped in decades, rather than years, improvement in capability being gained through installation of new engines and equipment, in place of retirement and replacement. Cost, too, has been the raison d'être of new design and manufacturing companies for the RAF's front-line aircraft: SEPECAT and Panavia are international concerns formed to

Epitomising the skill and professionalism of the RAF, the famous 'Red Arrows' aerobatic team of the Central Flying School fly their British Aerospace Hawk T.Mk 1s over the top of a loop.

The aircraft of the 1980s and 1990s, as far as the RAF is concerned, are the Panavia Tornado GR.Mk 1 and F.Mk 2. The GR.Mk 1 is shown here, and this version is already in service with three squadrons of Strike Command. The aircraft has swing-wings (here fully swept) and carries all its offensive load on external hardpoints.

share the financial burden and to pool acquired technology for the mutual benefit of several European nations.

This international outlook extends to the RAF's primary role – participation with Britain's other armed services in the combined forces of the North Atlantic Treaty Organization (NATO). Most closely associated with the European commitment is RAF Germany, comprising a dozen squadrons of strike and interceptor aircraft and helicopters, but the majority of home-based units are also declared to NATO for overseas 'rapid intervention' deployment, transport, or defence of the United Kingdom itself. In the event of a new European war, as in the last, Britain will become the rearward supply base, holding 40 per cent of NATO's forces. Long-range radar coverage and far-reaching all-weather interceptors (exemplified by the BAe Nimrod AEW.Mk 3 and Panavia Tornado F.Mk 2) are thus a vital necessity to secure the home base from bomber attack.

Outside NATO, the RAF's former global deployment has virtually evaporated, leaving a mere handful of aircraft permanently based outside Britain and Germany. Withdrawal from the Gulf states by the early 1970s has more recently been followed by abandonment of Malta, from which Nimrod MR.Mk 1s and photo-reconnaissance BAC Canberras were removed during 1977-8, and even Gibraltar now has no resident squadron, in order not to upset the Spaniards. Only the detachment of BAe Harriers and Aérospatiale/Westland Pumas in the central American country of Belize perpetuates Britain's long-established role as protecting power to smaller independent states, although helicopter squadrons in Cyprus and Hong Kong are assigned humanitarian and policing tasks appropriate to the particular demands of their areas and the Falklands garrison remains.

As always, the roles assigned to the RAF are not of its own making; rather, they are duties assigned by the government of the day in furtherance of policies it believes to be in the country's interests. Differences of opinion between the Chiefs of Staff and the government have occurred in the past, and doubtless will continue from time to time, but conjecture is invariably restricted to anticipated conflicts between the task given and the resources allocated by the government for the task's execution. Naturally, changes of political direction in Westminster have their effects on the armed forces, touching anything from a basic recruit's pay to the future of a multi-million pound equipment programme, and predictions of the shape of the RAF even half a dozen years hence hinge entirely on the verdict of the ballot box.

Political questions

Clearly, election of a government opposed to nuclear weapons and membership of NATO would bring fundamental changes in the RAF, whilst one perceiving no threat from the Soviet bloc would be unlikely to follow the Swedish and Swiss policy of well-armed neutrality. Neither of the main parliamentary parties can claim an unblemished record in its dealings with the RAF since the end of World War 2, particularly now that choice of equipment has become a political matter, rather than a subject left to the service to decide.

Governmental participation (stronger words might appropriately be used) in weapons selection has become more apparent as rocketing costs have forced collaboration with neighbouring countries, or even outright purchase of foreign equipment. Whether the motive is to buy British and so to save jobs, or to obtain from overseas and so to cut costs, political direction may be expected to increase rather than decline. Some evidence of this may perhaps be seen in the dramatic reversal of officially-expressed opinion on the McDonnell-Douglas AV-8B in the year before it was ordered as the Harrier GR.Mk 5, it being difficult to accept that a modification marginally improving the manoeuvrability was sufficient to reconcile the very different operational demands of the US Marines (to whose needs it was specifically tailored) and the RAF.

Despite the highly detailed reports of defence expenditure issued annually, the true cost of the RAF is difficult to determine with accuracy. Typically, however, taking the £15,743 million 1983-4 defence budget as an example, general purpose forces of the RAF are allocated £3,207 million, including £579 million for air defence, £922 million for strike, attack and reconnaissance, and £118 million for offensive support; but other units and research and development substantially increase the RAF's share of resources. A stringent review of defence spending conducted early in 1981 left the RAF virtually unscathed in terms of financial allocations, and adherence (almost) to the NATO-agreed target of annual 3 per cent increments in defence up to 1985-6 (and 1 per cent thereafter until 1991) will go some way towards dispelling the belief held in some quarters that the RAF is 'the world's best trained, worst equipped air force'.

Value for money

Although Britain spends a creditable 46 per cent of its defence budget actually on equipment (compared, for example, with only 23 per cent in Japan), every penny of this is needed to meet escalating costs. At £17.1 million, a single Tornado F.Mk 2 costs in apparent terms over a thousand times more than a World War 2 Spitfire, and even allowing for inflation, the additional sophistication of a Harrier over its Hawker Hunter F.Mk 6/FGA.Mk 9 predecessor produced a four-fold increase in real-term cost. Viewed against the background of a generally diminishing proportion of gross domestic product being devoted to defence (currently 5.5 per cent), the need is readily apparent for maximum use to be made of each item of equipment.

The 'value for money' theme was taken up by John Nott on his appointment as Defence Secretary early in 1981, resulting in the unusual occurrence of aircraft retirement programmes being accelerated whilst defence expenditure was actually on the increase. Throughout the armed forces, the aim is to ensure efficient functioning of complete weapons systems (if necessary by reducing the total number of systems), and the early decision to double the number of air-to-air missiles (AAMs) in stock implies that there may be some truth in the US opinion that European countries devote considerable resources to major items of equipment and then find themselves unable to provide the necessary ammunition and/or fuel to make them effective in anything but the shortest of conflicts. In the light of experience gained during the Falklands war, stocks of ammunition and other stores will be increased even further.

Indeed, fuel costs have become a principal expense over the last decade, the RAF having consumed 1,344,000 tonnes of oil products for all purposes in the 1981-2 financial year, whilst all three services used 1,000,000 tonnes of aviation fuel alone, the greatest proportion attributable to the RAF. Economies resulted in a reduction of pilots' flying hours until the start of the Falklands war, only the training programme being exempt, together with newly-qualified pilots on their first tour of operational duty. Uniformed strength of the RAF is now some 89,900 (including 5,300 women), but a further 12,700 civilian staff are directly employed, excluding those in research and support organisations.

The 1,800 aircraft in the RAF inventory include 650 of front-line status, and these are assigned to 59 squadrons, 17 operational conversion units (OCUs), 8 flying schools, 12 miscellaneous flights and 57 reserve training units, with equipment ranging from Tornado to the 'stick and string' Grasshopper glider. Successive amalgamations of groups and commands have left the RAF with only three principal elements: Strike Command and RAF Germany for offensive operations and air defence; and Support Command, with training, logistic and maintenance functions.

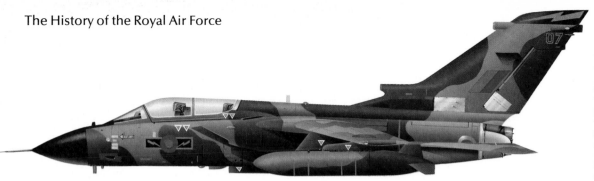

The second RAF squadron to receive the Panavia Tornado GR.Mk 1 was No. 617 Squadron, the successors to the original Dambusters squadron. This unit has been re-formed at RAF Marham and carries a red lightning flash on a black field as its new squadron insignia, shown here on aircraft ZA560, issued to the squadron in December, 1982. It carries the individual number '07' but the squadron has subsequently changed to carry the same aircraft letters as were used by the original Lancasters on the famous raid on the dams in May, 1943. ZA560 is now 'G' – using the same code letter as Guy Gibson's Lancaster.

Strike Command

Combining the proud traditions of the former Fighter and Bomber Commands, as exemplified by its motto 'Defend and Strike', Strike Command was formed on the RAF's 50th birthday, 1 April 1968, by the fusion of Nos 1 (Bomber) and 11 (Fighter) Groups, and established its headquarters at High Wycombe, from where, a quarter of a century earlier, 'Bomber' Harris directed the strategic assault on Germany. Gaining No. 18 (Maritime) Group the following year, it was further reinforced in 1972 by absorption of the short-lived Air Support Command in the form of No. 46 Group's transport aircraft and the fighter-support element of No. 38 Group (combined under the latter's title), although No. 90 (Signals) Group was shed simultaneously. Strike Command is tasked with long-range interdiction and strike using conventional and nuclear weapons; strategic and tactical reconnaissance; airborne early warning; strategic and tactical support for all three services; maritime reconnaissance and strike, plus anti-submarine warfare; and air defence of the UK, overseas bases and the Royal Navy's fleet.

Since April 1975, Strike Command's 45 squadrons have been allocated to NATO's Supreme Allied Commander Europe (SACEUR), some having a dual assignment. SACEUR's Strategic Reserve (Air), or SRR(A), comprises one Harrier and three SEPECAT Jaguar squadrons, plus elements of the USAF's 3rd Air Force based in Britain, although the Harrier unit is also dedicated to Allied Command Europe Mobile Force (AMF), together with half a squadron of Pumas. One Jaguar squadron is alternatively allocated to the United Kingdom Mobile Force, alongside more Pumas and Boeing Vertol Chinooks.

Popularly termed 'fire brigade' forces, AMF and UKMF are equipped for rapid deployment anywhere within the NATO area from Norway and Denmark to Italy, Greece and Turkey. Their dissimilarity lies in national composition, for whilst the UKMF is by definition wholly a United Kingdom unit (with ground elements mainly comprising 6 Field Force of the British Army), the AMF is an integrated international grouping whose very presence in a threatened member country serves to underline the unity of NATO.

From headquarters at Upavon, No. 1 Group administers the RAF's over-land strike, inflight refuelling, reconnaissance and transport forces, having taken over control of the 'mobility' units of the former No. 38 Group on November 1983. Major changes are taking place within No. 1 Group, of which the most profound is the working-up of its three Tornado GR.Mk 1 squadrons.

The story of how the RAF came to receive the Tornado may best be described as an affair 'on the rebound' which culminated in a happy marriage. In 1967, the UK was teamed with France in the design of an Anglo-French Variable Geometry aircraft (logically enough known as the 'AFVG'), whilst the Federal Republic of Germany and the United States were working on a V/STOL strike aircraft codenamed (what else?) 'US/FRG'. Almost simultaneously, the French and Americans withdrew from their respective projects, but it did not take long for the two jilted partners (Messerschmitt-Bölkow-Blohm and BAC) to come together in a new programme in which they were joined by Belgium, Canada, the Netherlands and Italy.

Panavia Aircraft GmbH was established in Munich on 26 March 1969 to manage design and construction of a Multi-Role Combat Aircraft (MRCA), and after the inevitable drop-outs, Britain, West Germany and Italy remained, represented by their aircraft firms BAC, MBB and Aeritalia. Programme leadership was awarded to MBB by reason of the German requirement for the largest proportion of production, but the FRG's quantity of 700 was reduced, first to 420, then to 324 (212 for the Luftwaffe and 112 for the Bundesmarine), compared with the RAF need for 220 strike and 165 interceptor versions, and the Italian order for 100 strike aircraft which were initially to have been single-seat variants.

Courageously, Panavia opted for a completely new engine for the MRCA, and thus was born the Turbo Union RB.199 reheated turbofan, currently rated at 16,920-lb (7675-kg) thrust in its Mk 103 form. Even the fuselage-mounted 27-mm cannon were specially designed by Mauser. The project moved smoothly through the 1970s, passing its second milestone on 14 August 1974 with the initial flight of the first of nine prototype and six pre-series test aircraft. From the outset of flight trials, it was obvious that the Tornado was 'a winner' – an opinion shared by several high-ranking air force officers from non-participating countries who have flown the aircraft.

The hope of the future

NATO has been criticised for its lack of weapon standardisation, but the Tornado neatly solves the problem by carrying every tactical weapon used by Britain, West Germany and Italy on three twin hardpoints beneath the fuselage, two tandem inboard wing pylons and two single outer pylons. Capable of lifting up to 16,000 lb (7258 kg) of stores, the Tornado is able to deliver its ordnance with pinpoint accuracy in all weathers thanks to an avionics fit more comprehensive than that of any other tactical aircraft. For low-level flying to evade radar acquisition, the Tornado is equipped with terrain-following radar which can guide the aircraft, completely 'blind', over ground contours. Similar aerodynamic ingenuity has provided the aircraft with Mach 2 performance at high level, allied to a remarkable short take-off and landing run, imparted by slats and double-slotted flaps in the variable-geometry wing, and augmented by thrust reversers incorporated in the variable-profile exhaust nozzles.

Each nation's Tornados are being assembled locally, the first of 644 IDS (Interdictor/Strike) models having made its initial flight at BAe's Warton plant on 10 July 1979. This, one of 36 dual-control GR.Mk 1T aircraft included in early RAF production, is little different from the Tornado GR.Mk 1, and indeed, all three participants' aircraft are virtually identical. Training, too, has been standardised, and all crew conversion is undertaken at RAF Cottesmore under the auspices of the Tri-national Tornado Training Establishment (TTTE), while technical personnel are trained at the co-located Tornado Ground Servicing School. The 'Triple-T E' received its first aircraft on 1 July 1980, and after initial instructor training and syllabus validation the first courses for both pilots and navigators began on 5 January 1981. At full strength in late 1982, the TTTE (or more precisely, its flying element, comprising 'A', 'B', 'C' and the Standards Squadrons of the Tornado OCU) – had 22 West German, 20 British and eight Italian air-

The Tornado is fitted with terrain-following radar which allows it to fly at ultra-low level at very high speed with great safety. This enables the aircraft to escape detection from enemy radars for most of its flight over enemy territory and this capability is enhanced by the 'Sky Shadow' electronic countermeasures pods which can also be carried. The aircraft shown here is one of the development prototypes, strikingly demonstrating its low-level capability.

Panavia Tornado

The Panavia Tornado GR. Mk 1 is now the standard strike aircraft of the RAF and is likely to remain so for several decades. It first entered operational service in 1982 with No. 9 Squadron at Honington, in whose markings this aircraft, serial number ZA590, appears. The aircraft carries a standard 'conventional' load of eight 1,000 lb bombs under the fuselage, long-range tanks and Sky Shadow ECM pods on the wing pylons. No. 9 Squadron's bat emblem appears on the fin in dark green, outlined in yellow, and the squadron also uses a dark green arrowhead through the fuselage roundel, also outlined in yellow. ZA590 is aircraft 'E' of the squadron as shown on the top of the fin.

Keith Fretwell

craft on strength, and was producing some 135 crews per year on three parallel 10-week courses. Pilot conversion to this advanced aircraft is quite straightforward despite its futuristic concept, and although a first solo is possible after six to eight hours, slightly longer time is allowed in the training syllabus.

After the Cottesmore course, foreign crews proceed to their own country for weapons training (although instructors receive an additional three weeks' training with the TOCU's Standards Squadron before posting), while RAF personnel proceed to the Tornado Weapons Conversion Unit at Honington. Receipt by the TWCU on 30 June 1981 of its first aircraft was a historic moment, representing the first Tornado delivery to a wholly RAF unit, and work began a few weeks later to train instructors, before induction of the first students early in 1982.

A comprehensive training programme for the use of laser-guided and cluster bombs, airfield denial weapons and internal cannon (plus the AIM-9 Sidewinder AAMs used for self-defence) is given at the TWCU before crews are assigned to an operational squadron, the first of which, No. 9 Squadron at Honington, formed on 1 June 1982. Though essentially a Vulcan replacement, the Tornado has a shorter unrefuelled range (980 miles/1577 km compared with 1,440 miles/2317 km), which dictates that it be based in Germany, and most of the six Vulcan squadrons to be converted will take the place of RAFG's Jaguars and Buccaneers. A Tornado reconnaissance squadron will be available to RAFG in 1986, the home-based users of the GR.Mk 1 version being restricted to one squadron at Honington, plus two at Marham. Tornado bases are among the first to be equipped with hardened aircraft shelters for protection from attack.

When the final Royal Navy Buccaneers were transferred with the paying-off of HMS *Ark Royal* in December 1978, the RAF's fleet of Martel-equipped Buccaneer S.Mk 2Bs and non-Martel

S.Mk 2As was increased to almost 100, these equipping Nos 15 and 16 Squadrons in Germany and four units at home. Until recently, the principal Buccaneer base was Honington, which housed Nos 12, 208 and 216 Squadrons, plus No. 237 OCU for training, but in July 1980 Nos 12 and 216 began moving to Lossiemouth, Scotland, a more convenient site from which to operate in their anti-shipping role, leaving No. 208 to its overland-strike duties at the East Anglian base for a further three years before joining them.

Buccaneer operations were suspended for a six-month period during 1980 following discovery that fatigue cracks in the mainplane had caused the mid-air break-up of an aircraft flying in a 'Red Flag' training exercise in the USA during February of that year. Despite their sturdy construction, many more aircraft were found to have similar defects, and the entire fleet was grounded until August when flying was resumed by those unaffected, or with easily remedied faults. Others beyond economical repair were scrapped, and No. 216 Squadron failed to survive the grounding. Its two former companions are now in No. 18 Group.

The Lossiemouth Buccaneers are assigned to NATO's SACLANT (Supreme Allied Commander Atlantic), towards which Britain also contributes part of the UK/Netherlands Amphibious Force, including naval helicopters. Their primary weapons are laser-guided bombs and the Anglo-French Martel air-to-surface missile but, fittingly, Buccaneers have been involved in trials of the latter's successor, the BAe Dynamics P3T Sea Eagle, built to specification AST (Air Staff Target) 1226. Dummy separation trials of the Sea Eagle began late in 1980, and were followed by unguided test round firings in mid-1981, from a Buccaneer in both instances. Powered by a miniature jet engine (and thus known as an 'air-breathing' missile), the Sea Eagle also will be issued to the Royal Navy's BAe Sea Harriers, but its intended application to the Tornado is now open to doubt. The original plan to re-equip SACLANT's two squadrons with Tor-

Two squadrons of Lightnings (Nos 5 and 11) are left, both based at Binbrook. They are equipped with F. Mk 3s and F. Mk 6s with Red Top missiles. The aircraft are painted in two-tone low visibility grey. This example is an F. Mk 6 of No. 5 Squadron, with an old F. Mk 2 visible in the background.

In 1982 the Hawker Siddeley (Avro) Vulcan B.Mk 2 was to be phased out of service. However, this was halted by the Falklands dispute and various alternative roles and fitments were developed. Now the tanker version of the Vulcan is the only one still in service and will help to cover the tanker shortage until the VC.10 and TriStar tankers enter service. These aircraft are operated by No. 50 Squadron, although when this photograph was taken they were still in the markings of their former operator, No. 101 Squadron.

nados has been abandoned, and instead the two naval strike Buccaneer units will be given an extended lease of life, equipped with the long-range, surface-skimming Sea Eagle and revised avionics.

The majestic Vulcan is also making its way to the scrap-heap in ever-increasing numbers now that Tornado deliveries are in full swing, and disposal of the first aircraft began in February 1981, the same month in which the aircraft clocked up its 500,000th flying hour with the RAF. Conceived as a high-level strategic bomber, the Vulcan has served with distinction in the low-level role since the mid-1960s, suffering few ill-effects from the rigours of beneath-the-radar flying. Together with USAF General Dynamics F-111s based at Lakenheath and Upper Heyford, the Vulcan B.Mk 2 has provided NATO's land-based, long-range strike element, as the only aircraft in the RAF capable of undertaking deep penetration attacks in all weathers.

The smaller, faster and less vulnerable Tornado will represent a major upgrading of offensive capability, although even in its declining years the Vulcan was updated with fin-top threat-sensors to augment its extensive, but dated avionics. Visual detectability was reduced from late 1979 by the repainting of some aircraft in darker grey/green camouflage, this extending over the entire lower surfaces, as well as the original upper surfaces – an impressive spectacle on such a large aircraft.

With the withdrawal of Nos 9 and 35 Squadrons from Akrotiri, Cyprus, in January 1975, Vulcan B.Mk 2 operations were centred on Scampton and Waddington, only a few miles north and south respectively of Lincoln. At the former, training unit No. 230 OCU was disbanded in mid-1981, followed soon afterwards by Nos 35, 617 and 27 Squadrons, the last-mentioned being equipped with specially modified Vulcan B.Mk 2MRRs for the maritime radar reconnaissance role. The Waddington-based aircraft of Nos 9, 44, 50 and 101 Squadrons were due to disappear by June 1982, and although No. 9 disbanded in April, the remainder

received a reprieve for the Falklands War, No. 101 finally going in August and No. 44 in December of that year. Six Vulcan K.Mk 2 tankers, hastily converted in mid-1982 to alleviate the pressure on RAF airborne refuelling resources, will remain in operation with No. 50 Squadron at Waddington until 1984 when sufficient VC10 K.Mk 2s and K.Mk 3s and TriStars are available to assume their duties.

Whilst the Vulcan's days may be numbered, its predecessor, the Canberra, soldiers on – albeit in roles far removed from its original concept. Canberra operations have been centralised at Wyton, where accommodation was provided by disbandment of the RAF's last two operational Canberra squadrons. Assigned to photo-reconnaissance roles, Nos 13 (Canberra PR.Mk 7) and 39 (Canberra PR.Mk 9) Squadrons withdrew in January and May 1982 respectively, leaving the PR.Mk 9-equipped No. 1 Photographic Reconnaissance Unit to continue with survey and mapping work, but the venerable Canberra is destined to continue in second-line operations until, the early 1990s. To this end, 54 RAF and Royal Navy Canberras received lengthy rebuilds at BAe Samlesbury during 1976–82 their number including 13 T.Mk 17s of the joint-service No. 360 Squadron. Easily distinguished by its unusual nose ('a bulge with bulges on'), the Canberra T.Mk 17 simulates ECM-equipped intruding aircraft for the training of air defence system operators.

No. 100 Squadron moved to Wyton in January 1982 with Canberra B.Mk 2s and E.Mk 15s previously operated from Marham in the banner-towing and radar target roles, simultaneously adding specialist sleeve and 'solid' target-towing TT.Mk 18s from the disbanded No. 7 Squadron at St Mawgan, and later accepting a quartet of PR.Mk 7s. Crew training for the Canberra fleet is provided by No. 231 OCU, which was installed at Wyton in July 1982 with B.Mk 2s and T.Mk 4s.

Wyton also houses more publicity-shy units in the form of No. 51 Squadron and the Electronic

Warfare Avionics Unit. The latter has the use of a single BAe (HS) Andover C.Mk 1 for flight-testing of new electronic countermeasures (ECM) equipment and similar 'black boxes', whilst No. 51 Squadron uses three Nimrod R.Mk 1s for the gathering of electronic intelligence. Entering service in May 1974, the Nimrod R.Mk 1 lacks the MAD tailboom of its maritime compatriots. Little is known of their precise role, but sightings in the Baltic indicate that they regularly operate around outside the Warsaw Pact boundaries noting radar frequencies and eavesdropping on radio traffic, the traditional Elint (electronic intelligence) duties.

The equipment of No. 1 Group is completed by its flight-refuelling force, comprising 22 BAe (Handley Page) Victor K.Mk 2s and (soon) nine BAe (BAC) VC10s and six Lockheed TriStars. Based at Marham, the Victors of Nos 55 and 57 Squadrons operate for the benefit of suitably equipped aircraft from any RAF unit. Apart from training sorties, the Victor's principal operational role is in support of fighters intercepting Soviet Elint aircraft off the British coast. Augmentation of the heavily-worked Victors and their temporary Vulcan assistants is at hand through AST 406, calling for tanker conversion of five VC10s and four Super VC10s, bought in 1978 from Gulf Air and East African Airways respectively. To be known as VC10 K.Mk 2s and Super VC10 K.Mk 3s, the aircraft have undergone lengthy overhaul at BAe Filton and are being delivered to No. 101 Squadron at Brize Norton.

Much discussion took place during 1980 between the RAF and British civilian airlines on the possibility of installing the necessary 'plumbing' in new wide-bodied airliners then on order, to allow rapid conversion to flight-refuelling tankers in an emergency. Nothing came of the proposal, but as a result of the severe shortage of airborne refuelling aircraft exposed by the Falklands war, it was announced late in 1982 that the RAF would obtain six former British Airways Lockheed TriStar 500 airliners, each of which would have a fuel transfer capability equal to three VC10s or nine Victors. Conversion work on the aircraft began early in 1983, although four TriStars are later to be modified with a large freight door and strengthened floors for dual-role tanker/transport operations.

Adoption of the TriStar 500 may result in changes to the VC10 tanker programme, for apart from the nine VC10s and Super VC10s initially obtained, the RAF bought 14 surplus British Airways 'Supers' in the following year, of which four were stripped for spares and the others earmarked for possible tanker conversion.

In November 1983, No. 1 Group moved HQ from Bawtry to Upavon, taking over the accommodation and aircraft of the former No. 38 Group. However, this was far more than an administrative change, for several aircraft of the 'old' No. 1 have been dis-

tributed to other groups and the new formation is essentially No. 38 Group's strike-fighters, transports and helicopters with the home-based Tornado fleet and the Victor tankers grafted on. No. 18 Group received the Canberra force in December 1982 and added the maritime strike Buccaneers based at Lossiemouth in July 1983, significantly enhancing its combat potential.

Strike Command's offensive capability would be of little value without the security afforded to its bases by the air defence elements of No. 11 Group. With headquarters at Bentley Priory, Stanmore (famed nerve-centre of fighter operations in the Battle of Britain) No. 11 Group is tasked with early warning of missile and aircraft threats to the United Kingdom, investigation of airspace violations, and all air defence operations within the UK Air Defence Region. Defences are organised on an omni-directional basis to counter the ability of Soviet Tupolev Tu-26 'Backfire' and Sukhoi Su-24 'Fencer' aircraft to enter through the 'back door' (i.e. from the west), and in 1977 the RAF announced a 10-year defence modernisation programme under which 25 per cent of equipment funds will be devoted to SAMs, interceptors and radar, in addition to hardening of airfield infrastructure.

Distribution of air defence

ADR organisation comprises three key sector operations centres grouped around radar units at Boulmer, Buchan and Neatishead, and fed with information from 12 UK Air Defence Ground Environment (UKADGE) stations via digital data links from other air defence centres and reporting posts. NATO funding has been provided for modernisation of the 12 stations with new three-dimensional L- and S-band radars, display and communications equipment, in a programme due for completion in 1986. When finished, the new system will permit total cross-operability between ground radar and control units through a secure communications network. At present, in the event of one site being eliminated, neighbouring units have only limited ability to assume its functions.

SAM defences rely principally on the ageing Bloodhound Mk 2s of No. 85 Squadron, deployed along the coast at West Raynham ('A' Flight), North Coates ('B' Flight) and Bawdsey ('C' Flight). Designed for high-altitude defence, the Bloodhound is now used for medium-and low-level interception, but efficiency is limited by the lack of IFF (Identification Friend or Foe) and dated 'valve-technology' ground equipment. Nevertheless, No. 25 Squadron has recently moved from Germany to strengthen home SAM defences with detachments at Barkston Heath, near Cranwell ('A' Flight), Wyton ('B' Flight) and Wattisham ('C') Flight, the first of which was established in January 1982 using newly-built accommodation. Although the weapon

Operated by No. 51 Squadron at Wyton are three Hawker Siddeley Nimrod R.Mk 1s. Little can be said about their task though it is known that they are fitted out for radar reconnaissance. XW665 is one of the three, landing here at Wyton and displaying the squadron's flying goose emblem on the fin.

Right: The British Aerospace (Hawker Siddeley/Blackburn) Buccaneer S.Mk 2A and S.Mk 2B perform as the main heavy strike aircraft in the RAF today. With a very long range capability, rock steady at low level and carrying a potent armoury of weapons, the Buccaneer still provides a considerable measure of effectiveness in this role, even though it first entered service with the Royal Navy in the early 1960s. Two squadrons serve in Britain, No. 208 (one of whose aircraft is seen here in Norwegian surroundings) and No. 12, both at Lossiemouth in the anti-shipping strike role.

Far left: The remarkable English Electric Canberra continues to serve in the RAF more than 30 years after it entered service. Most of those now flying are older than the pilots who fly them! One unit still using them is No. 360 Squadron at Wyton, which flies the T.Mk 17 version to train ECM operators for all branches of the services and is crewed by naval as well as RAF personnel.

Above: Just about to enter service is the RAF's flying command post, the Nimrod AEW.Mk 3, which will take over from the obsolescent Shackleton the task of airborne radar picket, picking up enemy aircraft long before they approach British shores and directing intercepting fighters on to them.

has a separate squadron numbering system.) Backed by Marconi Blindfire radar, the mobile and highly accurate Rapier is capable of all-weather operation, and will shortly be installed at USAF bases in Britain, although also manned by the Regiment.

A great advance in detection capability will be provided to No. 11 Group when deliveries begin of its 11 Nimrod AEW.Mk 3 airborne early warning and control aircraft, but in the meantime, low-level threats are monitored by the aged Shackleton AEW.Mk 2s of No. 8 Squadron at Lossiemouth. A dozen Shackleton MR.Mk 2s were modified to AEW standard by the expedient of grafting to their undersides the radar equipment of redundant Royal Navy Fairey Gannet AEW.Mk 3s, but half the fleet was withdrawn early in 1981 as an economy measure. Nimrod AEW.Mk 3s are being produced by extensive conversion of MR.Mk 1s, the first of three prototypes flying on 16 July 1980 as an aerodynamic test vehicle.

The heart of the Nimrod AEW.Mk 3 is its GEC-Marconi Mission System Avionics, outwardly distinguished by aerials mounted in large bulbous fairings in the nose and tail. Sweeping in synchronisation, the aerials provide 360° coverage uninterrupted by the aircraft's structure, in contrast to the similarly-tasked Boeing E-3A Sentry and its mast-mounted scanner. In addition to a flight crew of four, the Nimrod AEW.Mk 3 carries a six-man tactical team, comprising a tactical air control officer, communications control officer, electronic warfare support measures operator (EWSM sensor pods are mounted on the wingtips), and three air direction officers. From their base at Waddington (where the first is expected in 1984) the Nimrod

is to receive a limited systems update, its replacement, probably in a European SAM programme, is becoming a matter of urgency.

Outside the English Bloodhound belt, the Scottish bases of Leuchars and Lossiemouth are protected by the short-range Rapier SAMs of Nos 27 and 48 Squadrons of the RAF Regiment. (It should be noted that the Regiment, which also provides ground defence for RAF bases and has recently received Scorpion and Spartan armoured vehicles,

A detachment of Westland Sea King HAR. Mk 3s of No. 202 Squadron was sent out to the Falklands from Coltishall to provide long-range SAR facilities and to relieve the Royal Navy helicopters to get on with their more essential tasks. They were repainted in overall grey markings, with the squadron badge in outline on the crew door, as shown on XZ587 here. The detachment still serves on the Falklands and became No. 1564 Flight in August 1983.

AEW.Mk 3s will be capable of mounting a standing patrol of six or seven hours' duration far out to sea and co-ordinating the attacks of friendly fighters on incoming threats. Such capability is urgently required, not only to bolt the 'back door' but to provide adequate opportunity for interceptors to destroy enemy aircraft well before they achieve landfall.

Phantom bases

The interception task is assigned to eight squadrons based at airfields along the eastern coast of Britain, backed by the flight-refuelling fleet of No. 1 Group. Predominant in this force is the American Spey-engined McDonnell Phantom, of which some 130 remain, including those assigned to two further interceptor squadrons in RAF Germany. At Leuchars, No. 43 Squadron operates the F-4K Phantom FG.Mk 1s diverted on delivery from the naval order for 52, whilst the co-located No. 111 Squadron standardised on this variant when HMS *Ark Royal*'s Phantom squadron disbanded late in 1978. Remaining units are equipped with the F-4M Phantom FGR.Mk 2, from 118 such aircraft supplied to RAF requirements. Wattisham now houses only No. 56 Squadron, but the Phantom's 'home' is Coningsby, where No. 29 Squadron operates alongside No. 228 OCU, which is responsible for all pilot and navigator training on both Phantom marks. In an emergency, the OCU instructors would form a front-line squadron, and thus their aircraft are marked with the insignia of No. 64 Squadron, the OCU's 'shadow' unit.

In October 1982, No. 29 Squadron transferred from Coningsby to Port Stanley to provide air defence for the British garrison on the Falkland Islands, but soon afterwards it was announced that the resultant deficiency in UK-based forces would be rectified by purchase of at least 12 F-4J Phantoms (later increased to 15) from the US Navy. Formerly at Wattisham, No. 23 Squadron replaced No. 29 in the Falklands in April 1983.

During 1973, trial installation was made in a Phantom FG.Mk 1 of threat-warning sensors mounted in a fin-top pod, and this modification is gradually finding incorporation in all aircraft. Similarly, slow progress is being made in re-painting Phantoms in overall light grey tones (following the first experimental application late in 1978) for medium-altitude camouflage, replacing the standard grey/green upper-surface colours hitherto worn for low-level operations. In addition to the formidable M61 Vulcan cannon, Phantoms are equipped with four infra-red AIM-9D/G Sidewinder and four radar-guided AIM-7E2 Sparrow AAMs, but units are now being issued with the improved AIM-9L and Sky Flash versions of these weapons. The AIM-9L comes from a European production group for the US-designed Sidewinder, headed by Bodenseewerke and utilising components produced in Britain, Germany, Italy and Norway, but Sky Flash is a wholly-British modification of the Sparrow, incorporating indigenous guidance and fusing mechanisms, giving 'snapdown' capability to as low as 200 ft (61 m). Development of a Sky Flash Mk 2 was halted early in 1981 as an economy measure.

Four Phantom squadrons will be retained until the end of the 1980s, some time after their compatriots have been replaced by Tornados, but a mid-decade retirement is planned for No. 11 Group's oldest interceptor, the BAe (BAC) Lightning. Armed with two Firestreak or Red Top AAMs, the dated but still effective Lightning is operated from Binbrook by Nos 5 and 11 Squadrons, plus their associated unit, the Lightning Training Flight. A large reserve of Lightnings is held at Binbrook, and some 60 single-seaters (one third

After serving in the fighter/ground-attack reconnaissance role in the RAF until supplanted by the Jaguar in the mid-1970s, the Phantom FGR.Mk 2 has since then formed the main fighter defence both of the RAF Germany (two squadrons) and Britain (five squadrons). Since the Falklands episode this miniscule fighter force has been stretched even thinner by one of the squadrons being detached there, and the RAF is imminently receiving 15 ex-US Navy Phantoms of a dissimilar version, to boost the UK air defence until the arrival of the Tornado F.Mk 2 in service. The No. 29 Squadron Phantom shown here was one of the first to take up defence duties at Port Stanley airfield.

The Tornado F.Mk 2 (carrying four Sky Flash AAMs) employs the advanced Foxhunter radar system, which necessitates the longer nose compared to the GR.Mk 1. Also only one 27-mm Mauser cannon is carried (on the starboard side of the fuselage).

Eagerly awaited in service, to replace both Phantoms and Lightnings, is the Tornado F.Mk 2, the third prototype being seen here. This swing-wing fighter is fitted for flight-refuelling and for Sky Flash missiles (and subsequent newer missiles). Its task will be to meet enemy raiders far out from British shores and destroy them long before they come near Britain. Some 165 such aircraft will eventually be built, the first coming into service in 1985.

F.Mk 3s and the remainder F.Mk 6s) and 10 T.Mk 5 trainers are used in rotation by the resident units. A third squadron was to have formed in 1981–2, but instead, the LTF has been given a 'shadow' operational role. The first light-grey overall Lightnings began to appear in mid-1981.

Air defence will receive a significant boost from 1986 onwards, when the Tornado F.Mk 2 enters service. An exclusively British version of the international strike aircraft, the F.Mk 2 (known to its manufacturers as the ADV, or Air Defence Variant) retains 80 per cent commonality, but is externally differentiated by its longer forward fuselage, which houses additional fuel. Equipped with a retractable refuelling probe, the F.Mk 2 has as its prime sensor the Ferranti-Marconi Foxhunter multi-target intercept radar, the range of which is reportedly in the region of 100 miles (161 km). Essentially a long-range, all-weather interceptor, operating far from base, supported by Nimrod AEW.Mk 3 command posts and aerial tankers, the Tornado F.Mk 2 makes no pretence at being in the General Dynamics F-16's dogfighter category. However, it is an agile aeroplane for its class (more so than the Tornado GR.Mk 1), and has demonstrated a low-altitude level speed of 920 mph (1481 km/h), well above the 805–865 mph (1295–1392 km/h) to which potential adversaries are limited by aerodynamic and structural factors.

The first of three Tornado F.Mk 2 trials aircraft made its initial flight on 27 October 1979, although it was not until June 1981 that Foxhunter was airborne in its intended recipient. Early days were beset by reports in overseas journals suggesting that the RAF would cancel the F.Mk 2 in favour of US fighters (even ex-Iranian Grumman F-14 Tomcats were mentioned) but the service never wavered from its commitment to the aircraft, and placed a firm order for 18 in 1980 as part of the fourth trinational production contract with Panavia. A further 52 F.Mk 2s were the subject of a 1982 contract, and additional orders will follow to increase the total to 165.

Coningsby will house the Tornado F.Mk 2 OCU, to be formed late 1985 or early 1986, and replacement of Lightnings will begin some 18 months later, three squadrons being assigned to Leeming and others probably to Lossiemouth and Wattisham. Tornado armament will include new-generation AAMs now in the early stages of development under a NATO agreement. The advanced short-range weapon (ASRAAM) is being produced by Britain, Germany and Italy to replace the Sidewinder, whilst the medium-range AMRAAM will be a US-designed Sparrow follow-on which will replace the cancelled Sky Flash Mk 2 in RAF service. Production of the two missile types will be undertaken on both sides of the Atlantic.

A late addition to air defence roles is the BAe Hawk T.Mk 1 advanced trainer, 95 of which will be modified to carry two AIM-9L Sidewinders, allowing a force of 72 to be declared to NATO, including those of the Red Arrows aerobatic team, which is to receive a 'shadow' squadron identity. By 1985 these will be augmented by 36 Sidewinder-equipped Jaguars, withdrawn from Germany with the coming of the Tornado and allocated a secondary defence role. No. 11 Group is responsible for the Hawks of Nos 1 and 2 Tactical Weapons Units at Brawdy and Chivenor respectively, the aircraft being readily distinguishable from the Support

Command Hawks by application of camouflage in place of red and white livery. The TWUs provide weapons courses for students graduating from flying training to an OCU, and No. 1 TWU (which also has a 'refresher' element for officers returning to flying duties after a ground tour) additionally operates a handful of Hunter F.Mk 6As, T.Mk 7s and FGA.Mk 9s, and three forward air control (FAC) Jet Provost T.Mk 4s. No. 1 TWU has the 'shadows' of Nos 79 and 234 Squadron, whilst No. 2 TWU comprises Nos 63 and 151 Squadrons, most aircraft being appropriately marked in squadron insignia. Hawk deliveries were completed in 1982 after 175 aircraft, a further order for 18 having fallen victim of the late-1980s defence economies.

Responsible for tasks formerly assigned to Coastal Command, No. 18 (Maritime) Group comprises only six squadrons and an OCU up to 1983, with peacetime duties of patrol and surveillance of the Eastern Atlantic, North Sea and home waters (230 miles/370 km from the coastline), fishery and oil rig protection, and a large international SAR (search and rescue) commitment. No. 18 Group possesses strong NATO affiliations, its commander-in-chief holding joint posts of Maritime Air Commander Eastern Atlantic and Maritime Air Commander Channel Command from headquarters at Northwood, Middlesex. Perhaps the most 'operational' of all groups, No. 18 is in constant touch with Soviet forces through its primary role of submarine shadowing. Vessels leaving Murmansk are first tracked by the Norwegian air force, and then 'handed over' to RAF Nimrods (amongst other NATO elements) before, in turn, they are followed by US carrier- and shore-based aircraft. It is a matter of pride amongst squadrons to hand their plot on to the next unit in the chain, for accurate knowledge of submarine deployments can yield vital knowledge of Soviet intentions should there be any sudden change in its pattern.

Far left: Like the Canberra, the Hawker Hunter is also in its fourth decade of RAF service. It is now used in the training role, specially equipped two-seaters flying with the Buccaneer squadrons for instrument practice, and both single-seaters (as this F.Mk 6) and two-seaters with the Tactical Weapons Unit at Brawdy.

Live weapon firing is a feature of the course at the two Tactical Weapons Units of the RAF (Chivenor and Brawdy), equipped largely with the Hawk T.Mk 1. This Brawdy aircraft, carrying the markings of No. 234 Squadron, is rippling unguided rockets from the SNEB pod under the wing.

The RAF's standard anti-submarine, maritime reconnaissance and strike vehicle is the Hawker Siddeley Nimrod in its MR.Mk 1 and MR.Mk 2 versions, which are almost indistinguishable externally but very differently equipped within. Recently these aircraft have been repainted in a special matt finish to make them hard to observe over the grey-green Atlantic wastes.

The mantle of the RAF's search-and rescue squadrons now falls on No. 22 Squadron (equipped with Westland Wessex HC.Mk 2s) and No. 202 Squadron (with Westland Sea King HAR.Mk 3s). XZ597, a Sea King, belongs to No. 202 Squadron's D Flight at Lossiemouth, and is seen flying back to base over the town.

Of 46 Nimrod MR.Mk 1s built for the RAF, 11 are earmarked for AEW conversion, whilst the remaining 35 are in the process of MR.Mk 2 conversion with new Searchwater radar, advanced AQS-901 data processing equipment, Australian-produced Barra sonobuoys, and provision for Stingray torpedoes. The first MR.Mk 2 was delivered to the Kinloss Nimrod Wing (Nos 120, 201 and 206 Squadrons) in August 1979, and the conversion pro-

gramme will be complete by late 1984 with the re-equipment of No. 42 Squadron and No. 236 OCU ('shadow' No. 37 Squadron) at St Mawgan, Cornwall.

Publicly, the most well-known and appreciated service provided by No. 18 Group is its helicopter SAR operation which aids over 800 persons (the vast majority of them civilians) in the course of 800–900 calls-out per year. Replacement of the

redoubtable Westland Whirlwind HAR.Mk 10 was completed late in 1981 after 26 years of sterling service, and from combined headquarters at Finningley, Nos 22 and 202 Squadrons are now equipped with short-range Westland Wessex HC.Mk 2s and 16 long-range Westland Sea King HAR.Mk 3s respectively, backed by the SAR Training Squadron's Wessex at Valley. SAR flights are maintained around the coast in type rotation (integrated with similarly-tasked Royal Navy units): at Lossiemouth is No. 202 Squadron/'D' Flight, at Leuchars 22/'B', at Boulmer 202/'A', at Leconfield 22/'D', at Coltishall 22/'F', at Manston 22/'E', at Chivenor 22/'A', at Brawdy 202/'B', and at Valley 22/'C'.

New roles have been assumed by No. 18 Group with its absorption of elements from No. 1 Group, the two Buccaneer squadrons operating in the strike configuration with particular emphasis on over-water sorties, while Canberras are assigned a wartime role of maritime visual reconnaissance in addition to their daily training operations. The Falklands war saw Nimrods equipped with Harpoon anti-ship missiles (and self-defence Sidewinders) on wing pylons, and these weapons will doubtless be held in reserve for application in any future conflict.

Rapid deployment to Europe

It is obvious, and indeed logical, that each RAF group operates aircraft whose roles are to some extent related, but at first glance the system appears to break down with Upavon-based No. 1 Group. The connection between transport aircraft and strike-fighters is not immediately apparent until the role of tactical transport is considered in its operational context, for as the RAF's 'Mobility Group' No. 1 works closely with the Army, transporting its equipment to the scene of operations, bringing supplies to the front line by helicopter and augmenting its firepower by strike aircraft. Most units are equipped to be deployed from their home bases to Europe at short notice and operate as self-contained formations there, although this mobility is not shared by the Tornados and Victors which were added to the formation in November 1982.

Offensive support is provided by Jaguars and STOVL Harriers. At Coltishall, Jaguar GR.Mk 1s of Nos 6 and 54 Squadrons operate in the strike role, whilst the co-located No. 41 Squadron has a divided reconnaissance and strike function. Harrier GR.Mk 3s are based at Wittering in the form of No. 1 Squadron, mainly for close-air support of

ground forces, but with a secondary reconnaissance capability. Pilots are provided for No. 1 Group and RAF Germany by No. 226 OCU at Lossiemouth with some 15 Jaguar GR.Mk 1s and a similar number of T.Mk 2s, and No. 233 OCU at Wittering with Harrier GR.Mk 3s and T.Mk 4s.

No. 1 Group's transport effort falls into three categories: strategic, tactical and communications. No. 10 Squadron's 13 VC10 C.Mk 1s undertake long-range supply flights from their base at Brize Norton, but the Lockheed Hercules of the Lyneham Transport Wing is used in a dual role. A total of 30 Hercules C.Mk 1s (half the remaining force) are in the process of conversion to C.Mk 3 standard by the addition of 15 ft (4.57 m) to the cargo hold length, giving the equivalent of eight additional aircraft but without the corresponding demands of servicing and crew-training. Five units, including No. 242 OCU, draw their aircraft from the Lyneham pool, Nos 24 and 30 Squadrons specialising in scheduled route operation and inflight-refuelling with six Hercules K.Mk 1s, and Nos 47 and 70 Squadrons in tactical support including low-level dropping of supplies. Further modification is in prospect for the Hercules, involving installation of secondary radar for adverse-weather formation-keeping, the intention being that the RAF should be able to para-drop an entire battalion group within 15 minutes, in all weathers.

The forward troop-lift helicopter fleet of No. 1 Group includes Wessex and Puma types, but it received a substantial boost in December 1980 with the arrival of the first of 33 Boeing Vertol Chinook HC.Mk 1s at No. 240 OCU, Odiham. Twice postponed, the Chinook purchase gives the RAF a lifting capacity of 28,000 lb/12701 kg (eight times that of the Wessex), considerably increasing the range of tasks it can perform in support of the British Army. No. 18 Squadron formed with Chinooks at Odiham in August 1981 prior to taking up its operational station with RAF Germany at Gütersloh early in 1983, whilst No. 7 Squadron was established at Odiham in September 1982 as the UK-based Chinook unit, although one of its first tasks was to provide a detachment for the Falkland Islands garrison. Eight more Chinooks were ordered in 1982 to replace three lost during the Falklands war and boost the medium-lift helicopter (MLH) force.

In 1980, a further eight Westland-built SA 330L Puma HC.Mk 1s were delivered to the RAF to augment the 36 survivors of the 40 originally received, these serving No. 33 Squadron and No.

For many years the RAF has had a requirement for a medium-lift helicopter which can accommodate big and awkward loads in its fuselage or carry heavy underslung loads. Financial stringency prevented such aircraft until 1980, when Odiham received its first Boeing Vertol Chinook HC.Mk 1s. These equipped the first operational squadron, No. 18, which participated with one aircraft in the Falklands campaign. No. 18 Squadron transferred to RAF Germany in April 1983, and No. 7 Squadron is now the home-based Chinook squadron. The Falklands detachment became No. 130 Flight in August 1983.

A fine study of a Puma HC.Mk 1 on patrol along a river in Belize. The Pumas have been deployed several times on similar peacekeeping missions, such as the elections in Zimbabwe, after majority rule had been attained.

240 OCU at Odiham, plus a German-based squadron. The earlier aircraft are being brought up to SA.330L standard with plastic rotor blades, plus distinctive air intake filters. Only No. 72 Squadron remains with the Wessex HC.Mk 2, but with overseas deployment of the Chinook imminent, it was withdrawn from its NATO AMF assignment in November 1981 and re-deployed from Benson to Aldergrove for support of the British Army in Northern Ireland.

For the future requirements of its transport and other groups, the RAF has initiated a Large Aircraft Replacement Programme (LARP) to supplant no less than 198 of the present fleet. Hercules, Nimrods, VC10s and Victors were included at the upper end of the scale, but subsequent study showed the LARP net to have been cast too wide, and two distinct new types are now favoured as the solution. A variant of the Airbus Industrie A300 series has been proposed for the 'Large LARP', but the BAe 146 could also find favour. Rotary-wing requirements are expressed in AST 404, which calls for a 4/6 tonne helicopter in the early 1990s, but the proposed Super Puma order in satisfaction of AST 407 has failed to materialise.

VIP transport is also the responsibility of No. 1 Group, its most famous unit being The Queen's Flight at Benson with three BAe (HS) Andover CC.Mk 2s and two Wessex HCC.Mk 4s. Two squadrons at Northolt comprise No. 207 with 12 ageing de Havilland Devon CC.Mk 2s, including permanent detachments at Wyton and Turnhouse/Edinburgh, and No. 32 Squadron operating a mixed fleet of three Andover CC.Mk 2s and one passenger-converted Andover C.Mk 1, 10 HS Dominie CC.Mk 3s and three Westland Gazelle HCC.Mk 4s. Economies have forced the abandonment of plans to obtain two BAC One-Elevens for The Queen's Flight, and 18 (later reduced to 14) turboprop twins as Devon and Hunting Pembroke replacements under ASR (Air Staff Requirement) 408. RAF preference for the Beech Super King Air was overruled by the government instruction to buy the

more expensive BAe Jetstream 31, but ASR 408 became an academic exercise in 1980 when the brake was placed on defence spending for all except the front-line. However, late in 1982 the RAF announced its intention to purchase two BAe 146 Series 100 airliners for general-purpose duties and evaluation as possible replacements for The Queen's Flight Andovers. If the aircraft prove satisfactory, they will be exchanged for two new VVIP models.

The No. 38 Group inventory is completed by a handful of Andover E.Mk 3s, converted from the transport role for calibration of airfield navigation aids by No. 115 Squadron at Benson, its pilots being provided by the co-located Andover Training Flight. Both units transferred to their new location from Brize Norton in January 1983, the ATF

The Aérospatiale/Westland Puma HC.Mk 1 serves with two RAF squadrons, No. 33 at Odiham and No. 230 at Gütersloh in Germany for support of the British I Corps. XW223 'DG' is one of the latter unit's aircraft, here nose down in the high-speed low-level configuration.

It is a March morning and at breakfast time a cold front soaked the hard-standing at RAF Wittering. Now, as the concrete dries out, a two-seat Harrier T.Mk 4 and three single-seat GR.Mk 3s are lined up on No. 233 OCU's pad.

responsible for transport and tanker VC10, BAe 146 C.Mk 1 and TriStar K.Mk 1 training at Brize Norton. The first BAe 146 arrived in June 1983 and trooping flights with unconverted TriStars began in July with the transfer of soldiers to Canada for training.

Overseas deployment

The RAF's commitment to NATO is nowhere more clearly expressed than in the high degree of operational readiness demonstrated by its remaining overseas command, RAF Germany. In conjunction with Belgian, Dutch and northern German (including USAF) units, together forming the 2nd Allied Tactical Air Force, it is assigned to support of the Northern Allied Army Group. Specific roles are nuclear strike, interdiction, counter-air (airfield attack), air defence, close air support, tactical reconnaissance and helicopter support, for which 14 squadrons (plus SAM units) are permanently assigned. Most RAFG squadrons have a complement of 16 aircraft and enjoy priority in pilots (an average of 1.5 per aircraft, compared with 1.2:1 throughout the RAF) and equipment. Five airfields are assigned to the RAF in Germany, although Gatow, in West Berlin, houses only a couple of DHC Chipmunks for border patrol. The other aerodromes are 'toned-down', well defended installations, operating their aircraft from hardened shelters strong enough to withstand a 1,000-lb (454-kg) bomb.

Close air support for land forces is the primary role of the Harrier GR.Mk 3s of Nos 3 and 4 Squadrons at Gütersloh, operating in wartime from about six dispersed sites near the front line, although No. 4 Squadron has a parallel photo-reconnaissance role with an underfuselage pod of five optical cameras to augment the left-facing camera installed in the nose of all Harriers. Up to 5,000 lb (2268 kg) of ordnance can be carried on three underfuselage and four underwing strongpoints, this load normally comprising two podded 30-mm Aden cannon and cluster-bombs (CBUs). Earlier withdrawal of SNEB podded rockets has been reconsidered, and the installation is likely to return for low-profile attacks on armour, especially in areas of enemy air superiority. Fully loaded, the Harrier is unable to take off vertically, but it requires only a short strip of ground from which to operate in the STOVL (short take-off), vertical landing) mode.

The question of a Harrier replacement was resolved in 1981 when an agreement between the British and US governments was concluded for licensed production of up to 100 McDonnell Douglas AV-8Bs, locally to assume the designation Harrier GR.Mk 5. Developed from the US Marines' first-generation Harrier (AV-8A), the AV-8B was selected in preference to a parallel BAe project undertaken specifically to meet RAF requirements as expressed in AST 409. Initial British AV-8B orders will cover 60 aircraft, of which half will be delivered to Nos 3 and 4 Squadrons in Germany from mid-1986, following first flight of a BAe-built trials aircraft early in 1984. Apart from a few allo-

cations to the OCU and experimental establishments, remaining Harrier GR.Mk 5s will be stored against attrition. Older GR.Mk 3s are to be maintained in service at home for as long as possible, as will the two-seat T.Mk 4s, there being no requirement for a trainer equivalent of the GR.Mk 5 because of its close similarity in handling to earlier marks.

However, there are several differences in terms of equipment and aerodynamic refinement between the two Harrier generations. Fitted with a completely new supercritical wing of graphite-epoxy construction, plus re-designed air intakes, several lift and manoeuvrability devices and new avionics, the AV-8B/Harrier GR.Mk 5 can be armed with up to 8,000 lb (3629 kg) of weapons on one centre-fuselage and six wing strongpoints, the centre position being deleted if two podded Aden cannon are fitted.

Most numerous of RAFG's aircraft is the Jaguar GR.Mk 1, of which four squadrons (Nos 14, 17, 20 and 31) are based at Brüggen for strike, counter-air and interdiction, together with No. 2 at Laarbruch in the reconnaissance role. Brüggen Wing aircraft can carry nuclear weapons, 1,000 lb (454-kg) 'Iron' bombs, or BL755 cluster bombs, and have all been refitted with uprated Mk 104 versions of the Adour turbofan. Further improvements will stem from modernisation of the navigation and weapons aiming systems, involving installation of Ferranti FIN 1064 inertial navigation equipment, first flown in a trials Jaguar in July 1981.

For tactical reconnaissance duties, No. 2 Squadron Jaguars are equipped with a half-ton pod beneath the fuselage containing a fan of four F95 cameras, taking up to 12 photographs per second for horizon-to-horizon coverage; one forward-facing F95; and a single, downwards-looking infra-red linescan camera. The squadron is accompanied by its own mobile Reconnaissance Intelligence Centre at which films are processed and interpreted well inside an hour of landing.

The Jaguar's replacement within RAFG will be the Tornado GR.Mk 1, including a reconnaissance version which will enter service in 1986, but it is unlikely that Jaguar squadrons will receive new equipment when their aircraft are finally retired at the end of the 1980s. Under AST 403, the RAF was originally seeking a single Harrier and Jaguar replacement, but when this proved impracticable, the specification was rewritten as a Jaguar replacement only, and the Harrier GR.Mk 3 successor became AST 409 which was subsequently met by

the AV-8B. Discussions with France and West Germany during 1979–80 on the possibility of a joint-design 'Eurofighter' meeting all three nations' differing combat aircraft requirements failed to find common ground at Air Staff level, and the prospective programme came to an abrupt end when Germany declared itself unable to find the necessary development funds.

British Aerospace kept the concept alive, as did MBB in Germany, the UK private venture (P.110) incorporating several features and systems of the Tornado, including its two RB.199 engines. In collaboration with Aeritalia – the third Tornado programme participant – the best of the British and German aircraft were combined in the Agile Combat Aircraft (ACA), which was revealed at the 1982 Farnborough display, and the UK government promised development funding for a technology demonstrator. This limited commitment falls far short of an undertaking to order the ACA for RAF use, but it at least holds out the prospect of Britain acquiring a strike-fighter with manoeuvrability equal to the most advanced interceptors. Looking even farther ahead, AST 410 has been formulated for a STOVL strike-interceptor, but with an introduction date early in the next century. Current studies in this direction centre on the BAe P.1214.

Defence of those bases where aircraft need permanent installations has been greatly enhanced by the building of hardened aircraft shelters (HASs). These contain the aircraft on base and are impervious to all nuclear, biological and chemical warfare attacks except direct hits. The aircraft can be completely refuelled, rearmed and serviced in the shelter, which has accommodation for air and ground crews. The aircraft can even start up in the shelters and taxi straight out to take-off, thus minimising the risk of being hit.

Two squadrons of Phantoms defend the RAF Germany bases. They are both stationed at Wildenrath and keep a readiness flight to investigate any intrusions from the East. This Phantom FGR.Mk 2 is from No. 92 Squadron, taxiing out for take-off on Wildenrath's one runway.

Pulling something in excess of 4g, these two Jaguar GR.Mk 1s of No. 20 Squadron at Brüggen pull round one of the many German castles as they fly a realistic low-level profile in practice for the defence of West Germany.

First Tornado GR.Mk 1 arrivals in RAFG – from late 1983 – will replace Laarbruch's two Buccaneer S.Mk 2B squadrons, Nos XV (15) and 16. Undertaking similar roles to the Jaguar, but with the added advantage of radar and a two-man crew for all-weather operation, the Tornado can carry a nuclear weapon, four 1,000-lb (454-kg) bombs or BL755 cluster-bombs in its rotating weapons bay. Wing strongpoints carry two fuel tanks, or an AIM-9B Sidewinder for self-defence and either an ALQ-101(V)-10 ECM jamming pod or a 'Pave Spike' laser designator pod for use in conjunction with 'Pave Way'-equipped bombs. Known as 'smart' bombs, because they hit the mark every time (in theory, at least), these comprise a standard 1,000-lb (454-kg) weapon fitted with a clip-on seeker and guide unit which enables them to fly down a laser beam reflected from the target. Tornados will have additional recourse to the new Hunting JP233 airfield-denial weapon, whilst in the longer term, development is under way of an anti-armour weapon to ASR 1227, and an anti-radar missile to ASR 1228. The BAeD ALARM was chosen for the latter requirement in 1983 against competition from several systems, including the US-designed AGM-88A HARM.

Interception for RAF Germany is the responsibility of Nos 19 and 92 Squadrons and their Wildenrath-based Phantom FGR.Mk 2s. Together with the McDonnell Douglas F-15C Eagles of the USAF's 32nd TFS at Soesterberg in the Netherlands, the two units have the peacetime role of investigating all unauthorised aircraft (invariably off-course civilians) in the Air Defence Identification Zone running parallel to the East/West German border, and a Battle Flight of two Phantoms is perpetually at instant readiness. RAFG received its first Sky Flash AAMs in January 1981 and new AIM-9L Sidewinders shortly afterwards, but AIM-7E Sparrows and AIM-9Gs will continue to find a place in the Phantom's armoury.

SAM defences for RAFG are provided by No. 4 Wing of the RAF Regiment, with HQ at Wildenrath and four component squadrons of Rapiers at

Wildenrath (No. 16), Laarbruch (No. 26), Brüggen (No. 37) and Gütersloh (No. 63). Augmented by Marconi DN 181 Blindfire radar since the spring of 1981, fully mobile detachments, eight per squadron, would be deployed one or two miles from their airfield in wartime for short-range defence. Rapier has replaced the medium-range Bloodhound Mk 2 at the 'Clutch' airfields near the Dutch border, and No. 25 (RAF) Squadron recently completed transferring its missiles to sites in the UK from Brüggen ('A' Flight), Wildenrath ('B' Flight) and Laarbruch ('C' Flight).

Helicopter support facilities for I (BR) Corps have undergone rapid expansion since 1980, and the British Army can now call on a much enlarged force to transport troops, ammunition and supplies to the battlefront. Wessex HC.Mk 2s of No. 18 Squadron were replaced by No. 230 Squadron's larger Puma HC.Mk 1s at Gütersloh in December 1980, whilst No. 18 returned to its former base early in 1983, completely re-equipped with Chinook HC.Mk 1s. Both squadrons are to remain in Germany. Under operational conditions, helicopters fly from dispersed sites in the forward areas, but the Chinook is difficult to camouflage on the ground, and would have its operating base some 100 miles (161 km) to the rear to reduce vulnerability.

Providing back-up facilities for RAFG operations are No. 60 Squadron at Wildenrath and No. 431 Maintenance Unit at Brüggen. No. 60 is the only squadron not assigned to NATO, and is equipped with seven Pembroke C.Mk 1s (the last in military service anywhere in the world) for communications and light freighting duties, including medical evacuation. With little prospect of replacement in the near future, the Pembrokes fortunately are fit for several more years of service thanks to a re-sparring programme begun in the late 1960s. No. 431 MU is the major storage unit for RAFG requirements ranging from bombs to office furniture, and has distinguished itself in pioneering work into techniques of aircraft battle damage repair.

For many years the Jet Provost has proved itself the finest basic jet trainer for the needs of the RAF at the time, and has served in T.Mk 1, T.Mk 3, T.Mk 4 and T.Mk 5 versions. These four, silhouetted against the sunset, belonged to 'The Poachers' aerobatic team from the RAF College, Cranwell, one of the many aerobatic teams to use 'JPs' in the 1960s and 1970s, but now cut back for financial considerations.

Apart from RAFG, only three other flying units were based overseas until recently, comprising the four Harrier GR.Mk 3s of No. 1417 Flight (with a Puma detachment from No. 33 Squadron and a section of Rapier SAMs) defending Belize, in Central America; No. 28 Squadron in Hong Kong and No. 84 Squadron at Akrotiri, Cyprus, both with Wessex HC.Mk 2s. The requirement to maintain a garrison on the Falkland Islands after their re-capture in June 1982 saw the installation of several detachments at Port Stanley, and their status was regularised in August of the following year with the allocation of numbers: No. 1310 Flight operates Chinooks for heavy-lift support; No. 1312 Flight has Hercules tankers to refuel based fighters and visiting aircraft; No. 1453 Flight operates Harrier GR.Mk 3s; and No. 1564 Flight is the Sea King HAR.Mk 3 SAR and general purpose unit. In addition, No. 23 Squadron is now resident in the air defence role with Phantom FRG.Mk 2s, having moved in from Wattisham in April 1983.

Of vital important to the functioning of Strike Command, the support element of the RAF undertakes the myriad tasks required to keep its front-line counterpart supplied with requirements as diversified as trained pilots and nuts and bolts. Following its amalgamation with Training Command in 1977, Support Command HQ at Brampton, near Huntingdon, is responsible for all technical and flying training (except OCUs and TWUs), and logistic support operations. For the former duty it operates a fleet of some 400 training aircraft, including gliders of the voluntary cadet corps associated with the RAF.

In peacetime, as at the height of the Battle of Britain, aircrew are a more precious commodity than aircraft, and an acute shortage of pilots resulting from low forces' pay and prospects in the latter half of the 1970s has left the RAF with a deficiency that will not be rectified fully until the end of the present decade. Training operations were expanded in 1979 to meet shortages in pilots ranging from 3.5 per cent in the front-line to 15 per cent in transport and large-jet squadrons, but costs are great for the high standard of tuition given to prospective pilots. By the time he takes his place in an operational fast-jet squadron, a young pilot will have received training costing no less than £2,000,000 – far more than the original price of a new Vulcan in its day.

Flying instruction may begin in one of two ways: university or direct entry. An increasing number of men spend their first three years of 'RAF service' studying at university and learning the basic skills of flying at one of 16 University Air Squadrons serving 46 higher education establishments. Half of the RAF's pilot intake receive 70 hours' flying instruction to wings standard on UAS BAe (SA) Bulldog T.Mk 1s, each unit having an average establishment of five aircraft from 130 of the type delivered. Among direct-entry candidates for flying training, aptitude is assessed in 15 hours on Chipmunk T.Mk 10s of the Flying Selection Squadron at Swinderby, and it is not unusual for up to 25 per cent of applicants to be rejected at this stage.

Primary and basic instruction is undertaken on the BAC (Hunting) Jet Provost, of which 80 T.Mk 3As and 100 higher-powered, pressurised T.Mk 5As are in service. University graduates are trained on 'JP5s' at one of the world's most prestigious air establishments, the RAF College at Cranwell, whilst direct-entry pilots attend No. 1 Flying Training School at Linton-on-Ouse or No. 7 FTS at nearby Church Fenton, where they receive 100 hours on JP3s. Thereafter, personnel are streamed according to aptitude, those considered suitable for fast-jet flying (known as Group 1) remaining at their FTS for a further 50 hours on the JP5 before posting to No. 4 FTS at Valley. No. 4 FTS operates a fleet of 60 Hawk T.Mk 1s in standard red and white training colours and provides a further 85 hours of advanced instruction, after which pilots pass to Strike Command for weapons training on Hawks of Nos 1 or 2 TWUs, followed by an OCU and ultimately, after some three years 'in the pipeline', their first squadron.

The Scottish Aviation Jetstream T.Mk 1 serves as a pilot trainer in the Multi-Engined Training School as part of No. 6 FTS at Finningley. This fleet of 11 aircraft is responsible for the training of those pilots who are going to fly the Nimrod, Hercules and other 'heavy' aircraft.

Far right: The Aérospatiale/Westland Gazelle HT.Mk 3s at RAF Shawbury are used by No. 2 FTS to provide helicopter pilots with their first training in rotary-wing flying. They are also used by the helicopter element of the Central Flying School.

Those considered best suited to piloting multi-engine aircraft (Group 2), or helicopters (Group 3) transfer to appropriate schools on completion of basic Jet Provost flying. No. 6 FTS at Finningley is the parent unit of the Multi-Engine Training Squadron, where 80 hours are flown on a dozen Jetstream T.Mk 1s; and at No. 2 FTS, Shawbury, Group 3 students receive 75 hours' tuition on 25 Gazelle HT.Mk 3s and a further 50 hours on the nine Wessex HC.Mk 2s delivered to the unit early in 1981 to replace Whirlwinds.

Pilot re-training and aircrew instruction is assigned to several other units, including No. 3 FTS at Leeming, whose Refresher Flying Squadron Jet Provost T.Mk 3As are used for re-orientation of officers returning to piloting duties after a tour of 'flying a desk' – and those transferring from large to small jet operations. Co-located at Leeming are 22 Bulldog T.Mk 1s of the Royal Navy Elementary Flying Training Squadron, which is also administered by No. 3 FTS with RAF aircraft despite its obvious nautical function. Remaining training for RN helicopter pilots is on the Navy's own aircraft, however. All other RAF fixed-wing aircrew training takes place at No. 6 FTS, which also operates a dozen Jet Provost T.Mk 5As, two Bulldogs and the entire RAF complement of 20 Dominie T.Mk 1s. Navigators fly 85 hours at high level in 'classroom' Dominies, followed by 30 hours' low-level training on the Jet Provost. (No. 6 FTS's JPs are the only Mk 5As permanently fitted with tip-tanks for long-range sorties.) Air Electronics Officers undergo 48 hours' flying on Dominies as part of their training, and Air Engineers have 25 hours on the same type of aircraft. Helicopter crewman training for tactical operations is undertaken on the Wessex of No. 2 FTS, and rescue winchmen are instructed by the SAR Training Flight's Wessex at Valley.

Perhaps the most renowned of training units is the Central Flying School – the world's oldest military flying training establishment. Despite its title, the one duty which the CFS does not perform is flying training, for all its students are experienced pilots who are being taught how to teach. CFS graduates become instructors at flying training schools, and whilst they follow a syllabus similar to that at an FTS, the accent at the CFS is on learning training procedures and not aircraft piloting as such. For economy reasons the flying side of the CFS has been split into three compo-

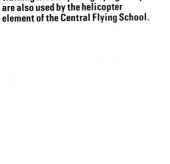

One of the most pleasant RAF aircraft to fly today is the Scottish Aviation Bulldog T.Mk 1. It serves in various roles, with the Central Flying School for instructor training, at Leeming where the RAF provided all basic training for the Fleet Air Arm, in the RN EFTS and with the university air squadrons around the country, giving university cadets a taste for flying and for the service. These two belong to the RN EFTS at Leeming.

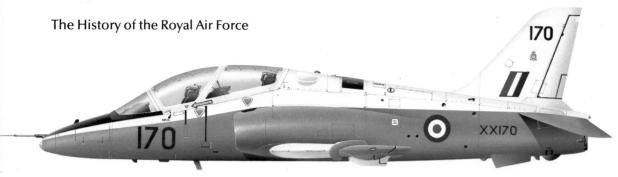

XX170 is one of nearly 60 BAe Hawk T.Mk 1s belonging to No. 4 FTS at RAF Valley in Anglesey. They are used to graduate all fast jet pilots for the RAF, and their red and white markings differentiate them from the weapons training Hawks used at the Tactical Weapons Units.

nents, and thus its Jet Provost and Bulldog element was pooled with the similar aircraft of No. 3 FTS at Leeming, the Hawks with No. 4 FTS's aircraft at Valley, and the Gazelles at Shawbury, alongside No. 2 FTS.

In what may be the first step towards re-integration, the Leeming element (including CFS Headquarters and the Standard Flight) will move to Scampton in 1984, a year after the arrival there from Kemble of the remaining CFS component, one which is without doubt the most well-known to the public of all RAF units: the Red Arrows. Having flown Folland Gnat T.Mk 1s since its inception in 1965, the RAF's premier aerobatic team re-equipped with Hawk T.Mk 1s from August 1979, giving its first public performance with the new aircraft in April 1980. Appreciated by millions for their skilful performances, the Red Arrows have contributed in no small measure to the esteem in which the RAF is held at home and abroad.

Air traffic control training

One final instructional unit deserves mention: the flight of 13 Jet Provost T.Mk 4s attached to the Central Air Traffic Control School at Shawbury. Local and area air traffic management (with the exception of specialist fighter-interception control) is taught by the CATCS, mostly by simulators and computers, but the civilian-manned JP unit gives trainees experience in directing 'real live' aircraft in the final stages of their course. The RAF also finds a use for many of its time-expired aircraft, and considerable numbers are in use for ground instruction at several bases, notably Nos 1 and 2 Schools of Technical Training at Halton and Cosford, and the Civilian Craft Apprentices' School at St Athan.

Support Command responsibilities extend to provision of aircraft and gliders for the two voluntary youth movements associated with the RAF, the controlling authority for which is HQ Air Cadets at Newton, Nottinghamshire. The Air Training Corps and units of the Combined Cadet Force provide their young members with flying experience through 13 Air Experience Flights and 27 Gliding Schools, all of which employ RAF aircraft at military or civilian airfields throughout the country. A total of 51 Chipmunk T.Mk 10s is attached to Nos 1 to 12 AEFs, of which No. 5 at Cambridge additionally operates a donated Beagle Husky, and No. 13 at Sydenham, Belfast, has a single Bulldog T.Mk 1. Gliding training, including the instructors' Central Gliding School at Syerston underwent a change in 1977 with first deliveries of 40 Slingsby Venture T.Mk 2 powered gliders for operation by 10 Volunteer Gliding Schools, and the momentum was maintained in 1983 when the first 10 of an anticipated 85 or so Schleicher ASK 21 Vanguard T.Mk 1s arrived to begin replacement of some 60 Sedbergh TX.Mk 1s and 70 Cadet TX.Mk 3s at the remaining 17 VGSs. At the same time, the CGS took delivery of further modern, high-performance equipment in the form of five ASW 19 Valiant T.Mk 1s and two Schempp-Hirth Janus Cs. CCF units at secondary schools have 60 Grasshopper TX.Mk 1 primary gliders and six Cadets.

Lacking the 'glamour' associated with flying formations are the RAF's Maintenance Units, of which the largest are the Engineering Wing at St Athan, dealing with major overhauls and modification of most front-line types; and the Abingdon-based Jaguar MU, the latter having expanded its responsibilities following closure of No. 5 MU at Kemble early in 1983. Several other MUs store ordnance, missiles and other equipment.

No review of the RAF would be complete without mention of external organisations whose task it is to perfect military aircraft and weapons, ensuring not only that they enter service in optimum condition, but also that development and refinement continues throughout their operational career. Air equipment of all three services is represented at the Aeroplane and Armament Experimental Establishment, Boscombe Down, the operational trials centre for all new military aircraft, which has among its veried equipment an airworthy Hawker Sea Fury and the last two North American T-6 Harvards in service. At the same base, the RAF Handling Squadron examines aircraft from the service pilot's point of view, recording performance and operating procedures in the 'Pilot's Notes' for issue to all those who will fly the particular aircraft in service. Boscombe Down is also the home of the Empire Test Pilots' School, another unit with a wide variety of equipment, training experienced pilots in the special skills required for trials work. Farnborough (forever to be remembered as the birthplace of British military aviation) is the headquarters of the Royal Aircraft Establishment, and hosts the Meteorological Research Flight and its much-modified Hercules W.2, plus the Institute of Aviation Medicine's Jaguar T.Mk 2. RAE bases elsewhere comprise Bedford (including the Radar Research Squadron and Flight Systems Squadron), Larkhill, Aberporth, Llanbedr and West Freugh, the establishment's role being scientific advancement, rather than solely military-oriented research. (Interestingly, the RAE transport fleet includes the last military Douglas C-47 Dakota in British military service together with five Devon C.Mk 2s. Following an administrative error at the time of its purchase, this veteran was recently issued with a new serial number; in fact, one which is newer than those applied to many of the RAF's Tornados. The late Donald Douglas would have approved!)

It is fitting to leave until last a small fleet of RAF aircraft whose appearance at air displays must have jerked more than a few nostalgic tears from those old enough to remember them, and their deeds, in days gone by. Lovingly maintained in pristine condition, and limited to a small number of flying hours each year, nine truly historic aircraft remain on RAF charge in airborne perpetuation of its fine traditions. Based with the CFS, the 'Vintage Pair' comprises the RAF's first and second jet aircraft, a Gloster Meteor and a de Havilland Vampire, but older still are the four Supermarine Spitfires, two Hawker Hurricanes and single Avro Lancaster stationed at Coningsby with the Battle of Britain Memorial Flight.

The roar of the Merlin and the whine of the early jets not only serve to stir memories in men's hearts; they are a living reminder of the firm basis on which today's RAF is built. It was Lord Trenchard's avowed intention to construct a solid foundation upon which the structure of his air force could be laid, and though initially it supported nothing more than a cottage, from it sprang the castle inside which Britain was secure when she stood alone against tyranny. Though undoubtedly far-sighted, the 'Father of the RAF' would be at a loss to comprehend the high level of technology now employed at every level of the RAF, but he would nevertheless feel immediately at home among present-day personnel, for though the 'jargon' has moved with the times, the RAF's unique esprit de corps remains unchanged from that of its earliest days.

INDEX

335